THE ONE YEAR BOOK OF
Family Devotions

VOLUME 2

THE ONE YEAR BOOK OF
Family Devotions

VOLUME 2

Tyndale House Publishers, Inc.
Wheaton, Illinois

Stories written by Katherine Ruth
Adams, Brenda Benedict, Judi
Boogaart, Carol Brookman, Daniel
A. Burns, V. Louise Cunningham,
Brenda Decker, Jorlyn Grasser, Jan
Hansen, Ruth Jay, Dean Kelley,
Beverly Kenniston, Nance E. Keyes,
Phyllis Klomparens, Sherry Kuyt,
Agnes Livezey, Deborah Marett,
Hazel Marett, Sara Nelson, Mary
Rose Pearson, Raelene Phillips,
Victoria Reinhardt, Phyllis Robinson,
Deana Rogers, Catherine Runyon,
Lynn Stamm-Rex, Tom VandenBerg,
Charlie VanderMeer, Geri Walcott,
Linda Weddle, Barbara Westberg,
and Carolyn Yost. Authors' initials
appear at the end of each story. All
stories are taken from issues of *Keys
for Kids,* published bimonthly by the
Children's Bible Hour, Box 1, Grand
Rapids, Michigan 49501.

Scripture quotations marked NIV are
taken from *The Holy Bible, New
International Version.* Copyright
1973, 1978, 1984 International Bible
Society. Used by permission of
Zondervan Bible Publishers.
    Quotations marked NKJV are from
The New King James Version.
Copyright 1979, 1980, 1982, Thomas
Nelson, Inc., Publishers.
    Quotations marked TLB are from
The Living Bible, copyright 1971
owned by assignment to Illinois
Regional Bank N.A. (as trustee). All
rights reserved.
    Quotations marked KJV are from
the King James Version of the Bible.
    The One Year is a trademark of
Tyndale House Publishers, Inc.

Library of Congress Catalog
Card Number 88-71950
ISBN 0-8423-2511-5, cloth
ISBN 0-8423-2510-7, kivar
Copyright © 1989,
Children's Bible Hour
All rights reserved
Printed in the United States
of America

2   3   4   5   6   93   92   91   90   89

CONTENTS

YOU HAVE in your hands a year's worth of delightful stories, all taken from *Keys for Kids,* a devotional magazine published by the Children's Bible Hour. For years the Children's Bible Hour has made *Keys* available free of charge to any family requesting a copy. Their fine ministry to families has been much appreciated over the years, and Tyndale House was proud to present *The One Year Book of Family Devotions.* So well-received was that book that Tyndale now presents this second volume of the many stories from *Keys for Kids.*

Each day's story provides a contemporary illustration of the day's Scripture reading. Following each story is a "How About You?" section that asks children to apply the story to themselves. Following this is a memory verse, usually taken from the Scripture reading. Many of these memory verses are taken from the King James Version, but in many cases another version has been used for the sake of clarity. Each devotion ends with a "key," a 2-5 word summary of the day's lesson.

The stories here are geared toward families with children ages 8 to 14. Children can enjoy reading these stories by themselves, but we hope that you will use them in a daily devotional time for the whole family. Like the many stories in the Bible that teach valuable lessons about life, the stories here will speak not only to children but to adults. They are simple, direct, and concrete, and, like Jesus' parables, they speak to all of us in terms we can understand. Like all good stories, they are made for sharing, so look at them as the basis for family sharing and growth.

This book includes a Scripture index and a topical index. The Scripture index is helpful if you want to locate a story related to a passage that you want to draw your family's attention to. The topical index is here because certain concerns arise spontaneously and unexpectedly in any family—illness, moving, or a new baby, for example. We hope you will use the book faithfully every day, but the indexes are here so that you will not just be locked into the daily reading format. Feel free to use any story at any time it relates to a special situation in your family.

R YAN DROPPED the weight he was holding. His face was covered with beads of sweat. "Mother has dinner ready, Champ," Dad said. "You need food as well as exercise, you know."

When Ryan finished his meal, he announced his plans for the evening—more weightlifting and exercise. Dad frowned. "You've been spending more than enough time working out," he said. "As a matter of fact, Son, you've been neglecting your chores. And what about homework?"

"Yes," added Mother, "and what about your devotional life? When you came back from the youth retreat, you told me God had shown you that you should spend some time each day with Him. Have you been doing that?"

Ryan looked down at the floor in embarrassment. "There's nothing wrong with wanting to have a strong body, is there?" he asked.

"Not at all," replied Dad, "but a well-exercised body is only part of a complete person. The Apostle Paul knew about exercise and training. He spoke often of running races and disciplining our bodies."

"He did?" Ryan's eyes widened in interest.

"Yes. He wrote to Timothy that bodily discipline or exercise could not compare with the benefits he obtained from spiritual exercise," replied Dad. "Just as you work hard to build up your muscles, so you must work at living God's way to build up your Christian life. You need to practice such things as Bible reading and prayer and sharing Christ with others. It takes hard work."

Ryan looked thoughtful. Then he nodded and smiled. "Okay, Dad," he said. "I'll practice obeying my parents by doing my chores now. Then I'll take care of my devotions and my homework. After this, I'll try to keep a balance between my physical and spiritual exercise."

HOW ABOUT YOU? Is there a special activity that takes too much of your time? Perhaps you play sports or have a pet with which you spend your free time. Maybe you spend a lot of time with your best friend. These things are fine, but be sure you don't neglect your time with God. As you begin a new year, remember that you need to take time each day for your spiritual exercise!

□ L.S.R.

TO MEMORIZE: *For physical training is of some value, but godliness has value for all things, holding promise for both the present life and the life to come.* 1 Timothy 4:8, NIV

The Weight Lifter

FROM THE BIBLE:
If you point these things out to the brothers, you will be a good minister of Christ Jesus, brought up in the truths of the faith and of the good teaching that you have followed. Have nothing to do with godless myths and old wives' tales; rather, train yourself to be godly. For physical training is of some value, but godliness has value for all things, holding promise for both the present life and the life to come. This is a trustworthy saying that deserves full acceptance (and for this we labor and strive), that we have put our hope in the living God, who is the Savior of all men, and especially of those who believe. Command and teach these things. Don't let anyone look down on you because you are young, but set an example for the believers in speech, in life, in love, in faith and in purity. Until I come, devote yourself to the public reading of Scripture, to preaching and to teaching.
1 Timothy 4:6-13, NIV

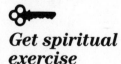

Get spiritual exercise

2

Still the Same

FROM THE BIBLE:

Your word, O LORD, is eternal;
it stands firm in the heavens.
Your faithfulness continues
through all generations; you
established the earth, and it
endures. Your laws endure to
this day, for all things serve you.
Psalm 119:89-91, NIV

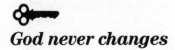

God never changes

DAD JUST walked out on us. Just plain walked out. No reasons, no apologies, no nothing, Andy thought. *I wonder why.* His mom tried to help him accept the situation, but he knew it was hard for her, too. He was sure she didn't really understand it herself.

One day Mom said, "Our house costs too much, Andy. We're going to move into an apartment. It will be a change, but you'll get used to it."

Moving was not something Andy had planned on. As long as he could stay in the same neighborhood and go to the same school, he could pretend things were still the same. But now—a new school and all new kids? Andy didn't like the sound of that at all.

Moving day came, and with it all the changes Andy dreaded. Their church was the only thing that stayed the same, but even there it seemed to Andy as if people acted differently—almost as if they were sorry for him. He didn't like that either.

In Sunday school one day, Mr. Robinson called on Andy to recite the memory verse. "For I am the Lord; I change not," Andy quoted. "Malachi 3:6."

Mr. Robinson nodded. "Even if the whole world seems upside-down, God is always the same," he said. "God loves us and will be with us, just as He was with Abraham in his journeys, with Daniel in the lions' den, and with Jonah in the whale." Mr. Robinson named the familiar Bible characters Andy had heard about all of his life. For the first time, it really meant something to Andy. He realized that, in all the changes that took place in their lives, God's people had found that He had been right there with them.

Andy breathed a quiet little prayer, just between himself and God. "Thank You for staying with Mom and me. I'm glad You're just the same as when Dad was with us. Please help me remember that in all of our changes, You will never go away."

HOW ABOUT YOU? Are you discouraged when changes come? The Bible gives many examples of people who had to learn about God's care during changing circumstances. Their stories are an example to you. God cares for you in difficult times just as He cared for them. □ P.K.

TO MEMORIZE: *I the LORD do not change.*
Malachi 3:6, NIV

"ROBBIE," Mother called. "I told you to get up long ago. Now hurry! We'll soon be leaving for church!" Robbie sleepily opened his eyes. It was so hard to get up in the morning! He put one foot on the floor, then the other. It was cold. He wrapped his blanket around him. "Robbie, are you hurrying?" Mother called from the hallway.

"Yeah, yeah, I'm hurrying," Robbie answered, but he didn't hurry at all. He put on his shirt and pants and then flopped down on the bed again. In fact, the next time Mom checked on him, he was fast asleep.

"You're just going to have to get to bed earlier," his mother sighed as she woke him again.

The following day was Robbie's birthday. All weekend his family had been giving him hints about a very special gift, and as soon as Robbie heard his dad and mom get up, he jumped out of bed, too. He didn't mind that it was early and cold. He threw his clothes on as fast as he could and then ran downstairs to open his gift.

"Hmmmm," Mother said. "This is funny."

"What's funny?" asked Dad.

"It's funny how easy it was for our sleepyhead to get out of bed this morning," said Mother.

"Today's a special day, Mom!" said Robbie, eyeing the big box standing in the center of the table. "Sundays are special days, too, Son," replied Mother. "Sundays are days we set apart to learn more about God's Word and to worship Him."

"Right," agreed Dad. "Going to church is a privilege we take too much for granted. We forget that it's special."

Robbie looked at his birthday present. He knew his parents were right. Then and there he decided he was going to take the ribbon from the birthday gift and pin it to his bulletin board. It would be a reminder that Sunday was a special day, and that it should be at least as important to him as his birthday.

HOW ABOUT YOU? Do you have trouble getting up for church? Maybe sometimes you don't get there at all! Or maybe Sunday morning is a hassle at your house because your dad and mom always have to be yelling at you to hurry up and get moving. Treat Sunday as a special day. Get to bed early on Saturday so you'll be ready to serve and worship the Lord on Sunday. □ L.W.

TO MEMORIZE: *This is the day which the LORD has made; we will rejoice and be glad in it.*
Psalm 118:24, NKJV

Time to Get Up!

FROM THE BIBLE:
I was glad when they said to me, "Let us go into the house of the LORD." Our feet have been standing within your gates, O Jerusalem! Jerusalem is built as a city that is compact together, where the tribes go up, the tribes of the LORD, to the Testimony of Israel, to give thanks to the name of the LORD. For thrones are set there for judgment, the thrones of the house of David. Pray for the peace of Jerusalem: "May they prosper who love you. Peace be within your walls, prosperity within your palaces." For the sake of my brethren and companions, I will now say, "Peace be within you." Because of the house of the LORD our God I will seek your good.
Psalm 122, NKJV

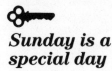

Sunday is a special day

The Old Mansion

FROM THE BIBLE:

So it was, when they came, that he looked at Eliab and said, "Surely the LORD's anointed is before Him." But the LORD said to Samuel, "Do not look at his appearance or at the height of his stature, because I have refused him. For the LORD does not see as man sees; for man looks at the outward appearance, but the LORD looks at the heart." So Jesse called Abinadab, and made him pass before Samuel. And he said, "Neither has the LORD chosen this one." . . . Thus Jesse made seven of his sons pass before Samuel. And Samuel said to Jesse, "The LORD has not chosen these." And Samuel said to Jesse, "Are all the young men here?" Then he said, "There remains yet the youngest, and there he is, keeping the sheep." And Samuel said to Jesse, "Send and bring him. For we will not sit down till he comes here." So he sent and brought him in. Now he was ruddy, with bright eyes, and good-looking. And the LORD said, "Arise, anoint him; for this is the one!"

1 Samuel 16:6-12, NKJV

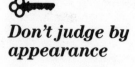

Don't judge by appearance

"I CAN HARDLY wait to see the old mansion!" exclaimed Ashley. She and her family were on their way to visit Grandma and Grandpa White, who had become caretakers of a large estate. As they drove, Ashley talked about her day at school. "There's a new girl in class, and her clothes are totally out of it. I was so embarrassed when our teacher asked me to show her around the school."

Mother frowned. "Sounds like you have an attitude problem," she said.

Several hours later, Dad turned down an overgrown lane. "This looks a lot more like a dump than a mansion!" Ashley exclaimed when she saw the house.

But when her grandparents welcomed them and led them in, Ashley could hardly believe her eyes. The floors glistened, and carpeted steps curved from the hallway to the second floor. "Oh, wow!" she said again and again. "This is so nice, and the outside's so awful."

Grandpa smiled. "Yes," he said. "The old place is being restored, but the firm which was hired for the outside work can't begin till next month. That's why there's such a difference between the inside and outside."

"Just like the inside and the outside of some people," commented Mother as she looked at Ashley.

"What do you mean?" asked Ashley.

"I was thinking of that new girl at school," Mother said. "Didn't you just assume she wasn't a nice person because of the way she dressed? The Lord tells us that the heart of a person is much more important than the way she looks."

Ashley looked around the beautiful house and then at the overgrown front yard. Her mother was right. She did judge people by the way they looked on the outside, and that was wrong.

"I'm going to get to know that new girl," she told her mother quietly.

HOW ABOUT YOU? Do you reject someone just because of the clothes he wears and the way he combs his hair? Think about that boy or girl in your class who's left out because of the way he or she looks. Remember, God says it's the inside that counts. Will you be a friend to that lonely boy or girl? Find out what he or she is really like. Do it for Jesus. □ L.W.

TO MEMORIZE: *Do not judge according to appearance, but judge with righteous judgment.* John 7:24, NKJV

I T WAS TIME to measure again. Bill was eager to see how much he'd grown. For four years now, Dad had marked the new height on his closet door.

"When Aunt Alice comes from the mission field," Bill said, "she'll see a big change in me!"

"Four years makes quite a difference," his dad agreed. "Just think, she'll be here next week."

Bill remembered the day Aunt Alice had left for the mission field. It was the same day he'd made his decision to live for Jesus Christ and let Him be Savior and Lord. Aunt Alice had been so pleased. She'd hugged him when they saw her off at the airport. "I suppose you'll be practically grown by the time I come home again," she had said. "Be sure to grow in grace, too!"

And now Aunt Alice was due to return. Bill knew she would see a difference in his physical growth. But would she see spiritual growth as well? He decided to ask Dad about it.

Dad smiled. "That's a good question," he said, "one we should all ask ourselves. Now, let's see— in what areas have you had problems? I seem to recall that you used to have a terrible time with your temper. Has that changed?"

"I got mad at Joe last week, and I told him off," Bill confessed. "But I did apologize later."

Dad nodded. "I'd say that's progress, wouldn't you? I'm also thinking of the boys you've been inviting to Sunday school. I think you've made progress in witnessing."

"I'll call Tom this afternoon and invite him to come along tomorrow," said Bill hastily, remembering a boy he had been avoiding.

"How about Bible knowledge?" asked Dad. "Do you know more about God than you did when Aunt Alice left?"

Bill nodded. "Quite a bit, I think. I've learned lots of verses and worked hard on my Sunday school lessons."

Yes, Bill thought, *maybe Aunt Alice would see some spiritual growth.*

HOW ABOUT YOU? Have you taken inventory to see if you've grown spiritually? Do you spend time with God, learning from His Word and talking to Him? Do you witness more than you once did? Are you more friendly, kind, and loving than you used to be? If marks could be put on the wall for spiritual growth, how would your chart look? □ R.J.

TO MEMORIZE: *Grow in the grace and knowledge of our Lord and Savior Jesus Christ.*
2 Peter 3:18, NIV

Growing Two Ways

FROM THE BIBLE:
And we pray this in order that you may live a life worthy of the Lord and may please him in every way: bearing fruit in every good work, growing in the knowledge of God, being strengthened with all power according to his glorious might so that you may have great endurance and patience, and joyfully giving thanks to the Father, who has qualified you to share in the inheritance of the saints in the kingdom of light.
Colossians 1:10-12, NIV

Grow spiritually

6

Unlimited Treasure

FROM THE BIBLE:

God's laws are perfect. They protect us, make us wise, and give us joy and light. God's laws are pure, eternal, just. They are more desirable than gold. They are sweeter than honey dripping from a honeycomb. For they warn us away from harm and give success to those who obey them.

Psalm 19:7-11, TLB

The Bible is valuable

"**O**H, MOM, what smells so good?" Christy asked as she put her schoolbooks on the kitchen table. "It smells like Grandma's backyard when the lilacs are blooming."

Mother smiled. "You're right, Christy. A friend at work gave me a bottle of perfume for my birthday. It's called Lilac Love. Her husband works at the cosmetic company where it's made, so she gets perfume at a discount."

Christy picked up the bottle. "Can I try some?"

"Sure," Mother agreed.

Every now and then during the next few weeks, Christy would smell lilacs and know her mother had been using the new perfume.

One day Christy and her mother were at a department store, looking for a new dress for Christy. "Mom, look." Christy pulled on her mother's hand as they were passing the perfume counter. "There's a bottle of Lilac Love."

"Sure enough!" Mother stopped to look at the display.

"Look at this!" Christy exclaimed. "It costs thirty-nine dollars and ninety-five cents!"

"Oh, my! I had no idea it cost that much!" groaned Mother. "Here I've been using it just about every day! If I had known how expensive it was, I would have saved it for special occasions."

Christy smiled. "It's just like my Sunday school teacher said about the Bible," she said. "Most people have a Bible, but they don't understand how valuable it is."

"You're so right, Christy," agreed Mother. "The Bible is even more valuable than expensive perfume! But the wonderful thing about the Bible is that we can use it every day and we'll never run out of it!"

HOW ABOUT YOU? Do you realize how important the Bible is? Do you realize that it explains how you can have eternal life? Do you know that it gives you guidelines for living your life? Some people don't know it's the inspired Word of God. Thank the Lord for giving you the Bible. Study it and find the hidden treasures inside. □ L.W.

TO MEMORIZE: *The law from your mouth is more precious to me than thousands of pieces of silver and gold.* Psalm 119:72, NIV

"MOM, LOOK! I've got an application to work at the corner store sweeping and stuff. See, here it is." Craig was so excited, he couldn't stop talking. This would be his first job. "Who can I give as references?" he asked.

Mother suggested the Ferrins from their church, but Craig looked a little sheepish. "I cut in front of Mrs. Ferrin at the store the other day," he said. "I was in a hurry, so I pretended I didn't see her, but I think she knew."

Looking disappointed, Mother next suggested the Days. Craig had to explain that Mr. Day had caught him hitting a little boy over the head with his empty lunch box. "I was just trying to look tough in front of the other guys," he admitted. "I didn't really hurt the kid."

"Craig," said Mother in a serious tone, "I think you're finding out how important all your actions are. But put the application away for now. It's time for supper."

After the evening meal, Craig's father took the big family Bible, and together they read from Acts 16. "Hmmmm. That's interesting," murmured Mother. "It seems that before Paul took Timothy with him on a missionary journey, he asked for references."

"Yeah," said Craig, "and I'll bet Timothy was relieved when he found that the men gave him a good report. It would be pretty exciting to go on a missionary trip with Paul!"

"It sure would," agreed Mother. "Can you imagine what would have happened if they'd said, 'Well, Tim's a pretty good kid, but we saw him hit a little kid over the head with his lunch box'?"

Craig laughed but quickly became serious. "You're right, Mom," he said. "I'm going to watch my behavior after this."

HOW ABOUT YOU? If you needed a good reference for something very important to you, would you have a difficult time finding one? Do you forget that people are observing your actions? Do you sometimes say unkind things or tease other kids? Little things that don't seem so bad to you at the time can affect other people's opinions of you. Ask Jesus to show you things you do that may be hurting your testimony to others. □ P.R.

TO MEMORIZE: *Don't let anyone look down on you because you are young, but set an example for the believers in speech, in life, in love, in faith and in purity.* 1 Timothy 4:12, NIV

References

FROM THE BIBLE:
Paul and Silas went first to Derbe and then on to Lystra where they met Timothy, a believer whose mother was a Christian Jewess but his father a Greek. Timothy was well thought of by the brothers in Lystra and Iconium, so Paul asked him to join them on their journey. In deference to the Jews of the area, he circumcised Timothy before they left, for everyone knew that his father was a Greek [and hadn't permitted this before]. Then they went from city to city, making known the decision concerning the Gentiles, as decided by the apostles and elders in Jerusalem. So the church grew daily in faith and numbers. Acts 16:1-5, TLB

All actions are important

JANUARY

8

Raging Waves

FROM THE BIBLE:

I felt I had to write and urge you to contend for the faith that was once for all entrusted to the saints. For certain men whose condemnation was written about long ago have secretly slipped in among you. They are godless men, who change the grace of our God into a license for immorality and deny Jesus Christ our only Sovereign and Lord. . . . These men are blemishes at your love feasts, eating with you without the slightest qualm—shepherds who feed only themselves. They are clouds without rain, blown along by the wind; autumn trees, without fruit and up-rooted—twice dead. They are wild waves of the sea, foaming up their shame; wandering stars, for whom blackest dark-ness has been reserved forever. . . . These men are grumblers and faultfinders; they follow their own evil desires; they boast about themselves and flatter others for their own advantage. But, dear friends, remember what the apostles of our Lord Jesus Christ foretold.
Jude 3-4, 12-13, 16-17, NIV

Learn what the Bible says

GREG WAS VISITING his grandparents in Florida. It was fun being outdoors in the sunshine, especially when he thought about the cold and snow at home in Minnesota. The neatest thing about visiting his grandparents was that they lived so close to the Atlantic Ocean. In fact, they could walk to the beach from their house.

One evening, Greg and his grandfather were playing catch. It was windy, and they could hear the waves beating against the rocks even though they were a couple of blocks away. "I've never heard the waves sound so loud," Greg said.

"They do get wild and noisy sometimes," Grandpa agreed. "Would you like to walk down and see them?"

"Sure." After Greg put his ball and glove in the house, he and his grandfather walked to the ocean. "Wow! Look at those waves!" Greg exclaimed. The water was crashing against the shoreline, sending spray high into the air.

"They're fun to watch," agreed Grandpa, "but the people who live in the houses along here are concerned because the water level is high, and it's washing away some of the soil from their yards. The waves are fascinating, but they're also quite destructive. Many homeowners have had to build stronger breakwaters to try to stop the erosion."

"And that probably costs a lot of money," said Greg.

"Right." Grandpa nodded. "By the way, Greg, did you know that the Letter of Jude uses waves to describe people who teach false doctrine? Jude says that those who twist and change what is writ-ten in the Bible are like raging waves of the sea, destroying the people who believe what they say."

"I'm glad I believe in the Lord Jesus," Greg said quietly, "and I'm glad I go to a church where the truth is preached."

HOW ABOUT YOU? Have you ever watched waves beat against the shore? They're interesting, but they can do a lot of damage. Remember, raging waves are a picture of false teachers who some-times use words that sound as if they come from the Bible. They may be interesting, but they're preaching their own doctrine, not God's. Learn what God's Word says so you will not be fooled by these "raging waves." □ L.W.

TO MEMORIZE: *Dear friends, remember what the apostles of our Lord Jesus Christ foretold.*
Jude 17, NIV

The Wax Figures

RENEE WAS HELPING her mother with some of the wax figurines that were to be displayed at the crafts fair. "Keep working on the figurines while the wax is still hot," encouraged Mother. "Remember, it's easier to form them while the wax is soft."

Renee nodded, but a few minutes later the telephone startled her, and she dashed off to answer it. It was Beth, her very best friend from school, and the girls talked for quite some time. By the time Renee hung up the phone, more than fifteen minutes had passed.

Back in the family room, Renee picked up her figurine. The wax had hardened, and it was almost impossible to form the figure as she wanted. Noticing this, her mother spoke. "That reminds me of something we've talked about before, Renee—the importance of giving yourself to Christ while you're young and allowing God to mold you as He wants. When people get older, they often become cold and hard, just as that wax did. Then they're often less interested in being saved. It concerns me very much that you have not yet accepted Jesus as your Savior."

Slowly Renee nodded her head. "You know, Mother, I was thinking of that, too. Beth just told me that her neighbor Mr. Jackson died. I remember hearing Grandpa tell us how he witnessed to old Mr. Jackson for years and years. I guess he never did accept the Lord." Renee paused and looked at the cold, hard wax. "I don't want to be like this. I want to accept Jesus now."

HOW ABOUT YOU? Have you accepted Jesus as your Savior? Maybe you think you'll do so later, when you're older. Remember, when you get older, you could become cold and hard toward the gospel of Christ. Come to Jesus today. □ R.P.

TO MEMORIZE: *Remember now your Creator in the days of your youth.* Ecclesiastes 12:1, NKJV

FROM THE BIBLE:
Rejoice, O young man, in your youth, and let your heart cheer you in the days of your youth; walk in the ways of your heart, and in the sight of your eyes; but know that for all these God will bring you into judgment. Therefore remove sorrow from your heart, and put away evil from your flesh, for childhood and youth are vanity. . . . Remember now your Creator in the days of your youth, before the difficult days come, and the years draw near when you say, "I have no pleasure in them." Ecclesiastes 11:9-10; 12:1, NKJV

Accept Jesus now

JANUARY

10

Never Again

FROM THE BIBLE:

For none of us lives to himself,
and no one dies to himself. For
if we live, we live to the Lord;
and if we die, we die to the
Lord. Therefore, whether we live
or die, we are the Lord's. For to
this end Christ died and rose
and lived again, that He might
be Lord of both the dead and the
living. But why do you judge
your brother? Or why do you
show contempt for your brother?
For we shall all stand before the
judgment seat of Christ. For it
is written: "As I live, says the
Lord, every knee shall bow to
Me, and every tongue shall
confess to God." So then each of
us shall give account of himself
to God.
Romans 14:7-12, NKJV

You're accountable
to God

"OKAY, KID. We've been watching you. Come with us." Cold fear chilled the back of Bob's neck. The woman who had spoken signaled a big man nearby, who immediately moved to Bob's side.

Where's Chuck? wondered Bob. *Taking a few candy bars was his idea, and now he's just disappeared into thin air.* Bob's thoughts raced through his mind as he walked with bent head between the two security guards.

In a small room the unsmiling woman said, "Open your jacket and put everything on the table." Then Bob was asked questions about everything: his name, address, school, parents, friends. Had he ever shoplifted before? Was he alone in the store? On and on. Bob thought it would never end. "Okay, Bob. Call your parents," the lady guard said finally.

"Oh no, please," protested Bob. "I'll never do—"

"You have to call them," interrupted the woman. "You're accountable to your parents."

When Bob heard his mother's voice on the phone, he tried not to cry while he explained the awful thing that had happened. "I'll be right there," said Mother.

Mother came, but Bob couldn't look at her. She spoke gently. "Why, Bob? You know better." The sadness of her tone made him feel like the lowest thing in the world. And the worst wasn't over yet. He still had to face his father.

When Bob's father heard about it, he said, "You've made your mother and me very sad today, Son, and you've made it necessary for us to punish you. But I want you to think about something else. How do you think God feels? As His child, you're accountable to Him too, you know."

Bob nodded solemnly. "I've told Him I'm sorry, too," he replied quietly. "I'll never do it again. I promise."

HOW ABOUT YOU? When you do something you know is wrong, is it hard to face people? When you know you've hurt your parents, is it hard to look them in the eye? Just as you are accountable to your parents, you are also accountable to God. Confess those things you've done wrong. Ask Him to help you live in such a way that your meeting with Him will be a joyful experience, not a fearful one. □ P.K.

TO MEMORIZE: *Each of us shall give account of himself to God.* Romans 14:12, NKJV

ERICA LOVED to entertain her little brothers, Bobby and Billy. "Lie down," she'd say, "and I'll read to you." The boys would lie wide-eyed and quiet as Erica read to them and showed them the pictures in the colorful books.

After reading one day, Erica took one of the books to her mother. "You know this book you bought at the garage sale?" she asked. "It says ponies are baby horses. Aren't baby horses called 'foals'?"

Mother nodded. She looked through the book. "Ponies are really a type of small horse," she said. "They're smaller than regular horses even when they're grown up. Whoever wrote this book made a mistake. I'm glad you're thinking about what you read because you can't always agree with everything people write. Just because something is in a book doesn't mean it's true." Then she handed Erica a bowl. "Let's bake some cookies," she said. "I have a new recipe that sounds great!"

They followed the directions carefully, but when they tasted the first batch of freshly baked cookies, both Erica and her mother frowned. "These don't taste quite right," Erica said.

"I think they have too much salt in them," said Mother. "I wondered about that while we mixed them, but I assumed the cookbook must be right."

"I guess cookbooks can be wrong just like kid's books," observed Erica.

"You have to be careful with any book written by people," counseled Mother. "Any time you read, you have to think, 'Is this true or false? Good or bad?' There's only one book you don't have to question."

"I know what that is!" Erica said. "The Bible."

Mom nodded. "That's right," she agreed. "The Bible is always true."

HOW ABOUT YOU? Do you believe everything you read? Remember, people aren't perfect and can make mistakes. People are also sinful and can write things the Bible says are wrong. The only book you can fully trust is the Bible. □ S.N.

TO MEMORIZE: *For the word of the LORD is right and true; he is faithful in all he does.* Psalm 33:4, NIV

Ponies and Cookies

FROM THE BIBLE:
And by that same mighty power he has given us all the other rich and wonderful blessings he promised; for instance, the promise to save us from the lust and rottenness all around us, and to give us his own character. . . . So we have seen and proved that what the prophets said came true. You will do well to pay close attention to everything they have written, for, like lights shining into dark corners, their words help us to understand many things that otherwise would be dark and difficult. But when you consider the wonderful truth of the prophets' words, then the light will dawn in your souls and Christ the Morning Star will shine in your hearts. . . . For no prophecy recorded in Scripture was ever thought up by the prophet himself. It was the Holy Spirit within these godly men who gave them true messages from God. 2 Peter 1:4, 19-21, TLB

Think about what you read

12

Secret Sin

FROM THE BIBLE:

The acts of the sinful nature are obvious: sexual immorality, impurity and debauchery; idolatry and witchcraft; hatred, discord, jealousy, fits of rage, selfish ambition, dissensions, factions and envy; drunkenness, orgies, and the like. I warn you, as I did before, that those who live like this will not inherit the kingdom of God. . . . Those who belong to Christ Jesus have crucified the sinful nature with its passions and desires. Since we live by the Spirit, let us keep in step with the Spirit.
Galatians 5:19-21, 24-25, NIV

Don't ever do wrong

"QUICK! Someone's coming." David's friend Brian whispered the warning, and David punched the button on the VCR remote control just in time.

"There it is," said Mom, coming into the den. She walked to the desk, picked up the dictionary, and left.

David knew he shouldn't turn the VCR back on. The movie Brian had brought over had violent scenes and bad language.

After supper, David's younger sister Carolyn was contentedly sucking her thumb. "What's that in your mouth?" Dad asked. Carolyn quickly took her thumb out of her mouth. Later that evening, David noticed Carolyn lying on the couch, her head buried under a pillow. He sneaked over and pulled the pillow off his sister's head. Carolyn was again sucking away on her thumb!

"Sucking your thumb may damage your teeth whether anyone sees you do it or not," Dad told her gently.

"That's right," said Mom. "Hiding while you do it won't make the damage any less." She paused, then added, "Hiding any damaging activity from others never lessens the damage done to your body—or to your mind and spirit."

It seemed to David that Mom looked right at him while she spoke. He didn't think she knew about the movie, but the damage was done anyway. He couldn't forget the violence he had seen or the bad language he had heard. Besides that, he was aware that God knew all about it.

As David prayed later that night, he confessed what he had done. He also asked God to give him courage to say no the next time he was tempted to do wrong things in secret.

The test came a few days later. "My dad has this great R-rated movie," Brian told him one day. "We can watch it before my folks get home."

"No, thanks," said David. "I don't care if our parents don't know. We know, and God knows."

HOW ABOUT YOU? Do you read magazines, watch movies, or listen to music in secret? If so, is it because you know it's wrong? You can't keep a wrong activity from hurting you by hiding it from others. And you can't hide what you do from God—He will hold you responsible, even for these things others don't know about. □ K.R.A.

TO MEMORIZE: *Anyone who does wrong will be repaid for his wrong, and there is no favoritism.*
Colossians 3:25, NIV

13

Don't Reap the Corners

TONY LIKED to hang around his father's small hardware store and watch as Dad worked on repair jobs. One Saturday he sat in the back room while Dad fiddled with a broken toaster. Finally Dad set the toaster down with a grin. "All finished," he said. On a small card he wrote, "Labor, one hour—$7.50." Then he took several minutes to clean and shine the toaster.

Tony frowned. "Dad, you counted wrong," he said. "I know you worked on that thing for at least an hour and ten minutes, besides the time you spent cleaning it." When his father just smiled, Tony continued. "And another thing, a lot of times I've seen you round off the amount somebody owes you. But you always make it lower, not higher. How are you ever going to make money that way?"

"Oh, I'm managing," Dad replied cheerfully. "I believe that if I give my customers good service and try not to charge any more than I have to, they'll keep coming back to my store. Besides, the Bible teaches that we shouldn't 'reap the corners.' "

Tony looked confused. "Huh? I don't get it."

"Well, in Leviticus, God told farmers to leave some of their crop behind when they harvested it, so that needy people could take what they wanted. I don't have a farm, but I figure that the principle applies to my business, too. It means that I shouldn't try to squeeze every nickel I can out of my customers. I should 'leave the corners' for them."

"If the farmer did all the work, he should get to keep all the harvest," objected Tony.

"But it's God who gives us the strength to work, and He blesses our efforts," Dad reminded him. "You've got a good head for business, Son, but you need to learn to be more generous. Even if nobody else notices, God will!"

HOW ABOUT YOU? Do you cheat others in little ways—practicing an instrument for twenty minutes instead of thirty, skipping chores when you think Mom won't notice, doing a sloppy job on your schoolwork because you know the teacher will accept it anyway? You should begin making an effort to do a little more than what is required of you. God will certainly reward your "extra" efforts, and it will earn you a good reputation in the eyes of others as well. □ S.K.

TO MEMORIZE: *One man pretends to be rich, yet has nothing; another pretends to be poor, yet has great wealth.* Proverbs 13:7, NIV

FROM THE BIBLE:
[The LORD said to Moses:]
"When you reap the harvest of your land, do not reap to the very edges of your field or gather the gleanings of your harvest. Do not go over your vineyard a second time or pick up the grapes that have fallen. Leave them for the poor and the alien. I am the LORD your God. Do not steal. Do not lie. Do not deceive one another. Do not swear falsely by my name and so profane the name of your God. I am the LORD. When you reap the harvest of your land, do not reap to the very edges of your field or gather the gleanings of your harvest. Leave them for the poor and the alien. I am the LORD your God."
Leviticus 19:9-12; 23:22, NIV

Be generous, not greedy

JANUARY

Dogs or Cats?

FROM THE BIBLE:

O Lord, what a variety you have made! And in wisdom you have made them all! The earth is full of your riches. There before me lies the mighty ocean, teeming with life of every kind, both great and small. And look! See the ships! And over there, the whale you made to play in the sea. Every one of these depends on you to give them daily food. You supply it, and they gather it. You open wide your hand to feed them and they are satisfied with all your bountiful provision. But if you turn away from them, then all is lost. And when you gather up their breath, they die and turn again to dust. Then you send your Spirit, and new life is born to replenish all the living of the earth. Praise God forever! How he must rejoice in all his work!
Psalm 104:24-31, TLB

Even animals can teach

"**W**HICH DO YOU like best, Grandma," asked Missy, "your dog or your cat? Mom says I can get either one, and I'm trying to decide which I'd rather have."

Grandma picked up Ashes, the cat, and sat with her pet on her lap. Ashes jumped down. "Well, Ashes can be quite aloof. Dusty, on the other hand, is always willing to accept my attention."

"I think I'd rather have a dog, then," Missy decided.

"Both animals can teach us lessons about ourselves and our relationship to God," Grandma continued. She picked up a ball and threw it down the hall. "Fetch, Dusty," she said. Dusty chased after the ball, brought it back, and laid it down. Dusty wagged her tail, waiting for the ball to be thrown again. "She'll fetch as long as I throw. She wants to do what pleases me."

"And we should want to please God, right?" asked Missy, as Ashes rubbed against her leg. "What do you learn from your cat?"

Suddenly a ball of gray fur landed on Grandma's lap. Grandma stroked the cat's head. "When Ashes does jump on my lap, it's special, because it's her choice to come to me," said Grandma. "Do you remember the robots we saw at the science fair that did whatever they were commanded to do? Would you like a hug from a robot?"

"No," giggled Missy. "It would be hard, and a hug from a robot wouldn't mean much."

"We aren't robots, either," said Grandma. "God created us with a free will. He is pleased when, on our own, we come to Him."

"So your dog shows us we should want to please God by doing what He wants," Missy said, "and your cat shows us how God wants us to give to Him our love and attention. But which do you like best?"

"God created each one special in its own way, and I like them both," Grandma said with a smile. "You'll just have to make up your own mind as to which you would rather have."

HOW ABOUT YOU? Do you have a pet? Do you like almost any animal? God made them all, and He often teaches lessons through them. Treat all animals with kindness and watch their behavior to see if the Lord will use some animal to teach you an important lesson. □ V.L.C.

TO MEMORIZE: *For every animal of the forest is mine, and the cattle on a thousand hills.*
Psalm 50:10, NIV

WHEN KENT'S Sunday school teacher suggested that the class go together to watch the space shuttle launch, Kent was thrilled. He had been wishing he could somehow have a really good view of the event. The week seemed to pass slowly, but finally Saturday arrived. Kent and six other excited boys met Mr. Marshall at church, and it was a wide-awake group that boarded the church van.

"Hope we're early enough to get a good view," exclaimed Kent—and they were! About an hour after they reached their viewing point the big space shuttle was launched. The bright red light and the trail that followed the lift-off was something Kent would never forget.

Back in the van, Mr. Marshall turned on the radio so they could listen to an announcer review what had taken place. They also heard the space control center talk with the astronauts.

"Well," said Mr. Marshall, "whenever you think of what you saw this morning, I want you to remember that all Christians will participate in a 'lift-off' someday."

"Hey, that's right," said Kent. "You mean when Jesus comes, don't you?"

"Exactly," answered Mr. Marshall. "When He returns, He'll be taking all Christians to live in heaven with Him."

"And we won't even need a spaceship, will we?" asked one of the boys.

"No," agreed Mr. Marshall. "It will all happen quick as a flash, or as the Bible puts it, 'in the twinkling of an eye.' " He looked at the boys. "I'm glad you all made it to the lift-off today. My prayer is that each of you will also be ready for that wonderful event when Jesus comes again."

HOW ABOUT YOU? When Jesus returns in the clouds, those who have confessed their sins and asked for God's forgiveness will rise to be with Him. Are you one who has done that? If not, you will not be "taken up" in that wonderful event that Christians look forward to. Prepare now by accepting Christ as Savior today. □ R.J.

TO MEMORIZE: *And if I go and prepare a place for you, I will come back and take you to be with me that you also may be where I am.* John 14:3, NIV

JANUARY

15

The Big Event

FROM THE BIBLE:
"Do not let your hearts be troubled. Trust in God; trust also in me. In my Father's house are many rooms; if it were not so, I would have told you. I am going there to prepare a place for you. And if I go and prepare a place for you, I will come back and take you to be with me that you also may be where I am. You know the way to the place where I am going."
Thomas said to him, "Lord, we don't know where you are going, so how can we know the way?"
Jesus answered, "I am the way and the truth and the life. No one comes to the Father except through me."
John 14:1-6, NIV

Be ready for Christ's return

JANUARY

16

I Remember

FROM THE BIBLE:
You have said, "It is futile to serve God. What did we gain by carrying out his requirements and going about like mourners before the LORD Almighty? But now we call the arrogant blessed. Certainly the evildoers prosper, and even those who challenge God escape." Then those who feared the LORD talked with each other, and the LORD listened and heard. A scroll of remembrance was written in his presence concerning those who feared the LORD and honored his name. "They will be mine," says the LORD Almighty, "in the day when I make up my treasured possession. I will spare them, just as in compassion a man spares his son who serves him. And you will again see the distinction between the righteous and the wicked, between those who serve God and those who do not."
Malachi 3:14-18, NIV

Build good memories

DANNY CARLSON had never been to a funeral, but now his grandfather had died. He felt nervous about attending the service. "Just keep remembering all the wonderful things Grandfather taught you," his mother said, "and keep in mind that this is only his body in the casket. He is with the Lord in heaven."

Danny nodded. He knew that everyone would die someday unless Jesus came back first. And he knew that when Christians die, they go to be with Jesus.

"Death is not to be feared if we are part of God's family," his mother was saying now. "Of course, we'll miss Grandfather, and that makes us feel sad. But we can be happy for him, and we can be thankful for the wonderful memories we have of him."

Danny's father put down his newspaper and joined the conversation. "Danny, what do you remember most about Grandfather?" he asked.

Danny thought for a minute. "I remember how nice he was to me and how he helped other people and . . ." Danny paused, then added, "And the way he prayed for me."

"Your grandfather would be so pleased to know he was remembered for those things," said Dad with a smile. "When the time comes for me to die, I want to leave good memories, too."

Those words stayed with Danny the rest of the day. When he went to bed, he prayed, thanking God for the years he had had with a godly grandfather and asking the Lord Jesus to help him be the kind of Christian who would leave good memories when his life was over.

HOW ABOUT YOU? When the time comes for God to call you home, what memories will you leave behind? More important, what will be written in God's "book of remembrance"? Will it be recorded that you were honest, kind, helpful, and loving? That you prayed for others and served the Lord? Live in such a way that you will be happy to have your deeds remembered by others and by God.
                                                                    □ R.J.

TO MEMORIZE: *A scroll of remembrance was written in his presence concerning those who feared the LORD and honored his name.* Malachi 3:16, NIV

It was Saturday morning, and Janet was hurrying to her Girl Scout leader's home. Her troop was going to make submarine sandwiches for the sale that afternoon. When she arrived, her Scout leader greeted her hurriedly. "Hello, Janet," she said smiling. "You're early. I was just going to go pick up one of the girls who needs a ride. Maybe you could wait here and let the others in."

After Mrs. Powers left, Janet decided to start making the sandwiches. She opened a long roll and piled it with ham, salami, and cheese. Then she wrapped each sandwich in waxed paper and stacked them all on a large tray. *Boy, is this fun!* she thought. *I've got almost a dozen made already.*

When the other girls began to arrive, they were surprised at Janet's progress. Even Mrs. Powers praised her when she returned. "How nice!" she began. Then her expression changed. "Uh-oh," she said. "Janet, you should have washed your hands before you started working."

When Janet looked down at her hands, she blushed. They were filthy. "I'll go wash them right now," she stammered.

"Yes, I think you should," agreed Mrs. Powers, "but we'll also have to set aside all these sandwiches that you made while your hands were dirty. It wouldn't be fair to sell them to the public."

As Janet went to wash her hands, she thought of last week's Sunday school lesson. It was about serving the Lord with unwashed hands. Now, as she turned on the faucet, she remembered that she had goofed off in Sunday school and had argued with her mother about which pew to sit in during church. Then she had sung a solo in church, and she had felt like a hypocrite while singing it. *I guess that was like trying to serve God with unwashed hands,* thought Janet. *Before I try to do anything for Jesus, I'm going to make sure to "wash my hands" first!*

HOW ABOUT YOU? Do you serve the Lord by singing in the choir, helping out in junior church, or working in the nursery? That's good, but being a willing worker is not enough. You need to "wash your hands" by confessing your sins and yielding yourself completely to God. Your heart must be right before God will accept your service. □ S.K.

TO MEMORIZE: *Come near to God and he will come near to you. Wash your hands, you sinners, and purify your hearts, you double-minded.* James 4:8, NIV

Unwashed Hands

FROM THE BIBLE:
Who may ascend the hill of the Lord? Who may stand in his holy place? He who has clean hands and a pure heart, who does not lift up his soul to an idol or swear by what is false. He will receive blessing from the Lord and vindication from God his Savior.
Psalm 24:3-5, NIV

Serve God with clean hands

18

True or False

FROM THE BIBLE:
Depart from evil, and do good; seek peace, and pursue it. The eyes of the LORD are on the righteous, and His ears are open to their cry. The face of the LORD is against those who do evil, to cut off the remembrance of them from the earth. The righteous cry out, and the LORD hears, and delivers them out of all their troubles. The LORD is near to those who have a broken heart, and saves such as have a contrite spirit.
Psalm 34:14-18, NKJV

Be truly sorry for sin

"THE ANSWER is no, Jason. That's final!" Mother was firm. As Jason flung himself out of the room, a swear word exploded from his lips. "Jason! Come back here this minute!" Mother ordered. "Did you say what I think you said?" Jason gritted his teeth and stared at the floor. Mother sighed deeply. "Son, what is the matter with you?" Jason did not answer, and tears filled Mother's eyes. "You will have to be punished for swearing. I'll talk to your father about it this evening."

"But, Mom, I didn't mean to," Jason pleaded. "It just slipped out. I'm sorry. Really I am. All the guys at school say those words, and they stick in my mind. I promise I'll never do it again. I'm sorry. Honest!"

Mother sighed and looked at him closely. "I believe you are," she decided. "Very well. We'll forget it this time."

Later than evening loud, angry words burst from Jason's room. "How many times have I told you to stay out of my stuff?" he roared.

As Mother started down the hall, she heard Tina cry, "But, Jason, I just wanted to borrow a pencil. I didn't mean to break your model. I'm sorry."

"That's what you said when you broke my watch. You're not really sorry! You're just sorry you got caught because you don't want to get in trouble. You cry and think I'll forget about it." Jason did not see his mother come into the room as he bent over to pick up the broken model, swearing softly.

"Jason!" At the sound of Mother's voice, Jason jumped and dropped the model. "Jason, look at me," Mother said. "Tina isn't the only one whose repentance is false. Didn't you tell me this afternoon you were sorry you swore?" Jason nodded slowly. Mother continued. "True repentance is more than saying, 'I'm sorry.' It's being sorry enough for what you have done to stop doing it. Now let's go talk to your father."

HOW ABOUT YOU? Do you ever say, "I'm sorry" simply to keep out of trouble? False repentance might fool others for a while, but it never fools God. □ B.W.

TO MEMORIZE: *Repent, and turn from all your transgressions, so that iniquity will not be your ruin.* Ezekiel 18:30, NKJV

BRENDA WAS in a bad mood. "I don't see why I have to go to that special service at the nursing home Friday night," she grumbled.

"But you told your youth leader you'd be there," said Mother. "When you joined the choir, you knew it would cost you some of your free time."

"What free time?" grumbled Brenda. "Church takes up most of Sunday. Then there's prayer meeting Wednesday night and choir practice Saturday mornings. Besides that, we have family devotions every day, and I pray and read my Bible before I go to bed—most days, anyway." Brenda turned to her little sister Tammy who had come into the room, holding a small box. "Is that your present for Grandma's birthday?"

"Yes—want to see it?" Tammy smiled and lifted the lid off the box. "I hope Grandma likes it."

"Oh, a scarf! That's pretty," Brenda said, "but take off the price tag before you wrap it."

Tammy shook her head. "I'm going to leave it on so Grandma will know it cost a lot!"

"Don't do that, silly," Brenda scolded. "It will seem like you're bragging about how much it cost."

Mother nodded. "I agree with Brenda," she said. "The important thing is not the price of your gift, but the fact that you love Grandma and want to please her."

As Tammy left the room, Brenda laughed. "If Tammy only knew how much Grandma has spent on gifts for her, she wouldn't think what she paid for that scarf was such a big deal." She glanced at Mother. "Why are you looking at me like that?"

"Tammy isn't the only one who leaves her 'price tag' showing," replied Mother. "I just heard you talking about how much you're doing for God and how much it cost you. Perhaps you need to remember just how much God has done for you and what it cost Him."

Brenda turned red. "You're right," she admitted. "He's done far more for me that I could ever do for Him. Going to sing at the nursing home Friday night is no big deal."

HOW ABOUT YOU? Do you think you've made a lot of sacrifices for God? Remember, everything you have was given to you by God. If you truly love Him, you'll serve Him willingly and cheerfully. Don't brag or complain. Just be thankful for all He has done for you. □ S.K.

TO MEMORIZE: *So let each one give as he purposes in his heart, not grudgingly or of necessity; for God loves a cheerful giver.* 2 Corinthians 9:7, NKJV

Price Tags & Presents

FROM THE BIBLE:
Take heed that you do not do your charitable deeds before men, to be seen by them. Otherwise you have no reward from your Father in heaven. Therefore, when you do a charitable deed, do not sound a trumpet before you as the hypocrites do in the synagogues and in the streets, that they may have glory from men. Assuredly, I say to you, they have their reward. But when you do a charitable deed, do not let your left hand know what your right hand is doing, that your charitable deed may be in secret; and your Father who sees in secret will Himself reward you openly. And when you pray, you shall not be like the hypocrites. For they love to pray standing in the synagogues and on the corners of the streets, that they may be seen by men. Assuredly, I say to you, they have their reward. But you, when you pray, go into your room, and when you have shut your door, pray to your Father who is in the secret place; and your Father who sees in secret will reward you openly.
Matthew 6:1-6, NKJV

Serve God cheerfully

JANUARY

20

Get Out of
the Dump

FROM THE BIBLE:
*But the day of the Lord will
come as a thief in the night, in
which the heavens will pass
away with a great noise, and the
elements will melt with fervent
heat; both the earth and the
works that are in it will be
burned up. Therefore, since all
these things will be dissolved,
what manner of persons ought
you to be in holy conduct and
godliness, looking for and
hastening the coming of the day
of God, because of which the
heavens will be dissolved being
on fire, and the elements will
melt with fervent heat? Nevertheless we, according to His
promise, look for new heavens
and a new earth in which
righteousness dwells. Therefore,
beloved, looking forward to these
things, be diligent to be found by
Him in peace, without spot and
blameless.*
2 Peter 3:10-14, NKJV

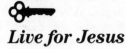

Live for Jesus

STEVE AND HIS FAMILY lived in an area where there was no trash pickup, so he and his dad would put the garbage cans in the back of their truck and take them to the county dump. One afternoon, as he was helping his dad unload the truck at the dump, Steve noticed some mice among the trash heaps.

"I can see why a mouse would love to nest in that trash," Dad said when Steve pointed them out. "There's always plenty of food and lots of papers and things for building materials. But those mice are in for a big shock. Tomorrow night some men from the county are going to burn all this trash. Most of the mice will escape, but their homes, their young ones, and everything else will be lost in the flames."

As Steve and his dad drove away, Steve couldn't resist one last look at the mice, who were cheer-fully scampering about as though they had nothing in the world to worry about. "That's too bad about the mice," he remarked, "but I guess they don't know any better."

When they arrived home, Steve went to his bedroom to change his clothes. As he opened the door, he glanced around. He saw his posters, his records, and his comic books. He saw his baseball mitt, his football, and his model ships. He saw his books and his Boy Scout manual. *Hmmm,* thought Steve. *This stuff won't last! I'd hate to be like those mice, spending all my life on things that are going to be burned up anyway. Maybe it's time I got out of the dump and started spending more time on things that really matter!* Steve swept a pile of comic books into the wastebasket, took his Bible from the dresser drawer, and placed it on his bed-side stand.

HOW ABOUT YOU? How do you spend most of your time? Are you involved in plans, projects, and ac-tivities of this life? These may be good, but they should not take up all your time. Remember, this life and this world are only temporary. Eternal things are what really matter. As the song says, "Only what's done for Christ will last." Get out of the dump! □ S.K.

TO MEMORIZE: *Therefore, since all these things will be dissolved, what manner of persons ought you to be in holy conduct and godliness?*
2 Peter 3:11, NKJV

"Mom, MAY WE buy this cereal today?" Stephanie asked. She held a brightly colored box over the grocery cart as though she were going to put it in. She giggled at Mother's raised eyebrow. "Just kidding, Mom," she said. "I know this one has too much sugar." She replaced it with a different kind. "Is this better?" she asked. Then, with a twinkle in her eye, she parroted Mom's often repeated words, "You are what you eat." Mom smiled and nodded.

When they arrived home, Stephanie flipped on the radio. They listened to a weather report, followed by a musical program. Stephanie hummed the melody of one of the numbers being sung, but Mom reached out and turned off the radio. "The words of that song encourage a kind of life that isn't pleasing to God," she said with a frown.

"But it has a nice tune," protested Stephanie. "Can't we just ignore the words?"

"Listening to that kind of music is like eating food that isn't good for us. Our minds 'eat up' the words whether we pay attention to them or not," Mom explained.

Stephanie thought hard while she helped Mom put the groceries away. She thought about how she often listened to the radio at Nancy's house. She and Nancy were always busy with something else while they listened, but Stephanie knew all the words to the songs they played on Nancy's favorite station, even though she seldom paid attention to them. Something about the music made the words stick in her mind.

"We are what we think about," added Mom. "We should fill our minds with thoughts that are pleasing to God so we'll grow spiritually."

Stephanie found the box of cereal she had chosen and put it in the cupboard. "From now on I'll choose music like I choose breakfast cereal," she decided. She chuckled at the idea. "No more junk food for my mind!"

HOW ABOUT YOU? Do you listen to music or anything else that encourages an unchristian way of life? God is pleased when you listen to things that are uplifting and that help you grow spiritually. What you hear gets into your mind whether you are aware of it or not. God sees what's there. Make sure He is pleased when you "become what you think." □

TO MEMORIZE: *I know what is going through your mind.* Ezekiel 11:5, NIV

Food for Thought

FROM THE BIBLE:
O Lord, you have examined my heart and know everything about me. You know when I sit or stand. When far away you know my every thought. You chart the path ahead of me, and tell me where to stop and rest. Every moment, you know where I am. You know what I am going to say before I even say it. You both precede and follow me, and place your hand of blessing on my head. . . . Search me, O God, and know my heart; test my thoughts. Point out anything you find in me that makes you sad, and lead me along the path of everlasting life.
Psalm 139:1-5, 23-24, TLB

Feed your mind good thoughts

JANUARY

22

All by Myself

FROM THE BIBLE:
*All this came upon King
Nebuchadnezzar. At the end of
the twelve months he was
walking about the royal palace
of Babylon. The king spoke,
saying, "Is not this great
Babylon, that I have built for a
royal dwelling by my mighty
power and for the honor of my
majesty?" While the word was
still in the king's mouth, a voice
fell from heaven: "King
Nebuchadnezzar, to you it is
spoken: the kingdom has
departed from you! And they
shall drive you from men, and
your dwelling shall be with the
beasts of the field. They shall
make you eat grass like oxen;
and seven times shall pass over
you, until you know that the
Most High rules in the kingdom
of men, and gives it to whomever
He chooses." That very hour the
word was fulfilled concerning
Nebuchadnezzar; he was driven
from men and ate grass like
oxen; his body was wet with the
dew of heaven till his hair had
grown like eagles' feathers and
his nails like birds' claws.*
Daniel 4:28-33, NKJV

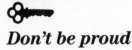

Don't be proud

"LOOK AT THAT neat tree house!"

Sitting on the carpeted floor of his new hideout, Mark heard the voices float up from the street.

"Yeah. That's Mark Patterson's. His dad is a carpenter, so Mark had all the tools and materials he needed. He claims he built it all by himself, but I don't believe him." Mark recognized Delbert's voice. "I could do twice as good with half as much," Delbert bragged.

Mark shook his fist at the backs of the two boys disappearing down the street. "Ha! You couldn't do half as good with twice as much, you mean!"

When his grandparents came the following week, Mark proudly showed Grandpa Patterson his work.

"You did a good job," approved Grandpa. "It's nice to have a carpenter dad to supply knowledge, materials, and tools, isn't it?"

Mark frowned. Delbert had said the same thing. "But I built it!" Mark insisted. "I built it all by myself!"

"There are very few things we can do entirely alone without assistance from anyone else," answered Grandpa.

"You drive a truck by yourself," Mark argued.

"I do and I don't," Grandpa replied. "The company I work for supplies the job and the truck. God gives me the strength and knowledge to drive it. The government builds the highways I drive on. So you see, I'm dependent upon a lot of people for my job. I could never do it all by myself."

Mark grinned. "All right, Grandpa, you win. Dad taught me how to build things. He loaned me his tools, God gave me the strength, and together we built this tree house."

HOW ABOUT YOU? Do you sometimes get proud of your work and forget to be thankful to those who help you? King Nebuchadnezzar bragged about his work and refused to give glory to God. Because he wanted all the credit for himself, God had to deal harshly with him. Don't make the same mistake he did. Take time right now to give thanks to God for helping you. And today be sure to thank some person who has helped you, too. □ B.W.

TO MEMORIZE: *Now I, Nebuchadnezzar, praise and extol and honor the King of heaven, all of whose works are truth, and His ways justice. And those who walk in pride He is able to abase.*
Daniel 4:37, NKJV

THE JOHNSONS—Becky, Bob, Mother, and Dad—had spent the past few days with Grandpa and Grandma Johnson. They treasured the long talks, the jokes, and the delicious food. They hated to leave. It was going to be a long good-bye, for it would be four years before they would meet again. In less than a week, the Johnsons were going to Peru as missionaries.

As they finally prepared to go home, fog settled in. "Oh, dear," moaned Mother, "I just knew we should have left earlier." Since they had brought several items to store in the grandparents' attic, she had driven the family car while Dad drove a truck they had borrowed. "John, how will I ever see the way home?" she murmured as she and the children got into the car.

"The fog lights on this truck will pierce through the mist pretty well, so I'll lead the way," said Dad. "Just follow me and keep your eyes on my taillights. I won't go very fast. Trust me."

Mother nervously gripped the steering wheel, but as the children prayed and sang, she gradually relaxed. It seemed like the trip home would never end, and it wasn't easy, either. When they got safely home, they thanked God for His protection.

"As I was driving, I couldn't help but think that God was using this fog to prepare us for Peru," said Dad. "We couldn't see very far ahead in the fog. Because we're going to an unfamiliar country, the future seems especially 'foggy' to us. The people, customs, and language are unknown to us, and we don't know just what's ahead, but God knows all about it. He'll take care of us."

"That's right," agreed Mother. "I had your taillights to guide me, and we have the Lord to guide us as we go to Peru. We can trust Him."

HOW ABOUT YOU? Does an unknown future upset you? Do you worry about a different school, an unfamiliar town, a new family or stepparent, or a new challenge awaiting you? God knows your fear and your future. Read His Word for instruction and encouragement. Pray to Him for wisdom. He'll guide you because He knows the path that you should take. □ J.H.

TO MEMORIZE: *For this is God, Our God forever and ever; He will be our guide even to death.* Psalm 48:14, NKJV

23

A Sure Guide

FROM THE BIBLE:
The Lord has paid me with his blessings, for I have done what is right, and I am pure of heart. This he knows, for he watches my every step. Lord, how merciful you are to those who are merciful. And you do not punish those who run from evil. You give blessings to the pure but pain to those who leave your paths. You deliver the humble but condemn the proud and haughty ones. You have turned on my light! The Lord my God has made my darkness turn to light. Now in your strength I can scale any wall, attack any troop. What a God he is! How perfect in every way! All his promises prove true. He is a shield for everyone who hides behind him. For who is God except our Lord? Who but he is as a rock? He fills me with strength and protects me wherever I go. He gives me the surefootedness of a mountain goat upon the crags. He leads me safely along the top of the cliffs. Psalm 18:24-33, TLB

Jesus will guide you

JANUARY

24

Part of the Team

FROM THE BIBLE:
And so, dear brothers, I plead with you to give your bodies to God. Let them be a living sacrifice, holy—the kind he can accept. When you think of what he has done for you, is this too much to ask? Don't copy the behavior and customs of this world, but be a new and different person with a fresh newness in all you do and think. Then you will learn from your own experience how his ways will really satisfy you. As God's messenger I give each of you God's warning: Be honest in your estimate of yourselves, measuring your value by how much faith God has given you.

Just as there are many parts to our bodies, so it is with Christ's body. We are all parts of it, and it takes every one of us to make it complete, for we each have different work to do. So we belong to each other, and each needs all the others.
Romans 12:1-5, TLB

Teamwork is important

"I'M TIRED of Bible club," complained Megan as she came into the kitchen. "I didn't feel like playing during game time today, but my leader said I had to, so I did. Then the other kids on my team got mad at me because they said I wasn't trying hard enough. Let them try hard if they like it so well. I didn't feel like it."

"Well," said Dad, "you can't blame them too much if they were unhappy with you. You were part of the team, and a team can't work well unless all the members participate enthusiastically. Besides, there may have been new clubbers there—perhaps even some unsaved kids who were wondering what being a Christian is all about—and your grouchiness is what they saw."

"Oh, Dad! They didn't need me," grumbled Megan as she went to her room. A moment later her dad heard her scream, "Jason, stop it! Stop it this instant!"

"What's going on?" asked Dad as he hurried down the hall.

"Jason broke my alarm clock," Megan answered, pointing to her two-year-old brother.

Dad examined the clock. "Well," he said, "it looks okay, except for the hour hand. But you don't need that!"

"Dad!" protested Megan. "That's ridiculous. I can't tell time without the hour hand. You know that!"

"Oh," Dad said with a smile, "you mean all the parts are important?"

"Of course." Megan looked at her dad. "You're tricking me! I know what you're saying. Just like a clock can't work unless all the parts are working, a team can't work without all the members playing."

Dad playfully tugged Megan's pigtail. "You're exactly right!" he agreed.

HOW ABOUT YOU? Do you play on a team? Do you help the team win, or are you a complainer, often whining that things are unfair or that you don't like the way the leader has told you to do something? As a Christian, you have a responsibility to be a joyful member of your team. The Lord wants you to work in unity with other Christians. Be a willing participant. Be a testimony by your attitude. □ L.W.

TO MEMORIZE: *If a kingdom is divided against itself, that kingdom cannot stand.* Mark 3:24, NIV

"JANICE," said Mother one Saturday afternoon, "I'm going down to the estate sale at the end of the block. Do you want to come?"

"Sure," Janice replied eagerly. "Is it like a garage sale?"

"In a way," answered Mother, "but in this case, the lady who lived in the house died, and her relatives are having the sale to dispose of all the things she's collected over the years."

The two walked down the block to a large brick house where a number of people were milling about, examining furniture, dishes, and other objects. After looking it all over, Mother paid for some glassware she had selected, and they walked out.

Janice was unusually quiet on the way home. "You know, Mom," she said finally, "I'd sure hate to think that someday people might be going through my things, and even taking some of them home."

"That idea does give one a strange feeling," agreed Mother, "and that makes me think of something else." She looked at her daughter seriously. "It's not only our worldly possessions that will be exposed when we die. The Bible says that someday the records in heaven will be opened, and all of our thoughts and actions will be exposed. We won't be able to keep any secrets as we stand before God."

"That makes me want to live as good a life as I can," mused Janice.

"Yes," Mother, nodding, said. "I feel that way, too. I'm so glad that I've accepted Jesus as my Savior. If I hadn't, some day I'd have to stand before God and admit that I refused His salvation. Wouldn't that be dreadful?"

"I never thought of it that way." Janice smiled. "I'm glad I know Jesus as my Savior, too!"

HOW ABOUT YOU? Do you ever wonder what it will be like to meet God someday? That day is going to come, and many of the things that seem important now will be meaningless then. Have you prepared for your eternal future? Be sure you know Jesus Christ as your Savior. If you haven't yet done so, accept Him today. □ S.K.

TO MEMORIZE: *Man is destined to die once, and after that to face judgment.* Hebrews 9:27, NIV

No More Secrets

FROM THE BIBLE:
The crowds grew until thousands upon thousands were milling about and crushing each other. He turned now to his disciples and warned them, "More than anything else, beware of these Pharisees and the way they pretend to be good when they aren't. But such hypocrisy cannot be hidden forever. It will become as evident as yeast in dough. Whatever they have said in the dark shall be heard in the light, and what you have whispered in the inner rooms shall be broadcast from the housetops for all to hear! Dear friends, don't be afraid of these who want to murder you. They can only kill the body; they have no power over your souls. But I'll tell you whom to fear—fear God who has the power to kill and then cast into hell."
Luke 12:1-5, TLB

No more secrets

26

World of Wars

FROM THE BIBLE:

Jesus answered: "Watch out that no one deceives you. For many will come in my name, claiming, 'I am the Christ,' and will deceive many. You will hear of wars and rumors of wars, but see to it that you are not alarmed. Such things must happen, but the end is still to come. Nation will rise against nation, and kingdom against kingdom. There will be famines and earthquakes in various places. All these are the beginning of birth pains. Then you will be handed over to be persecuted and put to death, and you will be hated by all nations because of me. At that time many will turn away from the faith and will betray and hate each other, and many false prophets will appear and deceive many people. Because of the increase of wickedness, the love of most will grow cold, but he who stands firm to the end will be saved. And this gospel of the kingdom will be preached in the whole world as a testimony to all nations, and then the end will come."

Matthew 24:4-14, NIV

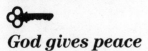

God gives peace

"**B**OY, HAVE I got a hard assignment tonight," Billy announced as he and his brother and sister sat down at the kitchen table to do their homework. "I have to memorize a bunch of dates about the Civil War. We're going to be tested on it tomorrow."

"And I'm learning about the different battles of the Revolutionary War," said John.

"All I have to do is go through the newspaper and cut out articles for our current events project," Joanie told her brothers. "That doesn't sound too hard compared to what you guys have to do."

"Just make sure you don't cut any of the comics," said Billy, grinning.

The three children worked quietly for awhile, then Joanie sighed. "Almost all the articles in this paper are about troubles and wars in one place or another."

"I wonder how come," said Billy. "Politicians are always talking about making the world a better place, but things just seem to be getting worse!"

"That's true," agreed Mother, who had just walked into the room, "but as Christians, we shouldn't be surprised. The Bible says there will always be wars and rumors of war. Men talk about peace, but their desire for power gets in the way. God is left completely out of the picture."

"It's kind of scary," Joanie said. "It makes me glad I'm a Christian."

"Right." Mom smiled. "As Christians, we can have peace of mind no matter what happens here on earth."

HOW ABOUT YOU? Do you ever wonder why the world is not getting better as so many politicians promise? Do you wonder why there are so many wars? Men, because they are human, cannot get along with each other. They refuse to listen to God and follow His way. Isn't it good to know that in spite of the chaos in the world around you, you can put your trust in God and have peace? □ L.W.

TO MEMORIZE: *The peace of God, which transcends all understanding, will guard your hearts and your minds in Christ Jesus.* Philippians 4:7, NIV

27

Peas or Peelings

IT WAS LUNCHTIME, and Karen watched in amusement as her little brother Kyle sat stubbornly shaking his head, refusing to eat the strained peas Mother was offering him on a spoon.

"Maybe you should give him some applesauce," suggested Karen. "He always like that."

"No," responded Mother, "he has to learn to eat what we give him and what he needs." Mother took Kyle out of his chair and set him on the floor. "Maybe he'll be more reasonable if we let him get good and hungry before we try feeding him again."

A short time later, Karen heard a rustling noise coming from behind the kitchen door. There was Kyle, rummaging in the trash bag. Paper towels and empty cans were strewn about, and clenched between his teeth was an old banana peel. "Oh, Mother! Look at this!" laughed Karen as she cleaned up the mess.

Mother rushed to the rescue, but Kyle cried when she took the banana peel out of his mouth. "Shame on you, rooting around in the garbage after refusing the good lunch I made for you!" Mother scolded. But little Kyle just didn't understand. He kept trying to get back into the trash, and finally Mother put him in his playpen.

"Wasn't that silly, Mom?" asked Karen. "Kyle sure doesn't know what's good for him, does he?"

"No," Mother replied, "he doesn't." She paused, then added, "Very often Christians don't, either. We neglect the things God has provided for our happiness and growth, and then try to fulfill our needs with earthly possessions and amusements. But those things are only so much 'garbage' compared with the things of the Lord. They are 'peelings,' not 'peas.' "

"You're right, we are like that," Karen agreed, turning off the TV. "I think I'll go do my Sunday school lesson."

HOW ABOUT YOU? Do you have a need in your life? A need for fellowship? For spiritual growth? For emotional fulfillment? For a sense of achievement? The things of this world will never satisfy these needs. Let God do it. Read His Word. Talk to Him. Sing His praises with other Christians. Whatever your need, give God the chance to satisfy it. □ S.K.

TO MEMORIZE: *My God will meet all your needs according to his glorious riches in Christ Jesus.* Philippians 4:19, NIV

FROM THE BIBLE:
The LORD is my shepherd; I shall not want. He makes me to lie down in green pastures; He leads me beside the still waters. He restores my soul; He leads me in the paths of righteousness for His name's sake. Yea, though I walk through the valley of the shadow of death, I will fear no evil; for You are with me; Your rod and Your staff, they comfort me. You prepare a table before me in the presence of my enemies; You anoint my head with oil; my cup runs over. Surely goodness and mercy shall follow me all the days of my life; and I will dwell in the house of the LORD forever.
Psalm 23, NKJV

God meets needs

28

Stop That Noise!

FROM THE BIBLE:

Though I speak with the tongues of men and of angels, but have not love, I have become as sounding brass or a clanging cymbal. And though I have the gift of prophecy, and understand all mysteries and all knowledge, and though I have all faith, so that I could remove mountains, but have not love, I am nothing. And though I bestow all my goods to feed the poor, and though I give my body to be burned, but have not love, it profits me nothing.
1 Corinthians 13:1-3, NKJV

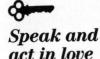

Speak and act in love

"**B**YE, MARCIE. See you tomorrow," said Paige. "And congratulations for getting the lead in the play." As soon as Marcie had gone, Paige mumbled, "I can't stand that girl! She's a snob."

"Why, Paige!" exclaimed her mother. "Didn't you tell me you've been witnessing to Marcie?"

"I'm trying," retorted Paige. "I did walk home with her, didn't I? I even invited her in for a snack." A horrible clanging noise started coming from her brother's room. "What's that noise?" she asked.

Mother laughed. "Pete borrowed Grandpa's antique dinner gong for his science project about sound."

"That thing!" Paige groaned. Grandpa collected brass antiques. Paige liked most of them, but the gong was ugly. Now Pete would probably be banging it all evening!

Pete banged the gong right outside Paige's door while she was doing her homework. "Mom!" Paige screamed. "Make him stop!"

Instead of saying anything to Pete, Mother came into Paige's room and sat down. "I don't like that noise any better than you do," she said, "but when I thought of our conversation about Marcie this afternoon, I decided to let Pete clang it a little. I thought it might teach you something." She handed Paige an open Bible. "Here, read the first verse of 1 Corinthians 13."

Paige knew that 1 Corinthians 13 was often called the "love chapter," but she didn't know what that had to do with the gong. When she saw the first verse, though, she simply said, "Oh."

"Do you understand?" Mother asked.

Paige nodded slowly. "Yes. Saying that I want Marcie to know the Lord and then treating her the way I do is like the sound of that brass gong Pete is clanging. It's just a bunch of noise without any value."

"That's exactly right," her mother agreed. "Now, why don't you think about those verses, and I'll go tell Pete to quit banging that gong!"

HOW ABOUT YOU? Do you pretend to like someone while inside you're really thinking mean thoughts? If there's someone who really bugs you, ask the Lord to help you sincerely care about that boy or girl so that you can show him or her God's love.
□ L.W.

TO MEMORIZE: *Though I speak with the tongues of men and of angels, but have not love, I have become as sounding brass or a clanging cymbal.*
1 Corinthians 13:1, NKJV

LEROY EAGERLY TORE the wrapping paper off the birthday present his parents had given him. "Oh, wow! Binoculars! Thanks!" he exclaimed, quickly pulling them out of the box. He turned them over and over in his hands. "Can we go to the state forest reserve? It has some good lookout points where I could try these out. I bet I can see a long way."

"Sounds great!" agreed Dad. "Let's go!"

Before long, LeRoy and his dad stood together on one of the park's lookout points and took turns looking through the binoculars. As LeRoy took a turn, he silently watched something for a moment. "Dad! I see a doe and twin fawns," he whispered. "They're so cute! Look!" Dad took the binoculars his son offered and soon located the animals. He watched them for a minute. "Aren't they neat?" whispered LeRoy.

Dad laughed and handed the binoculars back. "Yes, they are," he said out loud. "But you don't need to whisper."

LeRoy looked again. "Just think, those animals have no idea we're watching them," he said in awe. "We can see every move they make, but they're so far away that they don't even know we exist!"

"That is amazing," agreed Dad, "and it reminds me that we're being watched, too."

"We are? Who's watching us?" LeRoy wanted to know.

"God is. He's watching every move we make, whether it be right or wrong," explained Dad. "He sees the mistakes we make, and He sees the good things we do. Yet we're often unaware of His presence, just as the doe and fawns are unaware of us."

"I knew that, but I never thought about it quite that way," said LeRoy. "I think I'll be more careful of what I do if I remember that God is always watching."

HOW ABOUT YOU? Are you aware that God sees you twenty-four hours a day? Remembering that God's presence is always with you should help you make better decisions. Next time you're tempted to do something wrong, remember, God is watching! Next time you become discouraged in your efforts to do what is right, remember, God is watching! He sees you all the time. □ V.R.

TO MEMORIZE: *A man's ways are in full view of the LORD, and he examines all his paths.* Proverbs 5:21, NIV

The Binoculars

FROM THE BIBLE:
Does he not see my ways and count my every step? If I have walked in falsehood or my foot has hurried after deceit—let God weigh me in honest scales and he will know that I am blameless.
Job 31:4-6, NIV

From heaven the LORD looks down and sees all mankind; from his dwelling place he watches all who live on earth— he who forms the hearts of all, who considers everything they do.
Psalm 33:13-15, NIV

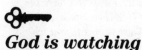

God is watching

30

False Labels

FROM THE BIBLE:

Everyone who believes that Jesus is the Christ is born of God, and everyone who loves the father loves his child as well. We accept man's testimony, but God's testimony is greater because it is the testimony of God, which he has given about his Son. Anyone who believes in the Son of God has this testimony in his heart. Anyone who does not believe God has made him out to be a liar, because he has not believed the testimony God has given about his Son. And this is the testimony: God has given us eternal life, and this life is in his Son. He who has the Son has life; he who does not have the Son of God does not have life. I write these things to you who believe in the name of the Son of God so that you may know that you have eternal life.

1 John 5:1, 9-13, NIV

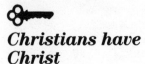

Christians have Christ

BARB'S SUNDAY SCHOOL class was having a slumber party at the Gordon's cottage. "Sleep well," said Mrs. Gordon, the teacher, "and be sure to bring your Bibles to breakfast tomorrow. We'll start the day with some spiritual food."

It was a sleepy looking bunch of girls that assembled in the dining room the next morning. Their eyes opened wider, however, as they surveyed the table. "Pickles? For breakfast?" Rhonda spoke for them all.

"Oh no," replied Mrs. Gordon. "Right after devotions we'll have bacon and eggs, cereal, sweet rolls—quite a variety this morning. And I want you all to be sure to try my own luscious strawberry jam!" She picked up a huge jar from the table and held it high for all to see.

"Jam!" exclaimed Barb. "That's a jar of pickles!"

Mrs. Gordon looked surprised. "Right here it says 'strawberry jam,' " she insisted.

Beth spoke up. "I don't care what the label says. What's inside is what counts, and I see pickles!"

Mrs. Gordon smiled. "You're right, of course. In order for this label to be correct, we would have to take out the pickles, wash the jar carefully, and fill it with strawberry jam." She looked at the girls around the table. "I hope none of you are like this jar of 'jam'—wearing a false label. Most of you girls wear the label 'Christian.' However, just as a jar of strawberry jam must have jam inside, a Christian must have Christ."

Mrs. Gordon picked up her Bible. "Turn with me to 1 John 5," she said. After they finished reading, Mrs. Gordon spoke again. "This passage tells us that if we do not have the Son, Jesus Christ, we do not have life. We can look inside this jar and see what's there. We can't look inside one another, however, but God can. Does He see Christ?"

HOW ABOUT YOU? Many people call themselves Christians. Do you? Calling yourself a Christian does not make you one. To be a Christian, you must admit that you are a sinner and believe on Jesus Christ, the Son of God. Believe that He died for you, that He rose again, and that He will forgive your sins. Ask Him to give you eternal life. He will.

□ H.M.

TO MEMORIZE: *He who has the Son has life; he who does not have the Son of God does not have life.*
1 John 5:12, NIV

"I STILL DON'T see why I have to go!" Shanna slammed the car door. "Why can't I take care of Shawn at home? Why do I have to baby-sit in a waiting room?"

Mother shook her head. "I've explained that we're going to Grandma's house right after we visit Aunt Ruth at the hospital. It would take too long to go back home for you."

Shanna snorted and then curled up in the corner and pouted. At the hospital, she rummaged through the magazines on a table and then picked up one she knew her parents would never allow her to read at home.

"Read your story out loud to me," Shawn begged.

Shanna grinned slyly. "I don't think so." She handed him another magazine. "Here, you look at the pictures." She was so engrossed in her reading that she jumped when a voice at her shoulder said, "Time to go, Shanna."

"Huh? Time to go?" Shanna asked in confusion. "Oh, time to go to Grandma's. Come on, Shawn." She saw Mother glance at the magazine she was hastily trying to slip under the stack on the table. "How was Aunt Ruth?" Shanna asked quickly. "What's wrong with her?"

"She has cancer," Dad replied. At Shanna's gasp, he continued, "But she'll probably be fine. Because she went to the doctor at the first warning symptom, they found it in the early stages."

Shanna let out a big sigh. "Oh, that's good."

"It's important to heed early warnings," Mother said as they entered the empty elevator. "I see some danger signals in your life, Shanna." Shanna hung her head, and Mother continued, "Your attitude for one thing, and your reading material for another, tell me that you need a spiritual checkup. Sin is like a dreadful cancer."

As Shanna wiped a tear from her cheek, Dad spoke up. "Heeding a physical warning symptom may have saved Aunt Ruth's life. Heeding the warnings your mother and I have given you could save you lots of trouble."

HOW ABOUT YOU? Have you been warned about your attitude or actions lately? Did you resent it? It could be a blessing in disguise. An early warning could save you from trouble later. Work on the problem area in your life today. □ B.W.

TO MEMORIZE: *If he had taken warning, he would have saved himself.* Ezekiel 33:5, NIV

31

Checkup Time

FROM THE BIBLE:
Here is a sample of John's preaching to the crowds that came for baptism: "You brood of snakes! You are trying to escape hell without truly turning to God! That is why you want to be baptized! First go and prove by the way you live that you really have repented. And don't think you are safe because you are descendants of Abraham. That isn't enough. God can produce children of Abraham from these desert stones! The axe of his judgment is poised over you, ready to sever your roots and cut you down. Yes, every tree that does not produce good fruit will be chopped down and thrown into the fire."
Luke 3:7-9, TLB

Heed early warnings

1

To Grandma, with Love

FROM THE BIBLE:

And being in Bethany at the house of Simon the leper, as He sat at the table, a woman came having an alabaster flask of very costly oil of spikenard. And she broke the flask and poured it on His head. But there were some who were indignant among themselves, and said, "Why was this fragrant oil wasted? For it might have been sold for more than three hundred denarii and given to the poor." And they criticized her sharply. But Jesus said, "Let her alone. Why do you trouble her? She has done a good work for Me. For you have the poor with you always, and whenever you wish you may do them good; but Me you do not have always. She has done what she could. She has come beforehand to anoint My body for burial. Assuredly, I say to you, wherever this gospel is preached throughout the whole world, what this woman did will also be spoken of as a memorial to her."

Mark 14:3-9, NKJV

Serve God in love

JOHN BUSILY worked on a picture for his grandmother, who would be coming for a visit soon. He finished drawing a house, then worked on trees and other objects. John enjoyed art, and his teacher had told him he had a talent for it. "There!" he said, checking the finished picture to make sure he had done it as well as he could.

Nearby John's younger sister, Sara, worked on a picture of her own. "Mine's done, too," she said, holding it up.

"Looks like scribbling to me," John scoffed.

When Grandma arrived, John gave her his drawing. "My, but this is good work, John," Grandma exclaimed. When Sara shyly held out her picture, Grandma exclaimed over it, too. But she noticed John's scowl.

Later, when John and Grandma were alone, she asked him about it. "You seemed displeased when I praised Sara for her picture. Why?"

"It wasn't as good as mine," replied John. "It was just scribbling. Why would you like it?"

"I saw the love that went into it," Grandma explained. "I saw that Sara had worked just as hard to please me as you had. Maybe it wasn't done with a practiced hand, as yours was, but the love was there."

John still looked a little doubtful, but he nodded slowly. "I guess that means you'd love me just as much if I couldn't draw well," he said. Then he added with a smile, "And that's good."

"That's right," agreed Grandma. "Shall I tell you something else that's good? God sees the things we do for Him out of love. We see some actions, or deeds, as being little or unimportant, but they're important to God because He notices the love put into them. Giving a helping hand, a friendly smile, or an encouraging word is just as important to God as any other job."

HOW ABOUT YOU? Do you sometimes feel that what you have done for God may be more important than what someone else has done? Or perhaps you feel your actions are less important. God sees the love in your deeds, no matter what they are. All acts done in love are precious in God's sight.

□ C.Y.

TO MEMORIZE: *She has done what she could.* Mark 14:8, NKJV

"BE QUIET, DAISY," murmured Ellen sleepily as she burrowed deeper into her bed. The barking continued, but Ellen scarcely heard it. Suddenly, *thump!* A hairy body landed on the bed beside her, still barking furiously. Annoyed, Ellen pushed the dog away. "Be still," she commanded again. Daisy ran down the hall toward Ellen's parents' room. Then *thump!* She was back again, pouncing on Ellen, dashing away, then pouncing again and again, all the while barking loudly. Ellen sat up, very much annoyed. "You stupid dog," she grumbled. "Let me sleep! You lie down and be still!" But the dog ran out the door, barking and looking back to see if Ellen was following.

Ellen sniffed the air. What was that smell? Smoke! It was smoke! She leaped from her bed and ran into the hall where her parents were just coming from their room. Soon they were all out in the yard, waiting for the fire trucks to arrive.

The next morning, Ellen read about the fire in the newspaper. "Dog Saves Home—Wakes Family before Much Damage Is Done," she read. She hugged Daisy. "Sorry I got mad at you," she apologized. "I'm glad you kept on pestering me even when I scolded you."

Mother looked over at Ellen. "Sometimes it's good to be awakened, isn't it?" she said thoughtfully. "That will be a good thing for you to keep in mind when you see your friend Alicia again."

"Alicia?" asked Ellen. "What do you mean?"

"You were just telling me that you thought maybe you shouldn't invite Alicia to Sunday school or try to witness to her anymore because it seems to annoy her. In a way she's saying, 'Let me sleep.' But she needs to be awakened to her need of accepting Jesus into her life," explained Mother. "Daisy loved you enough to keep after you even when you didn't like it. Maybe you need to love Alicia that way, too."

Slowly, Ellen nodded. "It's important enough to take a chance on annoying her a little, isn't it?"

HOW ABOUT YOU? Are you afraid to witness to your friends because they might be annoyed or angry? Even if they are, how serious will that be? Not nearly as serious as if they never awaken to their need of Jesus. Don't give up witnessing to them.

□ H.M.

TO MEMORIZE: *To the weak I became weak, to win the weak. I have become all things to all men so that by all possible means I might save some.*
1 Corinthians 9:22, NIV

Let Me Sleep

FROM THE BIBLE:
*The word of the L*ORD *came to me, saying, "Son of man, I have made you a watchman for the house of Israel; . . . When I say to the wicked, 'You shall surely die,' and you give him no warning, nor speak to warn the wicked from his wicked way, to save his life, that same wicked man shall die in his iniquity; but his blood I will require at your hand. Yet, if you warn the wicked, and he does not turn from his wickedness, nor from his wicked way, he shall die in his iniquity; but you have delivered your soul. Again, when a righteous man turns from his righteousness and commits iniquity, and I lay a stumbling block before him, he shall die; because you did not give him warning, he shall die in his sin, and his righteousness which he has done shall not be remembered; but his blood I will require at your hand. Nevertheless if you warn the righteous man that the righteous should not sin, and he does not sin, he shall surely live because he took warning; also you will have delivered your soul."*
Ezekiel 3:16-21, NKJV

Keep witnessing

3

In Shape

FROM THE BIBLE:

Anyone who wants to follow me must put aside his own desires and conveniences and carry his cross with him every day and keep close to me! Whoever loses his life for my sake will save it, but whoever insists on keeping his life will lose it; and what profit is there in gaining the whole world when it means forfeiting one's self? When I, the Messiah, come in my glory and in the glory of the Father and the holy angels, I will be ashamed then of all who are ashamed of me and of my words now.
Luke 9:23-26, TLB

Get daily spiritual exercise

DON HAD NEVER been so glad to see the end of a week. Band camp had been hard work! There had been fun times like the huge pillow fight the other night, but for the most part, this week of camp had been too much work. What a way to spend Christmas vacation!

On Monday, Don had played his trumpet so long and so hard that he'd split his lip, and the nurse had given him ointment to soothe it. He had to admit, though, that after all the hours of practice this week, his lips were stronger.

It wasn't just his lips that had been put to the test. Every morning the band had gotten up and done exercises at six o'clock. They had also marched two hours each day. After the first day, Don's legs had been so sore he felt like he never wanted to walk again! But his legs felt really strong and tough now that the week was over.

The very first day back at school, Don turned his ankle in gym and had to stay off it for several days. He was almost glad. At least he didn't have to march with the band! They were preparing for a long parade, and Mr. Artz, the band director, was really making them work hard.

Then just as Don was getting ready to rejoin the band, he got the flu. Now he began to get worried. He *did* want to march in that parade. He hoped nothing else would happen to him!

And nothing did. On the day of the parade he was feeling fine. Mr. Artz wasn't quite sure that Don would be up to marching, but he gave in to Don's pleas. Off Don marched with the band. He couldn't believe how tired it made him!

At church the next day, Pastor Stewart talked about being spiritually strong. "Our spiritual lives are like our physical lives," concluded the pastor. "We don't have to do anything to get *out* of shape, but we must exercise daily to stay *in* shape."

Don knew exactly what the pastor meant, and he knew that he had allowed himself to get out of shape spiritually, too. He asked the Lord to help him get his spiritual body back in shape and keep it that way.

HOW ABOUT YOU? Is your spirit out of shape from lack of exercise? Doing nothing will get you out of shape very quickly, so discipline yourself to read the Bible, pray, and live for Jesus every day.
□ R.P.

TO MEMORIZE: *I try with all my strength to always maintain a clear conscience before God and man.*
Acts 24:16, TLB

"**I** FEEL TERRIBLE," Tim complained. "I can hardly breathe, and my throat is so sore."

"I know," sympathized Mother. "Here's some juice for you. Just stay on the couch. In a few days your cold will be better."

A short time later Tim called his mother. "I still feel terrible," he said in a whining voice.

Mother brought a wet cloth for Tim's forehead, fixed his pillow, and tucked his cover around him. "Now you just rest," she said.

But Tim didn't feel like resting. He kept on moaning, sighing, and whining until finally Mother said, "Tim, I've done all I can for you. I know you're uncomfortable and that it's not fun to be sick. But you must learn not to complain. The Bible tells us to be patient in tribulation."

"What's tribulation?" asked Tim.

"It's a circumstance that makes you miserable or unhappy," said Mom. "That could mean not feeling well, or it could be other things that aren't pleasant."

"But I hate being sick. How can I be patient about that?" Tim argued.

"Complaining won't help you or anyone else. In fact, it will make you and those around you feel worse. If you learn to be cheerful and uncomplaining even when you're not feeling well, you bring glory to God," explained Mom. "Follow Jesus' example. He didn't complain when He suffered."

"Well, I never knew the Bible said anything about how to act when I have a cold," said Tim. "Okay, from now on I'll try to be more patient, but it's going to be hard."

"Asking the Lord for help will make it easier," Mom said.

HOW ABOUT YOU? When you're sick do you complain about your aches and pains all the time? It is necessary to let your parents know if you're not feeling well, but once you're getting treatment, there's no need to keep on complaining. Instead, think happy thoughts, and thank God for all the blessings you do have. □ C.Y.

TO MEMORIZE: *Be glad for all God is planning for you. Be patient in trouble, and prayerful always.* Romans 12:12, TLB

Aches and Pains

FROM THE BIBLE:
So now, since we have been made right in God's sight by faith in his promises, we can have real peace with him because of what Jesus Christ our Lord has done for us. For because of our faith, he has brought us into this place of highest privilege where we now stand, and we confidently and joyfully look forward to actually becoming all that God has had in mind for us to be. We can rejoice, too, when we run into problems and trials, for we know that they are good for us—they help us learn to be patient. And patience develops strength of character in us and helps us trust God more each time we use it until finally our hope and faith are strong and steady. Then, when that happens, we are able to hold our heads high no matter what happens and know that all is well, for we know how dearly God loves us, and we feel this warm love everywhere within us because God has given us the Holy Spirit to fill our hearts with his love.
Romans 5:1-5, TLB

Be patient in tribulation

FEBRUARY

5

A Cushion
for Chaos

FROM THE BIBLE:

*Love your enemies, do good to
those who hate you, bless those
who curse you, pray for those
who mistreat you. If someone
strikes you on one cheek, turn to
him the other also. If someone
takes your cloak, do not stop
him from taking your tunic.
Give to everyone who asks you,
and if anyone takes what
belongs to you, do not demand it
back. Do to others as you would
have them do to you. If you love
those who love you, what credit
is that to you? Even "sinners"
love those who love them. And if
you do good to those who are
good to you, what credit is that
to you? Even "sinners" do that.
And if you lend to those from
whom you expect repayment,
what credit is that to you? Even
"sinners" lend to "sinners,"
expecting to be repaid in full.
But love your enemies, do good
to them, and lend to them
without expecting to get anything
back. Then your reward will be
great, and you will be sons of
the Most High, because he is
kind to the ungrateful and
wicked. Be merciful, just as
your Father is merciful.*
Luke 6:27-36, NIV

*Cushion anger
with kindness*

DING, DONG! The doorbell had been ringing
for several minutes, but Jane and her family were
so busy arguing that they hadn't even heard it.
Loud, angry words were flying back and forth
when Jane finally noticed her friend Pam tapping
on the living room window. Embarrassed, she
quickly went outside and closed the door behind
her. "I'm sorry, Pam," she said. "I forgot you were
coming over. You see, I was kind of tied up in a—a
family discussion." She paused when she saw Pam
looking at her sympathetically. "Well," continued
Jane, "actually, it was a fight."

"Yes, I heard," said Pam softly. "I didn't mean
to eavesdrop, but I couldn't help overhearing."

Jane sighed. "I don't know why we can't get
along," she said. "We're all Christians, even though
none of us acts like it most of the time. I don't
want to argue with my parents and my brother.
And I don't think they like the fighting, either. But
what can I do about it?"

Just then Jane and Pam heard the squeal of
brakes and a crash. They rushed out to the street
and saw that a car had banged into the back of a
truck at a traffic light. The drivers looked the cars
over carefully. "I'm sorry I ran into you," said one
of them.

The other smiled and said, "I don't see any
damage. My rubber bumper guards cushioned the
impact."

As Jane and Pam walked back toward Jane's
house, Pam said thoughtfully, "That accident made
me think of something. The bumper guards were
like a cushion, so no damage was done. Maybe
you need to be like a cushion whenever someone
is grumpy with you. The Bible says, 'A gentle
answer turns away wrath.' Maybe if you answer
softly and kindly it will help the situation in your
house."

"I'll try it," Jane decided. "Something's got to
be done. Maybe if I act as a 'cushion,' it will help
to stop the 'chaos' at our house!"

HOW ABOUT YOU? When someone is angry with
you, do you reply sharply? Or do you keep your
temper and try to answer quietly and patiently?
The way you respond to anger can make a real
difference in your home and in your whole life.
□ S.K.

TO MEMORIZE: *A soft answer turns away wrath,
but a harsh word stirs up anger.*
Proverbs 15:1, NKJV

"ONE HUNDRED, two hundred, three, four, five," counted the dark-haired man as he placed green bills on the table in front of Ernie's father. A short time later, the man drove off with the family's older car.

Ernie was curious. "Dad," he said, "you let that man have our old car for only five hundred dollars. Is that all it's worth?"

Ernie's father smiled. "The money wasn't the total price of the car," he explained. "It was a down payment. He's going to pay the rest of it later."

"Oh, I see." Ernie nodded. "But, what if he changes his mind and decides not to buy it?"

"Then he'd lose the five hundred dollars," replied Dad, "but he wouldn't make such a down payment unless he honestly intended to buy the car." Dad grinned at Ernie. "In the old days, people used to call a down payment 'earnest money.' An 'earnest' is something that shows proof of a person's sincerity when he says he wants to buy something. It's a guarantee. In the Bible, the Holy Spirit is called the 'guarantee of our inheritance.' That means that God has given us His Holy Spirit to live inside us as proof that He will redeem us completely someday."

"That's neat, Dad," said Ernie. "Say, what if you change your mind and try to get the car back?"

"That wouldn't be honest," replied Dad. "When I accepted the down payment, I gave up my right to own the car." Ernie began to look uncomfortable as Dad continued. "I'm afraid we're not always that honest with God. Even though we've given ourselves to Jesus and received the Holy Spirit, we sometimes try to take our lives back and have our own way. God has been honest with us. We need to be honest with Him, too."

Ernie nodded. "From now on, I'm going to let my name remind me of the 'earnest' God gave me, and I'll be honest with Him."

HOW ABOUT YOU? Have you given your life to Jesus Christ? If so, the Bible says that God has given you His Holy Spirit as a "down payment" until you receive the rest of His wonderful blessings in heaven. God won't back out on His promise to you. So don't try to take over the control of your own life again after you've given it up to Him. Be honest with God! □ S.K.

TO MEMORIZE: *The Spirit's seal upon us means that God has already purchased us and that he guarantees to bring us to himself.* Ephesians 1:13-14, TLB

Honest Ernest

FROM THE BIBLE:
When the time is ripe he will gather us all together from wherever we are—in heaven or on earth—to be with him in Christ, forever. Moreover, because of what Christ has done we have become gifts to God that he delights in, for as part of God's sovereign plan we were chosen from the beginning to be his, and all things happen just as he decided long ago. God's purpose in this was that we should praise God and give glory to him for doing these mighty things for us, who were the first to trust in Christ. And because of what Christ did, all you others too, who heard the Good News about how to be saved, and trusted Christ, were marked as belonging to Christ by the Holy Spirit, who long ago had been promised to all of us Christians. His presence within us is God's guarantee that he really will give us all that he promised; and the Spirit's seal upon us means that God has already purchased us and that he guarantees to bring us to himself.
Ephesians 1:10-14, TLB

Be honest with God

7

The Broken Thumb

FROM THE BIBLE:

The body is a unit, though it is made up of many parts; and though all its parts are many, they form one body. . . . Now the body is not made up of one part but of many. If the foot should say, "Because I am not a hand, I do not belong to the body," it would not for that reason cease to be part of the body. And if the ear should say, "Because I am not an eye, I do not belong to the body," it would not for that reason cease to be part of the body. If the whole body were an eye, where would the sense of hearing be? If the whole body were an ear, where would the sense of smell be? But in fact God has arranged the parts in the body, every one of them, just as he wanted them to be. If they were all one part, where would the body be? As it is, there are many parts, but one body. The eye cannot say to the hand, "I don't need you!" And the head cannot say to the feet, "I don't need you!" On the contrary, those parts of the body that seem to be weaker are indispensable.

1 Corinthians 12:12, 14-22, NIV

Do your part

SHELLY WAS the junior high youth group secretary, but she had broken her thumb in gym class and was not able to write well. "Could you take notes for me this afternoon?" Shelly asked Sue as the officers met one Sunday.

"Sure," agreed Sue.

As ideas were discussed that afternoon, Doug, their president, offered a suggestion. "How about planning a missions program, giving everyone in the youth group something to do—you know, get everyone involved."

"Sounds like a good idea," commented their leader, Mr. Craig. "As a matter of fact, you'll see that it will fit in nicely with the Bible study I'm planning for the next several weeks. We'll be studying the church, which the Bible often refers to as 'the body' of Christ."

"What about kids who can't do anything?" asked Shelly. "I mean, let's face it, there are some kids in our group who don't seem to have anything to offer at all."

"Let me ask you something, Shelly," replied Mr. Craig. "How important is your thumb?"

"My thumb?" asked Shelly in surprise. "Well, if you had asked me last week, I'd probably have said I could easily live without it. But now that it's broken, I see how much I really need it. What does that have to do with our program?"

"God says that's exactly how it is with His body, the church," explained Mr. Craig. "Some members may seem less important than others, but each one is important for the total body to function properly."

"Oh, I see what you mean," said Shelly. She looked at her thumb. "We can find something for everybody to do," she said with a grin. "They're at least as necessary as a thumb."

HOW ABOUT YOU? Do you ever feel that you don't amount to much in God's family? You shouldn't feel that way because each Christian is an important member of God's body, the church. Can you show concern for others? Give your time? Organize? Make a card to encourage someone? Do your part, and don't forget to include others, too! □ D.R.

TO MEMORIZE: *Now you are the body of Christ, and each one of you is a part of it.*
1 Corinthians 12:27, NIV

KEN AND JESSIE were having a great time on a week-long visit to their grandparents' home. The ground was covered with snow, and they stayed outside for hours, building snow forts, walking on the ice-covered lake, and tramping through the woods. Then they would come in and sip hot chocolate in front of the fire.

One afternoon they persuaded Grandpa to go for a walk with them. They took off down the road, laughing and talking and occasionally even throwing a snowball at each other. Suddenly Grandpa whispered, "Stop, children! Don't move. Look over there!" Ken and Jessie looked where Grandpa was pointing. A huge bird sat on the branch of a tree. "It's an eagle," whispered Grandpa. The children were amazed. They had never seen such a big bird out in the wild. Suddenly, with a powerful flap of its wings, the eagle took off over the treetops.

"Wow!" Ken said. "That's one strong bird!"

"You're exactly right," agreed Grandpa. With a twinkle in his eye, he added, "You can be strong like that, too."

"How?" Kevin asked.

"Those who wait on the Lord shall renew their strength. They shall mount up with wings as eagles," replied Grandpa. "That's in the Bible."

"I've heard that verse, Grandpa," said Jessie, "but I never thought about what it meant before."

"It's a picture," said Grandpa, "a magnificent picture of the strength we have when we put our trust in God."

HOW ABOUT YOU? Do you have problems at school? Do you live in a tough home situation? Is it hard for you to make friends? Trust the Lord to help you. He doesn't promise to take problems away, but He does promise to give the strength needed to handle them. The next time you see a picture of an eagle, think of God's promise. □ L.W.

TO MEMORIZE: *But those who wait on the LORD shall renew their strength; they shall mount up with wings like eagles.* Isaiah 40:31, NKJV

What a Bird!

FROM THE BIBLE:
I plead with you to help me, Lord, for you are my Rock of safety. If you refuse to answer me, I might as well give up and die. Lord, I lift my hands to heaven and implore your help. Oh, listen to my cry. Don't punish me with all the wicked ones who speak so sweetly to their neighbors while planning to murder them. Give them the punishment they so richly deserve! Measure it out to them in proportion to their wickedness; pay them back for all their evil deeds. They care nothing for God or what he has done or what he has made; therefore God will dismantle them like old buildings, never to be rebuilt again. Oh, praise the Lord, for he has listened to my pleadings! He is my strength, my shield from every danger. I trusted in him, and he helped me. Joy rises in my heart until I burst out in songs of praise to him. The Lord protects his people and gives victory to his anointed king. Defend your people, Lord; defend and bless your chosen ones. Lead them like a shepherd and carry them forever in your arms.
Psalm 28, TLB

God gives strength

FEBRUARY

Who's Your Boss?

FROM THE BIBLE:

*Whatever you do, work at it
with all your heart, as working
for the Lord, not for men, since
you know that you will receive
an inheritance from the Lord as
a reward. It is the Lord Christ
you are serving. Anyone who
does wrong will be repaid for his
wrong, and there is no
favoritism.*
Colossians 3:23-25, NIV

Don't follow bad examples

BOB POUNDED his fist into his pillow. The whole thing was unfair! He was sent to his room for saying a bad word, but his father said those same words, and no one punished him.

Hearing noises, Bob glanced out his open window. Three men were working on the road in front of his house. "What do you say we have another little break?" suggested one.

"Sure thing, boss," answered the tallest one. The two men went to sit in the shade of a nearby tree, but the third, a dark-haired man, kept working. Soon the tall man came back and tried to persuade him to join them.

"I've already had my break this afternoon," answered the dark-haired man as he pushed his shovel.

"Haven't we all? But Harry says to take another one, and you know the foreman left him in charge," argued the tall man. "He's the boss this afternoon."

"I don't think he has authority to give us extra time off, though," said the third man. "Mr. Grant said he wanted the job finished today, and we'll have to push to get it done."

"You're crazy to turn down a chance to loaf on the job, especially when the boss invites you," snorted the other.

"Maybe it seems foolish," answered the dark-haired man pleasantly, "but it wouldn't be right for me to take something that isn't mine—time or anything else. Mr. Grant's my first boss, and I do my work for him."

Wow, what a man! Bob thought as he turned from the window. *That guy insists on working even when his temporary boss sets a bad example for him.* Then a new thought struck him. *I should do the same thing when it comes to using bad language. Even though other people say bad words, I should do what my first boss wants—and that's God.* Bob dropped to his knees. "Dear Lord, he prayed, "please help me to use only language that pleases You, even if others don't—including my dad."

HOW ABOUT YOU? It's hard to do what's right when someone you love and respect is setting a poor example. But remember that, first of all, you serve Christ. Do what He approves of, not what others are doing, even if they are parents, teachers, or relatives. □ C.Y.

TO MEMORIZE: *You know that you will receive an inheritance from the Lord as a reward. It is the Lord Christ you are serving.* Colossians 3:24, NIV

TIM AND DALE watched as the construction workers built a new apartment complex on the corner of their street. "It sure is tall and straight," commented Tim. "I wonder how they get a building so straight, especially when they build it on a hill like this."

"I don't know," Dale answered. "Let's go to the hardware store and ask Mr. Jacobs. He knows a lot about buildings."

The boys raced down the street, eager to hear what Mr. Jacobs would have to say. "I can tell that you boys have been thinking, as always," said Mr. Jacobs, who was their Sunday school teacher. "Tell me, do you know what a cornerstone is?"

Tim and Dale looked at each other, and then back at Mr. Jacobs. "No," Tim replied. Dale shrugged his shoulders.

"The cornerstone is a special stone or brick," said Mr. Jacobs. "Accurate instruments are used to lay the cornerstone right at the beginning of the building process. All the other bricks in the building are lined up with it. If the cornerstone is laid straight, the rest of the building will be straight, too, because the other bricks are laid one by one, using the cornerstone as a guide."

"Hey, that's neat!" said Dale enthusiastically.

Mr. Jacobs smiled. "You know, boys, the Bible tells us that Jesus is our cornerstone."

The boys looked surprised. "We aren't buildings," laughed Dale.

"No, but the Bible uses the word *building* when referring to the church—that is, all those who have accepted Jesus as Savior," answered Mr. Jacobs. "It says that Jesus is the cornerstone of His church. Our actions and attitudes must line up with His."

"So when we learn to act and think like Jesus, we help to build His church the way He wants it. Right?" Tim asked.

"It sure is!" replied Mr. Jacobs. "Always let Jesus be your guide."

HOW ABOUT YOU? Do you look to Jesus as your example when you are deciding how to act or think? Jesus was kind, friendly, honest, pure, loving, and everything else that is good and right. He loved God very much and prayed to Him daily. Line your actions up with Him so that you're helping to build God's church His way. □ D.R.

TO MEMORIZE: *Built on the foundation of the apostles and prophets, with Christ Jesus himself as the chief cornerstone.* Ephesians 2:20, NIV

The Cornerstone

FROM THE BIBLE:
Consequently, you are no longer foreigners and aliens, but fellow citizens with God's people and members of God's household, built on the foundation of the apostles and prophets, with Christ Jesus himself as the chief cornerstone. In him the whole building is joined together and rises to become a holy temple in the Lord. And in him you too are being built together to become a dwelling in which God lives by his Spirit.
Ephesians 2:19-22, NIV

Live as Jesus would

11

Surprise Dessert

FROM THE BIBLE:

I heard a loud shout from the throne saying, "Look, the home of God is now among men, and he will live with them and they will be his people; yes, God himself will be among them. He will wipe away all tears from their eyes, and there shall be no more death, nor sorrow, nor crying, nor pain. All of that has gone forever." The city itself was pure, transparent gold, like glass! The twelve gates were made of pearls—each gate from a single pearl! And the main street was pure, transparent gold, like glass. No temple could be seen in the city, for the Lord God Almighty and the Lamb are worshiped in it everywhere. And the city has no need of sun or moon to light it, for the glory of God and of the Lamb illuminate it.

Revelation 21:3, 18, 21-23, TLB

Heaven is wonderful

JIM TOOK a bite of his meat loaf, "We learned about heaven in Sunday school today," he said, "but there's something I don't understand." He frowned. "I know heaven is supposed to be wonderful and all that. But won't it be boring just walking around on the golden streets, singing hymns?"

"I'm sure we'll be doing more than that," Dad said with a smile, "though the Bible doesn't tell us a lot about it. But the wonderful part about heaven will be being together with Jesus."

"Right," agreed Mother. "I know it's hard to understand that at your age. Maybe it would help if you think about how glad you always are to see Grandpa and Grandma when they're able to come or when we can go to see them."

"I guess so." Jim shrugged as he ate the last bite of his mashed potatoes. "I wonder why God didn't tell us more about what heaven will be like."

"For one thing, it would be impossible for our minds to understand all the wonderful things He has planned for us," said Dad. He looked over at four-year-old Bobby. "Finish your carrots, Son. We're almost ready for dessert."

"What is it?" Bobby asked.

Mother just smiled. "It's a surprise," she said. "But I promise you'll like it."

"Can I have mine now, Mom?" asked Jim.

Mother shook her head. "Let's wait till Bobby's ready. It's his favorite. If he sees it, he'll get so excited that he won't want to finish his carrots."

A short time later they were all enjoying strawberry shortcake. "I just thought of another reason God didn't tell us exactly what heaven will be like," Jim announced with a grin. "If we knew, we'd get so excited, we'd never be happy on earth, doing the things God wants us to do now."

Dad and Mother smiled. "You may be right," agreed Mother. "We need to simply obey God and do His will now and trust that His 'dessert' will be just right!"

HOW ABOUT YOU? Do you ever wonder what heaven will be like? The Bible gives us some ideas about it, but we won't really know what God has in store until we get there. Trust Him and believe that He knows best how to make us happy. In the meantime, keep busy doing God's will on earth and telling others about Jesus so they can go to heaven, too! □ S.K.

TO MEMORIZE: *In Your presence is fullness of joy; at Your right hand are pleasures forevermore.* Psalm 16:11, NKJV

Valentine Project

PATSY WAS LOOKING through the box of valentine cards left over from last year. "I just don't know what to do, Mom," she sighed. "Mrs. Thompson said we should bring a valentine for everyone in our class."

"That's not such a bad idea," answered Mom, "although you don't sound very happy about it."

"Well, it's not that I don't want to be friendly, but some of these cards are so mushy!" Patsy wrinkled her nose. "None of us girls want to give these cards to the boys!"

Mother thought about it. "Why don't you *make* valentine cards to take to school? Then you could write whatever message you'd like. Come on, I'll help you get started."

Mom showed Patsy how to cut paper hearts by folding the paper in half. The table was soon full of pink, red, and white hearts. Next, they taped a piece of cinnamon gum to each heart. The red wrapper added just the right touch. They also used lace and little straw flowers to decorate the valentines. "This is fun, Mom! I think I know what I'd like to write on my valentines, too. I'll put 'God loves you! Happy Valentine's Day!' "

"That's a good idea," said Mom. "You've been concerned about witnessing to your classmates. This is a perfect opportunity."

"Yes," replied Patsy, "and it isn't mushy!"

HOW ABOUT YOU? What do you think of on Valentine's Day? Most people think of love—and God's love for us is the greatest example that we have of genuine love. He is the source of perfect love. Maybe you can write something on the valentines you distribute. Be sure to take advantage of this opportunity to share God's love with your friends.
□ D.R.

TO MEMORIZE: *Let us love one another, for love comes from God. Everyone who loves has been born of God and knows God.* 1 John 4:7, NIV

FROM THE BIBLE:
Dear friends, let us love one another, for love comes from God. Everyone who loves has been born of God and knows God. Whoever does not love does not know God, because God is love. This is how God showed his love among us: He sent his one and only Son into the world that we might live through him. This is love: not that we loved God, but that he loved us and sent his Son as an atoning sacrifice for our sins. Dear friends, since God so loved us, we also ought to love one another. No one has ever seen God; but if we love one another, God lives in us and his love is made complete in us.
1 John 4:7-12, NIV

Tell of God's love

FEBRUARY

13

True Love

FROM THE BIBLE:

*Love is very patient and kind,
never jealous or envious, never
boastful or proud, never haughty
or selfish or rude. Love does not
demand its own way. It is not
irritable or touchy. It does not
hold grudges and will hardly
even notice when others do it
wrong. It is never glad about
injustice, but rejoices whenever
truth wins out. If you love
someone you will be loyal to him
no matter what the cost. You
will always believe in him,
always expect the best of him,
and always stand your ground
in defending him. All the special
gifts and powers from God will
someday come to an end, but
love goes on forever. Someday
prophecy, and speaking in
unknown languages, and
special knowledge—these gifts
will disappear.*
1 Corinthians 13:4-8, TLB

Love one another

TINA SIGHED happily as she walked into the living room. "I'm in love!" she announced. "Gregg's such a wonderful guy! He's always so nice to me!"

Mother frowned slightly. "I'm glad you and Gregg are friends, but remember, *love is* a pretty strong word."

Tina's brother, Joel, laughed. "Tina thinks that just because she's fifteen, she knows everything about love." He reached down to pat his dog. "Now, me and Ralph here—that's love! He does whatever I tell him, he's always ready to play, and he doesn't talk my ear off like some drippy girl would. That's what I call true love."

Shortly afterwards, Tina had a phone call and came back looking upset. "That rotten Gregg!" she said. "He took another girl to the basketball game last night and never even asked me! I'll never speak to him again!"

"Ha, ha!" laughed Joel. "All that true love gone right down the drain!" Joel was laughing so hard that he didn't see Ralph sitting on the floor beside him. He stepped right on the dog's tail, and Ralph nipped him on the leg!

"Ouch! You bad dog!" scolded Joel. "Go away! I don't want you anymore!"

Hearing the commotion, Mother hurried in. "I overheard what you two were talking about. Each of you was certain that you had found 'true love.' What happened?"

"Well, I thought I loved Gregg, until he did something that made me mad," said Tina.

"Yeah, that's how I feel about Ralph," agreed Joel.

"I'm afraid that's the way it goes when we use the word *love* too loosely. Real love is constant. It doesn't change just because our feelings change. What if God stopped loving us just because we displeased Him?"

"It would be awful!" Tina exclaimed. "I'm glad He never stops loving us. I guess our love wasn't so real after all!"

HOW ABOUT YOU? Do you ever wonder what "true love" is? Some people think that love is a feeling, an emotional "high," something that just happens. But the Bible teaches that loving is something you decide to *do*. Today's Scripture passage is a good description of love. God commands you to love others. And He'll help you to do it! □ S.K.

TO MEMORIZE: *A new commandment I give to you, that you love one another.* John 13:34, NKJV

54

J UDY AND SANDI giggled as Judy slipped an envelope into the "valentine mailbox" their teacher had set up. "I've never seen such an ugly valentine!" laughed Judy. "I can hardly wait to see Dorrie's face when she opens it."

When Judy arrived home that afternoon, she didn't show her mother her valentines as she had done other years. When Mother asked about them, Judy silently emptied a big envelope of valentines onto the table. "Oh, my! This is a pretty one," said Mother, picking one up. "It even has a chocolate heart on it! I'll bet this is your favorite. Who is it from?" She turned it over. "Oh, from Dorrie."

To Mother's surprise, Judy burst into tears. "Oh, Mother," she sobbed, "I've been so mean to Dorrie! It always seems like our teacher likes her best, so I've been picking on her lately. I gave her an ugly valentine with a mean verse, and she gave me such a nice one. She was nice to me today, even after she got my valentine."

Mother put her arm around Judy. "I guess you're sorry for the way you've been acting, right?" she asked. Judy nodded. "Then isn't there something you should do?"

Judy wiped her eyes. "You mean apologize? Well, I suppose. But what can I say?" She sniffed. "Oh, this is so hard." She picked up her things and took them to her room.

When Mother called Judy to come set the table for supper, Judy bounced into the kitchen. She sang as she took plates from the cupboard. "You seem much happier now," observed Mother.

Judy smiled. "I called Dorrie, and she was so nice. Her feelings were hurt when she read the valentine, but she forgave me. We're going to play together tomorrow. I still can't get over how nice she was to me when I was being so mean to her."

"Well, I'm glad you've got that all settled," said Mother. "You know, Dorrie reminds me of Jesus. He loved us even though we were sinners. And He forgave us when we asked Him to. Let's be sure to thank Him for it."

HOW ABOUT YOU? Is it hard to admit you're a sinner? God says you are, but He loves you anyway. Why not confess your sin and receive His forgiveness. He wants to save you. Ask Him to do it today. □ H.M.

TO MEMORIZE: *But God demonstrates his own love for us in this: While we were still sinners, Christ died for us.* Romans 5:8, NKJV

Valentines

FROM THE BIBLE:
Let no debt remain outstanding, except the continuing debt to love one another, for he who loves his fellow man has fulfilled the law. The commandments, "Do not commit adultery," "Do not murder," "Do not steal," "Do not covet," and whatever other commandment there may be, are summed up in this one rule: "Love your neighbor as yourself." Love does no harm to its neighbor. Therefore love is the fulfillment of the law.
Romans 13:8-10, NIV

Jesus loves you

15

The Empty Cocoon

FROM THE BIBLE:
But someone will say, "How are the dead raised up? And with what body do they come?" Foolish one, what you sow is not made alive unless it dies. And what you sow, you do not sow that body that shall be, but mere grain—perhaps wheat or some other grain. But God gives it a body as He pleases, and to each seed its own body. All flesh is not the same flesh, but there is one kind of flesh of men, another flesh of beasts, another of fish, and another of birds. There are also celestial bodies and terrestrial bodies; but the glory of the celestial is one, and the glory of the terrestrial is another. . . . So also is the resurrection of the dead. The body is sown in corruption, it is raised in incorruption. It is sown in dishonor, it is raised in glory. It is sown in weakness, it is raised in power. It is sown a natural body, it is raised a spiritual body. There is a natural body, and there is a spiritual body.
1 Corinthians 15:35-40, 42-44, NKJV

Christians will have new bodies

"*Eeeek!*" Lisa ran up on the porch screaming.

Kyle followed laughing. "It's just a caterpillar," he said.

Lisa shuddered. "I don't like caterpillars." As she slammed the door behind her, she saw Mother wiping tears from her eyes. "What's the matter?" Lisa asked anxiously.

"I just got a phone call. Grannie Carter died."

"Oooohh!" Lisa wailed. "I don't want her to die!" Grannie Carter, a neighbor, was one of her favorite people.

Mother smiled faintly. "Grannie is happy. She wanted to be with Jesus and Grandpa Bob."

Lisa and Kyle dreaded the funeral service. It would be their first funeral. But when the time came, they found that, except for the casket and all the flowers, it wasn't so different from a regular church service. At the end, everyone walked out past the casket where Grannie lay. "She looks like she's asleep," Lisa whispered.

Later, at home, Lisa said, "I thought Grannie was in heaven, but she was put in the ground."

Before anyone could answer, Kyle jumped up. "Look!" He pointed at a brown object dangling from a branch.

"What is that?" Lisa asked.

"It's an empty cocoon," said Kyle. "At one time, it was a caterpillar. It spun a shell, or cocoon, around itself. After a while the shell burst open and a beautiful butterfly came out."

"That's a good example of what has happened to Grannie Carter," said Mother. "Remember how crippled Grannie was?" The children nodded. "She has left her old shell, her earthly body. Now it's like an empty cocoon. It was buried today, but the real Grannie has flown away to be with Jesus."

Just then a lovely butterfly fluttered past Lisa's nose. "Look!" she squealed. "A caterpillar in his new body."

HOW ABOUT YOU? Has someone you love died and gone to heaven? Don't worry about the old body that was buried in a grave. Remember that the real person has left his old body and gone to be with the Lord. God will give him a wonderful new body someday. □ B.W.

TO MEMORIZE: *It is sown in dishonor, it is raised in glory. It is sown in weakness, it is raised in power.*
1 Corinthians 15:43, NKJV

AT A MEETING at Jenny's church, Tommy, one of the roughest boys at school, was saved.

After the service, Jenny walked home with her friend Sandi, who had only recently started coming to their church. Jenny was surprised to hear Sandi's comments. "Maybe Tommy's behavior will improve now," said Sandi. "His family is very poor, you know, and his father drinks. I'm glad I don't have a family like that. I'm glad I was born a Christian."

"But *everybody* has to be saved," objected Jenny.

Sandi shrugged. "Oh, I know some people think that, but I don't. I come from a great family. My father is the mayor! In the church we used to attend, he was one of the deacons. I'm sure he'll soon be a deacon here, too." As Jenny began to protest, Sandi added, "Oh, forget it, will you? Come on, I'll race you home." Laughing, she ran ahead.

The circus had come to town, and Sandi invited Jenny to go with her after school on Tuesday. The girls arrived just in time. "Oh no!" groaned Sandi as the gatekeeper waited for their tickets. "I must have left the tickets in my math book!" She explained the situation to the gatekeeper, asking if they could please go on in and bring the tickets later. As he shook his head, Sandi squared her shoulders and looked him straight in the eye. "Do you know who I am?" she asked haughtily. "I'm the mayor's daughter!"

"Well, Miss Mayor's Daughter, when you show me your ticket you can get in. Not before!"

After walking in silence for a while, Jenny glanced at Sandi. "It didn't matter who you were, did it?" she asked timidly. "If the gatekeeper wouldn't let you into the circus even though you were the mayor's daughter, what makes you think God will let you into heaven for those reasons? You still need a ticket to get into the circus, and you need Jesus to get into heaven!"

Sandi looked startled. "Wow, I guess you're right," she decided. "Say, here's our Sunday school teacher's house. Let's stop in and talk to her about it. We've missed the circus anyway."

HOW ABOUT YOU? Do you think you were born a Christian? You weren't! The Bible says it makes no difference who you are. Whether you're from the best home in town or the worst, you are a sinner. You need Jesus. Ask Him to save you today. □ H.M.

TO MEMORIZE: *All have sinned and fall short of the glory of God.* Romans 3:22-23, NKJV

No Difference

FROM THE BIBLE:
As it is written: "There is no one righteous, not even one; there is no one who understands, no one who seeks God. All have turned away, they have together become worthless; there is no one who does good, not even one."
Romans 3:10-12, NIV

You are a sinner

17

A Heavy Burden

FROM THE BIBLE:
Come to Me, all you who labor and are heavy laden, and I will give you rest. Take My yoke upon you and learn from Me, for I am gentle and lowly in heart, and you will find rest for your souls. For My yoke is easy and My burden is light.
Matthew 11:28-30, NKJV

Be anxious for nothing, but in everything by prayer and supplication, with thanksgiving, let your requests be made known to God; and the peace of God, which surpasses all understanding, will guard your hearts and minds through Christ Jesus.
Philippians 4:6-7, NKJV

Give burdens to Jesus

"**M**OM, I WISH Dad still lived here," said Kyle as he finished getting ready for school. "If I had just behaved better, maybe he wouldn't have left."

"Honey, Dad's leaving had nothing to do with you. He loves you as much as ever," Mom said patiently, putting an arm around Kyle. She and Dad had told Kyle this many times. He wanted to believe them, but there was an ache in his heart that wouldn't go away. He was sure if he hadn't whined so much, or if he had minded more often, Dad wouldn't have moved out.

At school, thoughts of his dad often popped up between the sentences Kyle was reading. He finally got his mind off his problems when his teacher showed the class an interesting book. And he was thrilled when she said he could take it home for the evening.

Kyle tucked the heavy book under his arm and began walking home. As he walked, the book seemed to grow heavier and heavier. By the time he reached home, his arm ached.

Mother met him at the end of the driveway. "That book is too big," she said. "It's a burden too heavy for you to carry." She reached down and took it. "Feelings can also be a heavy burden," she continued quietly as she carried the book to the house. "The feeling that Dad's leaving is your fault is a burden too heavy for you to carry."

"I wish I didn't have that feeling," Kyle said. "It hurts."

"Yes, just like your arm hurts from carrying the book." Mother gently rubbed his aching arm. "Wouldn't you like Jesus to carry that burden of guilt for you?" Kyle nodded, and together they asked Jesus to carry Kyle's heavy burden. "Now," said Mom, "every time you feel Dad's leaving is your fault, remember Jesus is carrying that burden for you. Will you do that?"

Kyle nodded. His arm still hurt, but the ache in his heart felt better.

HOW ABOUT YOU? Do you have a burden too heavy for you? If your parents are separated, do you wonder if it's your fault? Or perhaps worries about school or friends constantly fill your mind. It's important to talk about heavy burdens to an adult who can help you turn them over to Jesus. Jesus loves you and wants you to be free of heavy burdens. □ K.R.A.

TO MEMORIZE: *Casting all your care upon Him, for He cares for you.* 1 Peter 5:7, NKJV

It WAS SATURDAY afternoon, and Mandy was slumped in the rocker, trying to read. Her mom knelt on the floor, surrounded by fabric, pattern pieces, tape measure, scissors, and pins. She was cutting out a blouse to sew for herself. Mandy glanced at her mom several times. Then she laid down her book and said, "I don't know how you do it, Mom. How do you turn all that confusion into the pretty blouse on the pattern envelope? It doesn't look anything like it right now!"

"That's true," Mom replied. "But I'll bet you could do it, too, if you wanted to."

"Oh, sure!" grunted Mandy.

"Really. You just need to follow the instructions." Mom held up a printed paper. "See, this paper says which pieces to use and how to cut and fit them together. If I do what it says, my blouse will turn out like the one in the picture."

"That's because you're a good sewer," Mandy answered. After a bit, she looked up again. "I wonder if that's what my teacher was talking about in Sunday school last week."

"What's that, Mandy?" asked Mother.

"She told us how God has in mind a plan of the wonderful person each of us could be. That's like the picture of the finished blouse on the pattern," explained Mandy. "Then she said that to become the person God wants us to be, we need to obey Him and do what He tells us in the Bible. That's like following the instructions in the pattern."

"That's right!" exclaimed Mother. "God is fashioning us into something special. Even when things look confusing or impossible—like this blouse does to you just now—we have to keep obeying Him, and He will make us into a beautiful finished product. That's a wonderful illustration, Mandy. You're a smart girl. Why, I'll bet you're even smart enough to figure out how to sew a blouse yourself."

"Maybe I am," said Mandy, "but I think I'll tackle something easier first—like finishing my book!"

HOW ABOUT YOU? Are you letting God fashion you into the person you could be? Do you look for His instructions in His Word and ask Him to help you follow them? A quiet and obedient spirit makes you beautiful to God. □ J.B.

TO MEMORIZE: *For we are God's workmanship, created in Christ Jesus to do good works, which God prepared in advance for us to do.* Ephesians 2:10, NIV

High Fashion

FROM THE BIBLE:

As for you, you were dead in your transgressions and sins, in which you used to live when you followed the ways of this world and of the ruler of the kingdom of the air, the spirit who is now at work in those who are disobedient. All of us also lived among them at one time, gratifying the cravings of our sinful nature and following its desires and thoughts. Like the rest, we were by nature objects of wrath. But because of his great love for us, God, who is rich in mercy, made us alive with Christ even when we were dead in transgressions—it is by grace you have been saved. And God raised us up with Christ and seated us with him in the heavenly realms in Christ Jesus, in order that in the coming ages he might show the incomparable riches of his grace, expressed in his kindness to us in Christ Jesus. . . . For we are God's workmanship, created in Christ Jesus to do good works, which God prepared in advance for us to do.
Ephesians 2:1-7, 10, NIV

Follow God's instructions

FEBRUARY

19

The Activity Box

FROM THE BIBLE:

God is at work within you, helping you want to obey him, and then helping you do what he wants. In everything you do, stay away from complaining and arguing, so that no one can speak a word of blame against you. You are to live clean, innocent lives as children of God in a dark world full of people who are crooked and stubborn. Shine out among them like beacon lights, holding out to them the Word of Life. Then when Christ returns how glad I will be that my work among you was so worthwhile.
Philippians 4:6-7, TLB

Work cheerfully

AS MOTHER put bread in the toaster, she sighed. "We have a lot to do today."

"We always do on Saturday," Jessica complained.

"Yeah," murmured Justin. "I hate Saturdays!"

Dad poured a cup of coffee. "I don't like them, either, because they're days of whining and grumbling," he said.

Justin scowled, "Stop the work and I'll stop grumbling."

Dad ignored him. "Please find me a shoe box, Justin. Jessica, you can bring me some paper and a pencil." When they returned, Dad said, "Let's write everything we have to do today on slips of paper and put them in this box."

"Change the sheets. Vacuum the carpet. Clean the bathrooms." Mother quickly named several tasks.

"Trim the hedge. Sweep the patio. Wash the car," added Dad. "Sweep the garage."

"Now," Dad said, "we'll take turns drawing out a slip."

"When the box is empty, we could pack a lunch and go to the park," suggested Mother.

"Yippee!" yelled the children.

"I want to draw first." Jessica reached for the box.

Dad held up his hand. "We forgot something," he said. "We need to give the Lord some time, too."

"Read a chapter in your Bible." Jessica wrote it on a slip of paper.

"Stop and give thanks for our family," wrote Justin.

"Memorize tomorrow's Bible verse," added Mother.

"Call Uncle John and invite him to church," Dad said as he wrote it down.

Then Dad held the box out to Jessica. "This is going to be the best Saturday we've had in a long time," she said as she drew out a slip and looked at it. Then she grinned. "Even if I do have to clean the bathrooms!"

HOW ABOUT YOU? If your tasks have become boring, make an activity box. If it won't work for your family, perhaps it will work for you. List everything you have to do today, and don't forget to include the Lord's work. Then do what your hands find to do—cheerfully! □ B.W.

TO MEMORIZE: *Whatever your hand finds to do, do it with your might.* Ecclesiastes 9:10, NKJV

TODD NEVER forgot the day his new baby sister, Megan, came home from the hospital. Dad and Mother had told him that her spinal cord was damaged before she was born and she would never be able to walk. Todd couldn't quite believe it. *Maybe if they all took real good care of Megan, her legs would become well,* he thought. When Todd mentioned this to Mother, she shook her head sadly. "No, the doctor said that unless God performs a miracle, her legs will never work. Instead of thinking about that, let's remember that this is somehow part of God's plan for Megan and our family—at least for now."

Todd slumped into the kitchen chair, his mind determined not to accept this "plan" Mother was talking about. "How can it be?" he asked, shaking his head.

Mother put down the potato peeler, wiped her hands on her apron, and sat down near Todd. "Megan is going to need special care because her legs have no feeling," she said. "She will not know whether they are hot or cold, or whether they have been cut or bruised."

"No feeling at all?" Todd blurted out. "She could hurt herself and not even know it!"

"That's where you and I fit into God's plan for her," said Mother. "It's going to take time and love to protect her from getting hurt and to help her learn about her handicap as she grows up."

"Oh," murmured Todd thoughtfully.

"Will you be part of God's plan for our family by helping us care for Megan?" Mother asked.

Todd was quiet for a long time before answering. "I wish Megan could walk someday," he said finally, "but since she can't, I want to help her as much as I can."

"Great!" Mother said. "God knew Megan would need a big brother like you."

HOW ABOUT YOU? Do you have a brother or sister who is handicapped? God has placed that person in your family as part of His plan for you. As you love and encourage him or her, God is using you to be a blessing. It will help both of you to grow in Him. Or, perhaps you have a handicap yourself. You may not realize it, but God wants to use you, too—to be a blessing to other members of your family. Cheerfully be part of God's plan for you.

□ J.G.

TO MEMORIZE: *I will set nothing wicked before my eyes.* Psalm 101:3, NKJV

God's Plan

FROM THE BIBLE:
Oh, the depth of the riches of the wisdom and knowledge of God! How unsearchable his judgments, and his paths beyond tracing out! "Who has known the mind of the Lord? Or who has been his counselor?" "Who has ever given to God, that God should repay him?" For from him and through him and to him are all things. To him be the glory forever! Amen.
Romans 11:33-36, NIV

Accept God's plan

21

Just Like Dad

FROM THE BIBLE:
So when He had washed their feet, taken His garments, and sat down again, He said to them, "Do you know what I have done to you? You call me Teacher and Lord, and you say well, for so I am. If I then, your Lord and Teacher, have washed your feet, you also ought to wash one another's feet. For I have given you an example, that you should do as I have done to you. Most assuredly, I say to you, a servant is not greater than his master; nor is he who is sent greater than he who sent him. If you know these things, happy are you if you do them."
John 13:12-17, NKJV

Imitate Jesus

BETHANY LAUGHED as she watched her little brother Nathan playing in the living room. He had climbed up into Dad's favorite chair and was pretending to read the newspaper. As he crossed his feet and tried to make them reach the footstool, he shouted, "Look at me! I'm just like Daddy!"

Bethany just couldn't resist giving Nathan a big hug. "Wait right there so we can show Mommy what a big boy you are!"

By the time Bethany returned to the living room with Mother, Nathan had put the paper down on his lap and was pretending to fall asleep. He was even leaning back with his hands behind his head, just like Dad did when he was finished reading the paper.

"Isn't that cute, Mom?" whispered Bethany, giggling. "He's trying to be just like Dad."

Mother nodded. "That's how children learn. They imitate the people they see."

"Did I ever do that?" asked Bethany.

"Sure you did," replied Mother. "You used to pretend you were making dinner. You would get the pots and pans out of the cupboard and tell me that you were making mashed potatoes." Bethany went over to pick up her brother as Mother continued to speak. "I'm reminded of an important lesson in the Bible, Bethany. As Christians, we're to be imitators of Jesus so we can learn how to live as mature Christians."

"But we can't see Jesus, so how can we imitate him?" Bethany said. "Oh, wait a minute! We have the Bible. That tells us how He lived!"

"Yes," affirmed Mother. "When we study His life faithfully, we learn how to live like Him."

HOW ABOUT YOU? Are you learning to imitate Jesus? To learn better how He would act and what He would say, study God's Word. Then when you are in a situation at school or at home, try to think of what Jesus would do if He were in your place. Imitate Him. □ D.R.

TO MEMORIZE: *Therefore be followers of God as dear children.* Ephesians 5:1, NKJV

BETHANY GAVE a lot of thought to Mother's words about learning to be like Jesus, and she was eager to be more like Him. She decided to read the Gospel of John. Every time she found an example of something Jesus did that she could follow, she wrote it down in a little notebook.

Thursday morning Mr. Singleton, the school principal, brought a new girl into Bethany's class. There was some snickering as Mr. Singleton introduced Kim to the class. Her clothes were worn and ill-fitting, and she had long straggly hair.

As Kim was finding a seat, Melissa slipped Bethany a note. On it was written a mean remark about Kim. Bethany smiled back at her friend, but inside she wished that she hadn't. She had just read the night before about how Jesus had been friendly to a Samaritan woman. Jesus was a Jew, and in those days people of Jewish descent didn't associate with people from Samaria! But Jesus talked with her anyway. Bethany had written in her notebook: "Be friendly to everyone, even when others are not." Here was her opportunity to put that principle into practice. "Dear Lord," she prayed quietly, "I think You would want me to be Kim's friend. Please give me courage to talk to her after class and to make her feel welcome."

As soon as the bell rang, Bethany made her way toward Kim. "Hi," she said, introducing herself. "Would you like to go to lunch with me?"

In the following days, Melissa and some of Bethany's other friends acted snobbishly toward Kim. But it wasn't long before all of the girls became good friends. Bethany was glad that she had followed the example of Jesus.

HOW ABOUT YOU? Do you hesitate to make friends with new kids or those that might seem different? It's especially hard when some of your other friends make fun of or laugh at a person. Jesus would be friendly, though, and he wants you to be kind to others, too. Follow His example. Be friendly even if others are not. □ D.R.

TO MEMORIZE: *Be devoted to one another in brotherly love.* Romans 12:10, NIV

Just Like Dad

(Continued from yesterday)

FROM THE BIBLE:
When a Samaritan woman came to draw water, Jesus said to her, "Will you give me a drink?" (His disciples had gone into the town to buy food.) The Samaritan woman said to him, "You are a Jew and I am a Samaritan woman. How can you ask me for a drink?" (For Jews do not associate with Samaritans.) Jesus answered her, "If you knew the gift of God and who it is that asks you for a drink, you would have asked him and he would have given you living water." "Sir," the woman said, "you have nothing to draw with and the well is deep. Where can you get this living water? Are you greater than our father Jacob, who gave us the well and drank from it himself, as did also his sons and his flocks and herds?" Jesus answered, "Everyone who drinks this water will be thirsty again, but whoever drinks the water I give him will never thirst. Indeed, the water I give him will become in him a spring of water welling up to eternal life."
John 4:7-14, NIV

Be friendly

23

Curiosity's Captive

FROM THE BIBLE:
Later on as Jesus left the town he saw a tax collector—with the usual reputation for cheating— sitting at a tax collection booth. The man's name was Levi. Jesus said to him, "Come and be one of my disciples!" So Levi left everything, sprang up and went with him. Soon Levi held a reception in his home with Jesus as the guest of honor. Many of Levi's fellow tax collectors and other guests were there. But the Pharisees and teachers of the Law complained bitterly to Jesus' disciples about his eating with such notorious sinners. Jesus answered them, "It is the sick who need a doctor, not those in good health."
Luke 5:27-31, TLB

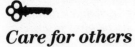

Care for others

"UNCLE PERRY makes me so mad!" said Jana as she slammed down the telephone. "That was Dee, and she was crying. The electric company threatened to turn off their electricity if Aunt Helen doesn't pay their bill by tomorrow. Uncle Perry's off drinking with his buddies."

Dad looked over the edge of the newspaper. "I feel sorry for Perry," he said.

"I feel sorry for his family! Uncle Perry is selfish and mean!" Jana ended in a sob.

"He hasn't always been an alcoholic," Dad reminded her. "We need to pray for him. He's bound by alcohol."

"He could get loose if he wanted to! He just—" Jana was interrupted by a banging sound from the garage. "What's that?"

"I don't know." Mother looked puzzled. "We had better find out. Buffy's out there." When they opened the door, the strangest sight met their eyes. A dog's body, with a plastic pitcher for a head, was bumping into everything.

Mother called softly to the frightened dog and gathered him in her arms. Holding his body, she tried to pull off the pitcher. She frowned. "I can't get it off."

Dad quickly got out his pocketknife and carefully cut the pitcher from the dog's neck. "Poor baby!" Jana crooned. "Your curiosity almost killed you that time."

"He must have stuck his nose in it, then pushed it up against something to hold it as he pushed his head farther inside," Mother reasoned.

Dad nodded. "Having us scold him and tell him how foolish he was wouldn't have helped him at all," he observed. "He was caught and couldn't do anything to help himself. He needed us to help him. Uncle Perry is like Buffy. Curiosity started him drinking. Now he is caught in a trap so powerful he cannot break loose. God can deliver him. It may be that God wants to use us to help Perry. If so, He will show us how."

HOW ABOUT YOU? Do you know people who are caught in the trap of sin? It might be alcohol or drugs or many other things. Are you tempted to dislike them? Ask God to give you compassion for them, and pray for them to be delivered. □ B.W.

TO MEMORIZE: *Live in harmony with one another; be sympathetic, love as brothers, be compassionate and humble.* 1 Peter 3:8, NIV

"MY NEW CAMERA says 'automatic focus.' What does that mean?" Jennifer asked.

"No matter how close or far you are from your subject, you won't have to adjust anything to make each picture come out clearly," Dad told her.

"Oh, good! My old camera gave me a lot of trouble with that," exclaimed Jennifer. "I also had trouble making the right adjustments for bright days and dark days."

"This one will work much better," Dad responded. "There's a little mechanism at the front of this camera that 'reads' how light it is. It automatically opens or closes the shutter to let in more or less light."

"My science teacher said that our eyes work a lot like a camera does," Jennifer said. "The colored part of the eye is like the shutter. When the light is real bright, it makes the pupil get smaller. When it's dark, the iris opens up wide to let more light through the pupil."

"That's right," Mom remembered. "I read somewhere that the eye also has a lens that allows things far away to be in focus, as well as things close up."

"The eyes God has given us are very unique," added Dad. "And just as the pictures you take with your camera are recorded on a film, so the pictures taken by your eyes are recorded on your brain. That's why your mother and I don't allow you to read certain books or watch many TV programs. We want your brain to be imprinted with better things."

"I hadn't thought about the eyes recording a picture on my brain," Jennifer admitted. "I'm going to be more careful to use the camera in my head to record good pictures."

"Good," said Mother with a smile, "and let's be sure to thank God for them, too."

HOW ABOUT YOU? What are your eyes seeing? Do you thank God for them? Close them for a moment and think how sad it would be if you could never open them again! You can thank God best by using your eyes to look at things that are good and wholesome and pure! □ C.V.M.

TO MEMORIZE: *I hate the work of those who fall away; it shall not cling to me.* Psalm 101:3, NKJV

Two Cameras

FROM THE BIBLE:
I will sing of mercy and justice; to You, O LORD, I will sing praises. I will behave wisely in a perfect way. Oh, when will You come to me? I will walk within my house with a perfect heart. I will set nothing wicked before my eyes; I hate the work of those who fall away; it shall not cling to me. A perverse heart shall depart from me; I will not know wickedness. Whoever secretly slanders his neighbor, him I will destroy; The one who has a haughty look and a proud heart, him I will not endure. My eyes shall be on the faithful of the land, that they may dwell with me; he who walks in a perfect way, he shall serve me. He who works deceit shall not dwell within my house; he who tells lies shall not continue in my presence. Early I will destroy all the wicked of the land, that I may cut off all the evildoers from the city of the LORD.
Psalm 101:1-8, NKJV

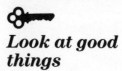

Look at good things

25

The Vacation

FROM THE BIBLE:

Sow for yourselves righteous-ness; reap in mercy; break up your fallow ground, for it is time to seek the LORD, till He comes and rains righteousness on you. You have plowed wickedness; you have reaped iniquity. You have eaten the fruit of lies, because you trusted in your own way, in the multitude of your mighty men.
Hosea 10:12-13, NKJV

Talk pleasantly

As THE JACKSON FAMILY traveled along, Trent and Traci seemed to quarrel constantly. It was a relief when thy reached Cripple Creek.

"This is an old gold mining town," Dad explained as he parked beside a railroad depot.

"May we ride the train?" Trent asked as they jumped from the car. Mother nodded, and soon they were seated on wooden benches in an open car behind an old steam engine. The engineer served as guide. As they entered a small valley, the train came to a stop. "This is Echo Valley," the engineer told them. "Listen."

He pulled the train's whistle. *Wwwwwooooooo.* A few seconds later they heard a faint reply, *Wwwwwooooooo!*

Traci laughed. "Let me try." She cupped her hands around her mouth and called loudly, "Hello!"

"Hello," came the faint reply.

"My turn," said Trent. "Good-byeee."

"Good-byeee," the echo repeated.

Later the tired and hungry family piled into the car. "Let's go to the motel and clean up before we eat dinner," Mother suggested.

"But I'm hungry now," whined Traci.

"Big baby," Trent mocked.

"Big baby yourself!" responded Traci.

"Listen to the echoes." Mother grimaced.

"Echoes? I don't hear any," Traci argued.

"I do," Mother insisted. "I hear ugly, hateful words echoing through this car. Echoes come back as they are sent. When Traci called out, 'Hello,' the echo did not reply, 'Good-bye.' When we send out nice, kind words, we get nice, kind words in return. When we spit out ugly, hateful words, we can only expect to hear ugly, hateful words in return."

"Let's make an agreement," said Dad. "For the rest of this vacation, let's agree to send out only words we would want returned to us."

Traci and Trent looked hesitantly at one another, then grinned. "Okay," they agreed. "We'll do it."

HOW ABOUT YOU? What kind of words have you been sending out? Would you like them returned to you? Life is an "Echo Valley." The words you send out will return. □ B.W.

TO MEMORIZE: *With the measure you use, it will be measured to you.* Luke 6:38, NIV

"AM I DOING this right, Grandma?"

Grandmother examined the strip of crocheted lace Sarah handed her. "Looks good to me," she said.

"This is going to be a pretty collar," Sarah said proudly. "What do I do next?"

"Make the next row exactly like this one," Grandmother replied. "By next week when I go to stay with your Aunt Denise, you should be able to follow the pattern by yourself."

"We wish you could stay with us all the time, don't we, Mittens?" Sarah brushed her bare toes over the fur of the cat at her feet. "Aunt Denise and Darci are so stuck-up. They may have more money, but they're not any better than we are! In fact, Darci is nothing but a spoiled brat. She tells lies to get what she wants, and she . . ."

"That's enough, Sarah Jane!" Grandmother said sternly. "Remember, Darci is my granddaughter, and I love her as much as I love you."

"But you don't know what she did . . . ," began Sarah.

"Dinner is ready!" Mother's call from the kitchen interrupted Sarah.

After dinner, Sarah and Grandmother returned to the family room. "I'm going to work on my—oh no! Look, Grandma!" Sarah pointed at the cat, who was playing with a mass of tangled thread. "Mittens unraveled all my hard work! I'll have to start all over."

Grandmother smiled sympathetically. "It takes time and careful thought to crochet a lace collar, but anyone—even a cat—can unravel one. It's like that with everything. It always takes more effort to build up than to tear down. It's easy to find fault with people and run them down, but it seems hard to find their good points and build them up. God commands us to do just that. He tells us to 'edify,' or build up, one another."

Sarah sighed as she started winding the thread around the spool. "You mean my remarks about Darci, I know. I guess I was just being catty, Grandma. I'm sorry."

HOW ABOUT YOU? Do you say catty things about others? Do you run them down? This would be a good day to stop tearing others down and start building them up as God wants you to do. □ B.W.

TO MEMORIZE: *Comfort each other and edify one another, just as you also are doing.*
1 Thessalonians 5:11, NKJV

Catty Remarks

FROM THE BIBLE:
But no man can tame the tongue. It is an unruly evil, full of deadly poison. With it we bless our God and Father, and with it we curse men, who have been made in the similitude of God. Out of the same mouth proceed blessing and cursing. My brethren, these things ought not to be so. . . . Who is wise and understanding among you? Let him show by good conduct that his works are done in the meekness of wisdom. But if you have bitter envy and self-seeking in your hearts, do not boast and lie against the truth. This wisdom does not descend from above, but is earthly, sensual, demonic. For where envy and self-seeking exist, confusion and every evil thing will be there. But the wisdom that is from above is first pure, then peaceable, gentle, willing to yield, full of mercy and good fruits, without partiality and without hypocrisy. Now the fruit of righteousness is sown in peace by those who make peace.
James 3:8-10, 13-18, NKJV

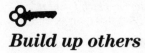

Build up others

27

Listen and Learn

FROM THE BIBLE:

Incline your ear, and come to Me. Hear, and your soul shall live; and I will make an everlasting covenant with you—the sure mercies of David. Seek the LORD while He may be found, call upon Him while He is near. Let the wicked forsake his way, and the unrighteous man his thoughts; let him return to the LORD, and He will have mercy on him; and to our God, for He will abundantly pardon. "For My thoughts are not your thoughts, nor are your ways My ways," says the LORD. "For as the heavens are higher than the earth, so are My ways higher than your ways, and My thoughts than your thoughts. For as the rain comes down, and the snow from heaven, and do not return there, but water the earth, and make it bring forth and bud, that it may give seed to the sower and bread to the eater, so shall My word be that goes forth from My mouth; it shall not return to Me void, but it shall accomplish what I please, and it shall prosper in the thing for which I sent it."

Isaiah 55:3, 6-11, NKJV

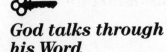

God talks through his Word

MOTHER CAME to tuck Wayne in, a nightly ritual in the Bronson home. "Wayne, you used to have your Bible propped on your lap when I came in to say good night," said Mother "What's happened the past few nights? Don't you still have devotions before you go to sleep?"

"Oh, sure. I pray after you leave," replied Wayne as he sat on the edge of his bed. "But I don't read anymore. I can't understand the Bible anyway." As he spoke, in came Heather, his golden retriever. She tipped her head and looked fondly at her master. "Hey, Heather, old girl," he greeted her. "Nice girl, Heather." As Wayne spoke, Heather inched closer and her tongue began to lick the air, itching to "slobber" her affection all over Wayne's face. Suddenly she could contain herself no longer. She leaped up, and all seventy pounds of Heather landed on Wayne's lap. Wayne fell back against the pillows laughing while Mother coaxed his pet out the door.

Mother came back and closed the door. "Wayne, why do you talk to Heather?" she asked. "Do you think she understands every word you say?"

"No, but I like to talk to her anyway," replied Wayne. "She always listens. And she does understand a lot of things—like *come, sit, fetch, walk, and roll over.* She keeps learning new words, too."

Mother picked up Wayne's Bible. "Wayne, do you know that God talks to us through His Word?"

Wayne looked at the Bible in his mother's hand. He grinned. "I get the point, Mom. God likes to talk to me even if I don't understand everything, just as I like to talk to Heather. And like Heather, I do understand some of God's commands, and I need to keep learning new things from Him."

Mother smiled, kissed Wayne good night, and handed him his Bible.

HOW ABOUT YOU? Have you stopped reading God's Word just because you can't understand everything? The more you let God speak to you, the more you will understand. He's pleased when you "listen." □ P.R.

TO MEMORIZE: *Continue in what you have learned and have become convinced of, because you know those from whom you learned it.*
2 Timothy 3:14, NIV

RICK AND SANDY were helping their dad in his meat shop. Part of their job was to take the trash out to the big bin behind the store. Together they carried out empty boxes and wastepaper. Rick lifted the trash bin cover, then he slammed it back down quickly. "Sandy, there's something in there. I saw it move!"

"You're just trying to scare me," laughed Sandy.

"I'm telling the truth," Rick persisted. Bravely he pulled up the lid and poked at the rubbish with a stick. A loud moan jarred the air, and Sandy screamed.

Dad rushed outside. "What's wrong?" he asked in alarm.

"Something's in the trash," Sandy choked out.

Looking doubtful, Dad approached the trash bin and looked inside "Why, it's a puppy!" he exclaimed. "Let's see if we can help him."

"Can we take him home, Dad?" Rick begged. "He looks like a stray."

"Ugh!" Sandy made a face. "He smells! I bet Mother won't want him."

"He's a mess all right," agreed Dad. "We'll clean him up and see if we can find him a home."

When they arrived home, the children told their mother all about the puppy. At her suggestion they named him Ragamuffin. "You know, children, Ragamuffin will make a good illustration for my Sunday school lesson tomorrow," said Mother as she looked at the bedraggled pup. "What you did for Ragamuffin, God did for us—and even more! God found us spiritually dirty, lost, and trapped in our sins. Yet He reached down to rescue us. He loved us when there was nothing lovable about us."

Ragamuffin barked and Sandy laughed. "He agrees with you, Mom. I think Ragamuffin is glad he's been found!"

HOW ABOUT YOU? Have you been "found"? Unlovely and sinful though you are, God loves you. He sent Jesus to rescue you from the penalty of sin, but you remain lost in sin unless you accept Him as Savior. Have you done that? □ J.H.

TO MEMORIZE: *At just the right time, when we were still powerless, Christ died for the ungodly.* Romans 5:6, NIV

Ragamuffin

FROM THE BIBLE:
You see, at just the right time, when we were still powerless, Christ died for the ungodly. Very rarely will anyone die for a righteous man, though for a good man someone might possibly dare to die. But God demonstrates his own love for us in this: While we were still sinners, Christ died for us. Since we have now been justified by his blood, how much more shall we be saved from God's wrath through him! For if, when we were God's enemies, we were reconciled to him through the death of his Son, how much more, having been reconciled, shall we be saved through his life! Not only is this so, but we also rejoice in God through our Lord Jesus Christ, through whom we have now received reconciliation.
Romans 5:6-11, NIV

Jesus loves sinners

FEBRUARY

29

Ragamuffin

(Continued from yesterday)

FROM THE BIBLE:
Praise the LORD! I will praise the LORD with my whole heart, in the assembly of the upright and in the congregation. The works of the LORD are great, studied by all who have pleasure in them. His work is honorable and glorious, and His righteousness endures forever. He has made His wonderful works to be remembered; the LORD is gracious and full of compassion. He has given food to those who fear Him; He will ever be mindful of His covenant. He has declared to His people the power of His works, in giving them the heritage of the nations. The works of His hands are verity and justice; all His precepts are sure. They stand fast forever and ever, and are done in truth and uprightness. He has sent redemption to His people; He has commanded His covenant forever: holy and awesome is His name. The fear of the LORD is the beginning of wisdom; a good understanding have all those who do His commandments. His praise endures forever.
Psalm 111, NKJV

Be devoted to God

RICK AND SANDY enjoyed romping with Ragamuffin, the stray puppy. They taught him tricks and took him on walks. They were delighted that no one answered the newspaper ad seeking Ragamuffin's owners.

But not everything was pleasant. Ragamuffin got into trouble. Sometimes he tracked mud into the house or knocked things over and broke them. Sometimes he chewed slippers and hid shoes. Though Rick and Sandy were patient, the puppy often had to be scolded or punished for misbehavior.

The children worried that Ragamuffin might not like them when they punished him, but he was always loyal. He ran to meet them, wagging his tail and jumping up and down with excitement. He followed them around and constantly wanted to be with them. He treated them as if they were the best thing that ever happened to him. "Ragamuffin makes us feel like we're really important to him," observed Rick one day.

"You are," Mother said. "You rescued him and you take care of him. Ragamuffin knows that, and he loves you in return."

"He's more appreciative than we seem to be," observed Dad. Seeing the children's puzzled looks, he continued, "Our heavenly Father loves us, He saved us, and He provides for us. Sometimes we sin, and He has to punish us to make us obey. But I wonder if we praise Him enough or show Him much admiration for all that He has done for us. Do we make God feel important to us?"

"I never thought of it like that," Sandy said. "I guess I sometimes act mad when God doesn't let things work out the way I want them to."

"And sometimes I get impatient when God doesn't answer my prayers right away," admitted Rick.

Mother nodded. "I'm afraid we're all guilty. We all need to learn to give to God the kind of unconditional devotion that Ragamuffin gives to you."

HOW ABOUT YOU? Is God important to you? Do you give Him your time? Your love? Your obedience? Your service? Do you praise Him with your lips and your life? Do you love and help others as He told you to? □ J.H.

TO MEMORIZE: *We love because he first loved us.*
1 John 4:19, NIV

BRENDA HUNG UP the phone. "We're trying to figure out what to do about Gerry," she told her mother. "She's being a 'sometimey' friend. She only wants to be our friend when she needs help with homework. She ignores us when she's doing something that's fun."

As Brenda crawled between the covers a little later, Mother appeared at her door. "Have you had your quiet time with the Lord today?" asked Mother.

Brenda yawned and glanced at the Bible on the nightstand. "I'll read in the morning," she said, "I'm too tired tonight." Mother prayed with her briefly, tucked her in, and left the room.

The next morning Brenda overslept. As she hurried downstairs, she tripped. "Mom!" she wailed. "My ankle!" Mother hurried to help. "Dear God," prayed Brenda silently while Mother wrapped her ankle and put ice packs on it, "please take this pain away. Make my ankle better."

Unable to walk, Brenda stayed home from school. "Honey," said Mother after making her comfortable on the couch, "you told me about the problem with your friend Gerry. How does it feel when she asks for your help but doesn't include you in her 'fun' times?"

Brenda sighed. "It bugs me, and it hurts, too. Friends should be friends *all* the time."

"Well," Mother continued, "last night I thought about how you talked so long to your friends on the phone but were too tired to talk to God."

Brenda squeezed her hands around the ice pack. "I prayed this morning," she defended herself.

"Did you?" asked Mother. "About what?"

"My ankle," said Brenda quickly.

Mother nodded. "You prayed because you needed help," she said. "God is an 'all-the-time' Friend. I think it hurts Him when we're 'sometimey' friends."

HOW ABOUT YOU? Do you talk to God as you do to a friend, or do you pray only when you have a need? You can chat with your heavenly Father anytime, not just in a crisis. Thank Him for the things you see on your way to school. Share your thoughts about people and things that happen. Praise Him for being Lord. Ask Him to help you with both the little and big tasks of the day. Live in an attitude of prayer all the time. □ N.E.K.

TO MEMORIZE: *Pray without ceasing.*
1 Thessalonians 5:17, NKJV

All-the-Time Friend

FROM THE BIBLE:
Rejoice always, pray without ceasing, in everything give thanks; for this is the will of God in Christ Jesus for you. Do not quench the Spirit.
1 Thessalonians 5:16-19, NKJV

Pray always

The Balloon That Burst

FROM THE BIBLE:
But he gives us more and more strength to stand against all such evil longings. As the Scripture says, God gives strength to the humble but sets himself against the proud and haughty. So give yourselves humbly to God. Resist the devil and he will flee from you. And when you draw close to God, God will draw close to you. Wash your hands, you sinners, and let your hearts be filled with God alone to make them pure and true to him. Let there be tears for the wrong things you have done. Let there be sorrow and sincere grief. Let there be sadness instead of laughter, and gloom instead of joy. Then when you realize your worthlessness before the Lord, he will lift you up, encourage, and help you.
James 4:6-10, TLB

Pride brings shame

"I WAS SURE I'd win the Bible quiz contest last night," said Gayle with a sigh. "I can't figure out what went wrong."

"Yeah," agreed Kristen. "You always win everything."

"Now Debbie will go to the state contest instead of me," Gayle added. "And she'll be honored at the church party tonight. I don't know what happened. I'm the smartest."

Miss Loveland held out some crepe streamers. "Hurry, girls," she urged. "The party begins soon. Hang up the rest of these while I blow up some balloons. Tell me about the contest while you work. I couldn't attend last night."

"I was awful," Gayle said as she fastened streamers to the ceiling. "I couldn't remember the answers, and I misquoted Bible verses."

"But she's smarter than Debbie," said Kristen.

"Sure I am," said Gayle confidently. "Besides, she just started going to church last year."

"Did you study for the contest?" asked Miss Loveland.

"Oh, I don't need to study much anymore," replied Gayle, "because I know the Bible so well."

"How much did you pray about the quiz?"

"Pray? Well, not much." Gayle was a little embarrassed.

Miss Loveland looked at the balloon she was blowing up. "Debbie told me she'd studied a great deal and had been asking the Lord to help her do well that she might honor Him," she said. She blew hard on the balloon. It grew bigger and bigger. Then, BANG! It burst into little pieces. "Well! The balloon was puffed up so much it burst," observed Miss Loveland. "You know, Gayle, I think that's your trouble, too. You were puffed up with pride. You thought you were so smart you didn't need any help. Debbie knew she had to depend on the Lord."

Gayle picked up a fragment of the balloon. "That's the difference, isn't it?" she said humbly. "My pride blew me up into little pieces. Next time I'll work hard and ask the Lord to help me."

HOW ABOUT YOU? Are there times when you think everything's going your way and then you fall flat on your face? Could pride be the trouble? Humbly depend on the Lord, and then He'll lift you up again. □ M.R.P.

TO MEMORIZE: *He who is devoid of wisdom despises his neighbor, but a man of understanding holds his peace.* Proverbs 7:8, NKJV

"PAM, IT'S TIME to leave for the missionary meeting at church," called Mother. "Are you ready?" When Pam didn't respond, Mother headed for her room. Hearing her mother's footsteps approaching, Pam slipped a book under her pillow and quickly changed the dial on her radio. "What were you listening to?" Mother asked. "I called and called, and you didn't seem to hear me."

"Oh, I was just looking for some good music," said Pam.

"Well, are you ready to leave for church?" asked Mother.

Pam reluctantly stood up. "I suppose," she muttered. But she was grouchy all the way to church because she really wanted to stay home and watch her favorite television program.

Pam expected to be bored, but when the missionary showed slides, she watched intently. "Many of our people worship idols, practice black magic, and dabble in the spirit world," the missionary said. "When they accept Christ as Savior and become new creatures in Him, they no longer want to do many of the things they did before. This last slide shows a big bonfire where they're burning their idols, magic books, and special potions. They're getting rid of anything that would keep them from living for God. They're often persecuted for their stand, but Jesus means more to them than worldly possessions or popularity." He turned off the projector and waited for the lights to come on. Then he asked, "Is there anything you need to 'burn'? Anything you need to get rid of so that it won't keep you from living for God?"

Pam thought about the heavy metal music she had listened to before her mom had come to her room. She remembered the book she didn't want her mom to see and the way she had wanted to put a television program above church attendance.

Pam bowed her head to pray. Just like those natives in Africa, she, too, had some idols to destroy in her life.

HOW ABOUT YOU? Does Jesus have first place in your life, or are you letting TV, video games, a new bicycle, or friends control your thinking and actions? Are they coming before God? Examine your life. If there are some "idols" you need to put away, take care of it today. □ J.H.

TO MEMORIZE: *Little children, keep yourselves from idols.* 1 John 5:21, NKJV

MARCH

3

No More Idols

FROM THE BIBLE:
You shall have no other gods before Me. You shall not make for yourself any carved image, or any likeness of anything that is in heaven above, or that is in the earth beneath, or that is in the water under the earth; you shall not bow down to them nor serve them. For I, the LORD your God, am a jealous God, visiting the iniquity of the fathers on the children to the third and fourth generations of those who hate Me.
Exodus 20:3-5, NKJV

Put away your idols

The Test

FROM THE BIBLE:

O LORD my God, if I have done this and there is guilt on my hands—if I have done evil to him who is at peace with me or without cause have robbed my foe—then let my enemy pursue and overtake me; let him trample my life to the ground and make me sleep in the dust. Arise, O LORD, in your anger; rise up against the rage of my enemies. Awake, my God; decree justice. Let the assembled peoples gather around you. Rule over them from on high; let the LORD judge the peoples. Judge me, O LORD, according to my righteousness, according to my integrity, O Most High. O righteous God, who searches minds and hearts, bring to an end the violence of the wicked and make the righteous secure. My shield is God Most High, who saves the upright in heart. God is a righteous judge, a God who expresses his wrath every day.

Psalm 7:3-11, NIV

Always be honest

"HERE'S TEN DOLLARS. That should be enough," said Mother as she put money and a shopping list into Joey's hand. "You may keep the change."

After Joey finished getting the items for his mother, he headed for his favorite candy shop. "I thought this was a dollar and twenty-seven cents," he mused as he pulled out the change, "but it's five dollars and twenty-seven cents! Mrs. Clemens gave me the wrong amount. Great! I'll buy some candy and save the rest for Saturday when I go to the amusement park with Steve."

After Joey got home, he worked on his model car while his mother ironed and listened to her favorite radio preacher. "I'd like to close my message today with a true story about integrity," said the speaker. Then he told about a pastor who noticed that he had been given too much change by a bus driver. As he rode along, he was tempted to put the extra money in his wallet without saying anything. But he knew that would be wrong. So, as he left the bus, he returned the extra money to the driver. "You made a mistake on my change," he said.

"That was no mistake," replied the bus driver. "That was a test. You see, I visited your church last Sunday when you were preaching on honesty, and I wanted to see if you practice what you preach. I think I'll come to hear you again."

Wow, thought Joey. *Maybe God is giving me a test, too. I'm going to take that extra money back to the store right now!*

HOW ABOUT YOU? Have you ever had the idea that no one would know when you did something dishonest? Be careful. You never know who may be watching you, perhaps even testing you. When you cheat, lie, neglect your work, or do other wrong things, you displease God, and you are a poor testimony for Him. □ P.R.

TO MEMORIZE: *Let the LORD judge the peoples. Judge me, O LORD, according to my righteousness, according to my integrity, O Most High.* Psalm 7:8, NIV

"JOSH, YOU SHOULD be ashamed," declared Christy when her brother gave a loud burp. "Your table manners are atrocious! And you've got syrup all over your mouth!"

Josh wiped his mouth with his napkin as Mother frowned. "Christy's right," she said. "If you must burp, you should at least ask those present to excuse you. Now, you kids hurry, or we'll be late for Sunday school."

After Sunday school, Christy joined her family for the church service. She enjoyed the singing and even listened quite well to the message. But then she got restless. The Lord's Supper was being served, and it seemed to Christy that Pastor Grayson said pretty much the same thing every time. Soon she was thinking of other things. She drew a few pictures on the back of the bulletin, and she even poked Josh and whispered to him. But she quickly sat up straight and folded her hands when she saw her father frowning at her. Both she and Josh snickered as they watched a fly crawl up the back of Mrs. Martin, two rows ahead of them.

At the dinner table that noon, Christy carefully placed her napkin on her lap. "It's not polite to put your elbows on the table," she scolded her brother.

Dad looked at Josh and then at Christy. "Seems to me you both need to learn some good table manners," he said.

"Me?" asked Christy. "I'm sitting properly."

"I was thinking of a different table," said Dad. "The Lord's Table." Christy blushed.

"That's right," agreed Mother. "Your manners there are more important than your manners here at home. I think we'd better talk about it."

HOW ABOUT YOU? How do you behave at the Lord's Table? Is it all so familiar that you don't pay much attention to it anymore? Even if you don't take Communion yet, remember Jesus at this special time. Listen to what the pastor says about what Jesus did on the cross for you. Thank God for what He did for you. Prayerfully examine your heart to see what sin may be in your life, and ask God to forgive you and help you forsake it. Listen to the music and think of the words to the songs being played. Have good "table manners."

□ H.M.

MARCH

5

Table Manners

FROM THE BIBLE:

For I received from the Lord that which I also delivered to you: that the Lord Jesus on the same night in which He was betrayed took bread; and when He had given thanks, He broke it and said, "Take, eat; this is My body which is broken for you; do this in remembrance of Me." In the same manner He also took the cup after supper, saying, "This cup is the new covenant in My blood. This do, as often as you drink it, in remembrance of Me." For as often as you eat this bread and drink this cup, you proclaim the Lord's death till He comes. Therefore whoever eats this bread or drinks this cup of the Lord in an unworthy manner will be guilty of the body and blood of the Lord. But let a man examine himself, and so let him eat of that bread and drink of that cup. For he who eats and drinks in an unworthy manner eats and drinks judgment to himself, not discerning the Lord's body.
1 Corinthians 11:23-29, NKJV

Behave at the Lord's Table

6

The Wrong Book

FROM THE BIBLE:

In the beginning God created the heavens and the earth. God said, "Let there be light" and there was light. Then God said, "Let there be a firmament in the midst of the waters, and let it divide the waters from the waters." Then God said, "Let the waters under the heavens be gathered together into one place, and let the dry land appear." Then God said, "Let there be lights in the firmament of the heavens to divide the day from the night." Then God said, "Let the waters abound with an abundance of living creatures, and let birds fly above the earth." Then God said, "Let the earth bring forth the living creature according to its kind." Then God said, "Let Us make man in Our image, according to Our likeness." Then God saw everything that He had made, and indeed it was very good. Genesis 1:1-3, 6, 9, 14, 20, 24, 26, 31, NKJV*

God made everything

GETTING OUT his science book, Todd sat down at the kitchen table to do some homework. *Wow!* he said to himself after reading a few pages. *This sure doesn't sound like what it says in the Bible.* Feeling confused, he went to talk to his dad, who was replacing some spark plugs in the car. "Dad, my science book doesn't teach creation like the Bible does," said Todd. "According to my book, many scientists believe that the earth and people and everything just 'happened' to come into existence."

"Well, Son," Dad responded, "you might as well know right now that some books are wrong. They have been written by man, and man can sometimes make mistakes. But the Bible has no errors!"

"Because the Bible was inspired by God?" Todd asked.

"That's right," Dad replied. "That's why we call it the Word of God, and it tells us that God created everything. In addition to that, our common sense tells us that man couldn't have just 'happened.' What if I told you this car just 'happened'—that nobody put the engine, the body, the seats, the wheels, and all the other parts of this car together, but they just all came together by themselves?"

"Why, I'd tell you that was the craziest thing I ever heard," said Todd with a smile.

"You'd be absolutely right," Dad replied. "And the human body is far more complicated than this car. We're not accidents. We are part of God's plan and creation."

HOW ABOUT YOU? Have you heard people talk about evolution as if it were fact? Don't you believe it! God made the whole world and everything in it. He made you, He loves you, and He has a wonderful plan and purpose for your life. □ C.V.M.

TO MEMORIZE: *In the beginning God created the heavens and the earth.* Genesis 1:1, NKJV

PATTY, a happy little girl in the second grade, had a pretty mom, a nice daddy, and a cat named Mittens. But one day, something happened that changed her whole life. "Daddy's very sick," Mom told her one day. "The doctors have done all they can to help him. We're praying that if it's God's will, he'll get better, but right now it seems that perhaps God will take him home to heaven instead."

One day when Patty came home from school, Daddy's bed was empty. "Daddy's in the hospital," Mom said, giving her a hug. "Aunt Ellie and Uncle Bud are taking you to their house. I'll come to get you in a few days."

So Patty went to Uncle Bud's house in the country. She felt afraid when she thought about Daddy. *He's going to die!* she thought, and she shivered.

One morning Patty awakened to see Mom sitting in the chair beside her bed. "Mom! You're here! I though you'd never come!" Patty jumped into Mom's warm arms. "Is Daddy better?"

Mom held Patty close. "Daddy has gone to be with Jesus, Honey," she said. "We won't be seeing him for a while, but he still loves us and will be waiting for us in heaven." With tear-filled eyes, Patty gazed up into her mother's face. "Patty, how did you feel when you awoke this morning and saw me here?"

Patty replied. "Surprised and happy."

"I think that's the way Daddy felt when he opened his eyes and saw Jesus." Mom's words were very quiet. "There's a Bible verse that says, 'Joy comes in the morning,' and that came true for Daddy. Now he's enjoying heaven. It must be a wonderful morning for him."

Patty squeezed her mom's hand. "Oh, Mom, I'll miss him so much, but I'm glad he's in heaven," she said, and they cried together.

"Daddy's with Jesus." Mom smiled through her tears, and Patty smiled back. "Someday we'll be with them, too."

HOW ABOUT YOU? God's plan for you may include sadness. It may even include death—for yourself or for someone you love. Does that frighten you? It's natural to feel sadness, but deep down there should also be joy. For a Christian, death is really a joyful experience. □ P.K.

TO MEMORIZE: *For his anger lasts only a moment, but his favor lasts a lifetime; weeping may remain for a night, but rejoicing comes in the morning.* Psalm 30:5, NIV

Joy in the Morning

FROM THE BIBLE:
Listen, I tell you a mystery: We will not all sleep, but we will all be changed—in a flash, in the twinkling of an eye, at the last trumpet. For the trumpet will sound, the dead will be raised imperishable, and we will be changed. For the perishable must clothe itself with the imperishable, and the mortal with immortality. When the perishable has been clothed with the imperishable, and the mortal with immortality, then the saying that is written will come true: "Death has been swallowed up in victory. Where, O death, is your victory? Where, O death, is your sting?" The sting of death is sin, and the power of sin is the law. But thanks be to God! He gives us the victory through our Lord Jesus Christ.
1 Corinthians 15:51-57, NIV

Death can be joyful

8

Can Right Be Wrong?

FROM THE BIBLE:

But food does not bring us near to God; we are no worse if we do not eat, and no better if we do. Be careful, however, that the exercise of your freedom does not become a stumbling block to the weak. For if anyone with a weak conscience sees you who have this knowledge eating in an idol's temple, won't he be emboldened to eat what has been sacrificed to idols? So this weak brother, for whom Christ died, is destroyed by your knowledge. When you sin against your brothers in this way and wound their weak conscience, you sin against Christ. Therefore, if what I eat causes my brother to fall into sin, I will never eat meat again, so that I will not cause him to fall.

1 Corinthians 8:8-13, NIV

Don't be a stumbling block

DARRELL BURST into the room. "Mom, guess what happened at Bible club!" he exclaimed. "Troy accepted Jesus as his Savior!"

"How wonderful!" Mother responded. "I'm happy Troy's a Christian, but I'm afraid he won't get much encouragement at home. His dad is an alcoholic and doesn't have much use for God or the church."

"I'll help Troy," Darrell said eagerly.

But a few weeks later, Darrell wasn't so sure about that. "I asked Troy to go with me to Don's house to play pool," he grumbled, "but you know what he said? He said, 'Darrell, I thought you were a Christian!' Then he walked away! I've been a Christian longer than he. Who does he think he is? What's wrong with playing pool?"

Mother was thoughtful. "Maybe Troy's father plays a lot of pool in the bars, so Troy associates playing pool with drinking, wasting money, and being away from home too much. He probably doesn't understand that a quiet game of pool in somebody's basement can be okay. Darrell, I think from now on you ought to stay away from playing pool so you're not a stumbling block to Troy."

"I don't see why I shouldn't play," objected Darrell. "I can't help it if he doesn't like it."

Mother thought for a moment. "Troy's a baby Christian. Seeing you do something he considers wrong might hurt him spiritually. Joining you might lead him to play pool in the wrong place. As he grows in his Christian life, he'll learn how to handle his actions. But right now, pool playing is a problem for him."

Darrell nodded thoughtfully. "I'll try not to do anything that would make Troy stumble in his faith."

HOW ABOUT YOU? Are there things you think are okay to do, but which bother other people? Remember, a Christian doesn't live for himself. His actions influence others. Do your activities draw people to Christ or turn them away? Refuse to be a "stumbling block," even if it means you have to give up something you enjoy. □ J.H.

TO MEMORIZE: *Be careful, however, that the exercise of your freedom does not become a stumbling block to the weak.* 1 Corinthians 8:9, NIV

Give and Get

PETE AND his brother Mike came into the house and hung up their coats. "How was Bible club?" asked Mother.

"I'm on the game committee for a party we're having next week," Mike replied. "We had a neat lesson, too. After I learn my verses for next week, I'm going to hunt up some games."

Mother looked at Pete as he turned on the TV. "Did you enjoy club, too?" she asked. "What was the lesson about?"

"Huh?" Pete looked up. "Oh . . . ah . . . something about some queen. I couldn't hear too good. I was in the back row." He turned his attention back to the TV.

"Are you on a committee for the party?" asked Mother.

"Naw," Pete mumbled. "They wanted me to help with decorations, but I'm not into that." He stood up. "Can I go over to Jim's house?"

"I guess so," agreed Mother, "but don't you have some Bible verses to learn?"

Pete shrugged. "I can do that later." He put on his coat and looked at himself in the hall mirror. His mother watched as he tipped his head and smiled. His reflection smiled back. Then he scowled, and the reflection scowled, too.

When Pete noticed Mother watching, he grinned at her. She smiled back. "Life is a little like a mirror," she said.

Pete's eyebrows shot up. "How's that?"

"Like a mirror, life gives back pretty much what you give to it," explained Mother. "If you give it a little, you get only a little out of it. If you put a lot into it, you'll find you enjoy it a lot more and get a lot out of it, too."

Pete's eyes fell on his Bible lying on the table. "You mean like Bible club?" he asked.

"Bible club," Mother, nodding, said, "and junior choir and school and your ball team and church and—"

"And everything," interrupted Pete. He picked up his Bible. I get the point," he said thoughtfully.

HOW ABOUT YOU? Are you giving your best to the activities in which you're involved? Do you do your part "heartily, as to the Lord"? When you do that, you are serving Him, and He will bless you for it.
□ H.M.

TO MEMORIZE: *And whatever you do in word or deed, do all in the name of the Lord Jesus, giving thanks to God the Father through Him.*
Colossians 3:17, NKJV

FROM THE BIBLE:
Let the word of Christ dwell in you richly in all wisdom, teaching and admonishing one another in psalms and hymns and spiritual songs, singing with grace in your hearts to the Lord. And whatever you do in word or deed, do all in the name of the Lord Jesus, giving thanks to God the Father through Him. Wives, submit to your own husbands, as is fitting in the Lord. Husbands, love your wives and do not be bitter toward them. Children, obey your parents in all things, for this is well pleasing to the Lord. Fathers, do not provoke your children, lest they become discouraged. Servants, obey in all things your masters according to the flesh, not with eyeservice, as men-pleasers, but in sincerity of heart, fearing God. And whatever you do, do it heartily, as to the Lord and not to men, knowing that from the Lord you will receive the reward of the inheritance; for you serve the Lord Christ.
Colossians 3:16-24, NKJV

Do things heartily

10

'Fess Up

FROM THE BIBLE:

Blessed is he whose transgressions are forgiven, whose sins are covered. Blessed is the man whose sin the LORD does not count against him and in whose spirit is no deceit. When I kept silent, my bones wasted away through my groaning all day long. For day and night your hand was heavy upon me; my strength was sapped as in the heat of summer. Then I acknowledged my sin to you and did not cover up my iniquity. I said, "I will confess my transgressions to the LORD"—and you forgave the guilt of my sin. Therefore let everyone who is godly pray to you while you may be found; surely when the mighty waters rise, they will not reach him. You are my hiding place; you will protect me from trouble and surround me with songs of deliverance.

Psalm 32:1-7, NIV

Confess your sins

TODD GASPED and choked. Quickly, he turned so Ned couldn't see his face. He knew he shouldn't be smoking, but he didn't want Ned to laugh at him.

"How'd ya like it?" Ned spoke to Todd's back.

"Great," Todd lied. "Just great." He glanced at his watch. "Hey, I gotta run. See you tomorrow." Guilt tugged at his heart as he hurried home.

When Todd entered the house, he heard his little sister's voice. "But, Mommy, I didn't do it! I didn't." Todd went down the hall toward his bedroom.

"Tiffany," Mother said, "I know you did."

As Todd passed his parents' room, the smell of perfume almost choked him. Looking in, he saw that the carpet was sprinkled with powder, and tiny footprints led from the vanity to the door. "You'd better 'fess up, little sister. You're caught for sure this time," Todd teased.

Tiffany sobbed, "I didn't mean to. I was only going to make me smell pretty for Daddy."

Mother tried to hide her smile. "Well, you certainly did that! The whole house is going to smell pretty for Daddy. Go sit in your room while I clean up this mess." She turned toward Todd. "And what have *you* been up to?"

Todd gulped. "I . . . I . . . nothing," he stuttered, a guilty look on his face.

Mother looked at him in surprise. She had been teasing, but now she realized Todd really had been up to something. "Better 'fess up, Son." She repeated the words he had used with his sister.

"I . . . I . . . Ned offered me a cigarette, and I tried smoking it," Todd confessed.

"Oh, Todd!" exclaimed Mother. "I'm sorry to hear that."

"It was terrible," admitted Todd. "I'm glad I confessed. I feel so much better, and I think it will help me to say no to Ned next time."

"I'm sure that's true," agreed Mother, "and don't forget to tell God about this and ask Him to help you."

HOW ABOUT YOU? Is there something bothering your conscience? Do you need to 'fess up? If so, right now tell God, your parents, or whoever is involved. A clean conscience is a priceless possession. □ B.W.

TO MEMORIZE: *If we confess our sins, He is faithful and just to forgive us our sins and to cleanse us from all unrighteousness.* 1 John 1:9, NKJV

SCHOOL BEGAN in the usual boring way for Roger—first math, then reading. *We need some action around here,* Roger thought. He peeked into his desk to check on the little mouse he had in a small box there.

A few minutes later, his teacher, Mrs. Madden, had to go to the office. She appointed Jennifer, one of the girls, to be class monitor in her absence. Jennifer proudly took her place behind the teacher's desk. Roger decided this was his chance. Quietly he took the mouse from his desk and released it. It scampered across the floor. "There's a mouse!" The girls screamed, and several of them ran to the back of the room.

"Take your seats," Jennifer instructed. "It won't hurt you." The mouse dashed across the floor, running right over Jennifer's foot. "Ahhhh!" she shrieked. She climbed onto her chair, and some of the other girls did the same.

"Quiet," Jennifer ordered. "Everyone sit down. There's nothing to worry about." But she remained on her chair.

Just then Mrs. Madden returned. She dismissed the class for an early lunch. While everyone was in the cafeteria, a janitor removed the little creature from the classroom.

After school, Roger told his mother about Jennifer and the mouse. He told her everything except how the mouse got there. "It was pretty funny," he said. "Jennifer told the class to sit down because there was nothing to worry about, but she stayed standing on her chair."

"That's a good example of what we discussed in my ladies' Bible study this morning," said Mother. "Just as Jennifer's actions didn't match her words, Christians' actions don't always match what they profess to believe. If we claim to love Jesus, yet do things in disobedience to Him, we're not putting our faith into action."

Roger felt guilty. He knew that disrupting the class was not Christ-like. When he reached his room, he asked God to forgive him for not living according to his faith.

HOW ABOUT YOU? Do you say you believe in Jesus but carelessly lie, cheat, or treat others unkindly? Or do you act out your faith by living a godly life? Ask God to help you act according to your faith.
□ N.E.K.

TO MEMORIZE: *Faith by itself, if it is not accompanied by action, is dead.* James 2:17, NIV

Roger's Mouse

FROM THE BIBLE:
What good is it, my brothers, if a man claims to have faith but has no deeds? Can such faith save him? Suppose a brother or sister is without clothes and daily food. If one of you says to him, "Go, I wish you well; keep warm and well fed," but does nothing about his physical needs, what good is it? In the same way, faith by itself, if it is not accompanied by action, is dead. But someone will say, "You have faith; I have deeds." Show me your faith without deeds, and I will show you my faith by what I do. You believe that there is one God. Good! Even the demons believe that—and shudder. You foolish man, do you want evidence that faith without deeds is useless?
James 2:14-20, NIV

Live what you believe

True Freedom

FROM THE BIBLE:

My son, keep your father's command, and do not forsake the law of your mother. Bind them continually upon your heart; tie them around your neck. When you roam, they will lead you; when you sleep, they will keep you; and when you awake, they will speak with you. For the commandment is a lamp, and the law is light; reproofs of instruction are the way of life.
Proverbs 6:20-23, NKJV

True freedom includes rules

CHRISTINA RAN into her bedroom and slammed the door. How unreasonable could her mother be! Christina wanted to go to the slumber party at Sarah's house, but her mother wouldn't let her go. "You know Sarah's family are not Christians," Mother had said, "and the girls are much older than you are and rather wild."

But Christina wouldn't listen. "You never give me any freedom," she had stormed. "I don't think you even want me to have any fun!"

She was still sniffling when she heard a sound at her window. Looking up, she saw a bird beating its wings against the glass. It seemed to be trying to get inside. As she watched, her Mother knocked on the door. "I have some clean laundry, Christina."

As Mother set the clothes on the dresser, she saw the bird beating at the glass. "Christina," Mother said softly, "open the window and let the poor bird in. It's cruel to keep him out when he desperately wants to get in."

"Mother, you've got to be kidding! He wouldn't know what to do once he got inside. He'd be trapped and frightened and wouldn't know how to get out again! He might get hurt."

"But, don't you want him to have his freedom?" asked Mother.

"He's got more space and freedom outside," Christina said grumpily.

Mother smiled and nodded. "So by saying no, you're really giving him freedom and protecting him," she said. "I know it doesn't make a lot of sense to you right now that I said no to the party, but God gave me the responsibility of protecting you. I don't want you to get caught in a situation where you might get hurt."

Christina looked at the foolish bird. Then she ran over and hugged her mother.

HOW ABOUT YOU? Do you feel that your parents are restricting your freedom by giving you rules and expecting you to obey? In love, they are actually protecting you from situations or things that could harm you. Trust their judgment and obey their decisions. True freedom includes living within bounds set up by God. □ J.H.

TO MEMORIZE: *For the commandment is a lamp, and the law is light; reproofs of instruction are the way of life.* Proverbs 6:23, NKJV

RACHELLE THREW her books on the couch and with a loud groan plopped down beside them. "Was it that bad?" Grandma asked as she laid down her needlepoint. Grandma always had time to listen.

Glumly, Rachelle nodded. "It was a terrible day, Gram. I can't do math. I've tried and tried, but I can't understand it. I got a D on my last test, and I'm so ashamed."

"Have you asked your teacher for help?" asked Grandma.

"Mr. Marker?" Rachelle snorted. "No way! He explains it in class, and if we don't understand, that's our problem. I'd be embarrassed to ask him for special help."

"I think you take after your grandpa," chuckled Grandma. "He hated to ask for help, too. We could be lost in some town, and he'd wander around for an hour before he'd stop and ask for directions. He was too proud."

"I brought you a glass of iced tea, Gram," said Troy as he came into the room carrying a tray that was almost too large for him to handle. As the glass wobbled, Rachelle reached out to help. The little boy jerked the tray out of her reach. "No! I can do it all by my—"

"Oh! Look what you did!" Rachelle cried as the glass toppled and tea splattered everywhere.

"Maybe I will ask Mr. Marker for help," Rachelle said thoughtfully when things had settled down. "I guess I've been acting like Troy and Grandpa, trying to do it by myself."

Grandma nodded. "And don't forget to ask God to help you, too."

HOW ABOUT YOU? Is there an area in which you need help? Does a subject in school seem too difficult? Is the minister too hard to understand? Are your memory verses too hard to learn? Is there a family situation you can't handle? Don't be too proud to ask for the help you need. Pride does not please God. Ask His help first, and then ask help of parents, friends, or teachers. God has given them to you, and He wants you to use their help.
□ B.W.

TO MEMORIZE: *When pride comes, then comes shame; but with the humble is wisdom.*
Proverbs 11:2, NKJV

MARCH

13

Too Proud

FROM THE BIBLE:
The LORD is far from the wicked, but He hears the prayer of the righteous. The light of the eyes rejoices the heart, and a good report makes the bones healthy. The ear that hears the reproof of life will abide among the wise. He who disdains instruction despises his own soul, but he who heeds reproof gets understanding. The fear of the LORD is the instruction of wisdom, and before honor is humility.
Proverbs 15:29-33, NKJV

Ask for help

14

Why Complain?

FROM THE BIBLE:

But godliness with contentment is great gain. For we brought nothing into the world, and we can take nothing out of it. But if we have food and clothing, we will be content with that.
1 Timothy 6:6-8, NIV

Enjoy what you have

IT WAS SPRING vacation, and Janie was bored. "Oh, Mom, what can I do?" she asked for the fourteenth time.

Her mother sighed. She had already made several suggestions, but nothing interested Janie. "I'll tell you what," Mother said finally. "I'll help you think of something that's fun to do, if you'll do some jobs for me first."

"Okay," Janie agreed. "Anything would be better than sitting around doing nothing." Mother wrote out a list of jobs. When Janie saw it, she groaned. First she had to vacuum the carpets and dust the furniture. Then she had to wash the bathroom tile. Finally, she folded some towels for her mother and put them away. "Is that enough?" she asked when she had finished.

"Not quite," said her mother. "I'd like you to take these cookies to Mrs. Gundy's house."

"All the way over there?" Janie grumbled. "Oh, okay!" By the time Janie got back, she was tired. She hoped her mother wouldn't think of any more jobs for her to do!

"Now, how about having a cookie?" invited Mother. "Then maybe you could read for a while."

"Good idea!" said Janie. Then she laughed. "Isn't that silly? You suggested the same thing before, and it sounded boring then. Now it sounds like fun."

"The activity hasn't changed. You have," said Mother. "An old saying says the 'grass is always greener on the other side of the fence.' It's all a matter of *attitude*. You didn't appreciate your free time when you had it. I took it away from you for a while, and now you want it again!"

"I'm sorry, Mom," said Janie. "I've been complaining and grumbling all morning. I know that's wrong. I think I will have that cookie now. After that, I'm sure I can find lots of interesting things to do!"

HOW ABOUT YOU? Are you a grumbler? Do you gripe and complain if you don't have some place to go or something exciting to do? Satan tries to make you want what you don't have, instead of being thankful for what you do have; God wants you to be happy with what He has given you.
□ S.K.

TO MEMORIZE: *But godliness with contentment is great gain.* 1 Timothy 6:6, NIV

"DAD SURE LOOKS tired lately," said Jenny to her brother, Steve. It was Saturday morning and the two children were playing catch in the front yard. Just a few minutes earlier, they had watched their dad slowly walk down the road to the bus stop. Even though it was the weekend, he had to go to the office.

"Dad's tired because of that big report he's writing for the convention next month," Steve explained.

"Mom's been busy, too," Jenny continued. "It's not easy teaching a Sunday school class and getting the house ready for company. Wish we could help them."

"Well, we have helped Mom with the cleaning," said Steve, "but there are some jobs kids just can't do!"

They threw the ball back and forth for a while, then Jenny spoke excitedly. "Steve, how much money do you have?"

Steve grinned. "I'm rich! All last week I helped Mr. Parker clean out the back room at his grocery store, remember? And he said he could use me later, too. Why?"

"I've got baby-sitting money saved up," said Jenny, "and I thought maybe we could take Dad and Mom out for dinner. We don't have to go to the most expensive place in town, but it would let them know how much we appreciate them."

And that's just what Jenny and Steve did! Their parents were very surprised. "You know," said Dad as they were eating, "this is the best hamburger I've ever tasted! The psalmist sure knew what he was talking about when he said, 'Children are a heritage from the Lord.'"

"I agree." Mom smiled. "It's terrific to know that our children care about us!"

Jenny and Steve grinned at each other. They were glad they had given their parents a special treat!

HOW ABOUT YOU? When was the last time you did something special for your dad and mom, or told them how much you appreciated the hard work they do? Dads and moms sometimes become very busy and therefore very tired. Read 1 Corinthians 13, a chapter in which the Apostle Paul talks about love. Then show that kind of love to your parents. □ L.W.

TO MEMORIZE: *"Honor your father and mother"— which is the first commandment with a promise.* Ephesians 6:2, NIV

MARCH

15

The Best Hamburger!

FROM THE BIBLE:
Though I speak with the tongues of men and of angels, but have not love, I have become as sounding brass or a clanging cymbal. And though I have the gift of prophecy, and understand all mysteries and all knowledge, and though I have all faith, so that I could remove mountains, but have not love, I am nothing. And though I bestow all my goods to feed the poor, and though I give my body to be burned, but have not love, it profits me nothing.
1 Corinthians 13:1-3, NKJV

Show love for parents

16

I Appreciate You!

Tell Priscilla and Aquila hello. They have been my fellow workers in the affairs of Christ Jesus. In fact, they risked their lives for me; and I am not the only one who is thankful to them: so are all the Gentile churches. Please give my greetings to all those who meet to worship in their home. Greet my good friend Epaenetus. He was the very first person to become a Christian in Asia. Remember me to Mary, too, who has worked so hard to help us. Then there are Andronicus and Junias, my relatives who were in prison with me. They are respected by the apostles, and became Christians before I did. Please give them my greetings. Say hello to Ampliatus, whom I love as one of God's own children, and Urbanus, our fellow worker, and beloved Stachys. Then there is Apelles, a good man whom the Lord approves; greet him for me. And give my best regards to those working at the house of Aristobulus.

Romans 16:3-10, TLB

Appreciate others— and tell them

EVERY MORNING Michael read a chapter of the Bible and prayed. One morning he read Romans 16. *This is kind of a different chapter,* he thought. *It's mostly a list of the people Paul appreciated.* He studied it for a moment. *Maybe this chapter is in the Bible to show us how important it is to let others know how much we appreciate them.*

So at breakfast Michael said to his mother, "Thanks for cooking these eggs for me, Mom." Then when his brother Steve came into the kitchen, Michael said, "Steve, I appreciate you for letting me use your markers for my report." Both Mom and Steve gave Michael such big smiles that he decided to keep on telling people how much they were appreciated.

At school, Michael said to his friend Keith, "Thanks for sticking up for me when those guys teased me yesterday. I appreciate that."

After class he told his teacher, "I appreciate the neat way you've been telling us about the Civil War. It makes studying so much more interesting."

On the way home from school, Michael walked by his church. Pastor Grey was standing in the parking lot, talking to the organist. "Pastor," Michael called, "I want you to know I appreciate your messages. And Mrs. Johnson, I appreciate you for playing the organ each week." Michael received two more big smiles.

That night as Michael was getting ready for bed, he thought once again about appreciation. People needed to be appreciated. He could tell that by the big smiles he had been getting all day. He was glad he had learned a lesson from the apostle Paul.

HOW ABOUT YOU? You probably do appreciate all the people who do things for you, but do you let them know it? Make a list of five people whom you appreciate, and then tell them. You'll feel good because you will be helping others feel good. And don't forget to include Jesus on your list. He deserves the most appreciation. □ L.W.

TO MEMORIZE: *I thank my God every time I remember you.* Philippians 1:3, NIV

"COME ON, SUE," Erika called. "It's time for choir. If we don't hurry, we'll be late."

Sue slowly put her books in her locker and shut the door. "I decided not to go, Erika. It's such a nuisance having to stay after school twice a week."

"But Sue, we planned on it!" Erika glanced at her watch. The girls were supposed to be in the music room in five minutes.

"Oh, come on! Let's forget choir this year," urged Sue. "Let's go to my house and play my new video game instead."

Erika hesitated. She wanted to stay, but she didn't want to go to choir alone. She knew Sue wouldn't change her mind, either. "Well, okay," she agreed slowly.

That night Erika's mom asked how choir was. "Sue and I decided not to join this year," Erika explained.

"Was that really your choice or Sue's?" Mother asked. "You have a talent, Erika, and you've always said you wanted to use it for the Lord. The training you get at school will help you develop your talent, and besides, you had a lot of fun singing at the concerts last year. The only person you're hurting by not joining is yourself."

Erika thought about her mother's words. This wasn't the first time Sue had discouraged her from doing something she wanted to do. In fact, by listening to Sue, she was becoming a very uninvolved, lazy person. She knew that was wrong. The Lord wanted her to do her best!

"Mom, I'll join the choir next week," she said firmly. "I'm not going to let Sue talk me out of doing things anymore! I'll ask the Lord to help me make my own decisions."

HOW ABOUT YOU? Do you let others tell you what you should or shouldn't do? Sometimes friends can sound pretty convincing, and if you're not careful, they'll make your decisions for you. The Lord tells you to do your best. Ask Him to help you stick to your principles. Don't let your friends sway you with persuasive words. Do what you know the Lord would want you to do. □ L.W.

TO MEMORIZE: *I can do everything through him who gives me strength.* Philippians 4:13, NIV

Her Own Decision

FROM THE BIBLE:

In the course of time, Absalom provided himself with a chariot and horses and with fifty men to run ahead of him. He would get up early and stand by the side of the road leading to the city gate. Whenever anyone came with a complaint to be placed before the king for a decision, Absalom would call out to him, "What town are you from?" He would answer, "Your servant is from one of the tribes of Israel." Then Absalom would say to him, "Look, your claims are valid and proper, but there is no representative of the king to hear you." And Absalom would add, "If only I were appointed judge in the land! Then everyone who has a complaint or case could come to me and I would see that he gets justice." Also, whenever anyone approached him to bow down before him, Absalom would reach out his hand, take hold of him and kiss him. Absalom behaved in this way toward all the Israelites who came to the king asking for justice, and so he stole the hearts of the men of Israel.
2 Samuel 15:1-6, NIV

Decide with God's help

MARCH

18

T-Shirt Day

FROM THE BIBLE:
Meanwhile, as Peter was sitting in the courtyard a girl came over and said to him, "You were with Jesus, for both of you are from Galilee." But Peter denied it loudly. "I don't even know what you are talking about," he angrily declared. Later, out by the gate, another girl noticed him and said to those standing around, "This man was with Jesus—from Nazareth." Again Peter denied it, this time with an oath. "I don't even know the man," he said. But after a while the men who had been standing there came over to him and said, "We know you are one of his disciples, for we can tell by your Galilean accent." Peter began to curse and swear. "I don't even know the man," he said. And immediately the cock crowed. Then Peter remembered what Jesus had said, "Before the cock crows, you will deny me three times." And he went away, crying bitterly.
Matthew 26:69-75, TLB

Don't be ashamed of Jesus

JENNY AND HER FAMILY were spending spring break at Mountain View Bible Camp, and Jenny was having a wonderful time. "Can I please buy a camp T-shirt?" she begged one day. "Everyone else has one." Mother agreed, and Jenny promptly put the shirt on. On the front was a picture of the chapel with the words "Proclaiming His Word to the World." On the back it said, "Mountain View Bible Camp." Jenny wore the shirt regularly, proud to be a part of the group.

Back home, Jenny stuffed the shirt in a drawer and forgot about it. Mother didn't forget, though. From time to time she suggested that Jenny wear it, but Jenny always refused. "I like it," she insisted, "but it just wouldn't look right here."

One Friday was declared T-Shirt Day at school. Again Jenny begged for a new shirt. "Not this time," Mother replied. "Wear your camp shirt. It's almost new."

"I can't wear that," protested Jenny. "It wouldn't look right. Everyone else will wear shirts with cute sayings on them or they'll be from exciting places like Fun Haven."

"Wasn't camp exciting?" asked Mother. "You loved your shirt before."

Jenny bit her lip. "It was different at camp," she said.

"Yes, it was," Mother admitted. "It was comfortable to be identified as a Christian then, because others shared your faith."

Jenny bristled. "Are you saying I'm ashamed now to let others see I'm a Christian?"

"Are you?" asked Mother softly.

Jenny thought about it. "I guess maybe I have been," she confessed. "I'll wear my camp shirt to school after all. Maybe I can interest my friends in attending Bible camp in the summer."

"Good," Mother said. "Then you'll be proclaiming God's Word, just like your shirt says!"

HOW ABOUT YOU? Do your friends and teachers know you're a Christian? Do you pray before you eat, witness when you can, and speak up for your faith in the classroom? Don't be ashamed of Jesus. Others need to know Him, too. □ J.H.

TO MEMORIZE: *So do not be ashamed to testify about our Lord, or ashamed of me his prisoner. But join with me in suffering for the gospel.*
2 Timothy 1:8, NIV

"I HATE this ugly nose!" wailed Heather as she looked into the mirror. "Why can't I have a nose like Sandy's? Hers is just perfect!"

"Let's not worry about noses now," said Mother. "We've got to get going if we want to stop at the zoo today."

It was a beautiful, sunny day. Heather and her mother enjoyed a leisurely stroll, looking at all the animals. "My! The elephants have long trunks, don't they?" commented Mother as they stopped to watch the great beasts. "I'm glad my nose isn't that long."

"Come on, Mom," protested Heather, "that's what makes an elephant an elephant!"

At the rhinoceros' cage, Mother laughed as she pointed to the horns on their noses. "Oh, dear! That kind of nose would be even worse!" Heather gave her a curious look, but said nothing. As they walked along, she noticed that Mother had a comment to make about almost every kind of animal's nose. When they reached the baboons, Mother turned to her. "Their noses are much too stubby, don't you think? Wouldn't they look better if they had noses more like the tigers'?"

Heather was annoyed. "No, they wouldn't!" she snapped. "I like them just the way they are. The animals wouldn't be very interesting if they were all alike. Besides, you've told me yourself that God made them the way they are and that He knows best how they should look."

"Exactly," nodded Mother. "He knows best how animals should look, and He knows best how people should look."

"Oh! exclaimed Heather as she clapped her hand over her nose. "I get it! I'm the way I am because God made me this way. I guess I should thank Him rather than question Him. Besides, if God likes my nose, who am I to say it isn't beautiful!"

HOW ABOUT YOU? Do you sometimes complain about the way you look? Do you wish you looked just like someone else? If everyone had the "perfect" nose, mouth, eyes, and teeth, we would all look alike! Wouldn't that be dull—and confusing! Remember, God made you, and He loves you just the way you are. □ P.R.

TO MEMORIZE: *The Spirit of God has made me, and the breath of the Almighty gives me life.* Job 33:4, NKJV

MARCH

19

The Right Nose

FROM THE BIBLE:

"I am the LORD, and there is no other; I form the light and create darkness, I make peace and create calamity; I, the LORD, do all these things. Woe to him who strives with his Maker! Let the potsherd strive with the potsherds of the earth. Shall the clay say to him who forms it, 'What are you making?' Or shall your handiwork say, 'He has no hands'? Woe to him who says to his father, 'What are you begetting?' Or to the woman, 'What have you brought forth?' " Thus says the LORD, the Holy One of Israel, and his Maker: "Ask Me of things to come concerning My sons; and concerning the work of My hands, you command Me. I have made the earth, and created man on it. It was I—My hands that stretched out the heavens, and all their host I have commanded."
Isaiah 45:6-7, 9-12, NKJV

God made me special

20

Grandpa Forgets

FROM THE BIBLE:
Remember these, O Jacob, and Israel, for you are My servant; I have formed you, you are My servant; O Israel, you will not be forgotten by Me!
Isaiah 44:21, NKJV

Are not five sparrows sold for two copper coins? And not one of them is forgotten before God. But the very hairs of your head are all numbered. Do not fear therefore; you are of more value than many sparrows.
Luke 12:6-7, NKJV

God never forgets you

"HI, GRANDPA!" exclaimed Denise. "Is Grandma here, too?" Denise had come to the supermarket with her father, who was picking up a cake mix and some ice cream for her birthday party the next day. But what was wrong with Grandpa? He didn't say anything. He just stared at her as if he didn't know her.

Just then Grandma appeared. She looked cross. "Robert, I told you to wait by the magazines," she scolded. Seeing Denise, she gave her a quick kiss. "Are you all ready for your birthday party?" she asked.

"Party?" asked Grandpa. "Who's having a party?"

"Denise is. We talked about it at breakfast," said Grandma patiently. "Don't you remember?" She took his arm. "Let's go buy a birthday present for a certain little girl, shall we?"

That night as Mother tucked her into bed, Denise told her about Grandpa's strange behavior. Mother looked concerned. "Grandpa isn't well," said Mother. "Do you remember when we took him to University Hospital not long ago?" Denise nodded. "The doctors discovered that he has a disease called Alzheimer's. It causes people to forget names, places, even people they love."

Denise swallowed hard. "But Grandpa and I are friends—he said so himself. And friends aren't supposed to forget each other."

"I know," said Mother, giving Denise a hug, "but I'm afraid that earthly friends do sometimes forget."

"But I thought I could always count on Grandpa," wailed Denise.

"Honey, Grandpa can't help it when he forgets," said Mother. "Thank God for the good times you've had together. Thank Him, too, that Jesus is always there for you—that He's a friend that sticks 'closer than a brother'—or even than a grandfather."

As Denise snuggled down, she thought about her mother's words. She thanked God that He would never leave her.

HOW ABOUT YOU? Do you feel sad because a friend moved away, chose someone else, or just simply forgot you? Aren't you glad that God will never forget His own? Thank Him for that, and let Him fill the empty place in your life. □ C.B.

TO MEMORIZE: *A man of many companions may come to ruin, but there is a friend who sticks closer than a brother.* Proverbs 18:24, NIV

PINK AND YELLOW balloons hung around the living room. A big sign saying "Happy Birthday, Denise" was over the sofa. Many of Denise's aunts, uncles, and cousins were already there when Grandpa and Grandma arrived. But Grandpa stood by the door, a lost, confused expression on his face. "Who are these people?" he asked.

"They're your children and grandchildren," said Grandma.

Denise noticed that she sounded like she was talking to a small child. *I guess that's because he has Alzheimer's disease and forgets a lot of things,* she thought. She went over and slipped her hand into his. "I'm glad you came to my party, Grandpa."

Grandpa looked down at Denise, and a soft smile spread over his face. He patted her head clumsily, and then he said, "Is this your house, little girl?"

"Of course, Grandpa," Denise replied. "I'm Denise, remember? You've been here lots of times."

When Denise and Daddy helped clean the kitchen after the party, Denise closed the dishwasher door with a bang. "Why does Grandpa have Alzheimer's?" she muttered. "It's an ugly disease. And I can't think of a single reason why God let it happen."

"Neither can I," said Daddy. Denise's eyes widened. "That surprises you, doesn't it?" he asked. Denise nodded. "In life we have to expect sad things to happen as well as good things," continued Daddy. "Grandpa's Alzheimer's disease is sad. And just as he often can't understand what's happening around him, we can't understand why such sad things happen. God doesn't ask us to understand, but He does ask us to believe in Him with all our hearts in spite of sad circumstances. He promises to be with us in difficult times."

"I guess I have to trust the Lord even when I feel like crying," agreed Denise. "I'm glad He'll help me through the sad times."

HOW ABOUT YOU? Are you puzzled, wondering why God has allowed some sad thing to happen? He wants you to trust Him, and He waits to give you comfort and help. As you believe in Him, this testing of your faith will strengthen you. You'll find that His grace and help is more than enough.

□ C.B.

TO MEMORIZE: *My grace is sufficient for you, for My strength is made perfect in weakness.*
2 Corinthians 12:9, NKJV

21

Grandpa Forgets

(Continued from yesterday)

FROM THE BIBLE:
I lift up my eyes to the hills— where does my help come from? My help comes from the LORD, the Maker of heaven and earth. He will not let your foot slip—he who watches over you will not slumber; indeed, he who watches over Israel will neither slumber nor sleep. The LORD watches over you—the LORD is your shade at your right hand; the sun will not harm you by day, nor the moon by night. The LORD will keep you from all harm—he will watch over your life; the LORD will watch over your coming and going both now and forevermore.
Psalm 121:1-8, NIV

Keep trusting God

22

Grandpa Forgets

(Continued from yesterday)

FROM THE BIBLE:
Let your conduct be without covetousness, and be content with such things as you have. For He Himself has said, "I will never leave you nor forsake you." So we may boldly say: "The Lord is my helper; I will not fear. What can man do to me?" Remember those who rule over you, who have spoken the word of God to you, whose faith follow, considering the outcome of their conduct. Jesus Christ is the same yesterday, today, and forever.
Hebrews 13:5-8, NKJV

God never changes

ONE SATURDAY, Denise woke up feeling grumpy and sad. When she got to the kitchen, she found Mother stirring the oatmeal. "How's Grandpa?" Denise asked. "Now that he's broken his hip, will he ever walk again?"

"I don't know," replied Mother. "Do you want to go with Daddy and me to the nursing home this afternoon?"

Denise nodded. She sat down to eat, but the oatmeal stuck in her throat. Life was turning out to be painful. First Grandpa had gotten Alzheimer's disease, and now, with a broken hip, he couldn't even be at home.

When they reached Grandpa's room that afternoon, Denise wished she hadn't come. Grandpa looked almost as white as his bedspread. His eyes were wild and frightened. "Help me. . . . please help me . . . Will someone please help me?" he cried over and over. A nurse came in, and Daddy took Denise's hand and led her from the room. He smiled at her with understanding. "It's pretty rough, isn't it?" he said.

"I wish things could be the way they used to be," cried Denise. "Grandpa's so different. I want him to stay the same."

Daddy patted her hand and sighed. "Everything in life changes," he said. "Why look at yourself—you've grown an inch since last summer. And Mother's gone on a diet and lost several pounds. As for me . . . well, I can't see it, of course, but they tell me I've gained a few."

Denise tried to smile. The transfer of weight from Mother to Daddy had been a family joke. Daddy squeezed her hand. "I'll tell you what helps me accept the changes," he said. "It's the knowledge that I have a Friend who never changes. The Bible says Jesus is the same yesterday, today, and forever. And in Malachi God says, 'I am the Lord. I change not.' He promises to stay the same."

Denise sniffed. "It's hard when things turn topsy-turvy," she said, "but I'm glad I can count on God not to change."

HOW ABOUT YOU? Are you frightened by the changes in your life? Perhaps someone close to you has died or moved away. Maybe someone you love is sick. Accept the changes—they're part of life—and trust God. He understands your confusion and hurt. And He's the God who never changes. □ C.B.

TO MEMORIZE: *Jesus Christ is the same yesterday, today, and forever.* Hebrews 13:8, NKJV

LAN CLOSED her locker and hurried toward the door. Her first day in the new school had been just as she expected. She felt as if everyone stared at her because she looked different from most of the girls in her class. But then, they had not been born in Korea, and she had. She sighed. She was glad there were at least a few other Asian girls in the class, and she hoped she'd soon get to know them better.

"Lan," someone called. "Wait for me." Lan turned abruptly and saw a short blonde girl coming toward her. "I was hoping I'd get to meet you," the girl said in a friendly voice. "My Sunday school teacher told me you and your folks had just moved next door to her."

Lan nodded. "She wanted me to go to church with her yesterday," the Korean girl confessed. "But . . . " She stopped again.

"My name is Gina Ellers," the other girl said. "I wish you had come to church yesterday. You would have liked it. There are lots of nice people there."

Lan shook her head. "No," she said shyly. "They would just look at me and say I'm different."

"Oh, I don't think so," Gina replied. "Most of them know nobody is really different."

Lan looked at the blonde girl in surprise. "That's silly. You sure look a lot different from me."

"Well, we look different on the outside," Gina admitted. "But it doesn't matter how different each one looks on the outside because God sees the heart, and He knows that we're all the same inside," she explained. "He knows we've all sinned, and we all need our sin taken away. So you see, you're not any different from me or anyone else. Jesus died for all of us."

"I never heard that before," Lan said thoughtfully. "Maybe I will come to your church and hear more about it. Or maybe you can tell me more."

HOW ABOUT YOU? Maybe you're a different color or nationality from others in your school. That makes no difference to God. He gave His Son for everyone, including you. Have you asked Him to take away your sin and make you His child? You can. Do it today. □ R.J.

TO MEMORIZE: *Everyone who calls on the name of the Lord will be saved.* Romans 10:13, NIV

Being Different

FROM THE BIBLE:

If you confess with your mouth, "Jesus is Lord," and believe in your heart that God raised him from the dead, you will be saved. For it is with your heart that you believe and are justified, and it is with your mouth that you confess and are saved. As the Scripture says, "Anyone who trusts in him will never be put to shame." For there is no difference between Jew and Gentile— the same Lord is Lord of all and richly blesses all who call on him, for, "Everyone who calls on the name of the Lord will be saved."

Romans 10:9-13, NIV

All have sinned

Being Different

(Continued from yesterday)

FROM THE BIBLE:
Then he called his disciples and the crowds to come over and listen. "If any of you wants to be my follower," he told them, "you must put aside your own pleasures and shoulder your cross, and follow me closely. If you insist on saving your life, you will lose it. Only those who throw away their lives for my sake and for the sake of the Good News will ever know what it means to really live. And how does a man benefit if he gains the whole world and loses his soul in the process? For is anything worth more than his soul? And anyone who is ashamed of me and my message in these days of unbelief and sin, I, the Messiah, will be ashamed of him when I return in the glory of my Father, with the holy angels."
Mark 8:34-38, TLB

Be different for Jesus

GINA AND LAN became good friends, and it wasn't long before Lan accepted Jesus as her Savior. She was beginning to feel more at home in her new school, too. The two girls talked about it one day. "You know something?" said Gina. "You've been afraid of being different, and so have I."

Lan looked at her in surprise. "You? Why would you be afraid of anything like that? You look just like all the other kids in school."

Gina nodded. "Maybe I look like most of them," she admitted, "but I've still been afraid of being different. I hardly ever talk to anyone about church or God or anything like that—all because I'm afraid they might laugh at me."

"You mean you've never talked to anyone like you talked to me?" Lan asked in surprise.

Gina shook her head. "I've been a Christian for three years," she said, "and I guess I've just been ashamed to let anyone know about it." She paused for a long time. "Yesterday in Sunday school, when our teacher read those verses about Jesus being ashamed of us before His Father if we are ashamed of Him down here on earth, I really felt terrible. I don't want Him to be ashamed of me anymore."

Lan was not sure she understood everything Gina was saying. It was still all so new to her. But she did know what it meant to be different. "Maybe we've both been wrong," she said slowly. "Maybe sometimes it's good to be different. I don't want Jesus to be ashamed of me either. Let's be different together."

HOW ABOUT YOU? Are you afraid to let your Christian testimony show for fear that someone will think you are a little different? Maybe "being different" in your actions and speech will be the very thing that will cause someone to see that you are a Christian. Perhaps it will give you the opportunity to win him for the Lord. □ R.J.

TO MEMORIZE: *If anyone would come after me, he must deny himself and take up his cross daily and follow me.* Luke 9:23, NIV

"WELL, GREG, what's on your schedule for tomorrow?" asked Dad as he sat down in an easy chair.

Greg snapped off the TV and picked up the paper. "Oh," he said, "tomorrow afternoon we have a youth group party." He quickly read through the comic page while his dad took off his shoes. Then, handing Dad the newspaper, Greg added, "We're having a Bible quiz at the beginning of the party. Maybe I'll just go late."

"Oh?" asked Dad. "You used to enjoy quizzes. Why don't you like them now?"

Greg leafed through a sports magazine. "Because Joel always wins, that's why. They're no fun anymore."

"Do you know what chapters the quiz will cover?"

"Yes," replied Greg, "but it doesn't matter what chapters they are. Joel will know everything in them. That guy really knows his Bible. The other day in science class, Joel and our teacher got into quite a discussion about creation, and Joel did really good. He quoted verses from the Bible and talked about why he believed it was true. He really knew what he was talking about."

"Good for Joel!" cheered Dad.

"I've heard him do the same kind of thing in history class. I wish I knew the Bible like that." Greg sighed and began reading an article.

Dad watched Greg for a moment, then he asked, "How do you suppose Joel learned so much?" Greg shrugged. "Well," said Dad, "I don't think it came from reading magazines or newspapers or watching TV. If you want to know the Bible, you have to study the Bible."

Greg looked at Dad thoughtfully. He looked down at his magazine. Then, putting it down, he got to his feet. "Excuse me, please." He grinned at his dad. "I have to go study a couple of chapters in my Bible. Joel's gonna get some competition tomorrow!"

HOW ABOUT YOU? Do you wish you had as much Bible knowledge as your pastor, your Sunday school teacher, or even a friend? It's available to you, too, but it won't come automatically. Listen carefully when God's Word is taught in church and Sunday school. Also, study it for yourself. □ H.M.

TO MEMORIZE: *Do your best to present yourself to God as one approved, a workman who does not need to be ashamed and who correctly handles the word of truth.* 2 Timothy 2:15, NIV

25

Study to Know

FROM THE BIBLE:
But as for you, continue in what you have learned and have become convinced of, because you know those from whom you learned it, and how from infancy you have known the holy Scriptures, which are able to make you wise for salvation through faith in Christ Jesus. All Scripture is God-breathed and is useful for teaching, rebuking, correcting and training in righteousness, so that the man of God may be thoroughly equipped for every good work.
2 Timothy 3:14-17, NIV

Study the Bible

MARCH

26

Are You Listening?

FROM THE BIBLE:
The boy Samuel ministered before the LORD under Eli. In those days the word of the LORD was rare. One night Eli, whose eyes were becoming so weak that he could barely see, was lying down in his usual place. Samuel was lying down in the temple of the LORD, where the ark of God was. Then the LORD called Samuel. Samuel answered, "Here I am." And he ran to Eli and said, "Here I am; you called me." But Eli said, "I did not call; go back and lie down." So he went and lay down. Again the LORD called, "Samuel!" And Samuel got up and went to Eli and said, "Here I am; you called me." "My son," Eli said, "I did not call; go back and lie down." The LORD called Samuel a third time, and Samuel got up and went to Eli and said, "Here I am; you called me." Then Eli realized that the LORD was calling the boy. So Eli told Samuel, "Go and lie down, and if he calls you, say, 'Speak, LORD, for your servant is listening.'"
1 Samuel 3:1-10, NIV

Listen for God's voice

"**I** HEARD THE LORD speak to me this morning," Dad said as the Jenkins family drove home from church.

"You did?" Four-year-old Jeremy was astonished. "I didn't hear Him."

"I didn't hear Him speak the same way you hear me," Dad explained, "but He spoke to my heart. I felt led to give more to missions."

Mother nodded. "I felt the same way. That certainly was a stirring message. Did you enjoy the part about the wheat harvest in Kansas, Phil?"

Phil looked blank. "Uhhh, I . . . well, I . . ."

In the rearview mirror Dad caught Phil's eye. "Did you even hear the sermon, Son?"

Phil looked at his feet.

Mother frowned. "Maybe you didn't hear the Lord because you weren't listening," she suggested.

Before Phil could defend himself, Dad said, "Here we are at home. I sure am hungry. I hope the roast is done."

As Mother prepared dinner, Dad watched the news on TV. The boys were sprawled on the living room carpet, and Phil read a Sunday school paper to Jeremy. "Ooohhh!" Dad gasped. "How terrible!" The boys looked up as the newscaster continued telling about a ten-year-old boy who was killed when he rode his bicycle in front of a train.

"That's odd," observed Phil as Dad turned off the TV. "Even if he was looking the wrong way, he should have heard it coming."

"He didn't hear the train because he wasn't listening for it. He was wearing headphones and was listening to his portable radio."

"Like Phil didn't hear the Lord speaking this morning because he wasn't listening?" Jeremy asked.

Phil frowned, "You didn't hear Him, either."

"But I will the next time," Jeremy answered positively. "Next time I'm gonna be listening."

HOW ABOUT YOU? The Lord very seldom shouts at you. He often speaks to your heart in a still, small voice, simply impressing you with what you should do. He speaks through sermons your pastor preaches, lessons your teachers teach, and the instructions your parents give. Don't let other things drown out the Lord's voice. □ B.W.

TO MEMORIZE: *Here I am! I stand at the door and knock. If anyone hears my voice and opens the door, I will come in and eat with him, and he with me.* Revelation 3:20, NIV

GARY SETTLED BACK in his seat as the shades were pulled. Today his science class was having a movie about Adelie penguins. Gary shivered as he saw the penguins swimming in the Antarctic. It was a cold and lonely place. How did they survive?

Gary watched as the penguins swam toward the coast in the spring. They slid and waddled across the icy land, searching for a nesting place. How funny they looked! Soon they stopped at a rocky place, which was called a rookery. Large numbers of penguins would lay their eggs and raise their young there. The rookery was very crowded. A million penguins could live in a single rookery, but each penguin had her own nest.

When the lights came on, Gary had several questions for his teacher. "If thousands of penguins live in one spot, how can a penguin tell which babies are hers?" he asked. "They all look dressed alike to me." The class laughed.

"That's a good question, Gary," his teacher said. "Each penguin has a different voice. The parents can pick out their own children from thousands of other penguins just by the sound of their voices. They know their own children, and they take care of their own children."

That evening Gary told his parents about the penguins. Dad smiled and nodded. "You know, God does the same thing for us," he said. "Millions and millions of people are scattered all over the world, but God knows those who belong to Him— those who have trusted Jesus as Savior. If they should stray away from Him, God will call them back to Himself by His Word. He knows His own children, and He takes care of them."

"I'm glad I belong to Jesus," Gary said to himself, "for I know God will always take care of me."

HOW ABOUT YOU? Do you sometimes worry about having food to eat or clothes to wear? Do you feel alone and forgotten? Do you wonder if God cares about you or your circumstances? If you've trusted Christ as your Savior, you belong to God. He knows you by name. He cares about every detail of your life. He has promised to care for you. Trust Him. □ J.H.

TO MEMORIZE: *The Lord knows those who are His.*
2 Timothy 2:19, NKJV

He Knows His Own

FROM THE BIBLE:
Anyone refusing to walk through the gate into a sheepfold, who sneaks over the wall, must surely be a thief! For a shepherd comes through the gate. The gatekeeper opens the gate for him, and the sheep hear his voice and come to him; and he calls his own sheep by name and leads them out. He walks ahead of them; and they follow him, for they recognize his voice. They won't follow a stranger but will run from him, for they don't recognize his voice. I am the Good Shepherd. The Good Shepherd lays down his life for the sheep. A hired man will run when he sees a wolf coming and will leave the sheep, for they aren't his and he isn't their shepherd. And so the wolf leaps on them and scatters the flock. The hired man runs because he is hired and has no real concern for the sheep. I am the Good Shepherd and know my own sheep, and they know me.
John 10:1-5, 11-14, TLB

God knows his own

28

He Knows His Own

(Continued from yesterday)

FROM THE BIBLE:

Let us draw near to God with a sincere heart in full assurance of faith, having our hearts sprinkled to cleanse us from a guilty conscience and having our bodies washed with pure water. Let us hold unswervingly to the hope we profess, for he who promised is faithful. And let us consider how we may spur one another on toward love and good deeds. Let us not give up meeting together, as some are in the habit of doing, but let us encourage one another—and all the more as you see the Day approaching.
Hebrews 10:22-25, NIV

Don't neglect church

AFTER SEEING the movie about penguins, Gary decided to do a report on them for extra credit. He was reading a book on penguins when his dad came into the family room. "How's your report coming, Gary?" Dad asked.

"Good, Dad. I'm learning some really neat stuff," Gary replied. "Did you know that when the penguins head for land and search for a nesting place, they march in single file for miles? They don't have any landmarks to guide them, but they never get lost. They use the sun to guide them. Aren't they smart?"

"Yes, and it's because God gave them certain instincts when He created them," Dad explained. "God cares about His creation."

"Listen to this," Gary continued. "When the penguin chicks are about three weeks old, they get so hungry that both parents must go out and hunt for food. Then the chicks gather into groups of fifty or sixty. Each group is called a crèche. In bad weather they huddle together to keep warm. They stick together for safety, too. If they wander off alone, a sea bird will try to capture them."

"That's a good illustration of Christians in a local church," Dad said. "They need to band together for warmth, fellowship, and protection. By themselves, they are more open to attacks of worldly living and false teaching. The church helps give them spiritual protection as they grow in the faith."

"Wow! I'm getting lots of lessons from the penguins. They sure are good teachers!" laughed Gary.

HOW ABOUT YOU? Do you attend a good Bible-believing church? Do you listen as the Word is taught? Do you make friends with the people there? These friends can encourage you as you live for Jesus. They can pray for you. Knowing they are there to help you makes it easier to stand up for Jesus in the world. □

TO MEMORIZE: *Let us not give up meeting together, as some are in the habit of doing, but let us encourage one another.* Hebrews 10:25, NIV

29

Be Still

AFTER DINNER one evening, Dad directed nine-year-old Phil, seven-year-old Tami, and Mother to three straight-backed chairs that stood in a row in the living room. The children looked puzzled, but followed instructions. Next, Dad took his position in front of them, holding the most sought-after book—the catalog of toys. Everyone listened attentively while Dad began describing a home computer in which Phil was especially interested.

Suddenly Mother began to kick her legs while leaning against Phil's arm. Then she nudged him gently as she turned around in her seat. Next she bent forward in front of him to pick up a fallen paper while rattling a bulletin.

Phil looked at Mother rather strangely as he tried to listen. He leaned forward so he wouldn't miss a word and so Mother's wiggling wouldn't bother him. Then Mother stood up and walked in front of him. She stopped at Tami's chair to ask in a loud whisper if Tami's friend Nancy would like to come home with Tami after church.

"Mother! How can I concentrate on what Dad's saying with all this going on!" Phil exploded.

Tami suddenly began to giggle. "I know what you're trying to do. You're showing us how we act in church during the sermon!"

"Oh," Phil groaned, "is that what you're doing?"

"You both are quiet in church," commented Dad, "but your wiggling and moving about can be just as disturbing as talking out loud."

Phil rolled his eyes and looked at Mother. "I see what you mean." He paused, then asked, "May we still read some more about the computer?"

"How about doing it after our Bible reading and prayer time?" Dad suggested.

HOW ABOUT YOU? Do you wiggle, rattle papers, turn around, or whisper during church services? If you do, your mind is not concentrating on the message, and you may be keeping someone else from listening, too. Ask God to help you to "be still" so you can learn more about Him. □ J.G.

TO MEMORIZE: *Be still, and know that I am God; I will be exalted among the nations, I will be exalted in the earth! Psalm 46:10, NKJV*

FROM THE BIBLE:
Now all the people gathered together as one man in the open square that was in front of the Water Gate; and they told Ezra the scribe to bring the Book of the Law of Moses, which the LORD had commanded Israel. So Ezra the priest brought the Law before the congregation, of men and women and all who could hear with understanding, on the first day of the seventh month. Then he read from it in the open square that was in front of the Water Gate from morning until midday, before the men and women and those who could understand; and the ears of all the people were attentive to the Book of the Law. And Ezra opened the book in the sight of all the people, for he was standing above all the people; and when he opened it, all the people stood up. And Ezra blessed the LORD, the great God. Then all the people answered, "Amen, Amen!" while lifting up their hands. And they bowed their heads and worshiped the LORD with their faces to the ground. So they read distinctly from the book, in the Law of God; and they gave the sense, and helped them to understand the reading.
Nehemiah 8:1-3, 5-6, 8, NKJV

Be still in church

30

The Solo Part

FROM THE BIBLE:

The third time he said to him, "Simon son of John, do you love me?" Peter was hurt because Jesus asked him the third time, "Do you love me?" He said, "Lord, you know all things; you know that I love you." Jesus said, "Feed my sheep. I tell you the truth, when you were younger you dressed yourself and went where you wanted; but when you are old you will stretch out your hands, and someone else will dress you and lead you where you do not want to go." Jesus said this to indicate the kind of death by which Peter would glorify God. Then he said to him, "Follow me!" Peter turned and saw that the disciple whom Jesus loved was following them. (This was the one who had leaned back against Jesus at the supper and had said, "Lord, who is going to betray you?") When Peter saw him he asked, "Lord, what about him?" Jesus answered, "If I want him to remain alive until I return, what is that to you? You must follow me."

John 21:17-22, NIV

Follow Jesus

"I'T'S NOT FAIR!" Troy whined. "It's just not fair! I go to children's choir practice every Saturday morning. I've never missed once. And I've been practicing the solo part for weeks, but now Mr. Widmark says that Joel gets to do the solo when we sing next Sunday." The nine-year-old boy was fighting tears as he rode home in the car with Mom.

"Now wait a minute, Troy," said Mom. "Did Mr. Widmark ever say that you were going to sing the solo?"

"Well, no," choked Troy, "but I'm the most faithful boy in the choir. I just took it for granted that I'd get to sing it. I've got the best voice in—"

"Stop it, Troy," Mom reprimanded. "You do have a nice voice, but evidently Joel does, too. Maybe Mr. Widmark is hoping that Joel's parents will come to church if he has the solo. Or maybe Joel has the better voice. Whatever the reason, it shouldn't matter to you who sings the solo part."

"But Mom, doesn't being faithful for all these weeks of practice count for anything?" asked Troy. "Joel has only been coming for a few weeks."

Mom sighed. "I can understand how you feel," she said gently, "but I think you need to remember the reason for being in the choir. You remind me a little of the Apostle Peter at the end of the Book of John. Peter had just been told by Jesus how he would die, and Peter immediately wondered how John would have to die. Jesus said, 'What is that to you? You follow me!'"

Now Troy was quiet for a long time. Finally he said, "So Jesus just wants me to follow Him and not worry about what Joel does. I hope Joel does a good job."

HOW ABOUT YOU? Have you ever been upset because, as you tried to serve the Lord, it seemed someone else got more glory than you or had an easier time of it? Peter had the same problem. He wondered if John was going to get to live a normal life, when he, Peter, was going to have to die for Jesus. You should not worry about what other people get to do. Your job is to follow Jesus.
□ R.P.

TO MEMORIZE: *Jesus answered, "If I want him to remain alive until I return, what is that to you? You must follow me." John 21:22, NIV*

ANDREA GLANCED around the Sunday school room. "Nina brought one visitor today," she whispered to Jana, "but that makes only five for her, and I brought six. I won!"

"I'm surprised to see Maria here." Jana looked at the lone figure in the back row. "Wouldn't she feel more comfortable in the class for special children?"

Andrea shrugged. "Maybe, but then she wouldn't count for me. Remember we have to bring visitors to *our* class."

"Well, aren't you going to sit with Maria?" asked Jana.

Andrea raised her eyebrows. "Are you kidding? I have to sit in front and help Miss Judy with the attendance list."

Just then Renee joined them. "Oh, Andrea, you look cute in my sweater," she gushed. "I only wore it once 'cuz it never did fit me right.

At that moment the bell rang. As Andrea took a front seat, her face felt like it was on fire. She was so humiliated! She wondered how many had heard Renee's announcement that she was wearing hand-me-down clothes. *I wish she'd never given me this stupid sweater! Andrea fumed inwardly. I'll certainly never wear it again!"*

". . . possible to do the right thing for the wrong reason." Miss Judy's words finally broke into Andrea's consciousness. "If we pray so others will think we're great Christians, our motive is wrong. If we give so others will praise us, it is wrong."

I hope Renee's listening! thought Andrea. *She just gave me her old clothes so she could act like Miss High-and-Mighty and put me down.*

". . . only invite others so we can win the contest, we should be ashamed." Miss Judy's voice broke into Andrea's thoughts again.

With a start, Andrea remembered Maria in the back row. She gulped as she realized she was no better than Renee. "I'm sorry, Lord," she whispered. "Starting now I'm going to do the right thing for the right reason." Rising quietly, she went to sit beside Maria.

HOW ABOUT YOU? Why do you give? Pray? Go to church? Witness? Do you do it so others will say nice things about you, or because you love the Lord? Do the right things for the right reasons and you will be blessed. □ B.W.

TO MEMORIZE: *Whatever you do, work at it with all your heart, as working for the Lord, not for men.* Colossians 3:23, NIV

31

Right But Wrong

FROM THE BIBLE:
Take care! Don't do your good deeds publicly, to be admired, for then you will lose the reward from your Father in heaven. When you give a gift to a beggar, don't shout about it as the hypocrites do—blowing trumpets in the synagogues and streets to call attention to their acts of charity! I tell you in all earnestness, they have received all the reward they will ever get. But when you do a kindness to someone, do it secretly—don't tell your left hand what your right hand is doing. And your Father who knows all secrets will reward you. And now about prayer. When you pray, don't be like the hypocrites who pretend piety by praying publicly on street corners and in the synagogues where everyone can see them. Truly, that is all the reward they will ever get. But when you pray, go away by yourself, all alone, and shut the door behind you and pray to your Father secretly, and your Father, who knows your secrets, will reward you.
Matthew 6:1-6, TLB

Have right motives

1

No Looking Back

FROM THE BIBLE:

Now it happened as they jour-
neyed on the road, that someone
said to Him, "Lord, I will
follow You wherever You go."
And Jesus said to him, "Foxes
have holes and birds of the air
have nests, but the Son of Man
has nowhere to lay His head."
Then He said to another,
"Follow Me." But he said,
"Lord, let me first go and bury
my father." Jesus said to him,
"Let the dead bury their own
dead, but you go and preach the
kingdom of God." And another
also said, "Lord, I will follow
You, but let me first go and bid
them farewell who are at my
house." But Jesus said to him,
"No one, having put his hand to
the plow, and looking back, is
fit for the kingdom of God."

Luke 9:57-62, NKJV

Look to Jesus

SCOTT HAD BEEN a Christian only a short time. His old friends kept after him to join them in things they used to do before he was saved, but he knew from experience that they often got into trouble. It was a real struggle for him.

"Scott, I need some help getting my garden ready for spring planting," said Mr. Lockwood, Scott's Sunday school teacher. "Would you care to come over after school tomorrow and help me?"

"Sure," responded Scott. He really liked Mr. Lockwood.

The next day Mr. Lockwood started the garden tiller and showed Scott how it worked. "Start here, and don't take your eyes off that post down there," said Mr. Lockwood, pointing to the other end of the garden. "Make a straight row toward it. When you come back this way, you follow the furrow you've just made."

Scott began eagerly, hoping he would do a good job. Soon his confidence began to build as row after row of neatly turned earth appeared. He was almost finished when he saw that his teacher had a big glass of lemonade for him.

"Shut it off and take a break," shouted Mr. Lockwood.

Grinning, Scott turned back to shut off the machine. To his dismay, he saw that the tiller had made a big swerve to the right while he had been looking back. Mr. Lockwood saw what had happened, too. "Come and have your lemonade," he said, "and then we'll see what can be done to straighten this last row."

As they sat under a tree and drank the lemonade, Scott mentioned the problems he was having with his old friends.

"Hmmm," murmured Mr. Lockwood thoughtfully as he gazed over the garden, "looking back messes up a field, and looking back often messes up a life, too. Sometimes we have to break friendships to serve the Lord. Don't look back on your old life, Scott. Look to Jesus."

HOW ABOUT YOU? Do you have old friends who want you to join them in doing things that would displease the Lord? Do those old ways seem attractive? Ask the Lord to help you not to look back. It may be necessary to replace old friendships and old habits with new ones. □ R.P.

TO MEMORIZE: *No one, having put his hand to the plow, and looking back, is fit for the kingdom of God.* Luke 9:62, NKJV

Doug WAS DELIGHTED when robins built a nest on a high ledge of the front porch. When the mother bird began sitting on it, he was sure there were eggs in it.

Doug waited eagerly for the eggs to hatch. Then one day, he saw the robins bringing worms to the nest and he heard peeping sounds, so he knew the babies were out of the eggs. He was so excited that he called Grandpa to tell him about it.

"I'll be over to see that little family soon," Grandpa said. "By the way, Doug, don't forget to have a little time with God every day."

"Oh, sure," mumbled Doug, remembering how Grandpa always seemed to bring up spiritual things. "I'm pretty busy, though."

"Nothing is more important than reading your Bible and praying," said Grandpa firmly.

"Yeah," agreed Doug. But he seldom got around to it.

A few days after the hatching, Doug saw three bald little heads bob up every time a worm was brought to the nest. The babies were getting stronger. Soon he heard louder cheeps, and the little heads, now fuzzy, shot up with beaks wide open for meals.

When Grandpa came over, Doug showed him the hungry little birds with their wide-open beaks just showing above the nest. "They've been getting stronger all the time," Doug said.

"What do you think would happen if they wouldn't open those little mouths for food?" asked Grandpa.

"Well, I guess they'd never get strong enough to fly," said Doug.

"Smart boy." Grandpa smiled. "Now, what do you think happens when Christians don't open up to take in God's Word—the spiritual food He gives to make us stronger Christians?"

Doug grinned. "Smart, Grandpa," he teased, then added, "I'm going to start 'opening wide' today by reading my Bible and praying."

HOW ABOUT YOU? Are you "opening wide" to take in the spiritual food God wants to give you? He has many good things in His Word for you to "eat"—promises, lessons, encouragement, warnings, and much more. Spend time with God daily and grow strong in your Christian life. □ C.Y.

TO MEMORIZE: *I am the LORD your God, who brought you up out of Egypt. Open wide your mouth and I will fill it.* Psalm 81:10, NIV

APRIL

2

Open Wide

FROM THE BIBLE:
I am the LORD your God, who brought you up out of Egypt. Open wide your mouth and I will fill it. But my people would not listen to me; Israel would not submit to me. So I gave them over to their stubborn hearts to follow their own devices. If my people would but listen to me, if Israel would follow my ways, how quickly would I subdue their enemies and turn my hand against their foes! Those who hate the LORD would cringe before him, and their punishment would last forever. But you would be fed with the finest of wheat; with honey from the rock I would satisfy you.
Psalm 81:10-16, NIV

Have daily devotions

3

Flying High

FROM THE BIBLE:

Do not fret because of evil men or be envious of those who do wrong; for like the grass they will soon wither, like green plants they will soon die away. Trust in the LORD and do good; dwell in the land and enjoy safe pasture. Delight yourself in the LORD and he will give you the desires of your heart. Commit your way to the LORD; trust in him and he will do this: He will make your righteousness shine like the dawn, the justice of your cause like the noonday sun. Be still before the LORD and wait patiently for him; do not fret when men succeed in their ways, when they carry out their wicked schemes. Refrain from anger and turn from wrath; do not fret—it leads only to evil. Psalm 37:1-8, NIV

Submit to God's control

ANDY WATCHED the red kite soaring in the bright sky. His brother Mike grinned. "Looks like fun, huh, Andy? Would you like to be able to fly high like that?" asked Mike.

"Sure would!" Andy grinned back. "But if I were that kite, I'd want to break loose and fly away, high into the sky." His small hands clutched the spool of kite string, trying to make sure his kite didn't do that.

Mike laughed. "But if you broke loose, you'd crash to the ground instead of flying away," he said. "Without the string, that kite would just fall down here on the field."

Andy turned to his father. "Would it, Daddy?"

"Yep." Dad nodded. "It only flies because the wind pushes it against the resistance of the string. Without that string, it would soon fall."

"Oh." Andy held the spool of string even more tightly.

"You know," Dad mused, "in a way, we're something like that kite. The string guides the kite, and God guides us. Sometimes it's hard to act the way He wants us to, and we pull against the discipline that He uses to direct us. We try to break loose and fly our own way. But if the bond that holds us to Him would ever break—if He'd let us go—we would plunge right down to destruction, like a kite whose string has broken."

"That's kind of scary," said Mike seriously.

"Would God ever let us go, Daddy?" asked Andy.

"No, Andy. If you trust Jesus as your Savior, He'll never let you go," Dad assured him. "The Bible says that nothing can ever separate us from His love. But it's important to submit ourselves to God's control, and not fight against it. He'll give us the power to be strong and graceful and beautiful for Him."

"Like the kite flying way up there," said Andy with a smile.

HOW ABOUT YOU? Do you sometimes resent the "strings" you feel God has put on your life? Do you feel you'd like to be free to go wherever you want, to choose your own friends, or to pick your own TV programs? Do you wish you could be rid of an illness, a teacher you dislike, or discipline from a parent? Everyone feels like that sometimes. But God has a reason for everything He allows to happen in your life. He wants what is best for you.
□ J.B.

TO MEMORIZE: *Commit your way to the LORD; trust in him and he will do this.* Psalm 37:5, NIV

WHEN THE SCHOOL BELL rang, Tyson pushed past several children and hurried to the drinking fountain. He edged in at the front of the long line. "No cuts!" called several children, but Tyson took a long drink. When he went to hang up his coat, he found a coat on the hook nearest the door. He moved it to a place down the line and put his own coat in his favorite spot. Somehow, he managed to be the last one to his seat.

It was the start of a typical day. Tyson spent a lot of time daydreaming instead of studying. At recess he tried to be the first one out the door and the last one back in. "No fair," he grumbled when he had to stay in to finish his work during the afternoon recess. He glared at his teacher.

After school, Tyson invited Jerry over to play. "I got a new detective set," he said. "Let's see if we can lift fingerprints."

The boys played until Tyson's dad came home from work. After Jerry left, Tyson told Dad about the "detective work" they had been doing. "You leave prints on everything you touch, you know," said Tyson.

"I know, Son. I know," said Dad. "And what kind of prints have you been leaving all day?"

Tyson squinted at his dad. "The same kind as always, of course," he said. "Your fingerprints don't change."

"True," agreed Dad, "but wherever you go, you leave other 'prints,' too. Let's call them 'lifeprints.' Everything you do makes an impression—or a 'lifeprint'—on other people. What kind of prints do you think you made today on your teacher and on the kids at school?" Tyson hadn't thought of that before! "Unlike fingerprints," Dad was saying, "we can change the kind of 'lifeprints' we make. But we need God's help."

Tyson nodded slowly. Changing his work and play habits wouldn't be easy. He would have to pray about that.

HOW ABOUT YOU? What kind of "lifeprints" are you making? Do others see selfishness and laziness in your prints, or do they see kindness, courtesy, faithfulness, and friendliness? Do they see Jesus? Ask God to help you live in such a way that the prints you leave are a good testimony for Him.
□ H.M.

TO MEMORIZE: *Therefore, as God's chosen people, holy and dearly loved, clothe yourselves with compassion, kindness, humility, gentleness and patience.* Colossians 3:12, NIV

Lifeprints

FROM THE BIBLE:
But now you must rid yourselves of all such things as these: anger, rage, malice, slander, and filthy language from your lips. Do not lie to each other, since you have taken off your old self with its practices. Therefore, as God's chosen people, holy and dearly loved, clothe yourselves with compassion, kindness, humility, gentleness and patience. Bear with each other and forgive whatever grievances you may have against one another. Forgive as the Lord forgave you. And over all these virtues put on love, which binds them all together in perfect unity. Colossians 3:8-9, 12-14, NIV

Witness through actions

APRIL

5

Just Outside Jill's Window

FROM THE BIBLE:

He who dwells in the shelter of the Most High will rest in the shadow of the Almighty. I will say of the LORD, "He is my refuge and my fortress, my God, in whom I trust." Surely he will save you from the fowler's snare and from the deadly pestilence. He will cover you with his feathers, and under his wings you will find refuge; his faithfulness will be your shield and rampart. You will not fear the terror of night, nor the arrow that flies by day, nor the pestilence that stalks in the darkness, nor the plague that destroys at midday. . . . If you make the Most High your dwelling—even the LORD, who is my refuge— then no harm will befall you, no disaster will come near your tent. For he will command his angels concerning you to guard you in all your ways; they will lift you up in their hands, so that you will not strike your foot against a stone. . . . "Because he loves me," says the LORD, "I will rescue him; I will protect him, for he acknowledges my name."
Psalm 91:1-6, 9-12, 14, NIV

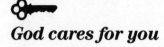

God cares for you

THE CARTER FAMILY lived in a two-story house with big trees surrounding it. Jill especially liked the maple tree that grew outside her window. She liked the sound of the leaves gently brushing against the glass.

One spring day Jill noticed a robin busily surveying the crook of a branch. Soon a second bird flew up. Jill stood absolutely still so she wouldn't frighten the birds. As she watched, they began to build a nest. The robins made many trips back and forth to the ground, gathering twigs and bits of leaves. Jill had to laugh when she saw one of the birds use a piece of hair ribbon that she had lost in the snow sometime during the winter.

Finally the nest was finished, and each day Jill checked to see if there was anything in it. Sure enough, one morning she saw four sky-blue eggs in the straw. After that she watched even more closely, waiting for the babies to hatch. Jill felt as if she had a front row seat when the tiny birds finally broke from their shells. After that, the parent birds were kept busy feeding them.

But one day there was a terrible thunderstorm. The branch swayed back and forth, and the nest swayed with it.

"How are the robins doing, Jill?" asked Dad, as he was passing her room.

"The branch is swaying in the wind, but the wings of the mother robin are covering the babies so they won't get hurt," Jill answered. "It's neat how God created her so she would know how to protect her babies."

"I'll tell you another neat thing," said Dad, coming in to take a look. "God uses that very picture— a mother bird spreading her wings to protect the babies—as an example of how He cares for us, His children."

"That is neat, Dad," agreed Jill. "I'm glad God cares for us, too."

HOW ABOUT YOU? Have you ever seen a mother bird protect her young? The Bible often uses "word pictures" to illustrate God's love for you. Remember a mother bird's care for her babies, and you'll know how carefully and completely God protects you. Keep that in mind and don't be afraid of storms, of dogs, or of anything else. □ L.W.

TO MEMORIZE: *He will cover you with his feathers, and under his wings you will find refuge.*
Psalm 91:4, NIV

"**H**URRY MOM,**"** Sam urged. He was eager to get to his Little League game. "Can't you drive any faster?"

"I'm driving the speed limit," Mother assured him. Moments later Sam's heart sank as she slowed down. "Oh, there's road construction ahead, and traffic's backing up," she said.

"Can't you drive on the shoulder or go across the median to get off and take another road?" asked Sam, sounding desperate.

"Sam, you're going to have to be patient," said Mother. "We can't do anything but sit here and wait."

"I don't believe this," Sam muttered as Mother turned off the engine. "Can't you do something?"

"Why don't *you* do something, Son?" answered Mother. "Why don't you ask Jesus to help?"

Sam decided that might be a good idea. "Dear Jesus," he prayed, "please get this traffic started so I can get to my game." After a while, people got out and stood by their cars. "See, it didn't do any good to pray. We're stuck here."

"Maybe you prayed the wrong prayer," suggested Mother. "Maybe the most important thing isn't getting to your game on time." Sam looked puzzled. "Maybe the Lord knows you need to work on patience and consideration of others," Mother added gently. "You're getting more upset by the minute, and you haven't been speaking very kindly to me." Then she asked, "Do you know why I turned the engine off when I saw we were going to be delayed?"

"So you don't waste gas."

"Right," Mother replied. "I didn't want to waste energy. But you're wasting a lot of energy getting all upset about something we can't do anything about."

Sam was quiet. Then he said, "I'm sorry, Mom. I'll try to be more patient." Silently he prayed a different prayer. "Dear God, forgive me for getting mad and losing my patience. And even if we're late, I know everything will be okay. Thank You."

HOW ABOUT YOU? Do you become upset when things don't go the way you planned? Do you get angry at people for things that aren't their fault? God wants you to develop patience. Decide right now to treat others kindly even when you're upset. Ask the Lord to help you. □ D.K.

TO MEMORIZE: *With all lowliness and gentleness, with longsuffering, bearing with one another in love.* Ephesians 4:2, NKJV

Road Construction

FROM THE BIBLE:
I, therefore, the prisoner of the Lord, beseech you to have a walk worthy of the calling with which you were called, with all lowliness and gentleness, with longsuffering, bearing with one another in love, endeavoring to keep the unity of the Spirit in the bond of peace.
Ephesians 4:1-3, NKJV

My brethren, count it all joy when you fall into various trials, knowing that the testing of your faith produces patience. But let patience have its perfect work, that you may be perfect and complete, lacking nothing.
James 1:2-4, NKJV

Be patient

APRIL

7

The Right Key

FROM THE BIBLE:

About midnight Paul and Silas were praying and singing hymns to God, and the other prisoners were listening to them. Suddenly there was such a violent earthquake that the foundations of the prison were shaken. At once all the prison doors flew open, and everybody's chains came loose. The jailer woke up, and when he saw the prison doors open, he drew his sword and was about to kill himself because he thought the prisoners had escaped. But Paul shouted, "Don't harm yourself! We are all here!" The jailer called for lights, rushed in and fell trembling before Paul and Silas. He then brought them out and asked, "Sirs, what must I do to be saved?" They replied, "Believe in the Lord Jesus, and you will be saved—you and your household."

Acts 16:25-31, NIV

Believe on Jesus

LET'S SEE," murmured Gary, looking at the keys he held. His grandparents had dropped him off at their house. They'd be home after Grandma had her checkup at the doctor's office. In the meantime, he planned to enjoy milk and cookies. "Grandpa said the silver key with the round top is his house key. But I can't find one like that."

Gary tried each key in the lock, and nothing worked. Now he walked around the house, checking every window and door. They were all locked securely.

After two long hours his grandparents arrived. "Hey, what took you so long?" Gary asked. "I've been outside the whole time. You didn't give me the right key."

"Oh no!" exclaimed Grandpa. "Now I remember I took it off that ring when I had a duplicate made. I must have forgotten to put it back. I'm sorry, Gary."

After they entered with Grandma's key, Gary said, "It sure was tough sitting out there with all those keys, and not one would work!"

Grandma nodded as she began to make supper. "Do you know there's something worse?" she asked. "It's expecting to get into heaven and then finding too late that you have the wrong key."

"What do you mean?" asked Gary. "You don't get into heaven with keys."

"No, not actual keys," agreed Grandma. "But many people think being in a Christian family or living a good life will get them into heaven. These things are a little like wrong keys. Jesus said, 'No man cometh unto the Father, but by me.' The right key is 'Believe in Lord Jesus Christ.'" She paused and then asked, "What key do you have, Gary? How do you expect to get into heaven?"

"Hey, I don't want to be left outside heaven's door!" exclaimed Gary. "And I won't be, either. I do believe in Jesus, and I'm trusting Him to save me."

HOW ABOUT YOU? What "key" are you counting on for entering heaven? Good works? A Christian family? Your church? These are useless in opening heaven's door. Jesus is the Door to heaven. Believing in Him as your Savior is the only key. □ M.R.P.

TO MEMORIZE: *Believe in the Lord Jesus, and you will be saved—you and your household.* Acts 16:31, NIV

SCOTT GLANCED nervously out the school window. All day it had looked stormy. He knew it was tornado season, and he hoped there wasn't going to be another tornado alert today. They always made him afraid. Sighing, he tried to concentrate on his math lesson.

As Scott began the first problem, a bell rang. "Tornado drill," said Miss Greely. "Take a large book and file quietly into the hall, children." Quickly they obeyed, taking their places in the school's inner hall and putting the books over their heads as they had done many times before. But there was something different today. Scott could hear a siren blowing, and as he listened, he knew it came from a nearby fire station. It was a signal that a tornado funnel had been seen nearby!

Scott had never been so scared before! But as he sat, trembling, he remembered something Dad had said just the weekend before. They had gone swimming, and as Dad walked out into the deep water, Scott's little brother Brian hung on to Dad's shoulders. "Are you scared in the deep water, Brian?" Scott had asked.

Brian had shook his head and said, "Nope, Dad's got me."

Dad had laughed as he replied, "Good boy! I'm in control here, and I'm glad you trust your father." Then he had added, "I hope both you boys will remember that you can always trust your Father in heaven, too. He's in control of all the circumstances of your lives." As Scott remembered that, he felt better.

A few minutes later, Scott heard a roaring sound. It began softly but got louder and louder. It almost sounded like a train rushing by. He had heard that a tornado sounded that way. *I'm still scared,* Scott thought, *but not so awfully scared. God's my heavenly Father, and He's in control.*

After the "all clear" whistle sounded, the children returned to their classrooms and were soon dismissed to go home. They learned that a tornado had indeed passed by, not far from their school. Much damage had been done, but no one had been hurt. With his family, Scott thanked God for watching over them.

HOW ABOUT YOU? Storms can be frightening, can't they? They are powerful and can cause a lot of damage. But God is even more powerful. Remember that God is in control. □ H.M.

TO MEMORIZE: *Who can this be, that even the wind and the sea obey Him!* Mark 4:41, NKJV

APRIL

8

God's Strentgh

FROM THE BIBLE:
Now when they had left the multitude, they took Him along in the boat as He was. And other little boats were also with Him. And a great windstorm arose, and the waves beat into the boat, so that it was already filling. But He was in the stern, asleep on a pillow. And they awoke Him and said to Him, "Teacher, do You not care that we are perishing?" Then He arose and rebuked the wind, and said to the sea, "Peace, be still!" And the wind ceased and there was a great calm. But He said to them, "Why are you so fearful? How is it that you have no faith?" And they feared exceedingly, and said to one another, "Who can this be, that even the wind and the sea obey Him!"
Mark 4:36-41, NKJV

God controls nature

APRIL

9

God's Strength

(Continued from yesterday)

FROM THE BIBLE:
*To keep me from becoming
conceited because of these
surpassingly great revelations,
there was given me a thorn in
my flesh, a messenger of Satan,
to torment me. Three times I
pleaded with the Lord to take it
away from me. But he said to
me, "My grace is sufficient for
you, for my power is made
perfect in weakness." Therefore
I will boast all the more gladly
about my weaknesses, so that
Christ's power may rest on me.
That is why, for Christ's sake, I
delight in weaknesses, in
insults, in hardships, in
persecutions, in difficulties. For
when I am weak, then I am
strong.*
2 Corinthians 12:7-10, NIV

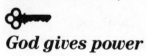

God gives power

THE TORNADO that passed close to Scott's town was the subject of conversation for many days. Scott and his family heard stories of strange things that had been caused by the strong winds.

One day Dad came home with a piece of a log. "What's that for?" asked Scott.

Dad held it out, and Scott saw that, sticking out from the wood, was a piece of straw. "One of the fellows at work found this on his property," said Dad. "His place was right on the edge of the storm. Isn't it amazing how the wind could take that little straw and drive it right into the wood without even bending it?"

"Wow!" marveled Scott. "I don't see how it could do that. It sure wouldn't work to try to pound it in."

"No," agreed Dad, "it took a stronger force than we could exert—a special kind of power. I've been thinking about that all afternoon, and I've decided to teach that class of boys I've been offered."

"What's that got to do with this wood?" asked Scott.

"Well, I wanted to take the class," said Dad, "but I was afraid I wouldn't be able to hold their interest. This afternoon the Lord showed me that I have a special kind of power available to me—the Holy Spirit. This straw was weak, but powered by the storm, it became very strong. I'm weak, too, but empowered by the Holy Spirit, I believe I can be of help to those boys. I thought about you, too."

"Me?" Scott was startled.

Dad nodded. "I heard Mrs. Jarvis, the choir director, asking you to sing a solo on youth night. She said she heard you sing and that you have a fine voice."

"But I get so nervous," began Scott, "and I . . . " He stopped. "But I have a special power available to me, too, don't I? I think I'll call Mrs. Jarvis. God will help me sing for Him."

HOW ABOUT YOU? Do you feel too weak to sing, give a testimony, make posters, or take part in some other activity for which God has given you a talent? If you're a Christian, a special power— God's power—is available to you. Are you using it? Ask Him to help you, and then say yes to the opportunities He gives to serve Him. He won't let you down. □ H.M.

TO MEMORIZE: *That is why, for Christ's sake, I delight in weaknesses, in insults, in hardships, in persecutions, in difficulties. For when I am weak, then I am strong.* 2 Corinthians 12:10, NIV

"WILL WE EVER get to Uncle Fred's?" Kristen whined.

Dad looked at his watch. "It's about another hour."

"If you're bored, Kristen, why don't you study the Ten Commandments?" Mother suggested. "You need to learn them for your Sunday school class, so I brought the list along."

"Okay. I guess I might as well," Kristen agreed, looking at the first one on the list. "'You shall have no other gods before me,'" she read. "Our teacher says that even in America people often worship false gods, but I never knew anybody who did that."

"Don't be so sure," answered Dad. "Another person, a job, money, clothes, popularity. Almost anything can become a god if we place it before the true God."

The miles passed quickly as Kristen studied. Almost before she knew it, they reached their destination. Uncle Fred and Aunt Jolene came to meet them, followed by Kristen's cousin Rita. Rita looked so different from the way she had looked before!

Kristen soon discovered the reason for the difference. Rita was doing her best to be just like the new rock star, Alicia. Rita walked like her, talked like her, and tried to sing like her. She fixed her hair like Alicia's, dressed like her, and even used the same toothpaste. Rita's room was plastered with posters of the rock star.

By the time Mom and Dad had said their good-byes the next day, Kristen was ready to leave. "I am so sick and tired of hearing about Alicia—the wonderful, the beautiful, the marvelous!" Kristen exploded as soon as they pulled out of the driveway. "Why, Rita worships that rock star! She's Rita's idol!"

"Now do you understand what the first commandment means?" Mother asked.

"I certainly do," Kristen replied.

HOW ABOUT YOU? What controls your thoughts, actions, and plans? Whom do you want to be like? It's normal to have someone you admire and look up to, but be careful to pick someone who is following Jesus. And remember, that person is only human. Don't make a "god" of him or her. If there are "other gods" in your life, now is the time to get rid of them. □ B.W.

TO MEMORIZE : *You shall have no other gods before Me.* Exodus 20:3, NKJV

Idol Worship

FROM THE BIBLE:
And God spoke all these words, saying: "I am the LORD your God, who brought you out of the land of Egypt, out of the house of bondage. You shall have no other gods before Me. You shall not make for yourself any carved image, or any likeness of anything that is in heaven above, or that is in the earth beneath, or that is in the water under the earth; you shall not bow down to them nor serve them. For I, the LORD your God, am a jealous God, visiting the iniquity of the fathers on the children to the third and fourth generations of those who hate Me, but showing mercy to thousands, to those who love Me and keep My commandments."
Exodus 20:1-6, NKJV

Worship the true God

11

The Red Cellophane

FROM THE BIBLE:

When we were utterly helpless with no way of escape, Christ came at just the right time and died for us sinners who had no use for him. Even if we were good, we really wouldn't expect anyone to die for us, though, of course, that might be barely possible. But God showed his great love for us by sending Christ to die for us while we were still sinners. And since by his blood he did all this for us as sinners, how much more will he do for us now that he has declared us not guilty? Now he will save us from all of God's wrath to come. And since, when we were his enemies, we were brought back to God by the death of his Son, what blessings he must have for us now that we are his friends, and he is living within us! Now we rejoice in our wonderful new relationship with God—all because of what our Lord Jesus Christ has done in dying for our sins—making us friends of God.

Romans 5:6-11, TLB

Jesus' blood covers sin

"**W**HAT'S THAT, GRANDPA?" Sammy pointed to some small cards and pieces of shiny red paper on the kitchen table.

Grandpa smiled. "Grandma found these when she was cleaning the attic the other day," he replied. "When I was a boy, we used to get these as prizes in cereal boxes."

"Wow!" Sammy was impressed. "They're really old! What are all the shiny red papers for?"

"Ah, that's what makes these cards interesting, Sammy," replied Grandpa. "Here, look at this one. It has a picture of Babe Ruth on the front. Now, see this question on the back of the card? It says, 'What was Babe Ruth's given name?' To find the answer, we put this shiny red paper—cellophane—right over the question, like this. Now what do you see?"

"It says 'George Herman Ruth,'" answered Sammy. "The question disappeared, and the answer showed up!"

"Right," said Grandpa. "This little piece of paper taught me a great lesson."

Sammy wrinkled his nose. "What do you mean?"

"When I was young, we had revival meetings at our church," began Grandpa. "I knew I was a sinner. I was the church rascal." Sammy laughed. "I had often heard that only the blood of Jesus could wash away sin," continued Grandpa, "One night, the evangelist called me up to the platform. He said he saw these cards sticking out of my pocket and wanted to use them as an illustration. Well, he took this Babe Ruth card, put the red paper over the question, and said, 'Bert, read the question for me.' I said I couldn't see the question, only the answer. Then he said, 'That's how it is with God. When you accept Jesus as Savior, the blood of Christ washes away your sin. Just as you can't see the question when it's covered by the red paper, God can no longer see your sin when it's covered by the blood of Christ. Just as you see only the answer on the card, God sees only Christ living in you'"

Sammy nodded. "I'm glad God sees only Jesus in me."

HOW ABOUT YOU? What does God see when He looks at you? Does He see your sins, or are they covered by Jesus' blood so that He only sees Christ living in you? If you haven't done so before, accept Jesus as your Savior today. □ P.R.

TO MEMORIZE: *I have been crucified with Christ.* Galatians 2:20, NIV

"MOM, CAN I bake a cake?" asked Cindy.

Mother smiled. "Sure, Cindy, but I'm going to be busy, so I won't be able to help. Follow the directions exactly."

"Oh, I will, Mom," promised Cindy eagerly.

Cindy did follow the directions. She carefully measured the correct amount of each ingredient she needed. But when the finished product looked and tasted awful, she was almost in tears.

"What's up?" asked Dad, walking into the kitchen, and Cindy explained about the ruined cake. "Oh no!" Dad exclaimed. "I know what happened. I stopped at the grocery store on the way home last night, remember? Well, the bag ripped and a few things fell out. Nothing broke, but the box of salt was leaking. When I saw that the sugar canister was empty, I poured the salt into it and threw the box away. I meant to mention it, but then the phone rang and I forgot."

"So what I thought was sugar was really salt?" Cindy asked. "I can't believe I wouldn't have noticed that!"

"I'm surprised, too, but it's my fault, and I'm sorry, Cindy." Dad gave her a hug.

"What a perfect illustration for the pastor's message last Sunday," commented Mother. "He talked about the verse in Isaiah where people called evil good, remember? And they said light was darkness and that bitter was sweet. Of course, salt isn't bitter, but the idea is still the same."

"Right." Dad nodded. "That jar said sugar, but it was really salt, and so the cake was ruined. That's not so bad because you can make another cake. But if people say a thing is good when God says it's evil—and if they say things are evil when God says they're good—that can ruin an entire life. That's not so easy to fix!"

HOW ABOUT YOU? Do you know what things God says are good? Do you know what things God says are evil? In today's world many people change it around so that the good seems to be evil and the evil seems to be good. It's sad that so many people think that things like dishonesty, immorality, and cheating are sometimes okay. That isn't true. Know what God says in His Word, and follow His guidelines. □ L.W.

TO MEMORIZE: *Woe to those who call evil good and good evil.* Isaiah 5:20, NIV

This Isn't Sugar!

FROM THE BIBLE:
Woe to those who draw sin along with cords of deceit, and wickedness as with cart ropes, to those who say, "Let God hurry, let him hasten his work so we may see it. Let it approach, let the plan of the Holy One of Israel come, so we may know it." Woe to those who call evil good and good evil, who put darkness for light and light for darkness, who put bitter for sweet and sweet for bitter. Woe to those who are wise in their own eyes and clever in their own sight.
Isaiah 5:18-21, NIV

Don't call evil "good"

APRIL

13

The Whistle

FROM THE BIBLE:

For the message of the cross is foolishness to those who are perishing, but to us who are being saved it is the power of God. For it is written: "I will destroy the wisdom of the wise, and bring to nothing the understanding of the prudent." Where is the wise? Where is the scribe? Where is the disputer of this age? Has not God made foolish the wisdom of this world? For since, in the wisdom of God, the world through wisdom did not know God, it pleased God through the foolishness of the message preached to save those who believe. For Jews request a sign, and Greeks seek after wisdom; but we preach Christ crucified, to the Jews a stumbling block and to the Greeks foolishness, but to those who are called, both Jews and Greeks, Christ the power of God and the wisdom of God. Because the foolishness of God is wiser than men, and the weakness of God is stronger than men.

1 Corinthians 1:18-25, NKJV

Hear God's voice

"**W**HERE'S MOLLY?" asked Dan. "I want to play with her." Dan had just come to spend a week with Grandpa, and he loved to play with Grandpa's big brown-and-white collie.

Grandpa took a whistle from his pocket, put it to his mouth and blew it. "It doesn't make any sound." said Dan. "It must be broken," But just then Molly came running from behind the barn.

Grandpa laughed, "No, the whistle's not broken. It emits a high-pitched sound that can't be heard by human ears, but a dog can hear it plainly," he explained.

Dan and Molly raced across the yard. Then Dan threw a stick for Molly to fetch. She brought it back and waited eagerly for him to throw it again. Grandpa sat on the porch and watched. When Dan was tired, he went to sit beside Grandpa, and Molly lay down nearby.

"May I play with the whistle, Grandpa?" Dan asked.

"No, Son." Grandpa shook his head. "It's not a toy. We only use it when we want Molly to respond. It gets her attention every time." He paused, then added, "While I was watching you and Molly play, I was thinking of some of the ways God calls us when He wants our attention."

"But God doesn't have a whistle," said Dan with a laugh.

Grandpa smiled. "No," he said, "but sometimes He speaks out loud to us through our parents, teachers, and pastors. Sometimes He speaks through the Bible as we read it or listen to it being read. And sometimes the Holy Spirit speaks silently through our consciences and minds."

"And we're the only ones who hear Him, aren't we?" Dan asked thoughtfully.

"That's right," agreed Grandpa. "Only God's children can hear and understand what He says to them."

Dan scratched Molly's ears, "I'll try to answer as quickly when God 'whistles' for me as you do when someone whistles for you," he told her.

HOW ABOUT YOU? Has God "whistled" for you? Has He spoken to you through His Word? Has He spoken through a parent, a teacher, or a pastor? Has He pricked your conscience regarding something you should or should not do? Pay attention. Do what He asks. It's the only way you can be truly happy. □ B.K.

TO MEMORIZE: *My sheep hear My voice, and I know them, and they follow Me.* John 10:27, NKJV

TAMMY LOVED to visit Grandpa Nelson's greenhouse. As far back as she could remember, she had worked with Grandpa among the flowers and plants, and she had learned how to care for them and keep them healthy. But today she was confused. Grandpa had sent her into the back room to get some more potting soil. There, on a shelf in the storage room, she saw some beautiful green plants. Grandpa had taught her that plants need light and water to grow, but these were being kept completely in the dark, and the soil in the pot was bone dry.

"Grandpa, those plants in the back room are going to die. Why did you put them where they aren't getting any light?" Tammy asked as she returned to the greenhouse.

"Those are Easter cactus plants," Grandpa replied. "If you keep that plant in the dark for a month, it almost immediately begins to bloom when you bring it out into the light. So, we can plan to have it blooming just when we want it to."

"How strange," murmured Tammy.

"Yes, it is," agreed Grandpa. He put down his trowel and smiled at Tammy. "You know, I think those plants are a picture of people. Sometimes God puts us in the dark so we can bloom, too."

"You mean like when you were in the hospital?" Tammy asked.

Grandpa was glad Tammy understood. "At first I couldn't figure out why I had to be so sick," he told her. "But while I had to lie still, I spent time praying and reading God's Word. I learned to be calm and just wait on God to work. You see, while I was 'in the dark,' the Lord gave me the 'bloom' of patience."

"And the 'bloom' of prayer, too?" asked Tammy.

"That, too." Grandpa smiled. "If we allow Him to teach us to bloom, the dark places are all worthwhile."

HOW ABOUT YOU? Have you ever wondered why you had to be "in the dark"—why you had to be sick, or face a death or divorce in your family, or struggle with school problems? Sometimes the Lord allows problems in order to bring the "bloom" of patience, or of prayer, or maybe of love into your life. Allow Him to work through problems in your life. □ R.P.

TO MEMORIZE: *You know that the testing of your faith develops perseverance.* James 1:3, NIV

APRIL

14

Blooms out of Darkness

FROM THE BIBLE:
Consider it pure joy, my brothers, whenever you face trials of many kinds, because you know that the testing of your faith develops perseverance. Perseverance must finish its work so that you may be mature and complete, not lacking anything. If any of you lacks wisdom, he should ask God, who gives generously to all without finding fault, and it will be given to him. Blessed is the man who perseveres under trial, because when he has stood the test, he will receive the crown of life that God has promised to those who love him.
James 1:2-5, 12, NIV

God works through problems

The Living God

FROM THE BIBLE:

But very early on Sunday morning they took the ointments to the tomb: and found that the huge stone covering the entrance had been rolled aside. So they went in—but the Lord Jesus' body was gone. They stood there puzzled, trying to think what could have happened to it. Suddenly two men appeared before them, clothed in shining robes so bright their eyes were dazzled. The women were terrified and bowed low before them. Then the men asked, "Why are you looking in a tomb for someone who is alive? He isn't here! He has come back to life again! Don't you remember what he told you back in Galilee—that the Messiah must be betrayed into the power of evil men and be crucified and that he would rise again the third day?" Then they remembered, and rushed back to Jerusalem to tell his eleven disciples—and everyone else—what had happened.
Luke 24:1-9, TLB

God is alive

KARLA STARED at the screen as the missionary pictures were being shown. She saw people dressed like those in her own church. There were businessmen and housewives, schoolchildren and toddlers, all kneeling before a strange idol! They were praying, telling this piece of sculpture about their problems. Karla knew that in some countries people worshiped wooden and stone gods, but these people were in a civilized area, a big city.

That evening she talked with her father and mother about it. "How do you know when you've got the right God?" she asked bluntly.

"What do you mean?" Karla's mother asked. "There is only one true God. The Bible tells us that."

"Sure," Karla replied, "but all those people I saw in the pictures—they think they've got the right God, too."

"Yes," Dad said, "But the Bible tells us there is only one God. He is the Creator of the earth. He made everything in it, including man."

Karla was quiet for a long time. Finally she spoke. "So that's why we believe in Him? Because He's so great?"

Dad shook his head. "Partly, but more than that."

Karla was thinking. "Like He sent His Son, Jesus, to die?" she suggested, already knowing the answer to her own question.

"There's still more," Dad told her. "Jesus did more than die for us, as wonderful as that was! He also arose. And no other religion in the world has a living Savior."

"And He hears and answers prayers," Karla's mother interjected quickly.

Karla thought about that for a minute. There were wooden gods, stone gods, golden gods, and probably every other kind. But her God was different. He was alive! Only He could hear and answer her prayers. She turned and went into her room. She was going to pray that her living God would help her to tell other people about Christ, the living Savior of the world.

HOW ABOUT YOU? Can you imagine what it would be like to pray to a stone or a piece of wood or to a person who is dead? If you are a Christian, give thanks for your risen, living Savior. Then tell others about Him, too. □ R.J.

TO MEMORIZE: *He isn't here! He has come back to life again!* Luke 24:6, TLB

WHEN ANGELA returned home from her friend's house, her hair was fixed a new way. "Kristine fixed it," Angela told her mother. "Do you like it?"

"It looks nice," said Mother. "It's fixed the same way Kristine wears hers, isn't it?" Angela nodded happily.

Her brother Dan snorted. "You two might as well be twins," he said. "You're together every spare minute. You're even beginning to look alike." Angela smiled. She was happy to be just like Kristine.

The next day things didn't go well for Angela. She found herself getting angrier than usual over unimportant things. *What's wrong with me?* she wondered after being rude to a teacher who had irritated her.

"You sounded like Kristine," the girl next to Angela whispered. "I guess it's because you two hang around together so much."

Angela looked at her in surprise. She knew one of Kristine's faults was a quick temper. Was Angela taking on that characteristic, too? Perhaps she didn't want to be like Kristine after all.

"Oh, well. No one is perfect," Angela reminded herself with a shrug. But then she suddenly remembered something. *There's one Person who's perfect—Jesus. He's the One I want to be like.* Angela knew she hadn't been "hanging around" with Him nearly enough lately. For quite some time, she had neglected her quiet time with Him. *I'm sorry, Lord. We'll have that special time as soon as I get home,* she promised.

HOW ABOUT YOU? A person often becomes like those with whom he spends the most time. It's easy to pick up dress, language, and even mannerisms of those with whom one "hangs around." Do you spend enough time with Jesus to become like Him? Are you faithful in prayer, Bible reading, and church attendance? Could someone ever tell you, "You acted just like Jesus would. I guess it's because you spend so much time with Him"?

□ K.R.A.

TO MEMORIZE: *Whoever claims to live in him must walk as Jesus did.* 1 John 2:6, NIV

APRIL

16

Just Alike

FROM THE BIBLE:

Take care to live in me, and let me live in you. For a branch can't produce fruit when severed from the vine. Nor can you be fruitful apart from me. Yes, I am the Vine; you are the branches. Whoever lives in me and I in him shall produce a large crop of fruit. For apart from me you can't do a thing. If anyone separates from me, he is thrown away like a useless branch, withers, and is gathered into a pile with all the others and burned. But if you stay in me and obey my commands, you may ask any request you like, and it will be granted! My true disciples produce bountiful harvests. This brings great glory to my Father. I have loved you even as the Father has loved me. Live within my love. When you obey me you are living in my love, just as I obey my Father and live in his love. I have told you this so that you will be filled with my joy. Yes, your cup of joy will overflow! I demand that you love each other as much as I love you. And here is how to measure it—the greatest love is shown when a person lays down his life for his friends; and you are my friends if you obey me.
John 15:4-14, TLB

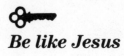

Be like Jesus

17

When the Tree Needs Help

FROM THE BIBLE:

My son, keep your father's commands and do not forsake your mother's teaching. Bind them upon your heart forever; fasten them around your neck. When you walk, they will guide you; when you sleep, they will watch over you; when you awake, they will speak to you. For these commands are a lamp, this teaching is a light, and the corrections of discipline are the way to life.
Proverbs 6:20-23, NIV

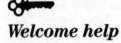

Welcome help

ROGER WATCHED his father pull out the stake that had been wired to a small tree ever since it had been planted.

"A small tree often doesn't have the strength or ability to stand alone," Dad said. "This stake acted as a support, but now I believe the tree is big enough to take any winds that may come along." He stood back and looked at the tree. It was growing tall and straight because it had been held in that position by the supporting stake. "That's pretty much like life," added Dad thoughtfully.

"What do you mean?" Roger asked.

"When you were small, your mother and I held on to your hand every time you took a step," Dad explained. "We didn't want you to fall and get hurt. Then as you began to grow and get control of your walk, we let you go by yourself, but we still watched you."

Roger nodded as he thought about it. Even now there were many times that he needed his parents' advice and help. He guessed maybe he would always depend on them. He mentioned that to his father.

"We'll be glad to help whenever you call on us," Dad replied smiling. "When the time comes that we are no longer here, you'll be ready to go on without us. There's a verse in the Bible that your mother and I try to follow as we raise you."

"Which one?" Roger asked.

"It's Proverbs 22:6," replied Dad. "Train up a child in the way he should go, and when he is old, he will not depart from it.' "

"Sort of like the tree, isn't it?" Roger asked. "When it was small and frail, you had to keep an eye on it all the time so it didn't grow wrong. But now that it's old enough, it will keep growing straight without the supporting stake."

Dad smiled broadly. "That's it," he agreed. "Exactly!"

HOW ABOUT YOU? How do you feel when you are restricted in some way by your parents' rules and guidance? Don't get angry. Every young tree needs help to grow big and strong and straight. Thank God for your "supporting stake"—your parents. □ R.J.

TO MEMORIZE: *Keep your father's commands and do not forsake your mother's teaching.*
Proverbs 6:20, NIV

"OH NO!" Gary groaned when he opened his dresser drawer and saw he had no clean socks. It didn't help to know it was his own fault. He had failed to throw his dirty things down the clothes chute the day Mother was going to do the washing. He groaned even louder when a button popped off his shirt. As he was tying his shoe, the shoelace broke. "Everything is going wrong!" he grumbled.

When Gary was finally ready, he went to the kitchen and got a bowl of cereal and milk. While carrying the bowl to the table, it slipped, and the contents spilled over the floor. His face grew red with anger, and he swore.

Mother looked up, shocked. Even before she said anything, Gary felt guilty about swearing over a bowl of spilled cereal. Swearing had only made him feel worse. He and his mother talked it over, and he told her about all the things that had gone wrong that morning.

"Instead of getting more and more angry each time something went wrong, what if you had stopped to pray?" Mother asked.

Gary stirred a new bowl of cereal, thinking that over. "If I had prayed, I probably wouldn't have gotten so angry," he said slowly. "Swearing didn't help. In fact, I felt worse."

Mother nodded. "I'm not surprised," she said.

"I'm going to pray right now for God's forgiveness," decided Gary. "And if anything else goes wrong today, I'm going to pray about it just as soon as it happens so I won't end up swearing again."

HOW ABOUT YOU? Does everything seem to go wrong some days? Do you get more and more upset until finally you're tempted to swear? A better way to handle your anger is to immediately talk to God about the things bothering you. Ask Him to take your anger away. Perhaps you'll even be able to laugh about some of the annoying things that happen. □ C.Y.

TO MEMORIZE: *He who guards his mouth and his tongue keeps himself from calamity.*
Proverbs 21:23, NIV

Everything's Wrong

FROM THE BIBLE:
He who pursues righteousness and love finds life, prosperity and honor. A wise man attacks the city of the mighty and pulls down the stronghold in which they trust. He who guards his mouth and his tongue keeps himself from calamity. The proud and arrogant man— "Mocker" is his name; he behaves with overweening pride.
Proverbs 21:21-24, NIV

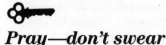

Pray—don't swear

APRIL

19

The Broken Watches

FROM THE BIBLE:
Listen to Me, O house of Jacob, and all the remnant of the house of Israel, who have been upheld by Me from birth, who have been carried from the womb: even to your old age, I am He, and even to gray hairs I will carry you! I have made, and I will bear; even I will carry, and will deliver you. Remember this, and show yourselves men; recall to mind, O you transgressors. Remember the former things of old, for I am God, and there is no other; I am God, and there is none like Me, declaring the end from the beginning, and from ancient times things that are not yet done, saying, "My counsel shall stand, and I will do all My pleasure."
Isaiah 46:3-4, 8-10, NKJV

Respect old people

CHARLES RAN into the house and slammed the front door. "Mom!" he called. "Is it true, what Betty said? Is Grandpa coming to visit again?"

"Yes, your sister is right," replied Mother. "Dad is going to get Grandpa on Saturday morning. You can probably go along if you like." She sighed. "My watch is broken, and I was hoping one of my old ones would still work. Look, Charles." She held up a small, gold wristwatch. "This is my high school graduation present from Grandpa and Grandma. This one with the leather strap was my official nurse's watch. And this lovely one I wear now—Dad bought this for me on our first wedding anniversary. And now it won't run, either."

Charles nodded, but he went back to the matter at hand. "I don't want to go get Grandpa," he whined. "Why does he have to come again? He spills things and talks funny. Why can't he just stay home?"

"I thought you loved Grandpa," Mother said quietly.

"I do," Charles said, "or I did before he had that stroke. He used to do stuff with me. Now he just sits around and . . . gets in the way."

Mother looked at the watches on the table. "These bring back precious memories of happy times, but none of them will run," she said. "I'm fond of them and hate to throw them out, but at least they don't have feelings. But people do." Charles looked at the floor. He knew she meant Grandpa. "My heart is full of memories of growing up with Grandpa and Grandma," added Mother. "Grandma is in heaven now, and age and illness have injured Grandpa. But he is still my father. I don't want to throw him out. I love him too much."

Charles hugged his mother. "I don't want to throw him out, either. I'm going with Dad to get him."

HOW ABOUT YOU? Do you value old people? Never "throw them away" just because they can't do all the things they once could. Use every opportunity to show them that you do love and appreciate them. As you give of yourself to them, you'll be surprised to find how much you still get back in return. □ B.K.

TO MEMORIZE: *The silver-haired head is a crown of glory, if it is found in the way of righteousness.* Proverbs 16:31, NKJV

"OUR CLASS is having a play," Tony told his parents one evening. "There's a scene with the devil in it, and Miss Clark gave me that part, but I really don't want to do it."

"Did you tell her?" Mother asked as she placed some food on Carrie's plate.

"No, I was going to, but—"

Tony's explanation was interrupted by Carrie. "I don't want that! I'm not going to eat it!"

"Then you will not get any dessert," said Mother sternly as she put some on Beth's plate, too.

"I was going to tell Miss Clark," Tony continued, "but Christi was talking to her. Christi was supposed to be a witch in the play, and she was telling Miss Clark she wouldn't do it. I was afraid—"

This time Tony was interrupted by Beth. "Mother, could I eat extra vegetables instead of this casserole, please?" Mother hesitated. "I suppose so."

"But what can I do about the play?" asked Tony.

He sighed as Carrie took over the conversation. "Why do I have to eat casserole if Beth doesn't?"

"Because your attitude is bad," Dad said sternly. "Beth asked politely if she could have a substitute. You declared rebelliously that you were not going to eat yours."

Mother turned to Tony. "Maybe that's your answer," she said. "Did Christi ask Miss Clark to excuse her from the play, or did she just say she wasn't going to do it?"

"She just said she wouldn't do it," replied Tony. "She was pretty hateful about it. I guess that might be why Miss Clark got mad."

"Whether or not our requests are granted often depends on how we ask than on what we ask," Dad said, as much to Carrie as to Tony.

The next day Tony came in from school wearing a big grin. "Guess what? I asked Miss Clark if I could be excused from the play, and she said, 'Certainly.' A right attitude does make a difference.

HOW ABOUT YOU? When you are asked to do something you feel is wrong, don't be afraid to say no, but say it in the right way. Daniel "purposed in his heart" (made up his mind ahead of time) that he would not do wrong. You need to do that, too, but don't be rebellious or super-holy about it. Be respectful but firm, as Daniel was. □ B.W.

TO MEMORIZE: *But Daniel resolved not to defile himself with the royal food and wine.* Daniel 1:8, NIV

20

The Right Way to Say No

FROM THE BIBLE:
Then the king ordered Ashpenaz, chief of his court officials, to bring in some of the Israelites from the royal family and the nobility—young men without any physical defect, handsome, showing aptitude for every kind of learning, well informed, quick to understand, and qualified to serve in the king's palace. He was to teach them the language and literature of the Babylonians. The king assigned them a daily amount of food and wine from the king's table. They were to be trained for three years, and after that they were to enter the king's service. But Daniel resolved not to defile himself with the royal food and wine, and he asked the chief official for permission not to defile himself this way.
Daniel 1:3-5, 8-9, NIV

Keep a pleasant attitude

APRIL

21

Good-for-Nothing Joe

FROM THE BIBLE:
*You are the salt of the earth.
But if the salt loses its saltiness,
how can it be made salty again?
It is no longer good for anything,
except to be thrown out and
trampled by men. You are the
light of the world. A city on a
hill cannot be hidden. Neither
do people light a lamp and put it
under a bowl. Instead they put
it on its stand, and it gives light
to everyone in the house. In the
same way, let your light shine
before men, that they may see
your good deeds and praise your
Father in heaven.*
Matthew 5:13-16, NIV

***Do good—
for nothing***

IN THE EXPRESS LANE at the store, Joe stood on one foot and then the other. *If I don't get home soon, Mother's going to be worried,* he thought, *but I promised Grannie Moore I'd bring her some brown sugar.*

The conversation of the two elderly men in front of him caught his attention. "I declare," complained one, "that grandson of mine is good for nothin'. His folks hire their lawn mowed while that kid sits in front of the TV all day."

"Yep," the other agreed, "this younger generation is spoiled rotten. Good for nothing is right." Joe fumed.

When Joe handed Grannie her brown sugar and change, she tried to return the money to him. "No. No." Joe put his hands in his pockets. "It was right on my way. I was glad to do it for you."

Mother was just getting her coat on when Joe arrived home. "Watch Sherrie for me, please, Son," she said. "I need to run a few errands." Joe nodded, and while Sherrie played on the swing set, Joe finished trimming a hedge.

At the dinner table that evening, Joe repeated the conversation he had heard at the supermarket. Just talking about it upset him. "Well, they did have a point," said Dad.

Mother almost dropped her fork, "Don, are you saying that Joe is good for nothing?"

"Well," said Dad, "today he ran an errand for Grannie Moore. What did you get paid for that, Son?"

Joe shrugged. "Nothing."

"And then you baby-sat Sherrie for your mother, and it looks like you trimmed the hedge for me. What did you get paid for those jobs?"

"Well, nothing," Joe responded.

"Then I guess you're good for nothing, Joe." Dad laughed. "And I reckon there are a lot more kids out there who are just as good for nothing as you are."

HOW ABOUT YOU? Do you expect to be paid for everything you do? Start doing at least one good deed a day for nothing. Don't expect anything, not even praise or thanks. God is pleased by such actions. In heaven you will be rewarded for the things done for nothing. □ B.W.

TO MEMORIZE: *But store up for yourselves treasures in heaven, where moth and rust do not destroy, and where thieves do not break in and steal.*
Matthew 6:20, NIV

"JUST BECAUSE the guys on that show use bad language, it doesn't mean I'm going to," complained Tony when his mother made him turn off the TV set.

As Tony headed outdoors, he considered asking Mother if he could have some candy from a plate he spied on the counter. But she had gone upstairs, and he was sure she'd say no anyway. He walked closer. *I'll just take a peek,* he thought. *Ummmm! It looks so good.* He reached out and picked up a green piece. *I wonder if this one's mint.* He broke off a tiny corner and tasted it. He nibbled another corner. Soon the whole thing was gone. *Guess I'll try a little piece of fudge.* The fudge was delicious, too, and when that was gone, he tried some peanut brittle.

After dinner that evening, Mother said, "Wait till you see what Mrs. Anders gave me." She got the plate of candies, but Tony noticed she looked a little puzzled. "I thought this plate was more full," she said. "But isn't it lovely? Everyone can choose a couple of pieces for dessert."

Tony felt so guilty! All evening he tried to forget it, but he couldn't. "What's the trouble, Son?" Mother asked when she noticed how unhappy he appeared.

Tears filled Tony's eyes. "I did it," he blurted out. "I ate the candy." And the story spilled out. "I'm sorry," he finished.

"Do you see how, little by little, you gave in to temptation?" asked Mother. "How one small peek led to handling and smelling and tasting and eating? That's how Satan works. He gets you to give in, just a little at a time, so it doesn't seem so bad."

Tony nodded. He thought of the TV show he had wanted to watch. Now he could see why it wasn't a good idea.

HOW ABOUT YOU? When you're not allowed to watch a certain TV show, do you like to see "just the beginning" to find out how it starts? When you pass a newsstand, do you like to peek at the pictures in some magazines that you would "never" buy? Would you like to take "just one puff" on a cigarette to see how it tastes or "just one sip" of an alcoholic drink? Satan wants you to try "just a little." He knows that next time you might try a little more. Follow God's advice. Say no right from the start. □ H.M.

TO MEMORIZE: *Submit to God. Resist the devil and he will flee from you.* James 4:7, NKJV

Just a Peek

FROM THE BIBLE:
But He gives more grace. Therefore He says: "God resists the proud, but gives grace to the humble." Therefore submit to God. Resist the devil and he will flee from you. Draw near to God and He will draw near to you. Cleanse your hands, you sinners; and purify your hearts, you double-minded. Lament and mourn and weep! Let your laughter be turned to mourning and your joy to gloom. Humble yourselves in the sight of the Lord, and He will lift you up.
James 4:6-10, NKJV

Resist temptation

23

A Fine-Free Day

FROM THE BIBLE:

And now you are free from your old master, sin; and you have become slaves to your new master, righteousness. I speak this way, using the illustration of slaves and masters, because it is easy to understand: just as you used to be slaves to all kinds of sin, so now you must let yourselves be slaves to all that is right and holy. In those days when you were slaves of sin you didn't bother much with goodness. And what was the result? Evidently not good, since you are ashamed now even to think about those things you used to do, for all of them end in eternal doom. But now you are free from the power of sin and are slaves of God, and his benefits to you include holiness and everlasting life. For the wages of sin is death, but the free gift of God is eternal life through Jesus Christ our Lord.
Romans 6:18-23, TLB

Jesus paid your fine

"OH, BOY! This is my lucky day," Steve shouted. "Listen to this, Mom." From the newspaper he read, "Wednesday has been declared Fine-Free Day at the local library. All overdue books may be returned without paying a fine."

Mother laughed. "The librarian will be sorry when she sees *you* coming. Think of all the money they'll lose!"

Very soon Steve was on his way to return all the overdue books. As he pedaled toward the library, old Mr. Burns staggered out of his house. "Drunk again!" Steve snorted in disgust.

"Hi ya, Steve," Mr. Burns slurred. "Where ya goin'?"

"To the library to return overdue books." Steve stopped his bike. "Today is Fine-Free Day."

"Sure wish they'd have Fine-Free Day at city hall. I've paid out a bundle of money down there." Mr. Burn's blurry eyes stared at the boy. "Hey, yer a good Christian. Ya suppose God has a Fine-Free Day?"

Steve blinked, then replied, "Sure He does, Mr. Burns. Today is Fine-Free Day with God, too. Jesus paid our fine at Calvary. If you'll turn your life over to Him, He'll forget the fine. He forgave me, and He'll forgive you!"

Mr. Burns shook his head. "Easy to say, boy. Ya only have *little* sins to yer charge. I've got a whole pack of 'em."

Steve pointed at his backpack, crammed with books. "It makes no difference to the librarian if I have one overdue book or ten. I don't have to pay a fine today. And it makes no difference to God if I have a few little sins or a whole pack of them. Jesus paid the fine."

"Ya really think so, Son?" As Steve nodded, Mr. Burns continued, "I'd sure like ta believe ya." He staggered toward his house, "I'll think that one over. Fine-Free Day, heh? Sounds pretty good ta me."

HOW ABOUT YOU? Are you carrying some sins for which you need to repent? It makes no difference if they're a "few little sins" or a "lot of big ones," they must be paid for. But, today is the day of salvation—Fine-Free Day! Tomorrow may be Judgment Day. Bring your sins to Christ while there's time. He paid your fine for you. □ B.W.

TO MEMORIZE: *Now is the time of God's favor, now is the day of salvation.* 2 Corinthians 6:2, NIV

SARAH RUBBED her stomach as she eyed the cake Mother had just finished frosting. "Christy and I sure are hungry!" Sarah's friend Christy had come to spend the night, and the girls were looking for an after-school snack.

Mother laughed. "Help yourself," she invited.

After cutting and serving the cake, Sarah sat down beside her friend. She watched as Christy picked at her piece. "Christy, are you just going to eat the frosting?" she asked. "The cake is full of nuts and goodies. In fact, it's the best part!"

"The frosting is all I ever eat," Christy responded. She glanced at Sarah's mother. "I hope you aren't offended."

"No," Mother answered, "but I'm afraid you won't find the frosting very satisfying, and dinner won't be ready for a while. But, as Sarah says, you're really leaving the best part. Why don't you take one taste and see if you like it?"

Christy grimaced, but she took a tiny bite. She grinned. "It *is* good! I think I'll eat the rest."

That evening the girls were right in the middle of a game when Dad called them for family devotions. "Can we just read the story and skip the rest?" Sarah asked.

Dad frowned. "Skip the Bible reading and prayer?"

"Well, just this once," Sarah murmured, "so we can finish our game."

"That would be like eating the frosting and leaving the cake, wouldn't it?" Christy asked. "Do you suppose the Lord would be offended if we read the story and skipped His Word?"

"He might not be offended," Mother answered, "but what we'd get wouldn't be very satisfying. We'd be missing the best part. If we don't have time for both the Scripture and the story, we had better read the Scripture."

"I see what you mean," Sarah admitted. "Well, let's just 'eat' the whole thing. It's all good!"

HOW ABOUT YOU? Are you tempted to skip the Bible reading and read only the story in this book? Don't do it. The Scripture is the most important part. "Eat" the whole thing, and enjoy every bite.

□ B.W.

TO MEMORIZE: *Taste and see that the LORD is good; blessed is the man who takes refuge in him.* Psalm 34:8, NIV

The Best Part

FROM THE BIBLE:

As Jesus and the disciples continued on their way to Jerusalem they came to a village where a woman named Martha welcomed them into her home. Her sister Mary sat on the floor, listening to Jesus as he talked. But Martha was the jittery type, and was worrying over the big dinner she was preparing. She came to Jesus and said, "Sir, doesn't it seem unfair to you that my sister just sits here while I do all the work? Tell her to come and help me." But the Lord said to her, "Martha, dear friend, you are so upset over all these details! There is really only one thing worth being concerned about. Mary has discovered it—and I won't take it away from her!"
Luke 10:38-42, TLB

Don't skip Bible reading

25

Needed: Time to Learn

FROM THE BIBLE:
*But the fruit of the Spirit is
love, joy, peace, patience,
kindness, goodness, faithfulness, gentleness and self-control. Against such things there is
no law. Those who belong to
Christ Jesus have crucified the
sinful nature with its passions
and desires. Since we live by the
Spirit, let us keep in step with
the Spirit. Let us not become
conceited, provoking and
envying each other. Brothers, if
someone is caught in a sin, you
who are spiritual should restore
him gently. But watch yourself,
or you also may be tempted.*
Galatians 5:22–6:1, NIV

Be patient with new Christians

"I T SEEMS TO ME that if Mary Jane really meant it when she said she accepted Jesus, she'd be a little nicer to the kids at school," Barbara told her mother as they finished the dishes. "We've been studying the fruits of the Spirit in Sunday school, but she acts like she never heard of them." As Barbara hung up the dishcloth, her yellow kitten jumped up on the counter. "Buddy! Get down from there!" screeched Barbara. Buddy jumped down and walked calmly across the room as if nothing had happened, "Oh!" sputtered Barbara. "That cat upsets me! Now I've got to wash the counter again!"

"Now, now," sympathized Barbara's mother. "No need to get so upset. Just keep after Buddy, and he'll eventually learn that he's not allowed up there."

Barbara quickly wiped the counter, then tromped outside and plopped down on the steps. "Sometimes I wish I didn't even have a cat," she pouted. "He can be such a pain!"

"Honey," said Mother, sitting down next to her daughter, "you know you wouldn't give Buddy up. But you have to remember that he's still a baby. You need to train him and teach him the rules."

Purring loudly, Buddy rubbed up against Barbara, and she softened a little. "Like you do for me?" she asked.

"Yes," agreed Mother, "and like older Christians do for new Christians. Those who are babes in Christ can't be expected to immediately know the whole Bible or to do everything right. We must have lots of patience and teach them. Then they'll learn to be strong Christians!"

Barbara reached down and picked up Buddy. "I guess I can't expect you to know the rules completely yet," she murmured to him, "and I guess I shouldn't expect quite so much of Mary Jane, either. I'll try to be more patient."

HOW ABOUT YOU? Do you expect too much from those who are new Christians? Remember that one of the fruits of the Spirit is patience. As you pray for new Christians, also be patient with them. As you develop patience, you will be growing in the Lord along with them. □ V.R.

TO MEMORIZE: *The fruit of the Spirit is love, joy, peace, patience, kindness, goodness, faithfulness.* Galatians 5:22, NIV

Brandon STRETCHED, yawned, and turned off the alarm. For several minutes he argued with himself. One voice said, "Get up. It's time for Sunday school." Another voice said, "Why? Your folks don't go. Sleep a little longer." In the end, the wrong voice won. "I'll never be missed," Brandon mumbled as he pulled the pillow over his head. "I'm the least important one in our class. I never do anything. I just go. And today I'll just *not* go."

Later that week Brandon tripped over a tree stump and broke a toe. How it hurt! When the doorbell rang on Saturday, he hobbled to the door. "Oh, hi, Mr. Newman," he greeted his Sunday school teacher. "Come in."

Mr. Newman followed Brandon into the living room. "I see you're limping, Brandon. Did you hurt your foot? Is that why you missed Sunday school?" Mr. Newman asked.

"I broke my little toe last Tuesday," Brandon answered. "I didn't come Sunday because . . . well . . . I just figured I'm not needed. I didn't think anyone would miss me."

Mr. Newman shook his head. "Oh, Brandon, you are needed. You're important to the Lord, to our church, and to me. When you're absent, there's a big gap in our class." He pointed to Brandon's foot and asked, "When you broke your little toe, did it just bother your toe, or did it affect your whole body?"

Brandon grimaced. "My whole body. I wasn't much good for anything for a couple of days."

"So it is with the body of Christ, the church," Mr. Newman explained. "Every member is important, even those who think of themselves as the 'little toe.' When one member hurts, we all hurt." He stood to leave. "You are important to our class, Brandon. Don't ever forget that."

As Brandon hobbled to the door with his teacher, he said, "I won't, Mr. Newman. Every time I take a step, I'll remember. See you tomorrow morning."

HOW ABOUT YOU? Do you feel little and unimportant? Or do you know someone else who feels that way and needs your encouragement? If you're a Christian, you're a member of the body of Christ. You're not only important, you're needed! □ B.W.

TO MEMORIZE: *The body is a unit, though it is made up of many parts; and though all its parts are many, they form one body. So it is with Christ.*
1 Corinthians 12:12, NIV

APRIL

26

The Littlest Member

FROM THE BIBLE:
The body is a unit, though it is made up of many parts; and though all its parts are many, they form one body. So it is with Christ. God has arranged the parts in the body, every one of them, just as he wanted them to be. If they were all one part, where would the body be? As it is, there are many parts, but one body. The eye cannot say to the hand, "I don't need you!" And the head cannot say to the feet, "I don't need you!" On the contrary, those parts of the body that seem to be weaker are indispensable, and the parts that we think are less honorable we treat with special honor. And the parts that are unpresentable are treated with special modesty, while our presentable parts need no special treatment. But God has combined the members of the body and has given greater honor to the parts that lacked it, so that there should be no division in the body, but that its parts should have equal concern for each other.

1 Corinthians 12:12, 18-25, NIV

Each member is important

27

A Way to Serve

FROM THE BIBLE:

But Samuel ministered before the LORD, even as a child, wearing a linen ephod. Moreover his mother used to make him a little robe, and bring it to him year by year when she came up with her husband to offer the yearly sacrifice. . . . And the child Samuel grew in stature, and in favor both with the LORD and men.

1 Samuel 2:18-19, 26, NKJV

Serve God by serving others

MELINDA LAY across her bed as she read an exciting missionary story. *Wow* she thought. *I wish I could serve God, but there's not much a kid can do.*

"Melinda, come here please," Mother called from the kitchen. "Mrs. Nelson is sick, and I want you to take this stew over there." Melinda sighed but did as Mother asked.

At the Nelsons' Melinda noticed that the breakfast and lunch dishes were still on the table. So she loaded them into the dishwasher and set the table for dinner.

When Melinda got back home, Mother asked her to run some magazines over to Grannie Wilson. Grannie was so pleased to see her that Melinda sat down and visited a while. "You're a sweet girl, Melinda," Grannie said. "Most young people these days don't have time for us old folks."

When Melinda arrived home once again, she was singing. "Well, you seem to be in a good mood," Mother remarked. "Would you feed Robbie?"

By the time Melinda finished feeding the baby, she was laughing. "He's such a clown," she said.

At dinner Melinda's mood became heavy. "I wish I could grow up fast so I could serve the Lord," she said, "like the missionary I've been reading about."

Mother looked up in amazement. "Why, Melinda, you've been doing things for the Lord all afternoon."

"Me? For the Lord?" Melinda asked.

"You helped Mrs. Nelson," Mother pointed out. "You visited with Grannie Wilson. You—"

"But, Mother, that was for *people*," sighed Melinda. "I want to do something for the *Lord*."

"How do you think missionaries serve the Lord?" asked Mother. "They do it by doing things for people. We serve God by serving others. And that's what you've been doing."

A big smile slowly spread over Melinda's face. "Well, in that case, would you like some help with the dishes?"

HOW ABOUT YOU? What have you done to serve God lately? You serve Him by serving others. Make a list of two or three things you can do today to help others. Then check at the end of the day to see if you've done them. □ B.W.

TO MEMORIZE: *Serve the LORD with gladness; come before His presence with singing.*
Psalm 100:2, NKJV

"THERE WAS A new girl at school today," remarked Gina as she helped clear the table.

Mother looked up from loading the dishwasher. "I hope you were kind to her. Remember how it feels to start at a new school?"

"But you should see this girl, Mother," Gina protested. "She's so backward. And she probably has lice!"

The front door burst open. "Look what I found, everybody!" called Jeremy. "Isn't he cute?"

Mother shuddered, "That pup is filthy! I'm sure he has fleas. Where did you find him?"

Jeremy patted the frightened, cowering animal. "He's been hanging around Stan's house, and his mother said they had to get rid of him. I'm sure he doesn't belong to anybody. Can I keep him, Mom? Please?" Jeremy begged.

Gina added her pleas. "We'll give him a bath and take good care of him, Mom. He won't be any trouble at all."

Mother laughed. "Oh, of course he won't!"

Jeremy jumped up and down. "Then we can keep him?"

"I didn't say that." Mother frowned. With dark, sad eyes the puppy looked at her and whined, and she weakened a little. "You'll have to ask your dad."

The children spent the next hour bathing, combing, feeding, and loving the pup. "He certainly looks better now," Mother remarked as she patted the playful puppy. "He's cute."

"I knew he was," Gina said. "All he needed was some tender, loving care."

"Hmmm," murmured Mother. "I wonder what the new girl in your class would look like if someone gave her tender, loving care." Gina's mouth fell open as Mother continued, "Maybe all she needs is a friend." Gina had no argument for that. She knew it was probably true. She intended to find out.

HOW ABOUT YOU? Do you know someone who needs tender, loving care? Will you love that one as Christ loved you? He loved you even when you were a sinner, ugly and dirty inside. He saw not only what you were, but what you could become. Your love can make a big difference in a person's life. Perhaps you will even have the opportunity to point him to Jesus. □ B.W.

TO MEMORIZE: *Do to others as you would have them do to you.* Luke 6:31, NIV

FROM THE BIBLE:
How thankful I am to Christ Jesus our Lord for choosing me as one of his messengers, and giving me the strength to be faithful to him, even though I used to scoff at the name of Christ. I hunted down his people, harming them in every way I could. But God had mercy on me because I didn't know what I was doing, for I didn't know Christ at that time. Oh, how kind our Lord was, for he showed me how to trust him and become full of the love of Christ Jesus. How true it is, and how I long that everyone should know it, that Christ Jesus came into the world to save sinners—and I was the greatest of them all. But God had mercy on me so that Christ Jesus could use me as an example to show everyone how patient he is with even the worst sinners, so that others will realize that they, too, can have everlasting life.
1 Timothy 1:12-16, TLB

Treat others with love

29

Better Than Apple Blossoms

FROM THE BIBLE:

Do you not know that in a race all the runners run, but only one gets the prize? Run in such a way as to get the prize. Everyone who competes in the games goes into strict training. They do it to get a crown that will not last; but we do it to get a crown that will last forever. Therefore I do not run like a man running aimlessly; I do not fight like a man beating the air. No, I beat my body and make it my slave so that after I have preached to others, I myself will not be disqualified for the prize.

1 Corinthians 9:24-27, NIV

Earn lasting rewards

THE APPLE BLOSSOM Festival was held each spring in Jill's town. She always looked forward to taking part in the games, and today was no exception. She especially loved the races, since she was a fast runner.

Jill did well. She came in second in the very first event. But she wanted to win a first-place ribbon so badly! In the third event, it happened—she came in first. Happily, she skipped up to the judge's platform. The mayor gave her a blue ribbon and placed a wreath of apple blossoms on her head. It was so exciting!

The excitement didn't last very long, though. By the next day, people were back to their regular routines, the booths were being taken down, and even Jill's wreath of blossoms was wilted and limp-looking. "I'm glad I won," Jill told her parents, "but look at my wreath. It's already dead! It sure wasn't very lasting. Oh, well—it was fun, and maybe I'll win another one next year."

For devotions that evening, Dad read 1 Corinthians 9. "The wreath you won at the races yesterday was a 'corruptible crown,'" he said when he finished reading. "It was just a passing glory. Paul reminds us that the race we run in life is for an 'incorruptible crown.' Things we do for the Lord will have lasting results. And there won't be just one winner. God will reward each of us according to how we have lived for Him."

"Yes." Mother nodded. "The race you run as you live your life for the Lord is the most important race."

HOW ABOUT YOU? Have you won a ribbon or a trophy? It's fun and exciting to win, isn't it? If you're a Christian, don't forget that you're running another kind of race, too. A "race" is the picture used by the Apostle Paul to describe the Christian's life. Follow God's guidelines, and live for Him so you can look forward to the lasting reward the Lord will give you. □ L.W.

TO MEMORIZE: *The man who plants and the man who waters have one purpose, and each will be rewarded according to his own labor.* 1 Corinthians 3:8, NIV

"OH NO! It looks like rain," Bob exclaimed, looking anxiously up at the sky one Saturday morning.

"It surely does," Dad agreed. "I think we'd better postpone our picnic until next week."

Bob was most unhappy about the delay. As the raindrops began to fall, his eyebrows drew together in a frown. And when the rain poured down, he grew downright grumpy. "My whole day is spoiled," he complained over and over.

"Shhhhh. Listen," his sister Becky held up her finger. A clear, pure song came from a treetop outside. A robin was singing in the rain.

"Well, let the dumb bird sing. My day is ruined," Bob grumped. He knew grumbling didn't please God, but he was so disappointed.

"Why don't you get out one of your games, Bob? We may as well have some fun in spite of the rain," suggested Dad.

Bob grudgingly went to get a game, and soon he and Becky and Dad and Mom were all busy playing and laughing. The time flew by, and Bob forgot all about the rain spoiling his fun. Suddenly Dad looked up at the clock. "Can you believe it's nearly dinner time?" he asked.

"We'll have a picnic right here on the floor," decided Mother. "Becky and I will get things ready, and you guys can clean up."

When the food was brought in, they all sat on a blanket on the floor while they ate. "This is fun!" declared Bob. "The whole day was so much fun I forgot about the rain. That robin had the right idea about singin' in the rain. My grumbling didn't stop the rain from coming, and I had as much fun as if I had gone on a picnic—well, almost, anyway. I'm sorry I grumbled."

Dad put his arm around Bob. "You've got the right idea, Son," he said. "That robin was a good example for us. There's always cause to sing, even when it rains."

HOW ABOUT YOU? Do you grumble when it "rains" in your life—when things don't go your way? There are plenty of reasons to be happy and sing in spite of rain or other disappointments. And best of all, you please God by being cheerful even when you're disappointed. □ C.Y.

TO MEMORIZE: *And do not grumble, as some of them did—and were killed by the destroying angel.* 1 Corinthians 10:10, NIV

Singing in the Rain

FROM THE BIBLE:
But they continued to sin against him, rebelling in the desert against the Most High. They willfully put God to the test by demanding the food they craved. They spoke against God, saying, "Can God spread a table in the desert? When he struck the rock, water gushed out, and streams flowed abundantly. But can he also give us food? Can he supply meat for his people?" When the LORD heard them, he was very angry; his fire broke out against Jacob, and his wrath rose against Israel, for they did not believe in God or trust in his deliverance.
Psalm 78:17-22, NIV

Sing to the Lord always

MAY

1

A Safe Place

FROM THE BIBLE:

Shout for joy, O heavens;
rejoice, O earth; burst into
song, O mountains! For the
LORD comforts his people and
will have compassion on his
afflicted ones. But Zion said,
"The LORD has forsaken me,
the LORD has forgotten me."
Can a mother forget the baby at
her breast and have no compas-
sion on the child she has borne?
Though she may forget, I will
not forget you! See, I have
engraved you on the palms of my
hands; your walls are ever
before me.

Isaiah 49:13-16, NIV

Accept Jesus as Savior

"**W**HAT DO YOU NEED, Mom?" asked Darla. She was going to the store for her mother.

"A gallon of milk, a loaf of bread, and a package of cheese," replied Mother. "Can you remember that?" She glanced at her daughter. "What are you doing?"

Darla lifted her head and grinned at her mother. She turned her hand to show her mother what she had done. "I wrote the list on my palm with this pen," she said. "That way I'll be able to remember what you need."

"That's a unique idea, but you could have used a piece of paper instead of your palm," suggested Mother.

Darla shook her head. "This is better. I might lose paper, but I can't lose my hand."

Mother laughed and gave Darla a hug. "You're right," she agreed. "Wait a minute. I want to show you an interesting verse in the Bible." Walking over to her desk, Mother picked up her Bible and opened it to Isaiah. "Read this," she said, pointing to a verse.

Darla read it aloud. "I have engraved you on the palms of my hands." She looked up at her mother. "Hey, that's neat! God writes on His palms, too."

Mother nodded. "Actually, He does more than just write. After all, that writing will wash off your palm—at least I certainly hope it will. But God said Israel was engraved on His palms, and I believe we can apply that to Christians, too. Engraving goes deeper than writing. It won't ever come off."

Darla looked down at the black writing on her hand. "That makes me feel good," she said. She closed her hand over the writing. "It's a safe place to be, isn't it?"

HOW ABOUT YOU? Have you ever written on your palm to remember a school assignment or someone's phone number? Your palm is a safe place for such things, isn't it? Are you engraved on God's palms? If not, why not ask Jesus to be your Savior today? God's palm is the safest place to be. □
L.S.R.

TO MEMORIZE: *See, I have engraved you on the palms of my hands; your walls are ever before me.* Isaiah 49:16, NIV

CHUCK LOVED FISHING. He went almost every Saturday and had read just about every book there was on the subject. Every time he went fishing, he took a long time getting ready. He would check his tackle box to make sure all his lures and hooks were in order. And he always checked his rod thoroughly. All his care paid off. It was very seldom that Chuck didn't come home with a string of fresh fish.

One day he invited his friend Kenny to go with him. Kenny had never been fishing before and could hardly wait.

As they spent the day together, Chuck taught his friend all he could about fishing. Kenny was a fast learner, and soon both had caught several fish.

That evening Chuck's mother noticed that he was unusually quiet at the supper table. When she asked if something was wrong, he replied, "Well, when Kenny and I were eating the picnic lunch you sent with us today, he asked me why I always bow my head and close my eyes for a few minutes before I eat. I told him I was praying, and he asked what praying was and why I did it."

"And what did you tell him?" asked Mother.

"I told him that praying was talking to God, and I was thanking Him for the food. Then he started asking me about church and God, and I didn't know what to say! I never thought about why we go to church, or how I know that God loves me. I just know, that's all!"

"Oh, I see." Mother was thoughtful. "Do you know what it means to be a 'fisher of men,' Chuck?"

"Sure," answered Chuck, "it means to try to bring others to Jesus."

"Well," said Mother, "before you go fishing for fish, you're always very careful in making your preparations. You should be that way about fishing for men, too. You need to be familiar with God's Word in order to be a successful fisher of men."

HOW ABOUT YOU? Have your friends ever started asking you questions that you didn't know how to answer? Praying, reading your Bible, and memorizing Scripture will help prepare you for unexpected questions. Be familiar with your Bible and know where to locate passages about salvation. Be an effective "fisher of men." □ D.M.

TO MEMORIZE: *Let me understand the teaching of your precepts; then I will meditate on your wonders.* Psalm 119:27, NIV

A Good Fisherman

FROM THE BIBLE:
One day as he was walking along the beach beside the Lake of Galilee, he saw two brothers—Simon, also called Peter, and Andrew—out in a boat fishing with a net, for they were commercial fishermen. Jesus called out, "Come along with me and I will show you how to fish for the souls of men!" And they left their nets at once and went with him. A little farther up the beach he saw two other brothers, James and John, sitting in a boat with their father Zebedee, mending their nets; and he called to them to come too. At once they stopped their work and, leaving their father behind, went with him. Matthew 4:18-22, TLB

Be ready to witness

MAY

3

Wrong Instructions

FROM THE BIBLE:

You slaves must always obey your earthly masters, not only trying to please them when they are watching you but all the time; obey them willingly because of your love for the Lord and because you want to please him. Work hard and cheerfully at all you do, just as though you were working for the Lord and not merely for your masters, remembering that it is the Lord Christ who is going to pay you, giving you your full portion of all he owns. He is the one you are really working for. And if you don't do your best for him, he will pay you in a way that you won't like—for he has no special favorites who can get away with shirking.

Colossians 3:22-25, TLB

Follow God's instructions

"I CAN DO IT, Dad. I know how." Gene was eager to help trim the hedge at the back of the yard.

"Okay, Son," agreed Dad. "I've got it started, so you can see how much I want cut off. Keep it nice and even. I'm going to run to the store for some grass seed. If you finish the hedge before I get back, you may cut just a little bit off those bushes at the side of the house."

Dad disappeared, and Gene took over the trimming. As he carefully cut the hedge to the same level Dad had started, his friend Barry, who lived in the house behind Gene's, came out. He eyed Gene's work. "You know what?" he said. "If you'd cut that down a little bit more, we'd be able to jump over it and wouldn't have to walk all the way around when we want to go to each other's house."

Gene thought about that. "You're right!" he said. And he proceeded to follow Barry's advice.

Next Gene trimmed the bushes beside the house. Deb, his sister, came out of the house and surveyed his work. "I've always wished we could have these bushes trimmed so they go in points, like in formal gardens," she said. "Can you do them that way?"

"Sure," said Gene confidently, and he proceeded to show her. The results were not quite what he expected.

When Dad got home, he looked from Gene to the hedge, to the bushes, and back at Gene. "What happened?" he asked. "You didn't do things the way I told you." Gene explained about Barry's and Deb's suggestions. "Who are you working for?" Dad asked quietly. "Them or me?"

Gene was embarrassed and ashamed. "I'm sorry, Dad," he said. "After this, I'll follow your instructions very carefully." And he did.

HOW ABOUT YOU? Did you know that you are a servant of Christ? As His servant, you need to follow His instructions. Your friends may say, "It doesn't hurt to cheat just a little." But God says, "Be honest." The world says, "A little white lie is okay." God says, "You shall not lie." Unbelievers may tell you, "God won't send anyone to hell." God says, "The soul that sins will die. Be witnesses for Me." What worldly advice is someone giving you? Shut it out and follow God's instruction.

□ H.M.

TO MEMORIZE: *Oh, that my ways were steadfast in obeying your decrees!* Psalm 119:5, NIV

The Most Dangerous Animal

JASON and his parents were visiting the zoo, and Jason especially enjoyed seeing the lions, bears, and other dangerous animals. "Wow! Look at the bear yawn!" he exclaimed at one cage. "See all those teeth? I'll bet he could really do some damage if he came after you!" A short time later, he was equally impressed with a large tiger who scowled warily at them. Jason shivered. "Imagine something like that sneaking up on you in the jungle!" he exclaimed. When they started for home, he asked, "Dad, which of the animals do you think is the most dangerous?"

"That's a good question," replied Dad as they drove away. "I think I'll vote for the lion, but there's something even more dangerous to people. Look out the window, Son. What do you see?"

"Well, we're right in the middle of the city!" replied Jason. "There are a bunch of old bars and theaters. Over there, a cop is talking to some drunk. And it looks like there's an accident up ahead, next to that burned-out building with the broken windows."

"This surely has become a poor section of town," murmured Mother. "It would be nice if we could avoid it, but it's the shortest route to the highway."

"But there aren't any animals here, Dad." Jason wanted to get back to the subject.

"Literally speaking, you're right," admitted Dad. "But this street shows the effects of sin in the heart of man, and it's all the work of Satan. More people die and more hearts and homes are broken because of man's sin than from all the animals put together. As much as we need to beware of dangerous animals like the ones we saw in the zoo, we need to be far more cautious about getting close to sin. Sin in the heart of a man, woman, or child is the most dangerous 'animal' there is!"

HOW ABOUT YOU? Would you be frightened if a lion or bear crossed your path? You should be much more frightened of that dirty book or movie, the beer or pot your friend wants you to try, or even that "little white" lie that seems so harmless. These are things Satan uses to destroy you and others as well. Be smart. Stay away from sin! S.K.

TO MEMORIZE: *Be self-controlled and alert. Your enemy the devil prowls around like a roaring lion looking for someone to devour.* 1 Peter 5:8, NIV

FROM THE BIBLE:

As the Scriptures say, "No one is good—no one in all the world is innocent." No one has ever really followed God's paths, or even truly wanted to. Every one has turned away; all have gone wrong. No one anywhere has kept on doing what is right; not one. Their talk is foul and filthy like the stench from an open grave. Their tongues are loaded with lies. Everything they say has in it the sting and poison of deadly snakes. Their mouths are full of cursing and bitterness. They are quick to kill, hating anyone who disagrees with them. Wherever they go they leave misery and trouble behind them, and they have never known what it is to feel secure or enjoy God's blessing. They care nothing about God nor what he thinks of them.

Romans 3:10-18, TLB

Beware of sin

5

The Lighthouse

FROM THE BIBLE:

For God is at work within you, helping you want to obey him, and then helping you do what he wants. In everything you do, stay away from complaining and arguing, so that no one can speak a word of blame against you. You are to live clean, innocent lives as children of God in a dark world full of people who are crooked and stubborn. Shine out among them like beacon lights, holding out to them the Word of Life. Then when Christ returns how glad I will be that my work among you was so worthwhile. Philippians 2:13-16, TLB

Be a prism for God

JEFF'S CLASS was on a field trip to a lighthouse, and the caretaker took them up to the top room to see the powerful light. "This big light runs on electricity," he said, indicating the heavy cables that went into the light. Walking over to a counter, he pointed to an old lamp that was about one-fourth the size of the modern one. "This lamp was used before they had electricity," he continued. "It ran on kerosene, and the caretaker's most important job was to make sure it didn't run out of fuel."

"But that light is so much smaller," one of the kids piped up. "I guess it didn't shine very far over the ocean, did it?"

"Actually, the old lamp shone just as far as the modern one does," the caretaker answered. He picked up two odd-shaped pieces of glass from the counter. "These are prisms. They are specially cut to bend the rays of light that hit them and reflect them back—not once, but several times. By using prisms, the beam of the kerosene lamp could be magnified up to a thousand times. A sailor far out at sea could see the beam of reflected light."

That night at supper all Jeff could talk about was his visit to the lighthouse. "They used a small kerosene lamp in the old days," he was saying. "They used prisms to reflect the beam of light to make it just as strong as the big light they use now."

Mother smiled. "Your story about the prisms reminds me of something I read in my Bible today. The passage was talking about Christ and how He is the light of the world. And because we are Christians, it's our job to reflect that light for the rest of the world to see. Each one of us is important, just like each of those prisms was important. If one of God's 'prisms' isn't doing his job, the beam is weakened."

HOW ABOUT YOU? What are you doing to reflect the light of Jesus? Are you using the talents He has given you to glorify Him? Are you telling others about Him? Are you kind and loving as He wants you to be? God holds you responsible to let your light shine for Him in the world. □ D.M.

TO MEMORIZE: *. . . so that you may become blameless and pure, children of God without fault in a crooked and depraved generation, in which you shine like stars in the universe.* Philippians 2:15, NIV

JENNY AND JANE. Bystanders thought they were twins, but their friends knew them as best buddies. They seemed inseparable. But one day that all changed.

"Jenny, aren't you going to stay for pep assembly?" Jane asked.

"No, I don't feel too well," Jenny said. "I called my mom to come and get me."

"See you tomorrow then," said Jane.

But Jenny didn't come to school the next day. Jane stopped to see her at home, but she was resting. Jenny did come back to school the next week, but she seemed very tired. And before long, she was in the hospital.

Jane immediately went there to see Jenny. She brought their favorite flower, a pink rose. Jane could tell Jenny liked the rose by the smile in her eyes, but Jenny didn't say much. She was hooked to several tubes, and nurses kept checking her.

The longer Jenny stayed in the hospital, the less Jane visited her. Finally Jane stopped visiting.

"Jane, who's your best friend now?" asked Mother one day.

Jane looked puzzled. "Jenny, of course!"

"I thought best friends like to be together," Mother answered, "and you haven't seen Jenny in days."

Jane burst into tears. "Mom, I can't go there. Jenny can barely talk. And she looks so different. I'm sure she's going to die. What can I say?"

"You don't need to say anything," answered Mother. "Just be there. Jenny really needs a friend now. She misses you so much, Jane. Her mom told me that. She thinks you no longer care about her."

"But I do, Mom!" exclaimed Jane. "I care so much it hurts!"

"Then go be with her," encouraged Mother. "Show her you still care. Let her know you're praying for her."

Jane got her coat. How could a real friend stay away?

HOW ABOUT YOU? Do you know someone who is ill? Be a comfort. Visit if possible. Read a few comforting Bible verses. Send a card, a note, flowers, or a favorite item. Let your friend know he is still important to you. □ J.H.

TO MEMORIZE: . . . *who comforts us in all our troubles, so that we can comfort those in any trouble with the comfort we ourselves have received from God.* 2 Corinthians 1:4, NIV

6

A Comforter

FROM THE BIBLE:

Praise be to the God and Father of our Lord Jesus Christ, the Father of compassion and the God of all comfort, who comforts us in all our troubles, so that we can comfort those in any trouble with the comfort we ourselves have received from God. For just as the sufferings of Christ flow over into our lives, so also through Christ our comfort overflows. . . . And our hope for you is firm, because we know that just as you share in our sufferings, so also you share in our comfort.

2 Corinthians 1:3-5, 7, NIV

Comfort the ill

MAY

7

Tried and True

FROM THE BIBLE:

Great are the works of the LORD; they are pondered by all who delight in them. Glorious and majestic are his deeds, and his righteousness endures forever. He has caused his wonders to be remembered; the LORD is gracious and compassionate. He provides food for those who fear him; he remembers his covenant forever. He has shown his people the power of his works, giving them the lands of other nations. The works of his hands are faithful and just; all his precepts are trustworthy. They are steadfast for ever and ever, done in faithfulness and uprightness. He provided redemption for his people; he ordained his covenant forever— holy and awesome is his name. The fear of the LORD is the beginning of wisdom; all who follow his precepts have good understanding. To him belongs eternal praise.

Psalm 111:2-10, NIV

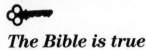

The Bible is true

LORI CAREFULLY measured a cup of sugar into a bowl. "I like making cookies," she said, "and Dad says my cookies are second only to yours." She grinned at her mother as she cracked an egg.

"You do a good job," agreed Mother, "and I appreciate your taking that task off my hands today. I need time to prepare for my Bible study."

"Yeah," murmured Lori. She looked thoughtful as she stirred the mixture. "Mom, how do you know the Bible is true, anyway? I mean, couldn't it have some mistakes?"

Mother looked surprised. "No, it couldn't."

"Well, Janie's father is a preacher, and they believe most of the Bible," said Lori, "but her father says some of the things just couldn't have happened. Like some of the miracles. He says God has set up certain laws of nature, and those things don't fit in."

"God did establish laws of nature," agreed Mother, "and He can also set them aside as He sees fit." She paused as she watched Lori take the baking soda from the cupboard. "Lori," said Mother, "why don't you put in a few extra teaspoons of soda today?"

Lori stood still. "How come?"

Mother shrugged. "It might make the cookies taste even better. And if you'd add an extra cup of milk to make a nice soft dough, you should get some nice soft cookies."

Lori stared at her mother, then she laughed. "Either you've gotta be kidding, or you're afraid Dad will like my cookies better than yours, so you're trying to ruin them," she teased. "Won't work, Mom! I've used this recipe often enough to know it's just right the way it is."

"In other words, you've tested it and found it to be accurate," said Mother, "just as I've tested many recipes in that cookbook." Then she pointed to the Bible lying on a kitchen shelf. "There's another book that's been tried and proven to be accurate. You can be sure that all it says is true."

HOW ABOUT YOU? Have you wondered if the Bible is really true? It is. Many events the Bible said would come to pass have already happened. The Bible has changed the lives of people throughout the world. Even science, as it has developed, proves the truth of the Bible. The Bible has stood the test of time. □ H.M.

TO MEMORIZE: *The grass withers and the flowers fall, but the word of our God stands forever.* Isaiah 40:8, NIV

JOEY LIKED to visit Great-Uncle Hank's dairy farm. He liked to throw down feed from the silo. He liked to swing on ropes in the hayloft. He liked to ride on the tractor. But most of all, he liked to work with Uncle Hank on the old Model T car in the shed behind the tractor barn.

The old car had been Uncle Hank's first, and he was working to restore it to its original condition. It had been taken apart piece by piece, then each piece had been cleaned. Worn parts had been repaired or replaced. The old paint had been stripped off the body, the rust removed, and a new coat of paint had been applied. Now the work was nearly done. Joey would polish the car until it shone as Uncle Hank put the engine back together.

As they were working on the car one day, Uncle Hank turned to Joey and asked, "How would you like to have this car?" Joey grinned, and his eyes lit up. Uncle Hank smiled. "Someday it will be yours," he said. "It's going to be your inheritance from me."

That evening Joey excitedly told his parents about Uncle Hank's decision. Mom smiled. "What a nice thing for Great-Uncle Hank to do," she said.

Dad nodded. "It certainly is," he agreed. After a moment he added, "You know, this reminds me of what God has done for us. He has promised that whoever trusts in His Son, Jesus Christ, will someday enjoy all the blessings of heaven, just as you'll someday enjoy owning that car. Aren't you glad you belong to Him?"

HOW ABOUT YOU? Is there an inheritance waiting in heaven for you? There is if you've asked Jesus Christ to save you from your sins. If you haven't yet done that, why not do it today? □ T.V.B.

TO MEMORIZE: *God, . . . according to His abundant mercy has begotten us again to a living hope through the resurrection of Jesus Christ from the dead.* 1 Peter 1:3, NKJV

MAY

8

An Inheritance

FROM THE BIBLE:
Blessed be the God and Father of our Lord Jesus Christ, who according to His abundant mercy has begotten us again to a living hope through the resurrection of Jesus Christ from the dead, to an inheritance incorruptible and undefiled and that does not fade away, reserved in heaven for you, who are kept by the power of God through faith for salvation ready to be revealed in the last time.
1 Peter 1:3-5, NKJV

Receive God's inheritance

9

An Inheritance

(Continued from yesterday)

FROM THE BIBLE:

Moreover, because of what Christ has done we have become gifts to God that he delights in, for as part of God's sovereign plan we were chosen from the beginning to be his, and all things happen just as he decided long ago. God's purpose in this was that we should praise God and give glory to him for doing these mighty things for us, who were the first to trust in Christ. And because of what Christ did, all you others too, who heard the Good News about how to be saved, and trusted Christ, were marked as belonging to Christ by the Holy Spirit, who long ago had been promised to all of us Christians. His presence within us is God's guarantee that he really will give us all that he promised; and the Spirit's seal upon us means that God has already purchased us and that he guarantees to bring us to himself. This is just one more reason for us to praise our glorious God.

Ephesians 1:11-14, TLB

Christians have the Holy Spirit

AS SOON AS he could, Joey visited Great-Uncle Hank and helped him work on the Model T again. After a while, Uncle Hank stuck his head out from under the hood and looked at Joey. "I thought you might like to know that I had your inheritance of this car added to my will," he said. "I'd like you to have a set of keys for it now."

"Wow!" Joey's eyes glistened as he thanked his uncle.

That night Joey happily showed his parents the keys. "So you're really going to own that car," said Dad with a smile.

Joey nodded, but he had a question. "You said Christians will receive the blessings of heaven as an inheritance from God. How can we be sure of that?"

"Well," replied Dad, "how can you be sure Uncle Hank will really give you the Model T?"

Joey answered quickly. "I trust him to do what he said because I've never seen him lie to anyone. He even gave me a set of keys to prove that he intends to give me the car."

"That's right," answered Dad, "and it's much the same with God. We know we can trust Him to do what He said, too, because He has never lied. He also sends the Holy Spirit to live in us to prove that we really belong to Him."

"But how can we know the Holy Spirit is living in us?" asked Joey.

"Well, one way is by the fruit of His presence in our lives," Dad answered. "Galatians 5:22-23 says the fruit of the Spirit is love, joy, peace, long-suffering, gentleness, goodness, faith, meekness, and temperance—or self-control."

"Another way I know I'm God's child is that His Spirit somehow tells me so," added Mother. "He causes me to be interested in the things of God, and He gives me an inner peace and assurance in my heart." Joey looked at the keys he held. They were a good reminder of a very important "proof" of an inheritance.

HOW ABOUT YOU? Has the Holy Spirit given you assurance that you are a child of God? Is He changing your life? Is there evidence of His presence there? There should be. Make sure that you've accepted Jesus as Savior. Then ask God to make you sensitive to the promptings of the Holy Spirit.

□ T.V.B.

TO MEMORIZE: *The Spirit himself testifies with our spirit that we are God's children.* Romans 8:16, NIV

"**W**HERE'S YOUR BIBLE, Jeff?" asked Dad as Jeff and his sister, Jenny, climbed into the car one Sunday morning.

"I dunno," mumbled Jeff. "I can't find it."

"If you had been doing your daily Bible reading, you'd know where it is," whispered Jenny. Jeff glared at her. "Do you know your memory verse?" Jenny continued.

Jeff shook his head. "I was too busy this week."

The next evening Jeff was going with his dad to play golf. They had just started backing out of the driveway when Jeff noticed Dad's golf bag standing in the garage. "Hold it!" he called. "You forgot your golfing equipment!"

"Oh, that," said Dad. "I thought we'd try golfing without all that stuff."

"Dad, that's crazy!" protested Jeff.

"Think so?" asked Dad. He looked at Jeff. "Is it any crazier than you saying you want to be a good testimony for the Lord but not taking the time to memorize His Word or read the Bible or pray?"

"Well," mumbled Jeff weakly, "I guess not."

"After the special youth services a few weeks ago, you told us that you went forward to dedicate your life to the Lord," Dad reminded Jeff. "The Bible says we are to be 'thoroughly equipped for every good work.' That means we are to be properly outfitted. I can't be properly equipped for golf without my clubs and golf balls. You can't be properly equipped to be a good testimony without a knowledge of God's Word. You need to study it regularly and spend time in prayer."

"I guess I never thought of it that way, Dad," admitted Jeff. "I know you're right."

"Tell you what," said Dad as he put his golf bag into the car. "Take your Sunday school book along, and we'll both learn your memory verse while we drive to the golf course." Jeff nodded and ran into the house.

HOW ABOUT YOU? Are you properly equipped to be a testimony for the Lord? Do you study and memorize God's Word so you can share His love with others? Do you spend time talking to the Lord? Don't try to "play the game"—to live a Christian life—without the equipment you need. □ L.W.

TO MEMORIZE: *That the man of God may be complete, thoroughly equipped for every good work.* 2 Timothy 3:17, NKJV

MAY

10

Equipped and Ready

FROM THE BIBLE:

But as for you, continue in the things which you have learned and been assured of, knowing from whom you have learned them, and that from childhood you have known the Holy Scriptures, which are able to make you wise for salvation through faith which is in Christ Jesus. All Scripture is given by inspiration of God, and is profitable for doctrine, for reproof, for correction, for instruction in righteousness, that the man of God may be complete, thoroughly equipped for every good work.

2 Timothy 3:14-17, NKJV

Be prepared to serve God

11

Twenty-Twenty Vision

FROM THE BIBLE:

Children, obey your parents; this is the right thing to do because God has placed them in authority over you. Honor your father and mother. This is the first of God's Ten Commandments that ends with a promise. And this is the promise: that if you honor your father and mother, yours will be a long life, full of blessing.

Ephesians 6:1-3, TLB

Honor your parents

"HEY, DAD, I went to the eye doctor today, and he said my vision was twenty-twenty," announced David at dinner. "That's perfect, you know!"

"That's right," agreed Mother as she passed the salad. Loud voices, slamming door, and squealing tires next door interrupted her. When it was quiet again, she murmured, "Poor Mrs. Marler."

"Yes, I'm afraid Chad is worrying her to death," Dad said with a nod.

"I don't know why everybody's on Chad's case," David protested. "I like him. He gave me a ride on his cycle."

"Well, you are not to get on his cycle again," Dad ordered.

"Aw, Dad, he's okay," argued David.

"In some ways he's a nice boy," said Mother, "but I don't approve of the way he's been acting lately. The way he talks to his parents is disgraceful!"

"He called his mother 'stupid old woman' the other day," little Cheri reported. "That's not nice."

"It certainly isn't," agreed Dad. "It's too bad Chad doesn't have twenty-twenty vision. He seems to be going blind."

"Chad's going blind?" David was horrified.

"Well, the Bible talks about the person who curses his parents. It says 'his lamp will be snuffed out in pitch darkness,' " Dad told him. "That means he will go blind—not physically, but spiritually. And a spiritually blind person can get into lots of trouble. Incidentally, that's Proverbs 20:20."

As Mother cleared the breakfast table the next morning, she told David, "Chad wrecked his folks' car and was charged with drunken driving last night."

"Ooooooh!" David exhaled. "Maybe he is going blind like Dad said." Before leaving for school, David paused long enough to hug his mother. "I'm going to work at keeping my vision twenty-twenty—spiritually as well as physically."

HOW ABOUT YOU? How's your spiritual eyesight? One way to check it is to take a look at your attitude toward your parents. Do you honor and obey them? To curse them—to speak disrespectfully of them or to them—is a warning of serious problems. □ B.W.

TO MEMORIZE: *If a man curses his father or mother, his lamp will be snuffed out in pitch darkness.* Proverbs 20:20, NIV

"**I**'M THE ONLY GIRL in my class who has to ride a bicycle!" Kim stormed as she picked up her library book. "The other girls' parents take them whenever they have to go somewhere! And the other girls get to date, too."

Mother looked up. "Kim, we've been through all this before. Why don't you sit down and let's talk about it."

But Kim headed for the door. "I have to get to the library," she grumbled. She went out to the garage, slamming the door behind her.

Mother sighed. "Well, we might as well enjoy a few minutes of quiet," she said. "Jason's taking a nap."

Dad nodded. "Might be a good time to clean the garage," he suggested, and the two of them got busy.

For an hour they worked in companionable silence. Then, just as a fuming Kim rode her bike into the garage, a voice rang out from the house. "Mommie?"

"Peace and quiet just went out the door." Mother grinned at Dad. She lifted her voice. "Jason, we're—"

"MOMMIE!" The little boy's scream drowned out her words.

Mother tried again. "Jason," she called, "we're in—"

"MOMMIE!" A terrified wail split the air. Mother and Dad, followed by Kim, flew into the house. Jason, looking wild-eyed, was standing in the kitchen. "I thought you left me," he sobbed.

"If you'd listened a minute, you could have heard Mother," Kim scolded crossly. "She was trying to answer you, but you were so busy yelling, you couldn't hear her."

Dad nodded. "That's true, Kim. Looks like we have two children not listening to their parents." Kim blushed. "We ask the Lord daily to help us make the right decisions concerning you," Dad continued, "and it's time you learned to listen."

HOW ABOUT YOU? Do you feel that your parents don't understand you? Have you tried to understand them? Have you really listened to what they have to say? God has given them the responsibility of using their wisdom in guiding you. He has given you the responsibility of listening to them and obeying them. They're worth listening to. □ B.W.

TO MEMORIZE: *My son, hear the instruction of your father, and do not forsake the law of your mother.* Proverbs 1:8, NKJV

MAY

12

Worth Listening

FROM THE BIBLE:
The fear of the LORD is the beginning of knowledge, but fools despise wisdom and instruction. My son, hear the instruction of your father, and do not forsake the law of your mother; for they will be graceful ornaments on your head, and chains about your neck.
Proverbs 1:7-9, NKJV

Listen to your parents

MAY

13

Thanks!

FROM THE BIBLE:

Who can find a virtuous wife? For her worth is far above rubies. . . . She opens her mouth with wisdom, and on her tongue is the law of kindness. She watches over the ways of her household, and does not eat the bread of idleness. Her children rise up and call her blessed; her husband also, and he praises her.
Proverbs 31:10, 26-28, NKJV

Thank God for your mother

THE STUDENTS in Mrs. Green's fifth-grade class were planning a party for their teacher's birthday. They wanted to surprise her with cake and ice cream. "But who will make the cake?" Fred asked his friends. "One of our mothers will have to do it."

"Count my mom out." Ricky spoke up. "She hates to cook!"

"My mom can't do it, either," Jessica said. "She works. The last time I asked her if I could bring cookies to school, she got really angry! She said she didn't even have time to go to the store to buy cookies!"

"Well, I guess it's up to my mom, then," said Fred when no one else offered. His mom worked as secretary in the family business and was busy, too. She wouldn't have time to make a fancy masterpiece, but Fred thought she'd probably be willing to make a cake from a mix.

Fred was right. Even though his mother was in the midst of organizing tax records, she said she'd make a cake for the class. In return, Fred agreed to do the dishes and to help in any way he could. "You're special, Mom." Fred gave her a hug. "None of the other mothers would take time to bake for us."

"Don't be too critical," Fred's mother told him. "Sometimes parents are too busy to take on an added responsibility." She paused and then continued. "Not all children are as helpful as you are, either, nor as appreciative. Maybe that makes a difference."

"Well, thanks for being such a great mother," Fred said.

HOW ABOUT YOU? When was the last time you thanked your mom for doing something special for you? When was the last time you told her how much you liked the supper she cooked? And did you thank God for her? You're very special to her, but sometimes it takes a great deal of effort to be a mom. Let her—and God—know how much you appreciate her. □ L.W.

TO MEMORIZE: *Her children rise up and call her blessed; her husband also, and he praises her.* Proverbs 31:28, NKJV

14

The Alarm

GREG FUMBLED for the snooze button on the alarm clock. As soon as the ringing stopped, he burrowed deeper into his blanket. It seemed to be only a minute later when the alarm again roused him. Once more he hit the snooze button and nestled back in his bed. Before the alarm could sound again, Mother was at his door. "Get up at once, Greg," she ordered. "You'll have to hurry or you'll miss your bus."

Greg sat up quickly, then stumbled from his bed. "I'll hurry." He did, and he was ready just in time to catch the bus.

"My alarm didn't go off this morning," Greg complained at the dinner table that evening. "I almost missed my bus."

Mother laughed. "It went off all right," she assured him. "I heard it. But you just kept hitting the snooze button and going back to sleep. So I finally called you myself."

"You sound like some Christians I know," said Dad. He grinned at Greg's quizzical look and reached for his Bible. "Let's read tonight from Romans 13. It tells us that Christians need to 'wake up.' Why don't you read for us, Greg?"

When Greg finished reading, Dad nodded. "In a way, God is sounding an 'alarm' here," he said. "He says we'd better wake up and live as we should because our time here is getting shorter and shorter. Soon it will be too late to win people we love to Jesus or to do the things we know God wants us to do. But so often we hit the 'snooze button' and ignore the warning. We often don't even realize what's happening. We need to wake up and live for the Lord."

HOW ABOUT YOU? Have you hit the "snooze button" in your Christian life? Do you go about day by day pleasing yourself? Time is passing quickly. It's time to wake up and start pleasing the Lord. Look over today's Scripture once again and see how many practical commands God gives in just this short passage. Ask Him to help you obey each one. □ H.M.

TO MEMORIZE: *The hour has come for you to wake up from your slumber, because our salvation is nearer now than when we first believed.* Romans 13:11, NIV

FROM THE BIBLE:
Give everyone what you owe him: If you owe taxes, pay taxes; if revenue, then revenue; if respect, then respect; if honor, then honor. Let no debt remain outstanding, except the continuing debt to love one another, for he who loves his fellowman has fulfilled the law. The commandments, "Do not commit adultery," "Do not murder," "Do not steal," "Do not covet," and whatever other commandment there may be, are summed up in this one rule: "Love your neighbor as yourself." Love does no harm to its neighbor. Therefore love is the fulfillment of the law. And do this, understanding the present time. The hour has come for you to wake up from your slumber, because our salvation is nearer now than when we first believed. So let us put aside the deeds of darkness and put on the armor of light. Let us behave decently, not in orgies and drunkenness, not in sexual immorality and debauchery, not in dissension and jealousy. Rather, clothe yourselves with the Lord Jesus Christ, and do not think about how to gratify the desires of the sinful nature.
Romans 13:7-14, NIV

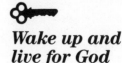

Wake up and live for God

15

Just Like Dorcas

FROM THE BIBLE:
In the city of Joppa there was a woman named Dorcas ("Gazelle"), a believer who was always doing kind things for others, especially for the poor. About this time she became ill and died. Her friends prepared her for burial and laid her in an upstairs room. But when they learned that Peter was nearby at Lydda, they sent two men to beg him to return with them to Joppa. This he did; as soon as he arrived, they took him upstairs where Dorcas lay. The room was filled with weeping widows who were showing one another the coats and other garments Dorcas had made for them. But Peter asked them all to leave the room; then he knelt and prayed. Turning to the body he said, "Get up, Dorcas," and she opened her eyes! And when she saw Peter, she sat up! He gave her his hand and helped her up and called in the believers and widows, presenting her to them. The news raced through the town, and many believed in the Lord. And Peter stayed a long time in Joppa, living with Simon, the tanner.
Acts 9:36-43, TLB

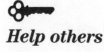

Help others

"**W**HAT ARE YOU MAKING, Mom?" Jody asked as she looked up from her book.

"I'm making a baby sweater for one of the ladies at church," answered Mom. "Mrs. Pauley is having a baby next month."

"How come you do so many things like that for other people?" Jody asked.

"I enjoy making things, and I enjoy giving them away." Mother smiled. "When you make something special at school you enjoy bringing it home to me, don't you?"

Jody nodded. "Sure, but that seems a little different," she said. "I mean, you're my mom! But you do a lot of things for people you hardly know."

"Not as much as Dorcas did," Mother answered.

"Dorcas?" Jody asked. "Who's she?"

"The Book of Acts tells about a lady named Dorcas," explained Mother. "She was probably one of the first women inspired by Christ to be active in works of love. She knew how to sew, and she devoted time to making clothes for widows and poor people. She was also their friend and listened to them."

"Oh, I remember hearing about her in Sunday school," Jody said thoughtfully.

Mother smiled. "When Dorcas died, everyone was very sad. Do you remember what happened then?"

Jody thought for a moment, then her face brightened. "Was she raised from the dead?"

"That's right," said Mother. "The Apostle Peter was in town at the time, and when he was told about it, he prayed, and God used him to raise her to life."

"When I get older I'm going to do things for other people, too—like Dorcas and you," Jody decided.

"You don't have to wait that long," said Mom. "Let's think of something you can do for others right now."

HOW ABOUT YOU? What can you do for someone? Could you draw a picture, or make a small gift, and give it to your grandparents? Help them by dusting or cleaning? Help your mother make cookies for someone who is ill? Make a card for a shut-in? Mow the lawn for an elderly neighbor? When you help others, you please the Lord, too.
□ V.L.C.

TO MEMORIZE: *She opens her arms to the poor and extends her hands to the needy.*
Proverbs 31:20, NIV

"I HOPE you don't get upset with me, Dad," said Trent, "but, well, I really like my science teacher, and he believes what Darwin says about evolution. Sometimes it sounds pretty logical."

Dad smiled. "I'm not at all upset with you, Son," he said. "I gave that a lot of thought when I was young, too." As he talked, he walked over to the bookshelves and pulled out a book. "Most kids your age don't get to see this book," he said as he held it out to Trent. "It's about evolution, and it's pretty hard to understand. But I'd like you to look through it and see how many times you can find such words as *let us assume, perhaps,* or *probably*—words indicating uncertainty. I'll come back in a few minutes to see what you've found."

Trent opened the book as he sat down in a nearby chair. Soon he was busily reading. He looked up as his dad walked into the room sometime later. "Nine times, Dad," Trent said, even before his dad could ask a question. "Nine times in ten minutes."

Dad took the book. "Imagine how often you'd find such words if you read this from cover to cover," he said. "To *assume* means to suppose or pretend. Trent, wouldn't you rather *know?*" Dad handed him another book. "Here's the world's best textbook, the Bible! It tells how we can know our Creator. We can know where we came from and where we're going."

HOW ABOUT YOU? Do you know the God who created you? You can know Him through His book, the Bible. It proves itself through fulfilled prophecy and changed lives. It has stood the test of time. It tells how you can have a personal relationship with God through His Son, Jesus Christ. □ P.R.

TO MEMORIZE: *That is why I am suffering as I am. Yet I am not ashamed, because I know whom I have believed, and am convinced that he is able to guard what I have entrusted to him for that day.* 2 Timothy 1:12, NIV

MAY 16

Now Let Us Assume

FROM THE BIBLE:
[God] ... who has saved us and called us to a holy life—not because of anything we have done but because of his own purpose and grace. This grace was given us in Christ Jesus before the beginning of time, but it has now been revealed through the appearing of our Savior, Christ Jesus, who has destroyed death and has brought life and immortality to light through the gospel. And of this gospel I was appointed a herald and an apostle and a teacher. That is why I am suffering as I am. Yet I am not ashamed, because I know whom I have believed, and am convinced that he is able to guard what I have entrusted to him for that day. What you heard from me, keep as the pattern of sound teaching, with faith and love in Christ Jesus. Guard the good deposit that was entrusted to you— guard it with the help of the Holy Spirit who lives in us. 2 Timothy 1:9-14, NIV

You can know God

MAY

17

Grow, Grow, Grow

FROM THE BIBLE:

When Jesus was twelve years old he accompanied his parents to Jerusalem for the annual Passover Festival. After the celebration was over they started home to Nazareth, but Jesus stayed behind in Jerusalem. When they couldn't find him, they went back to Jerusalem to search for him there. Three days later they finally discovered him. He was in the Temple, sitting among the teachers of Law, discussing deep questions with them and amazing everyone with his understanding and answers. His parents didn't know what to think. "Son!" his mother said to him. "Why have you done this to us? Your father and I have been frantic, searching for you everywhere." "But why did you need to search?" he asked. "Didn't you realize that I would be here at the Temple, in my Father's House?" But they didn't understand what he meant. Then he returned to Nazareth with them and was obedient to them. So Jesus grew both tall and wise, and was loved by God and man.

Luke 2:42-52, TLB

Check your spiritual growth

"**W**ILL YOU MEASURE me, Mary Jo?" Jeff asked his older sister.

"Again? I measured you every day this week," protested Mary Jo. At his pleading look, she gave in. "Well, all right. Stand straight."

"Have I grown any?" Jeff asked anxiously.

"Nope, you're still the same height," said Mary Jo. Jeff looked puzzled and unhappy.

In Sunday school the next day, Jeff sang with the other kids, but there was one song he didn't really want to sing. He joined in, but the words seemed to stick in his throat. "Read your Bible, pray every day . . . and you'll grow, grow, grow," went the words of the song. *It's just not true,* thought Jeff. *I've read my Bible every day, but I haven't grown even a little bit.* He was tempted to quit reading, but what if the other verse of the song were true? It went, "Neglect your Bible, forget to pray . . . and you'll shrink, shrink, shrink." He sure didn't want that to happen!

That afternoon Jeff went with his parents to visit his great-grandmother at the nursing home where she lived. "Jeff, you're growing more like your father every day," Grandma Owens said, patting his arm. "You stand like him, and you talk like him."

Jeff thought about that on the way home. Maybe there were more ways to grow than just getting taller. His great-grandma had said Jeff was growing more like his father. Maybe the words in the song meant growing in another way. He decided to ask his parents. Mom smiled, and Dad answered. "Reading the Bible and praying should make a person grow more like Jesus."

Jeff thought, *This week I'll measure myself in a different way. I'll see if I've grown to be more like Jesus.*

HOW ABOUT YOU? How much have you grown this year? It's fun to get measured and see how much you've grown physically, but have you checked to see if you've grown in your Christian life? By reading your Bible, thinking carefully about what you've read, and then obeying it, you'll grow to be more like Jesus every day. □ C.Y.

TO MEMORIZE: *Instead, speaking the truth in love, we will in all things grow up into him who is the Head, that is, Christ.* Ephesians 4:15, NIV

"**H**I THERE, KENNY. What are you doing?" The booming voice startled Kenny, and he glanced up to find his uncle looking over his shoulder. Quickly, Kenny hid the magazine he was reading behind his back.

"Uncle Walter! I didn't hear you coming."

Uncle Walter raised his eyebrows. "So I noticed. Would you like to go with me to the construction site of the new bank? I have some business with the contractor."

"Would I ever!" Kenny jumped up. Uncle Walter turned toward the car. Kenny started to follow him, then remembered the magazine in his hand. "Uncle Walter, wait a minute. I've . . . I've . . . ahhhh, I'm thirsty." Quickly, he slipped into the house. After hiding the magazine under the pillow on his bed, he stopped by the kitchen for a drink.

Later, at the construction site, Kenny and his uncle put on hard hats. Shielding his eyes, Kenny looked up, up, up the steel frame. "Wow!" he exclaimed. "Look, Uncle Walter. See those men working on the steel beams? That looks scary!"

"It is, " Uncle Walter agreed. "You'll never see a steel worker doing gymnastics on his job."

"I guess not!" Kenny couldn't keep his eyes off the men above him. "They have to watch every step."

"Watching these steel workers reminds me of a Bible verse. 'See then that you walk circumspectly.' That means to walk very, very carefully," Uncle Walter explained. "The verse ends by saying, 'not as fools, but as wise.' It's foolish for Christians not to be careful. The road we are walking is very narrow."

Kenny slowly lowered his gaze and saw that Uncle Walter was watching him closely. Kenny's face turned red. "I know what's coming. You saw the magazine I was reading. I can't hide anything from you."

"Or from God," Uncle Walter reminded him.

HOW ABOUT YOU? When the Bible talks about your "walk," it is often referring to your life. As a Christian, you should walk very carefully. Careless Christians stumble and fall into sin. Remember, one wrong step can get you into lots of trouble. Watch your steps—your reading material, your habits, your language, your friends, every part of your life! □ B.W.

TO MEMORIZE: *See then that you walk circumspectly, not as fools but as wise.* Ephesians 5:15, NKJV

MAY

18

Watch Your Step!

FROM THE BIBLE:
Do for others what you want them to do for you. This is the teaching of the laws of Moses in a nutshell. Heaven can be entered only through the narrow gate! The highway to hell is broad, and its gate is wide enough for all the multitudes who choose its easy way. But the Gateway to Life is small, and the road is narrow, and only a few ever find it.
Matthew 7:12-14, TLB

Walk carefully

MAY

19

Sin Bugs

FROM THE BIBLE:

Then I will turn to those on my left and say, "Away with you, you cursed ones, into the eternal fire prepared for the devil and his demons. For I was hungry and you wouldn't feed me; thirsty, and you wouldn't give me anything to drink; a stranger, and you refused me hospitality; naked, and you wouldn't clothe me; sick, and in prison, and you didn't visit me." Then they will reply, "Lord, when did we ever see you hungry or thirsty or a stranger or naked or sick or in prison, and not help you?" And I will answer, "When you refused to help the least of these my brothers, you were refusing help to me."

Matthew 25:41-45, TLB

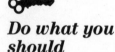

Do what you should

AS JANIE TURNED over a rock in the backyard, she drew back. "Yuck, Mom! Look at all these icky bugs hiding under this rock!"

Mother watched the bugs scurry around. "Those are sowbugs—or pillbugs," she said.

"They don't seem to like the sun. I think they're looking for a dark place to hide," observed Janie.

"They're a little like us then, aren't they?" Mother said thoughtfully.

Janie glanced at her mother in surprise. "Huh?"

"Well, just as these bugs are scrambling for hiding places, we sometimes scramble to find hiding places for the sin in our hearts," explained Mother. "We try to keep it in the dark, but God sees it."

"My Sunday school teacher was talking about sin last week. She says there are two kinds, sins of 'commission' and sins of 'omission.' "

"And do you know what that means?" said Mother, smiling.

"The sins of commission are the bad things we think or do," answered Janie. "It's sin to fight or lie or say something to hurt somebody."

"That's right." Mother nodded. "And what are the sins of omission?"

"That's when we don't do things we should do," answered Janie, "like not calling a friend when we know she's sad, or not telling a friend about Jesus when we get the chance."

"Good for you!" said Mothers. "You remembered that lesson very well. It's even more important to remember that God sees every sin."

Janie nodded as she watched the last of the insects disappear. "I'll think of these as 'sin bugs' from now on." She shuddered. "They'll be a reminder that I don't want sin in my heart."

HOW ABOUT YOU? Are *sins of commission* and *sins of omission* new terms to you? It's sometimes easy to recognize the things we do wrong, but it's harder to realize that "not doing" something may be a sin, too. Check your life. Is there something you should do for a friend? Are there things you should do around your home, even though no one has told you to do them? Do you think nobody will notice if you fail to do those things? God will know. Confess them to Him. Then get busy and do the things He wants you to do. □ V.L.C.

TO MEMORIZE: *Anyone, then, who knows the good he ought to do and doesn't do it, sins.*
James 4:17, NIV

"I'M NEVER going to speak to Michelle again!" stormed Tonya, slamming the door behind her. "I told her so, too!"

Mother frowned. "Never is a long time."

"I don't care how long it is," Tonya snapped. "Michelle is so selfish. She won't share . . . " Tonya's words faded as she ran down the hall to her room.

"Tonya!" Mrs. Bryant called after her. "Get your sweater. Let's go visit my Aunt Margaret!"

A short trip across town brought Tonya and her mother to the Colonial Plaza Nursing Home. As she walked beside her mother down the hall, Tonya's mind was still churning with angry thoughts about Michelle.

"Why, Aunt Margaret, what's the matter?" Mother's startled cry brought Tonya back to reality. Mother was kneeling beside the old lady's wheelchair.

In Aunt Margaret's hand was a crumpled letter. Tears were streaming down her cheeks. "Oh, Betty," she sobbed.

"Too late for what?" Mother questioned.

"Too late to say, 'I'm sorry.' " Aunt Margaret's voice quavered.

It was some time before Tonya and her mother made sense out of what Aunt Margaret was saying. When they finally left, Tonya was wiping her eyes. In the car she turned to her mother. "You mean Aunt Margaret and Aunt Sarah had not spoken to one another for twenty years?"

Mother nodded sadly. "Yes, and now Aunt Sarah is dead. Aunt Margaret can't even remember why they quarreled. Each was too proud and stubborn to say, 'I'm sorry.' So the wall between them grew and grew." She looked at her silent daughter. "One day Aunt Margaret said to Aunt Sarah, 'I'll never speak to you again!' Little did she realize what she was saying."

Tonya gulped. "When we get home, I'd better call Michelle. Never is a long time—too long."

HOW ABOUT YOU? Do you sometimes say things you don't really mean? Is there someone to whom you need to apologize? It will never be any easier than it is right now. So do it. You will always be glad you did. □ B.W.

TO MEMORIZE: *Bear with each other and forgive whatever grievances you may have against one another. Forgive as the Lord forgave you.* Colossians 3:13, NIV

Never Is a Long Time

FROM THE BIBLE:
But now you must rid yourselves of all such things as these: anger, rage, malice, slander, and filthy language from your lips. Do not lie to each other, since you have taken off your old self with its practices and have put on the new self, which is being renewed in knowledge in the image of its Creator. Here there is no Greek or Jew, circumcised or uncircumcised, barbarian, Scythian, slave or free, but Christ is all, and is in all. Therefore, as God's chosen people, holy and dearly loved, clothe yourselves with compassion, kindness, humility, gentleness and patience. Bear with each other and forgive whatever grievances you may have against one another. Forgive as the Lord forgave you. Colossians 3:8-13, NIV

Forgive others right away

21

A Difficult Move

After the death of Moses the servant of the LORD, the LORD said to Joshua son of Nun, Moses' aide: "Moses my servant is dead. Now then, you and all these people, get ready to cross the Jordan River into the land I am about to give to them—to the Israelites. I will give you every place where you set your foot, as I promised Moses. Your territory will extend from the desert to Lebanon, and from the great river, the Euphrates—all the Hittite country—to the Great Sea on the west. No one will be able to stand up against you all the days of your life. As I was with Moses, so I will be with you; I will never leave you nor forsake you."

Joshua 1:1-5, NIV

Accept God's leading

AT THE CLOSE of the church service, Carrie listened in disbelief as Pastor Allen said, "After much prayer, we feel the Lord is calling our family to serve Him at an Indian reservation. We will be leaving in a month." Carrie was horrified at the news. Her best friend was Becky, the pastor's daughter. That meant Becky would move, too.

When the service ended, Carrie dashed out to the car. She was too upset to even speak to Becky. "How could Pastor Allen do this?" Carrie sobbed on the way home.

"He must obey the Lord's leading," Dad said gently.

"But I don't want him to leave," Carrie wailed. "Becky's my best friend. They belong here!"

"Not if the Lord is calling them somewhere else," Dad replied.

Carrie was upset all day. At bedtime Mother gave her a hug. "Honey," she said, "your old crib is set up in the guest room. Why don't you sleep in it tonight?" Carrie stared at her mother. "I remember how you fought against the idea of moving out of it when you got your first bed," Mother continued, "so I thought maybe it would make you feel better to sleep in it again tonight."

Carrie laughed. "You can't be serious, Mother! I don't want to sleep in a crib anymore. Besides, I wouldn't fit."

Mother smiled. "That's true," she agreed. "Part of growing up means leaving behind old things and adjusting to new ways. People may change or move away, but God is still with us, planning things for our good. And keeping the Allens here apparently doesn't fit into God's plan."

"Right," said Dad. "Let's thank God for the good years we've had with them and make their last days at our church extra special."

"I guess you're right," Carrie said slowly. "It won't be easy for Becky, either, but I'll help her all I can."

HOW ABOUT YOU? Are you faced with a move, a new family member, or a new church or school? Are you angry about changes or new circumstances in your life? It isn't easy to let the familiar go, but God will still be with you in your new situation. □ J.H.

TO MEMORIZE: *As I was with Moses, so I will be with you; I will never leave you nor forsake you.* Joshua 1:5, NIV

"CAN I GET the prize out?" Geri asked Dad eagerly, pointing to the back of her cereal box. The picture showed a colored candy pouring out of a package.

Dad shook the box. He reached in and brought out the prize—a small, sample-size package of candy. He tossed it to Geri.

When Geri tore open the package a little later, she poured out the candy. She counted every piece—only twenty-six. She started to count the pieces in the picture on the cereal box. She stopped counting at one hundred, and there were still more. "I thought I would get as much candy as there was in the picture," she told Dad.

"The people who make the cereal wanted you to think that so you'd buy the cereal," explained Dad. "They deceived you."

Geri frowned. "What does *deceive* mean?"

"It means leading someone to believe something that isn't true," explained Dad, and Geri sighed.

That afternoon Geri's friend Ashley came to play. Geri had recently begun taking piano lessons, and she showed Ashley what she had been learning. "I'll be your pupil," said Ashley, so they pretended that Geri was the teacher.

Soon Beth, who lived down the street, came to the door. "Do you want to play?" Beth asked.

Geri didn't. She wanted Ashley all to herself. "We're having a piano lesson," Geri said, choosing her words carefully. This sent Beth on her way.

"Did you tell Beth the truth?" asked Dad.

Geri shrugged. "I didn't lie about it," she said.

"What picture did Beth get about the piano lesson?" persisted Dad. "Do you think you deceived her?"

Geri knew Beth thought her piano teacher was there. The picture she'd given Beth was just as deceiving as the picture on the cereal box. She hurried to the front door. "Come back, Beth," she called. "You can be in on our piano lesson, too."

HOW ABOUT YOU? Do you ever deceive someone by giving him the wrong idea? Do you give your parents the impression you're one place when you're actually somewhere else? Do you get out of doing something by making excuses that aren't quite accurate? You can lie in ways other than *saying* something that isn't true. God is as displeased with one kind of lie as with another.
□ K.R.A.

TO MEMORIZE: *Do not steal. Do not lie. Do not deceive one another.* Leviticus 19:11, NIV

The Lying Cereal Box

FROM THE BIBLE:

A truthful witness gives honest testimony, but a false witness tells lies. Reckless words pierce like a sword, but the tongue of the wise brings healing. Truthful lips endure forever, but a lying tongue lasts only a moment. There is deceit in the hearts of those who plot evil, but joy for those who promote peace. No harm befalls the righteous, but the wicked have their fill of trouble. The LORD detests lying lips, but he delights in men who are truthful.
Proverbs 12:17-22, NIV

Don't deceive

23

Too Much Foot

FROM THE BIBLE:

Then Job replied: "I have heard many things like these; miserable comforters are you all! Will your long-winded speeches never end? What ails you that you keep on arguing? I also could speak like you, if you were in my place; I could make fine speeches against you and shake my head at you. But my mouth would encourage you; comfort from my lips would bring you relief. Yet if I speak, my pain is not relieved; and if I refrain, it does not go away. Surely, O God, you have worn me out; you have devastated my entire household."

Job 16:1-7, NIV

Don't become a pest

"HEY, HOLLY, can you play today?" asked Karen.

Holly hesitated. "Well, I don't know. I have quite a few things to do."

"Aw, come on," begged Karen. "What do you have to do? I could help you."

Holly shook her head. "Not really. I have to practice the piano, and you can't help me do that."

"I could just come in and listen," persisted Karen.

"Karen," said Holly, "we were together last night after school and Monday night, too. And we spent a lot of time together over the weekend. I like playing with you, but I really will be busy."

"Well, okay," agreed Karen glumly.

Holly breathed a sigh of relief as she walked up the steps to the house. She found her mother in the kitchen starting supper. "Karen wanted to play again today, but I told her I had a lot of things to do. I hope she's not mad."

"Why would she be mad?" asked Mother. "You've been spending most afternoons with her lately."

"I know," sighed Holly. "I'm glad she's my friend, but sometimes I like being alone. I like to read and draw and write letters. It's hard to do those things with a friend."

Mother nodded. "Did you know there's a verse in the Bible about this very situation?"

"In the Bible? What verse?" asked Holly in surprise.

"Proverbs 25:17 says, 'Seldom set foot in your neighbor's house—too much of you, and he will hate you,'" quoted Mother. "See, Holly, the Lord who created friendship understands your problem. Friends do need to give each other time to develop different interests."

"Thanks, Mom!" exclaimed Holly. "I feel better about it now! I wish Karen could understand that verse, too."

HOW ABOUT YOU? Do you spend lots of time with only one friend? Reach out to other people and make new friends, too. Spend time alone and do a creative project or read a book. Often arguments start between two people because they spend too much time together. Listen to the Lord's advice concerning friendship! □ L.W.

TO MEMORIZE: *Seldom set foot in your neighbor's house—too much of you, and he will hate you.*
Proverbs 25:17, NIV

"MOM, HOW COME Christians have such different ideas about right and wrong?" asked Joan one day. "You and Daddy won't let me go to movies, but Stacey's parents think it's okay. Why can't Christians agree on what's right or wrong?"

Mother was silent for a while. "That's not an easy question to answer," she replied. "Let's see . . . we're having Uncle Phil and Aunt Sue over for dinner tonight, right? We'll all eat quite differently. Aunt Sue has diabetes and can't have food with sugar in it. Uncle Phil is on a low-cholesterol diet for his heart, so I'm cooking chicken without the skin for him."

"And Daddy needs to lose weight," giggled Joan, "so he'll eat a big salad and not too much of the other stuff. I'm glad I can eat anything!"

"But do you see what I'm getting at, Honey?" asked Mother. "People have different conditions, so they have different dietary needs. Christians have different backgrounds and different levels of maturity, so they have different spiritual needs."

Joan nodded seriously. "You mean, what's right for one person may not be right for another?"

"In a way that's true," agreed Mother. "God may convict one believer about a certain activity because it would cause those around him to stumble. Or someone may have a tender conscience about a particular activity because he's had a bad experience relating to it or because of the way he was brought up."

Joan was thoughtful. "Then it's just up to each person to decide what he may and may not do?"

"Well," said Mother, "some things are spelled out so clearly in the Bible that there's no room for argument. And even those things that aren't specifically forbidden may not always be the best choice for a Christian. We must avoid anything that would hurt God's cause or harm others. We need to follow the principles God has established and ask Him to teach us what is right."

HOW ABOUT YOU? Do you ask God to show you what things you should not do? Don't be critical of others regarding issues not spelled out in the Bible. On the other hand, don't do something if you have doubts about it. Accept your parents' guidance while you form your own convictions. □
S.K.

TO MEMORIZE: *One person esteems one day above another; another esteems every day alike. Let each be fully convinced in his own mind.*
Romans 14:5, NKJV

24

A Special Diet

FROM THE BIBLE:
Receive one who is weak in the faith, but not to disputes over doubtful things. For one believes he may eat all things, but he who is weak eats only vegetables. Let not him who eats despise him who does not eat, and let not him who does not eat judge him who eats; for God has received him. Who are you to judge another's servant? To his own master he stands or falls. Indeed, he will be made to stand, for God is able to make him stand. One person esteems one day above another; another esteems every day alike. Let each be fully convinced in his own mind. He who observes the day, observes it to the Lord; and he who does not observe the day, to the Lord he does not observe it. He who eats, eats to the Lord, for he gives God thanks; and he who does not eat, to the Lord he does not eat, and gives God thanks. . . . Why do you judge your brother? Or why do you show contempt for your brother? For we shall all stand before the judgment seat of Christ.
Romans 14:1-7, 10, NKJV

Develop convictions

25

A Special Diet

(Continued from yesterday)

FROM THE BIBLE:

Therefore let us not judge one another anymore, but rather resolve this, not to put a stumbling block or a cause to fall in our brother's way. I know and am convinced by the Lord Jesus that there is nothing unclean of itself; but to him who considers anything to be unclean, to him it is unclean. Yet if your brother is grieved because of your food, you are no longer walking in love. Do not destroy with your food the one for whom Christ died. Therefore do not let your good be spoken of as evil; for the kingdom of God is not food and drink, but righteousness and peace and joy in the Holy Spirit. For he who serves Christ in these things is acceptable to God and approved by men. Therefore let us pursue the things which make for peace and the things by which one may edify another. Do not destroy the work of God for the sake of food.

Romans 14:13-20, NKJV

Respect convictions of others

"C'MON, LET'S PLAY catch with my new softball," suggested Joan's brother, Rick, one Sunday afternoon.

After the children had thrown the ball back and forth for just a few moments, they heard a voice from next door. "I'm surprised at you children—playing ball on Sunday!" said their neighbor, Mrs. White. "And your parents call themselves Christians!" With that, she stalked off into her house.

Joan and Rick looked at each other in dismay and then hurried in to ask their parents what they should do. "Can you believe that?" grumbled Rick.

Mother sighed. "Don't be disrespectful, Son," she said. She was brought up to believe any kind of outdoor recreation is wrong on Sunday."

Joan scowled. "Wow! I'm glad you and Dad don't feel that way," she said. Then she added, "That reminds me of what you told me about 'special diets,' Mom—that what's wrong for one person may be right for someone else."

"Yes, but it's important to respect the 'special diets,' or convictions, of others," Mother replied.

Dad nodded. "Since Mrs. White feels rough and loud playing on Sunday is wrong, I think you should tone it down—maybe even confine your ball-playing to other days of the week."

"Why should we have to change what we do, just because of what she believes?" grumbled Rick.

"I can think of one good reason," Dad replied. "Although the Bible doesn't say, 'Don't play ball on Sunday,' it does say, 'Let not your good be evil spoken of.' So even though you may think it's good to play catch, if it offends Mrs. White, you may have to change your actions."

Rick replied, "I guess you're right."

"Of course they're right," added Joan. "From now on, I'll try not to remember that the convictions of other people are important, too."

HOW ABOUT YOU? Do you respect the convictions of others? You don't have to agree with what everyone else believes, but you can modify your actions, whenever possible, so that you don't offend people unnecessarily. You may feel free to participate in some "fun" activity, but if it hinders your witness to others, it's just not worth it. Remember how much Christ gave up for you! □ S.K.

TO MEMORIZE: *Therefore let us not judge one another anymore, but rather resolve this, not to put a stumbling block or a cause to fall in our brother's way.* Romans 14:13, NKJV

"**I** WANT a volunteer to sign this paper." Miss Sheryl showed her Sunday school class a blank sheet. "When you sign it, you will be agreeing to obey whatever I write on the paper." Eyebrows raised and eyes widened. "I could ask you to mow my lawn, or to give me your allowance next week, or to invite five people to Sunday school. I can write anything I want on this paper. Now who will sign it?" There were several giggles but no volunteers. "Don't you trust me?" asked Miss Sheryl.

Finally Gina raised her hand. "I'll sign it, Miss Sheryl."

After Gina signed her name, Miss Sheryl took the paper again and began writing. Everyone waited breathlessly. When she finished, she handed the paper to Gina. "Read it out loud," she instructed.

"Go to the table in the corner," Gina read. "Pick up the Bible, and keep whatever you find under it. It's yours." Quickly, Gina obeyed. "Ooohhh," she squealed as she lifted the Bible. On the table was a dollar bill. She picked it up and smiled at her teacher. "Thank you, Miss Sheryl."

"Thank you, Gina, for trusting me," Miss Sheryl replied.

When Gina had taken her seat, Miss Sheryl spoke. "When we give our lives to the Lord Jesus, it's like signing a blank sheet of paper. We say, 'Lord, I am surrendering my life to You. You write in the orders.' Before Gina could receive her prize, what did she have to do?"

"She had to sign the paper," said Tiffany.

"And she had to do what it said," Brent added.

"Right." Miss Sheryl nodded. "She had to trust me, and she had to obey me. So we must trust God and obey God. We don't have to be afraid to hand our lives over to Him. He has many rewards for those who surrender to Him."

HOW ABOUT YOU? Are you afraid to yield your life to God? Are you worried that He will ask you to do something hard? Don't fret. Give your life to Him in unconditional surrender. Do whatever it is that you know He wants you to do. You'll be surprised at all the good things He has in store for you.
□ B.W.

TO MEMORIZE: *How great is your goodness, which you have stored up for those who fear you, which you bestow in the sight of men on those who take refuge in you.* Psalm 31:19, NIV

26

The Blank Piece of Paper

FROM THE BIBLE:
So, dear brothers, you have no obligations whatever to your old sinful nature to do what it begs you to do. For if you keep on following it you are lost and will perish, but if through the power of the Holy Spirit you crush it and its evil deeds, you shall live. For all who are led by the Spirit of God are sons of God. And so we should not be like cringing, fearful slaves, but we should behave like God's very own children, adopted into the bosom of his family, and calling to him, "Father, Father." For his Holy Spirit speaks to us deep in our hearts, and tells us that we really are God's children. And since we are his children, we will share his treasures—for all God gives to his Son Jesus is now ours too. But if we are to share his glory, we must also share his suffering. Yet what we suffer now is nothing compared to the glory he will give us later. Romans 8:12-18, TLB

Trust and obey

27

A Promise Is a Promise

FROM THE BIBLE:

Now listen, you who say, "Today or tomorrow we will go to this or that city, spend a year there, carry on business and make money." Why, you do not even know what will happen tomorrow. What is your life? You are a mist that appears for a little while and then vanishes. Instead, you ought to say, "If it is the Lord's will, we will live and do this or that."
James 4:13-15, NIV

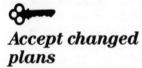

Accept changed plans

"It's SO SUNNY out today, I wish we could go to our cabin," said Maggie at the breakfast table.

"I was thinking the same thing," answered Dad. "Let's do it. We'll plan to leave as soon as I get home from work tonight—if you help Mom pack."

"Sure thing!" Maggie gave her dad a big kiss as he left.

While Maggie was helping her mother prepare for the trip, she thought about the fun they would have at the cabin. It was four o'clock when her dad called from the office. "I'm so sorry," he apologized, "but we have a big project that has to be completed by tomorrow afternoon. It was coming along fine, but there was a computer error, and now all the figures have to be rechecked. We'll have to postpone our trip till another day."

Maggie slammed down the receiver. "It's not fair!" she stormed, tears streaming down her face. "Dad promised we could go, and a promise is a promise!"

"When Dad's boss asks him to work longer, there's nothing he can do," Mother answered.

"But he promised!" wailed Maggie.

"Now just a minute," interrupted Mother. "He didn't exactly promise. He did say we'd plan to go, but you have to realize that sometimes it's difficult, or even impossible, to carry out our plans. We get sick, or circumstances change, and there's nothing we can do about it."

Maggie scowled. "Well, if I can't count on my own dad, who can I count on?"

"You can always count on God. He has made many promises to us, and because He is God, we know that we can trust Him completely." Mom smiled. "I know you're disappointed, but I'm sure Dad is disappointed, too."

Maggie was quiet. "I never thought about that. I really do know he would go if he could. Hey, may I bake one of his favorite chocolate cakes?"

HOW ABOUT YOU? Are you careful to make no promises that you may not be able to keep? Are you careful not to accuse Mom and Dad of "promising" things when they are merely "planning" them? And when they have to change their plans, do you become upset or do you try to understand the circumstances? Learn to accept changing circumstances and changing plans. □ L.W.

TO MEMORIZE: *You ought to say, "If it is the Lord's will, we will live and do this or that."*
James 4:15, NIV

PETER AND PAM tucked pansies and geraniums into the soil. They were helping Dad decorate their grandparents' graves. "Look at all the flags waving in the breeze," said Peter as he glanced around the cemetery.

Pam looked up from her work. "Daddy, how come only some graves have flags flying beside them?" she asked.

"Those flags honor the soldiers who gave their lives to protect our country's freedom," Dad explained. "We remember them by decorating their graves with flowers and flags. Some places have special services and parades to honor them, too."

"They paid a big price to keep us free, didn't they?" Peter asked thoughtfully.

"Yes, they did," agreed Dad. He gathered the tools they had been using. "Someone else paid a greater price for our freedom than the soldiers did," he observed as they started toward the car.

Peter and Pam looked puzzled. "Who?"

"The Lord Jesus. He died on the cross to free us from the penalty of sin," answered Dad. "He arose from the dead and is alive in heaven now, so there's no need to decorate a grave for Him. But there is a special way we can remember Him and His sacrifice."

"How?" Peter asked.

"By participating in the Communion service in church," Dad explained. "When a believer takes Communion, he remembers Christ's sacrifice on the cross. He is also looking forward to Christ's return, for Jesus told His followers to remember Him by taking Communion until He comes again. The Communion service and all that it means should fill our hearts with thanksgiving."

The children nodded. "That's lots better than decorating a grave!" exclaimed Pam happily.

HOW ABOUT YOU? Before you take Communion in church, make sure you are a Christian. Then examine your heart by asking yourself these questions: Am I obeying the Lord in my life? Have I confessed all known sin? If you have done anything that would hurt your fellowship with the Lord, confess it to Him before you take Communion. Then participate with a joyful and grateful heart.

□ J.H.

TO MEMORIZE: *For whenever you eat this bread and drink this cup, you proclaim the Lord's death until he comes.* 1 Corinthians 11:26, NIV

MAY

28

In Remembrance

FROM THE BIBLE:
For I received from the Lord what I also passed on to you: The Lord Jesus, on the night he was betrayed, took bread, and when he had given thanks, he broke it and said, "This is my body, which is for you; do this in remembrance of me." In the same way, after supper he took the cup, saying, "This cup is the new covenant in my blood; do this, whenever you drink it, in remembrance of me." For whenever you eat this bread and drink this cup, you proclaim the Lord's death until he comes. Therefore, whoever eats the bread or drinks the cup of the Lord in an unworthy manner will be guilty of sinning against the body and blood of the Lord. A man ought to examine himself before he eats of the bread and drinks of the cup.
1 Corinthians 11:23-28, NIV

Remember Christ's sacrifice

29

Weight Watchers

FROM THE BIBLE:

In a race, everyone runs but only one person gets first prize. So run your race to win. To win the contest you must deny yourselves many things that would keep you from doing your best. An athlete goes to all this trouble just to win a blue ribbon or a silver cup, but we do it for a heavenly reward that never disappears. So I run straight to the goal with purpose in every step. I fight to win. I'm not just shadow-boxing or playing around. Like an athlete I punish my body, treating it roughly, training it to do what it should, not what it wants to. Otherwise I fear that after enlisting others for the race, I myself might be declared unfit and ordered to stand aside.
1 Corinthians 9:24-27, TLB

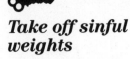

Take off sinful weights

"**M**AY I HAVE another piece of cake?" Brian asked.

"You've been unusually quiet," Mother remarked as she cut the cake. "Is something bothering you?"

"I came in third in track today," Brian blurted out. "I was always first last year. I don't know what's the matter with me."

"I do," said Stephanie. "You're too fat."

"Stephanie!" Dad reprimanded. "That was not kind."

"Is she *ever* kind?" Brian asked sarcastically.

"That's enough! You are both wrong—and right," Mother sighed. "It's wrong to say hateful things about one another, but it's true Brian has gained weight. And Stephanie, you're not the kind, sweet girl you used to be."

"Yes," Dad agreed. "You have changed in the last couple of months, Stephanie. I think you may be letting bitterness defeat you. I've noticed that you still seem to be resentful that Jill was chosen as captain of the sixth-grade basketball team."

"But Jill's new in town," Stephanie protested. "If it weren't for her sneaky ways, I'd be the captain. She stole all my friends, too. It's not fair."

"I suspect it's your bitter attitude that has affected your friendships," said Mother softly.

"Stephanie, even as Brian needs to take off weight to run well, so you need to lay aside that weight of bitterness," said Dad. "It's hindering you from being a winner in your life as a Christian. A diet of praise and thanksgiving would be good for you—in fact, good for all of us."

"Let's go on a diet," Mother suggested. "Let's be 'weight watchers'—both physically and spiritually."

HOW ABOUT YOU? Are you carrying some "weights" that are hindering your Christian race—a bad attitude, a sharp tongue, a bitter or rebellious spirit? These are things that bring defeat into the life of a Christian. Anything that keeps you from praying, reading your Bible, and overcoming sin needs to be "laid aside." Check your life now for "weights."
□ B.W.

TO MEMORIZE: *Therefore we also, since we are surrounded by so great a cloud of witnesses, let us lay aside every weight, and the sin which so easily ensnares us, and let us run with endurance the race that is set before us.* Hebrews 12:1, NKJV

WITH HANDS in his pockets, Tony stalked toward home. His teeth were clenched and his jaws tight. He was having trouble with Butch and his gang. Looking over his shoulder, he saw the four boys about a half a block behind him. They were pointing at him and laughing.

Tony's heart shifted gears. What could he do? He was six blocks from home. If he ran, they would pounce on him. He knew they wanted him to run. They had been teasing him about being a sissy Christian. But how could he fight four big bullies?

He quickened his steps as the voices behind him grew closer. "O, Lord, what can I do? Help me," he pleaded. Then he remembered the Scripture his dad had read that morning. The children of Judah had been outnumbered, too. The Lord had told King Jehoshaphat not to be afraid. "Would You fight my battle, too?" Tony asked God.

Then he remembered what the children of Judah did. They sang praises. Tony gulped. "Okay, Lord, I'll praise you," he whispered softly. Quietly, he started singing, "Bless the Lord, O my soul. Bless the Lord, O my soul; and all that is within me, bless His holy name."

He took a deep breath. He did feel better singing than worrying. Glancing back, he saw the bullies were getting closer. He sang louder, "And forever I will praise Him. And forever I will praise Him. . . . " When he looked around again, he was surprised to see that Butch and his gang had stopped. They were shouting at one another. Suddenly Butch grabbed one boy by the collar and a fight was on. Tony watched in amazement for a minute. Then with a big grin, he ran home singing, "And forget not His blessings, and forget not His blessings . . . "

He ran into the house. "Mom," he called, "you're not going to believe this!"

HOW ABOUT YOU? Are there times when you are outnumbered? Does it seem like everyone is against you? Don't worry. Praise the Lord. Let Him fight your battles. He may not cause your enemies to fight one another, but He has a way of solving your problems when you praise Him.
□ B.W.

TO MEMORIZE: *The battle is not yours, but God's.* 2 Chronicles 20:15, NIV

MAY

30

Praise the Lord

FROM THE BIBLE:

After this, the Moabites and Ammonites with some of the Meunites came to make war on Jehoshaphat. Some men came and told Jehoshaphat, "A vast army is coming against you from Edom, from the other side of the Sea. It is already in Hazazon Tamar" (that is, En Gedi). Alarmed, Jehoshaphat resolved to inquire of the LORD, and he proclaimed a fast for all Judah. The people of Judah came together to seek help from the LORD; indeed, they came from every town in Judah to seek him. . . . Then the Spirit of the LORD came upon Jahaziel son of Zechariah, the son of Benaiah, the son of Jeiel, the son of Mattaniah, a Levite and descendant of Asaph, as he stood in the assembly. He said: "Listen, King Jehoshaphat and all who live in Judah and Jerusalem! This is what the LORD says to you: 'Do not be afraid or discouraged because of this vast army. For the battle is not yours, but God's.' "
2 Chronicles 20:1-4, 14-15, NIV

Don't worry— praise God

MAY

31

Aunt Joy's Garden Gate

FROM THE BIBLE:

I tell you the truth, I am the gate for the sheep. All who ever came before me were thieves and robbers, but the sheep did not listen to them. I am the gate; whoever enters through me will be saved. He will come in and go out, and find pasture. The thief comes only to steal and kill and destroy; I have come that they may have life, and have it to the full. I am the good shepherd. The good shepherd lays down his life for the sheep. The hired hand is not the shepherd who owns the sheep. So when he sees the wolf coming, he abandons the sheep and runs away. Then the wolf attacks the flock and scatters it. The man runs away because he is a hired hand and cares nothing for the sheep. I am the good shepherd; I know my sheep and my sheep know me—just as the Father knows me and I know the Father—and I lay down my life for the sheep.
John 10:7-15, NIV

Enter heaven through Jesus

MEGAN SKIPPED up the sidewalk to Aunt Joy's home. She liked the way her aunt treated her—like a friend rather than just a child—although she did feel that sometimes Aunt Joy talked about God a bit too much. Megan rang her doorbell. Then after chatting with her aunt a few minutes, she asked, "May I go see the flowers?"

"Of course," agreed Aunt Joy.

Megan especially liked going into the flower garden, which was surrounded by a white fence. The only way to get in was through a charming gate. When she lifted the latch on the gate, hanging chimes sweetly tinkled, promising wonderful scenes inside. And just inside the gate, flowers of every color seemed to nod hello as they gently bobbed in the breeze, and honeysuckle vines perfumed the air.

After a little while, Megan ran back to the porch where her aunt was pouring tea and had set out some cookies. "Well, did you like my flowers?" Aunt Joy asked.

"Oh, I love your garden!" Megan exclaimed. "I love the gate, too. I like to hear the chimes when it opens."

Aunt Joy smiled. "What if you didn't go through the gate?" she asked. "What if you just stood outside?"

"Then I'd miss hearing the bell and seeing all the beautiful flowers," answered Megan promptly. She bit into a cookie. "That would be silly."

"Remember what I've been telling you about God's home in heaven?" asked Aunt Joy. "It's even lovelier than my garden. But you can get into God's beautiful heaven only through a special gate, the Lord Jesus—only by having your sins forgiven through Him. When you die, do you want to be outside, never able to enjoy heaven, or would you like to come in through Jesus?"

Megan looked thoughtful. "I'd be silly not to come in, wouldn't I?" she asked slowly. "Please tell me about it once more."

HOW ABOUT YOU? Are you going to get into heaven? The Bible often uses an illustration that helps you understand a truth. When Jesus says He's a "door" or "gate," He means that you can get into heaven by believing in Him. Do you believe? Trust Jesus right now to be your "gate." □ C.Y.

TO MEMORIZE: *I am the gate; whoever enters through me will be saved. He will come in and go out, and find pasture.* John 10:9, NIV

THE MURRAYS were concluding their family devotions by reading from an exciting missionary book. "The jungle closed in around Pedro," read Dad. "He knew his enemies were looking for him. Since Pedro had become a Christian, other members of his tribe were determined to kill him. There seemed no escape. Pedro prayed as he ran."

"This is so scary," Mary whispered.

Dad continued reading. "Suddenly a dark-skinned man stepped out of the bushes just ahead. He motioned for Pedro to follow him and started moving deeper into the jungle. *Should I follow him?* Pedro thought. *Is this man an enemy, too? I've never seen him before.* Pedro didn't know what to do." Dad looked up, put a marker in the book and closed it. "End of chapter," he said. "Bedtime!"

"Oh no!" groaned Kurt.

"Just one more page?" pleaded Mary.

Mother shook her head. "There's school tomorrow."

Kurt stretched. "Boy, some people live such exciting lives, and mine is so ordinary. School, practicing trumpet, studying, eating, sleeping, and school again."

"Well, I suspect Pedro was glad when his life became somewhat ordinary after he escaped from his enemies," Dad said.

"Then he does get away!" Kurt laughed heartily at his unexpected discovery. "Well, I still think my days are pretty dull."

"God planned for ordinary days in our lives," said Dad. "He knows we need them to grow and learn about Him. Even men of the Bible had ordinary days. Daniel didn't face lions every day. He also worked in the king's court doing many ordinary jobs. And Paul was a tentmaker. He no doubt spent many days sewing, measuring, and cutting. We need to see all those ordinary days as gifts from God."

With a yawn Kurt stood up. "Yeah. Now I better get to bed, so I can be rested for another ordinary day."

HOW ABOUT YOU? Do you sometimes feel all the exciting things are happening to everyone else? These days of school, eating, sleeping, and more school are a part of God's plan to prepare you for the future. See each day as a gift from God. □ J.G.

TO MEMORIZE: *There is a time for everything, and a season for every activity under heaven.* Ecclesiastes 3:1, NIV

JUNE

Ordinary Days

FROM THE BIBLE:
He has made everything beautiful in its time. He has also set eternity in the hearts of men; yet they cannot fathom what God has done from beginning to end. I know that there is nothing better for men than to be happy and do good while they live. That everyone may eat and drink, and find satisfaction in all his toil—this is the gift of God. I know that everything God does will endure forever; nothing can be added to it and nothing taken from it. God does it so that men will revere him. Ecclesiastes 3:11-14, NIV

Thank God for each day

JUNE

2

Pumped Up

FROM THE BIBLE:

Therefore, brothers, since we have confidence to enter the Most Holy Place by the blood of Jesus, by a new and living way opened for us through the curtain, that is, his body, and since we have a great priest over the house of God, let us draw near to God with a sincere heart in full assurance of faith, having our hearts sprinkled to cleanse us from a guilty conscience and having our bodies washed with pure water. Let us hold unswervingly to the hope we profess, for he who promised is faithful. And let us consider how we may spur one another on toward love and good deeds. Let us not give up meeting together, as some are in the habit of doing, but let us encourage one another—and all the more as you see the Day approaching.
Hebrews 10:19-25, NIV

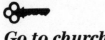

Go to church

EVERY SUNDAY morning Keith grumbled about going to church. He complained about having to get up early, about his clothes, and about anything else he could think of. "Why can't we stay home once in a while?" he whined. "Why must we always go to church and Sunday school?"

Dad rumpled Keith's hair as he walked by. "It's good for you," he said, "and it pleases the Lord."

That afternoon Keith and his dad decided to take a bike ride. "My tires are a little soft," said Keith as they started out. "I meant to pump them up at the gas station yesterday, but I forgot. I think they'll be fine though."

"We could pump them up before we go," suggested Dad.

"I don't feel like bothering," replied Keith. "They'll be fine. Let's go."

Before long, Keith began to get tired. "Whew, it's hard to peddle with soft tires," he exclaimed. He was glad when they finally reached home. He ran and got the tire pump. After the tires were filled, Keith tried the bike. "It pedals easy as pie now," he said.

Dad nodded. "Good," he said. "But now it's time to put your bike away and get ready for church."

"Aw, Dad," whined Keith, "seems like we just got back from church. I was thinking of taking another spin on my bike."

"I was thinking, too," said Dad. "Just as it's hard work to ride a bike with soft tires, it's hard work to live for God without the things we learn in church and Sunday school. It's hard work to live without the encouragement we get from other Christians. We need to get 'pumped up' regularly with God's Word and with Christian fellowship. It pays to take time to do that."

HOW ABOUT YOU? Do you sometimes complain about having to go to church or Sunday school? You need constant encouragement to live as God wants you to live. □ C.Y.

TO MEMORIZE: *And let us consider how we may spur one another on toward love and good deeds.* Hebrews 10:24, NIV

"I'LL HOOK UP the hose to rinse off the suds," offered Ted as he helped his dad wash the car one day. He screwed the end of a hose onto the faucet. "All set," he called.

"Turn it on harder," instructed his father. "I'm not getting much water here."

"But it's on all the way," objected Ted.

Dad looked up and laughed as he saw a row of tiny fountains all along the length of the hose. "I intended to throw that old hose away," he said. "Look at all the leaks!"

"Maybe we can fix it," suggested Ted. He ran into the house and returned carrying a roll of tape. Leaving the water on so he could see the leaks, he tried to patch one of the biggest holes. But when he wrapped tape around it, all the other "fountains" jumped several inches higher!

"That's not going to work," Dad said smiling, "even if you can find all the leaks. By the time you fixed the last ones, the first ones would be leaking again around the tape." Then he added thoughtfully, "This reminds me of something, Ted. You've been getting into a lot of trouble lately. Although you're always sorry, you're soon in some other trouble."

"I know," sighed Ted. "I try to be good. But what's the leaky hose got to do with that?"

"Trying to 'be good'—trying to get rid of all the sins in your life through your own efforts—is like trying to plug up all these holes with tape," explained Dad. "It just won't work! What we really need is a new hose. And what you need, Son, is a new heart."

"What does that mean?" asked Ted.

"I'm not talking about a flesh and blood heart," replied Dad. "I mean a new spiritual heart—a new nature that makes you want to obey God. Only Jesus can give it to you."

Ted was thoughtful. "I know you're right, and I do want to accept Jesus as my Savior from sin. I'm tired of trying to patch up my life all by myself."

HOW ABOUT YOU? Have you been trying to get rid of sin through your own efforts? It will never work. Come to Jesus just as you are. Let Him cleanse you and give you a new heart"—a new desire and ability to do His will. □ S.K.

TO MEMORIZE: *Therefore, if anyone is in Christ, he is a new creation; old things have passed away; behold, all things have become new.* 2 Corinthians 5:17, NKJV

3

The Hose with Holes

FROM THE BIBLE:

For the love of Christ constrains us, because we judge thus: that if One died for all, then all died; and He died for all, that those who live should live no longer for themselves, but for Him who died for them and rose again. Therefore, from now on, we regard no one according to the flesh. Even though we have known Christ according to the flesh, yet now we know Him thus no longer. Therefore, if anyone is in Christ, he is a new creation; old things have passed away; behold, all things have become new. Now all things are of God, who has reconciled us to Himself through Jesus Christ, and has given us the ministry of reconciliation, that is, that God was in Christ reconciling the world to Himself, not imputing their trespasses to them, and has committed to us the word of reconciliation. Therefore we are ambassadors for Christ, as though God were pleading through us: we implore you on Christ's behalf, be reconciled to God.

2 Corinthians 5:14-20, NKJV

Let Jesus remove your sin

JUNE

The Hose with Holes

(Continued from yesterday)

FROM THE BIBLE:

I don't understand myself at all, for I really want to do what is right, but I can't. I do what I don't want to—what I hate. I know perfectly well that what I am doing is wrong, and my bad conscience proves that I agree with these laws I am breaking. But I can't help myself, because I'm no longer doing it. It is sin inside me that is stronger than I am that makes me do these evil things. I know I am rotten through and through so far as my old sinful nature is concerned. No matter which way I turn I can't make myself do right. I want to but I can't. When I want to do good, I don't; and when I try not to do wrong, I do it anyway. . . . So you see how it is: my new life tells me to do right, but the old nature that is still inside me loves to sin. Oh, what a terrible predicament I'm in! Who will free me from my slavery to this deadly lower nature? Thank God! It has been done by Jesus Christ our Lord. He has set me free.

Romans 7:15-19, 23-25, TLB

Turn away from sin

ONE EVENING shortly after Ted accepted Jesus as Savior, his dad found him slumped on the couch in the living room, frowning. "What's wrong?" asked Dad.

Ted looked up and sighed. "Well, I thought you said that after I accepted Jesus, I would have a new nature that wouldn't want to sin," he explained. "But when Joe and Ralph started teasing some of the girls at school today, I went right along, even though I knew I shouldn't. If I have a new nature, why do I still sin?"

Dad thought for a moment. "I have to wash the car again. Want to help? We can talk while we work." Ted nodded, and they got busy. "Here," said Dad, handing Ted the hose. "Hook this up."

Ted's mind was still on his troubles as he attached the hose to the faucet. But when he turned the water on, he couldn't believe his eyes. "Hey, Dad," he laughed. "This is that same beat-up old hose we tried to use last time! Did you think it was the new one?"

Dad smiled. "Not exactly," he admitted, as he watched the familiar "fountain display" of the leaky old hose. "I handed it to you just now to help you understand why a Christian can still sin. You see, even though we bought a new hose, it's still possible to pick up the old one and try using it. In the same way, it's possible for a Christian to turn back to his old sin nature occasionally. When that happens, we need to admit our sin to God and turn from it. We'll have to fight our old nature until we get to heaven."

Ted sighed. "It sounds like a lot of work to me."

Dad nodded. "Sometimes it is," he agreed, "but we can have victory if we rely daily on the Lord to help us. And when we get to heaven, we'll be completely free from the temptations we face now. Just as I'm going to get rid of this hose, someday we'll get rid of our sinful old natures—for good!"

HOW ABOUT YOU? Do you wonder why you still have a problem with sin even though you're a Christian? It's because you sometimes fail to rely on the fact that, in Jesus, you are dead to sin. You fail to ask Him for help in overcoming it. Remember, your old nature has been crucified with Jesus so you can have victory. □ S.K.

TO MEMORIZE: *For we know that our old self was crucified with him so that the body of sin might be done away with, that we should no longer be slaves to sin.* Romans 6:6, NIV

"Is GREAT-GRANDPA wearing his shoes?" asked eight-year-old Linda. Mother patted Linda's arm and went on talking. The room was full of people talking. And, of course, there was Great-Grandpa. He lay, with his eyes closed and his hands folded, in a long box lined with satin—a casket. The funeral home was filled with the smell of flowers. Linda felt out of place. Then someone put a hand on her shoulder. It was Daddy. His face was kind as he took her hand and led her to a sofa where they sat down. Linda tried to smile, but her lips trembled. "Does Great-Grandpa have his shoes on?" she asked again.

"Yes, he does," said Daddy. Linda felt a teeny bit better. Daddy didn't act like she'd asked the wrong thing at all. He seemed to understand how strange she felt. "Remember when you helped me plant the garden last spring?" Daddy asked. Linda nodded. She had planted all the radishes and half the beans. "Tell me, what happened to the seeds you planted?" asked Daddy.

Linda smiled. "Beans and radishes grew where I planted them," she answered.

Daddy nodded. "Those tiny seeds died, but when they did, vegetables grew. There was new life in the garden. Great-Grandpa was a Christian, and when his body died, he went to be with Jesus. Now he has new life, too," Daddy explained. "His body is here, but the real person is in heaven with Jesus."

Linda thought about it. "Does he need his cane there?"

Daddy shook his head. "No, nor his shoes, either. Heaven is a perfect place where he has everything he needs or wants."

Linda felt better as she looked toward the casket where Great-Grandpa's body lay. "I'm glad he's in heaven," she said simply.

HOW ABOUT YOU? Have you visited a funeral home or seen someone who has died? Did it give you a strange feeling? Death is hard to understand, but it helps to remember that it's only the body that has died. The real person—the life—has moved on. For a Christian, that life goes to heaven to be with Jesus. □ C.B.

TO MEMORIZE: *He will swallow up death forever. The Sovereign LORD will wipe away the tears from all faces.* Isaiah 25:8, NIV

No Need of Shoes

FROM THE BIBLE:
I tell you this, my brothers: an earthly body made of flesh and blood cannot get into God's Kingdom. These perishable bodies of ours are not the right kind to live forever. But I am telling you this strange and wonderful secret: we shall not all die, but we shall all be given new bodies! It will all happen in a moment, in the twinkling of an eye, when the last trumpet is blown. For there will be a trumpet blast from the sky and all the Christians who have died will suddenly become alive, with new bodies that will never, never die; and then we who are still alive shall suddenly have new bodies too. For our earthly bodies, the ones we have now that can die, must be transformed into heavenly bodies that cannot perish but will live forever. When this happens, then at last this Scripture will come true: "Death is swallowed up in victory."
1 Corinthians 15:50-54, TLB

Only bodies die

JUNE

6

The Guest Book

FROM THE BIBLE:

No temple could be seen in the city, for the Lord God Almighty and the Lamb are worshiped in it everywhere. And the city has no need of sun or moon to light it, for the glory of God and of the Lamb illuminate it. Its light will light the nations of the earth, and the rulers of the world will come and bring their glory to it. Its gates never close; they stay open all day long—and there is no night! And the glory and honor of all the nations shall be brought into it. Nothing evil will be permitted in it—no one immoral or dishonest—but only those whose names are written in the Lamb's Book of Life.

Revelation 21:22-27, TLB

Accept Jesus as Savior

MEGAN WAS all aflutter because she was in charge of the guest book at her Aunt Sally's wedding. As the guests filed past, she very politely asked each one, "Will you sign the guest book, please?"

Suddenly a big, deep voice boomed out, "Well, here's my little niece, nearly all grown up." It was Megan's Uncle Joe, who was in the army. He was her favorite relative, and today he looked more handsome than ever in his uniform. "I see they have you on guest book duty today," said Uncle Joe with a smile. "That's a mighty important job. Here's a riddle for you: Where is the most important 'guest book' of all?" He tweaked her chin. "You have until after you get off duty to think about it."

After the wedding, Megan looked for her uncle and sat down beside him. "I've got the answer," she said. "The most important guest book is in the White House."

Uncle Joe laughed and shook his head. "Good try," he said, "but wrong. The most important guest book is in heaven."

"In heaven?" asked Megan. "There's a guest book there?"

"The Bible tells us of a Book of Life," replied Uncle Joe. "It says that to enter heaven, our names must be written in that book."

"Do we write them in when we get there?" Megan asked.

"Oh no," said Uncle Joe. "Your name has to be there you can get into heaven."

"Well, how do we get it written there?" asked Megan.

"By believing in the Lord Jesus Christ," replied Uncle Joe. "Have you asked Jesus to be your Savior from sin?" Megan nodded and Uncle Joe smiled. "Then it's there," he said. "As an old song says, your name is 'written down in glory.' That's great!" Megan's face broke into a big smile. It was great, and she felt happy—even happier than when she had been hostess for the guest book.

HOW ABOUT YOU? Have you asked Jesus to forgive your sin and be your Savior? He wants to write your name in the Book of Life so that you may some day join Him in heaven and be happy forever. Will you admit your need and ask Him to save you today? □ C.Y.

TO MEMORIZE: *However, do not rejoice that the spirits submit to you, but rejoice that your names are written in heaven.* Luke 10:20, NIV

WHEN HIS MOTHER called, John left his game reluctantly. "What do you want?" he asked irritably.

"Please sweep up the cookie crumbs you left on the floor," said Mother. "And don't help yourself to any more cookies. I have just enough for the meeting at church."

John scowled. "Well, don't leave them out in the open if you don't want them eaten."

"John! That was rude!" exclaimed Mother.

"I'm sorry," John muttered as he got the broom. His sister, Kara, came into the room while he was sweeping. Surprised, she asked why he was doing that. "Scram!" John growled. "Who asked you to stick your nose in?"

"Excuse me!" said Kara dramatically. "I came to tell you something, but now I don't know if I will." When John punched her in the shoulder, she ran behind the table. "Mr. Williams, your coach, called today," she said. "He wants to hire you to do some yard work. Guess what? He said to be sure to tell Mom he appreciated your respectful attitude at school! What a laugh!"

"What's so funny?" John asked. "I make a real effort to show I'm a Christian at school."

"Well," retorted Kara, "don't invite any of your friends or teachers home. If they saw how you act around here, they'd know what a phony you are."

After Kara left, John felt badly. *Could Kara be right?* he wondered. At school he tried to be an example of Christian living. But when he got home, he seemed to forget about kindness. After all, his family members knew he loved them and that he was saved. He didn't have to prove it to them. So why did he feel so guilty? He knew it was the Holy Spirit convicting him. "Lord, forgive me," he prayed. "Help me to behave like a Christian all the time, especially with the people who love me most." Then he went to apologize to his mother and sister.

HOW ABOUT YOU? Are you as kind to your brothers and sisters as you are to your friends? Do you speak as respectfully to your parents as you do to your teachers? Sometimes we can fool people with nice words and good deeds, but our families know whether or not we are really letting Christ's love flow through us. □ C.R.

TO MEMORIZE: *In the same way, let your light shine before men, that they may see your good deeds and praise your Father in heaven.* Matthew 5:16, NIV

JUNE

7

A "Sometimes Christian"

FROM THE BIBLE:

If I had the gift of being able to speak in other languages without learning them, and could speak in every language there is in all of heaven and earth, but didn't love others, I would only be making noise. If I had the gift of prophecy and knew all about what is going to happen in the future, knew everything about everything, but didn't love others, what good would it do? Even if I had the gift of faith so that I could speak to a mountain and make it move, I would still be worth nothing at all without love. If I gave everything I have to poor people, and if I were burned alive for preaching the Gospel but didn't love others, it would be of no value whatever. Love is very patient and kind, never jealous or envious, never boastful or proud, never haughty or selfish or rude. Love does not demand its own way.
1 Corinthians 13:1-5, TLB

Live for Christ at home

8

Waiting Too Long

FROM THE BIBLE:

Remember now your Creator in the days of your youth, before the difficult days come, and the years draw near when you say, "I have no pleasure in them": while the sun and the light, the moon and the stars, are not darkened, and the clouds do not return after the rain; in the day when the keepers of the house tremble, and the strong men bow down; when the grinders cease because they are few, and those that look through the windows grow dim; when the doors are shut in the streets, and the sound of grinding is low; when one rises up at the sound of a bird, and all the daughters of music are brought low; also when they are afraid of height, and of terrors in the way; when the almond tree blossoms, the grasshopper is a burden, and desire fails. For man goes to his eternal home, and the mourners go about the streets.
Ecclesiastes 12:1-5, NKJV

Accept Christ now

GLEN PULLED a brightly colored paper from his pocket. *What's this?* he thought. It was a coupon for a free candy bar. He had cut it out of the newspaper and then forgotten about it. Eager to get that candy, he hurried to the store, picked up the candy bar, and handed the coupon to the sales clerk.

The clerk smiled at Glen and looked at the coupon. "Oh, I'm sorry, but this coupon isn't good anymore," she said. "It's expired—it's past the date printed on it." She showed him the expiration date. Disappointed, he put the candy back.

On the way home, Glen decided to stop at his Aunt Carrie's house. He told her about the expired coupon.

"Too bad you didn't cash it in before," she sympathized, "but why don't you sit down and have some lemonade with me?" As she handed him a glass, she said, "Your experience reminds me of a story I read called 'Now Is the Time.' It's about a young man who often heard an invitation to be saved, but he always put off making a decision. At first he said he was too young, then he was too busy. And then he died in an accident before ever receiving Christ as his Savior."

"That's sad," said Glen.

"It certainly is," Aunt Carrie agreed solemnly. She looked intently at her nephew. "What about you, Glen?" she asked. "You waited too long to cash in the coupon for a free candy bar. What have you done about cashing in on God's offer for salvation?"

Glen suddenly realized that, just like the young man in the story, he had been putting off the decision to accept Jesus, and he didn't know when God's offer might "expire" for him. That afternoon as he and Aunt Carrie knelt by the sofa, he asked Jesus to be his Savior.

HOW ABOUT YOU? Have you been putting off your decision for Christ? There's no guarantee you'll be able to accept Him later. Do it now before the opportunity expires—before it's too late. □ C.Y.

TO MEMORIZE: *There is a judge for the one who rejects me and does not accept my words; that very word which I spoke will condemn him at the last day.* John 12:48, NIV

Todd QUICKLY scribbled a note for his mother—"Gone fishin'. Todd." That done, he grabbed his pole and bait and hurried out the door. As Todd reached the river, he saw a boy sitting in his favorite fishing spot. "Catchin' anything?" he asked.

The boy looked up, shrugged his shoulders and mumbled, "Naw, this isn't a very good spot."

Todd couldn't believe his ears! This was the best spot on the whole river! "Well, you gotta be patient when you're fishin'," he reminded the boy.

"Patient! I've been sitting here all morning without any bites," the boy complained, giving his pole such a jerk that his line popped completely out of the water.

"How often do you keep popping your line out of the water like that?" Todd asked.

"Oh, every few minutes—just to see if a fish has eaten the worm yet," the boy replied.

"You fish much?" asked Todd, sure that he already knew the answer.

"My first time," the boy answered without looking up.

"What's your name?" Todd asked.

"Pete Fisher," came the reply.

Todd sat down. "Pete," he said, "we've gotta talk."

At dinner that night, Todd told his family about Pete. "We sure had fun! He's learnin' to fish so he can live up to his name."

"That's funny," Dad said, smiling. "It reminds me of the Peter in the Bible. He was a fisherman too, you know. And one day Jesus came to Peter and said, 'Follow Me, and I will make you fishers of men.' Todd, you have a perfect opportunity to 'fish' for Pete. Your friendship can be the bait, God's Word can be the hook and line. Be a fisher of men, Todd, rather than just an ordinary fisherman."

HOW ABOUT YOU? Do you go fishing? You should if you're following Jesus. This kind of fishing doesn't even require handling wiggly worms or slippery fish! It requires a smile, some time, perhaps an invitation to play with you. It requires prayer and knowledge of God's Word. And it's more satisfying than fishing for ordinary fish. □ L.W.

TO MEMORIZE: *"Come, follow me," Jesus said, "and I will make you fishers of men."* Matthew 4:19, NIV

Gone Fishin'

FROM THE BIBLE:
From that time on Jesus began to preach, "Repent, for the kingdom of heaven is near." As Jesus was walking beside the Sea of Galilee, he saw two brothers, Simon called Peter and his brother Andrew. They were casting a net into the lake, for they were fishermen. "Come, follow me," Jesus said, "and I will make you fishers of men." At once they left their nets and followed him. Going on from there, he saw two other brothers, James son of Zebedee and his brother John. They were in a boat with their father Zebedee, preparing their nets. Jesus called them, and immediately they left the boat and their father and followed him.
Matthew 4:17-22, NIV

Be a fisher of men

Gone Fishin'

(Continued from yesterday)

FROM THE BIBLE:
Therefore be patient, brethren,
until the coming of the Lord.
See how the farmer waits for the
precious fruit of the earth,
waiting patiently for it until it
receives the early and latter
rain. You also be patient.
Establish your hearts, for the
coming of the Lord is at hand.
James 5:7-8, NKJV

Witness with patience

TODD LAY IN BED, thinking of what his dad had said about being a fisher of men. He knew that if he was going to use God's Word he would need to have much of it in his heart and mind, memorized and understood. He worked hard the following weeks at learning Scripture so he would be ready to share with his new friend, Pete.

Every day he asked Pete to go to church or to a church party, but Pete always refused. Pete never seemed interested when Todd tried to share Scripture verses either. Todd was frustrated. "I give up, Dad," he said. "Pete never wants to come to church, and he's getting sick of me asking all the time. I'm gonna quit!"

"Todd," Dad reminded him, "you have to be patient when you're fishing, remember? You can't keep popping your line out of the water to see if a fish has taken the bait."

"Huh?" grunted Todd. "What are you getting at?"

"You don't have to ask Pete every day to go to church with you," said Dad. "I suggest that you first strengthen your friendship with Pete. Share with him what you enjoy at church and the fun you have at the parties. Then maybe Pete will become interested enough to come sometime. Remember, though, don't lie to make it sound like it's just all fun. You must be honest."

For the next three weeks, Todd practiced what his dad had suggested. Finally, he felt the nibble he'd been waiting for. "Dad!" he shouted as he burst into the house. "Guess what happened today!"

"I found your note about going fishing, so I'd say you caught a fish." Dad smiled.

"Did I ever!" Todd beamed. "And his name is Pete! You were right, Dad. A good fisherman must be patient if he really wants to catch a fish."

HOW ABOUT YOU? Are you an impatient "fisher of men"? Does it seem as though you're never going to get a bite? Don't give up. Check the bait. Are you being a genuine friend? Do you have good times together? Do you pray for your friend? Are you prepared to share God's Word? Then, if you don't get a nibble right away, be patient. The salvation of a friend is worth waiting for. □ L.W.

TO MEMORIZE: *You also be patient. Establish your hearts, for the coming of the Lord is at hand.*
James 5:8, NKJV

"LOOK BEHIND YOU, Mom," said Rhonda as she and her mother picked raspberries. "Down low there are some berries you missed."

"Oh, and they're nice ones." Mother bent to pick them.

"There are more in the bush behind them," said Rhonda.

Mother looked as Rhonda pointed, but she shook her head. "No, those aren't ripe yet. But I see some in the bush you just finished."

"I guess we should pick each other's bushes," laughed Rhonda. "This is fun. Remember when Carla and her mom used to come with us?"

"Yes, I miss them." Mother sighed. "How is Carla doing since her mother left home?"

"Oh, she whines all the time about how she would rather live with her mother than with her dad. We girls get sick of hearing about it," said Rhonda. "After all, this way she's still in the same house and the same school. But she doesn't see that she's better off with her dad."

"I guess it all depends on your viewpoint," suggested Mother. "You see Carla's problems from a distance, so you see things she doesn't see. But don't forget that she also can see things you can't see. It's like these berries—we miss some good ones and mistake others for good, depending on how we view them."

Ronda nodded slowly. "I see what you mean."

"As Christians, we need to be more understanding and less critical of others," added Mother. "Tell me, what bothers Carla most now that her mother's gone?"

Rhonda thought for a minute. "Well, for one thing, her father is dating. I can see how that would be hard to take. And she says she misses her mom. They were so close. She could tell her mom anything."

"God can use you to help make this change easier for her," said Mother. "Show her good things about her situation and help her with the hard ones. She needs understanding."

HOW ABOUT YOU? Are you annoyed when our friends talk about their troubles? Does it bug you because it spoils your fun when you hear about the sad things happening to them? Remember, the Bible says, "a friend loves at all times." □ A.L.

TO MEMORIZE: *So give your servant a discerning heart to govern your people and to distinguish between right and wrong.* 1 Kings 3:9, NIV

JUNE

11

The Viewpoint

FROM THE BIBLE:
Since you have been chosen by God who has given you this new kind of life, and because of his deep love and concern for you, you should practice tender-hearted mercy and kindness to others. Don't worry about making a good impression on them but be ready to suffer quietly and patiently. Be gentle and ready to forgive; never hold grudges. Remember, the Lord forgave you, so you must forgive others. Most of all, let love guide your life, for then the whole church will stay together in perfect harmony. Let the peace of heart which comes from Christ be always present in your hearts and lives, for this is your responsibility and privilege as members of his body. And always be thankful. Remember what Christ taught and let his words enrich your lives and make you wise; teach them to each other and sing them out in psalms and hymns and spiritual songs, singing to the Lord with thankful hearts. And whatever you do or say, let it be as a representative of the Lord Jesus. Colossians 3:12-17, TLB

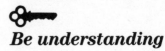

Be understanding

JUNE

12

Jana's Passport

Salvation is a personal choice

TED AND JANA were going to spend the summer in England with their older sister. "Did you forget anything?" Dad asked when they were on their way to the airport. "If so, now is the time to remember before we get too far from home."

"Have you got the tickets and passports?" Mother asked.

"Right here." Jana patted her purse. "I sure hate to show my passport to anyone, though. My picture is terrible."

"Let me see it again." Ted held out his hand.

"No way!" Jana held her purse tightly.

"Well, give me my ticket and passport," Ted insisted. "I would feel better carrying my own."

Jana opened her purse and took them out. "Oh no!"

Dad took his foot off the accelerator. "What's wrong?"

"I have Mother's passport instead of mine," wailed Jana. "They were in the same drawer, and I picked up the wrong one."

"It's a good thing you discovered it now!" Dad looked for a place to turn around. "Mother's passport wouldn't get you into England."

Mother looked thoughtful. "Hmmmm," she mused. "I'm going to have to tell Mrs. Lewis about this experience. I've had a couple of opportunities to witness to her, and whenever I ask if she has accepted Christ, she tells me about the wonderful Christian parents she has. She seems to think that makes her a Christian, too."

"I see what Mother's getting at," said Dad as he completed a turn and headed back home. "Maybe when Mrs. Lewis hears about this, she'll see that just as Mother's passport won't get Jana into England, the salvation of her parents won't get her into heaven. The decision to accept Christ is a decision everyone has to make for himself.

HOW ABOUT YOU? Do you have your "passport" to heaven? If your parents are Christians, you are blessed, but do not depend on that to get you to heaven. Your own righteousness—your fine family, your Christian parents, your own good works—will not get you to heaven. You must receive God's righteousness by accepting Jesus as your Savior. It's a decision you must make for yourself. □ B.W.

TO MEMORIZE: *Not having a righteousness of my own that comes from the law, but that which is through faith in Christ—the righteousness that comes from God.* Philippians 3:9, NIV

"IT'S TOO HOT to mow the lawn," groaned Josh one day.

"Well, it's not going to get any cooler, so you'd better start now," advised Mother.

"Mom, the Bible says, 'Provoke not your children to wrath,' and I feel angry right now," grumbled Josh.

"You're taking that verse out of context, Son," said Mother firmly. "The same chapter says, 'Children, obey your parents.'"

After finishing his work, Josh played with his little brother, Nick. Soon Mother heard Nick crying, so she went outside. "Josh pushed me down," sobbed the little boy.

"Well, he ran into me," Josh defended himself. "The Bible says, 'An eye for an eye, and a tooth for a tooth.'"

"There you go again, taking a verse out of context. The Bible also says, 'Be kind to one another,'" Mother replied sternly.

That evening Mother overheard the boys as the were playing in their room. "Leave Goldy in the fishbowl!" ordered Josh.

"I just want to pet him," whined Nick.

Mother went to check. "Don't take Goldy out of the water," she told Nick. Then turning to Josh she smiled and said, "Or should I say, 'Don't take Goldy out of his context'?"

"What does that mean?" Josh asked. "You said that about the verses, and now about the fish."

"Taking something out of its context means to take it out of its proper surroundings," Mother explained. "If you do that to a fish—you take it out of water—it will soon die. If you take a Bible verse out of its proper surroundings—that is, if you use it any way you want, without considering other Bible verses—you can make it seem like the verse is saying something different from what it really means."

"Okay, Mom, I'll try not to take verses out of context anymore," Josh promised. He grinned. "I hope Nick leaves Goldy in his 'context,' too."

HOW ABOUT YOU: Do you use Bible verses to try and get your own way? God's Word is sacred, and you should never use it in a wrong way. Don't use it in a way that doesn't agree with principles taught in the Bible. □ S.N.

TO MEMORIZE: *But when he, the Spirit of truth, comes, he will guide you into all truth.* John 16:13, NIV

JUNE

13

Lesson in a Fishbowl

FROM THE BIBLE:

The law of Moses says, "If a man gouges out another's eye, he must pay with his own eye. If a tooth gets knocked out, knock out the tooth of the one who did it." But I say: Don't resist violence! If you are slapped on one cheek, turn the other too. If you are ordered to court, and your shirt is taken from you, give your coat too. If the military demand that you carry their gear for a mile, carry it two. Give to those who ask, and don't turn away from those who want to borrow. There is a saying, "Love your friends and hate your enemies." But I say: Love your enemies! Pray for those who persecute you! In that way you will be acting as true sons of your Father in heaven. For he gives his sunlight to both the evil and the good, and sends rain on the just and on the unjust too. If you love only those who love you, what good is that? Even scoundrels do that much. If you are friendly only to your friends, how are you different from anyone else?
Matthew 5:38-47, TLB

Use God's Word carefully

JUNE

14

A Sad Story

FROM THE BIBLE:

So they seized him and led him to the High Priest's residence, and Peter followed at a distance. The soldiers lit a fire in the courtyard and sat around it for warmth, and Peter joined them there. A servant girl noticed him in the firelight and began staring at him. Finally she spoke: "This man was with Jesus!" Peter denied it. "Woman," he said, "I don't even know the man!" After a while someone else looked at him and said, "You must be one of them!" "No sir, I am not!" Peter replied. About an hour later someone else flatly stated, "I know this fellow is one of Jesus' disciples, for both are from Galilee." But Peter said, "Man, I don't know what you are talking about." And as he said the words, a rooster crowed. At that moment Jesus turned and looked at Peter. Then Peter remembered what he had said: "Before the rooster crows tomorrow morning, you will deny me three times." And Peter walked out of the courtyard, crying bitterly.

Luke 22:54-62, TLB

Put confidence in God

DAVID'S Sunday school teacher was Bob Carson, a young man who had recently graduated from college. He was lovingly called "Mr. Bob" by his class of sixth-grade boys, and he enjoyed teaching them. He often spent his Saturdays taking them fishing, miniature golfing, or doing some other activity. David constantly talked about the neat things Mr. Bob did. Through his teaching, David had grown spiritually, and his parents were thankful for such a good teacher. Sometimes they were concerned, however, that David talked about "Mr. Bob" too much.

One Sunday another man taught the class, and the boys were restless. Where was Mr. Bob? No one seemed to know.

That afternoon the pastor called David's father. David could tell it was about something serious because of the tone of his father's voice. When he got off the phone, Dad put his hand on David's shoulder. "Son, I have very sad news for you. Last night Bob Carson was arrested for drunk driving."

At first David refused to believe the news, but he finally realized it must be true. "How could he do such a thing!" he exclaimed angrily.

"David, we all have sinful natures within us," Dad replied. "Because we are human, we sometimes let people down. That's why the Bible tells us to put our confidence and trust in God rather than in another person. People fail. God doesn't! Be thankful for the help Mr. Bob has given you through his teaching. At the same time, recognize that he has a serious problem. Help him by praying that he will seek the Lord's help to overcome this."

HOW ABOUT YOU? Has a Sunday school teacher, a pastor, or perhaps a parent, let you down by doing something that is contrary to God's teaching? Because they are human and still have a sin nature, Christians do sometimes sin. Even Peter, who walked with Jesus for three years, denied Him. It's good that we can learn about God through other Christians, but our final authority and pattern for life should be the Lord. He won't let us down. □ L.W.

TO MEMORIZE: *It is better to take refuge in the LORD than to trust in man.* Psalm 118:8, NIV

PEARL SHOT from her chair and raced out to the pool. Her younger brother had just run in and reported that a small neighbor boy had fallen into the water. "Bobby can't swim," Leo had gasped, "and neither can I."

Without a thought for herself, Pearl dove into the pool. Bobby was thrashing around, trying in vain to stay above the water. His life was in Pearl's hands. She knew she had to rescue Bobby or he would probably drown.

By the time Mother ran out, Pearl and Bobby were lying on the cement, exhausted. Because of her quick action, he had swallowed only a little water and would be fine.

That evening they were still quite excited about what had happened, but Pearl was rather quiet. "Were you scared?" Leo asked for at least the sixth time.

Pearl shook her head. "I took that life-saving course, so I knew what to do," she said. She looked thoughtfully at her parents. "Last Sunday my teacher said that people are 'drowning in sin,' and that Christians know how they can be saved. I've been thinking about that. I didn't worry about whether Bobby would like the methods I used to save him. If I had, he might have died. But so often I don't tell my friends about Jesus because I'm afraid they won't like me to do that. I've got to start helping them, too—before it's too late."

HOW ABOUT YOU? If you could save someone from drowning, would you do it? Of course you would. How about if you could tell someone how to be saved from sin? Do you realize that those who don't know Jesus are headed for punishment in hell? What will you do about it? Perhaps you could show someone the ABCs of salvation. Do it today.

□ V.R.

TO MEMORIZE: *Go therefore and make disciples of all the nations, baptizing them in the name of the Father and of the Son and of the Holy Spirit.* Matthew 28:19, NKJV

JUNE

15

Life-saving

FROM THE BIBLE:
This being so, I want to remind you to stir into flame the strength and boldness that is in you, that entered into you when I laid my hands upon your head and blessed you. For the Holy Spirit, God's gift, does not want you to be afraid of people, but to be wise and strong, and to love them and enjoy being with them. If you will stir up this inner power, you will never be afraid to tell others about our Lord, or to let them know that I am your friend even though I am here in jail for Christ's sake. You will be ready to suffer with me for the Lord, for he will give you strength in suffering. It is he who saved us and chose us for his holy work, not because we deserved it but because that was his plan long before the world began—to show his love and kindness to us through Christ. And now he has made all of this plain to us by the coming of our Savior Jesus Christ, who broke the power of death and showed us the way of everlasting life through trusting him. And God has chosen me to be his missionary, to preach to the Gentiles and teach them. 2 Timothy 1:6-11, TLB

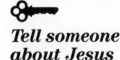

Tell someone about Jesus

JUNE

16

Still More Sanding

FROM THE BIBLE:
Praise our God, O peoples, let the sound of his praise be heard; he has preserved our lives and kept our feet from slipping. For you, O God, tested us; you refined us like silver. You brought us into prison and laid burdens on our backs. You let men ride over our heads; we went through fire and water, but you brought us to a place of abundance.
Psalm 66:8-12, NIV

Let God smooth you out

GREG WATCHED as his father began refinishing the old table. It was pretty—or at least his father said it would be when it was refinished. Dad put a new piece of sandpaper in his electric sander and began to work.

"You're spoiling it," Greg said when Dad finally stopped the sander. "You're making it look like it has all kinds of scratches."

"I'm not through with it yet," Dad answered, turning on the sander once more.

Greg watched for a long time. His father finally stopped sanding and began applying stain. When he had finished staining the wood the table did look pretty. But the next day he put a new piece of sandpaper in the sander and once again began sanding the table top.

"Dad," Greg called out, "you've already put the stain on."

Dad turned off the machine and began to explain. "It still has some flaws in it," he said taking Greg's hand and rubbing it over the table top so he could feel the rough spots. "I'll just keep sanding until it's perfect."

Greg wasn't sure he understood all there was to know about sanding, but by the time the table was finished, he had learned a lot. As he was admiring the finished product, he was surprised to hear Dad say, "We're a lot like this table."

Greg laughed. "I sure hope you're not planning to use the sander on me!"

Dad smiled. "Just as I worked on the table, God keeps working with us, sometimes using difficult situations to knock off the rough places and make us more beautiful Christians," Dad explained.

Greg nodded. He thought of the time he broke his arm. God had used it to teach him patience as he learned to write with his left hand. He would ask God to always help him grow and become a better Christian through whatever circumstances came into his life.

HOW ABOUT YOU? Have you had difficult experiences? Perhaps there has been a death or a divorce in your family. Maybe you or someone you love has been sick a lot. Whatever your experience, have you let God use it to make you a better, sweeter Christian? □ R.J.

TO MEMORIZE: *But he knows the way that I take; when he has tested me, I will come forth as gold.* Job 23:10, NIV

ROBERT WATCHED as his dad pounded a post into the ground close to the tree and then ripped old pieces of cloth into strips, getting ready to tie the tree to the post. "Why do you have to do that?" Robert asked.

"If I don't," Dad answered, "this tree will not be tall and straight when it grows up." He put his hand on the small tree trunk. "See how it's beginning to lean to the left? If I don't correct that now, it will keep on leaning until it'll be too late to correct."

When Dad finished the job, Robert patted the tree, a grin on his face. "Don't take it too hard, little tree," he said playfully. "It might hurt now, but you'll be glad later."

"Is that the way you feel when I have to straighten you out on certain things?" his father asked with a smile.

"What do you mean?" Robert asked in surprise.

"Well, when I see you doing things that aren't very Christ-like, it's my responsibility to correct you and help you to change your ways," explained Dad. "Are you glad I do that?"

Robert did not answer immediately. He could remember several spankings he had received when he was younger. He hadn't liked that, but, he guessed they had worked. Remembering the sting of the spankings had been enough to keep him from repeating his wrong doings. Now that he was older, he feared other types of punishment, too—being grounded, not being allowed to watch TV, being assigned extra duties. Those things still helped to keep him from doing wrong.

"I don't particularly like to discipline you," Dad was saying, "but if I'm going to be the kind of father you can be proud of, and if you're going to be the kind of son I can be proud of—and the kind of person God wants you to be—it's sometimes necessary."

Robert knew his dad was right. "Yeah, I'm glad you correct me," he said grinning, "only just don't ask me how I feel about it when it's happening!"

HOW ABOUT YOU? How do you feel when one of your parents must correct you for wrong doing? Do you get angry and resentful? God says correction is necessary to make you what you ought to be. After the discipline is over, see if you can't be thankful for what happened. □ B.W.

TO MEMORIZE: *Discipline your son, for in that there is hope; do not be a willing party to his death.* Proverbs 19:18, NIV

Reason for Discipline

FROM THE BIBLE:
And have you quite forgotten the encouraging words God spoke to you, his child? He said, "My son, don't be angry when the Lord punishes you. Don't be discouraged when he has to show you where you are wrong. For when he punishes you, it proves that he loves you. When he whips you it proves you are really his child." Let God train you, for he is doing what any loving father does for his children. Whoever heard of a son who was never corrected? If God doesn't punish you when you need it, as other fathers punish their sons, then it means that you aren't really God's son at all—that you don't really belong in his family. Since we respect our fathers here on earth, though they punish us, should we not all the more cheerfully submit to God's training so that we can begin really to live? Our earthly fathers trained us for a few brief years, doing the best for us that they knew how, but God's correction is always right and for our best good.
Hebrews 12:5-10, TLB

Be thankful for discipline

18

Like Jinx

FROM THE BIBLE:

Children, obey your parents in the Lord, for this is right.
"Honor your father and mother,"
which is the first commandment
with promise: "that it may be
well with you and you may live
long on the earth."
Ephesians 6:1-3, NKJV

Obey parents immediately

SARA OVERHEARD Mother telling Dad that she had failed to clean out her closet. "I even gave her a box to put the outgrown clothes into," said Mother.

Sara didn't listen to the rest of her parents' conversation. She went outside, feeling dejected, and sat on her swing. Her collie, Jinx, came over to her, but Sara ignored her pet. She thought of all the things she did do right. She considered herself to be a very obedient daughter. She made her bed before school. She set the table for dinner each afternoon. And she dried the dishes her mother washed each evening. Why was Mother now complaining to Dad? What was it her parents wanted from her anyway? She would clean that closet later. Why did it have to be done right now?

Soon Dad was sitting on the other swing. "Sara, what about cleaning your closet?" he asked.

"I'm going to do it, Dad," replied Sara. "I wanted to see that special on TV first."

Dad picked up a stick and threw it. "Get it, Jinx," he said. The dog was off at a gallop to retrieve the stick. Dad turned his attention back to Sara. "Now that is immediate obedience. Jinx didn't say, "'I'll do it when I get around to it.' He just obeyed." After a pause, Dad added, "A truck collecting clothing for needy people stopped here today, Sara. None of your outgrown clothes got put on it because you didn't obey Mother immediately."

Now Sara felt badly. "Why didn't Mother tell me the truck was coming?" she asked. "I would've cleaned the closet right away if I'd known."

"We want you to be willing to obey us without always asking for reasons," said Dad quietly. "God didn't say, 'Children, obey your parents when you understand why.' He said, 'Children, obey your parents.' To be truly obedient, you must be immediately obedient."

"Like Jinx," murmured Sara, giving her dog a hug.

HOW ABOUT YOU? When your parents tell you to do something, do you put them off? Do you demand reasons? Or do you try to argue that you will do it later when you've nothing else to do? The only true obedience is *immediate* obedience.

□ R.P.

TO MEMORIZE: *Children, obey your parents in the Lord, for this is right.* Ephesians 6:1, NKJV

"DAD, MY FISHING LINE is pulling!" shouted Ron.

Dad laughed. "That's because there's a fish on the end. Start reeling him in."

Soon the little sunfish was lying on the sand, but it was too small to keep. Reluctantly Ron put it back into the water. It flipped its tail, and in a moment it had disappeared.

"Whoa!" said Dad as Ron tossed his line back into the lake. "Aren't you forgetting something?" Ron looked at him with a question in his eyes. "The bait," Dad explained.

Ron laughed. "Oh, yeah," he said pulling his line back in. "I guess no fish would be dumb enough to bite on the bare hook, would he? I'll disguise it and make it look good with this juicy worm. The fish won't know there's any danger, and he'll open his big mouth and swallow the hook. Then I'll have him!" With a grin he returned the line to the water once more.

"This reminds me of the way Satan works," Dad mused.

Ron was curious. "What do you mean, Dad?"

"Well, Satan tries to make sin look attractive," explained Dad. "Sometimes we're uneasy about something, or maybe we've been warned that it's wrong. Yet it looks good. Or it feels good. Or our friends are doing it, and we're tempted to try it, too. Satan is a master at disguising sin. He knows how to make bad things look good to us. So when you're tempted by a questionable activity, remember the fish. He wouldn't have gotten caught if he had stayed away from the hook."

HOW ABOUT YOU? Does Satan use an interesting story on TV to get you accustomed to hearing bad language so that it doesn't bother you anymore? Does he catch your attention with a "good" movie so that you become careless about what you watch? Does he make playing games at the arcade so much fun that you do it even if you know you're spending too much money? What other methods does he use? Be careful. Ask God daily to help you stay away from the attractive bait Satan uses.

□ P.R.

TO MEMORIZE: *Put on the full armor of God so that you can take your stand against the devil's schemes.* Ephesians 6:11, NIV

JUNE

Attractive Bait

FROM THE BIBLE:
Be careful—watch out for attacks from Satan, your great enemy. He prowls around like a hungry, roaring lion, looking for some victim to tear apart. Stand firm when he attacks. Trust the Lord; and remember that other Christians all around the world are going through these sufferings too. After you have suffered a little while, our God, who is full of kindness through Christ, will give you his eternal glory. He personally will come and pick you up, and set you firmly in place, and make you stronger than ever. To him be all power over all things, forever and ever. Amen.
1 Peter 5:8, TLB

Avoid Satan's bait

20

Whiner or Winner?

FROM THE BIBLE:

In the land of Uz there lived a man whose name was Job. This man was blameless and upright. . . . One day when Job's sons and daughters were feasting and drinking wine at the oldest brother's house, a messenger came to Job and said, "The oxen were plowing and the donkeys were grazing nearby, and the Sabeans attacked and carried them off." . . . While he was still speaking, yet another messenger came and said, "Your sons and daughters were feasting and drinking wine at the oldest brother's house, when suddenly a mighty wind swept in from the desert and struck the four corners of the house. It collapsed on them and they are dead, and I am the only one who has escaped to tell you!" At this, Job got up and tore his robe and shaved his head. Then he fell to the ground in worship and said: "Naked I came from my mother's womb, and naked I will depart. The LORD gave and the LORD has taken away; may the name of the LORD be praised."

Job 1:1-2, 13-15, 18-22, NIV

Have right attitudes

"YOU HAVE SCOLIOSIS, which is a curved spine, Debi," Dr. Bryant said. He turned toward Mother. "A specialist will decide how it should be treated. Exercises may help, or Debi may have to wear a brace or possibly have surgery."

In the following days Debi prayed and prayed. Oh, how she wanted God to straighten her spine. "God can heal you, Debi," Mother said one night, "but if He doesn't, it's because He loves you and wants to make you a better person."

"How can wearing an ugly brace do that?" Debi sobbed.

"By teaching you discipline and compassion," Mother answered.

To her dismay, Debi did need the brace. "This will restrict your physical activities some, but not much," Dr. Roberts told her. "You'll be able to do almost everything you've always done."

A few days later, Mother noticed that Debi had allowed her room to become messy. "Go clean your room right now!" Mother scolded.

"But my brace is so awkward," whined Debi, "I can't."

Mother frowned. "I'm sorry, Honey, but you will have to adjust. Go clean your room."

Later Mother heard Debi on the telephone. "Oh, I couldn't do that, Pam. I might hurt my back," she whined.

"What can't you do?" Mother asked later.

"I can't go hiking," Debi answered.

"You certainly can," Mother insisted. "Debi, a brace on your back does not make you an invalid. Your physical problem can make you a whiner or a winner."

Debi sniffed. "How can I be a winner?"

"By having the right attitude," answered Mother. "Remember Job? Everything went wrong in his life—everything but his attitude. He came out a winner. Now, call Pam back and tell her you're going hiking."

HOW ABOUT YOU? The question is not, What's your problem? The question is, How's your attitude? Everyone has problems. You can become a whiner or a winner. It's up to you. What's your choice? Will you say with Job, "Blessed be the name of the Lord"? □ R.J.

TO MEMORIZE: *The LORD gave and the LORD has taken away; may the name of the LORD be praised.* Job 1:21, NIV

JEREMY AND ALICIA were watching a television show when their parents arrived home. "What's on?" Dad asked as he sat down in his easy chair.

"Oh, some show about an undercover policeman who's trying to break the mob's secret code." Jeremy kept his eyes glued to the television set as he answered.

"Oh, wow! Look at that, Jeremy!" Alicia, too, kept her eyes fastened on the TV. "He's breaking into the mob's warehouse where they store their drugs. He's got a gun, and he's going to blast the bad guys."

"Wait! There's his girlfriend. I wonder if they're going to kill her?" Jeremy sat up straight.

"I hope not! They just fell in love at the beginning of the show," replied Alicia. Just then a loud burst of gunfire pierced the stillness of the living room, followed by a torrent of machine gun fire. The mobsters began to fall to the ground while the hero continued to shoot around the warehouse.

Dad got up, walked over to the TV, and turned it off. "I thought you two knew better than to watch such a program," he said. "Doesn't that violence bother you?"

"It's not real," Alicia protested weakly.

"Real or not, this is wrong," replied Dad. "In fact, just this morning I read some verses in Psalm 101 that talk about these kinds of television shows."

"Aw, Dad, the Bible doesn't mention TV shows," protested Jeremy.

"Well," said Dad, "Psalm 101 says, 'I will set nothing wicked before my eyes.' Wouldn't you say that could be applied to programs like the one you were watching?"

Mother nodded in agreement. "Drug dealing and murder certainly is wickedness."

Jeremy and Alicia looked ashamed. "I guess you're right," Jeremy said soberly. "We didn't make a wise choice when we picked that show."

"I think we all need to be more careful about such things," said Dad.

HOW ABOUT YOU? Are the TV programs you watch filled with violence or inappropriate suggestions? Do they make sin look glamorous and desirable? Do they make you forget God and His principles? Be very careful about what you "set before your eyes"! □ L.S.R.

TO MEMORIZE: *I will be careful to lead a blameless life.* Psalm 101:2, NIV

No Wicked Thing

FROM THE BIBLE:
I will sing of your love and justice; to you, O LORD, I will sing praise. I will be careful to lead a blameless life—when will you come to me? I will walk in my house with blameless heart. I will set before my eyes no vile thing. The deeds of faithless men I hate; they will not cling to me. Men of perverse heart shall be far from me; I will have nothing to do with evil. Whoever slanders his neighbor in secret, him will I put to silence; whoever has haughty eyes and a proud heart, him will I not endure. My eyes will be on the faithful in the land, that they may dwell with me; he whose walk is blameless will minister to me. No one who practices deceit will dwell in my house; no one who speaks falsely will stand in my presence. Every morning I will put to silence all the wicked in the land; I will cut off every evildoer from the city of the LORD.
Psalm 101, NIV

Watch only good TV

JUNE

22

How to Beat Boredom

FROM THE BIBLE:
Then I, the King, shall say to those at my right, "Come, blessed of my Father, into the Kingdom prepared for you from the founding of the world. For I was hungry and you fed me; I was thirsty and you gave me water; I was a stranger and you invited me into your homes; naked and you clothed me; sick and in prison, and you visited me. When you did it to these my brothers you were doing it to me!" Then I will turn to those on my left and say, "Away with you, you cursed ones, into the eternal fire prepared for the devil and his demons. For I was hungry and you wouldn't feed me; thirsty, and you wouldn't give me anything to drink; a stranger, and you refused me hospitality; naked, and you wouldn't clothe me; sick, and in prison, and you didn't visit me. When you refused to help the least of these my brothers, you were refusing help to me."
Matthew 25:34-36, 40-45, TLB

Serve one another

MATT SAT IDLY on the porch swing. When Jerry came riding by on his bicycle at top speed, Matt almost didn't see him. "Hey, Jerry," he called to his friend's back, "where's the fire?"

Jerry slammed on his brakes. "No fire," he responded. "I've just got a lot to do today."

"Boy, I don't," Matt grumbled. "I'm so bored. There's nothing to do around here."

"Nothing to do?" echoed Jerry. "I'm really busy! I'm on my way to mow Gramp Norton's lawn. Want to help me?"

"Sure," Matt answered. "How much will we get paid?"

"Nothing." Jerry grinned. "I'm doing it for the Lord and for fun."

"For the Lord and for fun?" Matt slapped his forehead. "You're mowing a lawn for fun? Does Gramps have a riding mower or something?"

Jerry shook his head. "No. I'm doing it because it's fun to do things for other people. And, besides, Jesus said when I do something for others, I'm doing it for Him. I've decided to spend this summer working for Jesus."

Matt raised his eyebrows and moaned. But because he didn't have anything else to do, he went with Jerry. He also went with him the next day—and the next day, too—as Jerry "worked for the Lord."

"Say, this is fun," Matt told Jerry as they cleaned his dad's garage without having been asked to do so.

"My mom says we get bored because we think about ourselves too much," Jerry told Matt. "She says it's less likely to happen when we're busy helping others."

"Well, I sure haven't been bored the last few days," Matt said grinning. "Maybe this summer won't be so dull after all."

HOW ABOUT YOU? Is "I'm bored" your theme song? Could that be because you're thinking too much about yourself? There are many things you can do to keep busy and help others. Ask the Lord to show you some way you can help another person each day. Then do it. When you do something for someone else, you are doing it for Jesus too.
□ B.W.

TO MEMORIZE: *When you did it to these my brothers you were doing it to me!* Matthew 25:40, TLB

MARCIE CLIMBED slowly into the car. "Hi, Honey," said her dad. "It sure was a beautiful day for your picnic."

"Yeah," mumbled Marcie.

"Did you have a good time?" Dad asked.

"Uh, sure," she answered after a moment of silence.

Dad glanced at her curiously. "You don't sound very convincing. What's wrong?"

"Oh, Dad," moaned Marcie, "I blew it! While we were on the swings, Joni asked me about Jesus and being a Christian, and I couldn't answer her questions very well. I feel awful!"

"Oh, I see," Dad said thoughtfully. As they pulled into the driveway, he spoke again. "I've got something in the garage I want to show you."

"All right," Marcie agreed, still sniffling.

Dad walked to his workbench and handed Marcie a knife and a piece of wood. "Here," he said. "This is one of my wood-carving knives. Would you cut this stick in half for me, please."

Marcie tried to do as he directed. "I can't use this knife," she complained. "It's dull!"

"You're right," agreed Dad. "It is dull. It's been away from the sharpener a long time."

"Well, it's not much good like this," grumbled Marcie.

Dad smiled at her. "You know, Honey, this knife has to be sharpened often to be of much use. And if we want God to be able to use us, we have to be 'sharpened' by spending time daily with Him."

Marcie looked from her dad to the knife. "You gave me a dull knife on purpose, didn't you, Dad?" she asked. "You want me to see that I'm like this knife—I'm dull! You're right, too. I haven't been reading my Bible very often or even praying for my friends, and now when I had a chance to witness to Joni, I couldn't think of anything to tell her. I'm going to do better on my devotions from now on. Maybe I'll be 'sharper' the next time she asks questions."

HOW ABOUT YOU? Are you faithful in spending time with the Lord and studying His Word? Are you ready to answer when someone asks you questions? If not, it's time to "sharpen up." You never know when the chance will come, so prepare daily. □ S.N.

TO MEMORIZE: *Always be ready to give a defense to everyone who asks you a reason for the hope that is in you, with meekness and fear.* 1 Peter 3:15, NKJV

23

Be Sharp

FROM THE BIBLE:
Oh, how I love your law! I meditate on it all day long. Your commands make me wiser than my enemies, for they are ever with me. I have more insight than all my teachers, for I meditate on your statutes. I have more understanding than the elders, for I obey your precepts. I have kept my feet from every evil path so that I might obey your word. I have not departed from your laws, for you yourself have taught me. How sweet are your words to my taste, sweeter than honey to my mouth! I gain understanding from your precepts; therefore I hate every wrong path.
Psalm 119:97-104, NIV

Be ready to witness

24

Just the Shell

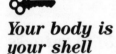

Your body is your shell

DAVID ALWAYS LIKE IT when the family went to the beach. He had been able to get a good-sized collection of shells from their trips. And now, here they were again, he and his father, walking up and down the sandy beach, looking for more shells. Suddenly he stopped and called, "Dad, come here! I found something, but I don't know what it is."

Dad soon joined David, who pointed at a strange-looking sea creature. At least that is what David thought it was. Dad knelt down and looked carefully at David's find. As he did so, David begged him to be careful. He didn't want his father to be bitten or snapped at by some dangerous sea animal. "This one will never bite," Dad said. "There's no life in him."

"How come?" David wanted to know.

David's father picked it up in his hands. "Because this is just a shell," he explained, turning it over and over so David could see what it looked like. "It's a lobster shell. There comes a time in the lobster's life when he squeezes out and leaves his shell."

Before David could ask any more questions, his father asked if he remembered when Grandpa Jones died. "Do you remember how I explained that Grandpa had gone to heaven?" Dad asked.

David nodded. "But I didn't understand how he could be in the casket and be in heaven, too," David replied.

"It's very much like this shell that you just found. The lobster is gone," Dad said. "This is just his shell. In the same way, when Grandpa died, he left his body and went to live with Jesus because he was a Christian."

Suddenly David seemed to understand. "Oh!" he exclaimed. "That's why Grandpa couldn't talk to us anymore. He was gone. It was just his shell that was left."

Dad smiled. "That's right," he said, "and though it made us sad because we knew we would miss him, we're glad that he's with Jesus."

HOW ABOUT YOU? Do you have a Christian relative or friend who has died recently? If so, that Christian has simply left his body and has gone to be with Jesus. Your body is just the house in which you live. □ R.J.

TO MEMORIZE: *We are confident, I say, and would prefer to be away from the body and at home with the Lord.* 2 Corinthians 5:8, NIV

DAVID SHOWED his mother the shells he and his dad had found on the beach. Then he told her about the lobster that had gone away and had left his shell behind. All that evening David was very quiet.

Just before he went to bed, he had more questions. "Doesn't Grandpa miss us?" he wanted to know. "Is he happy in heaven?"

"Absolutely," replied Dad. "Grandpa isn't sick like he was here because there's no sickness in heaven. Heaven is a perfect place. There's no sin, and no one even cries!"

"Mom cried at Grandpa's funeral," David reminded his father.

"That's right," Dad admitted. "That's because she knew she would miss him very much."

"But she wanted him to go to heaven, didn't she?" David asked.

David's father nodded. "That's right. She knew he would be happier there than he was here," he explained. "Here he had lots of pain. There he wouldn't have any pain. Mom also knew that she would be going to heaven someday, so she would see Grandpa again. Jesus gave her comfort in knowing these things."

Again David was quiet, thinking.

"Remember," Dad added, "if Grandpa had not accepted Jesus as his Savior, he wouldn't have gone to heaven."

David nodded. He knew what his father was saying. "I should be sure to accept Jesus now," he said, "so I'll be ready for that day." David was quiet for a long time. Finally he spoke again, "Will you help me to get ready?" he asked.

HOW ABOUT YOU? Would you be ready if God should ask you to leave your "shell"? Or would you "die in your sins"? If you have not already done so, accept Jesus as your Savior now. □ R.J.

TO MEMORIZE: *For God so loved the world that He gave His only begotten Son, that whoever believes in Him should not perish but have everlasting life.* John 3:16, NKJV

JUNE

25

Just the Shell

(Continued from yesterday)

FROM THE BIBLE:
These words Jesus spoke in the treasury, as He taught in the temple; and no one laid hands on Him, for His hour had not yet come. Then Jesus said to them again, "I am going away, and you will seek Me, and will die in your sin. Where I go you cannot come." So the Jews said, "Will He kill Himself, because He says, 'Where I go you cannot come'?" And He said to them, "You are from beneath; I am from above. You are of this world; I am not of this world. Therefore I said to you that you will die in your sins; for if you do not believe that I am He, you will die in your sins."
John 8:20-24, NKJV

Be saved

JUNE

26

Special Servants

FROM THE BIBLE:
I will extol the LORD at all times; his praise will always be on my lips. My soul will boast in the LORD; let the afflicted hear and rejoice. Glorify the LORD with me; let us exalt his name together. I sought the LORD, and he answered me; he delivered me from all my fears. Those who look to him are radiant; their faces are never covered with shame. This poor man called, and the LORD heard him; he saved him out of all his troubles. The angel of the LORD encamps around those who fear him, and he delivers them. Taste and see that the LORD is good; blessed is the man who takes refuge in him. Psalm 34:1-8, NIV

Angels protect Christians

AS SANDY and her brother, Jim, raced across the field, something suddenly moved in the long grass ahead of them!

"Oh!" exclaimed Sandy. "What is it?"

Jim came up, panting from the run. "Its only a bird, silly. But, look! It's hurt. I think its wing is broken."

They watched the bird slowly hop away, dragging one wing. "Let's catch it," suggested Sandy. As she reached down to touch the bird, it ran ahead, crying piteously.

Again and again the children got almost close enough to catch it, and each time it struggled forward, just out of reach. At the edge of the field, it suddenly flapped both wings and soared into the air. Sandy's mouth dropped open in surprise. "I thought it was badly hurt," she muttered.

At the dinner table that evening, Sandy and Jim told their parents what had happened. "That bird was probably a killdeer," said Dad. "More than likely, it had a nest in the grass and was leading you away from its babies."

"Well, I'd say it did a good job of protecting them, then," laughed Jim. "It sure had us fooled!"

"God provided a unique way for those young killdeer to be protected," observed Mother. "And did you know that both of you are protected in a special way, too? Angels watch over you. Can you think of any examples from the Bible where angels protected people?"

"Daniel in the lions' den!" shouted Sandy, just as Jim said, "Peter in prison!"

"You're both right," approved Dad. "Of course, Jesus is with us at all times, too, but it's hard for us to understand how He can be everywhere at once. It's comforting to know we have angels watching over us, also."

"Yeah," agreed Jim, "that's neat."

HOW ABOUT YOU? Did you know that God has provided angels to watch over His children? They are special servants of His. They give comfort to Christians, and they are very happy when people come to God through Jesus Christ. Angels also protect Christians, which means that nothing can happen to you unless God allows it. Thank Him today for the special protection He has provided. □ C.Y.

TO MEMORIZE: *The angel of the LORD encamps around those who fear him, and he delivers them.* Psalm 34:7, NIV

MARY AND HER MOTHER were busy in the garden. "Ouch!" yelled Mary as she trimmed a dead branch off a rose bush. "How come dead branches can still hurt like that? They should lose their thorns when they die!"

"But they don't," said Mother. "Even though they're dead, they can still inflict pain." She looked at Mary and then asked, "Have you heard of William Shakespeare?"

"Oh, sure, Mom," said Mary. "Miss Abbott read some of his poetry in English class. Sometimes it's hard to figure out what he means, though. They talked so funny back then."

"In one of Shakespeare's plays, someone said, 'The evil that men do lives after them.'"

"What does that mean?" Mary asked.

"Even after someone dies, the bad things he has done live on and continue to inflict pain," explained Mother. "I had an aunt who had a terrible temper. Shortly before she died in an accident, I heard her arguing with my mother—her sister. She said some terrible things that were not true. She died without ever being able to correct what she had said or to ask my mother to forgive her. Even now, my aunt's words still hurt Mother."

When Dad got out the Bible for family devotions that evening, Mary shared the things she and her mother had talked about. Dad turned in the Bible to Ecclesiastes 10. "King Solomon had some wise things to say about our speech, too," he said. "I believe he's telling us that a fool speaks without thinking sometimes, and no one can say what will happen to those words. But the words of a wise man are gracious."

"I just thought of something," said Mary with a smile. "I have a pressed rose in my Bible. It's dead, but it's still pretty. I want my words to be like that—something nice to remember for a long time, not something that keeps hurting people, like the dead thorns."

HOW ABOUT YOU? Listen to yourself today. Are your words pleasant to remember, or are they barbs that will hurt someone through the years? Words are often repeated and long remembered. They help or harm people, even people you may never meet. Let your words today be gracious and pleasing in God's sight. □ A.L.

TO MEMORIZE: *The words of a wise man's mouth are gracious, but the lips of a fool shall swallow him up.* Ecclesiastes 10:12, NKJV

Thorny Words

FROM THE BIBLE:
A serpent may bite when it is not charmed; the babbler is no different. The words of a wise man's mouth are gracious, but the lips of a fool shall swallow him up; the words of his mouth begin with foolishness, and the end of his talk is raving madness. A fool also multiplies words. No man knows what is to be; who can tell him what will be after him?
Ecclesiastes 10:11-14, NKJV

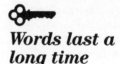

Words last a long time

28

Some Friend!

FROM THE BIBLE:

I tell you, whoever acknowledges me before men, the Son of Man will also acknowledge him before the angels of God. But he who disowns me before men will be disowned before the angels of God. And everyone who speaks a word against the Son of Man will be forgiven, but anyone who blasphemes against the Holy Spirit will not be forgiven. When you are brought before synagogues, rulers and authorities, do not worry about how you will defend yourselves or what you will say, for the Holy Spirit will teach you at that time what you should say.
Luke 12:8-12, NIV

Speak up for Jesus

THE POLICE CAR drew quickly to the curb where Todd was standing with some other children. "Do you kids know Jason Conner?" the officer asked.

"No, sir," answered one of the children.

"I've got to find him in a hurry," the policeman said, looking straight at Todd. Todd said nothing, and the officer drove away.

When Todd later told his friend Kurt what had happened, Kurt frowned. "I think you should have told him that you know Jason," said Kurt. "Jason's our friend, and he's probably playing ball at the park."

"I know, but what if he's in trouble?" asked Todd.

"Well, some friend you are!" scolded Kurt. "Seems like you should stand by him, not act like you don't know him."

Later both boys were sorry to learn why the police were looking for Jason. His parents had been badly injured in a car accident and were hospitalized.

As Kurt and Todd stood in a checkout lane at the supermarket the next day, two men behind them began talking. "I hear your neighbors, the Connors, were in a really bad accident," said one.

"They sure were," replied the other. "They both were really battered. Be out of work at least a month. That will give them plenty of time to wonder where their God was when they got hit. They've been on my back for years about trusting in their God." He glanced down at Kurt, who was staring at him. "Don't let anybody fool you about a loving, caring God, kid. There isn't any."

Kurt looked away and said nothing, but Todd looked up and smiled at the man. "Sir, I know the Connors," he said. "And God *is* their friend, and mine, too. He was with them when they got hurt, and He'll take good care of them. Right, Kurt?"

"Right, Todd," Kurt agreed nervously. With shame he thought of how he had scolded Todd for not admitting he knew Jason. Now by his silence, Kurt had denied his very best friend, the Lord Jesus.

HOW ABOUT YOU? Do you speak up for the Lord when you have a chance? Or, by your silence, do you deny that you even know Him? Ask God to give you the courage to speak up for Him. □ A.L.

TO MEMORIZE: *The Holy Spirit will teach you at that time what you should say.* Luke 12:12, NIV

JEAN WATCHED in horror as elderly Mrs. Carlson tripped over the curb and fell to the ground. Jean ran out of the house to see if her neighbor was hurt. "Don't move," she said when she saw that Mrs. Carlson was in great pain. "I'll get a blanket and call an ambulance." With that she ran into the house.

When Jean returned, Mrs. Carlson looked up and smiled weakly. "I'm so glad you were here," she said. "You seem to know exactly what to do. Thank you."

Soon the ambulance arrived, and Jean watched as the rescue workers carefully lifted Mrs. Carlson into the vehicle. As Jean turned to go back into the house, she uttered a silent prayer for the injured woman.

The next Sunday Jean told her Sunday school teacher about the incident. "I'm sure glad I took a first-aid class," she said. "I knew enough to put a blanket on her so she wouldn't go into shock."

"Great!" exclaimed Miss Berry. "It's good to know what to do in emergencies." She paused briefly. "There's a good spiritual lesson in this," she added. "Just as we should be prepared to give physical help, we should also be prepared to help someone find Christ when we see a need."

Jean was quiet. She had lots of firends who didn't know Jesus as Savior, but she didn't know what to say or how to talk with them about accepting Christ. Actually, she was embarrassed to talk with them about it. She admitted this to her teacher. "I know how you feel," Miss Berry replied. "But you've experienced salvation, and so have I. We need to tell our friends and neighbors what happened to us, as well as show them what a change Christ has brought into our lives. I know the Lord will help us find the right words to use."

Jean thought about Mrs. Carlson again and wondered if she had ever accepted Jesus as her Savior. She decided to go to the hospital and talk to her about it.

HOW ABOUT YOU? Do your friends know that you are a Christian? Have you ever talked with any of them about the new life you have in Christ? Don't be ashamed of sharing your testimony with those who do not believe in Christ. They need Jesus, too. He wants to use you to help those in need.

□ R.J.

TO MEMORIZE: *For I am not ashamed of the gospel of Christ, for it is the power of God to salvation for everyone who believes.* Romans 1:16, NKJV

Ready to Help

FROM THE BIBLE:

I desire to do your will, O my God; your law is within my heart. I proclaim righteousness in the great assembly; I do not seal my lips, as you know, O LORD. I do not hide your righteousness in my heart; I speak of your faithfulness and salvation. I do not conceal your love and your truth from the great assembly.
Psalm 40:8-10, NIV

Be ready to help

JUNE

30

The Mysterious Witness

FROM THE BIBLE:

Blessed is he whose transgressions are forgiven, whose sins are covered. Blessed is the man whose sin the LORD does not count against him and in whose spirit is no deceit. When I kept silent, my bones wasted away through my groaning all day long. For day and night your hand was heavy upon me; my strength was sapped as in the heat of summer. Then I acknowledged my sin to you and did not cover up my iniquity. I said, "I will confess my transgressions to the LORD"—and you forgave the guilt of my sin. Therefore let everyone who is godly pray to you while you may be found; surely when the mighty waters rise, they will not reach him. Do not be like the horse or the mule, which have no understanding but must be controlled by bit and bridle or they will not come to you. Many are the woes of the wicked, but the LORD's unfailing love surrounds the man who trusts in him.
Psalm 32:1-6, 9-10, NIV

God's Spirit convicts

THE RED NUMBERS on the watch flashed eerily in the darkness. Carl sighed and stuffed it under his pillow. Oh, why had he ever stolen it?

Carl had never owned a watch, and when he saw this one displayed on the store counter, it seemed he couldn't resist slipping it into his pocket. Now he realized what a foolish thing he had done. He couldn't wear the watch for fear his folks would notice it. Already he had begun to wonder if anyone at the store had seen him steal it.

Maybe things will seem better today, he thought. But twice on the way to school, he was sure he saw someone following him. At lunchtime he noticed several teachers talking together, and one of them seemed to glance in Carl's direction.

That night as he lay in his bed, Carl heard footsteps in the hallway. "Who's there?" he whispered hoarsely.

The door swung open, and Carl's father stepped in. "I just got up for a drink of water, Son. Is everything all right?"

Something inside Carl seemed to snap. "It's in my top drawer, so go ahead and take it," he sobbed.

Carl poured out the whole story, ending with his impression that everybody seemed to know what he had done. Dad nodded. "I think I know what you mean," he said. "Actually, someone did witness your theft of that watch, and He has been bothering you about it ever since."

"But who, Dad?" Carl wondered.

"The Holy Spirit, Son," explained Dad. "When the Spirit begins to convict people of sin, they often have the miserable feeling that someone is chasing them. You'll have no rest until you stop running from God and do the right thing."

So, on his knees, Carl asked for God's forgiveness. He would take the watch back the very next day and accept the consequences.

HOW ABOUT YOU? Do you ever feel that someone is "out to get you"—that people dislike you or that they don't trust you? Perhaps there is some sin in your heart about which God's Spirit is convicting you. Stop running from Him. Seek the perfect peace of His forgiveness? □ S.K.

TO MEMORIZE: *The wicked flee when no one pursues, but the righteous are bold as a lion.*
Proverbs 28:1, NKJV

"**H**I, MOM!" Tina hugged her mother, who had come to the scout leader's home to pick her up.

"It's great to have you back from camp," Mother said warmly. There was a sudden blast of music from the scout leader's porch. "What's all the noise?"

"Oh, somebody's radio," answered Tina. "We listened to it a lot, especially on the bus ride."

Mother raised her eyebrows. "You know, Tina, your father and I don't approve of that kind of music."

"Oh, Mom!" Tina frowned. "It's just music. No one pays any attention to the words."

Later that day Tina told her mother all about camp. "We sang a lot of song's around the campfire," Tina went on. "But one song was strange! The scout leader said it was a 'Bible song' about Abraham, Isaac, and Jacob, but the song said they were 'fishermen' who 'sailed to Jericho'!"

"So? What's wrong with that?" Mother asked, to Tina's surprise. "I've heard that song, and the tune is catchy. It's fun to sing."

"Mom!" Tina couldn't believe her ears. "Those men weren't fishermen. The song's not true."

"Does it matter?" asked Mother.

"Of course it matters," replied Tina, wondering what had gotten into her mother.

Mother smiled. "Well, I'm glad you realize that the words of the songs we use are important. That goes for all music, not just campfire songs."

Tina was quiet. "You mean that stuff on the radio, don't you?" she said finally.

Mother nodded. "Many of those songs talk about drugs, committing suicide, Satan worship, and all kinds of things the Bible teaches against. Often they have bad language in them as well. As Christians, it's our responsibility to avoid all of that as much as possible."

HOW ABOUT YOU? Are you careful about the music you hear? There are many songs with "nice tunes," but the words or messages may be evil. Listen to the words. If they are not good or true, turn them off. The music you listen to must please the Lord.
□ S.N.

TO MEMORIZE: *Speaking to one another in psalms and hymns and spiritual songs, singing and making melody in your heart to the LORD.*
Ephesians 5:19, NKJV

Abraham, a Fisherman?

FROM THE BIBLE:
Sing to the LORD *a new song, for he has done marvelous things; his right hand and his holy arm have worked salvation for him. The* LORD *has made his salvation known and revealed his righteousness to the nations. He has remembered his love and his faithfulness to the house of Israel; all the ends of the earth have seen the salvation of our God. Shout for joy to the* LORD, *all the earth, burst into jubilant song with music; make music to the* LORD *with the harp, with the harp and the sound of singing, with trumpets and the blast of the ram's horn—shout for joy before the* LORD, *the King. Let the sea resound, and everything in it, the world, and all who live in it. Let the rivers clap their hands, let the mountains sing together for joy; let them sing before the* LORD, *for he comes to judge the earth. He will judge the world in righteousness and the peoples with equity.*
Psalm 98:1-9, NIV

Choose music carefully

2

Once Is Too Often

FROM THE BIBLE:
*Wisdom calls aloud in the street, she raises her voice in the public squares; at the head of the noisy streets she cries out, in the gateways of the city she makes her speech: "How long will you simple ones love your simple ways? How long will mockers delight in mockery and fools hate knowledge? If you had responded to my rebuke, I would have poured out my heart to you and made my thoughts known to you. But since you rejected me when I called and no one gave heed when I stretched out my hand, since you ignored all my advice and would not accept my rebuke, I in turn will laugh at your disaster; I will mock when calamity overtakes you—when calamity overtakes you like a storm, when disaster sweeps over you like a whirlwind, when distress and trouble overwhelm you. Then they will call to me but I will not answer; they will look for me but will not find me."
Proverbs 1:20-28, NIV

Don't try drugs

"UNCLE BOB was in a car accident," said Mother as she hung up the phone. "He and some friends had apparently been taking drugs, and they hit another car. That driver was killed, and Uncle Bob is in a coma." Lisa and Kristen didn't know what to say, and after a moment, Mother continued. "The first time Uncle Bob took drugs he said he just wanted to get high once. He promised not to do it again, but he never quit." Mother turned to leave the room. "Can you play quietly? I'd like some time alone."

"Sure, Mom," they answered sympathetically.

After a few moments, Mother heard a crash. When she went to investigate, she saw pieces of china dolls on the floor. "What happened?" she asked. "You know you're not to handle those dolls. They're antique and very fragile."

"Lisa said it wouldn't hurt to play with them just once," murmured Kristen, looking at the floor, "and I bumped the shelf trying to get them down."

Lisa picked up the pieces. "Can't we fix them?" she asked anxiously. "There aren't many pieces."

"We'll try," said Mother, "but they'll never be the same. And it won't change your punishment for disobeying."

Mother got the glue, and they went to work. "The cracks still show," observed Lisa. "Can't you push the pieces tighter together?"

"They look like scars," Kristen added.

"I'm doing my best," Mom answered. "You know, girls, as I try to repair these, I keep thinking of Uncle Bob. His life is full of scars because of drugs. He never finished school, he lost several jobs, and he had this accident." As she set one doll down to dry, she turned to her daughters. "I'm disappointed that you girls disobeyed and tried to play with these dolls," she said. "When you look at them from now on, I hope you'll be reminded of the results of doing wrong—even one time."

HOW ABOUT YOU? Have you been tempted to try drugs "just once" to see what it's like? Once is too often. In Revelation 9:21 God condemns people for sorceries. Bible scholars say this can also mean drugs. "Doing drugs" for pleasure is evil in God's sight. It's destructive to the body, and taking them "once" could hurt you for life.
□ S.N.

TO MEMORIZE: *You were bought at a price. Therefore honor God with your body.* 1 Corinthians 6:20, NIV

THE HAMILTONS were moving. Beth came into the bedroom just as her mother pulled a box from the closet shelf. "What's in that box, Mother?" she asked.

Mrs. Hamilton smiled. "This box is full of old keepsakes—letters from your dad, school albums, report cards, things like that."

"What else is in there?" Beth poked around in the closet. She pulled a tattered piece of red and white cloth from a metal box. "Look at this old flag. Why don't you throw it away, Mother?"

A faraway look came into her mother's eyes. "That flag was draped over my grandfather's casket when he was shipped home from the war, Beth. He died for that flag."

"Died for this flag?" Beth squealed. "That was foolish."

"I mean he died so we would have the right to fly the flag," replied Mother. "He died for the freedom of our country. For years my grandmother flew that flag on every holiday. It was her most valuable possession. My mother was just a little girl when her father died. All she ever had of him was this flag. It meant a lot to her, and it means a lot to me. Someday I hope you will realize the value of that tattered piece of cloth."

"I know something we have that's even more valuable than this flag, Mother," Beth said quietly. "It's the Bible. We talked in Sunday school about how many of God's children have died so we could have His Word."

"You're right, Beth," Mother agreed. "Even today there are people in prison because they obeyed the Bible."

Mother picked up the flag and lovingly folded it. "How blessed we are to live in a free country where we have the Word of God in our homes and in our hearts. We would lose our freedom if men like Grandpa had not been willing to die for our flag," said Mother, "but we would lose more if we didn't have the Word of God. We would lose our souls and our hope of eternal life in heaven."

HOW ABOUT YOU? Do you realize the value of your Bible? It cost more than dollars and cents. It cost some people their lives. Do you take good care of your Bible or do you toss it around carelessly? Do you read it or lose it? Treasure it. It's valuable!

□ B.W.

TO MEMORIZE: *How can a young man keep his way pure? By living according to your word.* Psalm 119:9, NIV

3

The Tattered Treasure

FROM THE BIBLE:
Even his disciples said, "This is very hard to understand. Who can tell what he means?" Jesus knew within himself that his disciples were complaining and said to them, "Does this offend you? Then what will you think if you see me, the Messiah, return to heaven again? Only the Holy Spirit gives eternal life. Those born only once, with physical birth, will never receive this gift. But now I have told you how to get this true spiritual life. But some of you don't believe me." (For Jesus knew from the beginning who didn't believe and knew the one who would betray him.) And he remarked, "That is what I meant when I said that no one can come to me unless the Father attracts him to me." At this point many of his disciples turned away and deserted him. Then Jesus turned to the Twelve and asked, "Are you going too?" Simon Peter replied, "Master, to whom shall we go? You alone have the words that give eternal life, and we believe them and know you are the holy Son of God."
John 6:60-69, TLB

Treasure your Bible

JULY

No Limit

FROM THE BIBLE:

Come to me and I will give you rest—all of you who work so hard beneath a heavy yoke. Wear my yoke—for it fits perfectly— and let me teach you; for I am gentle and humble, and you shall find rest for your souls; for I give you only light burdens.
Matthew 11:28-30, TLB

Become a citizen of heaven

THE WIND whipped through Sam's hair, and salt water washed his face as the boat approached Liberty Island. "Look! There she is," he yelled. "Get your camera ready, Dad."

"The Statue of Liberty is beautiful!" exclaimed Mother.

"She certainly is some lady," Dad replied warmly.

As they docked, Sam skipped down the gangplank. He couldn't wait to get inside the Statue of Liberty.

After they had enjoyed a guided tour, they headed back to their hotel. "I can remember my grandparents telling what it was like to come to America from Holland," said Dad. "They said the Statue of Liberty was the first sight to welcome them in a strange land."

"I'll bet they were glad to get here," said Sam.

"Yes, they were," Dad replied, "and they were also glad when they became citizens of this country and could finally call America their home."

"Do immigrants still come to America?" Sam wondered.

"Yes," Dad answered, "but not as many as in times past."

"Why?" asked Sam. "Aren't many people interested in peace and freedom anymore?"

"Sure they are," said Dad, "but things have changed now. The poem on the statue says, 'Give me your tired, your poor, your huddled masses yearning to breathe free,' but the door is no longer open to everyone. Since so many people have wanted to come to America, our government has had to put restrictions on the invitation. Criminals and the insane aren't accepted, and there's a quota now on the number that can come each year from any one region. It seems rather sad, but I suppose it's necessary."

"That reminds me of another gateway to freedom," said Mother, "and it is open to everyone. Jesus invites all to come to Him. He offers freedom from sin, and He grants citizenship in heaven to anybody who will come. He won't turn away anyone who asks for salvation."

HOW ABOUT YOU? Have you accepted the invitation of Jesus? Is your citizenship in heaven? His offer is open to everyone. There's no limit to the number of people He will accept. □ J.H.

TO MEMORIZE: *Our citizenship is in heaven. And we eagerly await a Savior from there, the Lord Jesus Christ.* Philippians 3:20, NIV

"I TOLD ALL my friends I was going to Niagara Falls and Canada," sniffed Mindy, "and now—"

"Dad said he was sorry," interrupted twelve-year-old Jeff. "He can't help it that his job made it necessary to change our plans."

"I think we have two choices here," said Mother. "We can mope around all summer feeling sorry for ourselves, or we can be thankful for the things we *are* able to do. We can have a 'celebration summer' with mini-vacations."

"How?" Jeff and Mindy wanted to know. "What would we celebrate?"

"We can celebrate having good health and being together," suggested Dad. "We can enjoy the beauty of God's creation around us."

"And we can do special little things—things we have always planned to do 'someday,'" added Mother.

"Things like touring the pottery factory?" Mindy asked.

Mother nodded. "Yes, and the museum and the bakery."

"And this year we'll make time to go to the Indian powwow and the steam engine show," Dad promised.

"Let's take Granddad James with us," Mindy added. "He would love it."

Mother smiled. "That's a splendid idea. Why don't we include someone on each one of our mini-vacations? Let's share with someone else the good times God gives us."

"Boy, this sounds like lots more fun than riding for days in the car," Jeff told them.

"And this year it won't be just a two-week vacation. Our celebration summer is going to be the best summer ever," said Mindy as she went to find a calendar.

HOW ABOUT YOU? Is your family unable to take a big vacation this year? Why not have mini-vacations? And even if that doesn't work out, you'll be surprised at the good times you can have in your own neighborhood. Enjoy the things around you. And in your planning, don't forget to include someone who may be lonely. Most of all, don't forget to thank God for the many good things He has provided for you to enjoy. □ B.W.

TO MEMORIZE: *Praise be to the LORD, to God our Savior, who daily bears our burdens.*
Psalm 68:19, NIV

JULY

5

Celebration Summer

FROM THE BIBLE:

Praise the LORD, O my soul; all my inmost being, praise his holy name. Praise the LORD, O my soul, and forget not all his benefits—who forgives all your sins and heals all your diseases, who redeems your life from the pit and crowns you with love and compassion, who satisfies your desires with good things so that your youth is renewed like the eagle's. The LORD works righteousness and justice for all the oppressed. He made known his ways to Moses, his deeds to the people of Israel: The LORD is compassionate and gracious, slow to anger, abounding in love. He will not always accuse, nor will he harbor his anger forever; he does not treat us as our sins deserve or repay us according to our iniquities. For as high as the heavens are above the earth, so great is his love for those who fear him; as far as the east is from the west, so far has he removed our transgressions from us. As a father has compassion on his children, so the LORD has compassion on those who fear him. Psalm 103:1-13, NIV

Enjoy blessings around you

6

Patch It Up

FROM THE BIBLE:

The mouth of the righteous is a well of life, but violence covers the mouth of the wicked. Hatred stirs up strife, but love covers all sins. Wisdom is found on the lips of him who has understanding, but a rod is for the back of him who is devoid of understanding. Wise people store up knowledge, but the mouth of the foolish is near destruction. The rich man's wealth is his strong city; the destruction of the poor is their poverty. The labor of the righteous leads to life, the wages of the wicked to sin. He who keeps instruction is in the way of life, but he who refuses reproof goes astray. Whoever hides hatred has lying lips, and whoever spreads slander is a fool. In the multitude of words sin is not lacking, but he who restrains his lips is wise. The tongue of the righteous is choice silver; the heart of the wicked is worth little. The lips of the righteous feed many, but fools die for lack of wisdom.
Proverbs 10:11-21, NKJV

Don't make problems worse

ANGELA LOOKED at her brother in disgust. "There's a hole in your pants!" she exclaimed. "Go change them."

Mother shook her head and sighed. "His only good pair is in the wash, so he'll just have to wear these," she said. "Just make sure you don't pick at the hole, Jason. That will make it bigger."

Angela pouted. "Why do we have to wear such worn-out clothes to school, Mom? I'm sick of being poor!"

Mother sighed again. "You know we can't afford new clothes since the divorce, Honey," she said. "I could work more hours, but then I wouldn't have much time left for you kids. I think family life is more important than material things. Maybe I can get something nice at the Salvation Army store next week."

"Maybe if you had been a better wife to Dad, he wouldn't have left us," grumbled Angela. She tried not to see the tears that came to her mother's eyes.

On the way home from school, Angela noticed that the hole in Jason's pants was bigger. "You've been picking at that hole, haven't you?" she scolded. "Every time you pick at it, you only make it harder for Mom to patch it up."

Jason looked truly ashamed. "I do it without thinking," he said. "I don't want to make things harder for Mom." He paused, then added, "You do the same thing, you know."

"I do not!" retorted his sister.

"I'm talking about the way you treat Mom," explained Jason. "You know how awful she feels about the divorce and not having much money. But you always pick at her about it."

Angela was silent for a few moments. "I guess I do," she admitted. "I know it's not her fault."

"Mom will patch my jeans tonight," Jason said, "and I think we should do some patching, too. Let's try to 'patch up' Mom's problems rather than making them worse."

HOW ABOUT YOU? Do you have a problem at home? Instead of feeling angry or discouraged, do what you can to make the situation better. Pray about it, be as cheerful as possible, and be supportive and loving toward others. The Lord may use you to improve your home life. Most important, you'll be pleasing Him! □ S.K.

TO MEMORIZE: *In the multitude of words sin is not lacking, but he who restrains his lips is wise.*
Proverbs 10:19, NKJV

BEING a pastor's daughter didn't make it any easier for Bette to move to a new home, but her father felt the Lord wanted them on an Indian reservation in Florida. She felt discouraged and out of place. She longed to return to the city where her father's church had been filled every Sunday with people eager to hear the Word of God. Here, only one Indian family seemed interested in church, and they didn't come regularly.

One Saturday Bette's family went to the beach for the day. They were all amazed to see numerous starfish lying on the beach. "Perhaps they got stranded by the tide," suggested Dad, "or maybe they got washed up during the storm last night."

As they walked, they saw a man pick up something and put it into the water. When they approached the stranger, they greeted him. "What are you doing?" Dad asked.

"I'm putting starfish back into the ocean," the man told them. "If they don't get into the water, they'll die!"

Bette looked at all the starfish on the sand. "But there are so many!" she exclaimed. "You can't save them all, so what difference will it make if you save just a few?"

The man smiled. "It will make a difference to this one," he said, as he picked up a starfish and put it in the water.

That evening as Bette sat on the front steps, she saw an Indian girl coming down the path. *I suppose I should invite her to Sunday school,* she thought, *but even if she does come, church still will be practically empty.* Suddenly she sat up straight, remembering the starfish. Jumping up, she ran toward the girl. "Hi," she said with a smile. "I'm Bette. My dad preaches in that church over there, and we have such a good time in Sunday school. Will you come tomorrow?"

Maybe this was the one person to whom her invitation would make a difference.

HOW ABOUT YOU? Do you ever complain about being the lonely Christian at home? In your neighborhood? In your classroom? Does winning others to the Lord seem like too big a task? Maybe God has put you there because He wants to use you to make a difference in just one life. If only one person trusts the Lord as a result of your witness, it will be worth it. □ J.H.

TO MEMORIZE: *There is joy in the presence of the angels of God over one sinner who repents.* Luke 15:10, NKJV

JULY

7

Starfish and People

FROM THE BIBLE:
So He spoke this parable to them, saying: "What man of you, having a hundred sheep, if he loses one of them, does not leave the ninety-nine in the wilderness, and go after the one which is lost until he finds it? And when he has found it, he lays it on his shoulders, rejoicing. And when he comes home, he calls together his friends and neighbors, saying to them, 'Rejoice with me, for I have found my sheep which was lost!' I say to you that likewise there will be more joy in heaven over one sinner who repents than over ninety-nine just persons who need no repentance. Or what woman, having ten silver coins, if she loses one coin, does not light a lamp, sweep the house, and seek diligently until she finds it? And when she has found it, she calls her friends and neighbors together, saying, 'Rejoice with me, for I have found the piece which I lost!' Likewise, I say to you, there is joy in the presence of the angels of God over one sinner who repents."
Luke 15:3-10, NKJV

Every person is important

JULY

8

The Missing Piece

FROM THE BIBLE:

Out of the depths I cry to you, O LORD; O LORD, hear my voice. Let your ears be attentive to my cry for mercy. If you, O LORD, kept a record of sins, O LORD, who could stand? But with you there is forgiveness; therefore you are feared. I wait for the LORD, my soul waits, and in his word I put my hope. My soul waits for the LORD more than watchmen wait for the morning, more than watchmen wait for the morning. O Israel, put your hope in the LORD, for with the LORD is unfailing love and with him is full redemption. He himself will redeem Israel from all their sins.
Psalm 130, NIV

My heart is not proud, O LORD, my eyes are not haughty; I do not concern myself with great matters or things too wonderful for me. But I have stilled and quieted my soul; like a weaned child with its mother, like a weaned child is my soul within me. O Israel, put your hope in the LORD both now and forevermore.
Psalm 131, NIV

Don't insist on your own way

KAREN HUNG UP the phone and went into the den where her parents were assembling a jigsaw puzzle. "That was Cindy Lawson," she announced glumly. "She called to tell me she got a job for the summer baby-sitting the Tyler kids. Isn't that awful?"

Mother looked puzzled, "I think it sounds like a nice opportunity for Cindy."

"But I wanted that job," grumbled Karen. "Why does Cindy get all the breaks?"

"You sound just a little bit jealous," said Dad. "Cindy's your friend. You should be glad for her. Besides, you'll find other things to do this summer."

"No, I won't," Karen pouted. Then her face brightened. "Maybe if I call Cindy back and tell her how much I wanted the job, she'll let me have it. I've done plenty of things for her."

"I think you ought to let the matter drop," said Mother.

"But I'm sure God wants *me* to have this job," whined Karen. Then she glanced at her father curiously. He had picked up a puzzle piece and had gotten out a pair of scissors. He seemed to be considering cutting the piece of puzzle. "Dad, what are you doing?" Karen asked.

"I'm trying to fit this piece into this empty spot," explained Dad. "If I cut off this bump here and glue it onto the other side, I can make it fit."

"You know that won't work," scolded Karen. "Besides, you need that piece somewhere else in the puzzle."

Mother laughed. "I think I know what your father is trying to say, Karen. That puzzle piece represents you."

"Right," said Dad. "Trying to jam that piece into a place where it doesn't fit is like you trying to get your own way about that job. Even if you succeeded, you would miss out on whatever God had planned for you."

"I see." Karen grinned. "I know you're right, of course. And I love the way you point things out to me."

HOW ABOUT YOU? Do you get upset when things don't go the way you want? Remember that God is in control, and He knows what's best for you. Let Him put you in the right place at the right time. Be patient and wait for Him. □ S.K.

TO MEMORIZE: *My soul waits for the LORD more than watchmen wait for the morning, more than watchmen wait for the morning.* Psalm 130:6, NIV

As PAULA PACKED her suitcase, memories came flooding into her mind of her wonderful week at church camp the previous summer. She remembered new friends she had made—Becky and Elsa. She remembered the fun of swimming, ball games, and craft times. But the best memory of all was of the night she had truly understood the gospel for the first time and had asked Jesus to come into her heart. She started to sing the camp theme song at the top of her lungs.

"Whoa, little sister! You sure are happy today." It was Paula's big brother, Bob, who was home from Bible college for the summer. "Looking forward to camp, eh? The place where we meet the Lord is often special to us."

That evening Bob led in family devotions. Paula thought his choice of Scripture seemed a little strange. He read about Jacob's two trips to Bethel. And he explained that the name Jacob called the place on the second trip—El Bethel—meant "God of Bethel." When he prayed, he asked the Lord to give Paula a wonderful time and great blessing at camp. "But help us all to learn, like Jacob did, that it's the *God* of the place, not the *place*, that we serve," he finished.

When Paula arrived at camp the next day, everything seemed wrong. The tabernacle had been torn down and replaced with a new chapel. Becky and Elsa hadn't come back. There was a different speaker. Paula didn't feel close to God as she had thought she would. She wished she could go home.

It wasn't until they sang "Into My Heart" at the close of the evening service that Paula realized something. It was the God of Camp Carlson, not the camp, that had changed her life. Camp was a place where she would learn more about Him and have many more wonderful times. But it was God she worshiped, and He was still the same. She bowed her head and thanked Him.

HOW ABOUT YOU? Is there a special place where you feel close to God? Perhaps the place you found Him as your Savior? While it's nice to remember and go back to that place, be sure that you worship God, not the place. □ R.P.

TO MEMORIZE: *Jesus answered, "It is written: 'Worship the Lord your God and serve him only'."* Luke 4:8, NIV

The God of Camp Carlson

FROM THE BIBLE:
Then Jacob awoke from his sleep and said, "Surely the LORD is in this place, and I did not know it." And he was afraid and said, "How awesome is this place! This is none other than the house of God, and this is the gate of heaven!" Then Jacob rose early in the morning, and took the stone that he had put at his head, set it up as a pillar, and poured oil on top of it. And he called the name of that place Bethel; but the name of that city had been Luz previously. . . . Then God said to Jacob, "Arise, go up to Bethel and dwell there; and make an altar there to God, who appeared to you when you fled from the face of Esau your brother." And he built an altar there and called the place El Bethel, because there God appeared to him when he fled from the face of his brother. Genesis 28:16-19; 35:1, 7, NKJV

Worship God, not a place

10

A Fish out of Water

FROM THE BIBLE:

There are different kinds of gifts, but the same Spirit. There are different kinds of service, but the same Lord. There are different kinds of working, but the same God works all of them in all men. Now to each one the manifestation of the Spirit is given for the common good. To one there is given through the Spirit the message of wisdom, to another the message of knowledge by means of the same Spirit, to another faith by the same Spirit, to another gifts of healing by that one Spirit, to another miraculous powers, to another prophecy, to another distinguishing between spirits, to another speaking in different kinds of tongues, and to still another the interpretation of tongues. . . . For we were all baptized by one Spirit into one body—whether Jews or Greeks, slave or free—and we were all given the one Spirit to drink. Now the body is not made up of one part but of many.
1 Corinthians 12:4-10, 13-14, NIV

Worship God with others

AS THE SMALL ROWBOAT rocked with the gentle motion of the water, Billy watched his father cast his fishing line. "Dad," said Billy, "I don't want to go to the new church tomorrow."

"Really?" asked Dad. "Why not?"

"All my friends are back at our old church," replied Billy. "I know we had to move because of your job, but I'm going to miss our pastor and my friends."

Billy's dad slowly reeled in his line a little and looked at his son. "I'm going to miss everybody, too," he said, "but we still need to worship God and learn more about Him."

"But can't we just have church by ourselves at home?" asked Billy. "You could play your guitar, and we could sing. Then you and Mom could teach us from the Bible."

"Hold on a minute," said Dad. "I've got a bite." In a few moments he held up a small bluegill. "What would happen if we just threw this fish in the boat and left it there?"

"It would die," said Billy.

"And if we throw it back?" asked Dad as he threw the fish back into the lake.

"Well, now it will live."

"What if we took the fish to another lake and let it loose?" Dad asked next. "Would it be able to live there?"

Billy thought a moment. "I think so," he said.

"Well," said Dad, "our family is a little like a fish that's taken from one lake and put into another. We're in a new place, but we have everything we need to go on living—food, clothes, a home." He paused. "As Christians, there is one more thing we need," he added. "We need to be around other Christians. In a church, we worship God together. Oh, if we don't go, we don't actually die—like a fish out of water—but by going and caring for one another, we show the world that there is a living God. And it's something Christians need in order to keep on living for Him."

Billy was silent. "Dad," he said finally, "this is one 'fish' you've convinced."

HOW ABOUT YOU? Have you felt out of place when you had to change churches? If you're a Christian, you're really out of place—like a fish out of water—when you don't attend church. Meeting with other Christians is an important part of worshiping God. □ D.A.B.

TO MEMORIZE: *Now the body is not made up of one part but of many.* 1 Corinthians 12:14, NIV

SANDY WAS so happy! When she opened her birthday present, she found a beautiful doll! Every day after that, Sandy played with her doll. She pretended it was a real baby, and she treated it like one, pretending to feed it and put it to bed.

One day as Sandy was playing with her doll, she felt as though she needed to be with her mother for a while. Mother was always so busy with the new baby, and it had been a long time since Sandy and her mother had played a game together. "Please, Mother," begged Sandy, "will you play this game with me?"

"Not now, Dear," answered Mother. "I'm giving the baby her bath. Just play with your doll until I get finished. Then I'll play with you."

So Sandy sat and pretended to rock her doll to sleep. But she felt lonely. She still loved her doll, but she wanted someone to talk with her. Though she often talked to her doll, it couldn't answer her.

It seemed like a long time before Mother finished taking care of the baby. Finally Mother said, "Ready, Sandy?" Together they sat down on the floor and began the game. Sandy was happy now. It felt so good to be able to talk and laugh with Mother. She gave a contented sigh.

Mother put her arms around Sandy and said, "You were feeling lonely, weren't you, Honey?"

"Yes, I was. But I'm not now," answered Sandy.

"But don't you love your doll anymore?" asked Mother.

"Oh yes," said Sandy, "I still love her as much as I ever did. But I needed someone to love me back."

"Oh, Sandy," said Mother giving her a kiss, "I love you very much. You know, I think God must feel the same way you do. He could have made us just like dolls, to do whatever He makes us do. But He made us real people so we'd be able to love Him back. Let's tell God right now that we're glad He loves us, and that we love Him, too."

HOW ABOUT YOU? God shows you every day how much He loves you. Do you show Him that you love Him back? One way to do this is by obeying His commands. Another is by telling Him in prayer that you love Him. If you do love God, tell Him right now. □ C.Y.

TO MEMORIZE: *God is love, and he who abides in love abides in God, and God in him.*
1 John 4:16, NKJV

Love Returned

FROM THE BIBLE:
And we have known and believed the love that God has for us. God is love, and he who abides in love abides in God, and God in him. Love has been perfected among us in this: that we may have boldness in the day of judgment; because as He is, so are we in this world. There is no fear in love; but perfect love casts out fear, because fear involves torment. But he who fears has not been made perfect in love. We love Him because He first loved us. If someone says, "I love God," and hates his brother, he is a liar; for he who does not love his brother whom he has seen, how can he love God whom he has not seen? And this commandment we have from Him: that he who loves God must love his brother also.
1 John 4:16-21, NKJV

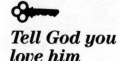

Tell God you love him

JULY

12

More Than Sand

FROM THE BIBLE:

Many, O LORD my God, are the wonders you have done. The things you planned for us no one can recount to you; were I to speak and tell of them, they would be too many to declare.
Psalm 40:5, NIV

I praise you because I am fearfully and wonderfully made; your works are wonderful, I know that full well. My frame was not hidden from you when I was made in the secret place. When I was woven together in the depths of the earth, your eyes saw my unformed body. All the days ordained for me were written in your book before one of them came to be. How precious to me are your thoughts, O God! How vast is the sum of them! Were I to count them, they would outnumber the grains of sand. When I awake, I am still with you.
Psalm 139:14-18, NIV

You are special

"NINE, TEN, ELEVEN." Julie painstakingly separated tiny pieces of sand from the pile she held in her hand and dropped them, grain by grain, into her pail.

"Are you just going to sit on this beach blanket, trying to count sand?" asked her brother Rick. "You could've stayed home in the sandbox."

"There must be more sand than anything else in the whole world," Julie exclaimed, ignoring her brother's remark. Rick rolled his eyes, picked up his float, and headed toward the water.

Julie stayed on the blanket, counting sand. After a little while her father looked up from the book he was reading. "How's the counting? Do you think you'll be able to finish the whole beach this afternoon?" he teased.

Julie sprinkled the remaining sand she held over her feet. "I give up," she said. "I can't even count one handful. There's so much sand on this beach, and it goes down deep, too. How much sand is there, Dad?"

Dad laughed. "There is no way we could begin to count all the sand in the world," he said. "Isn't that wonderful?"

Julie was puzzled. *"Wonderful?"* she asked. "Why is that wonderful?"

Dad reached into the tote bag packed with books, towels, and lotion. He took out a small Bible and turned to Psalm 139. "It says here that God's thoughts concerning us outnumber the grains of sand," he said. "Just think of that!" He scooped up a handful of sand. "God's love for us is endless."

Julie filled her bucket to the top with sand. Then she tipped it over and watched the millions of particles pour out. "Yes," she agreed. "It is wonderful, isn't it?"

HOW ABOUT YOU? Do you sometimes wonder if you matter? Do your brothers or sisters or classmates say things that leave you feeling worthless? God made each person very special to Him. The next time you feel less than special, think about how much sand there is over the entire earth. Then thank God that you are so special to Him that His thoughts for you are far more than all the grains of sand in the world. □ N.E.K.

TO MEMORIZE: *How precious to me are your thoughts, O God! How vast is the sum of them!* Psalm 139:17, NIV

THE SOUND of breaking glass brought Dale running into the dining room. "Ooohhh, Melissa! Look what you've done!" he gasped. Melissa stared in horror at the shattered pieces of crystal on the floor. "You broke Mom's favorite vase!" Dale exclaimed. "It's the one Uncle Don bought her just before he died. Boy, will she be mad!"

"I couldn't help it," said Melissa nervously.

"What's the matter?" The children both jumped at the sound of Mother's voice. Sorrow spread over her face as she realized what had happened.

Melissa burst into sobs. "I didn't mean to. I was just looking for a pencil, and it fell. Oh! I'm sorry."

Mother put her arm around Melissa. "There, there, Honey. Don't cry so!"

"Does she have to buy you another one?" asked Dale. "It'll probably take all her savings to replace it."

"No. Some things can't be replaced," Mother said sadly.

"Then are you going to ground her?" Dale wanted to know. Mother shook her head. "Spank her?" was Dale's next question. Again Mother shook her head. Dale was astounded. "Aren't you going to punish her at all?"

"No," Mother sighed. "Melissa has learned that she needs to be more careful."

Dale shrugged in disgust. "If I had broken it, I wouldn't have been able to sit down for a week!"

"That's not true!" Mother denied. Then she wisely added, "Don't be jealous when mercy is shown to someone else. Mercy is something for which we should all be very grateful. Except for the mercy of God, we would all receive the eternal punishment we deserve. So thank God for His mercy to you, and be glad when mercy is given to others, also. Who knows? Tomorrow you may need it again yourself."

As Dale was digesting this, Melissa began picking up pieces of the vase. "I'll get the trash can," Dale said. "I can help you."

HOW ABOUT YOU? Do you grumble when others are not punished as you think they should be? God tells you to "love mercy," even when it is given to others. If you are merciful, you will receive mercy. And you never know when you will need it. □ B.W.

TO MEMORIZE: *He has showed you, O man, what is good. And what does the LORD require of you? To act justly and to love mercy and to walk humbly with your God.* Micah 6:8, NIV

No Punishment

FROM THE BIBLE:

"Well," you may be saying, "what terrible people you have been talking about!" But wait a minute! You are just as bad. When you say they are wicked and should be punished, you are talking about yourselves, for you do these very same things. And we know that God, in justice, will punish anyone who does such things as these. Do you think that God will judge and condemn others for doing them and overlook you when you do them, too? Don't you realize how patient he is being with you? Or don't you care? Can't you see that he has been waiting all this time without punishing you, to give you time to turn from your sin? His kindness is meant to lead you to repentance.
Romans 2:1-4, TLB

Love mercy

JULY

14

Slivers and Sanding

FROM THE BIBLE:

Let God train you, for he is doing what any loving father does for his children. Whoever heard of a son who was never corrected? If God doesn't punish you when you need it, as other fathers punish their sons, then it means that you aren't really God's son at all—that you don't really belong in his family. Since we respect our fathers here on earth, though they punish us, should we not all the more cheerfully submit to God's training so that we can begin really to live? Our earthly fathers trained us for a few brief years, doing the best for us that they knew how, but God's correction is always right and for our best good, that we may share his holiness. Being punished isn't enjoyable while it is happening—it hurts! But afterwards we can see the result, a quiet growth in grace and character.

Hebrews 12:7-11, TLB

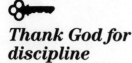

Thank God for discipline

"OUCH!" Ken stopped sanding the birdhouse he was making and looked at the sliver in his finger. He put down his tools and went to get help from his mother.

She met him at the kitchen door. "I was coming to look for you," she said. "I was just informed that you've been teasing Todd Berry and calling him names. Is this true?"

"Eric started it," murmured Ken. "Besides, Todd is such a sissy!" Suddenly he remembered the sliver. He held up his finger. "Look, Mom. The rough wood of my birdhouse did this to me."

"We'd better get that out before it starts to fester," Mother said. She got a needle and tweezers, and as gently as possible she worked on Ken's finger. The sliver went deep, but finally she held it up in triumph.

Ken looked at his sore finger. "Thanks, Mom," he said. "I'll go sand down that old birdhouse so it won't ever do that again!" He started for the door.

"Just a minute," said Mother. "It seems to me that just as the rough wood gave you a sliver, you gave Todd a 'sliver.' You hurt him by your words and actions. The things you said are probably still bothering him. They may be starting to 'fester.' Can you think of a way to remove that 'sliver'?"

Ken looked at his feet. He knew he had done wrong. "I'm sorry," he said finally. "I'll tell Todd I'm sorry, too."

"That should help some," said Mother. "You also need to confess what you've done to God and ask His forgiveness. But there's one more thing: Your father and I have talked with you about this problem before, and this time we'll have to do a little 'sanding' to help you avoid giving any more 'slivers.' That means being grounded for a few days."

Solemnly Ken nodded. "Okay," he said humbly. "My sore finger will remind me that I deserve what I'm getting."

HOW ABOUT YOU? Do you have rough edges that give "slivers" to other people? Do you say unkind things? Refuse to share? Snub others? Thank God for parents who help "sand you down" into a likable, useful person. Thank Him for the discipline you receive. Ask Him to help you improve your behavior. □ H.M.

TO MEMORIZE: *Being punished isn't enjoyable while it is happening—it hurts! But afterwards we can see the result, a quiet growth in grace and character.* Hebrews 12:11, TLB

"LOOKS GOOD, guys." Brent stood back and surveyed the side of the barn. "Be sure to brush the paint out nice and smooth." He and his younger brothers, Pat and Sam, were busy painting, and Brent was in charge. He had helped Dad paint before, so now he was showing his brothers how.

As they worked, the boys' conversation turned to their friend Keith, who lived nearby. "Keith asked me some questions about our church and what we believe," said Sam.

"Maybe we should ask the pastor to call on his family," suggested Brent.

"Yeah," agreed Pat. "They need to know about Jesus, and it's the pastor's job to tell them."

Soon Mother came out with a tray of cookies and milk. While the boys were eating, she talked with them. "Brent," she said, "since you were the only one who knew how to paint, why didn't Dad tell you to paint the barn alone?"

"Because the job was too big for one person," said Brent.

"Dad figured Brent could teach Sam and me to paint," Pat added. "Aren't we doing okay?"

"Oh, you're doing fine," Mother assured him. "But I overheard you say that it's the pastor's job to tell people about Jesus. He should do that, of course, but that job is too big for one person, too. The Bible says the pastor's primary job is to 'equip the saints for the work of ministry.' He is to teach Christians to serve God."

"He does lots of that in his sermons," observed Sam. "He teaches those special evangelistic training classes, too."

Mother nodded. "The pastor teaches us how to help tell others about Jesus, just like Brent taught the rest of you how to help him paint the barn."

"That makes sense," said Brent. "We better pay more attention so we'll be ready to answer Keith's questions."

HOW ABOUT YOU? Do you listen carefully to your pastor? Are you doing your best to serve God? It's not just the pastor's job. You need to be equipped, or prepared, to serve, too. The Lord uses pastors to help with much of that preparation. □ T.V.B.

TO MEMORIZE: *And He Himself gave some to be apostles, some prophets, some evangelists, and some pastors and teachers, for the equipping of the saints for the work of ministry.* Ephesians 4:11-12, NKJV

JULY

15

The Witness

FROM THE BIBLE:
And He Himself gave some to be apostles, some prophets, some evangelists, and some pastors and teachers, for the equipping of the saints for the work of ministry, for the edifying of the body of Christ, till we all come to the unity of the faith and the knowledge of the Son of God, to a perfect man, to the measure of the stature of the fullness of Christ.
Ephesians 4:11-13, NKJV

Learn from your pastor

JULY

16

The Witness

(Continued from yesterday)

FROM THE BIBLE:

About noon as I came near Damascus, suddenly a bright light from heaven flashed around me. I fell to the ground and heard a voice say to me, "Saul! Saul! Why do you persecute me?" "Who are you, Lord?" I asked. "I am Jesus of Nazareth, whom you are persecuting," he replied. "What shall I do, Lord?" I asked. "Get up," the Lord said, "and go into Damascus. There you will be told all that you have been assigned to do." My companions led me by the hand into Damascus, because the brilliance of the light had blinded me. A man named Ananias came to see me. He was a devout observer of the law and highly respected by all the Jews living there. He stood beside me and said, "Brother Saul, receive your sight!" And at that very moment I was able to see him. Then he said: "The God of our fathers has chosen you to know his will and to see the Righteous One and to hear words from his mouth. You will be his witness to all men of what you have seen and heard."
Acts 22:6-15, NIV

Tell how Jesus saved you

BRENT RAN excitedly into the house. "I'm going over to play with Keith pretty soon, Mom," he said. "How can I help him be sure he's going to heaven?"

"Well," said Mom, "how did you help your brothers know how to paint the barn? Did you tell them how some of the world's great artists mix colors? Or did you explain various types of strokes and painting techniques?"

"Of course not." Brent gave her a puzzled look. "I just told them what Dad told me and showed them how I did it."

Mother nodded. "You started with your own experience, didn't you? Why not do that when you talk to Keith about the Lord, too?" she suggested. "Tell him how you became a Christian. That's what the Apostle Paul often did."

"That's a great idea, Mom," agreed Brent.

Later that day Brent went over to Keith's house. "Hi, Brent," said Keith. "Come on in and see the model airplane I've been working on."

Brent looked at the model. "Wow!" he exclaimed. "That's a great model. Where did you get it?"

"My Uncle Fred gave it to me. He was going to help me build it, but he had his heart attack and died before we could get started," said Keith sadly. "I sure miss him."

"I'm sorry your uncle died," replied Brent. "Once you told me you were sure he went to heaven. Why did you say that?"

"He told me," Keith replied. "It had something to do with Jesus, but I never listened very well. I wish I had."

"I'm sure I'm going to heaven when I die," Brent replied. "Would you like me to tell you why?"

"Sure!" Keith exclaimed. "How can you be so positive?"

"When I was younger . . . ," began Brent. Keith leaned forward and listened carefully as Brent explained what had happened to him.

HOW ABOUT YOU? Do you tell your friends what you know about Jesus? Don't feel that you have to explain all the doctrines of the church. The words in today's memory verse were given to the Apostle Paul. Learn and apply them to yourself, too. Simply tell your friends what Jesus did for you. Then maybe they'll become Christians, too. □ T.V.B.

TO MEMORIZE: *You will be his witness to all men of what you have seen and heard.* Acts 22:15, NIV

"OH, THIS LETTER to Grandma is so messy," Sheila wailed.

Mother looked at the paper Sheila was holding up. "How did it get so messed up?" she asked.

"I erased a whole paragraph and did it over," explained Sheila. "I tried to erase carefully, but it still looks messy."

"Well, if you want to send it today, you'll have to leave it the way it is," replied Mother. "The mailman is coming down the street now. I think Grandma will understand." So Sheila reluctantly sealed the envelope and put it in the mailbox.

Later Sheila looked unhappy when she came in from playing outdoors. Mother glanced at her. "Is something bothering you, Honey?" she asked.

Sheila's voice shook as she replied, "I don't think Jane likes me anymore," she said. "Ever since I took her doll, she doesn't really want to play with me—I can tell. I took it back and told her how sorry I am. She said she forgave me, but she doesn't act like it." A tear rolled down Sheila's cheek. "I bet God hasn't forgiven me, either."

"Were you really sorry?" asked Mother. "Are you determined such a thing will never happen again?" Sheila nodded. "Then," said Mother, "God has forgiven you. And I believe Jane has, too, but it may take time to gain her trust again." She put an arm around Sheila. "Remember the letter to Grandma? You erased part of it, but it left the page a bit messy. Life is a little like that. We are writing a page in our lives each day. Sometimes we make mistakes—we sin. God has graciously provided a way to have those sins erased. But as far as people are concerned, that page in our lives is never quite the same again. Often it takes time before people can fully trust us. You see, sin—even though it's forgiven—leaves a mark on our lives here on earth. So be patient with Jane. Show her that you can be trusted."

HOW ABOUT YOU? Have you messed up a page in your life? If you're truly sorry and confess your sin to God, He will freely forgive you. As far as He is concerned, that sin is totally blotted out. Yet sin does leave its mark. Be patient when others need time before they can fully trust you again. Ask the Lord to help you live a pure life each day before Him and before others. □ H.M.

TO MEMORIZE: *Let us pursue the things which make for peace and the things by which one may edify another.* Romans 14:19, NKJV

FROM THE BIBLE:
For none of us lives to himself, and no one dies to himself. For if we live, we live to the Lord; and if we die, we die to the Lord. Therefore, whether we live or die, we are the Lord's. . . . for the kingdom of God is not food and drink, but righteousness and peace and joy in the Holy Spirit. For he who serves Christ in these things is acceptable to God and approved by men. Therefore let us pursue the things which make for peace and the things by which one may edify another.
Romans 14:7-8, 17-19, NKJV

Sin leaves its mark

18

Reflections

When Moses came down from Mount Sinai with the two tablets of the Testimony in his hands, he was not aware that his face was radiant because he had spoken with the LORD. When Aaron and all the Israelites saw Moses, his face was radiant, and they were afraid to come near him. But Moses called to them; so Aaron and all the leaders of the community came back to him, and he spoke to them. Afterward all the Israelites came near him, and he gave them all the commands the LORD had given him on Mount Sinai. When Moses finished speaking to them, he put a veil over his face. But whenever he entered the LORD's presence to speak with him, he removed the veil until he came out. And when he came out and told the Israelites what he had been commanded, they saw that his face was radiant. Then Moses would put the veil back over his face until he went in to speak with the LORD.

Exodus 34:29-35, NIV

Reflect Jesus

"**W**ELL?" Lisa looked at her sister, Beth. "Do I look like Tara?" Lisa held a picture in a magazine under her chin as she gazed into the mirror. She had worked long to get her hair arranged like that of the famous movie star.

Beth shrugged. "A little, maybe. Come on, we've got to go." They were on their way to the lake before Lisa mentioned the movie star again.

"Tara's so beautiful." Lisa sighed as she stared at the picture in the magazine.

"Why do you want to be like her?" asked Beth.

"Hasn't she been married several times?" asked Mom.

"Yes," said Beth, "and she's been arrested for drugs."

"This magazine says she has the most exciting life in the world," Lisa said.

When they reached the lake, everyone piled out of the car, and soon they were enjoying a picnic lunch. "The lake's lovely today. Look how blue it is," Mom observed.

The water isn't really blue, though," said Dad. "The lake is reflecting the sky."

After the picnic, they were busy with hiking, fishing, and other activities. "It looks like rain," said Dad when he noticed the gathering clouds. "We'd better go."

Soon they were on their way. "Look at the lake now." Mom pointed toward the water.

"Its not blue anymore—it's gray. It's reflecting the clouds," said Beth.

"And it isn't beautiful anymore," added Lisa.

"The lake doesn't have a choice about what it reflects," said Mom thoughtfully, "but in our lives, we can choose."

Lisa knew Mom was thinking about Tara Tarton. *Tara's life is gray compared to the beautiful life of Jesus,* Lisa admitted to herself. *I should be reflecting Him and no one else.* She shoved the magazine under the seat. She had better things to think about on the way home.

HOW ABOUT YOU? Is your life reflecting the beauty of Jesus? Compared to Him, the life of any singer or ball player, or of any friend or relative, is gray. Reflect Jesus and His way of life, not that of someone else. □ K.R.A.

TO MEMORIZE: *But we all, with unveiled face, beholding as in a mirror the glory of the Lord, are being transformed into the same image from glory to glory, just as by the Spirit of the Lord.*
2 Corinthians 3:18, NKJV

I WISH THIS feeling would never end, Julie thought as she sat near the campfire with her youth group friends. At this moment, as she and her Christian friends sang God's praises, she felt closer to Him than ever before. But the feeling would end. She'd been to retreats before, and she knew that on Monday morning she wouldn't feel nearly as close to God. *If I don't feel close to God on Monday, maybe this feeling of God's presence is just in my head. Maybe He isn't real at all.* Julie tried to forget these ideas, but she couldn't.

When Julie arrived home the next day, Mom was busy with dinner preparations. "My cousin, Pauline, is coming for dinner," Mom explained as she scurried about.

"I didn't know you had a cousin named Pauline," said Julie as she began to help.

Julie found Pauline delightful. She entertained them all during dinner with funny stories about Mom's childhood. "I'm glad I got to know you," Julie told her. "And just think, a few hours ago I didn't know you existed."

"Shame on your mom for not mentioning me," Pauline said with a wink. "But I've been here all along."

The words stuck with Julie. Cousin Pauline's existence wasn't dependent on Julie knowing about her or "feeling her presence." It was the same with God. *I've been a Doubting Thomas,* Julie told herself. Thomas doubted Jesus was really alive until he saw Him. Julie had doubted God was real because she didn't always feel His presence.

"Tell us about the retreat," suggested Mom.

"It was great," Julie said. "Really great."

HOW ABOUT YOU? Have you ever felt God to be especially close, only to be doubtful of His presence when you no longer felt that way? It's nice to feel God's presence, but it's important to know He is there whether you have the "feeling" or not. Don't rely on feelings. Rely on God's Word.
□ K.R.A.

TO MEMORIZE: *Blessed are those who have not seen and yet have believed.* John 20:29, NIV

No More Doubts

FROM THE BIBLE:
Now Thomas (called Didymus), one of the Twelve, was not with the disciples when Jesus came. So the other disciples told him, "We have seen the Lord!" But he said to them, "Unless I see the nail marks in his hands and put my finger where the nails were, and put my hand into his side, I will not believe it." A week later his disciples were in the house again, and Thomas was with them. Though the doors were locked, Jesus came and stood among them and said, "Peace be with you!" Then he said to Thomas, "Put your finger here; see my hands. Reach out your hand and put it into my side. Stop doubting and believe." Thomas said to him, "My Lord and my God!" Then Jesus told him, "Because you have seen me, you have believed; blessed are those who have not seen and yet have believed." Jesus did many other miraculous signs in the presence of his disciples.
John 20:24-30, NIV

Trust God's Word, not feelings

20

Drip-Dry Giver

FROM THE BIBLE:

But this I say: He who sows sparingly will also reap sparingly, and he who sows bountifully will also reap bountifully. So let each one give as he purposes in his heart, not grudgingly or of necessity; for God loves a cheerful giver. And God is able to make all grace abound toward you, that you, always having all sufficiency in all things, have an abundance for every good work. As it is written: "He has dispersed abroad, He has given to the poor; His righteousness remains forever."

2 Corinthians 9:6-9, NKJV

Give cheerfully

"CAMPING IS FUN, but it's sure easier to do the washing at home, isn't it?" observed Jody. She continued to slosh the clothes around in a bucket.

"Yes," agreed Mother as she wrung out a shirt, twisting it tightly. "Would you hang this up for me, please?"

"Sure." Jody hung the shirt on the clothesline. "Can I wring out this sweater now?" she asked.

"Oh, don't wring that," said Mother. "Just squeeze it gently and then roll it in a towel. Wringing wouldn't be good for that material." She turned to a third bucket. "Now these," she said, "are drip-dry. We'll hang them up dripping wet. The water will just drip right off of them and leave them almost wrinkle-free."

"Sounds great," said Jody. "Wrinkle-free and work free!" Soon the washing was finished.

Later that day Dad gave Jody her allowance. She looked at the money in her hand. "Would it be okay if I put all of this in the special missionary offering in church tomorrow?" she asked suddenly. "Since we're camping, I don't really need any of it this week."

Mother smiled. "You've come a long way in your giving."

"What do you mean?" asked Jody.

"Remember when you first got your allowance? We insisted that you give a tenth to the Lord, so you did. But you weren't happy about it," Mother reminded her. "It was kind of 'wrung' out of you, like I wrung the water out of the cotton shirt this morning. Later, you gave your tenth willingly, but that's all you'd give. It was as though you were 'gently squeezed' into giving that much. I'm aware that now you often give extra money. That reminds me of the drip-dry clothes where the water freely runs off. And which material did we decide we preferred?"

"The drip-dry." Jody smiled.

"Right," agreed Mother. "That's the kind of giver God prefers, too."

HOW ABOUT YOU? What kind of giver are you? Do you give only because you have to? Or do you gladly give a small portion of your money to the Lord? Best of all, do you give generously and cheerfully? That's the kind of giver God loves. □ H.M.

TO MEMORIZE: *He who sows sparingly will also reap sparingly, and he who sows bountifully will also reap bountifully.* 2 Corinthians 9:6, NKJV

"VALERIE, OVER HERE!" Valerie looked up in surprise as she heard her mother's voice. Why was Mother picking her up after school? "I thought you might like to go to the gift shop with me," said Mother as Valerie got in the car.

They had gone several blocks when Valerie blurted out, "Mother, I'm the only one in my class who doesn't watch those horror cartoons on Saturday morning. It's no fun being the oddball."

"I know it's not easy to be different, Val," agreed Mother as she drove into the parking lot, "but sometimes it's necessary in order to please God."

"I know." Valerie sighed. "Our Bible verse on Sunday was about being 'a peculiar people,' and I feel peculiar sometimes."

Mother laughed. "I'm sure you know it doesn't mean 'weird' in that verse. It means 'a special purchase'—a rare treasure to God," she explained as they got out of the car. Inside the shop, Mother said, "Let's look at the vases. I'd like to make a new flower arrangement for the piano."

Valerie immediately saw the vase she wanted. "Look at this one, Mother. It's so pretty!"

After looking at the price tag, Mother laughed. "Leave it to you to pick out the most expensive one in the shop. It costs four times more than this one beside it."

"Why is it so much more expensive?" asked Valerie.

"It's handcrafted," Mother explained. "These others were made in molds, and basically they're all alike. This one is special. It's one of a kind. There will never be another one made exactly like it. It's a 'peculiar' vessel."

"Just like me." Valerie grinned. "A rare treasure—a special purchase."

"Right. Just keep being peculiar, Honey. Don't let the world squeeze you into its mold." Mother picked up the vase. "Let's buy this vase even if it is expensive. It will be a constant reminder of how special we are to God."

HOW ABOUT YOU? Do you ever feel like an oddball because you have to take a stand for right? Just remember you are God's peculiar vessel, a special treasure unlike everybody else. It's okay to be different. □ B.W.

TO MEMORIZE: *You are a chosen people, a royal priesthood, a holy nation, a people belonging to God.* 1 Peter 2:9, NIV

A Special Purchase

FROM THE BIBLE:
But God's truth stands firm like a great rock, and nothing can shake it. It is a foundation stone with these words written on it: "The Lord knows those who are really his," and "A person who calls himself a Christian should not be doing things that are wrong." In a wealthy home there are dishes made of gold and silver as well as some made from wood and clay. The expensive dishes are used for guests, and the cheap ones are used in the kitchen or to put garbage in. If you stay away from sin you will be like one of these dishes made of purest gold—the very best in the house—so that Christ himself can use you for his highest purposes. Run from anything that gives you the evil thoughts that young men often have, but stay close to anything that makes you want to do right. Have faith and love, and enjoy the companionship of those who love the Lord and have pure hearts.
2 Timothy 2:19-22, TLB

Dare to be different

22

Vacation Lessons

FROM THE BIBLE:
Thus, by their fruit you will recognize them. Not everyone who says to me, "Lord, Lord," will enter the kingdom of heaven, but only he who does the will of my Father who is in heaven. Many will say to me on that day, "Lord, Lord, did we not prophesy in your name, and in your name drive out demons and perform many miracles?" Then I will tell them plainly, "I never knew you. Away from me, you evildoers!"
Matthew 7:20-23, NIV

"Christian" actions can't save you

KAREN HAD LOOKED forward to spending part of her summer vacation with her aunt in Colorado. Not only was Aunt Dee her very favorite aunt, but she owned a jewelry store where Karen loved to roam around, looking at all the beautiful gems. "Is this a ruby?" Karen asked the first day she visited the store. "It looks like the one you gave Mom for her birthday."

"It's not exactly the same," Aunt Dee replied. "Your mother's is the real thing. This one is synthetic."

Taking the ring, Karen looked at it carefully. "What's synthetic?"

Aunt Dee laughed. "Well, I guess you could call it a fake. It's not a real ruby. It looks like a ruby, and most people can't tell the difference. But a trained eye will tell you that it's not the real thing."

"Lots of people could be fooled," commented Karen, as she put the ring back.

"That's the idea," said Aunt Dee, smiling. After a moment she asked, "Did you know that there are synthetic Christians?"

"Synthetic Christians?" Karen repeated. "What do you mean?"

"The Bible tells us that some people are not really born again," explained Aunt Dee. "They just pretend to be Christians. They act like it on the outside, but there has not been a change inside. They are fakes—synthetic. But God knows who's real and who's faking it."

Karen thought about that. She was glad she could say she was really a Christian and not just a synthetic. She knew that when she confessed that she was a sinner and asked Jesus to forgive her sin and make her His child, He did. And she became the real thing!

HOW ABOUT YOU? Do you think you're a Christian because your parents are Christians? Or because you live a "good" life and do all the things you see other Christians do—attend church, read your Bible, pray, give? That won't do it. You have to be born again, and that's a personal commitment. Have you ever made that decision? □ R.J.

TO MEMORIZE: *Not everyone who says to me, "Lord, Lord," will enter the kingdom of heaven, but only he who does the will of my Father who is in heaven.* Matthew 7:21, NIV

"**W**E'RE GOING to have company tonight," Aunt Dee called to Karen, "so take out the good silver and set the table, will you, please?"

Karen went to the closet, where she knew her aunt kept the good silverware tray, and took it out carefully. A look of surprise came over her face when she opened the box. "Aunt Dee," she called in concern, "it's all black and ugly looking."

Aunt Dee came into the dining room and looked at the silverware. "Oh, of course," she said. "It hasn't been used for some time. We'll have to clean it before we can use it. I'll help you."

Karen and her aunt began to polish the tarnished silverware. "If silver is such a precious metal, how come it turns black like this?" Karen asked.

"I don't know exactly why it does that," answered Aunt Dee, "but I do know that the longer it sits around in a box or drawer without being used, the more likely it is to tarnish. Fortunately, it can be polished again."

"Sort of like Christians," Karen said softly. She recalled a sermon about how Christians should be kept clean and shining, ready for the Lord to use. She mentioned the illustration to her aunt.

"That is so right," Aunt Dee agreed. "When we allow sinful things to stain our lives, we can hardly expect God to use us in His service. We should be careful to keep ourselves from becoming soiled by the things of this world. And we should go daily to the Lord, confessing our sin and asking Him to help us keep from becoming tarnished."

HOW ABOUT YOU? Are you fit for the Master's use? If God wants you to do something for Him, are you clean and ready for His work? Don't allow sin to come into your life and stay there. You need to confess your sin and receive God's forgiveness. You must not go back to that sin, but rather turn from it. Then you're ready to witness to a friend, to sing in the choir, to help in the nursery, or to be used in whatever task God has for you. ▢ R.J.

TO MEMORIZE: *Encourage one another daily, as long as it is called Today, so that none of you may be hardened by sin's deceitfulness.*
Hebrews 3:13, NIV

Vacation Lessons

(Continued from yesterday)

FROM THE BIBLE:
What harmony is there between Christ and Belial? What does a believer have in common with an unbeliever? What agreement is there between the temple of God and idols? For we are the temple of the living God. As God has said: "I will live with them and walk among them, and I will be their God, and they will be my people." "Therefore come out from them and be separate, says the Lord. Touch no unclean thing, and I will receive you." "I will be a Father to you, and you will be my sons and daughters, says the Lord Almighty." . . . *Since we have these promises, dear friends, let us purify ourselves from everything that contaminates body and spirit, perfecting holiness out of reverence for God.*
2 Corinthians 6:15–7:1, NIV

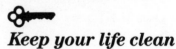

Keep your life clean

24

Vacation Lessons

(Continued from yesterday)

FROM THE BIBLE:

Now when the people saw that Moses delayed coming down from the mountain, the people gathered together to Aaron, and said to him, "Come, make us gods that shall go before us; for as for this Moses, the man who brought us up out of the land of Egypt, we do not know what has become of him." And Aaron said to them, "Break off the golden earrings which are in the ears of your wives, your sons, and your daughters, and bring them to me." So all the people broke off the golden earrings which were in their ears, and brought them to Aaron. And he received the gold from their hand, and he fashioned it with an engraving tool, and made a molded calf. Then they said, "This is your god, O Israel, that brought you out of the land of Egypt!"
Exodus 32:1-4, NKJV

God first— things later

KAREN CONTINUED to spend a lot of time in her aunt's jewelry store, and she read several books about gems. "Did you read this book?" her aunt asked one evening. "I think it's my favorite."

Karen shook her head. "What's it about?"

Aunt Dee began to turn the pages of the book. "It's sort of a history of gems," she explained. "For instance, in this chapter it tells how gems became so important in ancient days. It tells how carvings and inscriptions were made in the harder stones—those that would not chip or break easily. That made them very valuable. But then something terrible happened."

"What happened?" Karen asked.

"People started using these gems in their worship," Aunt Dee explained. "In fact, they began to worship the gems rather than worshiping God."

"Oh, that is terrible," agreed Karen. "It's kind of hard to imagine ever doing that."

Aunt Dee nodded. "Yes, but sometimes Christians still worship things instead of God."

Karen could hardly believe that. "I wouldn't put anything before the Lord, would you?"

Her aunt shook her head. "I don't mean to," she said, "but I must admit that sometimes things become so important to me that I get my priorities mixed up. Often the things themselves are not evil, but sometimes I let work, television, clothes, or a lot of other things become so important to me that I forget Whose I am and to Whom I should give my allegiance."

That was a new thought to Karen. She decided she had better examine her own life to see if she was really putting God first.

HOW ABOUT YOU? It's unlikely that you would ever make an idol that you would actually worship in the way the Israelites did. And you probably won't choose any objects to bow down to, either. But do things in your life become so important that you forget God? If you let friends, fads, styles, or other things become too important, there is a danger of neglecting God. Check yourself! □ R.J.

TO MEMORIZE: *The world and its desires pass away, but the man who does the will of God lives forever.* 1 John 2:17, NIV

KAREN HAD ENJOYED her vacation with Aunt Dee, but now it was time to go back home. The day before she left, her aunt gave her a special present—a little gold pendant with a real diamond chip! Karen squealed in delight.

"There's no gem with quite so much sparkle as the diamond," said Aunt Dee as Karen gave her a hug. As she spoke, the ring on her own finger sparkled brilliantly in the light.

Karen had seen Aunt Dee's diamond ring, but she had never really examined it carefully. Now she held her aunt's hand, turning it until the light made the diamond sparkle even more. "My mom has a diamond, too," she said, "and that's what I want when I get engaged!"

"Well, I hope that won't happen for a long time to come," laughed Aunt Dee. "But it's true that a young man often does show his great love for a young lady by giving her a diamond." She paused in thought. "God gave us more, much more, than a diamond. He gave us His Son. That's how much He loved us."

Karen had learned a special verse a long time ago, and right now it seemed to fit with what her aunt was saying. "For God so loved the world, that He gave His only begotten Son, that whoever believes in Him should not perish, but have eternal life." She quoted it to her aunt. "That's John 3:16," she finished.

"Yes, and that shows how much God loves us," Aunt Dee added. "Men give beautiful diamonds to the women they love, but God gave His very own Son for everyone."

Karen looked once again at the lovely diamond on her aunt's finger. Yes, diamonds were precious, but they couldn't compare with God's gift.

HOW ABOUT YOU? Do you ever think seriously about what God gave to this world? To you? It wasn't something man-made. It wasn't something you have to buy. It wasn't something that only had a sparkle. It was His own Son, Jesus. How much does that mean to you? Have you accepted His gift of love? Have you ever really thanked Him for that wonderful and priceless gift? Do so now.
□ R.J.

TO MEMORIZE: *This is love: not that we loved God, but that he loved us and sent his Son as an atoning sacrifice for our sins.* 1 John 4:10, NIV

Vacation Lessons

(Continued from yesterday)

FROM THE BIBLE:
And as Moses in the wilderness lifted up the bronze image of a serpent on a pole, even so I must be lifted up upon a pole, so that anyone who believes in me will have eternal life. For God loved the world so much that he gave his only Son so that anyone who believes in him shall not perish but have eternal life. God did not send his Son into the world to condemn it, but to save it. There is no eternal doom awaiting those who trust him to save them. But those who don't trust him have already been tried and condemned for not believing in the only Son of God. John 3:14-18, TLB

God gave us Jesus

26

Balancing the Account

FROM THE BIBLE:

The law of Moses says, "If a man gouges out another's eye, he must pay with his own eye. If a tooth gets knocked out, knock out the tooth of the one who did it." But I say: Don't resist violence! If you are slapped on one cheek, turn the other too. If you are ordered to court, and your shirt is taken from you, give your coat too. If the military demand that you carry their gear for a mile, carry it two. Give to those who ask, and don't turn away from those who want to borrow. There is a saying, "Love your friends and hate your enemies." But I say: Love your enemies! Pray for those who persecute you! In that way you will be acting as true sons of your Father in heaven. For he gives his sunlight to both the evil and the good, and sends rain on the just and on the unjust too. If you love only those who love you, what good is that? Even scoundrels do that much. If you are friendly only to your friends, how are you different from anyone else? Even the heathen do that. But you are to be perfect, even as your Father in heaven is perfect.
Matthew 5:38-48, TLB

Return good for evil

"Oooohhhh! I just can't get this checkbook to balance with the bank statement," moaned Mother.

Dad looked over her shoulder. "Last week I wrote a check for twenty dollars to Hanson's Hardware," he said. "Is it listed in the checkbook?"

Mother quickly scanned the check register. "No, it's not. That helps, but it still doesn't balance."

"Mother! Mother!" Stephen burst into the room. "Melissa hit me!"

"But he hit me first," yelled Melissa.

"Well, I owed you one from last time," Stephen roared. "The Bible says if someone hits you, you have the right to hit him back!"

Mother gasped. "Why, Son! That's not what the Bible teaches at all."

"Yes, it is," replied Stephen firmly. "The Old Testament says, 'An eye for an eye, and a tooth for a tooth.'"

"Sit down," ordered Dad. "That passage isn't talking about personal vengeance. It was meant as a civil law, to insure justice in the nation of Israel. People who return blow for blow find the score is never settled. Someone always owes someone else a blow."

Mother sighed. "That sounds like my checkbook. The account never balances."

Dad nodded. "Jesus did away with the law of revenge. He told us to return good for evil. That's the only way to settle the score."

"You mean when Stephen hits me, I'm supposed to do something good for him?" Melissa asked. "That'd be hard!"

Dad nodded. "God says to overcome evil with good."

Stephen and Melissa looked at each other. "We'll try," they said in unison. "Hey, this might be fun," added Stephen. "It'll sure be different."

Mother smiled. "Great. That balances one account. Now, if I could just get this checkbook to balance."

HOW ABOUT YOU? Are you keeping score of the wrongs others do to you? Are you figuring out how you can get back at them? God's way to settle the score is to do something good for them. Try it. You'll feel a lot better when the account is balanced that way. □ B.W.

TO MEMORIZE: *Do not be overcome by evil, but overcome evil with good.* Romans 12:21, NIV

CARLA STIRRED Jell-O into boiling water, added some ice cubes, and put the bowl with the watery mixture in the refrigerator to set. "What can I do now?" she asked her mother after a while. "I wish I had a real good Christian friend to play with."

"Isn't Dana a Christian?" asked Mother.

Carla nodded. "Yeah, but I'm beginning to think she's hopeless. She always wants her own way, and she says mean things about other kids."

"That's too bad," said Mother. "Well maybe it's time to check your Jell-O."

Carla went to the refrigerator. "It's getting there," she said. "It's ready for the fruit." She added apples and bananas while she continued to complain about Dana.

"Tell me something," said Mother. "Has she improved at all since she became a Christian?"

"Oh, sure." Carla nodded, "but not enough. She used to be just awful. Nobody liked her. Now she's not so bad, but she still has a long way to go."

"Like the Jell-O," said Mother.

"The Jell-O," repeated Carla. "What do you mean?"

"The Jell-O has improved since you started it, but it has a long way to go, too," explained Mother. "In time it will be set and ready to eat. It reminds me of Christians. They don't usually 'set' all at once. It takes time. As they grow in the Lord, they improve in outward behavior. We need to be patient with them."

"Maybe we can add some 'fruit' to help them." Carla was enjoying the comparison. "We can pray for them, and we can be friendly."

"Good," approved Mother, "and let's remember that you and I aren't finished yet, either. Let's grow together."

HOW ABOUT YOU? Do you know Christians who need a lot of improvement? Are you praying for them? Are you helping them by being friendly and encouraging them to attend church and study God's Word? Do you set a good example for them? God finishes what He starts. He'll finish what He has begun in them—and in you. □ H.M.

TO MEMORIZE: *He who has begun a good work in you will complete it until the day of Jesus Christ.* Philippians 1:6, NKJV

Not Hopeless

FROM THE BIBLE:
I thank my God upon every remembrance of you, always in every prayer of mine making request for you all with joy, for your fellowship in the gospel from the first day until now, being confident of this very thing, that He who has begun a good work in you will complete it until the day of Jesus Christ; just as it is right for me to think this of you all, because I have you in my heart, inasmuch as both in my chains and in the defense and confirmation of the gospel, you all are partakers with me of grace. For God is my witness, how greatly I long for you all with the affection of Jesus Christ. And this I pray, that your love may abound still more and more in knowledge and all discernment, that you may approve the things that are excellent, that you may be sincere and without offense till the day of Christ, being filled with the fruits of righteousness which are by Jesus Christ, to the glory and praise of God. Philippians 1:3-11, NKJV

God finishes what he started

28

Where's Jenna?

FROM THE BIBLE:

*O LORD, you have searched me
and you know me. You know
when I sit and when I rise; you
perceive my thoughts from afar.
You discern my going out and
my lying down; you are familiar
with all my ways. Before a word
is on my tongue you know it
completely, O LORD. You hem
me in—behind and before; you
have laid your hand upon me.
Such knowledge is too wonderful
for me, too lofty for me to attain.
Where can I go from your
Spirit? Where can I flee from
your presence? If I go up to the
heavens, you are there; if I
make my bed in the depths, you
are there. If I rise on the wings
of the dawn, if I settle on the far
side of the sea, even there your
hand will guide me, your right
hand will hold me fast. If I say,
"Surely the darkness will hide
me and the light become night
around me," even the darkness
will not be dark to you; the
night will shine like the day, for
darkness is as light to you.*
Psalm 139:1-12, NIV

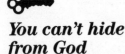

You can't hide from God

"**W**HERE IS JENNA?" called Marcia in a singsong voice as she played with her baby sister one afternoon. "Where is Jenna hiding?" Jenna peeked through the chubby little fingers she was holding in front of her face. Suddenly she dropped her hand. "There she is!" exclaimed Marcia. "There's Jenna!" The baby squealed in delight and promptly placed her fingers back over her eyes, ready to play the game again. Marcia laughed, too. "You really think you're hiding from me, don't you?" she said. "Babies are silly, aren't they, Mother?"

"Sometimes they are," agreed Mother. "Almost as silly as adults."

Marcia looked at her mother suspiciously. "What do you mean?" she asked.

"I was just thinking," said Mother, "of how we sometimes try to hide from God. We do something wrong, and we think nobody knows about it. Isn't that silly? We tend to forget that God sees and knows all about it."

Marcia nodded. "I know I try to hide sometimes," she admitted. She laughed as she saw Jenna once again peeking through her fingers. "Next time I'm tempted to think that way, I'll remember how silly it is."

HOW ABOUT YOU? Do you think nobody knows you broke that dish or toy? Told that lie? Snitched a cookie? Whatever you've done, God knows all about it. You may hide it from Mom and Dad, and your friends may never know. But God knows. Confess your sin to Him and to the person you've wronged. Ask for forgiveness. You'll be glad you did. □ H.M.

TO MEMORIZE: *"Can anyone hide in secret places so that I cannot see him?" declares the LORD. "Do not I fill heaven and earth?" declares the LORD.* Jeremiah 23:24, NIV

JULIE QUICKLY RAN to the telephone. It was her friend Susie. "I'm sorry, Susie, but I can't come over now," said Julie. "My mother needs my help with the laundry." Julie hung up the phone and began helping Mom fold clothes.

"Why, Julie," Mother said with a surprise, "I never mentioned needing help with the laundry. Why did you tell Susie I needed you?"

"Don't you want me to help you?" Julie asked.

"That would be nice," agreed Mother. "However, what you told Susie wasn't true, was it?"

"In a way it was true, even though you hadn't asked for my help," argued Julie. "If you needed me to help I would. Besides, a lot of people say things that aren't completely true, so is that so bad?"

"Julie," said Mother, "hand me that handkerchief from the top of the laundry basket, please. What color do you think it is?"

"It's white, Mom," replied Julie. "All of Dad's hankies are white."

"Now dig to the bottom of the basket and get me another handkerchief," Mother directed. Julie looked puzzled but did as she was told. "What color is that one?" asked Mother.

Julie looked at it. "It's white, too," she said, "but next to this one, the first one looks yellowish."

"That's right, Julie." Mother nodded. "Until you had a really white hankie, you couldn't tell the first one was actually old and yellowed. It's the same with our lives. If we compare them with the lives of people around us, it seems that we are doing all right. But when we compare ourselves with Jesus, we see how sinful we are. People may think it's all right to tell what they call 'little white lies,' but God says Jesus, the Son of God, never lied or sinned in any way. He left a perfect example for us to follow. Be careful to use Jesus as your example instead of watching how others play with sin."

HOW ABOUT YOU? Do you try to live like Jesus? Don't compare your life with anyone else. He is the only perfect pattern after which to shape your life. □ B.B.

TO MEMORIZE: *For to this you were called, because Christ also suffered for us, leaving us an example, that you should follow His steps.* 1 Peter 2:21, NKJV

The "White" Hand-kerchief

FROM THE BIBLE:

For to this you were called, because Christ also suffered for us, leaving us an example, that you should follow His steps: "Who committed no sin, nor was guile found in His mouth" who, when He was reviled, did not revile in return; when He suffered, He did not threaten, but committed Himself to Him who judges righteously; who Himself bore our sins in His own body on the tree, that we, having died to sins, might live for righteousness—by whose stripes you were healed. For you were like sheep going astray, but have now returned to the Shepherd and Overseer of your souls.

1 Peter 2:21-25, NKJV

Follow Jesus' example

30

Believe It or Not

FROM THE BIBLE:

*"What do you mean?"
Nicodemus asked. Jesus
replied, "You, a respected
Jewish teacher, and yet you don't
understand these things? I am
telling you what I know and
have seen—and yet you won't
believe me. But if you don't even
believe me when I tell you about
such things as these that happen
here among men, how can you
possibly believe if I tell you what
is going on in heaven? For only
I, the Messiah, have come to
earth and will return to heaven
again. And as Moses in the
wilderness lifted up the bronze
image of a serpent on a pole,
even so I must be lifted up upon
a pole, so that anyone who
believes in me will have eternal
life.*
John 3:9-15, TLB

God's Word is true

JEFF WAS SPENDING summer vacation with his cousin Rodney, and every day was action-packed. Jeff loved it. But each evening when they had family devotions, Jeff endured the Bible reading and prayer. "You don't really believe all that religious bunk, do you?" he asked Rodney one night.

"Sure I do, and it's not 'religious bunk'!" retorted Rodney.

Jeff shrugged. "Well, I don't see how anyone could believe some of those Bible stories. Imagine men walking in fire and not being burned, or a man walking on water, or people walking through the Red Sea and not getting wet." Jeff snorted.

One day as they drove into town, Rodney read a bumper sticker. "If Jesus said it, I believe it, and it's so."

"It should say, 'If Jesus said it, it's so,' " his dad commented. "It's so whether I believe it or not."

One day Rodney's dad took them on a canoe trip. "The water's not very deep," said Jeff as they floated peacefully downstream. "I can see the bottom."

"It's deeper than it looks, Jeff," chuckled Rodney's dad. "I'm sure it's over your head."

"Aw, I don't believe it," Jeff scoffed just as they went under a low-hanging branch. Over they went into the water. All three came up spitting and sputtering.

"Stand up, Jeff," said Rodney, grinning.

"I can't! I can't touch the bottom." Jeff swam toward the overturned canoe.

Soon the canoe was righted, and they again floated downstream. "The water was deep whether you believed it or not, Jeff," commented Rodney's dad. "Believing it or not believing it doesn't change it. The same is true of God's Word."

Jeff grinned sheepishly as he repeated, "If Jesus said it, it's so."

HOW ABOUT YOU? Do you believe the Word of God? Do you believe *all* of it? Your unbelief will not change God's Word, but it will change your life. God says if you do not believe on Jesus, you are "condemned already," but if you will believe, you are no longer condemned. Believe on Jesus. Ask Him to save you today. □ B.W.

TO MEMORIZE: *What if some did not have faith? Will their lack of faith nullify God's faithfulness? Not at all! Let God be true, and every man a liar.*
Romans 3:3-4, NIV

IT WAS Kurt's and Kristen's responsibility to see that the swimming pool got the proper amount of chlorine and other chemicals, but they hadn't done their job. Now the water was green. This meant they couldn't swim for two whole days.

"I'll bet these two days are going to be the hottest ones all summer," moaned Kurt, as he wiped the sweat off his forehead. "I can't believe that the water turned green so fast. It didn't look that bad yesterday."

"You're right," sighed Kristen, fanning herself. "We should have used the water tester. By the time we could see that the algae was growing, it was too late to prevent it with chemicals."

"Did you say you haven't been using the water tester to see whether or not you needed to add chemicals?" Mother asked.

"Yeah," replied Kurt. "We thought we'd be able to tell if the water was getting dirty just by looking at it."

"How could all of that green stuff get in the pool overnight?" asked Kristen.

"You didn't *see* it yesterday," responded Mom. "The algae was there all right, but you needed to use the water tester so that you would know that it was there. That reminds me of some sins," she remarked. "Some little actions hardly seem like sin at all, but given a chance to grow, they can become very ugly."

"Too bad we don't have a guide to tell us when there's a problem—like we have the water tester for the pool," observed Kristen.

"We do!" exclaimed Kurt. "We can use the Bible. It's our guide to help us know when our actions aren't right, so we can change them.

"Well, I think you two have learned some good lessons from this experience," said Mother.

Both children nodded, and Kurt grinned as he said, "C'mon, Kristen. No need to use the water tester for the pool today, but let's go use our other guide—the Bible."

HOW ABOUT YOU? Do you ever have trouble with "little" sins getting out of control? Do your actions measure up to God's standards? Do you know what God says about lying? Cheating? Loving? Forgiving? The Bible is the guide to test your actions. Use it daily. □ D.R.

TO MEMORIZE: *Direct me in the path of your commands, for there I find delight.* Psalm 119:35, NIV

The Water Tester

FROM THE BIBLE:
The law of the LORD is perfect, reviving the soul. The statutes of the LORD are trustworthy, making wise the simple. The precepts of the LORD are right, giving joy to the heart. The commands of the LORD are radiant, giving light to the eyes. The fear of the LORD is pure, enduring forever. The ordinances of the LORD are sure and altogether righteous. They are more precious than gold, than much pure gold; they are sweeter than honey, than honey from the comb. By them is your servant warned; in keeping them there is great reward. Who can discern his errors? Forgive my hidden faults. Keep your servant also from willful sins; may they not rule over me. Then will I be blameless, innocent of great transgression. May the words of my mouth and the meditation of my heart be pleasing in your sight, O LORD, my Rock and my Redeemer.
Psalm 19:7-14, NIV

**The Bible is
our guide**

1

Out of Tune

FROM THE BIBLE:

*Is there any such thing as
Christians cheering each other
up? Do you love me enough to
want to help me? Does it mean
anything to you that we are
brothers in the Lord, sharing
the same Spirit? Are your hearts
tender and sympathetic at all?
Then make me truly happy by
loving each other and agreeing
wholeheartedly with each other,
working together with one heart
and mind and purpose. Don't be
selfish; don't live to make a good
impression on others. Be
humble, thinking of others as
better than yourself. Don't just
think about your own affairs,
but be interested in others, too,
and in what they are doing.
Your attitude should be the kind
that was shown us by Jesus
Christ.*

Philippians 2:1-5, TLB

Get in tune
with God

"WHERE'S my guitar pick?" demanded James. "You've been in my room again, haven't you, Mandy?" His little sister shook her head. "You must have been," James argued. "I left my pick on my dresser, and now it's gone."

"I didn't take it," said Mandy. "Mama says to stay out of your room, and I do."

"Well, someone took it!" James stomped down the hall and slammed his bedroom door. Mandy felt sad as she thought about her brother. He had been acting like this often in recent weeks.

Later that evening James sat at the piano, tuning his guitar. "Where did you find your pick, James?" asked Mother. "Mandy told me you thought she had taken it."

"It was in my pocket," James muttered. He struck a piano key with one finger. *Plunk! Plunk!* Then he plucked a guitar string. *Ping! Ping! Plunk!* After a few more twists and turns, he ran his fingers across the strings and a harmonious chord sounded.

"You're getting pretty good, Son," said Dad.

"Why do you always listen to the piano and the guitar together?" asked Mandy.

"If all the strings aren't in tune with the piano, they don't sound good with each other, either," explained James.

Mother looked at James. "Just like each of your guitar strings has to be in tune with the piano, so every member of the family has to be in harmony with God, or they are out of tune with each other," she said thoughtfully. "Just one person out of tune can disrupt the whole family harmony."

Dad nodded. "I've been hearing some discord around here. Could it be someone is out of tune?"

James sighed. "All right—I know it's me," he admitted. "I'm sorry. Guess I'd better let the Lord do a little tuning on me. It's really no fun being out of tune, anyway."

HOW ABOUT YOU? Are you out of tune with God? Do you have trouble getting along with your family and friends? Now's the time to have a little "prayer meeting" all by yourself, and let God get you back in tune. □ B. W.

TO MEMORIZE: *How good and pleasant it is when brothers live together in unity!* Psalm 133:1, NIV

"YOUR HOT DOG'S almost done, Joey," Aaron told his little brother. Aaron twirled the long fork once more before withdrawing it from the fire. He placed the frankfurter on a roll, and handed it to Joey. Then he began to roast one for himself.

"Know what, Dad?" Aaron turned his attention to his father, who was roasting two hot dogs at a time. "I think Kendall is a Christian. He's the new boy in my class."

"Well, that's great," replied Dad. "And what makes you think he's a Christian?"

"Well, I know he goes to church, and he's just real nice. He never swears or blows his cool," Aaron replied. "He's not like most of the guys."

"Hmmmm. Sounds promising." Dad moved to the picnic table and handed one of the hot dogs to Mother.

Aaron followed. "Joey, you're not eating the hot dog I roasted for you," he complained, looking at the untouched meat on Joey's plate.

"Am, too. See?" Joey held up a half-eaten hot dog bun, thickly spread with catsup. "I like hot dogs."

"That's just bread," said Aaron. "It's not a hot dog unless the meat's in it." Joey just shrugged and went on eating.

"Aaron's right," said Dad. "And here's something else to remember—just as a frankfurter roll isn't a hot dog without the meat, a person isn't a Christian without Christ. He's like that empty roll. Take your friend Kendall, for instance. I'm glad he's such a nice young man, Aaron, but none of the things you mentioned make him a Christian. You need to find out if he's accepted Christ into his life. Only if he's done that is he a Christian."

Aaron nodded. "Thanks for reminding me, Dad. I'll find out," he promised. "If he isn't already a Christian, maybe he'd like to become one."

HOW ABOUT YOU? Have you asked Jesus Christ to come into your life? You may be a very nice person—but a very nice person without Christ is not a Christian. Don't be like an "empty roll." □ M.M.

TO MEMORIZE: *It is no longer I who live, but Christ lives in me.* Galatians 2:20, NKJV

2

The Empty Roll

FROM THE BIBLE:
A man is not justified by the works of the law but by faith in Jesus Christ, even we have believed in Christ Jesus, that we might be justified by faith in Christ and not by the works of the law; for by the works of the law no flesh shall be justified. But if, while we seek to be justified by Christ, we ourselves also are found sinners, is Christ therefore a minister of sin? Certainly not! For if I build again those things which I destroyed, I make myself a transgressor. For I through the law died to the law that I might live to God. I have been crucified with Christ; it is no longer I who live, but Christ lives in me; and the life which I now live in the flesh I live by faith in the Son of God, who loved me and gave Himself for me. Galatians 2:16-20, NKJV

A Christian has Christ

3

Christian Says

FROM THE BIBLE:

This is how we know what love is: Jesus Christ laid down his life for us. And we ought to lay down our lives for our brothers. If anyone has material possess- ions and sees his brother in need but has no pity on him, how can the love of God be in him? Dear children, let us not love with words or tongue but with actions and in truth. . . . And this is his command: to believe in the name of his Son, Jesus Christ, and to love one another as he commanded us. Those who obey his commands live in him, and he in them. And this is how we know that he lives in us: We know it by the Spirit he gave us.
1 John 3:16-18, 23-24, NIV

Don't just "say"— but "do"

"I'M SIMON—and remember, you must always do what Simon *says.*" Miss Elwood, Andy's teacher, was speaking.

Andy tried hard to concentrate. *I wish I could win this game just once,* he thought.

"Simon says, 'Thumbs up,' " called Miss El- wood. So Andy turned his thumbs up. "Simon says, 'Step forward,' " Miss Elwood instructed as she stepped forward. All the children followed her example. "Simon says, 'Snap your fingers.' " But Miss Elwood clapped her hands instead, and before Andy could stop himself, he clapped his hands, too. Andy sank into his seat. Once again he was out of the game.

After supper Andy's family learned a Bible verse during evening devotions. "We'll learn 1 John 3:18," said Dad. "Let us not love in word or in tongue, but in deed and in truth." They repeated it together several times, and Dad explained it. "Our actions should go along with our words," he said.

"Hey," laughed Andy, "Simon should learn this verse."

"Simon?" asked Mother. "What do you mean?" So Andy explained the trouble he had when "Simon" said one thing and did another.

"That brings up a good point," observed Dad. "As Christians, we sometimes act like we're playing a game. Maybe it could be called 'Christian Says.' Sometimes Christians say one thing and do another. Can you think of examples of that?"

"Christian says, 'Read your Bible,' and then he only opoens it on Sunday," suggested Mother.

"Christian says, 'Go to church,' and then he stays home to watch a football game," said Andy's brother.

"Christian says, 'Be helpful,' and then sneaks out of doing the dishes," added Andy.

"You've got the idea," said Dad. "Let's be careful not to say one thing while we're doing another."

HOW ABOUT YOU? Do you play "Christian Says"? No doubt you can think of many other ways to play the game. Which ones do you use? Remember that people will often follow what you do rather than what you say. So give up playing at living a Christian life. Listen to what God says, and love others in deed, not just in work. □ H.M.

TO MEMORIZE: *Dear children, let us not love with words or tongue but with actions and in truth.*
1 John 3:18, NIV

EVER SINCE SUNDAY, David had been thinking, off and on, about the pastor's sermon. He knew he should ask Jesus to be his Savior, and he had almost made that decision last Sunday. But right now he had other things on his mind—baseball, for instance. Getting saved could wait. He was determined not to worry about it!

David shook the thoughts from his mind as he got out of bed. Today was the big day! His team, the Lions, would be playing the Bears, a team from the south side of town, for the city championship. David was the shortstop for his team, and he was eager to play.

The coaches had been saying that the two teams were equal in ability, and it soon became obvious that this was true. First the Lions were ahead, then the Bears, then the Lions again. Unfortunately for David and his teammates, the Bears scored two runs in the bottom of the ninth inning and won the championship.

"That was a good game!" Dad said later.

"But Dad, we lost!" David protested.

"You still can feel good about it," Mother comforted. "You did end up the second-place team in the city. That's considered an honor, too!"

"Yeah, David," his sister agreed. "You almost won!"

"Almost isn't enough!" David was determined to be discouraged.

Dad gave him a thoughtful look. "That's true, David. Almost isn't enough—not in winning baseball games, nor in getting to heaven."

David was startled. He hadn't thought about it that way before! He knew he needed to make the decision to become a Christian, and he was almost ready to do it. Now, he realized that being almost a Christian wasn't enough. He had to make that decision to accept the Lord immediately!

HOW ABOUT YOU? Are you "almost" a Christian? Perhaps you listen to your parents, your pastor, and your Sunday school teacher talk about Christ, and you're almost ready to admit you are a sinner and ask Jesus to save you. It needs to be done now! The only way to have your sins forgiven is to become a Christian. Don't hesitate any longer. Do it now. □ L.W.

TO MEMORIZE: *Then Agrippa said to Paul, "Do you think that in such a short time you can persuade me to be a Christian?"* Acts 26:28 NIV

AUGUST 4

Almost!

FROM THE BIBLE:

Then Agrippa said to Paul, "You have permission to speak for yourself." So Paul motioned with his hand and began his defense: "King Agrippa, I consider myself fortunate to stand before you today as I make my defense against all the accusations of the Jews. . . . King Agrippa, do you believe the prophets? I know you do." Then Agrippa said to Paul, "Do you think that in such a short time you can persuade me to be a Christian?" Paul replied, "Short time or long—I pray God that not only you but all who are listening to me today may become what I am, except for these chains."

Acts 26:1-2, 27-29, NIV

Accept Christ today

AUGUST

5

No Longer Trash

FROM THE BIBLE:

Remind the people to be subject to rulers and authorities, to be obedient, to be ready to do whatever is good, to slander no one, to be peaceable and considerate, and to show true humility toward all men. . . . This is a trustworthy saying. And I want you to stress these things, so that those who have trusted in God may be careful to devote themselves to doing what is good. These things are excellent and profitable for everyone. . . . Our people must learn to devote themselves to doing what is good, in order that they may provide for daily necessities and not live unproductive lives.
Titus 3:1-2, 8, 14, NIV

You're saved to serve

"MOM, CAN YOU take me to my Bible club today?" asked Darci one afternoon. "I'm late."

"Okay," agreed Mother, "but you'll have to walk home." They went to the car. "Do we need to stop for anyone else?" asked Mother. "Have you invited any of your friends?" Darci shook her head. "The Carsons are coming over this evening," continued Mother. "Daddy and I hope we'll have a chance to witness to them, and I thought you could share some of your stories with Tina. I think she'd enjoy those."

Darci squirmed. *I wish Mother would quit suggesting stuff like that,* she thought. *I don't want the kids to think I'm weird.*

When Darci returned home late that afternoon, Mother asked her to empty the kitchen wastebasket. Darci took it out to the trash can in the garage. When she came back into the house, she was carrying a styrofoam meat tray. After putting the wastebasket in its place, she rinsed the tray and headed for her room. Mother frowned. "Hold it! What do you intend to do with that trash?" she asked.

"I need this for a Bible club craft," Darci explained. "We're going to use them as frames for our shell pictures."

"Okay," said Mother. "I don't want you to accumulate all kinds of junk, but I see you've rescued that tray for a purpose." She paused, then added thoughtfully, "It's a bit like us. We were worthless 'trash,' lost in sin, but God saved us for a purpose. We can worship Him and serve Him and bring others to Him. We should always live for His glory. Your picture will be a good reminder of that."

Darci looked at the tray and nodded slowly. She was a Christian, but she knew she hadn't done much about fulfilling the purpose for which she'd been saved. *Tonight will be a good time to start,* she thought. *I'll share those stories with Tina.*

HOW ABOUT YOU? Are you a Christian? Good works could never have saved you, but now that you are saved, God expects you to work for Him. God saved you for a purpose. What are you doing about it? □ H.M.

TO MEMORIZE: *Our people must learn to devote themselves to doing what is good.* Titus 3:14, NIV

"**L**INDA LOUISE LINCOLN, get down here!" called Mother. "Everyone is in the car, waiting for you." Linda hurried out to the car.

"What's in that box you're carrying?" asked Dad.

"My new necklace. I forgot to pack it, and I want to wear it when we get dressed up for the Sunday services," said Linda, holding the box securely on her lap.

"A necklace! You made us wait all that time for a stupid piece of jewelry?" bellowed her brother Rob. "We're going camping, not to a fashion show!"

A few hours later, the Lincolns arrived at the campground. The days that followed were filled with fishing, swimming, boating, and campfires. When Sunday came, they got ready to attend the church service held at the camp pavilion. "Grab your Bibles and let's head on over," said Dad.

"Bibles?" Linda looked startled. "I didn't bring mine."

Mom, Dad, and Rob all looked at her in surprise. "But we're all doing that 'Read through the Bible' program," Rob said.

"Let's go," urged Dad. "You can look on with one of us."

When the pastor got up to speak, he said, "I'm glad you folks have not taken a vacation from God this week. You'll sense from our text how grieved God must be when we forget to spend time with Him. I'm reading from Jeremiah 2, the New International Version. 'Does a maiden forget her jewelry, a bride her wedding ornaments? Yet my people have forgotten me, days without number.' "

Linda blushed when her brother poked her with his elbow and turned to look at her. She knew he was remembering, as she was, that she had brought her jewelry to camp but had forgotten her Bible. All week she had neglected to spend time with the Lord. Right then she made up her mind that she would copy that verse from her dad's Bible and memorize it. She didn't want to ever forget to spend time with God again.

HOW ABOUT YOU? Have you forgotten God "days without number"? Perhaps it isn't jewelry that you put ahead of the Lord, but how about TV? Or baseball? Or a bicycle? God wants you to put Him first. Spend time with Him daily. ☐ P.R.

TO MEMORIZE: *Does a maiden forget her jewelry, a bride her wedding ornaments? Yet my people have forgotten me, days without number.*
Jeremiah 2:32, NIV

Forgotten Jewel

FROM THE BIBLE:
Be careful that you do not forget the LORD your God, failing to observe his commands, his laws and his decrees that I am giving you this day. Otherwise, when you eat and are satisfied, when you build fine houses and settle down, and when your herds and flocks grow large and your silver and gold increase and all you have is multiplied, then your heart will become proud and you will forget the LORD your God, who brought you out of Egypt, out of the land of slavery. He led you through the vast and dreadful desert, that thirsty and waterless land, with its venomous snakes and scorpions. He brought you water out of hard rock. He gave you manna to eat in the desert, something your fathers had never known, to humble and to test you so that in the end it might go well with you.
Deuteronomy 8:11-16, NIV

Don't forget God

AUGUST

7

Fishers of Men

FROM THE BIBLE:

*One day as he was walking
along the beach beside the Lake
of Galilee, he saw two
brothers—Simon, also called
Peter, and Andrew—out in a
boat fishing with a net, for they
were commercial fishermen.
Jesus called out, "Come along
with me and I will show you
how to fish for the souls of
men!" And they left their nets at
once and went with him. A little
farther up the beach he saw two
other brothers, James and John,
sitting in a boat with their father
Zebedee, mending their nets;
and he called to them to come
too. At once they stopped their
work and, leaving their father
behind, went with him.
Matthew 4:18-22, TLB*

Keep witnessing

GRAMPS STRETCHED out lazily on the creek bank. Tad shifted restlessly. "The fish aren't biting here. Let's try another spot, Gramps," he suggested.

"This is the third spot we tried already," Gramps reminded him. "Relax."

Tad sighed. As his cork rocked on the gentle waves, he sighed again.

"Something bothering you?" asked Gramps.

"Yeah," said Tad. "I've invited six guys to Sunday school this week, and not one is going to come. I don't think I'll invite them again. I think I'll quit inviting anybody to church." Gramps wrinkled his brow as he looked at Tad. Then he sat up and started reeling in his line. Tad jumped up. "You got a bite?" he asked excitedly.

Gramps shook his head. "No. I'm quittin'."

"But Gramps, we've got all afternoon," Tad argued.

"Yeah, but we've been here long enough, and we haven't caught one fish. I'm giving up fishing for good." Gramps stood up. "Pull in your line."

"Please, let's wait a little longer," Tad pleaded.

As Gramps checked his bait, he gave his grandson a crooked grin. "Well, if you're sure. I just thought you were ready to quit. If you give up that easy fishing for men, I reckoned you would soon tire of fishing for fish, too."

Tad smiled. "I get the message, Gramps. When we get home, I'll call Cliff and invite him to Sunday school."

Gramps tossed his line back into the water. "That's more like it," he said. "Just because the fish aren't biting today, it doesn't mean we give up fishing."

Tad grabbed his rod. "Look, Gramps! Look! I've got a bite." Quickly he reeled in his line.

As a big bass broke the water, Gramps chuckled. "Yep, you gotta keep fishin'," he said. "Never know when you're gonna get a bite."

HOW ABOUT YOU? Does it seem like you're wasting your time inviting your friends to church or witnessing in other ways? Don't be discouraged. Sooner or later someone will "take the bait." Just keep on fishing. □ B.W.

TO MEMORIZE: *Then Jesus said to them, "Come after Me, and I will make you become fishers of men"* Mark 1:17, NKJV

"MOM, I FINISHED cleaning the front window for you," reported Keith, and he went off to play. A short time later, he heard Mother calling him.

"Keith, you didn't do a very good job on that window," she said. "Look at all those smudges! Please do that over. The Johnsons are coming for dinner, you know."

"I don't understand it," said Keith. He walked closer to the window. "Oh," he said, "the inside is clean. All those spots are on the outside. I'll hurry and finish the job."

As Keith was eating dinner, he saw Mother trying to catch his eye. Then she quietly advised him to use his napkin. A little later Dad frowned when Keith interrupted Mr. Johnson. Finally, Mother said, "If you're finished, Keith, you may be excused. You can play in your room." Keith knew that look of Mother's, so he went to his room.

After the visitors left, Mother came to talk with him. "Keith, your table manners were bad tonight," she frankly told him. "You forgot to use your napkin, you slurped your spaghetti, and you dropped your silverware twice. Besides that, you kept interrupting Dad and Mr. Johnson."

"I just wasn't thinking," he said. "I'm sorry. I know you and Dad have been witnessing to them, and I don't want to be a bad testimony."

Mother smiled. "I appreciate your attitude, Son," she said. "You know, this is like your window-cleaning today. It was important to clean the window inside, just like it's important for us to keep our life clean inside—to get rid of sins like selfishness, worry, and greed. But you also needed to clean the outside of the window, and we need to keep the outside of our lives clean—to overcome bad habits and manners that may offend others. It will help the light of our Christian testimony really shine through."

HOW ABOUT YOU? Do you have bad habits you need to overcome? Sloppy manners? Cracking knuckles? Failure to keep yourself clean? Using poor grammar? These things may not be sinful in themselves, but you should work at eliminating habits that bother others. Don't let anything get in the way of your witness. □ S.K.

TO MEMORIZE: *I am not seeking my own good but the good of many, so that they may be saved.*
1 Corinthians 10:33, NIV

Both Sides

FROM THE BIBLE:
"Everything is permissible"— but not everything is beneficial. "Everything is permissible"— but not everything is constructive. Nobody should seek his own good, but the good of others. . . . So whether you eat or drink or whatever you do, do it all for the glory of God. Do not cause anyone to stumble, whether Jews, Greeks or the church of God—even as I try to please everybody in every way. For I am not seeking my own good but the good of many, so that they may be saved.
1 Corinthians 10:23-24, 31-33, NIV

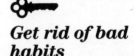

Get rid of bad habits

AUGUST

9

The Right Program

FROM THE BIBLE:
Always be full of joy in the Lord; I say it again, rejoice! Let everyone see that you are unselfish and considerate in all you do. Remember that the Lord is coming soon. Don't worry about anything; instead, pray about everything; tell God your needs and don't forget to thank him for his answers. If you do this you will experience God's peace, which is far more wonderful than the human mind can understand. His peace will keep your thoughts and your hearts quiet and at rest as you trust in Christ Jesus. And now, brothers, as I close this letter let me say this one more thing: Fix your thoughts on what is true and good and right. Think about things that are pure and lovely, and dwell on the fine, good things in others. Think about all you can praise God for and be glad about. Keep putting into practice all you learned from me and saw me doing, and the God of peace will be with you.
Philippians 4:4-9, TLB

Put right things in your mind

HANNAH'S SCREAMS brought Mother running. As she picked up the shaking little girl, Mother demanded, "What have you done now, boys?"

"Oh, she's such a baby," Josh said scornfully. "She's scared to death of a little old worm."

The sound of a car in the drive drew everyone's attention. "It's Dad," yelled Jeremy, "with our new computer!" The boys raced for the garage.

Dad brought the computer into the house and plugged it in. While he read the instructions, the boys pushed several keys, intending to play a game. But nothing happened. "Dad, this doesn't work like Uncle Dan's," complained Josh. He pushed more buttons. "It won't do anything."

Dad looked up. "Yes, it will." He slipped a disk into the computer and pushed a button. There was a *whirrr* and a *click,* and a game appeared on the screen. "A computer can only do what it's programmed to do," said Dad. "The program is on the disk."

"Look at the monster, Hannah. It's going to get you!" Jeremy teased, pointing at the screen.

Mother instantly turned off the computer, and the boys howled. "Before you play one game, listen to me," she said firmly. "When we are born, our minds are like this computer. We have great potential, but what we become depends entirely on how we are programmed. That is why we have family devotions and provide good, wholesome reading materials and tapes. That is why we talk about good things. But you, Jeremy and Josh, are programming fear into Hannah, and it has to stop."

Dad frowned and nodded. "Either you stop, or I'm going to put some fear into you!"

The boys knew what he meant—a spanking! "We're sorry," they said in unison.

"If you're truly sorry, you'll stop," Dad declared. "Now, with Mother's permission, we'll reprogram this computer."

HOW ABOUT YOU? Are you programming the wrong things into a little brother or sister? And what are you programming into yourself? What you read, watch, and hear "programs" your mind. If God checked on you today, would He be pleased with what He finds flashing on the screen of your mind? □ B.W.

TO MEMORIZE: *I will put my laws in their minds and write them on their hearts.* Hebrews 8:10, NIV

10

A Sick Friend

SCOTT SAT on the porch steps, his chin propped up in his hand. There was a baseball game on TV, but Scott didn't even care. All he could think about was Bobby Jonas! Just the week before, the boys had taken a hike around the park. Now Bobby was in the hospital, seriously sick. When Scott's mom had talked to Bobby's mom that morning, Mrs. Jonas said the doctors had told them Bobby might not get well. That was scary! Scott sat and thought about his friend. He didn't feel like doing anything else.

The screen door opened behind him, and Scott's mother brought out a glass of lemonade. "I thought you might be thirsty," she said.

Scott drank the lemonade without even noticing how good it tasted. "Mom, why did Bobby get sick?"

"Well," replied Mom, "all the bad things that happen to us are a result of sin entering the world. It's because of sin that the world is out of balance. Death will come to all of us sooner or later—sometimes through sickness, sometimes through car accidents, and sometimes other ways. The important thing is that God cares about us, and He cares about Bobby. He is there to give comfort to the Jonas family. He is there to help Bobby face the situation. We should pray that Bobby understands the comfort that the Lord can provide, and that God's will is done in regard to his health."

"Mom, could we pray right now?" Scott asked.

Mother sat on the step next to Scott, and together they talked to God about Bobby.

HOW ABOUT YOU? Has there been a time when one of your friends or a relative was very sick? When someone you loved died? Did you wonder why it happened? Sickness and death are a result of sin entering the world. But God gives comfort to Christians! He promises them an eternal home in heaven, where there is no sickness or death. Through Him you can have peace, even in the most difficult times. □ L.W.

TO MEMORIZE: *Our present sufferings are not worth comparing with the glory that will be revealed in us.* Romans 8:18, NIV

FROM THE BIBLE:

I consider that our present sufferings are not worth comparing with the glory that will be revealed in us. The creation waits in eager expectation for the sons of God to be revealed. For the creation was subjected to frustration, not by its own choice, but by the will of the one who subjected it, in hope that the creation itself will be liberated from its bondage to decay and brought into the glorious freedom of the children of God. We know that the whole creation has been groaning as in the pains of childbirth right up to the present time. Not only so, but we ourselves, who have the first fruits of the Spirit, groan inwardly as we wait eagerly for our adoption as sons, the redemption of our bodies.
Romans 8:18-23, NIV

God gives comfort

11

A Sick Friend

(Continued from yesterday)

FROM THE BIBLE:

Paul, an apostle of Christ Jesus by the will of God, and Timothy our brother, To the church of God in Corinth, together with all the saints throughout Achaia: Grace and peace to you from God our Father and the Lord Jesus Christ. Praise be to the God and Father of our Lord Jesus Christ, the Father of compassion and the God of all comfort, who comforts us in all our troubles, so that we can comfort those in any trouble with the comfort we ourselves have received from God. For just as the sufferings of Christ flow over into our lives, so also through Christ our comfort overflows. If we are distressed, it is for your comfort and salvation; if we are comforted, it is for your comfort, which produces in you patient endurance of the same sufferings we suffer. And our hope for you is firm, because we know that just as you share in our sufferings, so also you share in our comfort.
2 Corinthians 1:1-7, NIV

Encourage those in need

ONE DAY, Scott's mom again talked to Mrs. Jonas on the phone. After she hung up she said, "Bobby is feeling a little better and would like some company. How would you like to go to the hospital to see him?"

Scott hesitated. "But Mom, what would I say?"

"Talk about the things you usually talk about—baseball, school, or hiking," suggested Mother.

Scott still looked worried. "But what if Bobby wants to talk about being sick?"

"Let him," Mother advised. "Sometimes the kindest thing to do for someone in the hospital is to listen—to let him talk about how he is feeling."

Scott was thoughtful. "I'm glad Bobby is a Christian," he said finally.

"Yes, that is comforting." Scott's mother paused and then said, "Remember, you can't pretend to understand what Bobby is going through. You've never been faced with a serious illness. You can, however, remind Bobby that the Lord understands, and that the Lord loves him and cares for him very much."

Scott got his jacket. He was still scared to go, but he knew he should. He was certainly glad he knew the Lord as His personal Savior. The Lord could help him know what to say when he visited his friend.

HOW ABOUT YOU? Are you afraid to visit a sick person because you don't know what to say? Even adults are often nervous about visiting someone who is ill. But don't stay away! Let that person know you care. If you've been in the same circumstances, you can share that with him. If not, don't pretend to know what he is feeling. If he wants to talk about it, let him. If he doesn't, don't ask nosy questions. Share what's been happening in school and Sunday school. Share a memory verse with him. Encourage him to trust the Lord for strength to face tough situations. Share with him that God cares. □ L.W.

TO MEMORIZE: *For just as the sufferings of Christ flow over into our lives, so also through Christ our comfort overflows.* 2 Corinthians 1:5, NIV

"**S**PECIAL BULLETIN!" the radio blared. "There will be no school at Brookside today. The school was vandalized last night. Windows were broken, desks smashed, and rooms sprayed with paint. Damage is estimated to be . . ."

"Vandalized!" Norma exclaimed. "Who would want to destroy our beautiful school?"

"Whoever did it was really dumb," declared Eric. "What do they expect to gain by it?"

"I bet someone who hated school did it," Norma guessed.

"It's sad when someone has no respect for property or the rights of others," said Dad. "Unless that person changes his ways, I fear he is headed for real trouble. Well, enough of that. You have the day off from school, but I still have to go to work. I'd better be going."

Several days later the vandal was arrested. He was a fifteen-year-old named Keith. He had been in trouble with the law many times before. When his case was tried, he was found guilty.

"The judge sent Keith to reform school," Norma said that evening. "It must be awful to go to a place like that."

"Yes, but sin has a penalty," Dad reminded her. "In a sense, the judge didn't send Keith to reform school. Keith sent himself. He knew the rules, and he chose to disobey. Now he has to face the consequences. This reminds me of the way people say, 'How could a loving God send anyone to hell?' They forget that God is not only loving, He is holy, too, and the penalty for sin must be paid. Jesus paid for our redemption, but it's our choice to accept or reject what He did for us. God doesn't force His will on us, so if a person goes to hell, it's his own choice. He refused to accept Christ."

"I never thought of it that way," said Eric. "But you're right, Dad. We do have to make our own choice."

HOW ABOUT YOU? What choice have you made? You have sinned, but God doesn't want you to die in your sin. Jesus died so that you may have eternal life. You must confess your sins, ask forgiveness, and accept Christ as your Savior. Have you done that? □ J.H.

TO MEMORIZE: *As for me and my household, we will serve the LORD.* Joshua 24:15, NIV

Keith's Choice

FROM THE BIBLE:
And as Moses in the wilderness lifted up the bronze image of a serpent on a pole, even so I must be lifted up upon a pole, so that anyone who believes in me will have eternal life. For God loved the world so much that he gave his only Son so that anyone who believes in him shall not perish but have eternal life. God did not send his Son into the world to condemn it, but to save it. There is no eternal doom awaiting those who trust him to save them. But those who don't trust him have already been tried and condemned for not believing in the only Son of God. John 3:14-18, TLB

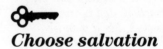

Choose salvation

13

No Room

FROM THE BIBLE:

Not all who sound religious are really godly people. They may refer to me as "Lord," but still won't get to heaven. For the decisive question is whether they obey my Father in heaven. At the Judgment many will tell me, "Lord, Lord, we told others about you and used your name to cast out demons and to do many other great miracles." But I will reply, "You have never been mine. Go away, for your deeds are evil." All who listen to my instructions and follow them are wise, like a man who builds his house on solid rock. Though the rain comes in torrents, and the floods rise and the storm winds beat against his house, it won't collapse, for it is built on rock. But those who hear my instructions and ignore them are foolish, like a man who builds his house on sand. For when the rains and floods come, and storm winds beat against his house, it will fall with a mighty crash.
Matthew 7:21-27, TLB

Be registered in heaven

"**A**RE WE almost there? It's been such a long ride!" exclaimed Jamie. She and her sister, Kellie, could hardly wait to get to Sea World and their motel.

"Two whole days in a motel with a pool!" Kellie giggled. "We're going to have a ball!"

"We're here, girls," announced Dad, and he turned off the highway toward the motel.

Inside, Dad approached the desk. "My name is Gardiner," he said. "We have reservations."

The receptionist whirled a large card file. "I'm sorry," she said uncertainly, "but I can't find your name here."

"Please look again," Dad said patiently. After another search, the receptionist shook her head slowly. "Well, do you have a room with two double beds?" asked Dad.

"No, I don't. I'm really sorry," the lady replied. "There's a convention in town, and all motels are full."

"It would be awful to go back home now," wailed Jamie.

Dad nodded. "There's been a mistake," he said, "but don't fret. Let's have a cup of coffee while we think about what to do next."

Seated in the restaurant, Dad said, "If this seems bad, think how it would be if we should arrive in heaven someday and discover that our names have never been registered there."

"But Daddy," Jamie said thoughtfully, "that won't happen. The Bible says Jesus has gone ahead of us and has already written our names down. He knows we love Him."

"You're absolutely right," said Dad with a smile. "We're already registered there, and God never makes a mistake. Shall we thank Him for that and then trust Him to find a place for us here?" The girls nodded, and they all bowed their heads.

HOW ABOUT YOU? Is your name registered in heaven? Or if you died today, would you hear the awful words, "Depart from me. I never knew you." If you're not absolutely sure about that, make sure today. Admit your sin and need of a Savior. Ask Jesus to forgive and save you. Then your name will be written in heaven, and you'll never be turned away there. □ P.K.

TO MEMORIZE: *And I saw the dead, small and great, standing before God, and books were opened. And another book was opened, which is the Book of Life.* Revelation 20:12, NKJV

WHEN THE DOORBELL rang, Marcia came to the door. The postman stood there, a letter in his hand. "Marcia," he said, "did you address this letter? You didn't put down the zip code or the city and state. It's going to end up in the dead letter office."

"Oops!" exclaimed Marcia. "I was going to ask Mother for Aunt Julia's address, but I forgot. What's the dead letter office?"

"It's a department of the post office. Mail that can't be delivered goes there," explained Mr. Zachary. "Then clerks open it and look for return addresses inside. If there is one, the mail is returned to the sender."

"What if there isn't any return address?" asked Marcia.

"Most of the letters are destroyed," said Mr. Zachary. "The contents of parcels are sold, and the money goes into the post office funds."

"Well, I don't want Aunt Julia's letter to end up there," declared Marcia. "Thanks, Mr. Zachary."

At family devotions that evening Marcia began her prayer: "Dear heavenly Father, thank You for a beautiful day and for my parents, and for . . ." She stopped. "I think my prayer is going to God's dead letter office," she said, right in the middle of her prayer. Her parents looked at her in surprise. "I know He won't hear my prayers until I make something right first," added Marcia tearfully. "Daddy, I took five dollars from your wallet last week. I know God hasn't heard my prayers since. Please forgive me. I'll pay you back from my allowance."

"Of course I forgive you, Marcia," said Dad. "But you must confess your sin to God, too."

Marcia nodded her head. "I know," she said. "I'm going to do that right now."

HOW ABOUT YOU? Isn't prayer a wonderful privilege? But is there unconfessed sin in your life? If so, the Lord says He won't hear you. Make things right with others and with God. Then learn and experience the following verse. □ M.R.P.

TO MEMORIZE: *God has surely listened and heard my voice in prayer.* Psalm 66:19, NIV

The Dead Letter Office

FROM THE BIBLE:
Come and listen, all you who fear God; let me tell you what he has done for me. I cried out to him with my mouth; his praise was on my tongue. If I had cherished sin in my heart, the LORD would not have listened; but God has surely listened and heard my voice in prayer. Praise be to God, who has not rejected my prayer or withheld his love from me!
Psalm 66:16-20, NIV

Pray with a pure heart

15

Susie and Her Shadow

FROM THE BIBLE:
But you are not like that, for you have been chosen by God himself—you are priests of the King, you are holy and pure, you are God's very own—all this so that you may show to others how God called you out of the darkness into his wonderful light. Once you were less than nothing; now you are God's own. Once you knew very little of God's kindness; now your very lives have been changed by it. Dear brothers, you are only visitors here. Since your real home is in heaven I beg you to keep away from the evil pleasures of this world; they are not for you, for they fight against your very souls. Be careful how you behave among your unsaved neighbors; for then, even if they are suspicious of you and talk against you, they will end up praising God for your good works when Christ returns.
1 Peter 2:9-12, TLB

You influence others

"LOOK, MOM!" Mary Jo pointed out the window. "Look at Susie." Mother looked, and she and Mary Jo laughed together as they watched three-year-old Susie play with her shadow in the bright sunlight. Susie ran as fast as she could, then she turned around and saw that her shadow had come right along with her. "Stay there," she commanded. Turning her back on her shadow, she took a big jump. She turned around again to find that her shadow had jumped, too.

At dinnertime Mother asked Mary Jo to set the table. "I'll help, too," piped up Susie—and she did, carefully watching to see how Mary Jo placed the dishes and the silver. She copied what she observed.

As they were eating, Mary Jo passed the lima beans to her younger brother, Jerry. He passed them on to Mother. "Help yourself first, Son," she said. "You need to try a few."

Jerry glanced at Mary Jo's plate. "Mary Jo doesn't have any." As Mother passed the lima beans back to her, Mary Jo scowled but put a few on her plate.

After dinner Dad got up from the table. "Who'd like to help me wash the car before it gets dark?" he asked.

Mary Jo spoke. "I will."

"I'll help, too," said Jerry quickly.

"Me, too," added Susie.

Mary Jo laughed. "What is this—'copy Mary Jo' night?"

Mother smiled. "Remember Susie and her shadow?" she asked. "Whether she liked it or not, Susie had her shadow with her. Wherever Susie went, her shadow went. There was no way she could get away from it. The influence we have over others is like that. Whether we like it or not, what we do and say influences other people. We can't get away from that fact. It's important to make sure we influence them in the right way—for good and not for bad."

HOW ABOUT YOU? What kind of influence do you have? As a Christian, it's important to be kind, honest, faithful. Live in such a way that your life will cause the unsaved to want to know Jesus and will help other Christians live for Him. Living close to the Son of God—the Lord Jesus—gives you a good, strong Christian influence. □ H.M.

TO MEMORIZE: *For none of us lives to himself, and no one dies to himself.* Romans 14:7, NKJV

"MOM, WHY do we have to go to church every Sunday?" Chad asked at breakfast. "Some of my friends don't go."

"Well, we do," Mother answered. "We go to be instructed from God's Word, so please get ready. We'll be leaving soon." This wasn't the first time Chad had complained about going to church recently. He once loved to go to church, but as he grew older, he sometimes didn't want to go.

That afternoon the subject came up again. "My friends are playing basketball tonight," said Chad. "May I go?"

"Chad," Dad answered this time, "we're going to church."

"I don't see why we can't just read the Bible for ourselves instead of having to sit in church all that time," Chad grumbled.

After supper the next day, Chad covered a table with newspapers. "I'm going to work on my new model car. It's going to be some car when I get it put together! Just look at all those pieces," he exclaimed. He began to work, but soon he looked up. "Can you help me with this, Dad?" he asked.

Dad shrugged. "I don't think you need me," he said. "Just put the pieces together. It should turn out just fine."

"Dad," Chad was discouraged, "how would I know how the pieces go when I can't understand it?"

Dad got up and walked over to the table. "Chad," he said, "trying to put this model together without my help is like trying to live your Christian life without help from God's servants. Lately you've not wanted to go to church, yet our pastor and Sunday school teachers help us understand how God wants us to live."

Chad thought about it. "I guess you're right. There are lots of things in the Bible that I don't understand by myself," he admitted. "I'll try to remember that. Now—do you think you could help me with this model?"

HOW ABOUT YOU? Do you think you don't need to go to church? It's great to read the Bible for yourself, and you should do that. But God has also provided godly men and women in your church and Sunday school who can help you understand His Word. Learn from them. □ D.K.

TO MEMORIZE: *Teach me your way, O LORD; lead me in a straight path because of my oppressors.* Psalm 27:11, NIV

Model Building

FROM THE BIBLE:
You are my hiding place; you will protect me from trouble and surround me with songs of deliverance. I will instruct you and teach you in the way you should go; I will counsel you and watch over you. Do not be like the horse or the mule, which have no understanding but must be controlled by bit and bridle or they will not come to you. Many are the woes of the wicked, but the LORD's unfailing love surrounds the man who trusts in him. Rejoice in the LORD and be glad, you righteous; sing, all you who are upright in heart!
Psalm 32:7-11, NIV

Go to church

17

Citizenship

FROM THE BIBLE:

Never forget that once you were heathen, and that you were called godless and "unclean" by the Jews. (But their hearts, too, were still unclean, even though they were going through the ceremonies and rituals of the godly, for they circumcised themselves as a sign of godliness.) Remember that in those days you were living utterly apart from Christ; you were enemies of God's children and he had promised you no help. You were lost, without God, without hope. But now you belong to Christ Jesus, and though you once were far away from God, now you have been brought very near to him because of what Jesus Christ has done for you with his blood. For Christ himself is our way of peace. He has made peace between us Jews and you Gentiles by making us all one family, breaking down the wall of contempt that used to separate us.

Ephesians 2:11-14, TLB

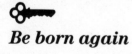

Be born again

CURT WAS GLAD to run an errand to Judge Patton's home. He always liked to hear the retired judge's stories about his days in court. Today, after he and Judge Patton had talked a while, the judge asked, "Are you a Christian?"

"Oh, I think so," replied Curt. "I try to be good. I obey my parents and teachers pretty well."

"So you'd say you belong to God's kingdom because you're good?" asked the judge. "Let me tell you a story. I used to sit on the bench as judge in southern California. One day a man was brought before me—a fine-looking, well-dressed man. He had been living in our town for a number of years. One day when he tried to buy some property, it was discovered that he was not a United States citizen. He was still a citizen of Mexico. 'But Your Honor,' he said to me, 'I obey the laws. I'm a good neighbor. I pay my bills.' Now, Curt, do you think I should have told him he had nothing more to do to become a citizen?"

Curt shook his head. "We studied about that in school," he said. "A foreigner has to be naturalized. He must renounce his allegiance to his own country and swear allegiance to the United States constitution."

"And who makes the rules for citizenship—a foreigner or the United States government?" asked Judge Patton.

"Why, the government, of course," said Curt.

The judge nodded. "Well, Curt," he said, "you expect God to make you a citizen in the kingdom of God based on *your* rules—by living a good, obedient life. But who has a right to set the rules for heavenly citizenship—you or God?"

"God does."

"Yes. The blood of His dear Son, Jesus, had to be shed on the cross to make our citizenship possible," said Judge Patton. "Do you think, then, that He would change His rules to suit you?"

"No," said Curt. "I must apply for citizenship by God's rules. Will you tell me what they are?"

HOW ABOUT YOU? Do you claim to be a citizen of God's kingdom? On what do you base your claim—doing good works, obeying the commandments, being a church member? Jesus said, "Except a man be born again, he cannot see the kingdom of God." □ M.R.P.

TO MEMORIZE: *I tell you the truth, no one can see the kingdom of God unless he is born again.* John 3:3, NIV

"**W**HAT ARE YOU DOING, Dad?" asked Nathan as he dropped his bike on the lawn and joined his father, who was half-hidden under the raised car hood. "There's nothing wrong with the car, is there?"

"No, and I want it to stay that way," came Dad's muffled reply. "Ever hear the saying, 'An ounce of prevention is worth a pound of cure'?"

Nathan shook his head. "No. What does it mean?"

"It means it's better to keep a car from breaking down than to repair it." Dad slammed down the hood and picked up his tools. "Looks like we might be in for a thunderstorm."

Dad was right. There was a storm that evening! The wind howled, and rain poured down! As hailstones began pounding the house, Nathan had a sudden thought. "Oh, my bike!" he exclaimed. "I forgot to put it in the garage!"

"Again," added Dad. "Too late now."

Later, when the storm had stopped, Nathan put his bicycle in the garage and found several dents in the fenders. "Too bad," Dad said. "Preventing those dents would have been a lot easier than fixing them." Nathan hung his head.

At bedtime Mom and Dad called Nathan into the den for family devotions. "Why do we have to have devotions every evening?" Nathan grumbled.

"An ounce of prevention is worth a pound of cure," Dad quoted. "I maintain the car to keep it in good condition. You should do the same for your bicycle. But it's even more important to take care of the soul, the most valuable possession we have. How much better it is to daily maintain our walk with God than to wait until we break down and then try to repair the damage."

Nathan picked up his Bible and grinned at his dad. "Where shall we read?" he asked.

HOW ABOUT YOU? Do you practice spiritual maintenance every day? Remember, it is much better to keep from disobeying God than to have to repent. Prayer and reading the Word of God will help you stay in tip-top spiritual condition. □ B.W.

TO MEMORIZE: *Then will I ever sing praise to your name and fulfill my vows day after day.* Psalm 61:8, NIV

AUGUST

18

An Ounce of Prevention

FROM THE BIBLE:
O God, you are my God, earnestly I seek you; my soul thirsts for you, my body longs for you, in a dry and weary land where there is no water. I have seen you in the sanctuary and beheld your power and your glory. Because your love is better than life, my lips will glorify you. I will praise you as long as I live, and in your name I will lift up my hands. My soul will be satisfied as with the richest of foods; with singing lips my mouth will praise you. On my bed I remember you; I think of you through the watches of the night. Because you are my help, I sing in the shadow of your wings. My soul clings to you; your right hand upholds me. Psalm 63:1-8, NIV

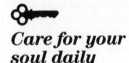

Care for your soul daily

A Perfect Solution

FROM THE BIBLE:

If you are wise, live a life of steady goodness, so that only good deeds will pour forth. And if you don't brag about them, then you will be truly wise! And by all means don't brag about being wise and good if you are bitter and jealous and selfish; that is the worst sort of lie. For jealousy and selfishness are not God's kind of wisdom. Such things are earthly, unspiritual, inspired by the devil. For wherever there is jealousy or selfish ambition, there will be disorder and every other kind of evil. But the wisdom that comes from heaven is first of all pure and full of quiet gentleness. Then it is peace-loving and courteous. It allows discussion and is willing to yield to others; it is full of mercy and good deeds. It is wholehearted and straightforward and sincere. And those who are peacemakers will plant seeds of peace and reap a harvest of goodness.
James 3:13-18, TLB

Don't fight

ONE LOOK at Randy's flushed face told Mother something was wrong. "How was school?" she asked.

"So-so." Randy drew a deep, ragged breath, then blurted out, "If Jeff doesn't leave me alone on the bus, I'm going to have to fight him!"

"Oh?" Mother responded. "If you do, you had better be prepared to take the consequences."

Randy looked up. "Will you whip me?"

"No," Mother said, "but Jeff might. There must be a better solution than a fight. Does Jeff bother you at school?"

"No. He knows Miss Jenkins won't allow it," Randy answered, "but it's different on the bus."

"Well, let's pray about it, Randy," Mother said. "The Lord will help you find a solution."

The next day Randy came home from school grinning from ear to ear. Before Mother could ask, he told her. "Jeff left me alone today."

"What did you do?" Mother asked.

Randy chuckled. "I sat in the front seat of the bus," he said. "With the driver right there, Jeff didn't dare make trouble." Together Randy and Mother celebrated with cookies and milk.

Randy was surprised when Mother came over and hugged him a little later. "You've taught me a lesson today, Randy. I've been having a little trouble with my temper lately," she confessed. "I haven't thought about having a fist fight with anybody, but there are a couple of people I've been tempted to tell off. I think the devil has been encouraging me to really give them a piece of my mind. But you have given me the perfect solution. Now I know how to keep Satan from bothering me."

Randy looked surprised. "How?"

"By getting just as close to Jesus as I can," Mother answered. "I've been sitting in the 'back of the bus.' I need to move up."

HOW ABOUT YOU? Are you tempted to go to "fist city" to solve your problems? Think again. A fight would probably make matters worse. Get close to Jesus through reading His Word, praying, and keeping your thoughts on Him. He can give you the perfect solution for solving your problems peaceably. □ B.W.

TO MEMORIZE: *If it is possible, as far as it depends on you, live at peace with everyone.*
Romans 12:18, NIV

DAVE EXCITEDLY helped Dad unpack the big box. The old black-and-white TV set had given out completely, and Dave looked forward to watching his favorite team in living color tonight. "I know how to hook up this baby," he told his father. "I helped Tony get his TV hooked up last Christmas." Dad smiled and let Dave work.

After twisting the small wires around the screws to the antenna lead, he finally plugged the TV cord into the wall socket. He waited for the picture to come into view. When it did, it was very blurred. "I know what's wrong," he said, moving the rabbit ears from one side to the other. But still the picture was out of focus.

"Are you sure you've got it hooked up right?" his father asked, offering to check it out.

Dave pushed his father's hand away. "Sure," he said. "This set is practically the same as Tony's, and we got it together okay. There's got to be something wrong with this one."

"Read the instruction sheet," Dad suggested. "This set could be different from Tony's."

Dave picked up the instructions that had come with the set and began to read them. Then he went back to the set and switched the wires of the VHF with the UHF. The improvement of the picture was outstanding.

Dave was embarrassed. "If all else fails," he said, "read the directions."

"Better yet," said Dad, "read the instructions *first*. That principle is true in our Christian lives, too. God's instruction book, the Bible, not only tells us how to accept Jesus Christ as personal Savior, it also tells us how to live the Christian life. But we won't know unless we read it."

HOW ABOUT YOU? Are you a Christian? Then God's Word, the Bible, should be your guide, your instruction book. It explains what a Christian should do if he falls into sin. It commands every believer to love, to give, to witness, and many other things. God's book is very important. But if it's going to be helpful, it has to be read. □ R.J.

TO MEMORIZE: *Your hands made me and formed me; give me understanding to learn your commands.*
Psalm 119:73, NIV

Follow the Manual

FROM THE BIBLE:
How can a young man keep his way pure? By living according to your word. I seek you with all my heart; do not let me stray from your commands. I have hidden your word in my heart that I might not sin against you. Praise be to you, O LORD; teach me your decrees. With my lips I recount all the laws that come from your mouth. I rejoice in following your statutes as one rejoices in great riches. I meditate on your precepts and consider your ways. I delight in your decrees; I will not neglect your word. Do good to your servant, and I will live; I will obey your word. Open my eyes that I may see wonderful things in your law.
Psalm 119:9-18, NIV

Follow God's Book

AUGUST

21

Out of Harmony

FROM THE BIBLE:

Is there any such thing as Christians cheering each other up? Do you love me enough to want to help me? Does it mean anything to you that we are brothers in the LORD, sharing the same Spirit? Are your hearts tender and sympathetic at all? Then make me truly happy by loving each other and agreeing wholeheartedly with each other, working together with one heart and mind and purpose. Don't be selfish; don't live to make a good impression on others. Be humble, thinking of others as better than yourself. Don't just think about your own affairs, but be interested in others, too, and in what they are doing. Your attitude should be the kind that was shown us by Jesus Christ, who, though he was God, did not demand and cling to his rights as God, but laid aside his mighty power and glory, taking the disguise of a slave and becoming like men. And he humbled himself even further, going so far as actually to die a criminal's death on a cross.

Philippians 2:1-8, TLB

Don't be a sour note

MELODY STOMPED down the hall and slammed the bedroom door. She flung herself down on the bed. "Someone is always on my back! Nothing I do is right, anymore," she muttered angrily. "Everyone is mad at me."

From the den came the sound of Mother playing the piano. Melody grimaced. Something was wrong! Melody had never heard Mother play like that! She usually played so beautifully, but now the music jarred her eardrums. It was terrible.

Jumping up, Melody ran into the den. "That sounds awful," she blurted out. "What's the matter?"

"Oh?" said Mother. "Does this sound any better?" She ran her fingers over the keyboard.

"It sure does," Melody answered.

"Sit down and let me show you something," invited Mother. She scooted over so Melody could join her on the piano bench. "When the music sounded so terrible, all I was doing was hitting one note wrong. Each time I hit it, it threw everything else out of harmony. Listen." She played several notes. "One wrong note in a chord causes a 'discord.' And one member of a family out of harmony with the other members causes discord in a home."

"Oh!" sputtered Melody, jumping up and walking out of the room. She stopped when she saw her own angry face in the hall mirror. Melody hung her head. She knew *she* was the wrong note. She had to admit that her attitude had been sour lately. She had tried to blame everyone else, but she knew she was the problem.

"I think you need to call on the Lord Jesus and ask Him to 'tune' your attitude," suggested Mother. "It would be nice for our family to be in harmony again."

Melody nodded and went to her room. This time she shut the door quietly behind her and knelt beside her bed.

HOW ABOUT YOU? Are you out of tune with everyone? Do you feel and sound off-key? Maybe you've been blaming everyone else when you are the one who needs tuning. Don't be a "wrong note." Get in tune with God and your family. Help produce a beautiful, harmonious home life.

□ B.W.

TO MEMORIZE: *He put a new song in my mouth, a hymn of praise to our God. Many will see and fear and put their trust in the LORD.* Psalm 40:3, NIV

"IT'S SO DARK OUT," said Kathy as she and her brother Josh stumbled along the path toward their campsite. They had been visiting the campsite of some friends.

"Yeah," agreed Josh, "but we're almost—" His words were cut off as he caught his toe on a tree root and fell.

Kathy reached down to help him up. "Are you okay?"

"Yes," said Josh, brushing himself off, "but we'd better not go quite so fast." Kathy agreed, and the two of them moved slowly and carefully along until they reached the camp where their parents were waiting.

"We could hear you two coming," Mother greeted them. "Did someone fall?"

"Josh did," replied Kathy, "but he's not hurt. It was so dark we couldn't see."

"Why didn't you use your flashlight?" asked Dad.

"Flashlight?" Kathy and Josh looked at each other. "Oh, our flashlight!" They began to laugh.

"Real smart, Josh," teased Kathy. "You've got the flashlight, you know. You stuck it in your sweater pocket."

"I forgot I had it," admitted Josh.

"You two remind me of a lot of people," observed Dad. "They have a light for their path, but they either forget to use it, or they just don't bother."

"Like who?" Kathy wanted to know.

"Like all the Christians who fail to read their Bibles," replied Dad, picking up his own. "God says His Word is a light to our path, but it doesn't do any good if we don't use it. Gather 'round now. It's time for devotions."

HOW ABOUT YOU? Do you read your Bible regularly? It contains many principles to help you in your daily life. It has a lot of practical advice. It offers comfort when you hurt. But unless you use it, it can't help you. Don't stumble along in the dark. Use your Bible every day. □ H.M.

TO MEMORIZE: *Your word is a lamp to my feet and a light for my path.* Psalm 119:105, NIV

AUGUST

22

Needed: A Light

FROM THE BIBLE:

Your word is a lamp to my feet and a light for my path. I have taken an oath and confirmed it, that I will follow your righteous laws. I have suffered much; preserve my life, O LORD, according to your word. Accept, O LORD, the willing praise of my mouth, and teach me your laws. Though I constantly take my life in my hands, I will not forget your law. The wicked have set a snare for me, but I have not strayed from your precepts. Your statutes are my heritage forever; they are the joy of my heart. My heart is set on keeping your decrees to the very end.

Psalm 119:105-112, NIV

Use your Bible daily

23

Needed: A Light

(Continued from yesterday)

FROM THE BIBLE:

Your word is a lamp to my feet and a light for my path. I have taken an oath and confirmed it, that I will follow your righteous laws. I have suffered much; preserve my life, O LORD, according to your word. Accept, O LORD, the willing praise of my mouth, and teach me your laws. Though I constantly take my life in my hands, I will not forget your law. The wicked have set a snare for me, but I have not strayed from your precepts. Your statutes are my heritage forever; they are the joy of my heart. My heart is set on keeping your decrees to the very end.

Psalm 119:105-112, NIV

Apply God's Word to yourself

"**W**HY DON'T you sleep at our camp tonight?" Josh asked his friend, Ben. "My mom said it was okay with her."

"Can I, Mom?" Ben looked over at his mother. "Then I won't wake you when I get up early to go fishing."

Ben's mother laughed. "Take your sleeping bag and run along," she agreed. "It's already dark."

Soon the boys were on their way. Josh snapped on his flashlight. "Last night I left this thing in my pocket all the way home, but I'm not going to make the same dumb mistake twice!" he said as he led the way, turning back to flash the light on Ben's path. He continued to leave the beam of light on the path behind him, making sure Ben could see. "Last night I fell over a tree roo—" Down went Josh, and the flashlight went flying into a bush.

"Are you okay?" asked Ben.

Josh got up and retrieved his flashlight. "Yeah," he mumbled. "Walk up here with me so we can both see where we're going."

When they arrived at Josh's campsite, his family was waiting. "We saw your light, and heard a crash," said Mother. "What happened?"

"Fell again, didn't you?" said Kathy with a smirk.

When they had heard the story, Dad grinned. "Do you know who you remind me of tonight?"

Josh shook his head. "I was using my flashlight."

Dad nodded. "Yep, and you were pointing it on somebody else's path. You remind me of people who hear God's Word preached, and they think, *I hope So-and-So is listening. He really needs this.* Or maybe they read something from God's Word and apply it to somebody else's life. They fail to see that they need it themselves."

HOW ABOUT YOU? Did you notice that today's Scripture is the same as yesterday's? Read it again, and emphasize the words *I, my,* and *me.* Then when you read other passages in the Bible, such as, "Children, obey your parents," apply that to yourself, not to your sister. When you read, "Be ye kind to one another," think of what you—not your neighbor—should do. Remember, it's for *you.*

□ H.M.

TO MEMORIZE: *My heart is set on keeping your decrees to the very end.* Psalm 119:112, NIV

MARCY SCREAMED and sat up in bed. She began to cry. Her parents quickly came to her bedside, and her mother held her tightly. "Won't it ever stop?" asked Marcy between sobs. "I had another nightmare about the accident when Karen died. I keep seeing the car wreck."

"Try to remember your sister the way she used to be—lively, loving, and beautiful," Marcy's father suggested.

"I try," said Marcy, "but I can't seem to remember her that way."

"Honey, you know that Karen was a Christian," Mother reminded her, "so she's alive in heaven. Can you picture her there?"

Marcy shook her head. "I can't see her that way, either," she said sadly.

"I want to show you something," said Dad. "I'll get it." He left the room, returning soon with a watch, which he placed in Marcy's hand.

Marcy shuddered. "Oh, take Karen's watch away," she begged. "It's all broken from the wreck—just like Karen."

Dad took the watch. "Yes," he said, "like Karen. The case is scratched, and the crystal's broken. But let's look inside." After some prying, Dad lifted the watch from the case. "Look, Marcy. It's still running," he said. "Only the outside was ruined. Karen is still living. Only the 'case' she lived in here—her body—is dead."

After a moment, Marcy looked up with a trembling smile. "Karen truly is still alive, isn't she?" she said. "That never seemed real before."

"I'll get a new case for this watch, and you may have it as a reminder," said Dad. "Remember, Karen will have a new body someday, too—her very same body, made over new.

"I'll always keep the watch near me," promised Marcy. "When bad thoughts or dreams come, I'll see the watch ticking, and I'll think of Karen still living in heaven and waiting for her new body—and for us to join her!"

HOW ABOUT YOU? Has death taken away someone you love? Does this seem very final? A person never really dies. He just lays aside the body for a while. If you and your loved one are Christians, you'll meet again, and you'll be together forever.
□ M.R.P.

TO MEMORIZE: *We know that when he appears, we shall be like him, for we shall see him as he is.*
1 John 3:2, NIV

24

The Ticking Watch

FROM THE BIBLE:
In the same way, our earthly bodies which die and decay are different from the bodies we shall have when we come back to life again, for they will never die. The bodies we have now embarrass us for they become sick and die; but they will be full of glory when we come back to life again. Yes, they are weak, dying bodies now, but when we live again they will be full of strength. They are just human bodies at death, but when they come back to life they will be superhuman bodies. For just as there are natural, human bodies, there are also supernatural, spiritual bodies. The Scriptures tell us that the first man, Adam, was given a natural, human body but Christ is more than that, for he was life-giving Spirit. But I am telling you this strange and wonderful secret: we shall not all die, but we shall all be given new bodies!
1 Corinthians 15:42-45, 51, TLB

The real person never dies

AUGUST

25

The Raft Rescue

FROM THE BIBLE:
For the Father loves the Son, and tells him everything he is doing; and the Son will do far more awesome miracles than this man's healing. He will even raise from the dead anyone he wants to, just as the Father does. And the Father leaves all judgment of sin to his Son, so that everyone will honor the Son, just as they honor the Father. But if you refuse to honor God's Son, whom he sent to you, then you are certainly not honoring the Father. I say emphatically that anyone who listens to my message and believes in God who sent me has eternal life, and will never be damned for his sins, but has already passed out of death into life.
John 5:20-24, TLB

Let Jesus save you

"HELP! HELP! Save me!" Todd screamed as his homemade raft rushed toward the falls. Todd had gone down the river's edge to play on the raft he and his friends had built. It was tied to a sturdy elm tree on the riverbank. Because the current was rough, the raft was never untied. Unknown to Todd, the once thick rope had become badly frayed from rubbing on a rock. When he jumped onto the raft to catch a frog that was sunning itself, the rope snapped, and the raft lunged out from the river's edge and went pell-mell downstream.

Oh no! Todd thought. *What am I going to do? I can't swim well enough to reach the shore, and just two miles downstream the river plunges fifty feet over Drop-Off Point.* The river ran right next to the road. Thinking someone might see him, he waved his arms and yelled loudly.

Todd's father was driving home from work on that very road, and he looked out at the river. Upstream in the distance, he could see the raft spinning around, and he saw that someone was on it. Quickly stopping the car, he kicked off his shoes and headed for the river. Being a strong swimmer, he stroked toward the middle of the river and waited for the raft to reach him. How surprised he was to see his own son on it! He called out, "Todd, jump! Jump! I'll save you!"

Todd looked at the sturdy raft, then at his father in the swirling waters. He wasn't sure he wanted to leave the raft, but he knew it would mean sure death if he didn't! As he leaped into the surging water, his father caught his arm. Todd's father made it back to the shore, with Todd in tow.

Later, as they were drying off at home, Dad said, "You know, what I did for you today is sort of like what Jesus did for us. We were headed for sure death, and we couldn't save ourselves. Just as you had to trust me to save you when you jumped, so we had to be willing to 'leap out' by faith and trust the Lord to save us from our sins."

HOW ABOUT YOU? Have you put your faith and trust in Jesus Christ? If not, you are headed for trouble. God says you are a sinner, and sin brings eternal death. But Jesus suffered that death for you, and by simply trusting Him you are rescued, and you receive life. □ C.V.M.

TO MEMORIZE: *For the wages of sin is death, but the gift of God is eternal life in Christ Jesus our Lord.* Romans 6:23, NIV

BLACKIE WAS a farm dog. He was born in a barn in a nest of hay. When he was just a little pup, he had a great time playing with his brothers and sisters and hunting for mice under the hay. As the puppies grew older, one by one they left for new homes, but Blackie stayed on the farm. He was the special pet of Jimmy, the farmer's son.

Jimmy taught Blackie to stay on their own land. "Stay, Blackie! Stay!" Jimmy would often command, as he crossed the road to get the mail or to visit his neighbor. And like a good puppy, Blackie would sit there, tail wagging, until Jimmy returned.

Like most dogs, Blackie liked to hunt for treasures—dog treasures. He would hunt for squirrels, chipmunks, and mice. What fun Blackie had hunting on his property! Then one day he saw something moving in the tall grass across the road. The temptation was more than he could bear, and soon he crossed the road. What a treasure he found—a rabbit! He could hardly wait to get home with it. He bounded out of the tall grass, rabbit in his mouth. Like a streak of lightning, he darted across the road—and he never saw the big car coming! The driver blew his horn and pressed his foot as hard as he could on the brake. But Blackie, treasure in his mouth, went under the wheels of the car.

Hearing the commotion, Jimmy rushed from the house. He gathered the little dog into his arms, and soon Dad was taking him to the veterinarian.

"He's badly hurt," the vet told them, shaking his head. "With your permission I'll keep him here so I can watch him. I'll do my best to save him."

"All for a rabbit," moaned Jimmy, on the way home. "Blackie considers rabbits to be great treasures, but I'm sure even Blackie would agree it wasn't worth it. It may cost him his life!"

HOW ABOUT YOU? Do you know that many young people have lost their lives running after "treasures" such as drugs, drink, cigarettes, money, and even popularity? These things may look attractive now, but they are not worth what they may cost in the end. Keep your thoughts on Jesus. Don't wander across any road of life without Jesus by your side. □ R.P.

TO MEMORIZE: *God is faithful; he will not let you be tempted beyond what you can bear. But when you are tempted, he will also provide a way out so that you can stand up under it.*
1 Corinthians 10:13, NIV

Treasures

FROM THE BIBLE:
Happy is the man who doesn't give in and do wrong when he is tempted, for afterwards he will get as his reward the crown of life that God has promised those who love him. And remember, when someone wants to do wrong it is never God who is tempting him, for God never wants to do wrong and never tempts anyone else to do it. Temptation is the pull of man's own evil thoughts and wishes. These evil thoughts lead to evil actions and afterwards to the death penalty from God. So don't be misled, dear brothers.
James 1:12-16, TLB

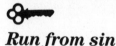

Run from sin

AUGUST

27

Overloaded

FROM THE BIBLE:

Calling the Twelve to him, he sent them out two by two and gave them authority over evil spirits. These were his instructions: "Take nothing for the journey except a staff—no bread, no bag, no money in your belts. Wear sandals but not an extra tunic. Whenever you enter a house, stay there until you leave that town. And if any place will not welcome you or listen to you, shake the dust off your feet when you leave, as a testimony against them." They went out and preached that people should repent. They drove out many demons and anointed many sick people with oil and healed them. . . . The apostles gathered around Jesus and reported to him all they had done and taught. Then, because so many people were coming and going that they did not even have a chance to eat, he said to them, "Come with me by yourselves to a quiet place and get some rest."

Mark 6:7-13, 30-31, NIV

Don't get too busy

THE TAYLORS were on their way to a cottage they were renting near Sunshine Lake. "It's already dark out," observed Sue as she stared out the car window. "I can hardly wait to get there. It seems like years since we've been on a real vacation!"

"I know," sighed Mother. "We've been so busy getting your father's business started and redecorating the house. It's hard to find a time when we're all free to take a vacation. I'm glad we're getting a few days together before school starts."

When they arrived at the cottage, Sue and her brother, Jimmy, helped Dad unpack the car while Mother swept and dusted inside. "Phew! This place sure is musty," Jimmy commented.

"It'll be all right once we've tidied up," replied Mother. "It's pretty rustic, but at least it has electricity. I'll plug in the coffeepot and put some water on the stove for hot chocolate." As soon as she did so, however, all the lights went off. "Oh no! I must have blown a fuse," she moaned.

"I'll check," said Dad, getting the flashlight and going to find the fuse box. A few minutes later he called, "Looks to me like there are too many things on one small circuit. You'll have to turn off a few lights before you can perk that coffee and use the stove." Mother hurried to do so, and soon the lights came back on.

Later, as they sat together near the fireplace, Mother said thoughtfully, "This incident reminds me of our family lately. We've been overloaded, too. We've all been so busy that we don't have much time to spend together anymore."

Dad nodded. "I think we should take some time during this vacation to evaluate our activities and see which ones we could cut out of our schedules," he said. Then he picked up the Bible from the magazine rack. "Let's have family devotions right now. That's one activity we should always take time for."

HOW ABOUT YOU? Have you been too busy lately? Make a list of things you do and put the really important ones first. Be sure to put daily devotions near the top, along with time spent with your family, proper rest, and meals. If there isn't time for everything else on your list, decide which ones can be omitted or done another time. Don't get overloaded. □ S.K.

TO MEMORIZE: *Come with me by yourselves to a quiet place and get some rest.* Mark 6:31, NIV

J IM ALWAYS DREADED going to the dentist. He didn't like the loud buzzing of the drill. He clenched the arms of the chair, hoping Dr. Jones was nearly done. It was a relief when the buzzing stopped and Dr. Jones checked the tooth.

"Are you finished yet?" Jim asked anxiously.

"Just a little more drilling, Jim," replied Dr. Jones. "I know this isn't pleasant, but I have to get all of the cavity out, or it would keep on decaying underneath the new filling. Then you'd probably have a toothache and could even lose the whole tooth."

Finally Dr. Jones finished drilling and began to put in the new filling. "When I drill out a cavity, I'm reminded of how I must 'drill' sin out of my life," said Dr. Jones. "I can't leave any decayed material in the tooth because that would cause too many problems later on. It's that way in my life, too. If I leave any sins alone, they'll cause problems later on." Jim's mouth was wide open, and he couldn't answer. He just nodded numbly. "If I find myself telling even a little lie, I try to correct it," continued Dr. Jones. "I ask God to forgive me and help me to always tell the truth."

Jim felt more relaxed now that the drilling was finished, and he thought about what Dr. Jones was saying. He thought about how he often said his homework or his chores around the house were all done when that wasn't quite true—it was almost true, but not entirely true. He thought about how he no longer used bad language very often—but he did use it occasionally. Lying in the dentist chair, Jim realized he had to make some changes.

"How do you feel?" asked Dr. Jones as he helped Jim out of the chair.

Jim looked at him soberly. "Great! I'm glad to be rid of that cavity," he answered. "I've got a couple of other 'cavities' I'm going to finish drilling out, too. They're getting much too big."

HOW ABOUT YOU? Are there some things in your life that you know aren't quite right? Maybe just a little lying, a little cheating, or a little talking back to parents or teachers? Get rid of those things completely before they grow bigger and become much harder to stop. Ask God's forgiveness and His help to drill the sin out of your life. □ C.Y.

TO MEMORIZE: *I hate double-minded men, but I love your law.* Psalm 119:113, NIV

28

Drill It Out

FROM THE BIBLE:

But Gehazi, the servant of Elisha the man of God, said, "Look, my master has spared Naaman this Syrian, while not receiving from his hands what he brought; but as the LORD lives, I will run after him and take something from him." So Gehazi pursued Naaman. When Naaman saw him running after him, he got down from the chariot to meet him, and said, "Is all well?" And he said, "All is well. My master has sent me, saying, 'Indeed, just now two young men of the sons of the prophets have come to me from the mountains of Ephraim. Please give them a talent of silver and two changes of garments.' So Naaman said, "Please, take two talents." Now he went in and stood before his master. And Elisha said to him, "Where did you go, Gehazi?" And he said, "Your servant did not go anywhere." Then he said to him, "Did not my heart go with you when the man turned back from his chariot to meet you? Therefore the leprosy of Naaman shall cling to you and your descendants forever." And he went out from his presence leprous, as white as snow.
2 Kings 5:20-23, 25-27, NKJV

Drill sin out

29

The Donkey's Tail

FROM THE BIBLE:

Therefore be followers of God as dear children. And walk in love, as Christ also has loved us and given Himself for us, an offering and a sacrifice to God for a sweet-smelling aroma. But fornication and all uncleanness or covetousness, let it not even be named among you, as is fitting for saints; neither filthiness, nor foolish talking, nor coarse jesting, which are not fitting, but rather giving of thanks. For this you know, that no fornicator, unclean person, nor covetous man, who is an idolater, has any inheritance in the kingdom of Christ and God. Let no one deceive you with empty words, for because of these things the wrath of God comes upon the sons of disobedience. Therefore do not be partakers with them. For you were once darkness, but now you are light in the Lord. Walk as children of light.
Ephesians 5:1-8, NKJV

Get rid of spiritual blindness

IT WAS the day of the Sunday school party, and Jack wiggled impatiently as Mrs. Gates, the teacher, tied a blindfold over his eyes. Against the wall was the big picture of a donkey without a tail. Each child had a turn to be blindfolded and turned around a few times before attaching a tail to the donkey.

"There you are," said Mrs. Gates, turning Jack around. "Where would you like to put that tail?"

Jack took an uncertain step. This wasn't as easy as he expected. He walked forward, wobbling just a little. He reached out with his hand and found he was close enough. He thought carefully for a moment, trying to remember just which way the donkey was facing and how tall it was. Then he reached out and—there! It was done. The other children laughed as he snatched off his blindfold. He couldn't believe his eyes. There stood the donkey with a tail growing right out of its nose!

When the game was over, Mrs. Gates called the group together for a few devotional thoughts before refreshments. "Think about the game we just played," she said. "It would be easy for any one of you to go right now and pin that tail in the right place. What made it hard during the game?"

"We were blindfolded," said one of the children.

"And dizzy from being turned around," added Jack.

"That's right," agreed Mrs. Gates. "As Christians, we're sometimes like that, too. We have spiritual blindfolds—things like laziness, selfishness, hate, or stubbornness. We shut our eyes to opportunities to serve the Lord. And we get turned around by worldly things such as TV, bad companions, or even a book or ball game that takes time we should be using for the Lord. Let's ask God to give us the desire and strength to get rid of 'blindfolds' and stay facing in the right direction."

HOW ABOUT YOU? Are you wearing a spiritual blindfold? Does something such as jealousy or wanting your own way keep you from doing the things you should? Are you being turned away from pleasing the Lord—by your friends, things you read, music you choose, an improper joke? Get rid of those things. Ask God to help you walk straight ahead—to live a life that is pleasing to Him. □ H.M.

TO MEMORIZE: *For you were once darkness, but now you are light in the Lord. Walk as children of light.* Ephesians 5:8, NKJV

CARL AND HIS FRIEND Jay burst into the living room. "Look, Dad. I've got a new model." Carl held up the box so his father could see the picture of the fighter plane.

"Nice!" approved Dad. "You must have quite a collection. You've brought home several models lately."

"Right! I've got a Tiger, and a Hornet and a B-52—"

"Can I see them?" interrupted Jay.

Carl hesitated. "Well, I haven't finished them yet. But I've got 'em all started. I'll finish them someday."

Dad looked up, frowning. "In that case I think I'd better hold this one for you until the others are done. Leaving things unfinished is a waste of time and effort."

"Aw, Dad," protested Carl, "it's just a model."

"Yes," agreed Dad, "but I'm afraid you're developing lifelong habits that will hurt you, Carl. Remember the garden last spring? You got the ground all prepared, but you never got it planted. And then there was the doghouse you started to build."

"Don't remind me," groaned Carl. "But don't worry. I'll do it tomorrow."

Jay laughed. "My dad always says, 'Tomorrow never comes.' "

"He's right," agreed Dad. "God tells us we are to be faithful in the things we have to do, big or small. Good work habits will help you serve the Lord better. If you can't finish the things you start for your own pleasure, you probably won't finish the things you start for Him, either."

Carl looked at the model he was holding. Then he handed it to Dad. "Here, don't put this too far away. I'll need it soon," he said. He looked at Jay. "I've got some models I need to get to work on. Wanna give me a hand?"

HOW ABOUT YOU? Do you lose interest in projects before you finish them? Have you ever promised the Lord you would be faithful in a certain area, such as praying or Bible reading, and then failed to do so? God has the power to help you keep on working when the job may seem uninteresting or difficult. Ask Him to give you His strength to complete any service you begin. Make up your mind not to quit before a job is finished. □ C.R.

TO MEMORIZE: *No! For unless you are honest in small matters, you won't be in large ones.* Luke 16:10, TLB

AUGUST

30

A Good Start, But…

FROM THE BIBLE:

No! For unless you are honest in small matters, you won't be in large ones. If you cheat even a little, you won't be honest with greater responsibilities. And if you are untrustworthy about worldly wealth, who will trust you with the true riches of heaven? And if you are not faithful with other people's money, why should you be entrusted with money of your own? For neither you nor anyone else can serve two masters. You will hate one and show loyalty to the other, or else the other way around—you will be enthusiastic about one and despise the other. You cannot serve both God and money. Luke 16:10-13, TLB

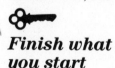

Finish what you start

31

No Rejects

FROM THE BIBLE:

I praise you because I am fearfully and wonderfully made; your works are wonderful, I know that full well. My frame was not hidden from you when I was made in the secret place. When I was woven together in the depths of the earth, your eyes saw my unformed body. All the days ordained for me were written in your book before one of them came to be. How precious to me are your thoughts, O God! How vast is the sum of them! Were I to count them, they would outnumber the grains of sand. When I awake, I am still with you.
Psalm 139:14-18, NIV

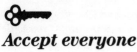

Accept everyone

"MOM, YOU SHOULD have seen the new kid at our Sunday school party last night!" said Tom as he reached for a freshly baked, chocolate chip cookie.

"What about him?" asked Mother as she pulled another batch from the oven.

"He's weird, really weird!" exclaimed Tom. "Nobody likes him."

"Oh?" Mother raised her eyebrows. "What's so different about him?"

"Well, for one thing, he dresses funny." Tom laughed as he remembered. "He had on these clothes that look twenty years old."

"Maybe his family is short on money," suggested Mother.

Tom shrugged. "His clothes aren't all that's weird about him," he said. "He has a goofy-looking nose that—" He stopped short as he watched his mother sort through the cookies she had just baked. She inspected each one closely and then separated them onto different plates. "What are you doing?" he asked.

Mother picked up the fullest plate and walked toward the trash can. "Some of these didn't turn out quite right," she said. "I'll just dump them."

"Don't throw them away!" exclaimed Tom in disbelief.

"But they're not perfect, Tom," explained Mother. "I examined each one, and only a few have the right color and the exact number of chips I like in a cookie."

"They're still good though," protested Tom. "You have to expect them to be different. . . ." He hesitated and then added quietly, "Just like the new kid, huh?"

Mom nodded. "Just like the new kid," she agreed. "Just like all kids—and all men and women. God made them all different—He made them all special. He loves them all, and we should, too." She held out the plate of "rejects" toward her son.

Tom took one. "No rejects," he said as he bit into it.

HOW ABOUT YOU? Do you have trouble liking people who dress or talk differently from you and your friends? Or who are different in other ways? Remember that God made them the way they are, and He loves them. Don't reject them. □ D.A.B.

TO MEMORIZE: *I praise you because I am fearfully and wonderfully made; your works are wonderful, I know that full well.* Psalm 139:14, NIV

JANA SIGHED as she sat down at the table one morning. "I wish I could do something important for the special services at church," she said. "Carl and Jack are going to play a trumpet duet, and Melanie and Sherri and Tara are singing a trio. Holly's playing the piano one evening, and Bonnie was asked to read her poem on prayer. Everybody's doing something but me."

"I thought you were helping in the nursery," said Mother.

"Oh, I always do that," said Jana, "but I'd like to do something really important for once."

Jana's older sister, Traci, limped into the room. "How's the toe you hurt yesterday?" asked Mother.

"Much better," reported Traci, pushing a strand of hair from her face. "Before long, I'll be able to walk normally." She stuck out her foot. "I never realized before how important a little toe is! I recommend that everyone pay more attention to their little toes."

Mother smiled. "Did you look at your little toes this morning, Jana?" she asked.

"Probably not," laughed Jana.

"Did you comb your hair?" asked Mother. "Did you look at your face?"

"Sure," said Jana. "What are you getting at, Mother?"

"Well," said Mother, "I'm just trying to point out that although we normally pay more attention to some parts of our bodies, like our hair and our face, every part is important. Even our little toes. Every member of the body of Christ—that is, every believer—is important, too. We tend to pay more attention to those who play or sing or speak. But those who work in the nursery or sweep the church or pray as they sit quietly in their seats are just as important. We often notice them only when they get 'hurt' and can't perform their jobs, but God notices them all the time. They're very important."

HOW ABOUT YOU? Do you feel unimportant? Some jobs seem more "glamorous" to us than others, but God won't reward you according to how glamorous your task is. He'll reward you according to how faithfully you perform the task He has given you to do. It's important in His sight, and so are you! □ H.M.

TO MEMORIZE: *Those parts of the body that seem to be weaker are indispensable.*
1 Corinthians 12:22, NIV

The Little Toe

FROM THE BIBLE:
There are many parts, but one body. The eye cannot say to the hand, "I don't need you!" And the head cannot say to the feet, "I don't need you!" On the contrary, those parts of the body that seem to be weaker are indispensable, and the parts that we think are less honorable we treat with special honor. And the parts that are unpresentable are treated with special modesty, while our presentable parts need no special treatment. But God has combined the members of the body and has given greater honor to the parts that lacked it, so that there should be no division in the body, but that its parts should have equal concern for each other. If one part suffers, every part suffers with it; if one part is honored, every part rejoices with it. Now you are the body of Christ, and each one of you is a part of it.
1 Corinthians 12:20-27, NIV

You are important

2

Not Worth It

FROM THE BIBLE:

The fear of the LORD prolongs days, but the years of the wicked will be shortened. The hope of the righteous will be gladness, but the expectation of the wicked will perish. The way of the LORD is strength for the upright, but destruction will come to the workers of iniquity. The righteous will never be removed, but the wicked will not inhabit the earth. The mouth of the righteous brings forth wisdom, but the perverse tongue will be cut out. The lips of the righteous know what is acceptable, but the mouth of the wicked what is perverse.

Proverbs 10:27-32, NKJV

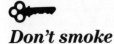

Don't smoke

DALE COUGHED violently, then rubbed the cigarette out. Ken, one of the other boys, noticed. "Anybody that wants to be in this club has to smoke," he stated firmly.

"Well, I have to go now," said Dale. Leaving the clubhouse, he set off for his uncle's home. Uncle Vern was a doctor, and Dale had some questions for him. "Is it really true that smoking causes cancer?" Dale asked. "I mean, I know some old people who have smoked for years, and they've never gotten cancer."

Uncle Vern looked serious. "That's true," he agreed. "Not everyone's body reacts exactly the same. One person may not smoke much but may get cancer at an early age. Another person won't develop cancer for a long time even though he may smoke more. And another may not get cancer at all."

"So it's a big chance?" Dale asked.

"It's a chance *not* worth taking," said Uncle Vern. "There's a much stronger possibility of getting lung cancer if you smoke than if you don't. And smoking also causes heart damage and other problems."

"But not for certain?" Dale asked, anxious to justify getting involved in smoking.

Uncle Vern frowned. "The problem is that no one knows how his body will react. You could be the person who gets cancer at an early age with light smoking. God made our bodies to work most efficiently when we don't overtax or abuse them. Remember, too, that smoking is habit-forming, and God is not pleased when we allow anything to control our actions in that way."

"Well, I guess smoking is out then," Dale concluded reluctantly.

Uncle Vern slapped him on the back. "I knew you were a smart guy!"

HOW ABOUT YOU? Are you a "smart guy or gal"? Smart enough not to smoke? God created your body to be of service to Him, and it cannot work at its best when it has to fight pollution like cigarette smoke. Decide right now not to smoke. That decision will glorify God, and it may result in a longer life for you. □ C.Y.

TO MEMORIZE: *The fear of the LORD prolongs days, but the years of the wicked will be shortened.* Proverbs 10:27, NKJV

"I AM THE DOOR. If anyone enters by Me, he will be saved." As Mr. Bates, Jerry's Sunday school teacher, read the words of Jesus, Jerry was puzzled. He wondered how Jesus could be a door, but as Mr. Bates began to explain the verse, Jerry's mind drifted to other things.

That night Jerry stayed at the home of his friend Tony because their Sunday school class was leaving on a camping trip early the next morning. After they had gone to bed, Jerry realized that he had forgotten to pack his fishing gear. "Let's run to my house and get it," he said.

"Isn't it too late?" Tony asked. "Everybody will be sleeping."

"We'll sneak in," said Jerry. "Come on."

Jerry tried the doors at his house, but they were all locked. He decided to pry the screen off his bedroom window and enter that way. He tried to be quiet, but the noise woke his parents. His dad grabbed a bat and went to investigate. Jerry had one foot in the window when his dad yelled, "Stop, or I'll hit you!"

Jerry froze. "Don't! It's me, Dad!" he said.

His father flicked on a light. "Jerry? Why are you sneaking in the window? Why didn't you come through the door?" he asked. "I would have let you in." Jerry gulped. He knew he had a lot to explain.

When the boys saw Mr. Bates the next morning, they told him about their adventure. "I didn't think it mattered how I got in," Jerry said, "But it did. My dad thought I was a burglar."

"That's a good example of the lesson I was teaching in club yesterday," said Mr. Bates. "Jesus is called 'the Door' because it's only through Him that we enter heaven. Some people think they can sneak into heaven by doing good works, attending church, or being baptized. But that won't work. You must enter heaven by the Door—by accepting Jesus as your Savior."

"I wasn't listening yesterday," confessed Jerry, "but I'm ready to listen now. Tell me more about it."

HOW ABOUT YOU? Are you trying to sneak into heaven? You can't do it. On earth, a person might be able to sneak into a house and get away with it, but the only way to get into heaven is through the Door, Jesus Christ. Come to Him today.

◻ J.H.

TO MEMORIZE: *I am the door. If anyone enters by Me, he will be saved, and will go in and out and find pasture.* John 10:9, NKJV

SEPTEMBER

3

No Sneaking In

FROM THE BIBLE:

"Most assuredly, I say to you, he who does not enter the sheepfold by the door, but climbs up some other way, the same is a thief and a robber. But he who enters by the door is the shepherd of the sheep. To him the door-keeper opens, and the sheep hear his voice; and he calls his own sheep by name and leads them out. Yet they will by no means follow a stranger, but will flee from him, for they do not know the voice of strangers." Jesus used this illustration, but they did not understand the things which He spoke to them. Then Jesus said to them again, "Most assuredly, I say to you, I am the door of the sheep. All who ever came before Me are thieves and robbers, but the sheep did not hear them. I am the door. If anyone enters by Me, he will be saved, and will go in and out and find pasture. The thief does not come except to steal, and to kill, and to destroy. I have come that they may have life, and that they may have it more abundantly.

John 10:1-10, NKJV

Enter heaven by the "Door"

Pencil Problems

FROM THE BIBLE:
I speak this way, using the illustration of slaves and masters, because it is easy to understand: just as you used to be slaves to all kinds of sin, so now you must let yourselves be slaves to all that is right and holy. In those days when you were slaves of sin you didn't bother much with goodness. . . . But there is something else deep within me, in my lower nature, that is at war with my mind and wins the fight and makes me a slave to the sin that is still within me. In my mind I want to be God's willing servant but instead I find myself still enslaved to sin. So you see how it is: my new life tells me to do right, but the old nature that is still inside me loves to sin. Oh, what a terrible predicament I'm in! Who will free me from my slavery to this deadly lower nature? Thank God! It has been done by Jesus Christ our Lord. He has set me free.
Romans 6:19-20; 7:23-24, TLB

You belong to God

EAGERLY, Chad tore open the large envelope he had received in the mail. "Here's the pencil I ordered," he said. "See—it has my name on it." He pointed to his name, stamped in gold, on the side of the pencil. His little sister Caryn, reached for the pencil, but Chad pulled it back. "You can't use it," he said. "This pencil cost me money, and nobody gets to use it but me."

"I can use it, too," insisted Caryn. "I'll ask Daddy." That evening she did just that. "Chad has to share with me, doesn't he?" she asked. "I can use the pencil, too!" But she was disappointed to see her father shake his head.

"It's Chad's pencil," said Dad. "He paid for it and his name is on it. He has the right to control that pencil."

"Hey, that's like my lesson last Sunday," said Chad. "My Sunday school teacher says God has the right to control us because we belong to Him."

Dad nodded. "Good point. This pencil can be a reminder of that. You bought and paid for it, so it's yours. God bought us. It cost the blood of Jesus to purchase our salvation. Now we are His. Your name is stamped on the pencil, marking it as your own. The Holy Spirit now lives within us, marking us as 'Christians.' We should always remember that our lives belong to God."

HOW ABOUT YOU? Do you belong to God? You do if you've accepted Jesus as your Savior. Yield yourself to be used of Him. Don't allow the world to "use" you. Don't be greedy, unkind, or selfish. Don't lie, cheat, or hate. In short, don't do the things Satan wants you to do. He has no claim on you. You are God's. Allow Him to control you. Live to please Him. □ H.M.

TO MEMORIZE: *Do you not know that your body is a temple of the Holy Spirit, who is in you, whom you have received from God? You are not your own.* 1 Corinthians 6:19, NIV

"ARE YOU READY for Bible club?" asked Chad's mother, "or should you learn your verse before you go out to play?"

Chad looked at the ball and mitt in his hand, then back at his mother. "Sometimes I get tired of having to go to Bible club and church and choir and everything," he grumbled. Then he quickly added, "Don't get me wrong. I'm glad I'm a Christian, but it seems like I always have to study while the other kids get to play. Sometimes I wish we could just go to church without getting so involved."

A few moments later, Mother heard angry voices. "Give that to me, Caryn," demanded Chad. "It's mine." Mother couldn't hear Caryn's reply, but she heard sounds of a scuffle. She hurried to see what was causing the problem.

"Caryn's got my pencil," explained Chad. His little sister looked guilty as she stared at him defiantly, hands behind her back.

"Give me the pencil," ordered Mother, and Caryn reluctantly handed it over. Mother looked at Chad's name stamped on it. "Well, Son," she said, "suppose I break this in half and give you each a piece."

"No way!" Chad answered quickly. "That would ruin it. I want my whole pencil."

"I can understand that," Mother agreed, handing it to him. "It's yours—the whole thing. I hope that seeing your name on it reminds you that you are God's. Not just half of you—half of your talents, money, and time—but all of you. It wouldn't be right to give Him only half."

Slowly Chad nodded. "So I shouldn't just go to church and Sunday school. I should become involved in Christian activities and in doing things for the Lord, right?" He grinned and waved his pencil at his mother as he opened his book to study.

HOW ABOUT YOU? Are you a "Sunday Christian"? Do you want to do things your own way the rest of the week.? Do you serve the Lord only when it's convenient for you? You belong wholly to Him, and He wants you to love and serve Him and your whole heart. Ask Him to help you do that each day. □ H.M.

TO MEMORIZE: *What does the LORD your God ask of you but to fear the LORD your God, to walk in all his ways, to love him, to serve the LORD your God with all your heart and with all your soul.* Deuteronomy 10:12, NIV

Pencil Problems

(Continued from yesterday)

FROM THE BIBLE:
One of the teachers of religion who was standing there listening to the discussion realized that Jesus had answered well. So he asked, "Of all the commandments, which is the most important?" Jesus replied, "The one that says, 'Hear, O Israel! The Lord our God is the one and only God. And you must love him with all your heart and soul and mind and strength.' The second is: 'You must love others as much as yourself.' No other commandments are greater than these." The teacher of religion replied, "Sir, you have spoken a true word in saying that there is only one God and no other. And I know it is far more important to love him with all my heart and understanding and strength, and to love others as myself, than to offer all kinds of sacrifices on the altar of the Temple." Realizing this man's understanding, Jesus said to him, "You are not far from the Kingdom of God." And after that, no one dared ask him any more questions.
Mark 12:28-34, TLB

Serve God all the time

6

A Puzzling Situation

FROM THE BIBLE:

Do not be yoked together with unbelievers. For what do righteousness and wickedness have in common? Or what fellowship can light have with darkness? What harmony is there between Christ and Belial? What does a believer have in common with an unbeliever? What agreement is there between the temple of God and idols? For we are the temple of the living God. As God has said: "I will live with them and walk among them, and I will be their God, and they will be my people." "Therefore come out from them and be separate, says the Lord. Touch no unclean thing, and I will receive you."

2 Corinthians 6:14-17, NIV

Be yoked with Christians

"CINDY!" exclaimed Josh. "You messed up our puzzle."

"I help," insisted Cindy, stirring the pieces around.

Beth took a simple puzzle from a shelf and helped four-year-old Cindy get started on it. "You work this puzzle. Ours is too hard for you."

Josh and Beth enjoyed watching their puzzle picture develop. Then trouble started again. "Cindy, that piece belongs in your puzzle, not in this one!" protested Beth as the little girl tried to fit a piece from her puzzle into theirs.

"Here, Cindy. Help me open the mail." Mother had just come in with several envelopes in her hand. While Cindy struggled with one envelope, Mother opened another. "Oh, dear," she sighed. "Your cousin, Paula, is getting married, and Dave, her fiancé, isn't a Christian."

"She thinks he'll attend church with her more often after they're married," remarked Beth.

"Well, I pray Dave will become a Christian," said Mother, "but they're starting out in opposition to God's command. He says Christians should not be 'unequally yoked' with unbelievers."

"Cindy, don't!" exclaimed Josh as his little sister tried to fit her piece into the wrong puzzle.

"You see," said Mother, "just as pieces from two different puzzles will never really fit properly together, a believer and an unbeliever do not fit together. This is especially true in marriage. But it's also true in business and in friendships."

"That's why you don't like me to get too chummy with Carl, isn't it?" asked Josh.

Mother nodded. "You can be friends, but your best friends should be Christians. And when you're old enough to date, all your dates should be Christians."

"Dates!" Josh made a face. "Forget it!"

Mother laughed. "That time will come before you know it," she said. "I hope you'll both decide that you'll follow God's plan in this matter."

HOW ABOUT YOU? Are your best friends Christians? Are you determined that, when the time comes, you will choose a Christian mate? Don't disobey God on this important issue. □ H.M.

TO MEMORIZE: *Do not be yoked together with unbelievers. For what do righteousness and wickedness have in common? Or what fellowship can light have with darkness?* 2 Corinthians 6:14-17, NIV

BETH AND JOSH raced to put in the last few pieces of their puzzle. Finally, Beth picked up the very last one on the table. "You're hiding a piece," she accused Josh when she saw that two pieces were still missing from the puzzle. "You always think you have to put in the last piece."

"I don't have it," said Josh. "Maybe it's on the floor." He looked under the table, but there was nothing there. The children began to search the rest of the room. Unwilling to give up, they had just removed several things from a shelf when Mother came into the room.

"What's going on?" asked Mother. They showed her the puzzle with a piece missing. "That's too bad," she said, "but I think you may as well forget it for now. If we come across it, we'll put it in the box."

"Forget it?" objected Beth. "But we need it to finish the picture." They continued their search, and finally they found the missing piece.

"You certainly were persistent," observed Mother when she saw the finished puzzle. "Good for you!"

"Yeah," agreed Josh, playfully patting himself on the back. "Hey, Mom, you always see neat little lessons in things that happen. Do you see one in this?"

Mother thought for a moment. "Actually, I do," she said. "I'm thinking of your friend Jim. I know you've been very disappointed in him since he was caught shoplifting. Although he's rebellious right now, I believe he really is a Christian. He's part of the 'puzzle.' You do need to be careful that he doesn't influence you or damage your reputation, but you can be persistent in 'finding' him and bringing him back to take his proper place. I hope you'll faithfully pray for him. And if you get a chance, lovingly rebuke him and encourage him to live for the Lord. He belongs in the picture."

HOW ABOUT YOU? Do you know a Christian who has strayed from the Lord? A Christian who won't come to church? A Christian who does things you know are displeasing in God's sight? Sometimes it's necessary to avoid close companionship with such a person. But never stop praying for him. Try to lead him back to the Lord. □ H.M.

TO MEMORIZE: *And if anyone does not obey our word in this epistle, note that person and do not keep company with him, that he may be ashamed. Yet do not count him as an enemy, but admonish him as a brother.* 2 Thessalonians 3:14-15, NKJV

7

A Puzzling Situation

(Continued from yesterday)

FROM THE BIBLE:
But we command you, brethren, in the name of our Lord Jesus Christ, that you withdraw from every brother who walks disorderly and not according to the tradition which he received from us. For you yourselves know how you ought to follow us, for we were not disorderly among you. . . . And if anyone does not obey our word in this epistle, note that person and do not keep company with him, that he may be ashamed. Yet do not count him as an enemy, but admonish him as a brother.
2 Thessalonians 3:6-7, 14-15, NKJV

Pray for straying Christians

8

God Counts

FROM THE BIBLE:
You shall not steal, nor deal falsely, nor lie to one another.
Leviticus 19:11, NKJV

Are not two sparrows sold for a copper coin? And not one of them falls to the ground apart from your Father's will. But the very hairs of your head are all numbered.
Matthew 10:29-30, NKJV

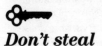

Don't steal

JASON AND BETH strolled past the booths at the crafts fair. "Look, Jason!" Beth squealed. "Isn't it beautiful?" She held up a handmade doll with a china face and hands.

"It's fine if you like dolls!" Jason shrugged. "Let's look at something more interesting."

"Where'd Mom go?" Beth asked as she searched the crowd.

"I don't know," Jason answered, "but she'll find us. Don't worry."

The two continued down the midway of the fairgrounds. "Mmmm. Do you smell what I smell?" Jason asked.

"Smells like a bakery," Beth replied, "and there it is!"

Jason walked up to the booth where delicious baked goods were displayed. "Look at those doughnuts, Beth. I sure would like one."

"We spent all our money, remember?" Beth reminded her brother.

"So?" Jason smiled. "No one's around. The vendor must be taking a break. He won't miss one little doughnut."

"No, Jason. Don't take one! You know that would be stealing," warned Beth.

"Oh, Beth, no one will ever know," Jason sneered, looking carefully around. "I'm sure they didn't count every single doughnut. They'll never miss it."

"Maybe not," Beth admitted. "But perhaps God counted them."

Jason gulped and looked at Beth. After a few minutes he replied, "You're right, Beth. God does count. The Bible says that even 'the hairs on our head are numbered'!" Jason and Beth walked away from the booth empty-handed, but happy.

HOW ABOUT YOU? Are you tempted to steal just "little" things because you think that no one will ever know? Do you think it won't matter if you take things that belong to a brother or sister or even your parents? Remember, God counts. Even little things matter to Him. □ B.D.

TO MEMORIZE: *But the very hairs of your head are all numbered.* Matthew 10:30, NKJV

IT WAS Grandparents' Day at Tommy's school. As usual, Tommy's Grandpa came for the program. Grandpa listened with interest as the children read essays they had written on what they liked about their grandparents. Katie told how much she liked her grandma because she gave her nice gifts. Bobby liked his grandpa because he always had candy for him. And Amanda liked her grandpa because he never scolded her. Tommy's report was quite different, and as he read it, he saw his grandpa smile with pleasure.

After school, Grandpa told Tommy how pleased he was with what Tommy had written. "Well, you always do have time for me," said Tommy. "You listen when I tell you something and take time to help me when I need you. And you're not afraid to say no to me, or to scold me. I don't always like it, but I know you're right, and so I'm glad you do it anyway."

"Ahhh, it pleases me to hear you say that, Tommy," Grandpa told him. "You know, the things you like about me are also some of the things I like about God."

"Really?" asked Tommy.

Grandpa nodded. "God always listens to me when I pray and is there when I need Him," he said. "He helps me say no to bad things. If I don't, He punishes me. Then He helps me admit I'm wrong and apologize to people. He not only saved me, but He always does what is best for me."

"Yeah, God is like that, isn't He?" Tommy said thoughtfully. "I'm even glad He doesn't always give us what we want. If he had, we wouldn't have moved to this town, and then I wouldn't have gotten to see so much of you."

Grandpa smiled. "I'm glad you like both God and me for the right reasons. I want to be a godly grandpa who does what's best for you. I'm so glad that's what you want, too."

HOW ABOUT YOU? Do you like people for what they give you or because you can get them to do what you want? You ought to love them for themselves, not for their gifts. You should even be glad for discipline because it makes you a better person. And you should love God, not only for giving you eternal life, but for always being there to help you. □ A.L.

TO MEMORIZE: *Now that you have purified yourselves by obeying the truth so that you have sincere love for your brothers, love one another deeply, from the heart.* 1 Peter 1:22, NIV

9
Grand-parents' Day

FROM THE BIBLE:
And have you quite forgotten the encouraging words God spoke to you, his child? He said, "My son, don't be angry when the Lord punishes you. Don't be discouraged when he has to show you where you are wrong. For when he punishes you, it proves that he loves you. When he whips you it proves you are really his child." Let God train you, for he is doing what any loving father does for his children. Whoever heard of a son who was never corrected? If God doesn't punish you when you need it, as other fathers punish their sons, then it means that you aren't really God's son at all—that you don't really belong in his family. Since we respect our fathers here on earth, though they punish us, should we not all the more cheerfully submit to God's training so that we can begin really to live?
Hebrews 12:5-9, TLB

Love people for themselves

263

10

Cantaloupe Episode

FROM THE BIBLE:

Do not steal. Do not lie. Do not deceive one another. Do not swear falsely by my name and so profane the name of your God. I am the LORD. Do not defraud your neighbor or rob him. Do not hold back the wages of a hired man overnight.
Leviticus 19:11-13, NIV

Don't steal

"LET'S GO," whispered Jack. "Mr. Brown just went into his house." He and his friend Tom, crept up to the garden. Jack grabbed a big, ripe cantaloupe, stuffed it under his shirt and ran in a bent-over position to the path leading to the road. Tom was right behind him, also keeping low. When they reached the road, they ducked into some bushes near Jack's house. Tom handed his pocketknife to Jack, who cut through the juicy cantaloupe.

"We must have gotten the best melon out of Mr. Brown's whole garden," Jack said as he wiped his mouth with the back of his hand.

After dinner that evening, Jack's father got out some heavy gloves. "I have to go clear out a patch of poison ivy," he said. "Want to help, Jack?"

"Sure," Jack agreed.

They got shovels and put on the gloves. To Jack's surprise, Dad headed straight for the bushes where the boys had eaten the melon! "Look," said Dad, "someone's been eating cantaloupe in this patch of poison ivy!"

Just then Mr. Brown came up. "Someone stole my best cantaloupe this afternoon," he said. His eyes grew wide when he saw the rinds and seeds on the ground.

"I'm terribly sorry to hear that," Jack's father replied. "It looks like the remains of your cantaloupe right here."

"That burns me up!" exclaimed Mr. Brown. "I was going to enter that big one in the fair tomorrow. I'm sure it would have won a prize."

Jack's heart was pounding as he began to help clear out the poison ivy. *I just meant to have some fun,* he thought. *But I guess taking that cantaloupe was really stealing.* Somehow he was sure the cantaloupe episode wasn't over yet.

HOW ABOUT YOU? Have you ever taken something that belonged to someone else just to tease that person or just to see if you could get away with it? It may seem like you're only having fun, especially when you're with someone else. But it's never fun for the person from whom you steal. It isn't fun in God's sight, either. Honor Him by obeying His command. □ C.Y.

TO MEMORIZE: *You shall not steal.*
Exodus 20:15, NIV

J ACK TOSSED and turned in bed. He just couldn't get to sleep. Oh, if only he hadn't taken Mr. Brown's prize cantaloupe! He knew now that taking the melon was not just "having a little fun." It was stealing. He needed help, and he wanted to talk with Dad about it. Even being punished was better than feeling like this!

Jack got out of bed and knocked on his parents' bedroom door. "Dad, Mom, may I talk to you?" he asked. Soon he was telling them all about it.

"Son, I'm sorry you took Mr. Brown's melon," said Dad, "but I'm very glad you've admitted it. Now you need to tell God you're sorry. And tomorrow you'll have to tell Mr. Brown you're sorry, too. And ask if you may help him in his garden or yard to pay for the melon."

"I will, Dad," said Jack as the three got on their knees. After Jack prayed, his parents gave him a hug. Jack squirmed. "Ouch," he said. "My skin feels like it's on fire. It itches terribly."

They took a closer look. "It's poison ivy!" exclaimed Mother, and she hurried away to get some soothing salve.

"You see, Jack, sin can have two results," said Dad. "It hurts our conscience, making us feel apart from God. We can remedy that by confessing our sin and receiving God's forgiveness. But sometimes sin hurts us in other ways, too. In this case, you'll have to suffer with poison ivy."

Jack nodded. "I gotta admit I'm getting just what I deserve. I think I'll remember this lesson a long time!"

HOW ABOUT YOU? Are you suffering as a result of sin in your life? Sin must be confessed to God and to those you've wronged. It's the only way to forgiveness and peace of mind. But you may still have to suffer as a result of your sin—perhaps physically, perhaps through the loss of something. If that's the case, accept it and learn from it. With God's help, never repeat that sin again. □ C.Y.

TO MEMORIZE: *Do not be deceived, God is not mocked; for whatever a man sows, that he will also reap.* Galatians 6:7, NKJV

Cantaloupe Episode

(Continued from yesterday)

FROM THE BIBLE:
Do not be deceived, God is not mocked; for whatever a man sows, that he will also reap. For he who sows to his flesh will of the flesh reap corruption, but he who sows to the Spirit will of the Spirit reap everlasting life. And let us not grow weary while doing good, for in due season we shall reap if we do not lose heart. Therefore, as we have opportunity, let us do good to all, especially to those who are of the household of faith.
Galatians 6:7-10, NKJV

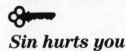

Sin hurts you

SEPTEMBER

12

The False Hood

FROM THE BIBLE:
Take care! Don't do your good deeds publicly, to be admired, for then you will lose the reward from your Father in heaven. When you give a gift to a beggar, don't shout about it as the hypocrites do—blowing trumpets in the synagogues and streets to call attention to their acts of charity! I tell you in all earnestness, they have received all the reward they will ever get. But when you do a kindness to someone, do it secretly—don't tell your left hand what your right hand is doing. And your Father who knows all secrets will reward you. And now about prayer. When you pray, don't be like the hypocrites who pretend piety by praying publicly on street corners and in the synagogues where everyone can see them. Truly, that is all the reward they will ever get. But when you pray, go away by yourself, all alone, and shut the door behind you and pray to your Father secretly, and your Father, who knows your secrets, will reward you.
Matthew 6:1-6, TLB

Be honest and obedient

"**D**AD, WHAT'S a falsehood?" asked Katie as she plunked herself in a chair beside her father.

"A falsehood?" Dad asked in surprise. "Well, a falsehood is a lie or untruth."

"That's what I thought," said Katie, "but it's a funny word. Why would a lie be called a falsehood?"

"Hmmm," pondered Dad. "Well, one explanation I've heard is that it comes from something done hundreds of years ago. It was during a time when people wore hoods instead of hats, and they wore cloaks instead of coats."

"Like Little Red Riding Hood?" asked Katie.

"Sort of," answered Dad. "A person like a doctor or lawyer—or whatever profession—wore a certain type and color of hood."

"Then if you saw someone with a certain kind of hood, you would know what he was?" asked Katie.

"Yes, and that's where the falsehood comes in," Dad answered. "Some dishonest people would go to a town where they weren't known, wear a hood they hadn't earned, and set up a practice. They were living a lie. They were wearing a false hood."

Katie nodded. "I can see how the word came to mean a lie," she said. "I think it's a good word to use to describe people who pretend to be something they're not today, too. Some kids cheat and swear at school, but pretend to be Christians on Sunday. It's like they're hiding under a false hood."

"That's right!" answered Dad. "On more than one occasion Jesus condemned the Scribes and Pharisees for making long prayers—pretending to be worshiping God when they were really just putting on a show to impress people. Be careful always to be honest before God and others."

"I will," Katie promised.

HOW ABOUT YOU? Are you pretending to be something you aren't? If you feel the need to pretend, ask yourself why. If you're honest and obedient as God wants you to be, you will not feel the need to hide under a "false hood." □ A.L.

TO MEMORIZE: *You reject all who stray from your decrees, for their deceitfulness is in vain.*
Psalm 119:118, NIV

ONE SATURDAY MORNING, Molly was moping around the house. Mother noticed and said, "Why is my favorite nine-year-old so sad today?"

"Oh, Mom," Molly whimpered, "I'm no good at anything! I can't sing high like Cheryl does, and I can't play the piano half as good as she does!"

"No good, huh?" her mother replied. "Well, I know one thing you're very good at, and that's helping me to get lunch on the table." Molly smiled and seemed to forget her blue mood while they ate.

After lunch, much to the surprise of Molly and her mother, Dad sat down on the piano bench. He began to bang on the piano keys as he playfully sang in an off-key voice. Soon Molly and Mother were laughing hard. Molly put her hands over her ears as she shouted, "Daddy, please! Give our ears a break!"

As Dad stopped playing, Mother said, "Remember, Molly, you said you couldn't play the piano very well. But it all depends on what you compare yourself to. Compared to Daddy, you play the piano very well."

Molly still wasn't convinced. "I see what you mean about the piano. But I'm not good at sports like Daddy is, and I can't sing high notes like Cheryl does either!"

"Oh, Molly," Mother chuckled, "don't compare yourself with others so much! You're much better at sports than I ever was! And Mrs. Pierce told me just last week that you are one of the best altos in the junior choir."

"Molly, I know a verse from the Bible that you need to learn," said Dad. As Molly looked at 1 Peter 4:10, Dad pointed out that God wants His children to develop their own talents and not waste their time comparing themselves with their friends. Molly promised to learn the verse, and Mother and Dad promised to pray for her.

HOW ABOUT YOU? Do you want to be like someone you know, and are you constantly comparing yourself with that person? God wants you to just be you! He expects you to be a good steward with the gifts He has given you. Use them to serve others—and Him! □ R.P.

TO MEMORIZE: *As each one has received a gift, minister it to one another, as good stewards of the manifold grace of God.* 1 Peter 4:10, NKJV

13

Compared with What?

FROM THE BIBLE:

And so, dear brothers, I plead with you to give your bodies to God. Let them be a living sacrifice, holy—the kind he can accept. When you think of what he has done for you, is this too much to ask? Don't copy the behavior and customs of this world, but be a new and different person with a fresh newness in all you do and think. Then you will learn from your own experience how his ways will really satisfy you. As God's messenger I give each of you God's warning: Be honest in your estimate of yourselves, measuring your value by how much faith God has given you. Just as there are many parts to our bodies, so it is with Christ's body. We are all parts of it, and it takes every one of us to make it complete, for we each have different work to do. So we belong to each other, and each needs all the others. God has given each of us the ability to do certain things well.
Romans 12:1-6, TLB

Be yourself

Phony Jackets

FROM THE BIBLE:
"For neither you nor anyone else can serve two masters. You will hate one and show loyalty to the other, or else the other way around—you will be enthusiastic about one and despise the other. You cannot serve both God and money." The Pharisees, who dearly loved their money, naturally scoffed at all this. Then he said to them, "You wear a noble, pious expression in public, but God knows your evil hearts. Your pretense brings you honor from the people, but it is an abomination in the sight of God. Until John the Baptist began to preach, the laws of Moses and the messages of the prophets were your guides. But John introduced the Good News that the Kingdom of God would come soon. And now eager multitudes are pressing in. But that doesn't mean that the Law has lost its force in even the smallest point. It is as strong and unshakable as heaven and earth."
Luke 16:13-17, TLB

You can't fool God

"**M**OM, I GOT IT," announced Kathy after school one day.

"Got what?" asked her brother, Ben. "Is it catching?" He moved to the other side of the room, pretending to be afraid of her.

"Silly!" Kathy held up a book. The picture on the jacket showed a girl in a long skirt cooking over an old-fashioned stove. "My teacher let me bring this home. It tells how to make 'vanity cakes' like they did years ago. Mom said she'd help me make some if I brought home the recipe." She turned to her mother. "Can we make them today?"

"Right after supper," Mother promised.

When they had finished the evening meal, Mother said Ben should do the dishes, and Kathy ran to get the book she had brought home. She eagerly opened it. Then she closed the book and looked at the cover. Once more she opened it. "Mother," she wailed, "this is the wrong book! This cover is a phony! It says *Old Time Cooking*, but it's a book about antique cars!"

Mother came to investigate. "Somehow this book got the wrong jacket on it," she said. "I guess this proves the old saying, 'You can't tell a book by its cover.' "

"That jacket fooled Kathy," observed Dad, "until she looked inside. I'm reminded of people who put on a good cover. They go to church and do all sorts of good deeds. Their phony jackets fool lots of people who think such fine folk must be Christians. But they never fool God. He knows whether or not they've accepted Jesus. He knows if they're pretending to be something they're not."

"Yeah," said Kathy. She sighed. "We won't be able to make those cakes tonight after all."

"Hey, does this mean I get out of doing dishes?" asked Ben hopefully.

"It means you get some help with them," answered Mother. "Let's all get at it."

HOW ABOUT YOU? Are you wearing a "jacket" that makes you appear to be something you're not? Others may think you're a Christian because you go to church, behave nicely, and talk about the Lord. But God is not fooled by some cover you might be wearing. He sees the real you. He knows if you've really accepted Jesus as your Savior. If you haven't done that, won't you stop pretending?
□ H.M.

TO MEMORIZE: *Deal with each man according to all he does, since you know his heart (for you alone know the hearts of all men).* 1 Kings 8:39, NIV

"GET OUT of my way," ordered Ben, reaching out to give his sister a shove. "I can't see."

"Who wants to watch this stupid program anyway?" retorted Kathy. "Baseball again!" Ben's sarcastic reply was wasted when Kathy went to answer the phone.

"I'm going to sing with a few other kids two weeks from Sunday," Kathy reported when she returned. "We're going to sing 'Get That Frown Off Your Face.' "

"Big deal," muttered Ben. This time Kathy's smart reply was wasted when Ben jumped up to answer the phone.

Soon Ben returned. "Guess what, Miss Smarty! I get to sing, too. Mrs. Snyder said she forgot she had two people to ask from this family."

Kathy turned to her mother who had just come into the room. "Mom, Ben has my book—the one with the wrong jacket on it. Make him give it to me."

Mother sighed. "What song did you say you were singing?"

"It's one we just learned," replied Ben. "It goes, 'Get that frown off your face. Put a smile in its place. . . .' "

"It sounds like a good song," said Mother, nodding. "I guess you're planning to wear your jackets that day."

"Our jackets?" Ben and Kathy were puzzled.

Mother nodded. "You know—like that book. Christians sometimes wear 'jackets,' too—jackets that say they're something they're not. In public, they act sweet, but in private they can't get along."

Kathy blushed. "That sounds like us," she admitted. "I'm sorry, Ben. You can read the book."

"I'm sorry, too," said Ben. "And you can turn off the ball game. I'm not really interested in those teams."

HOW ABOUT YOU? Do you say "please" and "thank you" only when you're away from home? Do you talk nicely when you're at church and use bad language when you're at school? That's called "hypocrisy," or being "two-faced." Ask God to help you live a pure, honest life wherever you are. □ H.M.

TO MEMORIZE: *But the wisdom that is from above is first pure, then peaceable, gentle, willing to yield, full of mercy and good fruits, without partiality and without hypocrisy.* James 3:17, NKJV

Phony Jackets

(Continued from yesterday)

FROM THE BIBLE:
Who is wise and understanding among you? Let him show by good conduct that his works are done in the meekness of wisdom. But if you have bitter envy and self-seeking in your hearts, do not boast and lie against the truth. This wisdom does not descend from above, but is earthly, sensual, demonic. For where envy and self-seeking exist, confusion and every evil thing will be there. But the wisdom that is from above is first pure, then peaceable, gentle, willing to yield, full of mercy and good fruits, without partiality and without hypocrisy. Now the fruit of righteousness is sown in peace by those who make peace.
James 3:13-18, NKJV

Don't be two-faced

16

A Dark Place

FROM THE BIBLE:

"Die?" asked the crowd. "We understood that the Messiah would live forever and never die. Why are you saying he will die? What Messiah are you talking about?" Jesus replied, "My light will shine out for you just a little while longer. Walk in it while you can, and go where you want to go before the darkness falls, for then it will be too late for you to find your way. Make use of the Light while there is still time; then you will become light bearers." After saying these things, Jesus went away and was hidden from them. . . . "I have come as a Light to shine in this dark world, so that all who put their trust in me will no longer wander in the darkness." John 12:34-36, 46, TLB

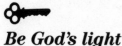

Be God's light

As CAMMIE listened to the cheerful voices singing choruses at Bible club, she wished she could stay there forever. She was glad she had come and heard about Jesus and that she had trusted Him as her Savior.

After Bible club was over, Cammie lingered to help Mrs. Steiner, the hostess, straighten the room. "Thank you, Cammie," said Mrs. Steiner. "Now, how about a nice dish of peaches before you go? Would you like to call your parents and make sure it's all right with them?"

"It'll be okay," Cammie answered. "Mom works late, and Dad will be passed out—I mean, sleeping on the couch."

"Well, then, would you mind getting a jar of my home-canned peaches from the basement?" Mrs. Steiner asked. "I'll get out the dishes and some milk." She told Cammie where to find the fruit. Cammie was limping when she returned with the peaches.

"The light didn't go on in the fruit cellar," Cammie explained, "so I couldn't see very well. I ran into a ladder, but I'm fine."

"Oh, dear, the bulb must have burned out," Mrs. Steiner said. "I'm sorry. A light is needed in a dark place like that." She opened the jar and dished up the golden fruit. "How are things going at home?"

Cammie sighed and told how her mom worked late hours and her dad was an alcoholic.

"It must be hard for you, Cammie," sympathized Mrs. Steiner, "but Jesus needs you there in your home. Just like the basement really needed a light so you could find the peaches more easily, you need to be a light in your home to help your parents find Christ as their Savior."

"I never thought about Jesus needing me in my home," Cammie said. "I'll try to be a good light in a dark place."

"Good," said Mrs. Steiner. "I'll be praying for you and for your parents, too."

HOW ABOUT YOU? Are you the only Christian in your home or in your classroom? It's difficult to stand alone, but it's in the dark that a light is needed the most. Jesus needs you to let your light shine for Him. □ J.H.

TO MEMORIZE: *So that you may become blameless and pure, children of God without fault in a crooked and depraved generation, in which you shine like stars in the universe.* Philippians 2:15, NIV

"**I** DON'T LIKE spiders, do you?" Ann asked her friend.

"Ugh! No, I hate them!" Jean shuddered. "They're creepy."

A spider had stretched its web across a section of fence in Ann's backyard, and the girls had gone over to look at it. "The web sure is pretty, though," observed Ann as they leaned closer. Each silvery strand of the beautifully constructed web connected to make a lacy pattern. Dewdrops on the web sparkled in the morning sun.

"I wonder how the spider knows how to make a web like that," said Jean.

"Since God made everything, He must have made spiders so they'd know how to make their webs," answered Ann.

Just then an insect buzzed around their heads. When Ann swatted at it, the bug flew into the web. Quick as a wink, the spider dashed out from a corner of the web and wrapped silk around the insect until it was held fast.

"Wow! Did you see how fast that spider moved?" marveled Jean.

"Yeah, and it sure made quick work of that bug," replied Ann. "Good thing, or the bug might have bitten us. Looks like spiders are good for something after all. Some bugs eat our garden plants, and some carry diseases. Every bug that's caught by a spider is one that can't hurt us any more."

"I never thought of that before," said Jean. "I guess God must have known we'd need spiders."

HOW ABOUT YOU? Have you ever thanked God for spiders? In their own quiet way, they are helping man every day. Stop and think how each creature fits into God's creation. It will help you appreciate the greatness of God and all of His creation.
□ C.Y.

TO MEMORIZE: *For everything God created is good, and nothing is to be rejected if it is received with thanksgiving.* 1 Timothy 4:4, NIV

Good for Something

FROM THE BIBLE:
Then God said, "Let the waters abound with an abundance of living creatures, and let birds fly above the earth across the face of the firmament of the heavens." So God created great sea creatures and every living thing that moves, with which the waters abounded, according to their kind, and every winged bird according to its kind. And God saw that it was good. And God blessed them, saying, "Be fruitful and multiply, and fill the waters in the seas, and let birds multiply on the earth." So the evening and the morning were the fifth day. Then God said, "Let the earth bring forth the living creature according to its kind: cattle and creeping thing and beast of the earth, each according to its kind"; and it was so. And God made the beast of the earth according to its kind, cattle according to its kind, and everything that creeps on the earth according to its kind. And God saw that it was good. Then God said, "Let Us make man in Our image, according to Our likeness." Genesis 1:20-26, NKJV

God made everything good

18

In Need of a Friend

FROM THE BIBLE:

My command is this: Love each other as I have loved you. Greater love has no one than this, that he lay down his life for his friends. You are my friends if you do what I command. I no longer call you servants, because a servant does not know his master's business. Instead, I have called you friends, for everything that I learned from my Father I have made known to you. You did not choose me, but I chose you and appointed you to go and bear fruit—fruit that will last. Then the Father will give you whatever you ask in my name. This is my command: Love each other.
John 15:12-17, NIV

To have a friend, be one

STACI CAME HOME in tears. "This is my third week at school, and I still don't have a friend," she wailed. "I wish we had never moved here!"

Mother ached for her. "I know you miss your old friends, Honey," she said. "I've been praying about this."

"Everyone just stares at me and walks right on by," Staci sobbed. "I'm so lonely."

The door flew open, and Tim blew in like a whirlwind. "Hey, Mom, is it all right if I go over to Paul's for a couple of hours? He needs help with his science project."

Mother nodded. "Just be home by five-thirty." The door slammed behind Tim. "Now, Staci, dry your tears and take this casserole to Mrs. Carson next door. She just came home from the hospital today."

Staci blew her nose loudly. "How do you know that?" she asked. "You seem to know everyone in this apartment building already. Why can't I make friends like you and Tim do?"

Mother took a deep breath. "Staci, you've been looking for someone to be a friend to you, and you haven't found anyone. But Tim and I have found people everywhere who need a friend. Stop looking for a friend, and start trying to be one instead." Mother hugged Staci gently.

An hour later Staci came skipping into the apartment. "Guess what, Mother?" She was beaming. "I found someone who needs a friend. Her name is Tara, and she's Mrs. Carson's granddaughter. May I go over there after dinner and help her clean her grandma's apartment?"

HOW ABOUT YOU? Are you lonely? Stop looking at yourself and look around you. There are lonely people everywhere. God's way for making a friend is to be one. Try it, and you will have lots of friends. □ B.W.

TO MEMORIZE: *This is my command: Love each other.* John 15:17, NIV

Don't Rush It

TEARS TRICKLED down Katrina's cheeks as she repeated her argument. "It wouldn't be a real date—just Jeff and Shana and Mark and me. I told you Jeff's folks would be there."

Mother sighed deeply. "Katrina, I'm sorry. But twelve is too young."

"I'm too young for everything!" Katrina wailed.

Mother put her arm around Katrina's stiff shoulders. "Not too young to make fudge for your entry in the pecan show. You'll find the pecans on the table. If you need help, I'll be in the backyard."

As Katrina cooked, she sniffed, snorted, and slammed pans. The fudge was in the refrigerator, and Katrina was cleaning up the kitchen when Mother came in carrying another pail of pecans. "Remember when we planted our pecan tree, Katie?" she asked. "You were just a little girl. It took a long time, but it's finally producing!"

Katrina ignored her mother and opened the refrigerator to check on the fudge. "It isn't getting hard!" she whined.

Mother looked over her shoulder. "I'm afraid you got in too big a hurry, Honey, and didn't cook it long enough."

Later as Mother helped Katrina pick pecans out of the shells for a second batch of fudge, Mother said softly, "A lot of things in life take time—things like fudge and pecan trees and growing up. When we rush them, we often ruin them. Be patient, Honey."

Katrina knew Mother was right. She gave Mother a tearful smile. "This time I'm going to let you help me decide when the fudge is ready," she said. "You've had more experience with it. And I'll let you help me decide when I'm ready to date, too. You also know a lot more about that than I do."

HOW ABOUT YOU? Are you fretting and stewing, wanting to do something your parents say you're not old enough to do? Ask the Lord to help you be patient. Whatever you're waiting for will be more enjoyable and valuable because of the wait. Meanwhile, use the experiences God is giving you right now to develop Christian virtues (including patience). Trust Him to give you opportunities. □ B.W.

TO MEMORIZE: *Since we are surrounded by so great a cloud of witnesses, let us lay aside every weight, and the sin which so easily ensnares us, and let us run with endurance the race that is set before us.* Hebrews 12:1, NKJV

FROM THE BIBLE:
Now as for you, dear brothers who are waiting for the Lord's return, be patient, like a farmer who waits until the autumn for his precious harvest to ripen. Yes, be patient. And take courage, for the coming of the Lord is near. Don't grumble about each other, brothers. Are you yourselves above criticism? For see! The great Judge is coming. He is almost here. [Let him do whatever criticizing must be done]. For examples of patience in suffering, look at the Lord's prophets. We know how happy they are now because they stayed true to him then, even though they suffered greatly for it. Job is an example of a man who continued to trust the Lord in sorrow; from his experiences we can see how the Lord's plan finally ended in good, for he is full of tenderness and mercy.
James 5:7-11, TLB

Be patient

20

The Pity Party

FROM THE BIBLE:
*Praise the LORD, O my soul;
all my inmost being, praise his
holy name. Praise the LORD, O
my soul, and forget not all his
benefits—who forgives all your
sins and heals all your diseases,
who redeems your life from the
pit and crowns you with love
and compassion, who satisfies
your desires with good things so
that your youth is renewed like
the eagle's. The LORD works
righteousness and justice for all
the oppressed. He made known
his ways to Moses, his deeds to
the people of Israel: The LORD
is compassionate and gracious,
slow to anger, abounding in
love. He will not always accuse,
nor will he harbor his anger
forever; he does not treat us as
our sins deserve or repay us
according to our iniquities. For
as high as the heavens are above
the earth, so great is his love for
those who fear him; as far as the
east is from the west, so far has
he removed our transgressions
from us. As a father has
compassion on his children, so
the LORD has compassion on
those who fear him.*
Psalm 103:1-13, NIV

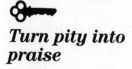

*Turn pity into
praise*

BILLY WAS POUTING in the backseat of the car. When Mother asked why, his sister Mary laughed. "He's just mad because Dad wouldn't let him buy that set of Indian arrowheads he saw at the gift shop," she said.

"I don't see why I couldn't have it," Billy scowled. "It was only six dollars. I never get to buy anything."

Dad raised his eyebrows. "Sounds like you're having a pity party," he said. "That's what we call it when someone feels so sorry for himself that he doesn't even want to be cheered up."

"Well," Billy grumbled, "you've only let me buy one souvenir, and we've already been on vacation four days. Besides, I always have to sit in the backseat."

"I've had to sit in the backseat, too," pouted Mary. "It's so hot, and you know I get carsick sometimes."

Dad and Mother exchanged glances. Mother's eyes twinkled. "Well, how about me?" she whined. "That mattress last night was so hard, I couldn't sleep, and the fried eggs I got for breakfast were cold and overdone. And I've got—"

"You think you've got it bad?" interrupted Dad in a complaining tone. "I've spent a whole lot more on this trip than I planned because the rain kept us from camping out the last two nights, and we had to stay in a motel."

The children stared. It surely seemed strange to have their parents whining! Dad and Mother laughed at the expression on their faces. "Look at that magnificent view," Dad said, pulling into a scenic turnoff. "We were so busy with our pity party that we've been forgetting about the good things around us."

"Yeah," Billy admitted. "Hey! Let's spend the next few minutes thinking of all the things we're thankful for. A praise party is more fun than a pity party, any day!"

HOW ABOUT YOU? Do you sometimes complain and feel sorry for yourself? Having this attitude makes you blind to the blessings of God and to the needs of others. Stop being selfish. Be thankful instead. Change your "pity party" into a "praise party."
                                        □ S.K.

TO MEMORIZE: *Praise the LORD, O my soul, and forget not all his benefits.* Psalm 103:2, NIV

SARA WAS IN a terrible mood. She sat at the kitchen table, criticizing and complaining. "I just hate school! Mr. Martin is a jerk. Luci and Jodi are stuck-up. They think they're so special." On and on she grumbled. Mother listened with a frown.

"Got anything to eat?" Jason's entrance into the room interrupted his sister's monologue. As he took an apple from a bowl on the counter, he talked excitedly. "Brad and I are doing a science project on air waves. Mr. Newkirk says scientists believe that everything that's ever been said is still around in space."

"Aw," Sara scoffed, "I don't believe that."

Jason pulled up a chair. "He read that on one of the first space flights, the radio picked up a program that had been aired twenty or thirty years before. Wouldn't it be neat to develop a device that could pull voices out of the air? How would you like everyone to hear everything you've ever said?"

Sara frowned at the idea of someone hearing a replay of her voice saying the things she had said only a few minutes ago. She shuddered. "I wouldn't."

"I don't know the method God uses," said Mother, joining the conversation, "but He keeps a record of everything we say. One day we'll give an account for every word we've spoken. Words, once they are spoken, never die."

"I didn't know that," said Sara. "Do you think you could invent a device that would stop me from saying things I shouldn't, Jason?"

Jason laughed, but Mother answered. "There already is such a device. It's called self-control. All you have to do is use it."

HOW ABOUT YOU? Do you often say things you should not say? Then you need to pray, like David did, "Lord, set a guard over my mouth." You need to ask the Lord to help you practice self-control. Remember you'll have to answer to Him for your words. □ B.W.

TO MEMORIZE: *Set a guard over my mouth, O LORD; keep watch over the door of my lips.* Psalm 141:3, NIV

21

Watch Your Mouth

FROM THE BIBLE:
You brood of snakes! How could evil men like you speak what is good and right? For a man's heart determines his speech. A good man's speech reveals the rich treasures within him. An evil-hearted man is filled with venom, and his speech reveals it. And I tell you this, that you must give account on Judgment Day for every idle word you speak. Your words now reflect your fate then: either you will be justified by them or you will be condemned.
Matthew 12:34-37, TLB

Don't speak thoughtlessly

22

Unarmed!

FROM THE BIBLE:

Put on the full armor of God so that you can take your stand against the devil's schemes. For our struggle is not against flesh and blood, but against the rulers, against the authorities, against the powers of this dark world and against the spiritual forces of evil in the heavenly realms. Therefore put on the full armor of God, so that when the day of evil comes, you may be able to stand your ground, and after you have done everything, to stand. Stand firm then, with the belt of truth buckled around your waist, with the breastplate of righteousness in place, and with your feet fitted with the readiness that comes from the gospel of peace. In addition to all this, take up the shield of faith, with which you can extinguish all the flaming arrows of the evil one. Take the helmet of salvation and the sword of the Spirit, which is the word of God. And pray in the Spirit on all occasions with all kinds of prayers and requests. With this in mind, be alert and always keep on praying for all the saints.
Ephesians 6:11-18, NIV

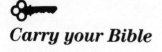

Carry your Bible

"OH NO!" Bobby exclaimed out loud, but not too loud. He didn't want Mom or Dad to hear. "I forgot my Bible again!" The Kerner family was on their way to Sunday school, and already they were too far from home to go back for the Bible. He had forgotten it the week before, too, and his teacher, Mr. Lawrence, had told him to be sure and bring it the next time. In class this Sunday Mr. Lawrence told the boys to turn to Ephesians 6. Bobby quickly scooted his chair over to his friend's, hoping his teacher wouldn't notice that he didn't have his own Bible.

Mr. Lawrence didn't seem to notice. He just started telling the boys a story. "Frederick was a soldier, and he was very proud of being a soldier. He loved his country and believed in the laws of his government. When it was necessary to fight to protect those laws, he immediately went to battle. One day Frederick came face to face with the enemy. But lo and behold, he cried out, 'I forgot my sword! I have nothing with which to fight!'" The boys laughed. It seemed funny for a soldier to forget his sword! Then Mr. Lawrence had one of the boys read Ephesians 6:17. "And take the helmet of salvation, and the sword of the Spirit, which is the Word of God."

Even before Mr. Lawrence explained it, Bobby knew why he had told that story. As a Christian, Bobby, too, was in a battle—a battle against Satan. The Word of God was what he needed to fight that battle! He needed the Bible to show him the difference between right and wrong. He needed the Bible in order to learn more about the men and women who served God. Now Bobby understood why it was important for him to remember his Bible. No longer would he be an unarmed soldier!

HOW ABOUT YOU? Do you often forget your Bible when you go to church? Do you take it other places? To school? To ball games? To parties? It is part of the armor you need to fight Satan. It's a good idea to have at least a New Testament that you can easily carry with you wherever you go. You never know when you may need it. □ L.W.

TO MEMORIZE: *Take the helmet of salvation and the sword of the Spirit, which is the word of God.*
Ephesians 6:17, NIV

23

Worse Than Onions

"**Y**UCK!" Dustin complained. "It smells terrible in here! What are you eating?"

"Just this hot dog," Ben answered with a shrug.

Dustin looked at Ben's paper plate on the counter. "Onions! You're eating onions. That's what stinks!"

"What's a hot dog without onions?" Ben asked, smiling.

"It'll give you bad breath!" warned Dustin.

"So?" laughed Ben. "If you don't like the smell, don't sit so close."

"Good idea!" Dustin said, taking a hot dog and moving to the other side of the room. "I'm not spoiling my hot dog with any stinky onions!"

"This conversation about onions reminds me of sin in our lives," observed Dad, who had been listening.

"Huh?" Ben mumbled with a full mouth.

Dad explained. "When a person feeds regularly on God's Word and obeys His commands, his life becomes as a fragrant sacrifice to the Lord. But, when a person refuses to follow God's commands and lives to please himself, his life is wretched and stinks of sin."

"But onions taste good," Ben stated.

"Sometimes sin tastes good, too," Dad said, "at least for a while. The guy who drinks or uses drugs or smokes probably feels good or important at the time, but often the end results are tragic. No matter how appealing sin looks, God hates it. To Him, it stinks."

"Even worse than onions," agreed Ben. "I can still eat them, can't I?"

"Just as long as you brush your teeth," Dustin suggested laughingly.

HOW ABOUT YOU? Consider your actions. How do you behave when Mother asks you to do something? When your younger brother breaks your things? When being honest is going to result in punishment? When someone tells a dirty joke? Is your behavior pleasing to God or does it "stink" before Him? Next time you're tempted to behave in a way you know is wrong, think about the smell of onions. Don't allow your behavior to "smell" even worse than that. □ B.D.

TO MEMORIZE: *Be imitators of God, therefore, as dearly loved children.* Ephesians 5:1, NIV

FROM THE BIBLE:

Be imitators of God, therefore, as dearly loved children and live a life of love, just as Christ loved us and gave himself up for us as a fragrant offering and sacrifice to God. But among you there must not be even a hint of sexual immorality, or of any kind of impurity, or of greed, because these are improper for God's holy people. Nor should there be obscenity, foolish talk or coarse joking, which are out of place, but rather thanksgiving. For of this you can be sure: No immoral, impure or greedy person—such a man is an idolater—has any inheritance in the kingdom of Christ and of God. Let no one deceive you with empty words, for because of such things God's wrath comes on those who are disobedient. Therefore do not be partners with them.
Ephesians 5:1-7, NIV

Choose to please God

SEPTEMBER

24

Happy to Serve

Is there any such thing as Christians cheering each other up? Do you love me enough to want to help me? Does it mean anything to you that we are brothers in the Lord, sharing the same Spirit? Are your hearts tender and sympathetic at all? Then make me truly happy by loving each other and agreeing wholeheartedly with each other, working together with one heart and mind and purpose. Don't be selfish; don't live to make a good impression on others. Be humble, thinking of others as better than yourself. Don't just think about your own affairs, but be interested in others, too, and in what they are doing. Your attitude should be the kind that was shown us by Jesus Christ, who, though he was God, did not demand and cling to his rights as God, but laid aside his mighty power and glory, taking the disguise of a slave and becoming like men. And he humbled himself even further, going so far as actually to die a criminal's death on a cross.

Philippians 2:1-8, TLB

Service brings joy

TIM HAD a minibike, a generous allowance, and lots of toys. When he came home from school each day, Mother was there with a listening ear. Tim went with his family to church regularly, and they always had daily devotions. Tim was a member of the Boy Scouts and played baseball. It seemed as though he had everything a boy could want, but he wasn't happy. He often moped and griped and asked for more and more things.

When Grandmother came to spend a few weeks, she didn't say much, but she listened and watched. She saw Tim throw a fit because his friends wouldn't do exactly as he ordered. She heard him demand a new baseball mitt because the old one had a little crack in it. She saw him become angry if anyone interrupted his video game.

One day Grandmother asked, "Tim, would you run this magazine over to Aunt Maude at the nursing home for me, please?" Tim did, and he came home whistling.

The next day Grandmother said, "Tim, today is your mother's birthday. Would you please help me fix a nice birthday dinner for her?" Tim did, and later went to bed smiling.

Then Grandmother had another idea. "The neighbors are going on vacation," she told Tim. "Why don't you offer to take care of their dog? Mrs. Wells mentioned how much Snoopy hates to go to the kennel." So Tim did, and for two weeks he romped and played with Snoopy.

At Grandmother's suggestion, Tim mowed the lawn for Mr. Nelson who had broken his leg. He weeded out the flower bed for his mother. He washed the car for his dad. And he moped and griped less and less—and smiled, laughed, and whistled more and more.

His parents noticed the difference. "What happened to Tim?" they wondered. "He's like a different boy."

Grandmother simply smiled and said, "To be happy we must serve, not be served. We must give, not get."

HOW ABOUT YOU? Are you unhappy and wondering why? Maybe you need to start serving others and giving to them. Giving yourself in service to others brings true happiness. Jesus became a servant. Can you do any less? □ B.W.

TO MEMORIZE: *You, my brothers, were called to be free. But do not use your freedom to indulge the sinful nature; rather, serve one another in love.* Galatians 5:13, NIV

ERIN and her brother, Greg, had been praying that some of their friends would be saved. Greg was overjoyed one Sunday when Chuck joined him at church. As the family returned home, Greg excitedly told them that Chuck had accepted Jesus during Sunday school.

"That's great," Dad said with a smile.

"Wonderful," added Mother enthusiastically. "Your prayers have been answered."

But Erin looked very discouraged. "I pray for Lynn," she said. "Why doesn't God answer my prayers, too?"

"Don't be discouraged," advised Dad. "Sometimes it takes a long time before a person will accept Christ."

"Yeah," added Greg, "I invited Chuck to Sunday school a whole year before he ever came."

"That's right," agreed Mother. She turned to Erin. "How often have you invited Lynn to go to church with you?"

"Why, I haven't actually invited her," stammered Erin, "but I let her know I was going."

"You didn't ask her to come?" said Greg. "Have you ever told her about Jesus?"

"Well, not exactly," admitted Erin. "I pray for her, though—all the time!"

"Hmmm," murmured Dad. "Remember the Bible story of Nehemiah and the people of Israel building a wall around Jerusalem? When they heard their enemies were coming, they prayed. But they also prepared to fight. It's great that you pray for Lynn, but sometimes the Lord wants to use us to answer our own prayers."

Erin was silent for a while. "May I be excused? I'd like to call Lynn and invite her to Sunday school this week, okay?"

Dad nodded. "Hurry back," he said. "It's almost time for family devotions, and we all want to pray for Lynn, too."

HOW ABOUT YOU? Are you praying about something special—for someone's salvation, for money you need, or perhaps for help with your lessons? Prayer is very important, but don't just pray if there's something you could also do to help. Maybe the Lord wants you to talk to somebody, to mow a lawn, to be a friend, to study hard. Pray, and then with the Lord's help, do all you can to accomplish the task. □ H.M.

TO MEMORIZE: *But we prayed to our God and posted a guard day and night to meet this threat.* Nehemiah 4:9, NIV

The Answer

FROM THE BIBLE:

So we rebuilt the wall till all of it reached half its height, for the people worked with all their heart. But when Sanballat, Tobiah, the Arabs, the Ammonites and the men of Ashdod heard that the repairs to Jerusalem's walls had gone ahead and that the gaps were being closed, they were very angry. They all plotted together to come and fight against Jerusalem and stir up trouble against it. But we prayed to our God and posted a guard day and night to meet this threat. Meanwhile, the people in Judah said, "The strength of the laborers is giving out, and there is so much rubble that we cannot rebuild the wall." Also our enemies said, "Before they know it or see us, we will be right there among them and will kill them and put an end to the work." Then the Jews who lived near them came and told us ten times over, "Wherever you turn, they will attack us." Therefore I stationed some of the people behind the lowest points of the wall at the exposed places, posting them by families, with their swords, spears and bows. Nehemiah 4:6-13, NIV

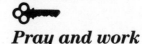

Pray and work

SEPTEMBER

26

Forgotten Combination

FROM THE BIBLE:

But very early on Sunday morning they took the ointments to the tomb: and found that the huge stone covering the entrance had been rolled aside. So they went in—but the Lord Jesus' body was gone. They stood there puzzled, trying to think what could have happened to it. Suddenly two men appeared before them, clothed in shining robes so bright their eyes were dazzled. The women were terrified and bowed low before them. Then the men asked, "Why are you looking in a tomb for someone who is alive? He isn't here! He has come back to life again! Don't you remember what he told you back in Galilee—that the Messiah must be betrayed into the power of evil men and be crucified and that he would rise again the third day?" Then they remembered.

Luke 24:1-8, TLB

Memorize God's Word

"OUR NEW LOCKERS are neat, but I can't get mine open." Amber frowned at the paper in her hand.

"Let me help you." Tonya took the paper, studied it, spun the dial, and the door opened.

"Oh, thanks. I don't know what I did wrong," said Amber as she closed the door again.

"You'd better memorize it," suggested Tonya.

"I don't need to. I'll just keep it here in my notebook." Amber dumped her books in her locker and closed the door.

The next morning Amber's family gathered around the table for devotions before breakfast. "What's the Bible verse for today?" Joey asked.

"I wish we didn't have to learn a verse every day," Amber grumbled.

Mother ignored her. "It's Colossians 3:16. 'Let the word of Christ dwell in you richly.' "

Joey grinned at Amber as he repeated the verse. He knew she hated memorizing. "Now it's your turn, Amber."

"I don't have time now. I'll learn it this evening." Amber changed the subject. "We have new combination lockers at school."

"What's your combination?" Dad asked.

"I don't remember, but I put it in my notebook." Amber reached for a piece of toast. "All I have to do is—" Her mouth dropped open. "All I have to do is look in my notebook. And my notebook is in my locker!" she wailed. "Oh, why didn't I memorize it like Tonya said? Say, maybe Tonya remembers it." She dashed for the phone. A few minutes later she returned smiling. "Tonya remembered it. I've written it down, and I'll memorize it on the way to school. But right now I need to learn Colossians 3:16. I just learned that it's not a good idea to postpone memorizing important things."

HOW ABOUT YOU? Do you complain about memorizing God's Word? The Word of God is a "combination" that will unlock many doors in life for you. It's important that you memorize it now. Someday you will need to know the combination for yourself. □ B.W.

TO MEMORIZE: *Let the word of Christ dwell in you richly in all wisdom, teaching and admonishing one another in psalms and hymns and spiritual songs, singing with grace in your hearts to the Lord.* Colossians 3:16, NKJV

"IT LOOKS LIKE these tomatoes will be just perfect for the fair next week," noted Mother as she stooped to examine Kara's vegetables. "You certainly have worked hard in the garden this summer, Honey."

"It was fun most of the time," said Kara with a smile. She moved the hose over to the carrots as she continued to think about the fair. "I wonder how Becky is doing on the quilt she's making for the sewing exhibit."

"I'd like to see it sometime," said Mother, picking up the weeds she had pulled from the garden. "She's such a sweet girl. Has she enjoyed coming to Sunday school with us?"

"I think so," replied Kara, turning to her mom with a look of concern. "I wish she'd get saved, though! I thought as soon as she heard about Jesus, she'd trust Him as her Savior."

"The Bible says that every time we tell someone about Jesus, it's like planting a seed," answered Mother. "Do you remember waiting for these vegetable seeds to grow?"

Kara nodded. "Some of them sprouted almost right away. Others didn't come up for several days."

"You didn't stop taking care of the seeds that didn't come up right away, did you?" asked Mother.

"No, that would have been silly," answered Kara. "I don't think I'll ever understand exactly what goes on inside the ground to change small, dry seeds into radishes or cucumbers! But I knew that if I kept on watering the ground where we planted the seeds, eventually they would grow. Some just took longer than others."

"As we keep 'watering' the gospel 'seeds' by continuing to witness to our unsaved friends, God will make these 'seeds' grow, too," said Mother.

"I'm going to keep 'watering the seeds' that we planted in Becky then," said Kara happily. "I'll ask God to turn them into Becky's decision to be saved."

HOW ABOUT YOU? Have you been discouraged because someone you've been witnessing to hasn't accepted Jesus as Savior yet? Don't give up! Keep at it! God will make your 'seeds' of testimony about Him grow. □ D.R

TO MEMORIZE: *I planted, Apollos watered, but God gave the increase.* 1 Corinthians 3:6, NKJV

SEPTEMBER

27

Seeds First

FROM THE BIBLE:
Here is another story illustrating what the Kingdom of God is like: A farmer sowed his field, and went away, and as the days went by, the seeds grew and grew without his help. For the soil made the seeds grow. First a leaf-blade pushed through, and later the wheat-heads formed and finally the grain ripened, and then the farmer came at once with his sickle and harvested it.
Mark 4:26-29, TLB

Keep witnessing

28

Buckle Up

FROM THE BIBLE:

*God's laws are perfect. They
protect us, make us wise, and
give us joy and light. God's laws
are pure, eternal, just. They are
more desirable than gold. They
are sweeter than honey dripping
from a honeycomb. For they
warn us away from harm and
give success to those who obey
them.*

Psalm 19:7-11, TLB

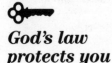

God's law
protects you

BOB BURST through the kitchen door. "You
oughta see this new rule we got. No one can leave
the lunchroom until they've been there at least
fifteen minutes!"

"What's so bad about that, Bob?" asked Mother.

"I could eat in five minutes and be out on the
playground if we didn't have that stupid rule."

"Exactly," said Mother, "and eating that fast
isn't good for your digestion."

"Seems like I should be able to decide how long
I need to eat," Bob argued. "It's my body."

"Come on, Bob," said Mother, changing the
subject. "I have to get Stevie's shoes from the repair shop. You can ride along. Put Stevie in the car
seat for me, would you?"

Bob picked up the baby. As he put Stevie in the
baby seat, Stevie fought him. He didn't want to
be strapped in! Bob stormed into the house.
"Stevie doesn't want to be buckled up. Can't he
just sit on my lap?"

"No, he must be buckled up," said Mother. "It's
the law here."

Later, as they were going through an intersection, another car ignored the yield sign and crashed
into them. Although the cars were damaged, no
one was hurt.

As the family had devotions together that evening, they again thought over the events of the
day. "Good thing Stevie was buckled up," Dad
commented. "You know, we've just been reading
in Psalm 19 that there is reward in following God's
commandments. I think He gave a practical object
lesson today to show us that laws are for our good."

"Yes," agreed Mother. "That 'buckle up' law
was made to protect lives, just like God gives us
rules for our protection. Sometimes we feel God's
laws strap us down, but they really keep us from
harming ourselves or others."

"I'll try to remember that the next time I want
to do things my way," Bob said. He grinned. "I'll
even sit quietly for fifteen minutes at lunchtime."

HOW ABOUT YOU? Do you complain about the rules
that God gives in His Word? Do you think they
are too strict or tie you down? Remember God
made you, and He knows what will keep you safe
and happy. Obey His rules. □ J.H.

TO MEMORIZE: *So then, the law is holy, and the
commandment is holy, righteous and good.*
Romans 7:12, NIV

DAVID SAT on the bench and waited for his turn at bat. His team was losing by just a couple of runs, and it was the last inning, their last opportunity to catch up with the other team. *I know,* David thought. *I'll pray that I get a home run.* He bowed his head and whispered a prayer.

Finally it was David's turn. Confidently, he picked up his bat and walked to home plate. The pitcher threw the ball, and David took a big swing—but missed. Again, the pitcher threw the ball. This time David hit it, and it slowly rolled toward the third baseman. An easy out to end the game!

David slowly walked over to meet his parents. How could he have missed? "I don't understand it," David said as they drove home. "I prayed that the Lord would give me a home run, but I hit the ball worse than all the other times I was up to bat today!"

"Hmmm," Dad said thoughtfully, "the Gray boys were on the other team, and they're Christians, too. I wonder what they were praying!" David smiled. That was true. There were Christians on the other team. "Seriously, David," his father went on, "sometimes our prayers are selfish. We want what we want now. That's not the purpose of prayer."

"But doesn't God care about the ball game?" David asked.

"Yes, God does care. He cares that you have a good, Christian attitude, whether you win or lose. Baseball is only a game. Sometimes we make ball games more important than they really are. The thing to remember is to ask for the Lord's will to be done."

"I'll remember, Dad." Next game, David was going to ask the Lord to help him be a good short whether he hit a home run or not.

HOW ABOUT YOU? Do you sometimes pray selfishly? Do you pray that you will hit a home run, or that you will receive an *A* on a test (when you haven't even studied), or that you will get a new bike? Remember, you need to ask that the Lord's will be done concerning all your requests. You also need to remember to have a Christian attitude, no matter what the outcome. The Lord knows what is best for you. □ L.W.

TO MEMORIZE: *This is the confidence we have in approaching God: that if we ask anything according to his will, he hears us.* 1 John 5:14, NIV

The Home Run That Wasn't

FROM THE BIBLE:

And in the same way—by our faith—the Holy Spirit helps us with our daily problems and in our praying. For we don't even know what we should pray for, nor how to pray as we should; but the Holy Spirit prays for us with such feeling that it cannot be expressed in words. And the Father who knows all hearts knows, of course, what the Spirit is saying as he pleads for us in harmony with God's own will. And we know that all that happens to us is working for our good if we love God and are fitting into his plans. For from the very beginning God decided that those who came to him— and all along he knew who would—should become like his Son, so that his Son would be the First, with many brothers. And having chosen us, he called us to come to him; and when we came, he declared us "not guilty," filled us with Christ's goodness, gave us right standing with himself, and promised us his glory.

Romans 8:26-30, TLB

Pray for God's will

30

Cure for Loneliness

FROM THE BIBLE:
Love each other with brotherly affection and take delight in honoring each other. Never be lazy in your work but serve the Lord enthusiastically. Be glad for all God is planning for you. Be patient in trouble, and prayerful always. When God's children are in need, you be the one to help them out. And get into the habit of inviting guests home for dinner or, if they need lodging, for the night. If someone mistreats you because you are a Christian, don't curse him; pray that God will bless him. When others are happy, be happy with them. If they are sad, share their sorrow. Work happily together. Don't try to act big. Don't try to get into the good graces of important people, but enjoy the company of ordinary folks. And don't think you know it all! Never pay back evil for evil. Do things in such a way that everyone can see you are honest clear through. Don't quarrel with anyone. Be at peace with everyone, just as much as possible.
Romans 12:10-18, TLB

Be friendly

"I'VE BEEN HERE a week, Mother, and I still don't know anyone," Paula complained. "The kids have their own friends. They don't need me."

"If you want to have friends you must be friendly," Mother reminded her.

"Don't start preaching at me, Mother. I'm so lonely! Oh, why did we have to move here?" Paula sobbed.

"Honey, I do understand. I'm having that problem, too." Mother sighed. "Let's try an experiment. Let's put Proverbs 18:24 into practice." She handed Paula a Bible.

Paula flipped through the pages and read, "A man who has friends must himself be friendly."

"We're the newcomers, and so we think others should make us welcome. But let's forget that. Let's go out of our way to be friendly," Mother suggested. "It will be fun. Every evening we can report our successes."

"Yeah—or our failures." Paula was doubtful, but she decided to give it a try.

The next evening Paula reported, "I loaned a pencil to Pat, the girl who sits next to me. She lives only a couple blocks away, and she's coming over tonight." Mother told how she had caught and returned the neighbor's runaway puppy. As a result, she had been invited for coffee.

The next day Paula helped another girl with spelling. While she was doing that, a boy she had seen at church came over and asked a couple of questions. Paula's eyes sparkled as she told her mother about it later.

Mother had called the church and volunteered to "give a hand" wherever needed. She was invited to the Ladies' Society workday the following afternoon.

After a week of showing themselves friendly, Mother and Paula were amazed at the results. "People here aren't like they were when we first came," Paula remarked. "They've changed." Then Paula realized who had really changed.

HOW ABOUT YOU? Are you lonely? Do you need friends? Do you think others are unfriendly? Maybe it's just that you are unapproachable. Smile and speak to others. Look for ways to help them. They need your friendship as much as you need theirs. Offer it to them. □ B.W.

TO MEMORIZE: *Perfume and incense bring joy to the heart, and the pleasantness of one's friend springs from his earnest counsel.*
Proverbs 27:9, NIV

"THERE WAS a new girl in our class today," Mary Ellen announced at the dinner table. "I don't like her, though. She's a snob. She sits just like this." Mary Ellen turned her nose up, pushed her shoulders back, and sat very erect. "When Debi asked her if she wanted to jump rope with us, she said, 'No, thank you,' so prissy."

"Hmmm," murmured Mother as she passed the chicken casserole. "Aren't you judging a little prematurely? God says we shouldn't do that."

Dad peered at the casserole. "What is this?"

"A new casserole," said Mother.

"I don't want any," stated five-year-old Matthew. "I don't like it."

Mary Ellen laughed. "You've never tasted it," she said.

"I know I won't like it," Matthew repeated.

"Well, I want you to try it," said Dad. "Take two bites, Matthew."

Matthew looked pleadingly at Mother. "You heard your dad," she said. "Two bites." Matthew put a tiny bit on the edge of his spoon. "That's not even enough to taste," Mother said as she filled his spoon. "Now taste it."

Matthew grimaced as he put the spoon to his mouth. He swallowed, then slowly grinned. "It *is* good!" he exclaimed.

When the laughter had died down, Mother looked at Mary Ellen. "You are acting about the new girl just like Matthew did about the casserole. You haven't given her a fair chance."

The next day Mary Ellen came bouncing in from school. "Guess what, Mother? I do like Jolene," she said. "She's nice. She sits like she does because she wears a back brace. That's why she couldn't jump rope. She just hated to tell anybody."

Mother smiled. "I'm glad you gave her a fair chance," she said. "I'm sure the Lord is, too."

HOW ABOUT YOU? Are you afraid to try new things or meet new people? If you judge them on the basis of first impressions, you may miss some wonderful experiences. Determine now to give everyone you meet a fair chance to be your friend. God warns about judging unfairly. □ B.W.

TO MEMORIZE: *Do not judge, and you will not be judged. Do not condemn, and you will not be condemned. Forgive, and you will be forgiven.* Luke 6:37, NIV

1

A Fair Chance

FROM THE BIBLE:
Don't criticize, and then you won't be criticized. For others will treat you as you treat them. And why worry about a speck in the eye of a brother when you have a board in your own? Should you say, "Friend, let me help you get that speck out of your eye," when you can't even see because of the board in your own? Hypocrite! First get rid of the board. Then you can see to help your brother.
Matthew 7:1-5, TLB

Give people a fair chance

OCTOBER

2

The Copybook

FROM THE BIBLE:
For this is commendable, if because of conscience toward God one endures grief, suffering wrongfully. For what credit is it if, when you are beaten for your faults, you take it patiently? But when you do good and suffer for it, if you take it patiently, this is commendable before God. For to this you were called, because Christ also suffered for us, leaving us an example, that you should follow His steps: "Who committed no sin, nor was guile found in His mouth"; who, when He was reviled, did not revile in return; when He suffered, He did not threaten, but committed Himself to Him who judges righteously; who Himself bore our sins in His own body on the tree, that we, having died to sins, might live for righteousness—by whose stripes you were healed. For you were like sheep going astray, but have now returned to the Shepherd and Overseer of your souls.
1 Peter 2:19-25, NKJV

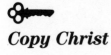

Copy Christ

AMANDA BOWED her head and closed her eyes to pray, just as she always did before eating her school lunch. When she opened her eyes, her lunch had disappeared, every eye was on her, and the children were snickering.

"Who has my lunch?" asked Amanda. "Will you give it back, please?" At that, everyone burst into laughter.

"Ask God where your lunch is, Miss Christian," said Butch. "You always talk to Him, don't you?"

Just then the teacher stood behind Amanda. "The person who has Amanda's lunch had better hand it over right now, or you'll all be in trouble," she said. Butch pulled his hands out from under the table. He had taken Amanda's lunch. But for the rest of the day, the children made fun of Amanda and called her "Miss Christian."

When Amanda arrived home, she told her mother what had happened. "I was so embarrassed, Mom," she said. "I don't know how to act when the kids make fun of me."

"Follow Jesus' example," advised Mother. "How did He act when He was persecuted?"

"Well, He didn't fight or talk back," replied Amanda.

Mother nodded. "Do you remember the copybooks you used when you were learning to write? There were letters and words printed on the top line. They were your example. You copied them the best you could."

"And now Jesus is my example," said Amanda thoughtfully. "But I can't be perfect, as He is."

"No. But look at one of your old copybooks," suggested Mother. "Your writing is much more like the letters at the top now than it was when you started. And as you follow Jesus' example, you'll become more and more like Him."

"I think I'll find an old book and tear a page out to keep in my notebook," decided Amanda. "It will remind me to keep on copying Jesus and not give up."

HOW ABOUT YOU? Has anyone made fun of you for being a Christian? How did you react? Were you angry or spiteful? Next time ask yourself, "How would Jesus act if He were in my place?" By copying Him, you may even be able to influence your persecutors to be saved. □ M.R.P.

TO MEMORIZE: *For to this you were called, because Christ also suffered for us, leaving us an example, that you should follow His steps.* 1 Peter 2:21, NKJV

BRAD HAD BEEN praying that his friend Ted would be saved. Now Ted had agreed to go with the church youth group to the amusement park, and Brad was delighted. Perhaps if Ted enjoyed himself, he'd come along to church sometime.

The group had a great time at the park, and all too soon it was over. On the way home the kids discussed their favorite rides.

"I'd never go on that roller coaster," Jenny said.

"Why not?" Ted asked. "That's my favorite! You don't know what you're missing."

"I sure do," said Jenny. "I'm missing a scary ride. What if something would break, and the whole thing fell off the track?"

"Aw, ya gotta have more faith, Jenny," Ted teased. "The roller coaster is safe. Isn't that right, Mr. Benson?" He turned to the youth leader.

"It's been tested for safety," Mr. Benson said, "but it isn't foolproof, of course. However, it doesn't matter how much faith a person has, but where his faith is placed."

"What do you mean?" Ted asked.

"Well, these rides are tested for safety, and people put their faith in them every day," Mr. Benson replied. "Yet occasionally the news reports tell of one breaking down and someone getting hurt. No matter how much faith they had in the ride, it didn't help. They just put their faith in the wrong thing that time."

"Yeah, I guess so," agreed Ted. "So there's nothing and nobody you can really trust, is there? I mean, everything and everybody fails some time or other." He laughed. "Well, so much for faith!"

"Ah, but there's an exception—the Lord Jesus." Mr. Benson smiled. "He will never fail you if you put your trust in Him."

Ted looked a bit doubtful, but he was listening. "Tell me more, Mr. Benson," he said.

HOW ABOUT YOU? Where have you put your faith? In good works? In baptism? In church attendance? All those things will fail you. Only by placing your faith in Jesus Christ will you receive salvation.
□ J.H.

TO MEMORIZE: *A man is not justified by observing the law, but by faith in Jesus Christ. So we, too, have put our faith in Christ Jesus that we may be justified by faith in Christ and not by observing the law.* Galatians 2:16, NIV

3

The Roller Coaster

FROM THE BIBLE:
Abraham was, humanly speaking, the founder of our Jewish nation. What were his experiences concerning this question of being saved by faith? Was it because of his good deeds that God accepted him? If so, then he would have something to boast about. But from God's point of view Abraham had no basis at all for pride. For the Scriptures tell us Abraham believed God, and that is why God canceled his sins and declared him "not guilty." But didn't he earn his right to heaven by all the good things he did? No, for being saved is a gift; if a person could earn it by being good, then it wouldn't be free—but it is! It is given to those who do not work for it. For God declares sinners to be good in his sight if they have faith in Christ to save them from God's wrath. King David spoke of this, describing the happiness of an undeserving sinner who is declared "not guilty" by God. "Blessed, and to be envied," he said, "are those whose sins are forgiven and put out of sight." Romans 4:1-7, TLB

Put faith in Christ

Marvin Gets Mad

FROM THE BIBLE:

If you are angry, don't sin by nursing your grudge. Don't let the sun go down with you still angry—get over it quickly; for when you are angry you give a mighty foothold to the devil. If anyone is stealing he must stop it and begin using those hands of his for honest work so he can give to others in need. Don't use bad language. Say only what is good and helpful to those you are talking to, and what will give them a blessing. Don't cause the Holy Spirit sorrow by the way you live. Remember, he is the one who marks you to be present on that day when salvation from sin will be complete. Stop being mean, bad-tempered and angry. Quarreling, harsh words, and dislike of others should have no place in your lives. Instead, be kind to each other, tender-hearted, forgiving one another, just as God has forgiven you because you belong to Christ. Ephesians 4:26-32, TLB*

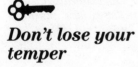

Don't lose your temper

*B*ANG! went Marvin's ankle against the dining room chair. *Crash!* went the chair as Marvin kicked it over with his bare foot. And "Ouch!" said Marvin as he sat down to rub his sore ankle and aching toes.

"That dumb chair!" Marvin shouted. "It always gets in the way." He continued to complain as he rubbed his bruises.

Just then Dad walked in. He quietly set the chair up, then asked, "Who are you mad at, Son?"

"At the chair," replied Marvin. "It hurt my foot!"

"I'm sorry you got hurt," Dad said. "But surely you're not really angry with the chair, are you? After all, it's only a thing. It didn't actually jump out in front of you."

Marvin pouted. "No, I guess not," he admitted. "But what's the big deal? Who cares if I yelled at the chair? It can't hear me."

"No, the chair can't, but God can," Dad replied. "Do you think He's pleased when you shout and kick the furniture whenever things don't go your way?" Marvin hung his head. This was not the first time Dad had spoken to him about his problem with anger. "You're responsible for your actions and for the words that come out of your mouth," continued Dad. "Displaying your temper won't make your anger go away. It only makes you, and everyone around you, more tense and unhappy."

"Well, what should I do?" grumbled Marvin.

"Deal with your anger God's way," Dad replied. "Pray immediately that God will help you get rid of it. Do what you can to solve the problem—like walking more slowly through the dining room, for example. Also, confess any feelings of self-pity or pride that may be causing your anger."

"I'll try, Dad," sighed Marvin. He turned toward the chair and smiled. "Sorry, chair. I'll think twice before I yell at you again. Even if you can't hear me, God can!"

HOW ABOUT YOU? Do you get angry when things don't turn out your way? Do you control your feelings of anger, or do you let them control you? People who lose their temper displease God and irritate those around them. Anger can easily lead to other kinds of sin as well. Don't lose your temper! □ S.K.

TO MEMORIZE: *Better a patient man than a warrior, a man who controls his temper than one who takes a city.* Proverbs 16:32, NIV

"LOOK AT all the people!" exclaimed Andy. "Yes," replied Dad. "This parade better be good, or I'll wish I'd stayed home." He inched forward with the traffic. "A lot of cars are turning here," he added. "Maybe they know of a place to park around the corner." He made a right turn, following the car in front of him.

Immediately the traffic speeded up, and instead of finding a place to park, they found themselves on a ramp leading to a freeway. "Oh no," groaned Dad. "I never saw the sign for the freeway! Now we'll have to go a few miles before we can get back off." He scowled at the car ahead of him. "Thanks a lot, mister," he growled. "You led me wrong!"

Mother laughed. "Oh, so it's his fault, huh?"

"What about the car behind you?" asked Andy. "I noticed that it followed along, too. Is that your fault?"

Dad grinned. "No," he said. "They should have watched where they were going."

Again Mother and Andy laughed. "Sounds a little like someone else I know," observed Mother, looking at Andy.

Andy blushed. Just the night before he had excused his rowdy behavior at a Sunday school picnic by saying that everybody else was doing the same thing. He was only following the example of some of the older boys. At the same time, he had insisted that he was not responsible for the way his little sister had copied his actions.

"At times we all tend to forget that God has given each of us intelligence. He intends for us to use it instead of blindly following the crowd," said Dad. "On the other hand, He expects us to live in such a way that others may follow us." They were approaching a ramp. "I don't know about that guy ahead of me, but I'm getting off here and turning around."

HOW ABOUT YOU? God gave you intelligence. Are you using it to think for yourself? Are you accepting your responsibility to be a good example to others? Don't use the excuse that "everybody's doing it." Instead, be able to say, "I believe this is what God wants me to do." Others are following you. Lead them in the right way. □ H.M.

TO MEMORIZE: *Don't let anyone look down on you because you are young, but set an example for the believers in speech, in life, in love, in faith and in purity.* 1 Timothy 4:12, NIV

Followers

FROM THE BIBLE:
May the Lord bring you into an ever deeper understanding of the love of God and of the patience that comes from Christ. Now here is a command, dear brothers, given in the name of our Lord Jesus Christ by his authority: Stay away from any Christian who spends his days in laziness and does not follow the ideal of hard work we set up for you. For you well know that you ought to follow our example: you never saw us loafing; we never accepted food from anyone without buying it; we worked hard day and night for the money we needed to live on, in order that we would not be a burden to any of you. We wanted to show you, firsthand, how you should work for your living. Yet we hear that some of you are living in laziness, refusing to work, and wasting your time in gossiping. In the name of the Lord Jesus Christ we appeal to such people—we command them—to quiet down, get to work, and earn their own living. And to the rest of you I say, dear brothers, never be tired of doing right.
2 Thessalonians 3:5-13, TLB

Follow Jesus, not the crowd

6

Joey Takes a Stand

FROM THE BIBLE:

Some sat in darkness and the deepest gloom, prisoners suffering in iron chains, for they had rebelled against the words of God and despised the counsel of the Most High. So he subjected them to bitter labor; they stumbled, and there was no one to help. Then they cried to the LORD in their trouble, and he saved them from their distress. He brought them out of darkness and the deepest gloom and broke away their chains. Let them give thanks to the LORD for his unfailing love and his wonderful deeds for men, for he breaks down gates of bronze and cuts through bars of iron. Some became fools through their rebellious ways and suffered affliction because of their iniquities. They loathed all food and drew near the gates of death. Then they cried to the LORD in their trouble, and he saved them from their distress. He sent forth his word and healed them; he rescued them from the grave. Let them give thanks to the LORD for his unfailing love and his wonderful deeds for men.

Psalm 107:10-21, NIV

Don't develop bad habits

"GUYS, LOOK what I found!" Joey picked up a short piece of chain from the sidewalk. "Bet you can't break it."

Bill and Andy examined it. "Bet you can't, either," said Bill. "No use even trying."

Another friend, Carl, didn't even look at the chain. "Come on, Joey, you're the smallest," he said. "Squeeze through this fence and get us some strawberries." Through the crack in the fence Joey could see Mr. Wilken's strawberry patch. He knew there were delicious berries hiding under the green leaves. "Go on," Carl urged.

Joey didn't want to go into Mr. Wilken's yard. But what would his friends think of him if he didn't go along with their plans? Would they make fun of him if he told them why he didn't want to do it? The length of chain he still held in his sweaty hand gave him an idea. Joey took a deep breath. "I'm a Christian," he said bravely, "and I'm afraid of getting into bad habits. Habits are hard to break, especially bad habits. We wouldn't be able to break the links in this chain no matter how hard we tried. And if we take stuff from people's gardens, we may get into the habit of stealing—a habit we can't break. I don't want to be a thief all my life."

"What's a few berries?" snorted Carl. "Come on, guys, let's leave this baby and see what old Mrs. Smith has in her garden."

Bill and Andy hesitated. Then Bill said, "We'll walk home with Joey." Joey smiled as they started off. He felt almost as big as the other boys.

HOW ABOUT YOU? Will you say no when someone suggests stealing, telling a lie, or making fun of another person? Ask God to help you "take a stand." Ask Him to keep you from developing a sinful habit you can't break. Maybe you already have a bad habit. God can give the strength you need to overcome it. You can't do it alone. □ B.B.

TO MEMORIZE: *Then they cried to the LORD in their trouble, and he saved them from their distress.* Psalm 107:13, NIV

EIGHT-YEAR-OLD HEIDI loved to crawl up on Grandpa Hohenberger's lap and listen to stories about his younger days back in Germany. Heidi thought her grandpa must have lived the most exciting life imaginable. Today Grandpa asked Heidi a question. "What did you learn in Sunday school, Little One?"

"We're studying Matthew 5," Heidi answered, "and we're learning some of the verses. My teacher calls them the Beatitudes."

"Oh, good!" responded Grandpa. "We can learn lots of good lessons from them. Have you learned any yet?"

"Yep!" replied Heidi. "The first one is 'Blessed are the poor in spirit, for theirs is the kingdom of heaven.' I didn't know you had to be poor to be a Christian."

"Ach, Heidi! You don't!" said Grandpa. "You have to be poor *in spirit!* To be poor in spirit is the opposite of being proud in spirit. If you're proud, you think you can get to heaven on your own. But if you're poor in spirit, you realize that you have a need! It reminds me of when I decided to leave Germany and come to America!"

"Goody!" Heidi giggled. "I love your stories!"

"Well," the old man began, "in a sense, I had to be 'poor in spirit' to want to leave Germany. In other words, I had to see my own need. Now, that step wasn't hard. Hitler had taken over the government, and it was plain to me that he was opposed to God and Christianity. Hitler's army was building up, and I knew if I didn't leave soon, I'd be forced to serve in it. Oh, I could have been proud and said, 'Hitler will never get me!' But, that would have been foolish!"

"I get it," Heidi responded. "You had to see your need to get out of Germany so you could be free from Hitler."

"That's right." Grandpa smiled. "And, being poor in spirit means to see our need of accepting Jesus to be free from sin."

HOW ABOUT YOU? Do you realize that you have a need for freedom from sin? Do you see that you cannot meet that need on your own? Because all are sinners (Romans 3:23), all need Jesus to take away that sin (Romans 6:23). Don't be too proud to admit that you are "poor in spirit"—in other words, that you have a need of Jesus! □ R.P.

TO MEMORIZE: *Blessed are the poor in spirit, for theirs is the kingdom of heaven.* Matthew 5:3, NIV

THE BEATITUDES
Poor in Spirit

FROM THE BIBLE:
I cried to him and he answered me! He freed me from all my fears. Others too were radiant at what he did for them. Theirs was no downcast look of rejection! This poor man cried to the Lord—and the Lord heard him and saved him out of his troubles. For the Angel of the Lord guards and rescues all who reverence him. Oh, put God to the test and see how kind he is! See for yourself the way his mercies shower down on all who trust in him.
Psalm 34:4-8, TLB

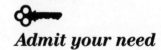

Admit your need

8

THE BEATITUDES

They That Mourn

FROM THE BIBLE:

*Hear me, Lord; oh, have pity
and help me." Then he turned
my sorrow into joy! He took
away my clothes of mourning
and clothed me with joy so that I
might sing glad praises to the
Lord instead of lying in silence
in the grave. O Lord my God, I
will keep on thanking you
forever!*

Psalm 30:10-12, TLB

Mourn over sin

"WHAT'S THE SECOND Beatitude, Heidi?" asked Grandpa Hohenberger.

"Blessed are they that mourn, for they shall be comforted," said Heidi promptly. "Does that mean it's good if somebody dies or something terrible happens to make us cry?"

Grandpa smiled. "No," he replied. "I think the mourning referred to here means mourning over *sin*. To mourn is to have a deep concern to the point of action. Let's go back to our comparison of getting out of Germany, shall we? There were many people who saw the need but didn't try to get away. They didn't care enough to do anything, but I did. I ran from the Nazi soldiers in the night. I even hid in a garbage truck so they didn't see me."

"That sounds awful," exclaimed Heidi.

"It was," agreed Grandpa. "You see, I cared so much that I would have done almost anything to get out of Germany. Sad to say, many people did not care that much. They didn't like what was happening in our homeland, but they didn't mourn like I did! Many died in concentration camps because they didn't care enough to try to escape!"

Heidi was thinking deeply. "I know some kids who are like that about heaven! They know they need to be saved, but they just don't care enough to do anything about it. I guess they don't mourn—right, Grandpa?"

"That's right." The old man nodded. "And if they don't mourn, they will never know the comfort salvation brings!" He paused a moment, then added, "There are also Christians who know of sin in their lives. They, too, need to mourn, or repent, and then they'll find the comfort of the full forgiveness that God has promised."

HOW ABOUT YOU? Do you mourn about the sin in your life? This means to care enough to want to change! If you're a Christian, you cared enough to call on Jesus, and He took away your sin and made you a citizen of His kingdom! But how about the disobedience, pride, carelessness, or other wrong things you still sometimes do? Do you mourn over them? You should! Ask God to forgive you and to help you change. He will forgive and comfort you.

□ R.P.

TO MEMORIZE: *Blessed are those who mourn, for they will be comforted.* Matthew 5:4, NIV

"GRANDPA, I learned another Beatitude," said Heidi the next day. "It's 'Blessed are the meek.' Everyone at school calls one of the third-grade teachers 'Meek Mr. Milton.' He's a little man with a high, whiny voice. He's a sissy, Grandpa! Why would Jesus give special blessings to sissies?"

"Heidi," said Grandpa sternly, "do not talk that way! Your teachers are your elders. That fact—and their position, too—demands your respect. Besides, *meek* doesn't mean weak. A person can be very strong and still be meek. I was meek when my ship from Germany landed in New York."

"I remember you told me you cried tears of joy when you saw the Statue of Liberty, Grandpa. But that didn't mean you were meek! You were just happy to be in a free land!"

"Heidi, I really was meek." Grandpa paused, then explained, "To be meek means you're willing to surrender your will to another and do what *he* wants. I was willing to do whatever was necessary to stay in this wonderful country! Later I gave up all allegiance to Germany and became a citizen here.

"Oh, I see. It's like you were switching your loyalty from Germany to America," said Heidi. "But what loyalty does a person switch when he becomes a Christian?"

"That's an easy one, Heidi," said Grandpa. "Before I was saved, I obeyed Satan most of the time because I belonged to him. But when I saw my need of Jesus, I surrendered my will to Him. That is being meek."

"I love Jesus, too, but sometimes I still want my own way," Heidi confessed.

"Ah, yes," said Grandpa. "We all struggle with that. After I became an American citizen, I sometimes missed Germany. But I had changed my loyalty, so I reminded myself that I was an American now. That's the way it is after we've given Jesus our loyalty. We must daily surrender our will to Him to be fully happy and blessed."

HOW ABOUT YOU? Do you love Jesus enough to surrender your will to Him and do whatever He wants you to do? That's what Jesus means by being meek! You'll be happiest when you give Him full control, and you will be rewarded in eternity as well. □ R.P.

TO MEMORIZE: *Blessed are the meek, for they will inherit the earth.* Matthew 5:5, NIV

THE BEATITUDES
The Meek

FROM THE BIBLE:
Do not offer the parts of your body to sin, as instruments of wickedness, but rather offer yourselves to God. For sin shall not be your master, because you are not under law, but under grace. What then? Shall we sin because we are not under law but under grace? By no means! Don't you know that when you offer yourselves to someone to obey him as slaves, you are slaves to the one whom you obey—whether you are slaves to sin, which leads to death, or to obedience, which leads to righteousness? But thanks be to God that, though you used to be slaves to sin, you wholeheartedly obeyed the form of teaching to which you were entrusted. You have been set free from sin and have become slaves to righteousness. I put this in human terms because you are weak in your natural selves. Just as you used to offer the parts of your body in slavery to impurity and to ever-increasing wickedness, so now offer them in slavery to righteousness leading to holiness.
Romans 6:13-19, NIV

Surrender your will

OCTOBER

10

THE BEATITUDES

Hunger and Thirst

FROM THE BIBLE:
So they asked him, "What miraculous sign then will you give that we may see it and believe you? What will you do? Our forefathers ate the manna in the desert; as it is written: 'He gave them bread from heaven to eat.' " Jesus said to them, "I tell you the truth, it is not Moses who has given you the bread from heaven, but it is my Father who gives you the true bread from heaven. For the bread of God is he who comes down from heaven and gives life to the world." "Sir," they said, "from now on give us this bread." Then Jesus declared, "I am the bread of life. He who comes to me will never go hungry, and he who believes in me will never be thirsty."
John 6:30-35, NIV

Learn about God

DISCUSSING THE BEATITUDES with her grandpa really helped Heidi understand them. One day she announced, "Guess what, Grandpa? My verse today is about hungering and thirsting after righteousness, and I think I understand it already. I think it means to want to know all about God. But can you tell me a story about it, anyway?"

"Let's see," said Grandpa. "Well, after I got to this country and decided to become an American citizen, I wanted to learn all I could about America!"

"You had to learn to speak English, right?" asked Heidi.

"Yes, and that was very hard for me, Heidi! But I wasn't content just to learn the language. I wanted to learn all there was to know about the country, too," explained Grandpa. "As soon as I could speak well enough, I went to high school at night and studied American history. Some boys in the class made fun of the way I talked, but even that didn't discourage me. I was so hungry to learn about my new country."

"Have you ever been disappointed in America, Grandpa?" Heidi asked.

"Sometimes, but I still believe this country is the greatest in the world," said Grandpa. "The more I learn about her, the more I love her! It's like that with God, too. I have hungered and thirsted for His righteousness for many years, ever since I was saved. And the more I study about God and learn about Him, the more I love Him. He never disappoints me." Grandpa hesitated. "We must not only thirst to know about Him, but also to be more like Him," he added.

HOW ABOUT YOU? Do you hunger and thirst after righteousness? God wants you to know all you can about Him. He has revealed Himself in His Word. Study it; learn to know God better; to know Him is to love Him. He wants you to show His righteousness in your life. □ R.P.

TO MEMORIZE: *Blessed are those who hunger and thirst for righteousness, for they will be filled.* Matthew 5:6, NIV

"BLESSED are the merciful for they will be shown mercy," read Heidi as she studied a a new verse. "Grandpa, what is mercy anyway?"

"Why don't you look in the dictionary?" suggested Grandpa. "I'll help you."

Heidi ran to get the dictionary, and together they found the word. "To show mercy means 'to forgive, spare, or pity,'" read Heidi, " 'or to show compassion.' "

"Yes," said Grandpa, "and God shows the most wonderful mercy of all. He's willing to forgive our sins instead of giving us the punishment we deserve. He wants us to follow His example and show mercy to others."

"Did anyone show you mercy when you came to America?" asked Heidi.

"Indeed they did," said Grandpa. "Did I ever tell you about my first job in America? Work was hard to find, and I applied many places. When I inquired at the grocery store near our apartment, the man I talked with showed me a list of boys who were ahead of me in line for a job. As I turned to leave, the owner of the store came in. He must have seen the discouraged look on my face, for he stopped me and asked a lot of questions. The next day—"

"You got the job," interrupted Heidi.

"Right," said Grandpa, "only it wasn't *the* job. There really were no openings. It was a job—one the owner made up for me. After hearing my story, he took pity on me. He showed me mercy by finding some work for me to do. I didn't deserve a job any more than all those boys who had applied before me."

"Did you work there long?" Heidi asked.

"Quite a while," answered Grandpa, "and the owner showed mercy more than once. It was all so new to me, and I made many mistakes, but he never fired me as I deserved. He was a Christian, and I'm sure God blessed him for being such a merciful man."

HOW ABOUT YOU? Are you a merciful Christian? Do you show mercy and forgiveness when you are wronged, or do you retaliate? If you see someone struggling with schoolwork, needing a friend, or too busy to get everything done, do you show mercy and help? If you show mercy to others, God says you will also have mercy shown to you.
□ R.P.

TO MEMORIZE: *Blessed are the merciful, for they will be shown mercy.* Matthew 5:7, NIV

THE BEATITUDES

The Merciful

FROM THE BIBLE:
Give to everyone who asks you, and if anyone takes what belongs to you, do not demand it back. Do to others as you would have them do to you. If you love those who love you, what credit is that to you? Even "sinners" love those who love them. And if you do good to those who are good to you, what credit is that to you? Even "sinners" do that. And if you lend to those from whom you expect repayment, what credit is that to you? Even "sinners" lend to "sinners," expecting to be repaid in full. But love your enemies, do good to them, and lend to them without expecting to get anything back. Then your reward will be great, and you will be sons of the Most High, because he is kind to the ungrateful and wicked. Be merciful, just as your Father is merciful.
Luke 6:30-46, NIV

Show compassion

OCTOBER

THE BEATITUDES

The Pure in Heart

FROM THE BIBLE:

As they were walking along the road, a man said to him, "I will follow you wherever you go." Jesus replied, "Foxes have holes and birds of the air have nests, but the Son of Man has no place to lay his head." He said to another man, "Follow me." But the man replied, "Lord, first let me go and bury my father." Jesus said to him, "Let the dead bury their own dead, but you go and proclaim the kingdom of God." Still another said, "I will follow you, Lord; but first let me go back and say good-by to my family." Jesus replied, "No one who puts his hand to the plow and looks back is fit for service in the kingdom of God." Luke 9:57-62, NIV

Look to Jesus

"**G**RANDPA, this Beatitude says the pure in heart will see God. What does it mean to be pure in heart?" asked Heidi.

Grandpa looked thoughtful. "To be pure in heart means to have the love of God so fill us that there is no room for sin," he answered. "We must center our thoughts and actions on Him, Heidi. We must not be double-minded."

"Double-minded?" Heidi asked, puzzled.

Grandpa nodded. "Peter, a friend who came from Germany with me, was double-minded. All he ever seemed to talk about was our homeland. He never did learn to like America because he always compared it to Germany. The mountains here were not as pretty, the cities were not as clean—on and on he would go. Often I tried to tell him to get his eyes off Germany so he could see America, but he never did. He died a very bitter man. He wanted to be citizen here, but he wanted to hold on to the old country, too."

"But you loved Germany, too, didn't you, Grandpa?" the little girl asked. "How did you forget about Germany?"

"I chose to!" said Grandpa emphatically. "I decided that America was my new home, and I would not look back!"

"That reminds me of a chorus we sing in Sunday school Heidi said, and she began to sing. 'I have decided to follow Jesus—no turning back, no turning back.' "

"That's exactly it, Heidi," agreed Grandpa. "If you are single-minded, with your thoughts centered only on Jesus, you will be pure in heart. You will not only be able to see God in heaven some day, but you will see Him working in your life now, too."

HOW ABOUT YOU? Can you see God at work in your life? If not, perhaps your eyes are clouded by looking at things other than God. If you read the wrong books, or watch the wrong TV programs, your heart can't remain pure. So decide now to follow Jesus without looking back at old sinful habits. □ R.P.

TO MEMORIZE: *Blessed are the pure in heart, for they will see God.* Matthew 5:8, NIV

"GUESS WHAT!" said Heidi as she took her Bible from the shelf and went to sit beside Grandpa. "Nancy and Sherri were mad at each other all day. For art class today we had to make a drawing of one of our favorite things. They both drew rainbows, and Nancy got mad. She said Sherri copied her, and then Sherri got mad. She said it was her idea in the first place." Heidi sighed as she opened her Bible to Matthew 5, ready to learn a new Beatitude.

"And what did you do?" asked Grandpa.

"Each of the girls wanted me to play with her at recess," answered Heidi, "so I told them I would if they'd quit fighting. But they both stayed mad, so I played with Alice. But Nancy and Sherri really like each other, so Mom says I may invite them both to stay overnight on Saturday and go to church and Sunday school with us. We'll have fun, and they'll see how silly they've been. Besides, maybe they'll like Sunday school and keep coming."

"Good!" approved Grandpa. "Maybe they'll accept Jesus as Savior as a result of your invitation. Now, Heidi, let's get to work on that next Beatitude. I think you'll find it interesting today because it applies to you."

Heidi looked at her open Bible. "Blessed are the peacemakers," she read slowly. A big smile lighted her face as she looked up at Grandpa. "Was I a peacemaker today, Grandpa?"

"I'd say so," he said. "You not only tried to bring peace between your friends, but you also did something to introduce them to Jesus. Only He can give lasting peace."

"This Beatitude is going to be easy to remember," declared Heidi. "And if Nancy and Sherri accept Jesus, I *know* I'll never forget it."

HOW ABOUT YOU? When friends are quarreling, do you eagerly listen to all the details and add a few biting comments of your own? Or do you heed Jesus' words and try to bring peace between them? Helping people to get along is great, but also be sure to point your friends to Jesus, the only source of lasting peace. Then you will truly be a peacemaker. □ R.P.

TO MEMORIZE: *Blessed are the peacemakers, for they will be called sons of God.* Matthew 5:9, NIV

THE BEATITUDES

Peace- makers

FROM THE BIBLE:
For the kingdom of God is not a matter of eating and drinking, but of righteousness, peace and joy in the Holy Spirit, because anyone who serves Christ in this way is pleasing to God and approved by men. Let us therefore make every effort to do what leads to peace and to mutual edification.
Romans 14:17-19, NIV

Be a peacemaker

OCTOBER

14

Nutcracker

FROM THE BIBLE:

He is despised and rejected by men, a man of sorrows and acquainted with grief. And we hid, as it were, our faces from Him; He was despised, and we did not esteem Him. Surely He has borne our griefs and carried our sorrows; yet we esteemed Him stricken, smitten by God, and afflicted. But He was wounded for our transgressions, He was bruised for our iniquities; the chastisement for our peace was upon Him, and by His stripes we are healed. All we like sheep have gone astray; we have turned, every one, to his own way; and the LORD has laid on Him the iniquity of us all. He was oppressed and He was afflicted, yet He opened not His mouth; He was led as a lamb to the slaughter, and as a sheep before its shearers is silent, so He opened not his mouth. He was taken from prison and from judgment, and who will declare His generation? For He was cut off from the land of the living; for the transgressions of My people He was stricken.
Isaiah 53:3-8, NKJV

Jesus took your punishment

"MOMMY, in Bible club today we had a lesson on hell." Mindy was troubled as she reached for a pecan and placed it between the jaws of the nutcracker. "It scared me. What if I would have to go there?" She squeezed the ends of the nutcracker, but the nut slid out.

"Hell is a scary subject," agreed Mother, "but have you asked Jesus to wash your sins away?"

Mindy nodded. "Yes, but I still worry about it sometimes," she confessed. She squeezed the nutcracker again, this time holding the pecan with her fingers. "Oh, ouch!" she wailed as the nut again slipped away and the jaws of the nutcracker closed on her finger. "Oweeee! It hurts!" Tears filled Mindy's eyes, and she put her finger to her mouth. "I'm keeping my fingers out of there," she declared when she was ready to crack nuts again.

"I'm not scared to put my finger in the nutcracker," boasted her brother, Bill. "Look!" True to his word, he put his finger in the nutcracker, but before squeezing down on it, he placed the thick handle of a knife beside his finger. When he squeezed down, the knife handle held the jaws of the nutcracker open, preventing them from touching his finger. "See," he laughed. "It doesn't even hurt."

Mindy made a face at her brother, but Mother spoke quickly. "You've given us a good illustration, Bill. Thank you," she said. She turned to Mindy. "You see, Honey," she continued, "Bill's finger deserves to be hurt, since he's being so cocky, right? But the handle of that knife is taking all the pressure—all the punishment—his finger deserves. We all have sinned, and we deserve to go to hell to be punished for our sins. Just as Bill has taken that knife handle as his protection from the nutcracker, we can accept Jesus into our lives as our protection from hell. Bill trusts the knife handle to keep his finger safe, and we can trust Jesus to keep us safe for all eternity. He went to the cross and took the punishment we deserve."

HOW ABOUT YOU? Do you worry about hell? You are right to be concerned. But Jesus took all the punishment you deserve. If you have accepted Him as Savior, you don't need to worry about going to hell. If you haven't accepted Him, don't wait any longer. Take Him as your Savior now. □ H.M.

TO MEMORIZE: *But He was wounded for our transgressions, He was bruised for our iniquities; the chastisement for our peace was upon Him, and by His stripes we are healed.* Isaiah 53:5, NKJV

JEREMY WAS GOING on his first airplane ride, but he was not excited about it. Inside, he felt as dark and gloomy as the day around him. His parents were getting a divorce, and he was going to live with his grandparents for a while.

As they boarded the plane, Jeremy choked down the lump in his throat. Grandmother gave him a reassuring smile. "Scared?" she asked.

Jeremy shook his head. Inside, he said, *Yes, I'm scared! I'm scared of everything.* But he didn't say anything. As the plane sped down the runway, huge drops of rain splattered the windows. *Just like tears,* Jeremy thought. When the plane lifted from the earth, Jeremy felt his heart fly up into his throat. All around them, dark clouds tumbled and rumbled, and so did Jeremy's stomach.

Grandmother reached for his hand. "Don't be afraid, Jeremy. God loves us. He'll take care of us." Jeremy knew Grandmother was talking about more than the plane ride. He wanted to believe her, but there was so much fear in his heart. "We'll go right through these dark clouds, Jeremy," she explained. "For a few minutes, we'll be in a thick fog, because that's what clouds are—fog. But just wait until we get above the clouds."

Suddenly they were in the clouds. The interior of the plane dimmed. Then, just as suddenly, a brilliant light came streaming through the windows. Jeremy squinted as he pressed his nose to the pane. "It's beautiful," he gasped.

Grandmother nodded. "Yes. Above the clouds, the sun is always shining." The tone of her voice caused Jeremy to turn and look at her. Grandmother smiled gently. "Our family is going through a storm right now, Jeremy. Things look pretty dark. But God is still in control. One day soon we'll break through the clouds, and life will be filled with beauty and happiness again."

Jeremy brushed a tear from his cheek as he turned to look at the sea of sparkling clouds.

HOW ABOUT YOU? Are you going through a storm in your life? Are you afraid of the future? Remember, even when you can't see the sun, it is shining. Even when you can't feel God, He is near. Trust Him, and He will lift you above the clouds. □ B.W.

TO MEMORIZE: *Surely God is my salvation; I will trust and not be afraid. The LORD, the LORD, is my strength and my song; he has become my salvation.* Isaiah 12:2, NIV

15

Above the Clouds

FROM THE BIBLE:
God is our refuge and strength, a tested help in times of trouble. And so we need not fear even if the world blows up, and the mountains crumble into the sea. Let the oceans roar and foam; let the mountains tremble! There is a river of joy flowing through the City of our God— the sacred home of the God above all gods. God himself is living in that City; therefore it stands unmoved despite the turmoil everywhere. He will not delay his help. The nations rant and rave in anger—but when God speaks, the earth melts in submission and kingdoms totter into ruin. The Commander of the armies of heaven is here among us. He, the God of Jacob, has come to rescue us. Come, see the glorious things that our God does, how he brings ruin upon the world, and causes wars to end throughout the earth, breaking and burning every weapon. "Stand silent! Know that I am God! I will be honored by every nation in the world!"
Psalm 46: 1-10, TLB

Don't fear— trust God

16

Who's Right?

FROM THE BIBLE:

I am not praying for these alone but also for the future believers who will come to me because of the testimony of these. My prayer for all of them is that they will be of one heart and mind, just as you and I are, Father—that just as you are in me and I am in you, so they will be in us, and the world will believe you sent me. I have given them the glory you gave me—the glorious unity of being one, as we are: I in them and you in me, all being perfected into one—so that the world will know you sent me and will understand that you love them as much as you love me.
John 17:20-23, TLB

Christians are one in Christ

"**D**AD, WE DO things differently at our church than they do at Clint's church," Kenny said one day. "We had an argument about it. He said his church is right, and I said my church is right. Whose way is really right?"

Before Dad could attempt an answer, Kenny's little sister and brother came into the kitchen, carrying a keyboard. They set it on the table. "We want to play a song Daddy taught us," announced Cathy, and they proceeded to do so. At first, they carefully pressed the keys, and Kenny thought he recognized "Twinkle, Twinkle, Little Star." But then it became obvious that they were playing two different songs.

"That sounds awful," declared Kenny. "I think you need a new teacher."

"Wait a minute!" protested Dad. "The teacher's not the problem. They're not following my instructions."

When the children were gone, Dad grinned at Kenny. "That sure wasn't the way I intended their music to turn out," he said. "But, what just happened reminds me of what happens to Christians. Can't you almost hear God saying, 'That wasn't what I intended,' as He watches us? Jesus intended for His followers to all 'play the same song.' He wanted all Christians to be unified—to be one."

"But which song should we be playing? Whose way is right—Clint's church or our church?" Kenny asked again.

"God's way is right," Dad answered. "I don't know what church Clint attends. But we believe the church we go to teaches what God says in His Word. That's why we go there."

"So that's what I should tell Clint the next time we argue about our differences?" Kenny persisted.

"Why argue? Why not agree to read your Bible and do your best to do what it says?" suggested Dad. "That's what Jesus would want you to do."

HOW ABOUT YOU? Do you argue with someone from another church? You should attend a church that you believe agrees with what God says in His Word, and then quit arguing. By reading the Bible and putting its teaching into practice, and by encouraging others to do the same, we can have the unity Jesus wants for us. □ K.R.A.

TO MEMORIZE: *There is one body and one Spirit, just as you were called in one hope of your calling; one Lord, one faith, one baptism; one God and Father of all.* Ephesians 4:4-6, NKJV

RYAN PLAYED the first page of his music. Then he thought about how the guys had snickered when his mother had called him to come in and practice. He played some more. Then he wondered if the guys would snicker when he played in church a week from next Sunday. He sat at the piano and stared at his music.

"Why did you quit?" Mom called from the kitchen. When he didn't answer, she came to see.

"I don't want to play in church," Ryan said finally. "Piano playing is for girls."

"That isn't true," protested Mom, placing her hands on Ryan's shoulders. "God gave you an exceptional talent, and He expects you to use it."

"I can't," Ryan cried. Mom didn't insist that Ryan keep on practicing his special number, but she asked him to think and pray about it.

That week Ryan diligently worked on a gift he was making for his sister Abby's birthday. It was a wrist band like those most of the kids at school were wearing. He carefully wove it, using brightly colored twine.

"Thank you. It's nice," Abby said politely when she opened it on her birthday. But she went on to unwrap the next present without even trying it on. Ryan felt bad.

"Abby, you never wear the wrist band I made for you," Ryan complained a few days later.

"Well, it's pretty, but it's not really like the ones the other girls are wearing," Abby explained.

After Abby left the room, Mom looked at Ryan. "It hurts when you take special care with a gift for someone, and then that person doesn't use it," she observed. Ryan nodded sadly. "God must be hurt, too, when we don't use the gifts He gave us, don't you think?" added Mom.

As Ryan considered his mother's words, someone knocked at the door. Ryan answered it. "Want to play ball?" invited Adam, who lived next door.

Ryan hesitated. "Pretty soon," he said. "I'm going to practice piano first. I have to play in church next week."

HOW ABOUT YOU? Do you have a gift you aren't using? Maybe you're embarrassed to use it. Maybe you don't want to take the time or make the effort to develop it. God gave you gifts. He wants and expects you to use them. □ K.R.A.

TO MEMORIZE: *Who once were not a people but are now the people of God, who had not obtained mercy but now have obtained mercy.* 1 Peter 2:10, NKJV

Unused Gifts

FROM THE BIBLE:
God has given each of us the ability to do certain things well. So if God has given you the ability to prophesy, then prophesy whenever you can—as often as your faith is strong enough to receive a message from God. If your gift is that of serving others, serve them well. If you are a teacher, do a good job of teaching. If you are a preacher, see to it that your sermons are strong and helpful. If God has given you money, be generous in helping others with it. If God has given you administrative ability and put you in charge of the work of others, take the responsibility seriously. Those who offer comfort to the sorrowing should do so with Christian cheer. Don't just pretend that you love others: really love them. Hate what is wrong. Stand on the side of the good. Love each other with brotherly affection and take delight in honoring each other. Never be lazy in your work but serve the Lord enthusiastically. Be glad for all God is planning for you.
Romans 12:6-12, TLB

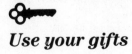

Use your gifts

OCTOBER

18

A Price to Pay

FROM THE BIBLE:

Then David said to Nathan, "I have sinned against the LORD." Nathan replied, "The LORD has taken away your sin. You are not going to die. But because by doing this you have made the enemies of the LORD show utter contempt, the son born to you will die." After Nathan had gone home, the LORD struck the child that Uriah's wife had borne to David, and he became ill. David pleaded with God for the child. He fasted and went into his house and spent the nights lying on the ground. The elders of his household stood beside him to get him up from the ground, but he refused, and he would not eat any food with them. On the seventh day the child died. David noticed that his servants were whispering among themselves and he realized the child was dead. "Is the child dead?" he asked. "Yes," they replied, "he is dead." Then David got up from the ground. After he had washed, put on lotions and changed his clothes, he went into the house of the LORD and worshiped.

2 Samuel 12:13-20, NIV

Sin brings sorrow

*T*HIS IS SO BORING, Brenda thought as she trudged along behind her mother at the grocery store. "May I walk around while you wait in line for cold cuts?" she asked. "I'll obey our shopping rules." Mother hesitated, but then agreed to let Brenda walk off some of her excess energy.

I'll see how many times I can circle up this aisle and down the next one before the man at the delicatessen calls the number on Mom's ticket, decided Brenda. She set a goal to complete her route five times. "Oh no!" Brenda murmured as she finished her fourth round. "Mom's up next!" She increased her speed, forgetting the "no running" rule. She raced around the bend, her arm swung out, and *splat!* Two large jars of applesauce smashed to the floor.

Mother came quickly, and Brenda dragged her feet as Mother propelled her to the service desk. Brenda could hardly hold back tears as she told the assistant manager what happened "Someone will clean up the mess right away," the man assured her.

"And Brenda will pay for the jars," said Mother firmly. As they walked to the checkout, Mother added, "I'll pay for the broken jars now, but you'll have to pay me back with your own money."

"But I don't have very much money. And I am sorry for what I did," whined Brenda. She sighed. "I wish I could make those jars go back up on the shelf, unsmashed."

"But you can't, can you?" said Mother, She wrapped her arm around Brenda. "I know you're sorry, but the jars are still broken, and you still need to pay for them." She paused. "That's the way it is with sin," she added. "When we're sorry and confess our sin, God forgives us. But sin still has consequences. When you're tempted to sin, it's good to remember that."

HOW ABOUT YOU? Do you find yourself doing things you know you shouldn't do? When that happens, it's your responsibility to tell God what you've done and to ask Him to remove the sin. But don't forget that even though you've been forgiven, there may still be a price to pay. Today's Scripture gives an example of that. Think about that the next time you're tempted to do wrong. □ N.E.K.

TO MEMORIZE: *Keep your servant also from willful sins; may they not rule over me. Then will I be blameless, innocent of great transgression.* Psalm 19:13, NIV

As THE NELSON family drove to Granddad's farm, Duane argued with his little sister about everything. Dad finally commanded, "If I hear one more cross word, you'll go straight to bed when we get there, and you'll miss the party."

When they arrived, the first person Duane saw was his cousin Paul. As the boys sat up in the branches of the old oak tree a little later, Duane said, "Granddad's birthday is almost as exciting as Christmas."

"Sure is," Paul agreed. "It's the only time, other than Christmas, when the entire Nelson family gets together."

Duane nodded as he scanned the crowd below him. "There's Uncle Ryan and Aunt Linda," he said, "but I don't see Uncle Joe and his family."

"Haven't you heard?" asked Paul. "They won't be here. Uncle Joe and Aunt Linda are mad at each other. Uncle Joe said he and his family weren't coming if she came. She said he could just stay away then, and it would suit her fine."

"Time to sing 'Happy Birthday' and open the presents," called Duane's mother. The boys scrambled to join the crowd on the big front porch.

After Granddad had opened the gifts and blown out all sixty-two candles, he stood up. Everyone was quiet. "Thank you, children, for coming. And thank you for the nice gifts. But what I really want . . ." Granddad gulped back a sob. "What I really wish is that my children would love one another. Can a father be truly happy if his children love him, but not each other?" With tears rolling down his cheeks, Granddad sat down.

For several minutes no one spoke. Then Aunt Linda stood. "I'm going to call Joe. I need to apologize. There's still time for him to come."

On the way home late that night there was no fussing, and everyone agreed with Duane when he said, "I'm glad Granddad's wish came true. And I'm going to try harder to get along with my sister."

HOW ABOUT YOU? Do you love your parents and want them to be happy? Then love your brothers and sisters. Show that love by making every effort not to fight with them. Do you love your Father in heaven and want Him to be happy? Then love His children—other Christians. ☐ B.W.

TO MEMORIZE: *And this commandment we have from Him: that he who loves God must love his brother also.* 1 John 4:21, NKJV

OCTOBER
19

A Father's Wish

FROM THE BIBLE:
If someone says, "I love God," and hates his brother, he is a liar; for he who does not love his brother whom he has seen, how can he love God whom he has not seen? And this command-ment we have from Him: that he who loves God must love his brother also.
1 John 4:20-21, NKJV

Love one another

OCTOBER

20

Danger! Contagious!

FROM THE BIBLE:

I only wish these teachers who want you to cut yourselves by being circumcised would cut themselves off from you and leave you alone! For, dear brothers, you have been given freedom: not freedom to do wrong, but freedom to love and serve each other. For the whole Law can be summed up in this one command: "Love others as you love yourself." But if instead of showing love among yourselves you are always critical and catty, watch out! Beware of ruining each other. I advise you to obey only the Holy Spirit's instructions. He will tell you where to go and what to do, and then you won't always be doing the wrong things your evil nature wants you to.
Galatians 5:12-16, TLB

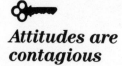

Attitudes are contagious

SHERRI DROPPED her books on the end table. As she slumped down on the sofa with a sigh, Mother looked up. "What's wrong?"

"I had a terrible day," Sherri whined. "Mrs. Carson doesn't like me. And Brenda got the solo part I wanted. And—"

"My, my!" Mother interrupted. "What is this, a pity party for Sherri?"

Sherri jumped up. "I knew you wouldn't understand. No one understands me!"

Soon Mother heard angry words coming from her daughter's bedroom. The door opened, and Stephanie came out, tears streaming down her cheeks. "Mother, make Sherri leave me alone. Everything was fine until she came home!"

"Sure! Sure! It's always my fault!" Sherri raged.

Mother frowned. "Girls," she began, but was interrupted by the telephone. A few minutes later she replaced the receiver and turned to the girls. "Amy is in the hospital. She is very sick."

"What's wrong?" Sherri asked. "Can we go see her?" Amy was her favorite cousin.

"No, but we must pray for her," answered Mother. "The doctor thinks she has hepatitis. They have her in isolation because it's highly contagious. Only her parents are allowed in the room, and they must wear sterile masks and gowns." She looked at Sherri as she continued "Diseases are not the only things that are contagious. Attitudes are, too."

"Attitudes?" Sherri frowned.

"Yes, attitudes," Mother repeated. "When you came home, Sherri, you had a bad attitude. It wasn't five minutes before that attitude had infected everyone in this family. If your attitude doesn't improve, I may have to put you in isolation—put you in your room alone for awhile."

Sherri hung her head. She knew what Mother said was true. "I'll try to do better," she promised.

"Good." Mother smiled and gave her a hug. "Now let's go pray for Amy."

HOW ABOUT YOU? Do you have a bad attitude that has infected your family? Or does someone else in your family have a bad attitude? How about counteracting it with a smile or a kind word? Don't catch it, resist it. Don't spread gloom, spread sunshine. □ B.W.

TO MEMORIZE: *Create in me a pure heart, O God, and renew a steadfast spirit within me.*
Psalm 51:10, NIV

304

"Hi, GORDY." Ken nervously greeted his longtime friend. He always felt guilty when he saw Gordy lately. That was because Ken had accepted Jesus as Savior, but he'd never told Gordy. He knew he should. In fact, he wanted to—it was just that he was afraid Gordy would laugh.

"What did you get for your birthday yesterday?" Gordy asked now. "Anything good?"

"You bet," replied Ken. He lifted his left hand and displayed a new baseball mitt. "How about this? No balls are going to get away from me now!"

"Neat," approved Gordy. "I could really use that."

"My grandparents gave it to me," said Ken, "and this shirt is from my brother. My folks gave me a skateboard."

"Wow!" Gordy let out a long whistle. "I could use all those things."

"Well, you can't have 'em," laughed Ken. Suddenly he thought about the gift of eternal life he had received a month ago. He'd told Gordy about all his other gifts. He knew he should tell him about that one, too. That was a gift Gordy could have. He took a deep breath. "A month ago I got . . ." He stopped, afraid to finish. "I got a gift from God. I got my sins forgiven."

"Huh?" Gordy looked startled. "What on earth are you talking about?"

"I'm a Christian now, and if you want to, you can have that gift, too." Ken finished in a hurry. "I gotta go. Bye." He hurried down the street as Gordy stared after him. Ken felt a little funny because he was sure he hadn't done that very well. At the same time, he felt lighthearted because he knew that at least it was a start. "I'm going to invite Gordy to Sunday school this week," he decided. "I'll ask him tomorrow. I'll pray that he'll be saved soon, too."

HOW ABOUT YOU? Do you talk with your friends about anything and everything except the Lord? Are you afraid to witness to them? If you're a Christian, God has given you a wonderful gift, and they can have it, too. Tell them about it. □ H.M.

TO MEMORIZE: *Speak these things, exhort, and rebuke with all authority.* Titus 2:15, NKJV

21
Gift to Share

FROM THE BIBLE:
For the grace of God that brings salvation has appeared to all men, teaching us that, denying ungodliness and worldly lusts, we should live soberly, righteously, and godly in the present age, looking for the blessed hope and glorious appearing of our great God and Savior Jesus Christ, who gave Himself for us, that He might redeem us from every lawless deed and purify for Himself His own special people, zealous for good works. Speak these things, exhort, and rebuke with all authority. Let no one despise you.
Titus 2:11-15, NKJV

Witness for Jesus

OCTOBER

22

Careless Words

FROM THE BIBLE:

Even if we believe that it makes no difference to the Lord whether we do these things, still we cannot just go ahead and do them to please ourselves; for we must bear the "burden" of being considerate of the doubts and fears of others—of those who feel these things are wrong. Let's please the other fellow, not ourselves, and do what is for his good and thus build him up in the Lord. Christ didn't please himself. As the Psalmist said, "He came for the very purpose of suffering under the insults of those who were against the Lord." These things that were written in the Scriptures so long ago are to teach us patience and to encourage us, so that we will look forward expectantly to the time when God will conquer sin and death. May God who gives patience, steadiness, and encouragement help you to live in complete harmony with each other—each with the attitude of Christ toward the other. So, warmly welcome each other into the church, just as Christ has warmly welcomed you.
Romans 15:1-7, TLB

Build others up

THE STUDENTS at Lakeview Christian Academy looked at each other in disbelief. They had just learned that one of the students had attempted to commit suicide the night before!

"I didn't think that Christian kids ever got that depressed," was Susan's reaction. "Eric knows God loves him. What made him do a thing like that?"

"It's not that simple," responded Kevin. "You have lots of friends." Kevin looked down at his desk as he continued, "I remember when we'd make fun of Eric in gym class. I never thought he took it seriously."

"But he's so smart," emphasized Brad. "We did laugh at him when he wasn't very coordinated, but I didn't think it hurt him that much. Didn't he know that we all wish we could be as smart as he is?"

"We don't always seem to recognize our good qualities," pointed out Mrs. Kelley. "Sometimes our weaknesses seem to get all of the attention." She picked up her Bible. "As Christians, we have the assurance of knowing that God loves us and accepts us just the way we are," she continued. "We also have the responsibility to love others the way God loves us. Listen to Ephesians 4:29. 'Do not let any unwholesome talk come out of your mouths, but only what is helpful for building others up according to their needs, that it may benefit those who listen.' "

Kevin looked up soberly. "I sure can't say that all of the things I said to Eric were intended to build him up. I'd like the chance again to really be his friend."

Mrs. Kelley smiled understandingly. "Let's pray you'll get that chance. Now, I think it's good to check up on ourselves and see if we're pleasing God in our treatment of others. Let's pray for God's healing in Eric's life, and let's also try to build each other up in our conversations."

HOW ABOUT YOU? Are you careful about the things you say to others? Sometimes careless words may seem harmless or funny, yet they may really be hurting someone inside. God wants your life to reflect His love to others. Accept people as they are. Show them God's love through your kind words. □ D.R.

TO MEMORIZE: *Let no corrupt communication proceed out of your mouth, but what is good for necessary edification, that it may impart grace to the hearers.* Ephesians 4:29, NKJV

CHRISTY WAS EXCITED about the birthday present Aunt Peggy had sent. It was a gift certificate to a beauty parlor so Christy could have her hair cut and permed. It sounded like fun. But that was before Christy knew what the outcome would be!

"Mother, I can't go to school like this!" she wailed after getting the perm. "All the kids will laugh at me!"

"Why should they laugh at you?" teased Christy's brother Joe. "You do look a little like a Brillo pad that got caught in the mud, but other than that, you look okay."

"Mother," Christy wailed again.

"That's enough, Joe," said Mother. "Christy feels bad enough without you kidding her. Actually, Christy, your hair looks nice. You just aren't used to it."

Christy looked in the mirror and scowled. She knew Mom would make her go to school tomorrow, and it was just too horrible to think about.

Mother looked at the grouchy expression on Christy's face. "Honey, remember that the Lord said it's not the outward appearance that counts, but what is on the inside. The fanciest hair style in the world isn't going to make up for a bad attitude and a grumpy look. On the other hand, if you'll be as kind and cheerful as you usually are, your hair will not be important."

Christy knew it was true. Her heart, not her hair, was what mattered. She would ask the Lord to help her give more attention to her inside appearance than to her outside appearance!

HOW ABOUT YOU? Do you care more about the latest hair styles and fashions than you do about your inner beauty? Yes, it is important to be neat and clean and attractive, but it is more important to share God's love through your actions, God is more concerned about your heart than He is about your curly hair or new shirt! □ L.W.

TO MEMORIZE: *The LORD does not see as man sees; for man looks at the outward appearance, but the LORD looks at the heart.* 1 Samuel 16:7, NKJV

Heart, Not Hair

FROM THE BIBLE:

Then the LORD said to Samuel, "How long will you mourn for Saul, seeing I have rejected him from reigning over Israel? Fill your horn with oil, and go; I am sending you to Jesse the Bethlehemite. For I have provided Myself a king among his sons." And Samuel said, "How can I go? If Saul hears it, he will kill me." And the LORD said, "Take a heifer with you, and say, 'I have come to sacrifice to the LORD.' I will show you what you shall do; you shall anoint for Me the one I name to you." So Samuel did what the LORD said, and went to Bethlehem. Then he sanctified Jesse and his sons, and invited them to the sacrifice. So it was, when they came, that he looked at Eliab and said, "Surely the LORD's anointed is before Him." But the LORD said to Samuel, "Do not look at his appearance or at the height of his stature, because I have refused him. For the LORD does not see as man sees; for man looks at the outward appearance, but the LORD looks at the heart."

1 Samuel 16:1-7, NKJV

Inside beauty counts

OCTOBER

24

What a Mess

FROM THE BIBLE:
*Show me your ways, O LORD,
teach me your paths; guide me
in your truth and teach me, for
you are God my Savior, and my
hope is in you all day long.
Remember, O LORD, your great
mercy and love, for they are
from of old. Remember not the
sins of my youth and my
rebellious ways; according to
your love remember me, for you
are good, O LORD. Good and
upright is the LORD; therefore
he instructs sinners in his ways.
He guides the humble in what is
right and teaches them his way.
All the ways of the LORD are
loving and faithful for those who
keep the demands of his covenant.
Psalm 25:4-10, NIV*

Follow God's direction

"**I** DON'T KNOW how I'm going to get every-thing done today," Mother said at the breakfast table. "I have several errands to run this morning, and somehow I'll have to find time to bake a birth-day cake for Tommy."

"I can make Tommy's cake!" said Julie. "You've told me before that it's easy. Besides, Tommy's only two, and he'll eat anything!"

"Well, okay," agreed Mother hesitantly. "The mix is in the cupboard. Be sure to read the instruc-tions. There's a can of frosting in the cupboard, too." Julie started the cake soon after Mother left. She read the directions and was about to pour the mix into the bowl when the phone rang. It was her friend Stephanie.

After Julie hung up the phone, she went about making her cake, remembering what she had read earlier. At least, she thought she remembered. But when the cake was done, it didn't look quite right to her. When it cooled, she frosted it carefully, but it was no use. The cake was dry, and Tommy, who was known to eat many strange things, wouldn't touch it.

"What a mess!" Mother exclaimed. "Didn't you follow the directions?"

"I read them, but then Stephanie called, and I didn't look at them again," explained Julie. "I thought I was doing it the right way."

"That's the way many people live their lives," observed Dad. Seeing the puzzled look on Julie's face, he continued. "They hear a sermon or read the Bible occasionally, and then they think they know all they need to know. But they forget what they heard. God gives directions, but some people ignore them, and their lives turn into big messes—just like that cake! Paying attention to directions is an important principle to learn."

"I see that." Julie smiled as she watched Tommy eat the frosting but leave the cake. "From now on, I'm going to follow directions and not do things my own way."

HOW ABOUT YOU? Do you ignore the directions the Lord gives in His Word, or do you follow what He says? Do you check up often to see if you are living the way you should and to see if God has further things for you to learn? It's important to spend time each day with God's Word and then to follow His directions. □ L.W.

TO MEMORIZE: *In all your ways acknowledge Him, and He shall direct your paths.* Proverbs 3:6, NKJV

B**RAD** STARTED toward the family room. "VAROOM!" sang out his little brother Kevin as he charged through the room, holding up his little plane. He crashed into Brad.

"Why don't you watch where you're going, you stupid jerk?" asked Brad angrily.

"You know very well that you are not to call people names," Dad said sternly.

Brad sighed. "I suppose I better go apologize." But just then the phone rang, and Brad picked it up. "Hello? Oh, hi, Jerry. Yeah, I heard what they're saying about Mrs. Simpson—that she comes to school looking so bleary-eyed because she's an alcoholic, right? Did you notice how she stumbled over her words in class? Oh, I have to go, Jerry. Dad wants me for something. Bye."

"You're going to have to call Jerry back and apologize for that gossip I just heard," said Dad. When Brad started to protest, Dad held up a hand. "Did you know that Mrs. Simpson's husband is dying?" he asked. "She has to stay up nights caring for him. No wonder she looks tired."

"Oh. I didn't know that." Brad looked truly sorry. "I'll call Jerry—after I apologize to Kevin."

"First come with me to my shop," said Dad, leading the way. He picked up a hammer and some nails. "I want you to pound these nails about half-way into this board." Brad obeyed with a puzzled look. "Now what?"

"Pull the nails out." Brad did so. "Brad, your words lately have been as sharp as these nails. They've been cutting and hurting. Saying you're sorry is fine. But look at this board. What do you see?"

"The nail holes," said Brad.

"Exactly," said Dad. "You can apologize and be forgiven, but you can never take back all the harm you've caused."

Brad picked up the board. "I get your point, Dad. I think I'll hang this in my room as a reminder to be more careful with my tongue."

HOW ABOUT YOU? Do you carelessly say things which hurt the feelings or reputations of others? An apology can bring forgiveness, but it can never erase all the harm. Ask the Lord to "keep the door of your lips." □ M.R.P.

TO MEMORIZE: *Though you probe my heart and examine me at night, though you test me, you will find nothing; I have resolved that my mouth will not sin.* Psalm 17:3, NIV

Nail Holes

FROM THE BIBLE:
If anyone can control his tongue, it proves that he has perfect control over himself in every other way. We can make a large horse turn around and go wherever we want by means of a small bit in his mouth. And a tiny rudder makes a huge ship turn wherever the pilot wants it to go, even though the winds are strong. So also the tongue is a small thing, but what enormous damage it can do. A great forest can be set on fire by one tiny spark. And the tongue is a flame of fire. It is full of wickedness, and poisons every part of the body. And the tongue is set on fire by hell itself, and can turn our whole lives into a blazing flame of destruction and disaster. Men have trained, or can train, every kind of animal or bird that lives and every kind of reptile and fish, but no human being can tame the tongue. It is always ready to pour out its deadly poison. Sometimes it praises our heavenly Father, and sometimes it breaks out into curses against men who are made like God. And so blessing and cursing come pouring out of the same mouth. Dear brothers, surely this is not right!
James 3:2-10, TLB

Think, then speak

OCTOBER

26

Mack, the Monkey

FROM THE BIBLE:

As the Scriptures say, "No one is good—no one in all the world is innocent." No one has ever really followed God's paths, or even truly wanted to. Every one has turned away; all have gone wrong. No one anywhere has kept on doing what is right; not one. . . . Now do you see it? No one can ever be made right in God's sight by doing what the law commands. For the more we know of God's laws, the clearer it becomes that we aren't obeying them; his laws serve only to make us see that we are sinners. But now God has shown us a different way to heaven—not by "being good enough" and trying to keep his laws, but by a new way (though not new, really, for the Scriptures told about it long ago). Now God says he will accept and acquit us—declare us "not guilty"—if we trust Jesus Christ to take away our sins. And we all can be saved in this same way, by coming to Christ, no matter who we are or what we have been like.
Romans 3:10-12, 20-22, TLB

Without Jesus, you're nothing

PATTI LISTENED eagerly as a man called Uncle Dan, the speaker for the evening, began to talk. "I'm glad to be here," said Uncle Dan, "and right now, I'd like to ask my friend Mack to join me here on the platform." Uncle Dan turned to look across the platform, and for the first time, Patti noticed a brown hairy puppet hanging by its arms from a corner of the piano. "Come here, Mack," called Uncle Dan, but Mack didn't move. Uncle Dan called to him a couple of times. "Well, I guess Mack is going to be uncooperative today," said Uncle Dan, going over to the piano and picking up the monkey. "I think I know what I need to do. I need to snap my fingers, let go, and Mack will spring to life." When Uncle Dan did this, Mack just ended up in a pile on the floor. The children laughed.

Uncle Dan kept talking to Mack, but it did no good. Mack wouldn't move. Finally Uncle Dan looked at the boys and girls in the front row where Patti was sitting. "Can someone help me? What has to happen before Mack will move?" he asked them.

Patti's hand shot into the air. "You have to put your hand inside and make him move," she said when Uncle Dan pointed to her.

"You are absolutely right, young lady," agreed Uncle Dan. "I could talk to Mack from now until it's time to go home, and he still wouldn't move. Without me, Mack can do nothing." He paused for a moment. "Did you know that the same is true of people? Jesus said to His disciples, 'Without Me, you can do nothing.' We might think we are really somebody, but unless we have trusted Jesus Christ as Savior and invited Him to be our Lord, we really cannot amount to anything. We can't get to heaven by ourselves. And we can't live the Christian life by ourselves. That's why I've come here today—to tell you more about Jesus and what He wants to do for you!"

Patti listened carefully to the rest of Uncle Dan's presentation. "I want Jesus as my Savior," she decided. "I don't want to be a 'nothing'!"

HOW ABOUT YOU? Do you realize that you are "nothing" without Jesus Christ living in your heart and life? If you've never done so before, invite Him to be your Savior right now. □ C.V.M.

TO MEMORIZE: *I am the vine, you are the branches. He who abides in Me, and I in him, bears much fruit; for without Me you can do nothing.*
John 15:5, NKJV

As JEFF TURNED the dial of his new radio, he counted the stations it could pick up. "Dad, how can there be so many stations inside my radio?" Jeff asked. "I counted thirty."

"I'm sure you know the stations aren't actually inside your radio," said Dad with a smile, "but sound waves from all those stations are right here in this room. Your radio is simply a 'receiver.' It picks out the various sound waves and then makes it possible for you to hear them."

"The man who invented the radio must have been pretty smart," Jeff said thoughtfully.

"Yes," agreed Dad, "but, you know, the One Who made your ear to hear the sounds is even smarter."

"You mean God, don't you, Dad?" Jeff asked.

"That's right," said Dad. "Just think about your ear for a moment. It can pick up the softest voice, but it can handle very loud noises as well. In a noisy room your ear can pick out a certain voice you want to hear while tuning out noises you don't want to hear. And since you have two ears, you can tell what direction a sound is coming from and also about how far away it is!"

"So the ear is something like a radio," said Jeff. "They both receive sound waves."

Dad nodded. "And even as your radio can be tuned to receive all kinds of sounds from different stations, so your ears can receive all sorts of different sounds. I don't think your ears have always been treated to the right kind of sounds lately. I've spoken to you about this before."

Jeff blushed. He remembered some programs and jokes he had listened to with his friends.

"Jeff," continued Dad, "be careful not to drown out God's voice with the sounds of the world. Let God speak to you. What He has to say is very important."

HOW ABOUT YOU? Are you using your ears to listen to the right kinds of things? Does the music you choose honor God? Do the jokes, stories, and programs you listen to please Him? Thank God right now for your hearing, and promise Him you'll use your ears to listen to good things! □ C.V.M.

TO MEMORIZE: *The hearing ear and the seeing eye, the LORD has made both of them.*
Proverbs 20:12, NKJV

27

The Right Sounds

FROM THE BIBLE:
How can a young man stay pure? By reading your Word and following its rules. I have tried my best to find you—don't let me wander off from your instructions. I have thought much about your words, and stored them in my heart so that they would hold me back from sin. Blessed Lord, teach me your rules. I have recited your laws, and rejoiced in them more than in riches. I will meditate upon them and give them my full respect. I will delight in them and not forget them.
Psalm 119:9-16, TLB

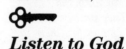

Listen to God

OCTOBER

28

In the Dark

FROM THE BIBLE:

For God loved the world so much that he gave his only Son so that anyone who believes in him shall not perish but have eternal life. God did not send his Son into the world to condemn it, but to save it. There is no eternal doom awaiting those who trust him to save them. But those who don't trust him have already been tried and condemned for not believing in the only Son of God. Their sentence is based on this fact: that the Light from heaven came into the world, but they loved the darkness more than the Light, for their deeds were evil. They hated the heavenly Light because they wanted to sin in the darkness. They stayed away from that Light for fear their sins would be exposed and they would be punished. But those doing right come gladly to the Light to let everyone see that they are doing what God wants them to.

John 3:16-21, TLB

Walk in God's light

THE CHURCH BUS rang with singing as the youth group traveled to Camp Macoma for a retreat. Arriving just before dark, they could see a storm brewing over the lake. They quickly carried their things to the cabins and then ran to the dining hall for supper. Suddenly the storm struck! A power line was hit by lightning, and the dining hall was enveloped in darkness.

"Just sit tight until the storm passes," Mr. Crane advised. "Then we'll see about getting the lights back on."

At first the children huddled where they were, but soon they got accustomed to the darkness and became braver. They ignored the leader's warning and started moving around. "Eva, there's a mouse on your leg," George called.

"Quit teasing me," Eva laughed. "Even if there were one, you wouldn't be able to see it." Just then Nancy brushed a paper plate against Sue's leg. Sue screamed loudly and jumped back, bruising her knee on a table.

"Enough of that!" Mr. Crane warned. "Let's all sit down before someone gets hurt."

Reluctantly the group settled down. "This would be a good time for devotions," suggested Mr., Crane. "Think about what happened tonight. When the lights first went out, you were scared and uncertain. You were afraid to be without the light. But then you got used to the darkness. Soon you delighted in it—scaring each other. You didn't think about the danger." Mr. Crane paused, then added, "As Christians, Christ is our light. If we walk in His light, we are safe, but if we wander off in the darkness of sin, there's danger. Often we'll get so used to the darkness that we actually like it because it hides what we are doing, We don't realize the danger until we get hurt, and we forget that someday everything will be brought to light. Let's ask God to help us walk in His light."

HOW ABOUT YOU? If everything you did were brought into the light, how would you feel? Pleased? Or would you be embarrassed to be caught in sin? Christ is your light. Don't stumble in the darkness of sin, when you can walk in the light. □ J.H.

TO MEMORIZE: *But if we walk in the light, as he is in the light, we have fellowship with one another, and the blood of Jesus, his Son, purifies us from all sin.* 1 John 1:7, NIV

CINDY WAS EXCITED. It was Sunday morning, the day she and her two friends, Shannon and Jill, were to sing in church. They had practiced their song several times the past two weeks. Now Cindy stood at the church door waiting for her friends. She hoped this would be the first of many times that the three girls would sing. She had also prayed that her aunt, who was not a Christian, would come to church that day.

"Are you nervous?" Jill asked as she ran up the church steps. "I could hardly sleep last night because I was so excited."

"Kind of," Cindy agreed, "but Mom prayed with me, and we asked the Lord to help all three of us to do our best."

Just then Shannon's brother, Dave, walked by. "Where's Shannon?" both girls asked at once.

"Oh, didn't you know?" Dave seemed surprised. "Our neighbors called last night, and Shannon went camping with them. She won't be back until tomorrow."

Cindy and Jill looked at each other! How could Shannon do this? They hurried to find the pianist, who assured them that they should sing anyhow.

Well, the girls did sing, and they did a good job. Even Cindy's aunt said so, but Cindy and Jill both knew that it would have sounded better if Shannon had been there. They were still somewhat upset by what had happened.

"This won't be the last time someone lets you down," Cindy's mother told her on the way home. "There are many people who just don't have a sense of responsibility. Remember this experience whenever you're tempted to back out of something at the last minute. God expects faithfulness from His servants. We owe it to Him and we owe it to others as well. If one person doesn't do his or her job, it hinders everyone."

"I guess there are times we all let other people down," Cindy admitted. "Maybe it's actually a good thing this happened. I know it will make me think twice before I break a promise to do something."

HOW ABOUT YOU? Do you take your responsibilities seriously? Or do you just not show up at the last minute if something better comes along? Remember, faithfulness is important in being a witness for Christ. □ L.W.

TO MEMORIZE: *Now it is required that those who have been given a trust must prove faithful.*
1 Corinthians 4:2, NIV

A Two-Member Trio

FROM THE BIBLE:
Again, the Kingdom of Heaven can be illustrated by the story of a man going into another country, who called together his servants and loaned them money to invest for him while he was gone. He gave $5,000 to one, $2,000 to another, and $1,000 to the last—dividing it in proportion to their abilities— and then left on his trip. The man who received the $5,000 began immediately to buy and sell with it and soon earned another $5,000. The man with $2,000 went right to work, too, and earned another $2,000. But the man who received the $1,000 dug a hole in the ground and hid the money for safekeeping. After a long time their master returned from his trip. The man to whom he had entrusted the $5,000 brought him $10,000. His master praised him for good work. "You have been faithful in handling this small amount," he told him, "so now I will give you many more responsibilities." Matthew 25:14-21, TLB

Take responsibility seriously

30

Whose Side?

FROM THE BIBLE:

Let love be without hypocrisy. Abhor what is evil. Cling to what is good. Be kindly affectionate to one another with brotherly love, in honor giving preference to one another; not lagging in diligence, fervent in spirit, serving the Lord; rejoicing in hope, patient in tribulation, continuing steadfastly in prayer; distributing to the needs of the saints, given to hospitality. Bless those who persecute you; bless and do not curse. Rejoice with those who rejoice, and weep with those who weep. Be of the same mind toward one another. Do not set your mind on high things, but associate with the humble. Do not be wise in your own opinion. Repay no one evil for evil. Have regard for good things in the sight of all men. Romans 12:9-17, NKJV

Witness by your life

"COME WITH ME Sunday. You'll hear more about Jesus, and . . ." Deb's voice reached the kitchen where her mother was working.

A little later Mother heard Deb and her brother talking as they played checkers. "Got caught peeking during a spelling test, didn't you?" asked Pete.

"Yeah," Deb admitted. "I'll be more careful if I ever try that again."

"Did you get a new kid in your class?" asked Pete.

Deb nodded. "She's a mess. Lives in that old rundown place on Cherry Street. My friends and I didn't play with her." Deb looked up as her mother and her little sister, Sally, came into the room.

"Which side are you on, Debbie?" asked Sally.

"The red," teased Deb as she moved a black checker.

"Are not," protested Sally. "You moved a black one."

Deb laughed, but Mother looked stern. "It's easy for Sally to see which side you're really on in spite of what you said," commented Mother. "I expect it's easy for Jan, too."

Deb stared at her mother. "What's that supposed to mean?"

"I heard your conversations," replied Mother, "both with Jan and with Pete just now. I was pleased that you were witnessing to Jan, but I doubt if she was impressed. Sally didn't believe what you said when she saw the move you made just now, and Jan won't believe your interest in things of the Lord as she observes the 'moves' you make at school. Your actions say you're on the side of wrong instead of on God's side."

Deb was troubled. "But I really am on God's side," she insisted. "I'm a Christian, and I want Jan to become one."

"Then she needs to see that Jesus makes a difference in your life," said Mother. "I'm afraid she couldn't tell that today. Now, about that spelling test. . . ."

HOW ABOUT YOU? When people see your actions will they believe you're on the Lord's side or on Satan's? Actions speak louder than words. Let your actions say that you belong to Jesus. □ H.M.

TO MEMORIZE: *Be of the same mind toward one another. Do not set your mind on high things, but associate with the humble. Do not be wise in your own opinion.* Romans 12:16, NKJV

"WHERE ARE WE GOING, Dad?" asked Kevin as his father turned at the intersection.

"Wait and see," Dad said with a wink.

"Madame Margarite, Spiritualist, Reader," Sarah read as they drove past a sign on Main Street. "Have your fortune told here."

"I'd sure like to know the future," Laura sighed. "Like, will Brad ask me to the youth banquet?"

"How much does it cost to have your fortune told, Dad?" Kevin asked.

"I don't know," Dad answered, "and I may never find out. God's Word warns against going to fortune-tellers."

"Why?" Sarah, Laura, and Kevin spoke in unison.

"It would be fun to know the future," Kevin argued. "Suppose we had known last Christmas that Grandma Snider was going to have a stroke the next week. Would we have enjoyed Christmas?" Dad asked.

"No, I guess not," answered Laura slowly.

"One young man was told by a fortune-teller that he would die when he was sixty-five," Dad said. "He began living very dangerously, thinking nothing could kill him. He took crazy risks. At the age of twenty-eight, he drowned."

"Then the fortune-teller was wrong!" Kevin exclaimed.

"Very often they are, but many people base their lives on false predictions. That's dangerous," Dad warned.

"Going to a fortune-teller is 'walking in the counsel of the ungodly.' That's in a psalm I learned," said Laura.

Dad pulled the car into the parking lot of a new ice cream store. "The future is God's secret. He wants us to trust Him, just as you trusted me today even though you didn't know where we were going. God wisely hides sorrows from us, and He provides many beautiful surprises."

"All we have to do is wait and see." Laura laughed as she got out of the car.

HOW ABOUT YOU? Do you worry about the future? Worry is unbelief and is not pleasing to God. Make up your mind to stop worrying about tomorrow. Trust God. He has everything under control.

□ B.W.

TO MEMORIZE: *Blessed is the man who does not walk in the counsel of the wicked or stand in the way of sinners or sit in the seat of mockers.* Psalm 1:1, NIV

OCTOBER

31

Wait and See

FROM THE BIBLE:

Look at the birds! They don't worry about what to eat—they don't need to sow or reap or store up food—for your heavenly Father feeds them. And you are far more valuable to him than they are. Will all your worries add a single moment to your life? And why worry about your clothes? Look at the field lilies! They don't worry about theirs. Yet King Solomon in all his glory was not clothed as beautifully as they. And if God cares so wonderfully for flowers that are here today and gone tomorrow, won't he more surely care for you, O men of little faith? So don't worry at all about having enough food and clothing. Why be like the heathen? For they take pride in all these things and are deeply concerned about them. But your heavenly Father already knows perfectly well that you need them, and he will give them to you if you give him first place in your life and live as he wants you to. So don't be anxious about tomorrow. God will take care of your tomorrow too. Live one day at a time. Matthew 6:26-34, TLB

Trust God for the future

NOVEMBER

1

THE TEN COMMANDMENTS

What's Important

FROM THE BIBLE:

I am the LORD your God, who brought you out of Egypt, out of the land of slavery. You shall have no other gods before me.
Exodus 20:1-3, NIV

Jesus replied, "'Love the Lord your God with all your heart, soul, and mind.' This is the first and greatest commandment. The second most important is similar: 'Love your neighbor as much as you love yourself.'"
Matthew 22:37-38, TLB

Put God first

WHEN ANDY became a Christian, he was thrilled with his newfound faith! He spent a lot of time reading God's Word and praying. He especially prayed that his parents would come to know Jesus. He loved his Sunday school class. He was memorizing Scripture and growing spiritually.

But all that was before Andy began his new hobby. Now it seemed all he could think about was BMX bike racing.

Andy's unsaved father was glad that Andy's new hobby took up so much of his time. "I was beginning to worry about you and your religion, Andy. You were taking it too seriously. But now that you're into BMX racing, you seem more normal."

Andy felt a stab of guilt. Was he allowing the racing to get too important in his life? But he ignored the feeling and helped Dad tighten the right-hand brake on his bike.

That Sunday morning Andy awoke to a terrible crash of thunder. It was pouring rain, and since Andy knew his BMX race would be cancelled due to the muddy track, he decided to go to Sunday school.

The lesson was on the Ten Commandments. Andy had memorized them, so when Mr. Helms asked someone to give the first one, he raised his hand. "You shall have no other gods before me," he stated when the teacher called on him. Then Mr. Helms asked what that meant. "It means the people in Africa and places like that shouldn't worship idols," replied Andy confidently.

"Yes," agreed Mr. Helms, "but it also means much more than that. It means none of us should allow anything to become more important to us than God is!" Andy was thinking of his father's words and of how important BMX racing had become to him. Silently he asked God to forgive him and to once again make him a good testimony before his parents.

HOW ABOUT YOU? Is there something in your life you have allowed to take first place over God? It could be a hobby or a TV show or another person. Even good things become wrong if you allow them to become "gods" in your life. As you memorize the first commandment, ask God to help you keep Him in first place where He belongs. □ R.P.

TO MEMORIZE: *You shall have no other gods before me.* Exodus 20:3, NIV

"SUSAN, "I've told you to quit looking at yourself in the mirror!" exclaimed Mrs. Morgan. "You make me want to take all the mirrors off the walls!"

"Oh, Mother, I just want to look my best. This new hairstyle makes me look years older, doesn't it?" Even as she said this, Susan was looking in the mirror again. Later Susan and her mother went shopping at the mall. Mother sighed when she noticed Susan constantly smiling at her reflection in the store windows.

After dinner Dad read the Ten Commandments. Then the family discussed what each one meant. "What do you think 'graven images' are?" asked Dad.

"Idols," answered Susan promptly, "like heathen people in other countries make to worship. And my Sunday school teacher said we should be careful, too, not to worship statues or pictures of Jesus. She said a lot of people worship the statue or picture instead of God Himself."

The smile on Mother's face turned to a frown as she saw that, even while Susan was speaking, she was admiring her reflection in the kitchen window across the table from her. Just then eight-year-old Bobby spoke up. "Well, I don't know what a graven image is, but I think some girls worship their own image!"

The whole family looked at Susan. She felt herself blushing as Mother said, "Technically, Susan's explanation of a graven image is more correct, but I think Bobby does have a point."

"I guess I have been too impressed by my own looks lately," admitted Susan. "I'll try to do better. I know—if I can't quit looking at myself all the time, I'll change back to my old hairstyle. I promise!"

The whole family was relieved to hear Susan say that. Mother laughed as she said, "Maybe we won't have to take all the mirrors down after all!"

HOW ABOUT YOU? Do you worship any "graven images"? Are you sometimes guilty of worshiping your own image? It's not wrong to want to look your best, but don't be guilty of "bowing down to" or "serving" yourself. God will not share His glory with anyone. Worship only Him. □ R.P.

TO MEMORIZE: *You shall not make for yourself an idol in the form of anything in heaven above or on the earth beneath or in the waters below.*
Exodus 20:4, NIV

THE TEN COMMANDMENTS
No Graven Images

FROM THE BIBLE:
You shall not make for yourself an idol in the form of anything in heaven above or on the earth beneath or in the waters below. You shall not bow down to them or worship them; for I, the LORD your God, am a jealous God, punishing the children for the sin of the fathers to the third and fourth generation of those who hate me, but showing love to a thousand generations of those who love me and keep my commandments.
Exodus 20:4-6, NIV

Worship God only

NOVEMBER

3

THE TEN COMMANDMENTS

Not in Vain

FROM THE BIBLE:
You shall not misuse the name of the LORD your God, for the LORD will not hold anyone guiltless who misuses his name.
Exodus 20:7, NIV

Keep my commands and follow them. I am the LORD. Do not profane my holy name. I must be acknowledged as holy by the Israelites. I am the LORD, who makes you holy.
Leviticus 22:31-32, NIV

God's name is holy

DEREK WAS WATCHING his favorite TV program as Mother worked on her knitting and Dad read the paper. The program was a comedy show about a family similar to their own. Derek laughed when an embarrassing incident took place in the story, and the star of the show said, "Oh, my God!"

Hearing this, Dad looked up from his paper. "Derek, how can you laugh when people use God's name in vain like that?" he asked. "You claim to love God and say He is your heavenly Father. Yet you seem to have forgotten that His name is holy."

"I know, Dad," Derek replied soberly. "I wish they didn't swear on TV so much, too, but what can I do about the swearing?"

"You can turn off the program," said Mother, "and then you could inform the TV station and those who sponsor the program that you turned it off, and tell them why."

"Good suggestion," agreed Dad. "Maybe you and your Christian friends can do something about it!"

Derek thought a lot about that. He discussed it with his friends and his youth leader at church. Soon Derek was heading up a campaign for "Cleaner TV." Many of the kids decided to do just what his mother had suggested. Through their local library they got the sponsors' addresses, and they wrote letters complaining about the program's foul language. They said if the companies continued to sponsor such programs, they and their families would quit buying the products. They also contacted the station they were watching and let them know how they felt.

It was hard to tell sometimes if their "Cleaner TV" campaign was doing any good. But they realized that it was reminding them over and over that God will not stand for His name being used in vain!

HOW ABOUT YOU? Have you heard people say, "Oh, my God!" or "Oh, my Lord!" so much that it doesn't even bother you anymore? It still bothers God! When you're talking with friends and they use God's name in vain, do you ask them not to do that? Perhaps you could begin a campaign of your own to promote cleaner language on TV.
□ R.P.

TO MEMORIZE: *You shall not misuse the name of the LORD your God, for the LORD will not hold anyone guiltless who misuses his name.*
Exodus 20:7, NIV

"Daddy," asked Heidi, "why do we have church on Sunday? Carolyn's church meets on Saturday. She said that the Bible says that Saturday is the Sabbath. She's wrong, isn't she?"

"Yes and no," answered Dad. "She's right about the Old Testament Sabbath being the same as our Saturday. But if she said our church is wrong to meet on Sunday, I can't agree with that. New Testament believers met on the *first* day of the week. This is mentioned in Acts 20:7 and 1 Corinthians 16:2."

"Why did they change?" asked Heidi.

"Because Jesus arose from the grave on Sunday," Dad explained. "When we meet on Sunday we're celebrating His resurrection. That's why we call it the Lord's Day, Heidi."

"Oh, well, I'll tell Carolyn," Heidi said as she skipped out of the room. But Heidi was a deep thinker, so in a few minutes she returned. "Daddy, do we still have to 'remember the Sabbath Day to keep it holy' like it says in the Ten Commandments?"

"Yes and no," chuckled Dad. "The people in the Old Testament lived under the Law. We don't, but we still believe that God wants us to set aside one day out of seven for Him. So we remember the Resurrection on Sunday, and we try to keep *that* day holy for God."

"You know what?" Heidi asked solemnly. "Sherri and her family had a picnic at the beach last Sunday, and they went swimming! They weren't keeping the day holy, were they?"

"Whoa!" cautioned Dad. "There are things that I believe our family should keep for other days of the week, but let's be careful. We don't have a strict set of rules like they had for the Old Testament Sabbath. Romans 14 says we shouldn't judge others on these matters."

Heidi stared at him for a moment. "Okay, Daddy. But at least I'll remember why you won't let us do some things on Sunday. It's because we're keeping that day for the Lord."

HOW ABOUT YOU? Do you set aside Sunday to worship and honor your Lord? Are there some things which you cannot do on that day if you wish to honor Jesus? Perhaps you will want to ask your parents or your Sunday school teacher to help you determine what you should or shouldn't do on the Lord's Day. □ R.P.

TO MEMORIZE: *Remember the Sabbath day by keeping it holy.* Exodus 20:8, NIV

THE TEN COMMANDMENTS

Keep It Holy

FROM THE BIBLE:
Remember the Sabbath day by keeping it holy. Six days you shall labor and do all your work, but the seventh day is a Sabbath to the LORD your God. On it you shall not do any work, neither you, nor your son or daughter, nor your manservant or maidservant, nor your animals, nor the alien within your gates. For in six days the LORD made the heavens and the earth, the sea, and all that is in them, but he rested on the seventh day. Therefore the LORD blessed the Sabbath day and made it holy.
Exodus 20:8-11, NIV

Keep Sunday special

5

THE TEN COMMANDMENTS

Father and Mother

FROM THE BIBLE:
Honor your father and your mother, so that you may live long in the land the LORD your God is giving you.
Exodus 20:12, NIV

Children, obey your parents; this is the right thing to do because God has placed them in authority over you. Honor your father and mother. This is the first of God's Ten Commandments that ends with a promise. And this is the promise: that if you honor your father and mother, yours will be a long life, full of blessing.
Ephesians 6:1-3, TLB

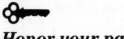

Honor your parents

BEFORE SUNDAY SCHOOL class began, all the sixth-grade boys gathered in a group outside. They didn't realize that a window was open near them, and their teacher was overhearing every remark they made.

Mark opened the conversation. "What did you guys do yesterday?"

"My old man made me help him paint our basement. I wanted to play football," Kyle grumbled.

"Well, my old lady had her parents over all day," said Terry, "and the Grams are both deaf. I spent the whole day saying things louder after they said, 'huh?'"

Mark had a complaint, too. "Helen and George made me wash their car. I told them I wasn't the one who got it dirty."

The others laughed. Then Kyle said, "Mark, how do you get away with calling your folks by their first names?"

Mark laughed. "Are you kidding? If I ever did that to their faces, old Baldhead would skin me alive. I have to call them *Sir* and *Ma'am* at home."

Just then a buzzer sounded and the boys filed into class. Mr. Beach asked, "How many of you know the Ten Commandments?" A few hands went up, and at Mr. Beach's nod, Mark recited them rapidly.

"Good," said Mr. Beach. "Now, how many of you realize you broke one of those commandments just a few minutes ago?" This time no hands went up, but there were many puzzled looks.

"Think about the Fifth Commandment," said Mr. Beach. "It says, 'Honor your father and your mother.' Then think about your conversation before class." The boys began to look ashamed. They really did love their parents but had thoughtlessly been disrespectful. After discussing it, Mr. Beach gave them a homework assignment for the next week. It was to put into practice the Fifth Commandment.

HOW ABOUT YOU? When you're away from your parents, do you call them the "old man" or "old lady"? Do you honor them to their faces and make fun of them behind their backs? If so, you're guilty of breaking the Fifth Commandment. Ask God to forgive you and to help you again to truly honor your parents! □ R.P.

TO MEMORIZE: *Honor your father and your mother, so that you may live long in the land the LORD your God is giving you.* Exodus 20:12, NIV

JUDY WOKE UP in a terrible mood. She had an oral book report to do at school today, and she wasn't well prepared. Besides, it was pouring rain! Her hair would get all kinky and fuzzy from the moisture!

Judy and her brother, Jerry, both reached the bathroom door at the same time. "Ouch!" cried Jerry as Judy grabbed his arm. "Mom, Judy pushed me against the wall!"

When Judy emerged from the bathroom, Mother was waiting. "I'm ready to hear an explanation from you, young lady. What did Jerry do to deserve this?" She showed Judy the long scrape on the little boy's arm.

"He got in my way, that's what!" exclaimed Judy. "My bus comes twenty minutes earlier than his. I've tried to tell the little fool that I should always be in the bathroom first, but he won't listen to me!"

"Judy, I'm ashamed of the way you're acting," scolded Mother. "Jerry hasn't done anything to you this morning. Now apologize, and get downstairs for breakfast!"

"I'm sorry," Judy spat. Then, as she headed for the kitchen, she whispered, "But I hate you, you big baby!"

After breakfast the family had devotions. At Mother's request, Dad read Matthew 5:21-22 and 1 John 3:15. "Jesus is teaching the Ten Commandments," Dad said. "Here He explains that being angry with no cause, or hating someone, or calling someone a fool is just as wrong in God's eyes as murder."

Judy looked shocked as she glanced at Jerry. She definitely didn't want to be a murderer! "I'm sorry," she whispered. "I didn't mean it. You can' even have the bathroom first after this."

HOW ABOUT YOU? Do you ever get angry at people for no good reason? Do you call them "fools"? Christ said anyone guilty of these things is like someone who has broken the Sixth Commandment. "I hate you" are words you should never use. □ R.P.

TO MEMORIZE: *You shall not murder.*
Exodus 20:13, NIV

THE TEN COMMANDMENTS

No Murder

FROM THE BIBLE:
You shall not murder.
Exodus 20:13, NIV

Under the laws of Moses the rule was, "If you murder, you must die." But I have added to that rule, and tell you that if you are only angry, even in your own home, you are in danger of judgment! If you call your friend an idiot, you are in danger of being brought before the court. And if you curse him, you are in danger of the fires of hell. So if you are standing before the altar in the Temple, offering a sacrifice to God, and suddenly remember that a friend has something against you, leave your sacrifice there beside the altar and go and apologize and be reconciled to him, and then come and offer your sacrifice to God.
Matthew 5:21-24, TLB

Hatred kills

NOVEMBER

7

THE TEN COMMANDMENTS

No Adultery

FROM THE BIBLE:
You shall not commit adultery.
Exodus 20:14, NIV

The laws of Moses said, "You shall not commit adultery." But I say: Anyone who even looks at a woman with lust in his eye has already committed adultery with her in his heart. So if your eye—even if it is your best eye!—causes you to lust, gouge it out and throw it away. Better for part of you to be destroyed than for all of you to be cast into hell. And if your hand—even your right hand—causes you to sin, cut it off and throw it away. Better that than find yourself in hell.
Matthew 5:27-30, TLB

Keep yourself pure

ONE DAY Carl Stone and his friend Brad went fishing with Carl's dad. They went to a lake and fished off a pier. Mr. Stone had gone back to the car for more bait, so the boys thought they were alone. As he returned to the pier, Mr. Stone overheard this conversation.

"Hey, Carl, did you see that girl lying on the beach back there?" asked Brad.

"D'ya mean the one in the pink bikini?" replied Carl. "She sure has a tan!"

"Who cares about the tan? Get a look at that body! If she looks that good in a bikini, I wonder what she'd look like with nothing on!" Brad snickered.

"Shh! Here comes Dad," answered Carl.

Mr. Stone was very concerned and prayed silently that God would show him how to teach the boys a special lesson. On the way home, he began, "Boys, do you know the Ten Commandments?"

"Most of them!" answered Brad. Then he and Carl began to recite them in unison.

When they got to the Seventh, Mr. Stone stopped them. "Do you know what that one means?" he asked.

"Our Sunday school teacher said adultery is referring to sexual sin," answered Carl. "He said it means we are supposed to have sexual love only with the person we're married to."

"That's right, Carl," replied his father. "But Jesus said in the New Testament that if a boy looks on a girl with lust in his heart, it's the same as committing the act of sex with her. To 'lust' means to want to do those things which we know are a privilege God reserves only for husbands and wives. It's important to ask God to help us keep our minds and bodies pure for Him."

Carl and Brad wondered how Mr. Stone knew what they had been thinking about on the pier. They finally decided it didn't matter how he knew, but they were glad that he did.

HOW ABOUT YOU? Do you ever wish you could have sexual contact with some boy or girl? Remember that God has reserved your body for the one person you will marry someday. The only time it is right to have sexual love with that person is after you are married. Ask God to keep your mind and body pure. Don't ever break the Seventh Commandment. □ R.P.

TO MEMORIZE: *You shall not commit adultery.*
Exodus 20:14, NIV

MIKE WAS SO GLAD when he learned that his partners on the science project would be Bart and Dean. Everyone knew that Bart was the smartest boy in the class, and Dean was the best artist. *I won't have to do a thing!* Mike thought to himself.

The groups met together each afternoon to plan their project and decide who would do what. The three boys finally decided to build a working model of a volcano. Bart would do the scientific part and figure out how to make it erupt. Dean would build the volcano. Mike, to his dismay, was to write a report. *Oh, well. I can probably get Bart to do it for me,* he thought.

The day of the science fair approached swiftly. The evening before it was to be held, Mike called Bart. "Help!" he cried into the telephone. "I forgot to do the report!" Bart was disgusted but agreed to do it himself.

The next afternoon Miss Pope announced the winners. "The best project this year is the volcano done by Bart, Mike, and Dean. You three boys will receive an *A* for your hard work."

Mike didn't feel as happy as he thought he would. He remembered that the Bible said a man has no right to eat unless he works. Mike knew that also meant he had no right to receive rewards for which he had not worked. He felt guilty.

The next day Mike approached Miss Pope. "Can I talk to you?" he asked. Then he explained what had happened. "I feel like a thief—like I stole an *A* from you. I didn't do the work, so I don't deserve an *A*." Miss Pope was quiet for what seemed to be a long time. "Mike," she finally said, "I really respect you for confessing this to me. I will have to give you an *F* on the project, but if I could grade you in honesty, it would be an "*A*-plus!""

HOW ABOUT YOU? Are you a thief? You don't have to *steal* things to be a thief. If you don't work when you are being paid to work, you're stealing time. If you take a grade you know you did not earn, you're stealing grades. As you memorize commandment number eight, remember all the various ways Satan can tempt you to steal. Determine, with God's help, not to yield to any of them.

□ R.P.

TO MEMORIZE: *You shall not steal.*
Exodus 20:15, NIV

THE TEN COMMANDMENTS
No Stealing

FROM THE BIBLE:
You shall not steal.
Exodus 20:15, NIV

If anyone is stealing he must stop it and begin using those hands of his for honest work so he can give to others in need.
Ephesians 4:28, TLB

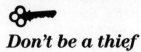

Don't be a thief

THE TEN COMMANDMENTS

No False Testimony

FROM THE BIBLE:
You shall not give false testimony against your neighbor.
Exodus 20:16, NIV

A good man is known by his truthfulness; a false man by deceit and lies. Some people like to make cutting remarks, but the words of the wise soothe and heal. Truth stands the test of time; lies are soon exposed. Deceit fills hearts that are plotting for evil; joy fills hearts that are planning for good! No real harm befalls the good, but there is constant trouble for the wicked. God delights in those who keep their promises, and abhors those who don't.
Proverbs 12:17-22, TLB

Do not lie

THE THIRD-GRADE Sunday school class was studying the life of Moses. When they came to the story of the Ten Commandments, they talked about one or two each week. After each one was discussed, Janice smiled and thought smugly, *I've never done that!*

Today's lesson began with the Ninth Commandment. "Who can tell me what this means?" asked Mrs. Bennett.

Tracy's hand shot up. "I was watching a new show on TV last night. It was called 'Live Courtroom.' There were witnesses there. They were people who had to tell what they knew about the case. What they told is their testimony."

"Yes, that's what a testimony is," said Mrs. Bennett. "But what is a *false* testimony?"

Molly raised her hand. "A false testimony would be when one of those people in the court was not telling the truth."

Janice smiled as she thought to herself, *I've never had to go to court and be a witness, so I'm okay on this commandment too. I don't think I've ever broken any of the Ten Commandments!*

"Bearing false witness doesn't just mean in court," Mrs. Bennett was saying. "Anytime we say anything that is not true, we are guilty of bearing false witness."

"Do you mean when we just fib a little?" asked Janice incredulously. Mrs. Bennett nodded. "Even if it's just a little white lie?" asked Janice again.

"To God, a lie doesn't have a color," stated Mrs. Bennett. "A lie is a lie." Even Janice had to admit that she had told lies. She knew she needed God's forgiveness just as all the other class members did.

HOW ABOUT YOU? Have you ever thought you were perfect and did not need to be saved? Maybe you never have killed anyone or worshiped idols, but if you've ever told anything that is not true, you have lied. Lying is sin. The Bible says that all people have sinned. So confess your sin, and let Jesus help you not to do it again. □ R.P.

TO MEMORIZE: *You shall not give false testimony against your neighbor.* Exodus 20:16, NIV

JIMMY'S BICYCLE was his favorite thing in all the world. It was a bright, shiny, silver color, and he rode it every day. He could even pop wheelies on it.

Then his neighbor, Tim, got a brand new ten-speed bike. It was metallic green, and it had a speedometer, a rearview mirror, and a headlight. Jimmy thought he had never seen anything so beautiful!

Mom and Dad began to notice that Jimmy didn't ride his bike so much any more. He used to be so proud of it that he waxed it till it gleamed, but now he didn't polish it anymore, either. One day Dad noticed Jimmy just staring next door where Tim was riding his new ten-speed.

"I think I found out what's wrong with Jimmy," Dad whispered to Mom. "He's almost sick with jealousy over Tim's bike. I hope this doesn't last too long."

At their time of family devotions that night, Dad read the Ten Commandments. Jimmy wondered why, but he didn't have to wonder long. When Dad came to the last one, he read it this way: "You should not covet your neighbor's wife, nor his manservant, nor his maidservant, nor his ox, nor his ten-speed bike, nor anything that is your neighbor's."

"It doesn't say that!" Jimmy exclaimed.

"No, but maybe it should," Dad suggested. Then he prayed that the Lord would forgive each of them for wanting or coveting anything belonging to someone else. He also asked God to make them content with what they had.

"May I go outside and ride my bike?" Jimmy asked after the dishes were done.

"You certainly may!" Dad smiled.

HOW ABOUT YOU? Have you ever wanted something that belonged to someone else—maybe a new bike, a video game, or clothes? The Bible calls that coveting, and coveting is sin! We all need to learn to be content with what we have. We should not try to keep up with the neighbors. As you memorize this last commandment, ask God to help you be content with what you have. □ R.P.

TO MEMORIZE: *You shall not covet.* Exodus 20:17, NIV

10

THE TEN COMMANDMENTS

No Coveting

FROM THE BIBLE:
You shall not covet your neighbor's house. You shall not covet your neighbor's wife, or his manservant or maidservant, his ox or donkey, or anything that belongs to your neighbor.
Exodus 20:17, NIV

Stay away from the love of money; be satisfied with what you have. For God has said, "I will never, never fail you nor forsake you." Hebrews 13:5, TLB

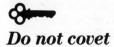

Do not covet

11

In the Ditch

FROM THE BIBLE:
*Vindicate me, O LORD, for I
have led a blameless life; I have
trusted in the LORD without
wavering. Test me, O LORD,
and try me, examine my heart
and my mind; for your love is
ever before me, and I walk
continually in your truth. I do
not sit with deceitful men, nor
do I consort with hypocrites;
I abhor the assembly of evildoers
and refuse to sit with the
wicked. I wash my hands in
innocence, and go about your
altar, O LORD, proclaiming
aloud your praise and telling of
all your wonderful deeds. I love
the house where you live, O
LORD, the place where your
glory dwells. Do not take away
my soul along with sinners, my
life with bloodthirsty men, in
whose hands are wicked
schemes, whose right hands are
full of bribes. But I lead a
blameless life; redeem me and
be merciful to me. My feet stand
on level ground; in the great
assembly I will praise the LORD.*
Psalm 26, NIV

Choose right friends

WHEN RYAN'S MOTHER picked him up at
school, he would not look at her. She had come
for him because the principal had called and asked
her to do so. Ryan and some other boys had been
caught smoking, and now he was being sent home.
He could see that his mother was very upset, and
he was too ashamed to say anything.

Rain pelted the windshield as they rode in silence. When they turned off the highway and
started up the hill toward their house, the car
slipped and skidded. Road repairs had been started
some time ago, and the street was a terrible mess!
"Be careful, Mom," Ryan exclaimed, "or we'll wind
up in the di—"

At that exact moment the car skidded again and
slid into a ditch! Mother shifted gears and rocked
the car, but it was hopeless. She looked at the
pouring rain and muddy street. "Nothing to do but
walk home and call a wrecker," she sighed. So
they trudged up the muddy hill toward home.

When Dad got home that evening, Ryan did his
best to keep Dad's attention on the matter of the
car. But the dreaded moment arrived when Dad
asked what had happened at school. "I didn't want
to smoke," Ryan said defensively. "It's just that I
couldn't have the other guys thinking I was a baby."

Dad frowned. "I thought you just told me you
didn't like walking on steep, muddy ground," he
said.

Ryan looked at him, puzzled. "What's that got
to do with it?"

"Well," said Dad, "when you spend a lot of time
with the wrong crowd, it's kind of like being on
steep, muddy ground and in danger of sliding. In
fact, I'd say you slid quite badly at school today.
You're a Christian, yet you've chosen friends who
pressure you into doing things that are not pleasing
to Christ. With the right kind of friends, life would
be a lot smoother."

Ryan nodded thoughtfully. With the punishment
his parents were sure to give him, life would not
be very smooth either. He knew it was his own
fault. Different friends—Christian friends—would
help!

HOW ABOUT YOU? Are you associating with the
wrong crowd? If so, you could be headed for a lot
of trouble. Choose close friends who will be a
help, not a hindrance, in living for Christ. □ B.W.

TO MEMORIZE: *I abhor the assembly of evildoers
and refuse to sit with the wicked.* Psalm 26:5, NIV

"**I** CAN'T STAND Christopher!" exploded Brandon. "He's a big bag of hot air, saying he met the mayor, they got a new car, they're going to Bermuda, his dad's on the city council. Bla-bla-bla!"

"Not jealous, are you?" asked Mother.

"No!" snorted Brandon, "just sick of his bragging. If he's not doing that, he's cussing. Mother, why does God let him have so many good things when he laughs at Christians and even curses God's name?"

"That's a good question," said Mother. "It used to bother me, too, when I saw wicked people being blessed." She was interrupted as Misty stomped into the room.

"Old Mr. Matlock is so hateful!" complained Misty. "He put barricades on the sidewalk in front of his house so Denise and I can't ride our bikes there. Denise said we ought to do something to get even with him."

"Oh no!" Mother shook her head. "Remember what we read from the Bible this morning? What did those verses tell you to do to Mr. Matlock?"

"Love him," mumbled Misty.

"That's not all," Mother reminded her. "What else?"

Brandon answered for Misty. "Bless him, pray for him, and do good to him."

"Would you like to make some cookies, Misty?" asked Mother. "You could take a few to Mr. Matlock."

"You've got to be kidding!" Misty was shocked.

Mother shook her head. "No, I'm not. The best way to destroy your enemies is to make them your friends." As she got out the cookbook, she turned to Brandon.

"God instructs us to bless our enemies and return good for evil," said Mother thoughtfully. "He's giving them every opportunity to change from enemies to friends."

A look of surprise spread over Brandon's face. He looked at Misty. "If I help you make cookies, can I have some to take to Christopher?"

HOW ABOUT YOU? Is there someone who is giving you a hard time? Try the formula Jesus used and watch them change. Don't be jealous when the Lord blesses those who do not love Him. Instead, see if there's some way you can help to make them His friends. □ B.W.

TO MEMORIZE: *Bless those who persecute you; bless and do not curse.* Romans 12:14, NKJV

Good for Evil

FROM THE BIBLE:
There is a saying, "Love your friends and hate your enemies." But I say: Love your enemies! Pray for those who persecute you! In that way you will be acting as true sons of your Father in heaven. For he gives his sunlight to both the evil and the good, and sends rain on the just and on the unjust too. If you love only those who love you, what good is that? Even scoundrels do that much. If you are friendly only to your friends, how are you different from anyone else? Even the heathen do that. But you are to be perfect, even as your Father in heaven is perfect.
Matthew 5:43-48, TLB

Love your enemies

13

The Wrong Way

FROM THE BIBLE:

Now therefore, thus says the LORD of hosts: "Consider your ways! You have sown much, and bring in little; you eat, but do not have enough; you drink, but you are not filled with drink; you clothe yourselves, but no one is warm; and he who earns wages, earns wages to put into a bag with holes." Thus says the LORD of hosts: "Consider your ways!"

Haggai 1:5-7, NKJV

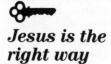

Jesus is the right way

"YOU SHOULD have seen Brianne today!" laughed Jim as the family began their dinner. His sister sent him a nasty look as he continued. "The girls think they're so smart! They insisted they could play touch football as good as us guys, so we let them play with us today. Know what Brianne did? When she got the ball, she ran toward the wrong goal line! Almost made a touchdown, too— for the wrong team. What a riot!"

Brianne reluctantly joined in the laughter at her expense. "You're in good company," Dad consoled her. "It's happened before—to professionals! Way back in 1929, a fellow named Roy Riegels played for the California Golden Bears. One time when he got the ball, he lit out for the wrong goal with 'do-or-die' determination. One of his teammates finally managed to bring him down just a yard from the goal line. But his team still lost the game."

"Good thing it was only a game," observed Mother. "There's an important lesson for us, though. Some people are running long and hard in the game of life, and they don't realize they're running in the wrong direction."

"That's true," said Dad. "Many people really are trying hard and doing their best to live a good life. In fact, their 'good deeds' sometimes put Christians to shame. But in spite of those 'good deeds,' they're still sinners, and they refuse to acknowledge Jesus as the only way to heaven. When all is said and done, they'll find that they went the wrong way. They'll spend eternity in hell instead of in heaven. What a tragedy!"

"That is sad," declared Brianne. "Maybe I didn't know which way to run in the football game, but I'm sure glad I know the way to heaven."

HOW ABOUT YOU? Are you running the wrong way in life? You are if you're trying to get to heaven by any other way than through the blood of Jesus Christ. Admit your need and trust Christ as Savior. □ H.M.

TO MEMORIZE: *There is a way that seems right to a man, but in the end it leads to death.*
Proverbs 14:12, NIV

"I'M SICK OF being ordered around!" Brad griped as he put his bike away. "Someone's always tellin' me it's time to get up, time to catch the bus, time for the bell. Just once I'd like to do what I want to do when I want to do it."

Dad looked up from his tool bench. "Suppose there were no rules or schedules, Brad?"

"That would be great!" Brad exclaimed.

Dad raised his eyebrows. "I'm not so sure. Just for fun though, let's imagine we woke one morning and everyone could do anything they wanted. What would you do?"

"I'd spend the day at the zoo," Brad answered.

"How would you get there?"

You would take me," Brad replied.

"Well, maybe. But remember, I don't have to do anything I don't want to do."

"Aw, you want to go to the zoo," pleaded Brad.

"Okay," agreed Dad, "so we get in the car and start for the zoo. I'm not sure we'd get there. There are no rules, remember? No traffic laws. Everyone drives exactly like he wants to—that is, until he runs into someone."

Brad whistled. "Well, we couldn't do away with traffic laws. We'll just get rid of all the other rules."

"So we keep the traffic laws," Dad conceded. "We arrive at the zoo, but we can't get in."

Brad looked startled. "Why not?"

"No schedules, so the gate attendant decided to sleep late," Dad explained.

Brad sighed. "If we didn't have rules and schedules, we'd just have confusion, wouldn't we?"

"Right!" agreed Dad. "When God created this world, He organized everything. The universe is run by laws and on a schedule. Even the sun has a schedule to keep." Dad looked at his watch. "According to my schedule, it's about time for lunch. How about a hamburger and a hot fudge sundae?"

Brad let out a whoop and ran for the car "Guess all schedules aren't bad," he said with a grin.

HOW ABOUT YOU? Do you often complain about having to do things "on schedule"? Would you rather put things off? Working with family and friends in an organized way makes life much smoother. Make up your mind to get "on schedule" and stay there. □ B.W.

TO MEMORIZE: *Whoever obeys his command will come to no harm, and the wise heart will know the proper time and procedure.* Ecclesiastes 8:5, NIV

Forgotten Schedules

FROM THE BIBLE:
There is a time for everything, and a season for every activity under heaven: a time to be born and a time to die, a time to plant and a time to uproot, a time to kill and a time to heal, a time to tear down and a time to build, a time to weep and a time to laugh, a time to mourn and a time to dance, a time to scatter stones and a time to gather them, a time to embrace and a time to refrain, a time to search and a time to give up, a time to keep and a time to throw away, a time to tear and a time to mend, a time to be silent and a time to speak, a time to love and a time to hate, a time for war and a time for peace. . . . He has made everything beautiful in its time. He has also set eternity in the hearts of men; yet they cannot fathom what God has done from beginning to end. Ecclesiastes 3:1-8, 11, NIV

Schedules aren't bad

15

Animal Charades

FROM THE BIBLE:
There was a man of the Pharisees named Nicodemus, a ruler of the Jews. This man came to Jesus by night and said to Him, "Rabbi, we know that You are a teacher come from God; for no one can do these signs that You do unless God is with him." Jesus answered and said to him, "Most assuredly, I say to you, unless one is born again, he cannot see the kingdom of God." Nicodemus said to Him, "How can a man be born when he is old? Can he enter a second time into his mother's womb and be born?" Jesus answered, "Most assuredly, I say to you, unless one is born of water and the Spirit, he cannot enter the kingdom of God. That which is born of the flesh is flesh, and that which is born of the Spirit is spirit. Do not marvel that I said to you, 'You must be born again.'. . . God so loved the world that He gave His only begotten Son, that whoever believes in Him should not perish but have everlasting life."

John 3:1-7, 16, NKJV

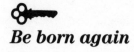

Be born again

AT THE SUNDAY SCHOOL class party, Lori listened eagerly as Miss Ellen explained the next game they would play. "Tom will be 'It' first," said Miss Ellen. "He'll pretend to be an animal. The first one to guess that animal will be 'It' next. You'll catch on. Go ahead, Tom."

Tom dropped to his hands and knees. He walked a few steps on all fours, then opened his mouth and barked. "You're a dog!" Pete shouted quickly. Tom nodded and got to his feet.

Pete thought for a moment. He got down on his stomach and wriggled his way across the room. "Are you a worm?" someone asked. Pete shook his head. As he crawled along, he rapidly stuck out his tongue several times. "A snake," squealed one of the girls, and it was her turn.

After several children had a turn, Miss Ellen was "It." The children watched as she began her act. She folded her hands and bowed her head. "You're a praying mantis," suggested Tom.

Miss Ellen shook her head. "I'll give you a clue," she said. "I'm a human, but what am I pretending to be?" She picked up her Bible and pretended to read. Next she stood up, tugged her clothes into place, and solemnly walked to a chair. She sat down and appeared to be listening to someone. She made motions as though she were opening a book. She also opened and closed her mouth several times, but no sound came out. "She's singing," whispered someone, and Miss Ellen nodded. Again she appeared to be listening. "She's in church," whispered someone else. Again Miss Ellen nodded.

Suddenly Lori knew the answer. "You're pretending to be a Christian!" she exclaimed.

"That's it," agreed Miss Ellen. "Boys and girls, it's time for you to be leaving. As you go, I want you to think about this: Pretending to be something doesn't make it so. You're not a dog unless you are born into the canine family, and you're not a Christian unless you are born into God's family. Jesus says you have to be born again by accepting Him as Savior."

HOW ABOUT YOU? Have you been born again? You may act like a Christian, but you're not one unless you've trusted Jesus and have been "born" into His family. Stop pretending and accept Him today.

□ H.M.

TO MEMORIZE: *Unless one is born of water and the Spirit, he cannot enter the kingdom of God.* John 3:5, NKJV

"THIS IS RIDICULOUS!" exclaimed Andy. He tapped his pencil impatiently on the paper in front of him. "Whoever thought up this assignment for Sunday school certainly doesn't know Jenny! I have to write down ten reasons why I like my sister, and I can't even think of one!"

"Thanks a lot!" Jenny called from the living room. "See if I ever bake cookies for you again!"

"Oops! I forgot about them." Andy wrote it down.

"How about the time last year when you were sick, and Jenny helped you with your homework?" suggested Mom.

"And how about the times I've played catch with you before a game?" Jenny asked. "Or last week when I let you ride my bike because yours was broken?"

Andy had forgotten all those things, too. He could see that Jenny really was a nice sister. He felt kind of guilty for all the times he had called her names or had purposely been a nuisance to her. It was hard to admit, but Andy said, "I guess I'm really kind of glad we had this assignment. It's made me appreciate my sister!"

"I can't believe I heard you say that," Jenny laughed. "In fact, I think it calls for a celebration. How about if I, being the wonderful sister that I am, make some popcorn?"

"Sounds great to me!" Andy said. He wrote one more thing on his paper. "She makes delicious popcorn!"

HOW ABOUT YOU? Do you appreciate the brothers or sisters the Lord has given you? Do you get along with them, or do you often create arguments just for the sake of arguing? Brother and sister conflicts are not new. They've been around since Cain and Abel! Brothers and sisters often overlook the good qualities in each other because they're so busy fighting. The Bible says that they are to help each other in times of trouble. Think about that verse, and then write down some reasons why you love your brothers and sisters! □ L.W.

TO MEMORIZE: *A friend loves at all times, and a brother is born for adversity.* Proverbs 17:17, NKJV

Sister Trouble

FROM THE BIBLE:
How wonderful it is, how pleasant, when brothers live in harmony! For harmony is as precious as the fragrant anointing oil that was poured over Aaron's head, and ran down onto his beard, and onto the border of his robe. Harmony is as refreshing as the dew on Mount Hermon, on the mountains of Israel. And God has pronounced this eternal blessing on Jerusalem, even life forevermore.
Psalm 133, TLB

Appreciate brothers and sisters

17

Not Hungry

FROM THE BIBLE:
But He knows the way that I take; when He has tested me, I shall come forth as gold. My foot has held fast to His steps; I have kept His way and not turned aside. I have not departed from the commandment of His lips; I have treasured the words of His mouth more than my necessary food.
Job 23:10-12, NKJV

Watch your mental diet

WHEN BRIAN came in from school, Mother was gone, so he raided the refrigerator and cupboards. When Mother returned, he was just finishing an after-school snack of potato chips, soda pop, ice cream, and cookies.

Mother frowned. "Next time don't eat so many snacks before supper," she said. As she started dinner, she added, "Mrs. Smith's grandson, Nicholas, will be going to Sunday school with us this week."

"I'm tired of Sunday school, and I'm tired of family devotions, too. That's kid stuff."

Brian took a comic book and settled down in front of the TV. The next thing he knew, Mother was calling him for dinner. At the table he wrinkled up his nose. "Hamburger casserole again? I don't want any."

"Mrs. Smith sent some cake for dessert," said Mother.

Brian grinned. "I might eat a little of that."

"Not until you eat some meat and vegetables," Dad ruled.

"But I'm not hungry," protested Brian.

"Because you filled up on junk food," Mother reminded him. As she passed the casserole to him, she added, "And that's exactly why you're not enjoying Sunday school and family devotions."

Brian snorted, "I don't enjoy Sunday school because I eat potato chips after school? Aw, Mom!"

"You know what your mother means," said Dad. "Unless we keep after you, you feed your mind junk food—TV programs, comic books, and loud music."

Mother passed Brian the vegetables. "If you aren't careful, you're going to be sick—spiritually and physically," she added.

Brian took a little from each dish. "It'll be nice to have Nicholas go along with us to Sunday school," he said sheepishly.

HOW ABOUT YOU? Are you filling your mind with junk food rather than wholesome spiritual food? Make up your mind to change your mental eating habits before you become spiritually sick. Read God's Word. Listen carefully to your Sunday school teacher and your pastor. Spend time with other Christians. ☐ B.W.

TO MEMORIZE: *I have treasured the words of His mouth more than my necessary food.*
Job 23:12, NKJV

As SOON AS Matt walked in the door, his mother knew something was wrong. He was quiet and thoughtful, not his usual happy self.

"How was school, Matt?" Mother asked.

Matt shrugged. "It was okay."

"You don't seem very happy," observed Mother.

Matt hesitated. "We had a discussion in social studies class. One of the kids started talking about nuclear war and how the whole world was going to end. Mr. Morgan, our teacher, agreed with him."

"What do you think, Matt?" asked Mother.

Matt gave his mother a little smile. "I think it's sort of scary. We talked about war at school. There are shows about it on TV." Matt paused. "Aren't you afraid, Mom?"

"Matt, this world is a messed-up place," answered Mother, "but when people tell frightening stories about nuclear war, I take time to thank the Lord that my future is in *His* hands. As Christians, we know that the Lord loves and cares for us. He is still in control. Only what He allows will happen, and we can trust Him to allow only what is best for us."

"But our teacher says that if everyone would stop making nuclear weapons, the world would be peaceful and no one would fight," offered Matt.

"That sounds good, Matt," answered Mother, "but it's not what the Bible says. Nations want to be powerful and will do anything to gain that power. It's unrealistic to think that all nations will suddenly decide to stop fighting. There will always be war. Again, we must remember to put our trust in the Lord."

Matt thought about it for a moment. Then he grinned at his mother. "It's good to be a Christian, Mom—and to trust the Lord to know what's best for me!"

HOW ABOUT YOU? Are you frightened when you hear stories about nuclear war? As a Christian, you don't have to be afraid. The Lord says that your future is in His hands. Whatever that future holds, He will be with you and help you through it. And isn't it nice to look forward to a wonderful future life in heaven? □ L.W.

TO MEMORIZE: *Do not let your hearts be troubled. Trust in God; trust also in me.* John 14:1, NIV

NOVEMBER

18

War!

FROM THE BIBLE:

And when you hear of wars and insurrections beginning, don't panic. True, wars must come, but the end won't follow immediately: for nation shall rise against nation and kingdom against kingdom, and there will be great earthquakes, and famines in many lands, and epidemics, and terrifying things happening in the heavens. But before all this occurs, there will be a time of special persecution, and you will be dragged into synagogues and prisons and before kings and governors for my name's sake. But as a result, the Messiah will be widely known and honored. Therefore, don't be concerned about how to answer the charges against you, for I will give you the right words and such logic that none of your opponents will be able to reply! Even those closest to you—your parents, brothers, relatives, and friends will betray you and have you arrested; and some of you will be killed. And everyone will hate you because you are mine and are called by my name. But not a hair of your head will perish! For if you stand firm, you will win your souls.

Luke 21:9-19, TLB

Don't fear—
trust God

Spend It Wisely

FROM THE BIBLE:
But the godly shall flourish like palm trees, and grow tall as the cedars of Lebanon. For they are transplanted into the LORD's own garden, and are under his personal care. Even in old age they will still produce fruit and be vital and green. This honors the LORD, and exhibits his faithful care. He is my shelter. There is nothing but goodness in him!
Psalm 92:12-15, TLB

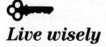

Live wisely

LINDA AND HER MOTHER went visiting in a nursing home one afternoon. First they saw Hattie Smith, who was always complaining.

"It's about time someone came to visit!" snapped Mrs. Smith. Then she grumbled about the food, the nurses, her doctor, and the rainy weather. "Oh, to be young again," said the old lady.

Linda felt sad as they walked down the hall, but when they got to Aunt Matilda's room, everything changed. The scrawny old woman in the wheelchair greeted them with a smile on her rosy, wrinkled cheeks. 'Praise the Lord! It's nice to see ye!" she said. "I've got so much joy bubblin' up in me today, that I've been prayin' for someone to share it with. This here's Lennie White. I've been talkin' to her about the Lord, and she asked Him into her heart a week ago last Tuesday."

After they left, Linda asked her mother, "Why are those ladies so different? They'll probably both die soon. But Aunt Matilda is happy, while Mrs. Smith is grumpy all the time."

"Let's think about it," Mother suggested. "Do you remember all the things we bought at the garage sale yesterday? We bought a shirt for your father, and a skirt and blouse for you. We got all that for ten dollars."

"That's a lot for only ten dollars!"

"Yes, I'm satisfied with the way we spent that money," said Mother. Then she said, "I think Aunt Matilda is happy because she has spent her life well. She's spent her whole life in loving service to others. She wouldn't have those years back for anything—just like I'd rather have the things I bought than the ten dollars that I spent for them. In addition, she's spending her remaining time well, witnessing and praising the Lord. I'm not sure about Mrs. Smith. Perhaps she looks back on her life with regret. Do you understand now?"

"I think so," Linda said. "I'm going to dedicate my life to God. Then, when I'm old, I'll be happy, too."

HOW ABOUT YOU? Are you afraid of growing old and dying? Don't be! Invest your life for God, and serve Him and others. He'll reward you in heaven someday. Whether your life on earth is long or short, you won't regret it when it comes to the end—if you've spent it wisely! □ S.K.

TO MEMORIZE: *The silver-haired head is a crown of glory, if it is found in the way of righteousness.* Proverbs 16:31, NKJV

"HELLO, RYAN," Grandpa Thompson said. "Is everything copasetic with my grandson today?"

"Copasetic? What does that mean, Grandpa?" Ryan asked, but he knew his grandfather wouldn't tell him. He'd make Ryan look it up in the dictionary.

Sure enough, Grandfather smiled and said, "That's what dictionaries are for, Ryan!"

Ryan quickly looked up the word *copasetic* and read that it meant "very satisfying." He was just closing the dictionary when his older brother (who was in high school and liked to think he was very smart) walked in the door.

"Hi, Bruce," Ryan greeted. "Everything copasetic?"

Bruce looked at Ryan strangely. "What are you talking about?" he asked.

Ryan looked at his grandfather and winked. "Look it up, Bruce. That's what dictionaries are for!"

While Bruce was flipping through the dictionary, Ryan went and sat down next to his grandfather on the couch. "You sure like using new words, don't you, Grandpa?"

Grandpa put his arm around Ryan. "Yes, I do. The way I look at it, the use of words is a gift from God. He gave man the ability to develop languages and to write words that express ideas and inventions. Communication is a vital part of life. Man can take that God-given ability and abuse it, or he can use it for good."

"Hmmm, I never thought about that before. I'm going to remember to thank the Lord for giving us the ability to use words," Ryan said as he got up to go to his room. "And, Grandpa, I hope you have a copasetic day!"

HOW ABOUT YOU? Have you ever thought about the importance of words? Without words you could not communicate with others. Without words there would be no books, no conversations, or radio programs! Are the words that come from your mouth pleasing to God? They should be. Thank God for words. And remember, the most important words are those found in God's Word, the Bible. □ L.W.

TO MEMORIZE: *A word fitly spoken is like apples of gold in settings of silver.* Proverbs 25:11, NKJV

A "Copasetic" Day

FROM THE BIBLE:
And moreover, because the Preacher was wise, he still taught the people knowledge; yes, he pondered and sought out and set in order many proverbs. The Preacher sought to find acceptable words; and what was written was upright—words of truth. The words of the wise are like goads, and the words of scholars are like well-driven nails, given by one Shepherd. And further, my son, be admonished by these. Of making many books there is no end, and much study is wearisome to the flesh. Let us hear the conclusion of the whole matter: Fear God and keep His commandments, for this is the whole duty of man. Ecclesiastes 12:9-13, NKJV

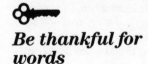

Be thankful for words

21

Taken for Granted

*A huge crowd, many of them
pilgrims on their way to
Jerusalem for the annual
Passover celebration, were
following him wherever he went,
to watch him heal the sick. So
when Jesus went up into the
hills and sat down with his
disciples around him, he soon
saw a great multitude of people
climbing the hill, looking for
him. Turning to Philip he
asked, "Philip, where can we
buy bread to feed all these
people?" (He was testing Philip,
for he already knew what he was
going to do.) Philip replied, "It
would take a fortune to begin to
do it!" Then Andrew, Simon
Peter's brother, spoke up.
"There's a youngster here with
five barley loaves and a couple
of fish! But what good is that
with all this mob?" "Tell
everyone to sit down," Jesus
ordered. And all of them—the
approximate count of the men
only was 5,000—sat down on
the grassy slopes. Then Jesus
took the loaves and gave thanks
to God and passed them out to
the people. Afterwards he did the
same with the fish. And everyone
ate until full!*
John 6:5-11, TLB

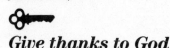

Give thanks to God

TIM BEGAN EATING his cereal. "You didn't
pray," his sister reminded him.

Tim shrugged. "I'm in a hurry."

It was Tim's turn to stack the breakfast dishes.
Usually Mother thanked him for his help, but today
she didn't say anything, even though Tim had done
a good job.

On the way to school, Tim saw a younger child
fall and drop several books. Tim hurried to help
him. The child grabbed the books and ran off without even looking at Tim. *What an ungrateful kid!*
thought Tim.

At recess, Tim offered to pass out papers. Up
and down the rows he went, putting the papers
on the desks. When he was finished, his teacher
glanced up. "You can go now," she said absently.
Didn't she even appreciate his help?

On Tim's paper route, there was an old man
crippled with arthritis. Since it was hard for him
to bend over, Tim always rang his doorbell and
handed the paper to him. Today the man grumbled,
"I've been looking for you. You're late!"

*I don't mind the extra trouble of waiting for him
to answer his door,* Tim thought, *but it sure would
be nice to know he liked what I do for him.*

"Why the sad face, Tim?" asked Mrs. Brown,
a nice lady who lived on his street.

"Oh, nothing big. But it just seems as though
everyone takes me for granted," complained Tim.

"I've felt that way myself," said Mrs. Brown.
"And I'm sure God must feel that way often."

"Why would He feel that way?"

"Well, I appreciate all He does for me," said
Mrs. Brown, "but so often I neglect to tell Him.
And I want to tell you, Tim, I appreciate having
you for a friend and neighbor."

Tim smiled and felt better, but he was thoughtful
as he walked home. The next morning he quietly
thanked God for his food before he began to eat.

HOW ABOUT YOU? Do you get tired of thanking God
for your food at every meal? Today's Scripture in-
dicates that Jesus took time to give thanks before
eating. How about all your other blessings? Maybe
you do appreciate them, but do you thank God in
your own words for all He gives you? God enjoys
hearing your "thank you." □ C.Y.

TO MEMORIZE: *Now therefore, our God, we thank
You and praise Your glorious name.*
1 Chronicles 29:13, NKJV

THE CARTER FAMILY was looking forward to a day at the beach. "Oh, I can hardly wait!" exclaimed Tamara. As the family sat down for breakfast, Dad asked her to lead in prayer. "Dear Jesus," Tamara prayed, "bless this food. Give us good weather and a good time. Give us safety. Keep Jeremy from fussing. Amen." Dad looked thoughtful when she finished, but said nothing.

After a quick breakfast, the family piled into the car for the trip. Soon they were enjoying the sun and sand. The children had just gotten into the water when a loud squawk interrupted their activities. A little way down the beach, sea gulls were fighting over some food they had found on the ground. "The birds are hungry," Tamara said. "I wish I had something to feed them."

Mother reached into the picnic basket. "Here, you can give them some of these crackers."

Tamara crumbled the crackers as she walked down the beach. When she threw them to the sea gulls, she was immediately surrounded by the screeching birds. They quickly gobbled up the pieces and squealed for more. They edged closer to Tamara, practically grabbing the crackers out of her fingers. "I think they like me," Tamara shouted happily. However, when the crackers were gone, the birds were gone, too.

"Oh, Daddy, the sea gulls didn't want me!" Tamara exclaimed. "They just wanted my crackers! When they got what they wanted, they left!"

Dad nodded. "I'm afraid we act somewhat like those sea gulls," he said. He smiled at her puzzled look and went on to explain. "Our prayers often express more 'gimmie' than gratitude for what Jesus has already done for us. We should seek the Lord Himself and not just the blessings or gifts that He gives us."

"I guess you're right," Tamara said thoughtfully as she remembered her prayer at the breakfast table. "The next time I pray I'm going to thank the Lord for the things He's given me before I ask for anything else."

HOW ABOUT YOU? Have you ever prayed a prayer of thanksgiving without asking for anything? Have you ever simply said, "Lord, I love You"? He wants to hear your requests, but sometimes you should just give Him your praise. He deserves it. □ J.H.

TO MEMORIZE: *Continue earnestly in prayer, being vigilant in it with thanksgiving.*
Colossians 4:2, NKJV

Gift or Giver

FROM THE BIBLE:
As they continued onward toward Jerusalem, they reached the border between Galilee and Samaria, and as they entered a village there, ten lepers stood at a distance, crying out, "Jesus, sir, have mercy on us!" He looked at them and said, "Go to the Jewish priest and show him that you are healed!" And as they were going, their leprosy disappeared. One of them came back to Jesus, shouting, "Glory to God, I'm healed!" He fell flat on the ground in front of Jesus, face downward in the dust, thanking him for what he had done. This man was a despised Samaritan. Jesus asked, "Didn't I heal ten men? Where are the nine? Does only this foreigner return to give glory to God?" And Jesus said to the man, "Stand up and go; your faith has made you well."
Luke 17:11-19, TLB

Give thanks before asking

23

It Takes Two

FROM THE BIBLE:

*For God did not appoint us to suffer wrath but to receive salvation through our L*ORD *Jesus Christ. He died for us so that, whether we are awake or asleep, we may live together with him. Therefore encourage one another and build each other up, just as in fact you are doing. Now we ask you, brothers, to respect those who work hard among you, who are over you in the L*ORD *and who admonish you. Hold them in the highest regard in love because of their work. Live in peace with each other. And we urge you, brothers, warn those who are idle, encourage the timid, help the weak, be patient with everyone. Make sure that nobody pays back wrong for wrong, but always try to be kind to each other and to everyone else.*

1 Thessalonians 5:9-15, NIV

Don't quarrel

MOTHER SIGHED deeply as she heard raised voices coming from the patio. Soon Brad came bursting into the house. "Mom, Tyler's being mean again! I wish he wouldn't even come over if he's going to act like that."

"I know you boys haven't gotten along very well lately," said Mother, "but why can't you be the one to stop all the quarreling that goes on between you?"

"Why me? Tyler's the one who always starts it." Brad defended himself.

"It takes *two* to quarrel," Mother pointed out. "If you refuse to fight, and if you ignore his teasing, there won't be any quarrel."

"If I don't stand up for my rights, he'll think I'm a sissy," protested Brad.

"Do you know what God thinks about all this?" asked Mother. "He says it's an honor for a man to avoid strife. Read it yourself in Proverbs—chapter twenty, verse three. Anybody can quarrel, you know, but it takes a wise person to stop a quarrel. The same verse says that it's a fool who is quick to quarrel."

"Tell that to Tyler!" demanded Brad.

"I'm not Tyler's mother. I'm yours, so I'm telling you," said Mother. "Do you choose to be an honorable man or a foolish kid?"

Brad took a deep breath. "All right, I'll try."

Several times in the next few days, Tyler tried to pick a quarrel. He rode Brad's bike without permission, he tossed pebbles at him, and he called him a sissy, but Brad ignored him. Whenever Tyler teased him, Brad just walked away. Finally Tyler could stand it no longer. "What's the matter with you?" he asked.

Brad grinned. "Read Proverbs 20:3," he advised. "If you follow its advice, it'll make a man—an honorable man—out of you." Brad walked away, laughing.

HOW ABOUT YOU? Do you often quarrel with your brothers and sisters or with friends? Remember what God says about someone who is quick to quarrel. Even if you think it's really the other person's fault, avoid arguing and fighting. It takes two to quarrel, so don't be one of the two. □ B.W.

TO MEMORIZE: *It is honorable for a man to stop striving, since any fool can start a quarrel.*
Proverbs 20:3, NKJV

STEPHANIE CLAPPED a hand over her mouth. As Mother took out the coffeepot, she looked at her daughter. "See that you don't use that word again," she said sternly.

"I'm sorry, Mom," apologized Stephanie. "I didn't mean to say it, but I hear it so often at school." She watched as Mother put a white paper into the coffeepot. "What's that thing for?"

"This is a filter," said Mother. "It lets the water through but keeps the coffee grounds from going into the coffee. I realize that you can't always help hearing bad words, but you need to learn to 'filter' all the things you hear and see and think. When we see someone do something wrong, we don't have to do it, too. Allow only the good things to settle down and stay with you. You'll need God's help, but you can do it."

"Okay, Mom," agreed Stephanie. "I'll try." She showed her mother a listing in the TV section of the paper. "Can I watch this program tonight?"

Mother read the description and shook her head. "I'm quite sure this isn't the type of program you should see," she said. "I'm sure the language and morals will be very ungodly."

"Oh, it'll be all right if I watch it, Mom," teased Stephanie. "I'll 'filter' out all the bad stuff."

Mother shook her head. "Would it be okay to put garbage in the coffeepot and expect the filter to make it fit to drink?"

"Yuck," exclaimed Stephanie. "I really did know that I shouldn't watch that program, but your illustration makes it more clear. We shouldn't dump 'garbage' in our minds on purpose. But when we can't help what we see and hear, that's when we should use our filters."

HOW ABOUT YOU? Do you find yourself automatically saying or doing something you know is wrong? The best policy is to avoid being where you will hear or see bad things. If that's impossible, ask the Lord to help you filter out the bad influences and to keep only the thoughts and ideas that are good and pleasing to Him. Then deliberately think about other things—wholesome things. □ H.M.

TO MEMORIZE: *Whatever is true, whatever is noble, whatever is right, whatever is pure, whatever is lovely, whatever is admirable—if anything is excellent or praiseworthy—think about such things.* Philippians 4:8, NIV

NOVEMBER

24

Christian Filters

FROM THE BIBLE:
And so, dear brothers, I plead with you to give your bodies to God. Let them be a living sacrifice, holy—the kind he can accept. When you think of what he has done for you, is this too much to ask? Don't copy the behavior and customs of this world, but be a new and different person with a fresh newness in all you do and think. Then you will learn from your own experience how his ways will really satisfy you. As God's messenger I give each of you God's warning: Be honest in your estimate of yourselves, measuring your value by how much faith God has given you. Romans 12:1-3, TLB

Keep thoughts pure

25

The Best Team

FROM THE BIBLE:

The sin of this one man, Adam, caused death to be king over all, but all who will take God's gift of forgiveness and acquittal are kings of life because of this one man, Jesus Christ. Yes, Adam's sin brought punishment to all, but Christ's righteousness makes men right with God, so that they can live. Adam caused many to be sinners because he disobeyed God, and Christ caused many to be made acceptable to God because he obeyed. The Ten Commandments were given so that all could see the extent of their failure to obey God's laws. But the more we see our sinfulness, the more we see God's abounding grace forgiving us. Before, sin ruled over all men and brought them to death, but now God's kindness rules instead, giving us right standing with God and resulting in eternal life through Jesus Christ our Lord.

Romans 5:17-21, TLB

Be on Jesus' team

"OUR TEAM WON!" shouted Eric as he dashed into the house. "Look what I got!" He held out a first-prize ribbon. "We had an archery competition at school today, and my team won!"

"And you always say you're no good at archery," said Mother. "How many points did you make?"

"None, but it didn't matter because Chet was on our team," replied Eric. "He's the best shooter in school, and he made enough points for all of us."

"So he really did the winning, but the whole team shared the victory, right?" asked Mother. "Well, I'm glad you had a good time today."

That evening Eric and his parents attended a special service at their church. "I know just what the preacher meant tonight when he talked about Christians being righteous in God's sight," remarked Eric on the way home. "After we accept Jesus, God sees His righteousness instead of our sin. I think we could say we're on Jesus' team."

"That's right," agreed Dad, "and just like Chet's points counted for all those on his team, the holiness of Jesus counts for everybody on His team. All Christians share in Jesus' victory over sin."

"And the prize we get is wonderful," added Mother. "We become children of God and heirs of all the riches of God."

Eric grinned. "That's really better than a blue ribbon."

HOW ABOUT YOU? Are you on Jesus' team? There's no way you can "win points" on your own. Jesus has already won the victory, and He invites you to share in it. Will you accept Him today? Then you'll be on the very best team! □ H.M.

TO MEMORIZE: *But thanks be to God! He gives us the victory through our Lord Jesus Christ.*
1 Corinthians 15:57, NIV

MATT WAS QUIET as he and his father raked the lawn one Saturday. "Dad," he said finally as he leaned on his rake, "I sometimes wonder if I'm really a Christian." Dad looked surprised. "Lately I . . . well, sometimes I have thoughts—bad thoughts—that I know a real Christian shouldn't have," added Matt, looking uncomfortable.

Dad was quiet for a moment. Then, motioning Matt to follow, he led the way to a cluster of small trees and moved back a branch to reveal a bird's nest. "I found this when I was pruning some branches," said Dad. "Do you notice anything strange about those eggs?"

"One is bigger than the others."

"That's because it wasn't laid by the bird who built this nest," explained Dad. "It was laid by a cowbird."

"A cowbird?" asked Matt. "Why would she lay her egg in another bird's nest?"

"So the other bird would think it was her own and care for the chick when it hatches," Dad replied. "The trouble is, the cowbird baby is usually bigger and stronger than the other baby birds and often takes their food or even pushes them out of the nest."

"What a mean trick!" exclaimed Matt. "Too bad the other bird can't tell that the big egg isn't her own. Then she could quick push it out before it hatches."

"That's right," Dad agreed. Then he added, "Satan is like that cowbird. He likes to put things into our minds that don't belong to us. We need to trust God to help us think and do the right things. We need to reject Satan's thoughts and push them out."

Matt nodded. "I'll watch out for thoughts like that. I'll ask God to help me push them out of my mind!"

HOW ABOUT YOU? Do you sometimes have thoughts that make you doubt God, or that make you feel like doing something you shouldn't? Don't dwell on these thoughts. Reject them in Jesus' name. This is easier to do when you read the Bible regularly and cut out bad influences—dirty TV shows or magazines, and friends who use foul language. Replace bad thoughts with good ones! □ S.K.

TO MEMORIZE: *Do not let the sun go down while you are still angry, and do not give the devil a foothold.* Ephesians 4:26-27, NIV

26

Bad Eggs

FROM THE BIBLE:
Always be full of joy in the Lord; I say it again, rejoice! Let everyone see that you are unselfish and considerate in all you do. Remember that the Lord is coming soon. Don't worry about anything; instead, pray about everything; tell God your needs and don't forget to thank him for his answers. If you do this you will experience God's peace, which is far more wonderful than the human mind can understand. His peace will keep your thoughts and your hearts quiet and at rest as you trust in Christ Jesus. And now, brothers, as I close this letter let me say this one more thing: Fix your thoughts on what is true and good and right. Think about things that are pure and lovely, and dwell on the fine, good things in others. Think about all you can praise God for and be glad about. Keep putting into practice all you learned from me and saw me doing, and the God of peace will be with you.
Philippians 4:4-9, TLB

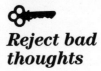

Reject bad thoughts

27

Wrong Impression

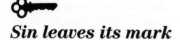

Sin leaves its mark

KEN AND HIS DAD went into the den to watch a football game. "Hmmm, that's funny," said Dad after turning on the set. "I know this is an old TV, but the picture's never been this bad before." After examining the screen a few minutes, he took a small booklet from a drawer and looked through it. "I thought so!" he said a moment later. "You've been playing video games a lot lately, haven't you?" Ken nodded. "According to this, if a video game is played for too long on a TV, it may begin to leave permanent marks on the screen," said Dad. Then he looked at Ken seriously and added, "Speaking of pictures, there's something I've been meaning to talk to you about."

"What's that?" asked Ken.

"Your mother told me she found a calendar in your room last week," replied Dad. "She said it had pictures that were definitely not honoring the Lord. Did you throw it out?" Ken nodded. "Good," said Dad, "but did it leave any permanent marks on your mind?"

Ken looked startled. "What do you mean?"

"Well," said Dad, "the overuse of that video game left an 'impression' that interferes with our ability to watch TV. The pictures you've been looking at might have left an impression on your life, interfering with your ability to live for the Lord."

Ken looked at the floor. "I do still think about them sometimes," he admitted, "especially when I look at a girl. I try not to, but I just can't help it."

Dad turned off the old TV. "It's important to be careful of what you do and hear and see," he said. "Let's talk about some things you can do to erase the impression that was made. After all, we can always get another TV, but you'll never get another chance to live your life for God."

HOW ABOUT YOU? Have you seen or heard something bad that made a lasting impression on you? Confess to God what has happened, admitting your fault. Spend time often in Bible reading and prayer. Avoid anything that makes you want to sin. Fill your life with books, friends, and programs that leave a good impression, not a bad one. □ S.K.

TO MEMORIZE: *Then, when desire has conceived, it gives birth to sin; and sin, when it is full-grown, brings forth death.* James 1:15, NKJV

I'D LIKE to do that, thought Melissa when Miss Baker asked for a volunteer to memorize Psalm 100 and recite it at the Thanksgiving program. *But if I made a mistake in front of all those people, I'd just die.* Some of the other girls in Melissa's Sunday school class expressed the same fear, and no one volunteered.

A little later Miss Baker told the Bible story of Peter walking on the water. She was such a good storyteller that Melissa could almost feel the water beneath her feet. The entire class seemed to relax when Peter and Jesus were finally in the boat with the other disciples, and the sea was calm. "Who in this story made the biggest mistake?" asked Miss Baker.

"Peter," was Dawn's quick reply.

"Why do you think it was Peter?" Miss Baker asked.

"I think it was because he was afraid," suggested Lucy.

"And he didn't trust Jesus," added Melissa.

Miss Baker shook her head. "Actually, Peter was the only one who *did* trust Jesus. He got out of the boat while the others sat and watched. The ones who made the biggest mistake were the eleven disciples who didn't have faith to do it. We're a lot like them. One of the worst mistakes we make is to allow fear to keep us from trying."

Melissa quickly raised her hand. "Miss Baker, I'll memorize Psalm 100 for the program," she volunteered.

Miss Baker smiled. "Thank you, Melissa."

At the Thanksgiving program two weeks later, Melissa trembled as she stood before the audience. Then she remembered Peter. *Lord Jesus, help me,* she prayed silently as she began to recite. Twice she forgot a word, and Miss Baker had to prompt her. But when she finished, Miss Baker gave her a big smile. Suddenly it was not so important that she had made a couple of mistakes. The important thing was that she had not let fear keep her from trying.

HOW ABOUT YOU? Is there something you want to do for the Lord Jesus, but you're afraid to try? Remember Peter. He tried, and when he began to sink, Jesus was there to lift him up. Trying and failing isn't a mistake, but it's a big mistake to fail to try. □ B.W.

TO MEMORIZE: *Though I have fallen, I will rise. Though I sit in darkness, the LORD will be my light.* Micah 7:8, NIV

NOVEMBER

28

A Big Mistake

FROM THE BIBLE:
Night fell, and out on the lake the disciples were in trouble. For the wind had risen and they were fighting heavy seas. About four o'clock in the morning Jesus came to them, walking on the water! They screamed in terror, for they thought he was a ghost. But Jesus immediately spoke to them, reassuring them. "Don't be afraid!" he said. Then Peter called to him: "Sir, if it is really you, tell me to come over to you, walking on the water." "All right," the Lord said, "come along!" So Peter went over the side of the boat and walked on the water toward Jesus. But when he looked around at the high waves, he was terrified and began to sink. "Save me, Lord!" he shouted. Instantly Jesus reached out his hand and rescued him. "O man of little faith," Jesus said. "Why did you doubt me?" And when they had climbed back into the boat, the wind stopped. The others sat there, awestruck. "You really are the Son of God!" they exclaimed.
Matthew 14:24-33, TLB

Dare to try

29

Important Work

FROM THE BIBLE:
Since you have been chosen by God who has given you this new kind of life, and because of his deep love and concern for you, you should practice tender-hearted mercy and kindness to others. Don't worry about making a good impression on them but be ready to suffer quietly and patiently. Be gentle and ready to forgive; never hold grudges. Remember, the Lord forgave you, so you must forgive others. Most of all, let love guide your life, for then the whole church will stay together in perfect harmony. And always be thankful. Remember what Christ taught and let his words enrich your lives and make you wise; teach them to each other and sing them out in psalms and hymns and spiritual songs, singing to the Lord with thankful hearts. And whatever you do or say, let it be as a representative of the Lord Jesus, and come with him into the presence of God the Father to give him your thanks.
Colossians 3:12-17, TLB

Express thankfulness

"MOM, MAY I GO to the park and play ball?" Andy asked.

"Are your thank-you notes finished?" asked Mom.

"I'll do them later," Andy said. He picked up the baseball glove his grandparents had sent for his birthday. Each of his three aunts had sent money, and he had spent some of it on a St. Louis Cardinal shirt.

"It's been a week since your birthday," Mom reminded him. "Don't wait too long."

"I won't," Andy assured her. "I promise!"

It was a hot day, perfect for ball. Andy's friends were waiting for him at the park. "Andy! Play shortstop," Michael yelled. Andy quickly got into position.

After playing about an hour, the boys were hot and tired. "Tell you what," said Andy, "let's go to the drugstore, and I'll buy you all a can of pop with the birthday money I still have left."

"Great!" they agreed.

The cooler air in the store felt good after the hot sun, and each boy chose a can of pop from the case. As Andy went to pay for them, a fire engine went racing down the street, its siren blaring. "Let's go see the fire," called one of the boys, and they all ran out the door.

"Wait!" called Andy, but no one paid attention to him. Andy paid for the pop, and then he walked home and went straight to his room.

His mother found him there a little later. "You're home? And writing thank-you notes?" She was surprised.

Andy explained how his friends had raced after the fire engine without waiting for him. "They didn't even thank me for the pop I bought them," he said. "It made me realize how important that is."

"You're right, Andy," agreed Mom. "We should have an attitude of thankfulness for all the Lord has done for us and also for what others do for us. And we should also express it."

HOW ABOUT YOU? Do you take time to let others know you appreciate what they've done for you? People often forget to be thankful and to show appreciation. Thankfulness should be a characteristic of a Christian. Let your thankfulness be a testimony to others. □ L.W.

TO MEMORIZE: *In everything give thanks; for this is the will of God in Christ Jesus for you.*
1 Thessalonians 5:18, NKJV

"**M**OM, HOW DO WE know that we didn't just evolve?" Timmy asked one day. "My science teacher believes that people evolved from monkeys. Sometimes he can make it sound so logical."

"Do be careful about believing everything you hear, Timmy," Mother warned. "Satan likes to make the wrong seem right sometimes, just to get us confused."

Timmy rested his chin in his hands. "Well, I know the Bible says God created everything. I've known that ever since I can remember. It's just that there are so many similarities between monkeys and humans.

"I can tell you have really been thinking," said Mother, handing Timmy some cookies and a glass of milk. "There are many people who are convinced that we evolved from other forms of life. Do you remember the time you took your hamster to school when it was going to have babies? Did anyone think they might come in one morning and find baby kittens in the cage instead of baby hamsters?"

"Of course not!" Timmy looked puzzled. "Mother hamsters always have baby hamsters."

"Aren't there quite a few similarities, though, between hamsters and kittens?" Mother asked. "Do you think they might have evolved from each other?" Timmy was beginning to see that what his science teacher was teaching might not be so convincing if looked at from a different angle.

Mother continued, "I like to think of the similarities we see in nature as a reminder of God's orderly fashion of creating the world. The Bible says God created everything to reproduce 'after his kind.' In other words, monkeys will always be monkeys, and people will always be people. God created it that way."

"Thanks for the talk, Mom," Timmy said gratefully. "I do believe that the Bible is true. I guess I just needed to be reminded of that."

HOW ABOUT YOU? Have you run into teachers at school who make evolution sound convincing? It's easy to get confused by the clever arguments of those who do not believe the truth of God's Word. The Bible tells us that nothing was ever made, except the things that God made. God made people to be people! □ D.R.

TO MEMORIZE: *All things were made through Him, and without Him nothing was made that was made.* John 1:3, NKJV

Never a Monkey

FROM THE BIBLE:
And God said, "Let the water teem with living creatures, and let birds fly above the earth across the expanse of the sky." And God saw that it was good. And there was evening, and there was morning—the fifth day. And God said, "Let the land produce living creatures according to their kinds: livestock, creatures that move along the ground, and wild animals, each according to its kind." And it was so. God made the wild animals. . . . And God saw that it was good. Then God said, "Let us make man in our image, in our likeness." So God created man in his own image, in the image of God he created him; male and female he created them.
Genesis 1:20-27, NIV

Christ himself is the Creator who made everything in heaven and earth, the things we can see and the things we can't; the spirit world with its kings and kingdoms, its rulers and authorities; all were made by Christ for his own use and glory.
Colossians 1:16, TLB

God created you

1

Hot Coals and Bare Feet

FROM THE BIBLE:

When the sentence for a crime is not quickly carried out, the hearts of the people are filled with schemes to do wrong. Although a wicked man commits a hundred crimes and still lives a long time, I know that it will go better with God-fearing men, who are reverent before God. Yet because the wicked do not fear God, it will not go well with them, and their days will not lengthen like a shadow. . . . Be happy, young man, while you are young, and let your heart give you joy in the days of your youth. Follow the ways of your heart and whatever your eyes see, but know that for all these things God will bring you to judgment. . . . Remember your Creator in the days of your youth, before the days of trouble come and the years approach when you will say, "I find no pleasure in them."

Ecclesiastes 8:11-13; 11:9; 12:1, NIV

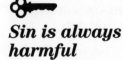

Sin is always harmful

"**H**I, MOM," said Tiffany as she came in the door.

"Hi," greeted Mom. "What did you do at Kay's?"

Tiffany hesitated. "Oh, nothing much."

Mom's brows creased. "You're hedging, Tiffany."

"Well, . . . Kay wanted to watch a movie on TV that had a lot of violence and swearing," confessed Tiffany. "I didn't really want to, but I was her guest. But don't worry, Mom. I don't let things like that affect me."

"Fooling around with sinful things is like playing with fire," replied Mother. "I was just thinking of my cousin, Annabel.

"I once went with Annabel and her folks on an outing in the woods. Her father built a bonfire. When the flames died down, her father threw water over the coals. They turned gray, and the fire seemed to be gone.

"Annabel and I played a game of tag. With her bare feet, Annabel ran right over those coals, not even noticing them, because they looked as gray as the sand. Oh, how she screamed! Inside, the coals were still very hot, and Annabel burned both her feet very badly."

"Oh, how awful!" exclaimed Tiffany.

"Yes," said Mom. "In Proverbs it says, 'Can one go upon hot coals, and his feet not be burned?' "

"Oh," said Tiffany, "that's what happened to Annabel."

"Yes. But God isn't warning here about real fire," said Mother. "He's talking about sinful things."

"Like bad TV and music?" asked Tiffany. "I didn't think a little would hurt."

Mom nodded. "Yes. Like the gray coals that looked harmless, sinful things often seem innocent. But sin always harms us."

"I like Kay," said Tiffany, "but from now on our friendship will be based on Christian principles, or we'll not be friends. I don't want to step on any hot coals."

HOW ABOUT YOU? Have you felt that a few worldly things wouldn't harm you? How much fire must you touch before you're burned? Treat every sin as though it's a red-hot coal of fire. □ M.R.P.

TO MEMORIZE: *Can a man scoop fire into his lap without his clothes being burned? Can a man walk on hot coals without his feet being scorched?* Proverbs 6:27-28, NIV

DANNY HARPER dragged his feet as he approached the small white house where Mr. Grant lived. He wouldn't be visiting the cross-looking old man if he hadn't been given that job as a "Christian work assignment" for his youth group. "Uh, I'm Danny Harper from church. I came to visit," he managed to say when Mr. Grant came to the door.

Mr. Grant swung the door open and invited Danny in. Soon the two were munching on cookies and drinking milk out of mugs. Mr. Grant started to talk about his past, and Danny learned that the old man had helped start the church they now attended. "That was back in the old days, when I was just saved," said Mr. Grant. "How well I remember going door to door, inviting people to come to our new church. My, how much energy and enthusiasm I had then! Oh, to be young again! That's when a person can really serve the Lord."

Danny laughed. "I never thought of it that way," he said. "I guess I figure that a kid like me can't do very much for Jesus. I keep thinking that when I'm older, then I'll really start working for the Lord."

Mr. Grant shook his finger in Danny's face. "Don't think that way, Son," he said. "Young people can do much for the Lord. They're so fresh and excited about life! Already you've done me a service by coming here today. You've made me realize that I ought to start serving God again like I used to. But I'll have to work pretty hard to keep up with a young whippersnapper like you!"

"Thanks, Mr. Grant!" said Danny. "You've helped me, too. Next time I won't be so afraid to visit someone just because he's got a few gray hairs!"

HOW ABOUT YOU? When was the last time you made friends with someone much older than yourself? You may feel that older people look down on you because of our youth. But actually you can do much for them by visiting, by helping with shopping or yard work, and by being enthusiastic about God and your church. You need the friendship of older Christians—and they need you! □ S.K.

TO MEMORIZE: *Let no one despise your youth, but be an example to the believers in word, in conduct, in love, in spirit, in faith, in purity.*
1 Timothy 4:12, NKJV

A Few Gray Hairs

FROM THE BIBLE:
But as for you, speak up for the right living that goes along with true Christianity. Teach the older men to be serious and unruffled; they must be sensible, knowing and believing the truth and doing everything with love and patience. Teach the older women to be quiet and respectful in everything they do. They must not go around speaking evil of others and must not be heavy drinkers, but they should be teachers of goodness. These older women must train the younger women to live quietly, to love their husbands and their children, and to be sensible and clean minded, spending their time in their own homes, being kind and obedient to their husbands, so that the Christian faith can't be spoken against by those who know them. In the same way, urge the young men to behave carefully, taking life seriously. And here you yourself must be an example to them of good deeds of every kind. Let everything you do reflect your love of the truth and the fact that you are in dead earnest about it.
Titus 2:1-7, TLB

Use the gift of youth

3

Worms of Sin

FROM THE BIBLE:

If we say that we have fellowship with Him, and walk in darkness, we lie and do not practice the truth. But if we walk in the light as He is in the light, we have fellowship with one another, and the blood of Jesus Christ His Son cleanses us from all sin. If we say that we have no sin, we deceive ourselves, and the truth is not in us. If we confess our sins, He is faithful and just to forgive us our sins and to cleanse us from all unrighteousness. If we say that we have not sinned, we make Him a liar, and His word is not in us.

1 John 1:6-10, NKJV

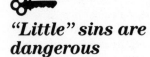

"Little" sins are dangerous

"**B**RRR!" CHATTERED SALLY as she slammed the front door and kicked off her boots. "It's freezing out there, Mom! Isn't there a warmer cap I can wear when I go out?"

"There should be one in this closet. All the winter things are here," Mother replied, opening the closet door. She rummaged around and pulled out some knitted hats, mittens, and scarves. She frowned when she saw that several contained large holes.

"Oh, no!" groaned Mother. "Moths got into them."

"Moths?" asked Sally.

Mother nodded. "Actually, it's not adult moths that eat cloth, but baby moths. They look like small worms. Each one can eat enough to permanently damage an article of clothing."

Sally made a face. "Who would have thought such little things could cause all this trouble?"

Mother glanced at her. "There's an important principle here," she said. "Sometimes we're tempted to think that the 'little' sinful things we do aren't so bad. We tell a 'little' lie or cheat just 'a little.' We don't hit anybody or knock anyone over, but we're a 'little bit' mean to them. We keep back just 'a little' of the money we know we should give to God. We forget that in God's sight, sin is sin. And we forget that just as each moth lays many, many eggs, one 'little' sin leads to other sins and causes much suffering and sorrow." She paused, then added, "I know the idea of worms eating your mittens sounds 'gross' to you. Remember that sin is gross, too!"

Sally nodded thoughtfully as she looked at the holes in a pair of mittens. "Maybe I should wear these to help me remember that lesson."

HOW ABOUT YOU? Do you sometimes feel that "little" sins won't really hurt anything? Sin always brings evil consequences. A "little sin" may make it easier for you to sin again in the future. It may encourage others to do wrong things. Or it may lead to hurt feelings and disappointment when others find out about it. Don't let sin "eat away" at your life. Confess your sin, and don't repeat it. □ S.K.

TO MEMORIZE: *If we say that we have no sin, we deceive ourselves, and the truth is not in us.*
1 John 1:8, NKJV

"GOD SURE HAS ANSWERED a lot of prayers for us lately, hasn't He?" Mark asked his big sister, Mary.

"He sure has," Mary agreed. "He healed Grandma, gave Daddy a job, and even sent us some new friends!"

"I guess God will give us anything we want. All we have to do is ask Him," five-year-old Mark reasoned. "What do you want, Mary?"

"I want a piano," Mary answered dreamily. "But Mother said I'd have to wait until I'm older. What do you want?"

"I want a new bicycle," exclaimed Mark. "Daddy said I'd have to wait until Christmas, but I want one now. Hey, let's ask God for what we want."

After Mother had tucked the children into bed that night, she returned to the living room, a frown on her face. "In their prayers tonight Mary asked God to send a piano right away, and Mark asked for a bike."

Dad grinned. "I guess they're taking their requests over our heads."

After a week of watching and waiting, Mark and Mary went to their mother. "I thought God always answered our prayers," Mary began.

"He does, Mary." Mother knew what was coming. "Did you ask for something you haven't received?"

Both children nodded. "We asked for a bicycle and a piano, but I guess God didn't hear us. Maybe we should pray louder," Mark said.

"I'm sure God heard you," replied Mother, "but I don't think you're hearing His answer. He's telling you the same thing Daddy and I told you. He's telling you to wait."

Mary frowned. "But we don't want to wait."

"Your daddy and I know that you need to wait, and God agrees with us," Mother explained.

Mary patted Mark's shoulder. "Well, Mark, we tried. Now I guess we'll just have to wait."

HOW ABOUT YOU? Are you asking God for something your parents have said you cannot have or will have to wait for? Perhaps what you want may not be good for you right now. When you pray, listen for God's answer. Sometimes He says, "Yes." Sometimes He says, "No." And sometimes He tells you, "Wait." God always answers your prayers. Do you always hear His answer?" □ B.W.

TO MEMORIZE: *And if we know that He hears us, whatever we ask, we know that we have the petitions that we have asked of Him.* 1 John 5:15, NKJV

God's Answer

FROM THE BIBLE:
Now this is the confidence that we have in Him, that if we ask anything according to His will, He hears us. And if we know that He hears us, whatever we ask, we know that we have the petitions that we have asked of Him.
1 John 5:14-15, NKJV

What is causing the quarrels and fights among you? Isn't it because there is a whole army of evil desires within you? You want what you don't have, so you kill to get it. You long for what others have, and can't afford it, so you start a fight to take it away from them. And yet the reason you don't have what you want is that you don't ask God for it. And even when you do ask you don't get it because your whole aim is wrong — you want only what will give you pleasure.
James 4:1-3, TLB

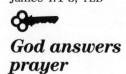

God answers prayer

DECEMBER

5

Snow Day

FROM THE BIBLE:
And so, dear brothers, I plead with you to give your bodies to God. Let them be a living sacrifice, holy—the kind he can accept. When you think of what he has done for you, is this too much to ask? Just as there are many parts to our bodies, so it is with Christ's body. We are all parts of it, and it takes every one of us to make it complete, for we each have different work to do. So we belong to each other, and each needs all the others. God has given each of us the ability to do certain things well. Don't just pretend that you love others: really love them. Hate what is wrong. Stand on the side of the good. Love each other with brotherly affection and take delight in honoring each other.
Romans 12:1, 4-6, 9-10, TLB

Don't waste a day

JANIE WEST was eating breakfast when the announcement came on the radio. "The following school closings have been reported due to the freezing temperatures and the icy condition of the roads: Springfield Public Schools . . . "

That was all Janie had to hear to get upset! "Why today?" she groaned. "I planned to go home with Karen after school. Now I won't be able to visit her. Besides, what's there to do at home? It's too cold to go outside, and it isn't any fun spending the day alone!"

Mother looked at Janie's scowling face. "That's not a very good attitude," her mother told her. "The Lord gave you this day." Janie knew that, but it didn't make her feel any better. Mother continued, "Since you can't think of anything you want to do today, why don't you dedicate the day to helping others?"

"How can I do that? I can't even go out of the house."

"You could bake cookies for Aunt Barb," suggested Mother. "She's not able to do much for herself because of her broken hip."

"Well, I guess I could do that," said Janie with a smile.

"And you could write a letter to Christy Blaine," added Mother. "The two of you had a lot of fun when her family was home on furlough last year. Missionaries enjoy receiving mail from home. And you could write to your grandma, too. She loves to get letters from her only granddaughter."

Janie thought about her mom's ideas. Maybe it could be a fun day! It was a day God had given. She would dedicate it to sharing His love with others.

HOW ABOUT YOU? What do you do when you have a free day? Do you waste it watching TV or fighting with your brother or sister? The next time you have a long day in front of you, see how many things you can do to share the Lord's love with others. You can start making a list now, so you will be prepared. □ L.W.

TO MEMORIZE: *Let us not love with words or tongue but with actions and in truth.* 1 John 3:18, NIV

"WHAT'S ON your mind, Johnny?" his mother asked. "You look so serious!"

Johnny sighed. "My Sunday school teacher says God is a trinity," he answered. "I don't get it."

"Yes," said Mother, "it is hard to understand."

"Mrs. Carroll said there's God the Father, God the Son, and God the Holy Spirit, and they're all one person," said Johnny. "How could that be true?"

"It seems impossible," agreed Mother, "but the Bible teaches that truth in many places." The ringing of the phone interrupted her reply. "That was your father," she said as she hung up. "He wants me to get his suit from the cleaners before—oh, dear! There's the phone again. Hello? . . . Oh, hi, Mom . . . Sure, I'll take you . . . Three-thirty? Okay, I'll be there by three. Good-bye."

Johnny grinned at his mother. "Grandma wants you, too, doesn't she?"

Mother nodded. "Yes, she needs to go to the doctor. I have to stop at Aunt Cindy's, too. I promised to take the baby for her this afternoon."

"Wow! What do people think you are?" asked Johnny. "Triplets?"

Mother laughed. "Sometimes it seems that way, but I don't mind. They all have a right to ask things of me. I'm Dad's wife, so he asks me to do things for him. I'm Mom's daughter, so she has a right to ask me to help her. And as Aunt Cindy's sister, she just asks me to be sisterly."

Johnny thought a while. "A sister, a daughter, and a wife—yet you're only one person. Maybe that's a little like God being more than one person?"

"Maybe a little, Johnny, though there's nothing you can really compare with the Trinity," answered Mother. "There are some things we believe because the Bible says so, not because we fully understand them. That's faith."

"Okay, Mom," agreed Johnny, "but this still helps me understand just a little."

HOW ABOUT YOU? Do you doubt what the Bible teaches because it "doesn't seem possible"? The Bible is the Word of God, and what it says is true. You think with a human mind, but God is far greater than that. Even if you can't understand something, you can believe it if God said it. □ A.L.

TO MEMORIZE: *All Scripture is given by inspiration of God, and is profitable for doctrine, for reproof, for correction, for instruction in righteousness.*
2 Timothy 3:16, NKJV

Not Impossible

FROM THE BIBLE:

"For my thoughts are not your thoughts, neither are your ways my ways," declares the LORD. "As the heavens are higher than the earth, so are my ways higher than your ways and my thoughts than your thoughts. As the rain and the snow come down from heaven, and do not return to it without watering the earth and making it bud and flourish, so that it yields seed for the sower and bread for the eater, so is my word that goes out from my mouth: It will not return to me empty, but will accomplish what I desire and achieve the purpose for which I sent it."
Isaiah 55:8-11, NIV

Believe all God says

7

The Wrong Friends

FROM THE BIBLE:

Don't be teamed with those who do not love the Lord, for what do the people of God have in common with the people of sin? How can light live with darkness? And what harmony can there be between Christ and the devil? How can a Christian be a partner with one who doesn't believe? And what union can there be between God's temple and idols? For you are God's temple, the home of the living God, and God has said of you, "I will live in them and walk among them, and I will be their God and they shall be my people." That is why the Lord has said, "Leave them; separate yourselves from them; don't touch their filthy things, and I will welcome you."

2 Corinthians 6:14-17, TLB

Choose Christian friends

ALAN'S LITTLE SISTER reached up. "Hold my hand, Alan," she said.

"I don't need to hold your hand," he answered. "You're not a baby, Melinda!"

"But Mama holds my hand when—oh! I 'most falled, Alan," Melinda exclaimed as she tripped over a crack in the sidewalk.

"If you'd look where you're going, you wouldn't trip!" Alan grabbed her hand. "Now hurry up!" Melinda chattered happily, but her big brother wasn't listening. He was still annoyed because Mother had insisted that he take Melinda to play in the park. He'd much rather be at the Get-N-Go, playing video games. But Mother didn't like him hanging around there, and she didn't like the boys he hung around with, either. Surely he was old enough to choose his friends! Steve and Klynt weren't so bad. Just because they had had a couple of brushes with the law didn't mean they should be treated like they had chicken pox!

When Alan and Melinda returned home, they saw Mother in the yard. Melinda dashed ahead, tripped on the water hose, and fell. "She never looks where she's going," Alan said in disgust.

Mother picked up the little girl. "She's not the only one," she said. "You need to open your eyes, too, and look where you're headed, Son. I just learned that Steve and Klynt were caught shoplifting this afternoon. I'm glad you weren't with them. But if you keep hanging around those two, you are headed for a big fall."

Melinda slipped out of her mother's arms. She reached up. "I'll hold your hand, Alan, so you won't fall."

Mother smiled at her. "I'm afraid you couldn't keep him from falling, but there's Someone who can. Alan had better let God hold his hand." Alan nodded soberly.

HOW ABOUT YOU? Have you looked down the road you're traveling to see what is ahead of you? If you're following the wrong crowd, you're headed for a fall. God says you cannot have real fellowship with unbelievers. In other words, they should not be your closest friends. Find someone who loves Jesus as you do to be best friends with, someone who will help you walk close to the Lord.

□ B.W.

TO MEMORIZE: *Move back from the tents of these wicked men! Do not touch anything belonging to them, or you will be swept away because of all their sins.* Numbers 16:26, NIV

"CARL!" CALLED DAD as he hung up the phone. Carl knew by the tone of Dad's voice that there was going to be trouble.

"That was your principal," said Dad with a frown. "He told me you were sent to his office today for goofing off in class and talking disrespectfully to your teacher."

Carl looked uncomfortable. "It wasn't my fault," he protested. "Jack started it. Besides, that class is boring!"

"Maybe it wouldn't be so boring if you studied your lessons more often," Dad replied sternly.

Carl shrugged. "Aw, Dad, if I studied all the time, I wouldn't have any fun!"

Dad was quiet for a moment. Then he said, "Come down to my workroom. I want to show you something."

After rummaging around in a box, Dad pulled out a small, thick piece of wood. "This belonged to Grandpa Williams," he said.

Carl looked at it curiously. "That can't be worth much," he said finally.

"Oh, but it is. It's solid cherry," said Dad. "Remember the hand-carved figure Mom has on the coffee table? Grandpa Williams used to carve those and sell them to collectors. They were made from the same kind of wood as this piece."

Carl whistled. "Wow! I guess that is valuable after all."

"On the other hand," said Dad, "if it were cut up into toothpicks, it would be worth only about fifty cents."

"That's not much," said Carl.

"No," agreed Dad. "The wood must be used properly. And the same thing is true of a human life. Life is a valuable gift from God, but it's important to use it well. Don't be careless with it and waste it. That would be even sadder than turning wood like this into toothpicks."

HOW ABOUT YOU? Do you think the most important thing in life is having fun? Are you careless in your schoolwork or lazy about prayer and Bible reading? Life passes quickly. Don't waste it. Make sure you know Christ as your Savior. Then determine to make use of every opportunity to serve Him. Fill your life with "treasure" instead of "toothpicks." □ S.K.

TO MEMORIZE: *Whatever your hand finds to do, do it with all your might.* Ecclesiastes 9:10, NIV

DECEMBER

8

Toothpicks or Treasure

FROM THE BIBLE:
No wonder the years are long and heavy here beneath your wrath. All our days are filled with sighing. Seventy years are given us! And some may even live to eighty. But even the best of these years are often emptiness and pain; soon they disappear, and we are gone. Who can realize the terrors of your anger? Which of us can fear you as he should? Teach us to number our days and recognize how few they are; help us to spend them as we should. O Jehovah, come and bless us! How long will you delay? Turn away your anger from us. Satisfy us in our earliest youth with your lovingkindness, giving us constant joy to the end of our lives. Give us gladness in proportion to our former misery! Replace the evil years with good. Let us see your miracles again; let our children see glorious things, the kind you used to do, and let the Lord our God favor us and give us success. May he give permanence to all we do.
Psalm 90:9-17, TLB

Use your life carefully

It's Hereditary

FROM THE BIBLE:
Behold what manner of love the Father has bestowed on us, that we should be called children of God! Therefore the world does not know us, because it did not know Him. Beloved, now we are children of God; and it has not yet been revealed what we shall be, but we know that when He is revealed, we shall be like Him, for we shall see Him as He is. And everyone who has this hope in Him purifies himself, just as He is pure.
1 John 3:1-3, NKJV

Reflect God's character

"OH, MOM! Why did I have to get freckles?" Becky complained as she studied her nose in the mirror.

"Be glad you don't have warts," consoled her younger brother, Jon. "Besides, what's wrong with freckles? Mom has freckles, and she's pretty."

"That's different," answered Becky. "She's a mother, and nobody cares if she has freckles."

"I'm not really surprised that you're getting freckles," Mother said. "After all, I've got them, and your grandma and great-grandma had freckles, too. They're one of the hereditary characteristics that I passed on to you."

"What does that mean, Mom?" Jon asked.

"It means that there's no hope for me," Becky moaned.

Mother smiled as she explained. "It means you have freckles because I have freckles. You and Becky have blue eyes because Daddy and I have blue eyes. We have blue eyes because our parents had blue eyes. What you are is a reflection of Daddy and me."

"I think I understand." Jon nodded. "We're a lot like you and Daddy because we were born into your family."

"Right," agreed Mother. "Becky may not appreciate all the characteristics she has inherited, but it's obvious that she's part of our family."

"Freckles and all!" Becky giggled.

"You know, kids," Mother mused, "as Christians, we're part of God's family, and that should be obvious, too. Our actions should show that we belong to God's family, and we should all reflect His character. Each day we should strive to be more and more like Him."

HOW ABOUT YOU? Do you belong to God's family? Then you should reflect His character. There should be less disobedience in your life, less laziness, fewer angry words. There should be more friendliness, more helpfulness, more kind acts. In other words, you should be growing more like Jesus every day. □ B.D.

TO MEMORIZE: *Beloved, now we are children of God; and it has not yet been revealed what we shall be, but we know that when He is revealed, we shall be like Him, for we shall see Him as He is.*
1 John 3:1, NKJV

J ANA PLOPPED down on the couch. "I don't think SueAnn will ever become a Christian. I've witnessed to her lots of times, but it doesn't do any good. She just keeps on going to R-rated movies and watching all those television shows you won't let me watch. I've told her what I think about all that, but she just laughs."

"She'll do those things until she has the Spirit of the Lord to give her power to overcome sin," Mother reasoned.

"But she doesn't want to overcome sin." Jana shook her head. "She enjoys it."

Mother nodded. "That's natural. There are pleasures in sin, but living for God is much better. Have you told Sue Ann how good—"

"Buffy! Come back with that!" Brian's cry rang down the hall. "Mother! Buffy has my crayon!"

The dog ran under the dining room table. "Give it to me, Buffy," ordered Mother. Buffy growled softly.

Mother reached for the crayon as she spoke. This time Buffy growled louder.

Jana laughed. "You two are doing that all wrong!" She took a small piece of cold meat from the refrigerator, then knelt beside the table. "Here, Buffy! Want some meat?" Immediately the puppy dropped the crayon and snatched up the food.

As Mother picked up the crayon, she grinned. "To get the crayon, all we had to do was offer him something better." As Buffy and Brian went romping down the hall, Mother turned to Jana. "Have you offered SueAnn something better than sin, Jana? You've told her all she shouldn't do, but have you told her all the good things she would receive as a Christian?"

Jana looked surprised. "No, I guess not. I just assumed she knew about the blessings of being a Christian. From now on, I'll offer her something better than what she has."

HOW ABOUT YOU? Do you witness by telling people all the things they are doing wrong and what they have to give up? Instead, tell them about the advantages of being a Christian. Make a list of the blessings you receive because you live for Jesus, and use it to help you witness. □ B.W.

TO MEMORIZE: *The blessing of the LORD brings wealth, and he adds no trouble to it.*
Proverbs 10:22, NIV

A Better Offer

FROM THE BIBLE:
Then Peter said to him, "We left everything to follow you. What will we get out of it?" And Jesus replied, "When I, the Messiah, shall sit upon my glorious throne in the Kingdom, you my disciples shall certainly sit on twelve thrones judging the twelve tribes of Israel. And anyone who gives up his home, brothers, sisters, father, mother, wife, children, or property, to follow me, shall receive a hundred times as much in return, and shall have eternal life. But many who are first now will be last then; and some who are last now will be first then."
Matthew 19:27-30, TLB

The Christian life is best

11

Song of the Wild

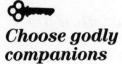

Choose godly companions

SARAH WAS SO excited she could hardly speak. "Look!" she exclaimed. "I caught a bird that can't fly. Can I keep it, Mom? I found this old cage in the garage."

Sarah's mother looked closely at the bird. "It's a sparrow, Sarah. I suppose you can keep it a few days to see if its wing will heal, but it's not a good idea to try to make pets of wild animals or birds."

"I know," Sarah said. "I'll let it go soon. I just want to watch it for a while. Do sparrows sing?"

Mother smiled. "Oh, they cheep and twitter, but they don't have the lovely call of a cardinal or dove."

"Well, I'll put it next to Biddy's cage," Sarah decided. "Biddy has a beautiful song. She'll teach the sparrow to sing."

A few minutes later, she added, "Angie asked me to play at her house for a while, okay?"

Mother frowned. "What do you have planned?"

Sarah shrugged. "She has lots of video games and records. She has her own television in her room, too. We'll find plenty to do."

"I'm sure that's true," said Mother, "but will it be the kind of activity we encourage in our family? Why don't you ask Angie to come over here more often?"

Sarah studied her tennis shoes. "Well, she doesn't like the Bible games I have, and she doesn't like my Christian records. She says our house is boring."

"You may go, but only for a short time," decided Mother. "Spending too much time with Angie may cause you to have less interest in spiritual things, Sarah. Instead, you should help her learn about Jesus."

A few days later, Sarah decided to release the sparrow. "Instead of this bird learning to sing like a canary, Biddy is starting to chirp and tweet like the sparrow!" she told her mother. She looked at the cage thoughtfully. "That's like Angie and me, isn't it?"

HOW ABOUT YOU? Do you think that by doing what unsaved people want you to do it will help them become Christians? Be very careful! Make sure your unsaved friends aren't influencing you. Your deepest friendships should be with Christians who will help you become more like Jesus. □ C.R.

TO MEMORIZE: *For the LORD watches over the way of the righteous, but the way of the wicked will perish.* Psalm 1:6, NIV

"I'LL PICK YOU UP after school and take you to see your grandpa in the hospital," Mother told Andy and Lisa. Andy tried to swallow the lump in his throat. "Is . . . is he doing to die?"

Mother took a deep breath. "I don't know. I only know Grandpa is in God's hands, and God will take care of him. Whatever is best for Grandpa is what we want, isn't it?"

Tears rolled down Andy's cheeks.

"Grandpa has been in a lot of pain lately," Mother reminded him. "And he hasn't been happy since Grandma died last spring. I think Grandpa wants to see Grandma and the Lord Jesus."

"But we need him," Andy protested, "and he doesn't want to leave us."

"Tie my belt, Mother," Lisa requested. As Mother did so, Lisa handed Andy a dollar. "Keep this for me until after school, will you, Andy? I might lose it, and I want to buy Grandpa a card before we go to the hospital."

Andy stuffed the dollar in his pocket. As they ran to catch the bus, Lisa said, "Take good care of my dollar, Andy."

The day crawled by for Andy. Every few minutes he reminded God, "Take good care of my Grandpa, Lord."

After school the children climbed into Mother's car. "Is Grandpa any better?" asked Andy.

Mother shook her head. "No. He's about the same."

"Where's my dollar, Andy?" Lisa asked, as they went in to buy Grandpa's card. Andy pulled it out of his pocket, and Lisa smiled. "Thanks for keeping it for me."

As Lisa paid for her card, Mother turned to Andy. "You know, Son, Grandpa is in God's hands. We can trust God to take care of him just as Lisa trusted you to take care of her money. Grandpa is in safekeeping."

Lisa came up to them and handed Andy a quarter. "Keep this for me, will you, Andy? I might lose it."

HOW ABOUT YOU? Is someone you love sick? Will you trust God to take care of him? Put him in God's hands. It's the safest place in the world to be. □ B.W.

TO MEMORIZE: *Let your face shine on your servant; save me in your unfailing love.* Psalm 31:16, NIV

In Safekeeping

FROM THE BIBLE:

In you, O LORD, I have taken refuge; let me never be put to shame; deliver me in your righteousness. Turn your ear to me, come quickly to my rescue; be my rock of refuge, a strong fortress to save me. Since you are my rock and my fortress, for the sake of your name lead and guide me. . . . But I trust in you, O LORD; I say, "You are my God." My times are in your hands; deliver me from my enemies and from those who pursue me. Let your face shine on your servant; save me in your unfailing love.
Psalm 31:1-3, 14-16, NIV

Trust God

13

It's Catching

FROM THE BIBLE:

Keep away from angry, short-tempered men, lest you learn to be like them and endanger your soul. . . . Don't envy godless men; don't even enjoy their company. For they spend their days plotting violence and cheating.

Proverbs 22:24-25; 24:1-2, TLB

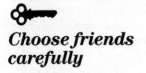

Choose friends carefully

"THE NEW GUY across the street is sharp!" Jason told his mother. "His name is Tim, and he's got a couple of bird dogs and some hamsters."

"I've noticed that Sam Wellman is often there," observed Mother. "Is Tim anything like Sam? I know Sam has often been in trouble at school."

"Oh, Mom," sighed Jason. "He's okay."

As the weeks passed, Tim and Jason spent more and more time together. Mother was concerned. "I'm glad you're friendly with Tim, but your close friends should be Christian friends," she said.

A few weeks later Jason and his family were out of town for a weekend. It was arranged for Tim to keep their dog, Midget, while they were away. When they returned from their trip, Jason brought the dog home. As he came in the door, he stubbed his toe. Mother was shocked when she heard what he said. "Do you think that kind of language is pleasing to the Lord?" she asked.

Jason hopped around on one foot, holding his toe. "I'm sorry. I didn't mean to say it, but it hurt. Tim says it all the time, and I guess I just picked it up."

"Then put it down!" Mother was upset.

That evening, Midget scratched and scratched. Dad looked up. "Has that dog got fleas?"

Jason began combing Midget's hair with his fingers. "She does have fleas! There's lots of them."

"Give her a bath immediately," Mother ordered. "Then sprinkle her with flea powder. She must have gotten those fleas from Tim's dogs."

As Jason got up to take care of the dog, Mother added, "And that, Jason, is why I have been so concerned about your friendship with Tim."

"You were afraid I'd get fleas?" Jason snorted.

"No, not fleas," replied Mother, "but sin is contagious, too. For instance, you can pick up things like bad words without even realizing it—until they slip out."

Jason was quiet for a minute. "I guess that's worse than fleas, huh? Midget and I had better be more choosy about who we spend time with."

HOW ABOUT YOU? Are you associating with the wrong crowd? Be careful. Your friends influence you by their talk and actions whether you realize it or not. Make sure they're the kind of friends whose influence makes you a better person, pleasing to your parents and to God. ☐ B.W.

TO MEMORIZE: *Do not be deceived: "Evil company corrupts good habits".* 1 Corinthians 15:33, NKJV

MEG WATCHED her big sister leave the house. "Why can't I go to the library with Tammy?" she asked. "I'll look at books while she studies."

"Meg," Mother said patiently, "Tammy will be gone a couple of hours. It's almost your bedtime."

"But I want to go with her," Meg argued.

"Of course you do, but you're eight years old. Tammy's in high school. When you're her age, you'll go to the library at night, too." Mother tried to soothe her daughter.

"Tammy has a stereo in her room, and she goes to the mall, and . . . " Meg's words tumbled over each other.

Mother got up from the couch. "Bedtime," she said. "Come on, I'll go up with you."

At the stairway, Mother stopped. "Meg," she said, "when you were a baby, you went up these stairs very carefully on your hands and knees. Later, you held onto my hand very tightly so I could help you. Do you remember that?"

Meg laughed and shook her head. "No, but the little kids at church do that. They're so cute."

"Now you're much bigger," Mother continued, "and you walk up the stairs. Physically, you become able to do more and more. That's the way God intends it to be. Gradually you'll be able to do more and more things. Why, look at all you do now! You stayed overnight with your friend Lisa last week. You ride your bicycle in the street now. You couldn't do those things when you were two, or even four, could you?" Slowly Meg shook her head. "God made us so we don't have to learn everything at once," Mother added. "We have to just take one step at a time. You'll be a much happier person when you learn to let God help you wait for the right time to do all the things Tammy can do."

HOW ABOUT YOU? Do you want to be grown-up right now? Do you think you should be allowed to do everything a big brother or sister is allowed to do? God has a time for everything. He has many things for you to learn right now. Other things are to be saved for later. Take just one step at a time with Him. □ D.K.

TO MEMORIZE: *He has made everything beautiful in its time.* Ecclesiastes 3:11, NIV

14

Just One Step

FROM THE BIBLE:
There is a time for everything, and a season for every activity under heaven: a time to be born and a time to die, a time to plant and a time to uproot, a time to kill and a time to heal, a time to tear down and a time to build, a time to weep and a time to laugh, a time to mourn and a time to dance, a time to scatter stones and a time to gather them, a time to embrace and a time to refrain, a time to search and a time to give up, a time to keep and a time to throw away, a time to tear and a time to mend, a time to be silent and a time to speak, a time to love and a time to hate, a time for war and a time for peace. . . . He has made everything beautiful in its time. He has also set eternity in the hearts of men; yet they cannot fathom what God has done from beginning to end. Ecclesiastes 3:1-8, 11, NIV

Be content to be a kid

DECEMBER

15

Out of Tune

FROM THE BIBLE:

Sprinkle me with the cleansing blood and I shall be clean again. Wash me and I shall be whiter than snow. And after you have punished me, give me back my joy again. Don't keep looking at my sins—erase them from your sight. Create in me a new, clean heart, O God, filled with clean thoughts and right desires. Don't toss me aside, banished forever from your presence. Don't take your Holy Spirit from me. Restore to me again the joy of your salvation, and make me willing to obey you. Then I will teach your ways to other sinners, and they—guilty like me—will repent and return to you.

Psalm 51:7-13, TLB

Follow God's standards

"**A**RE YOU COMING to the Christmas concert at school this afternoon?" asked Katie as she finished her breakfast. "Melanie and I are playing a flute duet, you know."

"I wouldn't miss it," Mother replied. As Katie stood up from the table, Mother gasped. "Where did you get that short skirt?"

Katie shrugged. "Cindy gave it to me. It was too small for her."

"Well, it's also too small for you!" declared Mother. "Please go up and change into something decent."

"Oh, Mother! You're so old-fashioned!" whined Katie as she stomped out of the room. "All the girls wear skirts like this. Why can't I be like everybody else?"

When Katie and Melanie began to play at the concert that afternoon, they realized at once that something was wrong. The notes they played just didn't sound right with the piano accompaniment. Embarrassed, the girls began to make mistakes. They were glad when the song was over and they could sit down.

"It was so humiliating," groaned Katie that evening. "Melanie and I made sure our instruments were in tune with each other, but we didn't tune them with the piano. I don't know how we could have forgotten to do that."

"Katie, this reminds me of what we were talking about this morning," said Mother. "You seemed to feel that going along with fads was okay because 'everyone was doing it.' But can you see that you might be 'in tune' with the standards of the world but 'out of tune' with God's standards?"

"You're right," said Katie with a sigh. "If I'm going to be out of tune with anybody, I guess it had better be with the other kids and not with the Lord."

HOW ABOUT YOU? Are your clothes in style? Do you listen to the same music and watch the same TV programs as everybody else? That's okay *if* they are in keeping with God's standards, too. He expects His children to live according to His rules and principles, not those of the world. Make sure you're "in tune" with Him! □ S.K.

TO MEMORIZE: *Do not be conformed to this world, but be transformed by the renewing of your mind, that you may prove what is that good and acceptable and perfect will of God.* Romans 12:2, NKJV

"**J**ERRY, IT'S TIME for bed," called Mother.

"Aw, Mom, can't I stay up just a little longer?" begged Jerry. "I'm reading my Bible, and I'm having trouble understanding what these verses mean." It was true. Jerry was reading his Bible, but he was also trying to get out of going to bed.

Mother came into the room. "Tell me what verses you're reading, Jerry."

"Well, I'm reading in John 3 right now," said Jerry. "Some of the verses have the words *verily, verily* in them. What does *verily* mean?"

"Remember what Dad told you to do when you don't know the meaning of a word in the Bible?" asked Mother.

Jerry thought for a moment. "Oh, I remember. He said to look it up in the dictionary—that often you don't even need a huge theological textbook, just a plainly written definition."

"That's right. You listened well." Mother smiled and added, "So, why don't you get the dictionary?"

Taking the dictionary out of his desk, Jerry turned to the *V*s. Sure enough the word *verily* was there. "It means 'truly' according to Mr. Webster," Jerry told his mother. "But why does Jesus use it so often?"

"I'd say He wanted the people to believe what He was saying," Mother answered. "He wanted to impress upon them that His words were true, so He would often start a sentence with 'truly, truly' to emphasize that."

"I guess I should look up words more often," Jerry said. "I've read the word *verily* in verses before, but I never took the time to figure out what it meant."

"Well, now that you know what it means," said Mother, "you'll understand this. Verily, verily, it is time for you to go to bed."

HOW ABOUT YOU? Do you sometimes have trouble understanding the words used in the Bible? It only takes a minute to look them up, and it will help you understand what God is saying to you. If you still don't understand, ask your parents, your Sunday school teachers, or your pastor. Learn about the Bible. □ L.W.

TO MEMORIZE: *No one can see the kingdom of God unless he is born again.* John 3:3, NIV

DECEMBER

16

This Is True!

FROM THE BIBLE:

Now there was a man of the Pharisees named Nicodemus, a member of the Jewish ruling council. He came to Jesus at night and said, "Rabbi, we know you are a teacher who has come from God. For no one could perform the miraculous signs you are doing if God were not with him." In reply Jesus declared, "I tell you the truth, no one can see the kingdom of God unless he is born again." "How can a man be born when he is old?" Nicodemus asked. "Surely he cannot enter a second time into his mother's womb to be born!" Jesus answered, "I tell you the truth, no one can enter the kingdom of God unless he is born of water and the Spirit. . . . Just as Moses lifted up the snake in the desert, so the Son of Man must be lifted up, that everyone who believes in him may have eternal life. For God so loved the world that he gave his one and only Son, that whoever believes in him shall not perish but have eternal life. For God did not send his Son into the world to condemn the world, but to save the world through him."
John 3:1-5, 14-17, NIV

Look up Bible words

17

Ask What You Can Do

FROM THE BIBLE:
*Sing to the LORD, all the earth;
proclaim his salvation day after
day. Declare his glory among
the nations, his marvelous
deeds among all peoples. For
great is the LORD and most
worthy of praise; he is to be
feared above all gods. For all the
gods of the nations are idols,
but the LORD made the heavens.
Splendor and majesty are before
him; strength and joy in his
dwelling place. Ascribe to the
LORD, O families of nations,
ascribe to the LORD glory and
strength, ascribe to the LORD
the glory due his name. Bring
an offering and come before
him; worship the LORD in the
splendor of his holiness.*
1 Chronicles 16:23-29, NIV

Be involved at church

CAROLYN WAS TIRED of her church. She couldn't even get excited about Sunday school. She told her mother, "Church bores me! The music seems so dull, and I can't follow Pastor Reese's sermons. I don't get anything out of the worship services. I wish I didn't always have to go!" Mother was very concerned and told Carolyn she would pray with her about it.

At school that week Carolyn was assigned to prepare an oral report on John F. Kennedy, and she found him to be a very interesting person. He was the youngest man ever elected president, and he was shot and killed while still in office.

When Carolyn finished her report, she asked her mom to listen as she practiced it. She ended with a quote from President Kennedy's inaugural address. "He is very famous for this line, 'Ask not what your country can do for you. Ask rather what you can do for your country.'"

Mom remained silent.

"Well, what do you think?" Carolyn asked.

"Oh, I'm sorry," said Mom. "It's good, dear, but that last line started me thinking. Remember what you told me about not being able to get anything out of the church service? Maybe we could apply President Kennedy's quote here. Ask not what your church can do for you; ask what you can do for your church."

"Hmmm, maybe so!" Carolyn responded. She thought a lot about it that week, and she decided to try it.

Within a very short time, Carolyn could hardly wait to get to church. She was singing in the junior choir. She played the piano for her Sunday school department's opening exercises. She took sermon notes to share with Grandma Miller at the nursing home. She also helped in the church nursery. Carolyn had learned a valuable lesson: True worship involves giving of ourselves as well as receiving blessings.

HOW ABOUT YOU? Do you just sit around expecting to receive blessings at church, or do you try to be a blessing to others? In church, as in the other areas, you generally get out of it as much as you put into it. Get involved in your church. True worship involves giving glory to God, giving offerings to God, and giving ourselves to God. □ R.P.

TO MEMORIZE: *Ascribe to the LORD the glory due his name. Bring an offering and come before him; worship the LORD in the splendor of his holiness.*
1 Chronicles 16:29, NIV

M ARYANN CAREFULLY DROPPED batter onto the cookie sheet. When it was filled, she put it in the oven and dropped down in a nearby chair. "There," she said. "The last ones. As soon as they're baked and cooled, I'll pack them in a box and take them to the school sale."

"You won't forget to clean up, will you?" asked Mother, entering the kitchen. "That's part of baking, you know."

Maryann nodded. "I'll do it later," she said, then added hesitantly, "unless you'll do it for me."

Mother shook her head. "No, Honey. I'm on my way to a church meeting. Anyway, you promised to clean up the kitchen if I let you bake those cookies after lunch."

"I didn't know I'd be running out of time," Maryann replied. "Can't we just leave the bowls and stuff and do them all with the supper dishes? I'll help you then." She peeked into the oven to see how the cookies were doing. "I hate the clean-up part," she added softly.

But Mother heard her. "Most of us do," she said, "but it has to be done."

Reluctantly Maryann dropped the messy bowls and spoons into the sink. "Can't I just soak them?" she persisted. "Everything is so sticky right now and . . . "

"Honey," said Mother, as she put her hand on Maryann's arm, "there are many times that I wish I could leave the unpleasant work for someone else to do. But that's not the way things work. I think it's especially important for Christians to be faithful in whatever we do. That means we must cheerfully do a complete job, including the less pleasant parts."

Maryann thought about her mother's words. She was glad Mother was faithful in doing her work and didn't leave it for Maryann! It wouldn't be fair to leave this for Mother, either. Besides, the Lord wouldn't be pleased. With determination Maryann began to clean up the work area.

HOW ABOUT YOU? Do you like to do all the fun things and leave the unpleasant jobs for someone else? When you do that you're only doing half a job. Next time you face an unpleasant task, remember that the Lord expects faithfulness in even the small things. Tackle that job and do it for Him.

□ R.J.

TO MEMORIZE: *Whatever you do, work at it with all your heart, as working for the Lord, not for men.* Colossians 3:23, NIV

DECEMBER

Only Half-Done

FROM THE BIBLE:
Unless you are honest in small matters, you won't be in large ones. If you cheat even a little, you won't be honest with greater responsibilities. And if you are untrustworthy about worldly wealth, who will trust you with the true riches of heaven? And if you are not faithful with other people's money, why should you be entrusted with money of your own?
Luke 17:10-12, TLB

"Half-done" is not done

Play It Again

FROM THE BIBLE:
*Pray along these lines: "Our
Father in heaven, we honor your
holy name. We ask that your
kingdom will come now. May
your will be done here on earth,
just as it is in heaven. Give us
our food again today, as usual,
and forgive us our sins, just as
we have forgiven those who have
sinned against us. Don't bring
us into temptation, but deliver
us from the Evil One. Amen."
Your heavenly Father will
forgive you if you forgive those
who sin against you; but if you
refuse to forgive them, he will
not forgive you.*
Matthew 6:9-15, TLB

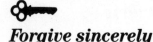

Forgive sincerely

"**W**HO USED my markers?" asked Peter.

"Mom says you're supposed to share," Tina retorted.

"And you're *supposed* to put the caps on tight so they won't dry out," grumbled Peter.

"Sorry," Tina said lightly.

"Well, you don't sound sorry," Peter snorted as he jumped up. Puzzle pieces scattered all over.

"Peter, look what you did!" screamed Melissa, who had been working on the puzzle.

"I didn't mean to. Besides, I was at the table first," Peter argued.

When Mother told all three of them to pick up the scattered puzzle pieces, Tina objected. "I'm just reading," she said. "They made the mess."

"You can all help," said Mother firmly. "And since you children don't seem to be able to talk nicely together, don't talk at all for a while. I'll put a record on, and you just listen and work silently until the entire record is finished."

Soon the words of Christmas carols were filling the air. As the children picked up the puzzle, they were quietly singing along on "Silent Night" until they came to the last line. "Christ, the Savior . . . the Savior . . . the Savior . . . the Savior . . ." sang the record. Peter laughed and went to fix it. "Guess we heard that often enough," he said.

"Yes," agreed Mother. "Like the words in our house."

"Huh? What do you mean?" asked Melissa.

"We say, 'I'm sorry,' 'I didn't mean to,' and 'It's not my fault' automatically, but we don't mean what we say," explained Mother. "We sound like a broken record."

The children were silent for some time. "I was wrong," Peter admitted finally. "I'm really sorry."

"Me, too," added Tina. "To prove it, I'll buy Peter some new markers."

Mother smiled. "Now that's something I'd like to hear played often!" she said.

HOW ABOUT YOU? Are you sincere when you say, "I'm sorry," or do you just mouth the words because you know it's expected of you? Perhaps you sometimes recite "The Lord's Prayer." It says, "Forgive us . . . as we forgive. . . ." Think about that. Then show by your actions that you truly forgive. ☐ J.H.

TO MEMORIZE: *This is how my heavenly Father will treat each of you unless you forgive your brother from your heart.* Matthew 18:35, NIV

CANDY CAME to the Village Bible Church shortly before Christmas. She had just moved to the area, and attending church was a new experience for her. She didn't know many Bible stories, and she couldn't understand the lessons on salvation, either. But she understood her teacher's love for her, and that drew her back each week.

One day Miss Weaver asked Candy to help her with decorations for the class Christmas party. "Could you get me some evergreen branches for the tables, Candy?" Miss Weaver asked. "They don't need to be big. Small twigs will do. I have some red candles to use with them."

Eager to please her teacher, Candy agreed to get the boughs, but she found it wasn't so easy. Some places that sold Christmas trees didn't have any boughs at all, and others would give her boughs only if she bought a tree. What could she do?

Walking home from school one day, Candy saw a pile of boughs at a Christmas tree lot. She had an idea. Instead of asking for free branches, she would buy some. *They* shouldn't cost much, she thought. Candy ran home to get money from her piggy bank, but when she offered it to the owner for the boughs, he said, "They're not for sale." Disappointed, Candy started to walk away. The man called her back quickly. "Honey, they're not for sale. They're free. Help yourself." Candy eagerly accepted all she could carry.

Later, while decorating the tables, Candy told Miss Weaver about her experiences. "That's a good illustration of salvation," Miss Weaver said. "Some people tell us we have to buy our salvation by doing good works. But the Bible says salvation is a gift. We can't earn it or buy it. It's not for sale. We can only receive salvation by accepting Jesus as Savior."

"Now I understand it," Candy said softly. "Will you pray with me, Miss Weaver? I want to accept the gift of salvation right now."

HOW ABOUT YOU? Are you trying to buy your salvation by being good, going to church, or getting baptized? It won't work! Salvation is a gift from God. You can have it only by accepting Jesus as your Savior. ☐ J.H.

TO MEMORIZE: *For by grace you have been saved through faith, and that not of yourselves; it is the gift of God.* Ephesians 2:8, NKJV

20

Not for Sale

FROM THE BIBLE:
When the apostles back in Jerusalem heard that the people of Samaria had accepted God's message, they sent down Peter and John. As soon as they arrived, they began praying for these new Christians to receive the Holy Spirit, for as yet he had not come upon any of them. For they had only been baptized in the name of the Lord Jesus. Then Peter and John laid their hands upon these believers, and they received the Holy Spirit. When Simon saw this—that the Holy Spirit was given when the apostles placed their hands upon people's heads—he offered money to buy this power. "Let me have this power too," he exclaimed, "so that when I lay my hands on people, they will receive the Holy Spirit!" But Peter replied, "Your money perish with you for thinking God's gift can be bought! You can have no part in this, for your heart is not right before God. Turn from this great wickedness and pray. Perhaps God will yet forgive your evil thoughts: for I can see that there is jealousy and sin in your heart."
Acts 8:14-23, TLB

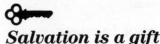

Salvation is a gift

DECEMBER

21

The Older Generation

FROM THE BIBLE:

I cannot count the times when you have faithfully rescued me from danger. I will tell everyone how good you are, and of your constant, daily care. I walk in the strength of the LORD God. I tell everyone that you alone are just and good. O God, you have helped me from my earliest childhood—and I have constantly testified to others of the wonderful things you do. And now that I am old and gray, don't forsake me. Give me time to tell this new generation (and their children too) about all your mighty miracles. Your power and goodness, LORD, reach to the highest heavens. You have done such wonderful things. Where is there another God like you? You have let me sink down deep in desperate problems. But you will bring me back to life again, up from the depths of the earth. You will give me greater honor than before, and turn again and comfort me. I will praise you with music, telling of your faithfulness to all your promises, O Holy One of Israel.
Psalm 71:15-22, TLB

Listen to your elders

"WE'LL MEET HERE at the church Saturday afternoon and go together," Mrs. Kendall announced. "Class dismissed."

As soon as the children were out the door, Marty groaned, "Who wants to go to the nursing home? What have I got in common with those old folks?"

Adam shrugged. "Not much! But we've got to go, or Mrs. Kendall will be disappointed." No one wanted that.

Coming up behind them, Natalie added, "Mrs. Kendall is the best Sunday school teacher we have ever had. But visiting a nursing home is a bum idea!"

Adam shrugged again. "Maybe we won't stay long."

The next Saturday afternoon, eight fifth-graders met at the church. "After we sing and read the Scripture, go around and introduce yourself," Mrs. Kendall instructed.

"What will we say to them?" Natalie asked.

Mrs. Kendall smiled. "You probably won't have to say much. Your main job will be listening."

Two hours later the boys and girls again piled into Mrs. Kendall's van. "That Mr. Wilson is sharp. He used to be the mayor," Marty said. "He offered to help me with my theme on the history of our town."

"Did you know that Mr. Rowland was once the foreman of the Flying W Ranch?" asked Adam. "He told me how the Lord saved him when he was lost in a blizzard."

"And Mrs. Baker is going to teach me how to crochet," Natalie said. "She made a beautiful bedspread to sell for missions. Next time we come, I need to bring . . . " Natalie paused, then continued, "We are going to come again, aren't we, Mrs. Kendall?"

Mrs. Kendall smiled as she started the van. "I'll leave that decision to you. Everyone that wants to come again say, 'aye.' " And a chorus of "ayes" filled the air.

HOW ABOUT YOU? Have you shunned older people because you didn't know how to talk to them? Many senior citizens need someone to listen to them. And you need to hear what they have to say. Plan to spend at least ten minutes today visiting with an elderly person. It will help you both.
□ B.W.

TO MEMORIZE: *One generation will commend your works to another; they will tell of your mighty acts.* Psalm 145:4, NIV

Mrs. KENDALL'S Sunday school class voted unanimously to visit the Greenwood Nursing Home on the fourth Saturday of every month. The next time they went, Natalie brought yarn and a crochet hook, Marty had a pencil and paper so he could take notes from Mr. Wilson on the history of Centerville, and Adam had a picture book of the Old West to share with Mr. Rowland. The others carried fruit, cookies, and books.

After they sang and read Scripture, they visited with the friends they had made the month before. Then their teacher called for their attention. "The activity director, Mrs. Nelson, has asked us to sing for some who are unable to get out of bed," she said. Jay picked up his guitar, and they went from room to room, singing and visiting.

As they prepared to leave later, Mrs. Nelson said, "Thank you so much. You don't know what this has meant to us. Some of these patients never have visitors."

As they piled into the van, Natalie spoke softly. "I learned more than how to chain stitch. I learned how important kindness is."

Mrs. Kendall nodded her agreement. "Compassion is a virtue all Christians should have."

"And I learned to be thankful for my health," Adam said. "Did you see that one man? He couldn't have been over twenty-five. Mrs. Nelson said he was born crippled."

"And I learned how blessed I am to be your Sunday school teacher." Mrs. Kendall smiled as she started the van.

HOW ABOUT YOU? When you see old people whose minds are no longer sharp, or when you see people who are crippled or retarded, do you make fun of them? Or do you have a desire to help them? If you are truly Christ-like, you'll be compassionate. That means you'll sympathize with them and want to help them. Pray right now for someone you know who needs your love and friendship. □ B.W.

TO MEMORIZE: *Live in harmony with one another; be sympathetic, love as brothers, be compassionate and humble.* 1 Peter 3:8, NIV

The Older Generation

(Continued from yesterday)

FROM THE BIBLE:
We know what real love is from Christ's example in dying for us. And so we also ought to lay down our lives for our Christian brothers. But if someone who is supposed to be a Christian has money enough to live well, and sees a brother in need, and won't help him—how can God's love be within him? Little children, let us stop just saying we love people; let us really love them, and show it by our actions.
1 John 3:16-18, TLB

Be compassionate

23

Denny's Party

FROM THE BIBLE:

That night some shepherds were in the fields outside the village, guarding their flocks of sheep. Suddenly an angel appeared among them, and the landscape shone bright with the glory of the Lord. They were badly frightened, but the angel reassured them. "Don't be afraid!" he said. "I bring you the most joyful news ever announced, and it is for everyone! The Savior—yes, the Messiah, the Lord—has been born tonight in Bethlehem! How will you recognize him? You will find a baby wrapped in a blanket, lying in a manger!" Suddenly, the angel was joined by a vast host of others—the armies of heaven—praising God: "Glory to God in the highest heaven," they sang, "and peace on earth for all those pleasing him." When this great army of angels had returned again to heaven, the shepherds said to each other, "Come on! Let's go to Bethlehem! Let's see this wonderful thing that has happened, which the Lord has told us about."

Luke 2:8-15, TLB

Christmas is Jesus' birthday

DENNY SPOKE into the telephone. "We're still at the shopping mall, Mom," he said. "The car won't start. A serviceman from a garage across the street is working on it now. Dad says to tell you we'll be there as soon as we can, but it'll be a while. He says to tell you the 'show must go on.' I don't know what he means by that."

Mother knew what Dad meant. He was talking about the surprise birthday party they had planned for Denny. Dad had taken Denny shopping just to get him out of the house while his mother got things ready. The guests were in the living room now, waiting for him to come home. Mother knew that Dad was telling her to go ahead with the games and entertainment.

When Denny finally burst into the house, he was greeted with cries of "Surprise! Surprise!" His friends were wearing party hats. He was surprised indeed!

"About time you got here," teased one of the children. "We were about to take the gifts and give them to somebody else."

"Uh-uh!" Denny's sister, Kelli, slipped her little hand into her big brother's. "They're Denny's. It's his birfday." Amid a lot of laughing and teasing, Denny opened the gifts his friends had brought.

Soon it was time for the children to leave. "Glad you finally made it," some told Denny as they went out the door. "Your birthday party just wasn't right without you."

After all his guests were gone, Denny sat down to eat a piece of his cake. "I wish I hadn't missed the games," he said, "but at least the car was fixed in time for me to see all the kids and open my presents. I'm glad of that!"

"I'm glad, too," said Mother. "As Kelli says, it's your 'birfday,' and a birthday party without the birthday person just isn't worth much."

HOW ABOUT YOU? Did you know that Christmas is celebrated in honor of Jesus' birthday? Do you remember this as you attend various Christmas parties and events? Does your behavior show that Jesus is with you? Christmas without Him isn't worth anything. Keep this in mind as you celebrate His birthday. □ H.M.

TO MEMORIZE: *And she gave birth to her first child, a son. She wrapped him in a blanket and laid him in a manger, because there was no room for them in the village inn.* Luke 2:7, TLB

JANE'S AUNT and uncle, who weren't Christians, were coming for Christmas dinner. Jane and her parents had prayed that somehow, this Christmas, God would help them show Aunt Ellen and Uncle Joe what they were missing. When they arrived, Uncle Joe held out a pile of presents. "Merry Christmas, Janie! See what Santa Claus brought!"

"We almost didn't come," said Aunt Ellen merrily. "Joe stayed late at the office party last night and came home even drunker than usual." She winked at her husband, but Jane felt badly. Was this all that Christmas meant to her aunt and uncle?

At dinner time the table was loaded with delicious food. After Dad gave thanks, Jane took helpings of several different things. Now all she needed to make a perfect meal was a drumstick. She looked around the table, then she looked again. "Where's the turkey?" she asked.

Startled, Mother stared at the table. "The turkey!" she cried. She ran to the kitchen and returned shortly with a large platter of meat. "The main part of the meal, and I forgot all about it!"

Jane giggled. "I guess we had so much other good stuff that we just didn't miss it at first," she said.

After dinner Uncle Joe stretched. "Now that was a good meal," he declared, "and I'm glad someone remembered the turkey! It wouldn't have been the same without it."

Dad nodded. "This dinner without the turkey would have been like Christmas without Christ," he said. "Many people think they can enjoy Christmas without paying much attention to Christ Himself. It's true that they may have some good times, but they're missing the 'meat.' They're not enjoying the best."

Uncle Joe and Aunt Ellen looked at each other, then settled back to listen as Dad began to read the Christmas story from the Bible. Jane couldn't help rejoicing at how God was using a missing turkey to answer prayer!

HOW ABOUT YOU? Are you missing the "meat" of Christmas? Have you gotten so involved in the "fun" things to do that you've forgotten all about Jesus Christ, God's Son? He came to be the sacrifice for your sins. Until you accept Him as Savior, you cannot enjoy Christmas at its best. □ S.K.

TO MEMORIZE: *He is before all things, and in him all things hold together.* Colossians 1:17, NIV

DECEMBER

24

The Missing Turkey

FROM THE BIBLE:

Before anything else existed, there was Christ, with God. He has always been alive and is himself God. He created everything there is—nothing exists that he didn't make. Eternal life is in him, and this life gives light to all mankind. The one who is the true Light arrived to shine on everyone coming into the world. . . . Christ became a human being and lived here on earth among us and was full of loving forgiveness and truth.
John 1:1-4, 9, 14, TLB

When this great army of angels had returned again to heaven, the shepherds said to each other, "Come on! Let's go to Bethlehem! Let's see this wonderful thing that has happened, which the Lord has told us about." They ran to the village and found their way to Mary and Joseph. And there was the baby, lying in the manger. The shepherds told everyone what had happened and what the angel had said to them about this child.
Luke 2:15-17, TLB

Don't forget Christ

369

25

Here I Am!

FROM THE BIBLE:

*Jesus was born in the town of
Bethlehem, in Judea, during
the reign of King Herod. At
about that time some astrologers
from eastern lands arrived in
Jerusalem, asking, "Where is
the newborn King of the Jews?
For we have seen his star in
far-off eastern lands, and have
come to worship him." King
Herod called a meeting of the
Jewish religious leaders. "Did
the prophets tell us where the
Messiah would be born?" he
asked. "Yes, in Bethlehem,"
they said, "for this is what the
prophet Micah wrote." Then
Herod sent a private message to
the astrologers, asking them to
come to see him; at this meeting
he found out from them the
exact time when they first saw
the star. Then he told them, "Go
to Bethlehem and search for the
child. And when you find him,
come back and tell me so that I
can go and worship him too!"
The star appeared to them
again, standing over Bethlehem.
Entering the house where the
baby and Mary his mother were,
they threw themselves down
before him, worshiping.*
Matthew 2:1-11, TLB

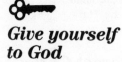

Give yourself
to God

VERY EARLY on Christmas morning, Mark
jumped out of bed, slipped on some clothes, and
went out into the hall, where he tapped lightly on
his sister's door. Betsy quickly opened it, took a
huge decorated box from her closet, and together
they went down the stairs. "Are you sure this isn't
a dumb idea?" whispered Mark as they went out
the front door.

"Mom and Dad will love it," Betsy assured him.
She lifted the cover off the box, and Mark stepped
inside. Then Betsy handed him an assortment of
signs. "I'm your errand boy," read one. "I'll clean
Timmy's room this month besides my own," read
another. "I'll clean the garage," read a third. Mark
put these, with several others, in a corner of the
box. Betsy put the cover on the box, and she put
a large red bow on the top.

"Sure hope the neighbors aren't up yet." Mark's
muffled voice reached Betsy as she rang the doorbell for him. He heard the loud, persistent ring as
she pushed the button again and again. Then he
heard the door close as Betsy disappeared inside
the house.

Soon the door reopened, and Mark heard Dad's
surprised voice. "Well! What have we here?
Mother!" he called. "Come quickly! I believe a
present has arrived for us." In no time, Mother
was there and the box was opened.

"Here I am. Merry Christmas!" called Mark
when they saw him. "You always do so much for
me, so I decided to give you myself this Christmas," he added, handing them the signs. "These
are just some of the things I can do for you."

There were tears in Mother's eyes as she
hugged him. Dad spoke for them both. "It's the
best present you could possibly give us. We love
it!"

HOW ABOUT YOU? Did you think today about the
fact that God gave His very best for you? What
have you given Him in return? What He wants
most of all is the gift of yourself. Will you give that
gift to Him? Only then can He use your talents,
time, and service. □ H.M.

TO MEMORIZE: *Their first action was to dedicate
themselves to the Lord.* 2 Corinthians 8:5, TLB

"THE TIME IS six twenty-one," announced Tim as he got up from the table.

"Well, thanks heaps for keeping us informed," said his sister, Meg. "I'll be glad when that digital watch of yours isn't so new. I don't need to know the exact time every minute of the day." She got up to answer the phone. "For you, Tim," she said.

Tim took the phone. "Hello? . . . oh, hi, George." He glanced at his mother. "I can't play tonight. I've got too many things to do. See ya later."

"Did I hear you tell George you can't play tonight?" asked Mother. "I thought you and some of your friends were going to the gym to play basketball for a while."

"Yeah, well. George is such a klutz," said Tim. "The time is now—"

"Don't change the subject," said Dad. "You lied to George, didn't you?"

"Oh, Dad, it was such a little thing," protested Tim. "I mean it's no big deal—just a little white lie." But Mother and Dad explained to Tim that God didn't see it that way, and though he refused to admit they were right, he agreed to call George back and invite him to join the game. "No answer," he said a few minutes later. "Well, at least I tried." He put on his jacket.

When Tim returned home, he wasn't quite so happy. "What's the problem?" asked Dad.

"I fell," replied Tim, holding out his arm. Across the face of the watch, Dad saw a small scratch.

"Oh, that's too bad," sympathized Dad. "But at least it's just a little scratch."

"Yeah," said Tim, "but it goes right across the numbers."

Mother had come to look. "A little scratch mars a watch," she murmured, "and a 'little' sin mars a testimony for the Lord. It matters."

Tim knew what she meant. "I guess you're right," he admitted. "I'll invite George to play with us tomorrow."

HOW ABOUT YOU? Have you told a "little" lie? Been a "little" unkind? Do you think a "little" sin doesn't matter? It does. It mars your testimony for the Lord. Confess even the "small" sins and ask the Lord to help you overcome them. □ H.M.

TO MEMORIZE: *For whoever keeps the whole law and yet stumbles at just one point is guilty of breaking all of it.* James 2:10, NIV

A Little Scratch

FROM THE BIBLE:
What a terrible thing it is that you are boasting about your purity, and yet you let this sort of thing go on. Don't you realize that if even one person is allowed to go on sinning, soon all will be affected? Remove this evil cancer—this wicked person—from among you, so that you can stay pure. Christ, God's Lamb, has been slain for us. So let us feast upon him and grow strong in the Christian life, leaving entirely behind us the cancerous old life with all its hatreds and wickedness. Let us feast instead upon the pure bread of honor and sincerity and truth.
2 Corinthians 5:6-8, TLB

"Little" sins matter

27

A Friend of Sinners

FROM THE BIBLE:

Later, as Jesus and his disciples were eating dinner [at Matthew's house], there were many notorious swindlers there as guests! The Pharisees were indignant. "Why does your teacher associate with men like that?" "Because people who are well don't need a doctor! It's the sick people who do!" was Jesus' reply. Then he added, "Now go away and learn the meaning of this verse of Scripture, 'It isn't your sacrifices and your gifts I want—I want you to be merciful.' For I have come to urge sinners, not the self-righteous, back to God."

Matthew 9:10-13, TLB

The church is for sinners

"**Y**OU DIDN'T INVITE Joy Blackburn to go to Sunday school with us, did you?" Jana already knew the answer before Mother nodded. "Ooohhhh, Mother!" she wailed. "Joy is dirty, and she talks loud and is so crude. She's everything you tell me not to be, then you turn around and invite her to come to Sunday school with us. I'm surprised you would want me to be friends with her." Jana picked up a knife and began to help her mother peel potatoes for dinner.

"I don't want you to be friends with her in the sense that you do what she does," said Mother, "but I want you to be kind to her."

"Ooohhhh!" Jana gasped. "I cut my hand!"

Mother grabbed a clean cloth and pressed it tightly against the cut. After examining it, she decided she had better take Jana to the emergency room. There a doctor examined Jana's hand, then he stitched and bandaged it. Soon they were ready to go home again. "Oh, dear, we've made quite a mess," Mother exclaimed as she looked around the room.

"Don't worry about that," the nurse said kindly. "We just want this little gal's hand to get better."

That evening Jana showed her father the bandaged hand. "We got blood all over the emergency room, but they didn't even care," she told him. "They were just concerned about me."

Dad smiled. "That's what hospitals are for, Honey—to take care of the sick and hurting."

"Something like church," mused Mother. "The church is a good place for sin-sick, hurting people who need Jesus. Jana, what if hospitals only allowed clean, well people in their emergency rooms?"

Jana sighed, "You're talking about Joy, I know. And you're right, Mom. I'm glad she's going to Sunday school with us, and I'm going to be just as nice to her as the doctor and nurse were to me!"

HOW ABOUT YOU? Do you invite only nice, clean kids to go to church with you? Do you shut the church door in the face of those who are sin-sick? This week, look for kids with special needs, and invite them to church with you. □ B.W.

TO MEMORIZE: *I have not come to call the righteous, but sinners, to repentance.* Luke 5:32, NKJV

As SHERRY AND TRUDY walked toward the gym, Sherry asked, "Trudy, do you expect to be in heaven some day?"

"Oh, sure," replied Trudy. "I try to be good."

"But no one is good enough," said Sherry. "Everyone has sinned, and sin can't enter heaven."

"Well, I'm sure I stand a lot better chance of getting in than a murderer does," insisted Trudy, as they arrived at the gym. "Here we are. Got your money ready?"

"Money?" asked Sherry. "My brother's on the team. I thought I could get in free."

"I doubt it," replied Trudy. "I brought a dollar."

At the ticket office, the girls found that they did need to pay, and tickets cost two dollars each. "Oh, no! What are we going to do now?" moaned Trudy. "I really want to see this game!"

"Trudy, this is like what I told you about getting into heaven," said Sherry thoughtfully. "You had a dollar, and I had nothing. Which one of us is getting into the gym?"

"Why, neither," answered Trudy. "Oh, I get it. I have some good works, but I'm no better off than a person who has none. I still can't pay my way into heaven."

They turned to see Sherry's father standing there.

"Oh, Daddy, I'm so glad to see you!" exclaimed Sherry. "We don't have enough money, so we can't buy our tickets."

"I can," answered her father.

The girls sat down in the bleachers just in time to see the teams take their places on the court. "You know, Trudy," said Sherry, "we both got here because my father paid for the tickets. That's like what Jesus did for us. He paid the price to buy our 'tickets' for heaven."

Slowly Trudy nodded. "I'll have to give that some more thought."

HOW ABOUT YOU? Do you expect to get into heaven because you're better than others are? Nobody is able to make it on his own goodness. Be sure you're not so proud of your "dollar"—your own goodness—that you refuse Christ's free "ticket." If you do, you'll end up outside heaven's gate. Accept His offer today. □ M.R.P.

TO MEMORIZE: *A man is justified by faith apart from observing the law.* Romans 3:28, NIV

The Free Tickets

FROM THE BIBLE:
Therefore no one will be declared righteous in his sight by observing the law; rather, through the law we become conscious of sin. But now a righteousness from God, apart from law, has been made known, to which the Law and the Prophets testify. This righteousness from God comes through faith in Jesus Christ to all who believe. There is no difference, for all have sinned and fall short of the glory of God, and are justified freely by his grace through the redemption that came by Christ Jesus. God presented him as a sacrifice of atonement, through faith in his blood. He did this to demonstrate his justice, because in his forbearance he had left the sins committed beforehand unpunished—he did it to demonstrate his justice at the present time, so as to be just and the one who justifies those who have faith in Jesus. Where, then, is boasting? It is excluded. On what principle? On that of observing the law? No, but on that of faith. For we maintain that a man is justified by faith apart from observing the law. Romans 3:20-28, NIV

Trust Jesus, not your "goodness"

29

A Citizen Now

FROM THE BIBLE:

These men of faith I have mentioned died without ever receiving all that God had promised them; but they saw it all awaiting them on ahead and were glad, for they agreed that this earth was not their real home but that they were just strangers visiting down here. And quite obviously when they talked like that, they were looking forward to their real home in heaven. If they had wanted to, they could have gone back to the good things of this world. But they didn't want to. They were living for heaven. And now God is not ashamed to be called their God, for he has made a heavenly city for them. Hebrews 11:13-16, TLB

Salvation isn't automatic

TAD LOOKED UP as his mother hung up the telephone. "I heard you tell Mrs. Lewis you'd be a witness. Did she have an accident?" he asked.

Mother smiled. "No, this is good news. Mrs. Lewis wants to become an American citizen. I'm going to be a *character witness* when she takes her examination."

"But she lives here," Tad said. "Isn't she an American citizen?"

"No," Mother replied, "living in America doesn't automatically make her an American. She was born in another country and came here when she married. But she has never applied for citizenship till now."

Mrs. Lewis was a good friend of Tad's family. When the big day arrived and she was sworn in as a United States citizen, they all went out for ice cream to help her celebrate. "Why did you decide to become an American citizen now?" Tad asked her.

"There was lots I couldn't do before," Mrs. Lewis explained. "I couldn't vote, hold a public office, or do some jobs. Now I can. I'm glad to give up my citizenship in the old country and become a citizen here."

"This reminds me of what happens when we become Christians," Dad said. "We renounce our allegiance to Satan and pledge our loyalty to Christ."

"That's right," Mother said. "No one is automatically a Christian because, in a sense, we're all born in a 'foreign country.' We're born in this world. To become a citizen of heaven, we each must accept Jesus as Savior."

"And being a Christian gives us certain privileges we wouldn't have under Satan's rule," added Dad. "Not only do we receive forgiveness from sin and a home in heaven, but God cares for our needs, Jesus prays for us, and the Holy Spirit guides us."

"I'm a citizen of the United States now," Mrs. Lewis said proudly. "But I'm a citizen of heaven, too. That's even better."

HOW ABOUT YOU? Where is your citizenship? Have you personally asked Jesus to forgive your sins and be your Savior? You must make that decision to become a citizen of heaven. □ J.H.

TO MEMORIZE: *For our citizenship is in heaven, from which we also eagerly wait for the Savior, the Lord Jesus Christ.* Philippians 3:20, NKJV

WITH A TWINKLE in his eye, Brad sneaked up behind Dad's armchair and plugged in the tape recorder. He pushed a button, and a moment later Dad's voice came from the machine. "Whew! This heat is unbearable! I guarantee you I'll never complain about the cold again. I'd give a lot for the sight of snow."

Dad looked up from his newspaper, startled to hear his own voice. A moment before, he had said almost the same thing—only this time he said the cold was unbearable and he wished for a good hot sun. "When did you record that?" he asked.

Brad laughed. "Last summer," he replied. "We hear the same thing every summer and every winter. I just wanted you to hear it yourself."

Dad laughed too. "How quickly we forget," he said.

Mother nodded as she listened from the dining room. "We often complain about what we don't have, instead of giving thanks for what we do have," she said. "We're hard to please, aren't we?"

"Oh, I don't know," said Brad. "I like summer, and I like winter. I'm an easy fellow to get along with."

"Good!" said Mother. "Then I assume you're going to do the lunch dishes for me without complaining? And you're going to remember with gratitude the good meal you just ate." Brad made a face, but he began to clear the table.

"And I'll shovel the driveway and give thanks that I don't have to pull weeds in the garden today," declared Dad. He patted Brad's shoulder. "Thanks for the good lesson, Son. And I hope you've recorded all this!"

HOW ABOUT YOU? Do you grumble about the rain or thank God that the grass is being watered? Do you murmur about someone who ignored you or thank the Lord for your friends? Do you long for a new shirt or give thanks for your new shoes? Be thankful for what you have. Don't always be wishing for something else. □ H.M.

TO MEMORIZE: *Godliness with contentment is great gain.* 1 Timothy 6:6, NKJV

Great Gain

FROM THE BIBLE:
But godliness with contentment is great gain. For we brought nothing into this world, and it is certain we can carry nothing out. And having food and clothing, with these we shall be content.
1 Timothy 6:6-8, NKJV

I bless the holy name of God with all my heart. Yes, I will bless the LORD and not forget the glorious things he does for me. He forgives all my sins. He heals me. He ransoms me from hell. He surrounds me with lovingkindness and tender mercies. He fills my life with good things! My youth is renewed like the eagle's!
Psalm 103:1-5, TLB

Be thankful always

31

Resolutions

FROM THE BIBLE:

O God, listen to me! Hear my prayer! For wherever I am, though far away at the ends of the earth, I will cry to you for help. When my heart is faint and overwhelmed, lead me to the mighty, towering Rock of safety. For you are my refuge, a high tower where my enemies can never reach me. I shall live forever in your tabernacle; oh, to be safe beneath the shelter of your wings! For you have heard my vows, O God, to praise you every day, and you have given me the blessings you reserve for those who reverence your name. You will give me added years of life, as rich and full as those of many generations, all packed into one. And I shall live before the LORD forever. Oh, send your lovingkindness and truth to guard and watch over me, and I will praise your name continually, fulfilling my vow of praising you each day.
Psalm 61, TLB

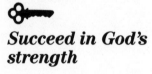

Succeed in God's strength

EVERY YEAR Jack cleaned out his desk on New Year's Eve. Usually he found lots of neat stuff that he had forgotten about, and this year was no exception. His desk top was soon piled high with old school papers, the birthday card he had gotten for his sister last summer and then lost, empty pop cans, and even a dollar bill. Jack was reading over a list of New Year's resolutions that he had found, when he was interrupted by a knock on his bedroom door. "May I come in?" It was Dad.

"Sure, if you don't mind a mess," answered Jack as he surveyed the contents of his desk. "I was just reading over the resolutions I made last year. I didn't follow through on many of them. Here's one that says 'Keep desk clean.' Look at all this stuff!"

Dad grinned as he sat down on the edge of the bed. "What else did you have on your list?"

"Read Bible every day," read Jack. "You know, I really tried to do that, Dad, but no matter how hard I tried, there were days when I just got busy or forgot about it. Maybe I'll skip making New Year's resolutions for next year. At least that way I won't break them."

Dad nodded understandingly. "When Mother and I were first married, we wrote out a list of goals," he said, "but it wasn't until we turned that goal list into a prayer list that we began to see real progress."

Jack glanced over the rest of last year's list. "So you think I should pray about my New Year's resolutions?"

"God wants us to depend on Him for strength and courage to accomplish our plans," stated Dad. "You can either quit, or you can ask God to give you His strength." Jack thought about Dad's suggestion. "This year, I'll talk to the Lord about my goals," he decided. "I can see that I need His help in meeting them."

HOW ABOUT YOU? Have you decided over and over again to read your Bible every day, or to tell someone about the Lord? Have you been determined to get your homework done every night, and then forgotten about it by the middle of the semester? Give your plans to God. Ask Him for the courage and strength to succeed. □ D.R.

TO MEMORIZE: *Commit to the LORD whatever you do, and your plans will succeed.*
Proverbs 16:3, NIV

INDEX
of Scripture in
Daily Readings

Matthew 18:35 *December 19*
Matthew 28:19 *June 15*
Matthew 25:40 *June 22*

Mark 1:17 *August 7*
Mark 3:24 *January 24*
Mark 4:41 *April 8*
Mark 6:31 *August 27*
Mark 14:8 *February 1*

Luke 2:7 *December 23*
Luke 4:8 *July 9*
Luke 5:32 *December 27*
Luke 6:31 *April 28*
Luke 6:37 *October 1*
Luke 6:38 *February 25*
Luke 9:23 *March 24*
Luke 9:62 *April 1*
Luke 10:20 *June 6*
Luke 12:12 *June 28*
Luke 15:10 *July 7*
Luke 16:10 *August 30*
Luke 24:5-6 *April 15*

John 1:3 *November 30*
John 3:3 *August 17*
John 3:3 *December 16*
John 3:5 *November 15*
John 3:16 *June 25*
John 7:24 *January 4*
John 10:6 *September 3*
John 10:9 *May 31*
John 10:9 *September 3*
John 10:27 *April 13*
John 12:48 *June 8*
John 13:34 *February 13*
John 14:1 *November 18*
John 14:3 *January 15*
John 15:5 *October 26*
John 15:17 *September 18*
John 16:13 *June 13*
John 20:29 *July 19*
John 21:22 *March 30*

Acts 16:31 *April 7*
Acts 22:15 *July 16*
Acts 26:28 *August 4*
Acts 24:16 *February 3*

Romans 1:16 *June 29*
Romans 3:3-4 *July 30*
Romans 3:22-23 *February 16*
Romans 3:28 *December 28*
Romans 5:6 *February 28*
Romans 5:8 *February 14*
Romans 6:6 *June 4*

Romans 6:23 *August 25*
Romans 7:12 *September 28*
Romans 8:16 *May 9*
Romans 8:18 *August 10*
Romans 10:13 *March 23*
Romans 12:2 *December 15*
Romans 12:10 *February 22*
Romans 12:12 *February 4*
Romans 12:14 *November 12*
Romans 12:16 *October 30*
Romans 12:18 *August 19*
Romans 12:21 *July 26*
Romans 13:11 *May 14*
Romans 14:5 *May 24*
Romans 14:7 *August 15*
Romans 14:12 *January 10*
Romans 14:13 *May 25*
Romans 14:19 *July 17*

1 Corinthians 3:6 *September 27*
1 Corinthians 3:8 *April 29*
1 Corinthians 4:2 *October 29*
1 Corinthians 6:19 *September 4*
1 Corinthians 6:20 *July 2*
1 Corinthians 8:9 *March 8*
1 Corinthians 9:22 *February 2*
1 Corinthians 10:10 *April 30*
1 Corinthians 10:13 *August 26*
1 Corinthians 10:33 *August 8*
1 Corinthians 11:24 *March 5*
1 Corinthians 11:26 *May 28*
1 Corinthians 12:12 *April 26*
1 Corinthians 12:14 *July 10*
1 Corinthians 12:22
  September 1
1 Corinthians 12:27 *February 7*
1 Corinthians 13:1 *January 28*
1 Corinthians 15:33
  December 13
1 Corinthians 15:43
  February 15
1 Corinthians 15:57
  November 25

2 Corinthians 1:4 *May 6*
2 Corinthians 1:5 *August 11*
2 Corinthians 3:18 *July 18*
2 Corinthians 5:8 *June 24*
2 Corinthians 5:17 *June 3*
2 Corinthians 6:2 *April 23*
2 Corinthians 6:14 *September 6*
2 Corinthians 8:5 *December 25*
2 Corinthians 9:6 *July 20*
2 Corinthians 9:7 *January 19*

2 Corinthians 12:9 *March 21*
2 Corinthians 12:10 *April 9*

Galatians 2:16 *October 3*
Galatians 2:20 *April 11*
Galatians 2:20 *August 2*
Galatians 5:13 *September 24*
Galatians 5:22 *April 25*
Galatians 6:7 *September 10*

Ephesians 1:13-14 *February 6*
Ephesians 2:8 *December 20*
Ephesians 2:10 *February 18*
Ephesians 2:20 *February 10*
Ephesians 4:2 *April 6*
Ephesians 4:4-6 *October 16*
Ephesians 4:11-12 *July 15*
Ephesians 4:15 *May 17*
Ephesians 4:26-27
  November 26
Ephesians 4:29 *October 22*
Ephesians 5:1 *February 21*
Ephesians 5:1 *September 23*
Ephesians 5:8 *August 29*
Ephesians 5:15 *May 18*
Ephesians 5:19 *July 1*
Ephesians 6:1 *June 18*
Ephesians 6:2 *March 15*
Ephesians 6:11 *June 19*
Ephesians 6:17 *September 22*

Philippians 1:3 *March 16*
Philippians 1:6 *July 27*
Philippians 2:15 *May 5*
Philippians 2:15 *September 16*
Philippians 3:9 *June 12*
Philippians 3:20 *December 29*
Philippians 3:20 *July 4*
Philippians 4:7 *January 26*
Philippians 4:8 *November 24*
Philippians 4:13 *March 17*
Philippians 4:19 *January 27*

Colossians 1:17 *December 24*
Colossians 3:12 *April 4*
Colossians 3:13 *May 20*
Colossians 3:16 *September 26*
Colossians 3:17 *March 9*
Colossians 3:23 *March 31*
Colossians 3:23 *December 18*
Colossians 3:24 *February 9*
Colossians 3:25 *January 12*
Colossians 4:2 *November 22*

1 Thessalonians 5:11
  February 26

1 Thessalonians 5:17 *March 1*
1 Thessalonians 5:18
  November 29

2 Thessalonians 3:14-15
  September 7

1 Timothy 4:4 *September 17*
1 Timothy 4:8 *January 1*
1 Timothy 4:12 *January 7*
1 Timothy 4:12 *October 5*
1 Timothy 4:12 *December 2*
1 Timothy 6:6 *March 14*
1 Timothy 6:6 *December 30*

2 Timothy 1:8 *March 18*
2 Timothy 1:12 *May 16*
2 Timothy 2:15 *March 25*
2 Timothy 2:19 *March 27*
2 Timothy 3:14 *February 27*
2 Timothy 3:16 *December 6*
2 Timothy 3:17 *May 10*

Titus 2:15 *October 21*
Titus 3:14 *August 5*

Hebrews 3:13 *July 23*
Hebrews 8:10 *August 9*
Hebrews 9:27 *January 25*

Hebrews 10:24 *June 2*
Hebrews 10:25 *March 28*
Hebrews 12:1 *May 29*
Hebrews 12:1 *September 19*
Hebrews 12:11 *July 14*
Hebrews 13:8 *March 22*

James 1:3 *April 14*
James 1:15 *November 27*
James 2:10 *December 26*
James 2:17 *March 11*
James 3:17 *September 15*
James 4:7 *April 22*
James 4:8 *January 17*
James 4:15 *May 27*
James 4:17 *May 19*
James 5:8 *June 10*

1 Peter 1:3-4 *May 8*
1 Peter 1:22 *September 9*
1 Peter 2:9 *July 21*
1 Peter 2:10 *October 17*
1 Peter 2:21 *July 29*
1 Peter 2:21 *October 2*
1 Peter 3:8 *December 22*
1 Peter 3:8 *February 23*
1 Peter 3:15 *June 23*
1 Peter 4:10 *September 13*

1 Peter 5:7 *February 17*
1 Peter 5:8 *May 4*

2 Peter 3:11 *January 20*
2 Peter 3:18 *January 5*

1 John 1:7 *October 28*
1 John 1:8 *December 3*
1 John 1:9 *March 10*
1 John 2:6 *April 16*
1 John 2:17 *July 24*
1 John 3:2 *August 24*
1 John 3:2 *December 9*
1 John 3:18 *August 3*
1 John 3:18 *December 5*
1 John 4:7 *February 12*
1 John 4:10 *July 25*
1 John 4:16 *July 11*
1 John 4:19 *February 29*
1 John 4:21 *October 19*
1 John 5:12 *January 30*
1 John 5:14 *September 29*
1 John 5:15 *December 4*
1 John 5:21 *March 3*

Jude 17 *January 8*

Revelation 3:20 *March 26*
Revelation 20:12 *August 13*